Sunset
Recipe Annual

2 0 0 3 E D I T I O N

Garlic Shrimp (page 139)

JAMES CARRIER; FOOD STYLING: BASIL FRIEDMAN

By the Editors of Sunset Magazine
and Sunset Books

Sunset Publishing Corporation ■ **Menlo Park, California**

SUNSET BOOKS

VP, General Manager
Richard A. Smeby

VP, Editorial Director
Bob Doyle

Production Director
Lory Day

Director of Operations
Rosann Sutherland

Sales Development Director
Linda Barker

Art Director
Vasken Guiragossian

STAFF FOR THIS BOOK
Managing Editor
Cornelia Fogle

Production Coordinator
Danielle Javier

SUNSET PUBLISHING CORPORATION

Senior Vice President
Kevin Lynch

VP, Administration and Manufacturing
Lorinda Reichert

VP, Marketing Director
Beth Whiteley

VP, Consumer Marketing Director
Christina Olsen

VP, General Manager
Mark Okean

VP, Editor-in-Chief, Sunset Magazine
Katie Tamony

Executive Editor/ sunset.com Editor
Carol Hoffman

Art Director
James H. McCann

Managing Director
Alan J. Phinney

Senior Editor, Food & Entertaining
Sara Schneider

Associate Art Directors
Dennis W. Leong
Keith Whitney

Chocolate Raspberry Shortcake (page 115)

Welcome to the 16th edition of the *Sunset Recipe Annual*, a collection of the recipes and food articles from the past year's issues of *Sunset Magazine*.

Again this year we discovered great recipes all over the West. They come from Pacific fishing ports and a Colorado guest ranch, from a Hawaiian wine and food festival, even a remote Montana cafe. Many chefs and innovative home cooks shared their special recipes, all of which have been tested in the *Sunset* kitchens.

Special sections focused on streamlined classic dishes in January, outdoor entertaining suggestions in July, and holiday entertaining recipes in November. Party ideas range from simple buy-and-serve buffets to holiday feasts—with make-ahead tips to simplify the effort. You'll find low-fat and quick-to-cook recipes, along with information on new products in the markets, and new tools that make food preparation easier.

Enjoy another year of great cooking!

Cover: Blueberry Buttermilk Pancakes (page 93). Cover design: Vasken Guiragossian. Photographer: James Carrier.

Back cover photographer: James Carrier (3).

Endsheets photographer: Tucker and Hossler.

First printing November 2002
Copyright © 2002 Sunset Publishing Corporation, Menlo Park, CA 94025. First edition. All rights reserved, including the right of reproduction in whole or in part in any form.

ISBN 0-376-02712-6 (hardcover)
ISBN 0-376-02714-2 (softcover)
ISSN 0896-2170
Printed in the United States

Material in this book originally appeared in the 2002 issues of *Sunset Magazine*. All of the recipes were developed and tested in the *Sunset* test kitchens. If you have comments or suggestions, please let us hear from you. Write us at Sunset Books, Cookbook Editorial, 80 Willow Road, Menlo Park, CA 94025.

Contents

A Letter from Sunset

DEAR READER,

Looking back over a year's worth of work naturally prompts a review. What happened to us in the last 12 months? How did we respond to our experience? And how are we doing now?

This time, such questions have a darker edge than usual. Our security has been challenged, at both personal and national levels. And many of us have worried about our investments for the future as we've watched financial markets falter.

Does this mean we should pull in, hold back, live less open-heartedly? Definitely not! Now, more than ever, we need to pay attention to the things that make life rich—shared pleasures such as dining together being among the most important.

As I appraise my own first year as the magazine's senior food editor, preparing this latest *Recipe Annual*, I also ask myself: Have we changed the ways we go about offering our readers great food from around the West? Has our editorial mission or method altered? Again, the immediate answer is, definitely not.

We have kept our commitment to explore markets, restaurants, and innovative home kitchens around the West to identify the best of established and emerging cooking styles. We are still honing techniques to make the resulting, research-honored dishes fit into the busy lives of both novice and experienced cooks. (And, of course, we are still testing each recipe meticulously to make sure it will succeed every time.)

We've continued to honor our territory's own resources, finding wonderful dishes grounded in specific places around the West: wine-country cooking from California's Santa Ynez Valley (page 76), specialties from working-harbor towns (page 174), fish from Hawaii (page 80), crab from the Mendocino coast (page 258).

We've also continued to celebrate the cooking of many cultures, reflecting the diversity of our population and our readers' enthusiasm for new flavors. Our ideas for entertaining took a decidedly ethnic turn. February brought a simple family dinner from China; March, noodle bowls from Vietnam; May, a Cinco de Mayo fiesta from Mexico; June, a small-plate party from the Caribbean; July, an authentic paella from Spain; August, chicken piri-piri from southern Portugal; September, a simple supper from Tuscany; and so on.

This year, our editors put their ingenuity to use to lighten and streamline comfort foods, which in the West can range from chicken cacciatore to sweet-and-sour pork (page 8). They've worked to achieve foolproof recipes for dishes involving some tricky cooking processes, such as making popovers (page 36).

The food-writing team, left to right: Sara Schneider (senior editor, food and entertaining), Charity Ferreira (food writer), Kate Washington (associate food editor), and Linda Lau Anusasananan (recipe editor).

The food-support team, front row, left to right: Bunnie Russell (retester), Dorothy Decker (retester), Bernadette Hart (test kitchen manager, editorial services), Marlene Kawahata (retester), and Michelle Hauf (photo editor, food). Back row, left to right: Laura H. Martin (senior designer), Keith Whitney (associate art director), Dennis W. Leong (associate art director), Leslie Smith (retester), Laura Berner (retester), and Sarah Epstein (retester). Retesters not pictured: Angela Brassinga, Wendy Connors, and Linda Tebben.

And as always, we've found ways to make the best possible use of seasonal treats—from fresh corn (page 144) to tree-ripe figs (page 188).

Steady as our editorial helm has remained, we've made a few adjustments I'm quite excited about. In June 2002, we premiered a new, front-of-the-book interdepartmental feature, Best of the West, giving our food writers a chance to report restaurant trends, offer timely news about produce developments, and share insights from chefs who are handling our region's bounty in fresh, creative ways.

Also in June, our Food Guide acquired a new voice—or rather, voices. Having been written for many years by my predecessor, Jerry Di Vecchio, who enjoyed more than 40 years of culinary adventure at *Sunset*, the guide now reflects the entire food staff's (exhilarating) discoveries: cooking techniques, tips on tools, and advice on products, to make your time in the kitchen interesting and easy—tidbits like preparing risotto ahead of time, to avoid all that last-minute stirring (page 209).

Happily, though, Jerry is still with us, through her own monthly column, Adventures in Cooking. This feature offers reminiscences and new thoughts that could only come from a veteran student and teacher of cooking. Sharing tuna salad with James Beard (page 149), cured salmon with M. F. K. Fisher (page 223), arroz con pollo with Native American cook and storyteller-potter Helen Cordero (page 202)—these are a few of Jerry's rich forays.

Wine writer Karen MacNeil is still sharing her lively and practical advice with us, too, from strategies for finding very good wines on a budget (page 27) to still wines that are great with brunch (page 54).

Continuity spiced with a little innovation: That's been my formula for carrying on *Sunset's* tradition of bringing you ways to live thoughtfully and well. Once in a while, that means breaking tradition, too. How about a vegetarian menu for Thanksgiving (page 224)? Or a picnic in the middle of winter (page 242)?

Looking back, I think we've done our part to make your own year-end review very satisfying.

Sara Schneider

Sara Schneider
Senior Editor, Food and Entertaining

TO USE OUR NUTRITIONAL INFORMATION

The most current data from the USDA is used for our recipes: calorie count; fat calories; grams of protein, total and saturated fat, carbohydrates, and fiber; and milligrams of sodium and cholesterol.

This analysis is usually given for a single serving, based on the largest number of servings listed. Or it's for a specific amount, such as per tablespoon (for sauces); or by unit, as per cookie.

Optional ingredients are not included, nor are those for which no specific amount is stated (salt added to taste, for example). If an ingredient is listed with an alternative, calculations are based on the first choice listed. Likewise, if a range is given for the amount of an ingredient (such as $1/2$ to 1 cup milk), values are figured on the first, lower amount.

Recipes using broth are calculated on the sodium content of salt-free broth, homemade or canned. If you use canned salted chicken broth, the sodium content will be higher.

Chicken Cacciatore and other classics have been lightened and streamlined for satisfying weeknight meals (see page 8).

January

cozy classics

Comfort foods from around the world—lightened, updated, and designed for weeknight dinners

What makes a dish a classic?

Longevity in a certain cuisine is one mark. France's coq au vin, for instance, qualifies—it has the power to evoke years of tradition. But the most enduring dishes evoke not only earlier days but also nostalgia for those times (high marks again for coq au vin). People take the most comfort, of course, from the foods they grew up eating, and in the West that list originates in many culinary traditions. Sweet and sour pork, fettuccine Alfredo, tamale pie, cassoulet—all these familiar dishes are our classics.

But "classic" doesn't necessarily entail long hours in the kitchen achieving feats with indulgent ingredients. We've lightened and streamlined some of our favorites—even those that seem defined by butter and cream (like fettuccine Alfredo)—replacing fat with other satisfying flavors to bring you a modern repertoire of classics for comforting weeknight meals.

Prosciutto and parmesan cheese keep the satisfaction factor high for lean fettuccine Alfredo.

Fettuccine Alfredo with Peas and Prosciutto

PREP AND COOK TIME: About 20 minutes
MAKES: 4 servings

- 3½ cups fat-skimmed **chicken broth**
- 2 cups **low-fat (1%) milk**
- ¾ pound **dried fettuccine**
- 1½ cups (10-oz. package) **frozen petite peas**
- 1 ounce **thin-sliced prosciutto**
- 1½ teaspoons **cornstarch**
- 1 cup **reduced-fat sour cream**
- ½ cup **grated parmesan cheese**
- ¼ teaspoon freshly grated **nutmeg** or ground nutmeg
- **Salt** and **pepper**

1. In a 5- to 6-quart pan, combine broth, milk, and fettuccine (break fettuccine if necessary to fit into pan); cover and bring to a boil over high heat, stirring occasionally. Reduce heat to medium-high and cook, uncovered, stirring often to separate noodles, for 5 minutes. Add peas and stir occasionally until pasta is tender to bite, 2 to 4 minutes longer.

2. Meanwhile, separate prosciutto slices and cut crosswise into ¼-inch-wide strips.

3. In a small bowl, mix cornstarch with 2 tablespoons water until smooth. Add to pasta mixture and stir until it boils and thickens. Add sour cream, parmesan cheese, nutmeg, and salt and pepper to taste; stir until well blended and heated through, about 1 minute. Stir in prosciutto. Spoon onto plates.

Per serving: 619 cal., 22% (135 cal.) from fat; 36 g protein; 15 g fat (7.2 g sat.); 84 g carbo (6.7 g fiber); 588 mg sodium; 39 mg chol.

By Linda Lau Anusasananan, Charity Ferreira, and Sara Schneider
Photographs by James Carrier • Food styling by Karen Shinto

Chicken Cacciatore

PREP AND COOK TIME: About 45 minutes

NOTES: To save time, you can use purchased cooked polenta, often sold refrigerated in cylinders in supermarkets (near the cheese). Skip step 4; instead, cut cylinder crosswise into ½-inch-thick rounds, lay on a baking sheet, brush with olive oil, and broil 4 to 6 inches from heat until lightly browned, or grill oiled rounds. In step 5, arrange polenta rounds on plates and top with chicken cacciatore.

MAKES: 4 servings

- 4 **boned, skinned chicken thighs** (5 oz. each)
- 1 teaspoon **olive oil**
- 1 **onion** (8 oz.), peeled and chopped
- 2 **carrots** (8 oz. total), peeled and chopped
- 8 ounces **sliced mushrooms** (about 3 cups)
- 2 cloves **garlic,** peeled and minced
- 1 can (14½ oz.) **diced tomatoes**
- 1 can (8 oz.) **tomato sauce**
- 1 teaspoon minced **fresh rosemary** leaves or crumbled dried rosemary
  Salt and **pepper**
- 1 quart fat-skimmed **chicken broth**
- 1 cup **polenta** or yellow cornmeal (see notes)
- 1 tablespoon chopped **parsley**
  Grated parmesan cheese

1. Rinse chicken and pat dry; remove and discard excess fat.

2. Pour olive oil into a 5- to 6-quart nonstick pan over high heat; when hot, add chicken and cook, turning once, until browned on both sides, 5 to 7 minutes total. Transfer to a plate.

3. Add onion, carrots, mushrooms, and garlic to pan; stir often until mushrooms begin to brown, 8 to 10 minutes. Add tomatoes and their juices, tomato sauce, rosemary, and the chicken with any accumulated juices; bring to a simmer, cover, reduce heat to low, and cook for 5 minutes. Turn chicken over and simmer, covered, until no longer pink in center of thickest part (cut to test), about 5 minutes longer. Season to taste with salt and pepper.

4. Meanwhile, in a 3- to 4-quart pan, stir broth and polenta until well blended. Bring to a boil over high heat, stirring often; reduce heat to low and stir often until polenta is creamy and smooth to bite, 8 to 12 minutes (about 3 minutes for cornmeal).

5. Spoon polenta into wide bowls or onto rimmed plates. Top with equal portions of chicken and sauce; sprinkle with parsley. Add parmesan cheese and more salt and pepper to taste.

Per serving: 560 cal., 13% (71 cal.) from fat; 46 g protein; 7.9 g fat (1.7 g sat.); 75 g carbo (12 g fiber); 735 mg sodium; 118 mg chol.

Boned chicken thighs make a quick, flavorful starting point for Chicken Cacciatore.

Quick-start tips

Partially prepared, high-quality ingredients can shave many minutes off the preparation time for most dishes. And more are available now than ever before. Consider these options:

■ **Fresh vegetables** that come rinsed, peeled, cut, or shredded can maintain the textures and flavors of fresh produce. Good choices: sliced mushrooms, peeled garlic cloves, salad mixes, shredded cabbage, broccoli florets, carrot sticks, celery sticks, and trimmed and cut greens such as mustard and spinach. For small quantities, check out your market's salad bar.

■ **Frozen vegetables,** which can eliminate labor-intensive steps, often retain high quality and can be used directly. Best bets: peas, corn kernels, pearl onions, artichoke hearts, sugar snap peas, and shelled soybeans.

■ **Some canned vegetables** rival fresh in quality during the winter. Wise picks: tomatoes and corn kernels. Others win because they simply save a lot of time: beans, roasted red peppers, roasted green chilies, and artichoke hearts and bottoms.

■ **Boned and trimmed meats** are ready to cook; many are sold sliced. Even more convenient and quick, some are already cooked. The best time-savers: boned and skinned chicken breasts and thighs, thinly sliced meats for stir-fries, cooked beef and chicken strips, and fully cooked beef pot roast.

■ **Good seafood counters and markets** offer well cleaned and prepared shellfish, needing, for the most part, only a quick rinse at home: cleaned, cracked cooked crab, for instance, and bearded and scrubbed mussels.

■ **Purchased sauces** add instant flavor: pasta, enchilada, sesame soy, teriyaki, peanut, curry, and chili.

■ **Ready-to-use cheeses**—sliced, shredded, or crumbled—can be used in small quantities to boost the satisfaction factor of dishes without adding too many calories.

■ **Canned broth** is a flavorful base for quick soups and sauces. Keep it on hand as a pantry staple.

■ **Cooked polenta,** sold in cylinders in a refrigerator case in most supermarkets, provides a great instant side dish.

Shrimp and Shallot Newburg

PREP AND COOK TIME: About 35 minutes
NOTES: This Newburg makes a great brunch entrée served over toasted English muffins or, more indulgently, spooned into hot popovers. Garnish servings with sprigs of fresh herbs such as tarragon.
MAKES: 4 or 5 servings

- 2 tablespoons **butter** or margarine
- 8 ounces **shallots**, peeled and slivered lengthwise
- ¼ cup **all-purpose flour**
- 2½ cups **low-fat (2%) milk**
- ¼ cup **dry sherry** or madeira
  Salt and **white** or black **pepper**
- 4 slices **firm-textured white bread** (about 4 oz. total; see notes)
- 1 pound **shelled cooked tiny shrimp**, thawed if frozen

1. Melt butter in a 4- to 5-quart pan over medium-high heat; add shallots and stir often until limp, about 3 minutes.
2. Sprinkle flour over shallots and stir until well mixed, about 1 minute. Whisk in milk and stir until mixture boils and thickens, about 5 minutes. Add sherry and salt and pepper to taste; reduce heat and simmer, stirring occasionally, to blend flavors, about 5 minutes.
3. Meanwhile, toast bread; trim off and discard crusts if desired. Rinse and drain shrimp. Add shrimp to sauce and stir often just until simmering again, about 2 minutes.
4. Set a slice of toast on each plate. Spoon hot shrimp Newburg equally over toast.
Per serving: 319 cal., 25% (79 cal.) from fat; 27 g protein; 8.8 g fat (4.8 g sat.); 29 g carbo (1 g fiber); 439 mg sodium; 199 mg chol.

Curried Mussels with Oven Frites

PREP AND COOK TIME: About 45 minutes
NOTES: These mussels were inspired by a dish prepared at Château Loudenne in the Bordeaux region of France, served near the big stone fireplace in the cozy harvesters' dining room. This version carries all the comfort of France's traditional mussels and *frites* (fries).
MAKES: 2 servings

- 2 **russet potatoes** (about 10 oz. each)
- 1 tablespoon **olive oil**
- ½ teaspoon **paprika**
  About ¼ teaspoon **salt**
  About ⅛ teaspoon **pepper**
- ½ cup diced (¼ in.) **onion**
- ½ cup diced (¼ in.) **carrots**
- ½ cup diced (¼ in.) **celery**
- ½ teaspoon **dried thyme**
- ½ teaspoon **curry powder**
- 1½ cups **dry white wine**
- 1 cup **canned diced tomatoes** or 1 cup chopped firm-ripe tomatoes
- ¼ cup **crème fraîche** or sour cream
- 1½ pounds **mussels**, beards pulled off, scrubbed

1. Coat a 10- by 15-inch pan generously with cooking oil spray. Peel potatoes and cut lengthwise into ¼-inch-thick sticks. In pan, mix potatoes with ½ tablespoon olive oil. Sprinkle with ¼ teaspoon paprika, ¼ teaspoon salt, and ⅛ teaspoon pepper; mix and spread level. Bake in a 450° regular or convection oven, turning occasionally with a wide spatula, until potatoes are crisp and browned on the outside and tender to bite on the inside, 25 to 30 minutes.
2. Meanwhile, in a 4- to 5-quart pan over high heat, stir onion, carrots, celery, thyme, curry powder, and remaining ¼ teaspoon paprika in remaining ½ tablespoon olive oil until vegetables are limp, about 5 minutes. Add wine and tomatoes and their juices; boil, stirring occasionally, to blend flavors, about 5 minutes. Stir in crème fraîche and season to taste with salt and pepper.
3. Discard any gaping mussels that don't close when you tap their shells.

Add mussels to pan; cover and cook until shells pop open, 8 to 10 minutes.
4. Ladle mussels and broth into wide bowls. Serve with oven frites.
Per serving: 637 cal., 30% (189 cal.) from fat; 20 g protein; 21 g fat (8.4 g sat.); 64 g carbo (7.6 g fiber); 666 mg sodium; 53 mg chol.

Shells and Cheese

PREP AND COOK TIME: About 40 minutes
MAKES: 4 servings

- 12 ounces **kale**
- 12 ounces **dried shell-shaped pasta** (about 1 in. long)
- 6 slices (about 4 in. long and ¼ in. thick) day-old **Italian-style bread**
- 1 clove **garlic**, peeled, plus 1 tablespoon pressed or minced garlic
- ½ teaspoon **hot chili flakes**
- 1 teaspoon **olive oil**
- 1 tablespoon **lemon juice**
  About ½ teaspoon **salt**
  Pepper
- 1½ cups **low-fat ricotta cheese**
- 2 tablespoons **shredded parmesan cheese**

1. In a 6- to 8-quart pan over high heat, bring 4 to 6 quarts water to a boil. Rinse kale; cut out and discard stems and tough centers of leaves. Add kale to boiling water and cook, stirring occasionally, until bright green and tender to bite, about 5 minutes. With a

Mussels cook quickly in a curry-wine broth and join crisp fries from the oven.

slotted spoon, transfer kale to a colander to drain. Add pasta to water and cook, stirring occasionally, until barely tender to bite, about 10 minutes. Drain pasta, reserving 1 cup cooking liquid; return pasta to pan.

2. Meanwhile, arrange bread slices in a single layer on a 12- by 15-inch baking sheet. Bake in a 350° regular or convection oven, turning once, until crisp and dry, about 15 minutes total. Rub one side of each bread slice with garlic clove; discard any remaining clove. Let bread cool, then seal in a heavy plastic bag and crush with a rolling pin or whirl in a food processor into coarse crumbs.

3. Coarsely chop kale. In a 10- to 12-inch frying pan over high heat, stir 1 tablespoon pressed or minced garlic and chili flakes in oil just until garlic is fragrant (but not brown), 1 to 2 minutes. Add lemon juice and kale and stir until liquid is evaporated, 2 to 3 minutes. Add salt and pepper to taste.

4. Stir kale mixture, ricotta cheese, ½ teaspoon salt, and reserved 1 cup pasta-cooking liquid into pasta. Divide equally among four bowls and sprinkle with bread crumbs and parmesan cheese.

Per serving: 537 cal., 18% (99 cal.) from fat; 26 g protein; 11 g fat (5.5 g sat.); 82 g carbo (3.7 g fiber); 569 mg sodium; 31 mg chol.

Skillet Tamale Pie

PREP AND COOK TIME: About 35 minutes

NOTES: If your frying pan is not big enough to add the topping in step 3, transfer hot meat mixture in step 2 to a hot, shallow 3-quart casserole (warm in oven as it preheats), then continue.

MAKES: 6 servings

- 1 **onion** (8 oz.), peeled and chopped
- 1 pound **ground lean** (7% fat) **beef** or turkey
- 1 tablespoon **chili powder**
- 1 teaspoon **cumin seeds**
- 2 cans (14½ oz. each) **salt-free diced tomatoes**
- 2 cups **frozen corn kernels**
- 1 can (2¼ oz.) **sliced black ripe olives,** drained
  About ¼ teaspoon **salt**
- 1 **large egg**
- 1 **large egg** white
- 1½ cups **shredded reduced-fat cheddar cheese** (about 6 oz.)
- 1 cup **nonfat milk**
- 1 cup **yellow cornmeal**
- ½ teaspoon **baking powder**

1. In an 11- to 12-inch ovenproof frying pan (2 to 3 in. deep, 2½- to 3-quart

capacity) over high heat, stir onion, beef, chili powder, and cumin seeds until beef is crumbled and lightly browned, 6 to 8 minutes.

2. Add tomatoes (including juices), corn, and olives; bring to a boil, stirring occasionally. Add salt to taste.

3. Meanwhile, in a bowl, whisk together egg, egg white, ½ cup cheese, milk, cornmeal, baking powder, and ¼ teaspoon salt until well blended (mixture will be thin). Pour evenly over hot meat mixture. Sprinkle evenly with remaining 1 cup cheese.

4. Bake in a 400° regular or convection oven until the top feels firm when lightly touched, about 15 minutes. Scoop out servings with a large spoon. Add salt to taste.

Per serving: 387 cal., 30% (117 cal.) from fat; 31 g protein; 13 g fat (5.5 g sat.); 39 g carbo (4.2 g fiber); 533 mg sodium; 96 mg chol.

Sweet and Sour Pork

PREP AND COOK TIME: About 45 minutes

NOTES: To save time, you can buy pork cut into thin strips for stir-frying, available in many supermarkets.

MAKES: 4 to 6 servings

- 2 cups **long-grain white rice**
- 1 pound **fat-trimmed boned pork loin** or sirloin (see notes)
- 2 tablespoons **soy sauce**
- 1 **onion** (8 oz.)
- 1 **red** or green **bell pepper** (8 oz.)
- 1 can (8 oz.) **pineapple chunks in juice**
- ¼ cup **catsup**
- 1 tablespoon **cornstarch**
- 1 tablespoon **sugar**
- 1 tablespoon **rice vinegar**
- ¼ teaspoon **cayenne** (optional)
- 1½ teaspoons **salad oil**
- 1 tablespoon minced **fresh ginger**
- 1 tablespoon minced **garlic**
  Salt

1. In a 2- to 3-quart pan over high heat, bring 3½ cups water and the rice to a boil. Reduce heat to medium-high and cook, uncovered, until most of the water is absorbed, 7 to 10 minutes. Turn heat to low, cover, and cook until rice is tender to bite, 10 to 15 minutes longer.

2. Meanwhile, rinse pork and pat dry; cut into 3-inch-long strips 1 inch wide and ¼ inch thick. In a small bowl, mix pork with 1 tablespoon soy sauce.

3. Peel onion and cut lengthwise into ¼-inch-wide slivers. Rinse, stem, and seed bell pepper; cut lengthwise into ¼-inch-wide slivers about 3 inches long.

4. Drain pineapple juice into a 1-cup

It's as fast to stir up this colorful Sweet and Sour Pork as to order out for Chinese.

Duck à l'Orange goes exotic with green olives but is on the table in no time.

1. Pour olive oil into a 10- to 12-inch nonstick frying pan over medium-high heat. Add duck breasts and cook, turning once, until well browned on the outside and barely pink in center of thickest part (cut to test), 12 to 15 minutes total. With tongs, transfer duck to a rimmed plate and cover with foil.

2. Add onion to pan and stir often until limp, about 5 minutes. Add orange juice, broth, marmalade, lemon juice, vinegar, and orange slices; boil, stirring occasionally, until mixture has thickened and is reduced by half, about 15 minutes.

3. Meanwhile, in a 1- to 2-quart pan over high heat, bring 1¼ cups water to a boil. Stir in couscous, cover, and remove from heat. Let stand 5 minutes.

4. Pull duck into 2-inch-long shreds, or cut into 2-inch pieces or ¼-inch-thick slices. Add to orange sauce along with any accumulated juices and the olives; stir until mixture is hot. Add salt and pepper to taste.

5. Gently fluff couscous with a fork. Spoon onto plates and top equally with duck and sauce.

Per serving: 567 cal., 5.6% (32 cal.) from fat; 43 g protein; 3.6 g fat (0.4 g sat.); 96 g carbo (4.9 g fiber); 478 mg sodium; 159 mg chol.

Italian Pot Roast

PREP AND COOK TIME: About 45 minutes
NOTES: Cooked pot roast is available in the refrigerated meat section of many supermarkets.
MAKES: 6 servings

- 1½ pounds **dried spaghetti**
- 1 **onion** (8 oz.), peeled and chopped
- 8 ounces **sliced mushrooms**
- 1 stalk **celery** (2 oz.), rinsed, ends trimmed, chopped
- ⅓ cup finely chopped **cooked ham**
- 1 teaspoon **olive oil**
- 1 cup fat-skimmed **beef broth**
- ½ cup **dry red wine** or more beef broth
- 1 can (6 oz.) **tomato paste**
- 1 package (2 lb.) **cooked boned beef pot roast with gravy**
  Salt and **pepper**
- 1 tablespoon chopped **parsley** (optional)

1. In an 8- to 10-quart covered pan over high heat, bring about 4 quarts water to a boil. Add spaghetti and cook until barely tender to bite, 8 to 10 minutes.

2. Meanwhile, in a 12-inch nonstick frying pan or 5- to 6-quart nonstick pan

glass measure. Add enough water to make ⅔ cup. Stir in remaining 1 tablespoon soy sauce, catsup, cornstarch, sugar, vinegar, and cayenne.

5. Pour ½ teaspoon oil into a 12-inch nonstick frying pan or 14-inch wok over high heat. When oil ripples when pan is tilted, add onion, bell pepper, ginger, and garlic. Stir often until bell pepper is tender-crisp to bite, 2 to 3 minutes. Pour from pan into a serving bowl.

6. Add remaining 1 teaspoon oil and the pork to pan; stir often until pork is no longer pink in the center (cut to test), 4 to 5 minutes. Return onion mixture to pan and add pineapple. Stir the pineapple juice mixture and add to pan. Stir until sauce boils and thickens, about 1 minute. Add salt to taste. Pour into a serving bowl and serve with hot cooked rice.

Per serving: 417 cal., 13% (54 cal.) from fat; 22 g protein; 6 g fat (1.7 g sat.); 67 g carbo (2.1 g fiber); 506 mg sodium; 45 mg chol.

Duck à l'Orange

PREP AND COOK TIME: About 40 minutes
NOTES: You may need to order duck breasts ahead from your meat market; thaw if frozen. If using chicken instead of duck, cook until well browned on the outside and no longer pink in the center of thickest part (cut to test), about 12 minutes.
MAKES: 2 to 3 servings

- ½ teaspoon **olive oil**
- 2 boned, skinned **duck breast halves** (about 8 oz. each) or 1 lb. boned, skinned chicken thighs (see notes)
- 1 **red onion** (7 oz.), peeled, halved, and thinly sliced crosswise
- 1 cup **orange juice**
- ⅔ cup fat-skimmed **chicken broth**
- ¼ cup **orange marmalade**
- 1 teaspoon **lemon juice**
- 1 teaspoon **red wine vinegar**
- 1 **orange** (8 oz.), rinsed, halved, and very thinly sliced crosswise (end pieces and seeds discarded)
- 1 cup **couscous**
- ¼ cup **medium-size green olives** such as Picholine, pitted and coarsely chopped
  Salt and **pepper**

over high heat, stir onion, mushrooms, celery, and ham in olive oil until onion begins to brown, 10 to 15 minutes. Add broth, wine, and tomato paste; stir until well blended.

3. Discard any solidified fat from pot roast and sauce. Scrape sauce from meat into onion-tomato mixture. Cut beef across the grain into ¼-inch-thick slices and lay over onion-tomato sauce; cover and simmer over low heat until beef is hot, 7 to 10 minutes. Add salt and pepper to taste.

4. Drain spaghetti well and pour onto a rimmed platter or into a wide, shallow bowl. With a slotted spatula, arrange beef slices over pasta. Spoon sauce over meat and pasta. Sprinkle with parsley.

Per serving: 751 cal., 19% (144 cal.) from fat; 46 g protein; 16 g fat (6 g sat.); 96 g carbo (4.7 g fiber); 1,125 mg sodium; 86 mg chol.

Shortcut Chicken Cassoulet

PREP AND COOK TIME: About 45 minutes
NOTES: Serve with a green salad and crusty bread.
MAKES: 4 servings

- 4 **boned, skinned chicken thighs** (4 oz. each)
- 8 ounces **turkey kielbasa** (Polish) **sausages**
- 1 ounce **French bread**
- 1 teaspoon **olive oil**
- 1 **onion** (8 oz.), peeled and chopped
- 2 **carrots** (8 oz. total), peeled and chopped
- ⅔ cup fat-skimmed **chicken broth**
- 2 teaspoons **fresh thyme** leaves or 1 teaspoon dried thyme
- 1 **dried bay leaf**
- 2 cans (15 oz. each) **cannellini** (white) **beans,** rinsed and drained
- 1 tablespoon chopped **parsley**
  Salt

1. Remove and discard excess fat from chicken; rinse thighs and pat dry. Cut sausages into ½-inch-thick slices.

2. Cut or tear bread into ½-inch chunks. Whirl in a food processor or blender into coarse crumbs; you should have ½ cup. In a 5- to 6-quart nonstick pan over medium-high heat, stir crumbs in ½ teaspoon olive oil until lightly browned and crisp, about 5 minutes. Scrape into a bowl.

3. Return pan to high heat; add remaining ½ teaspoon oil. When hot, add chicken and sausages; turn occasionally to brown on all sides, 4 to 6

minutes total. As chicken and sausages are browned, transfer to a plate. Add onion and carrots to pan; stir often until onion is limp, about 5 minutes.

4. Add broth, thyme, bay leaf, beans, chicken, and sausages; cover and bring to a boil. Reduce heat to low and simmer, stirring occasionally, until chicken is no longer pink in center of thickest part (cut to test), 5 to 7 minutes.

5. Spoon cassoulet into shallow bowls and sprinkle with toasted bread crumbs and parsley. Add salt to taste.

Per serving: 452 cal., 24% (108 cal.) from fat; 45 g protein; 12 g fat (4 g sat.); 40 g carbo (11 g fiber); 1,003 mg sodium; 125 mg chol.

Coq au Vin

PREP AND COOK TIME: About 45 minutes
NOTES: Serve with mashed potatoes or crusty bread to sop up juices.
MAKES: 4 servings

- 2½ pounds **chicken legs and thighs**
- 2 slices **turkey bacon** (1 oz. total), chopped
- 1 cup **frozen small whole onions** (about 5 oz.), thawed
- 12 ounces **sliced mushrooms** (about 4 cups)
- 2 cups fat-skimmed **chicken broth**
- 1 cup **dry red wine**
- 2 tablespoons Dijon mustard
- 2 sprigs **fresh thyme** (each about 2 in. long), rinsed
- 1 tablespoon **cornstarch**
  Salt and **pepper**

1. Remove and discard skin from chicken; rinse chicken and pat dry. Pull off and discard lumps of fat; with a sharp knife, separate legs and thighs.

2. In a 4- to 6-quart pan over high heat, stir bacon until browned, 2 to 3 minutes. Add onions and mushrooms and stir often until browned, 5 to 6 minutes. Add chicken, broth, wine, mustard, and thyme. Cover and bring to a boil, then reduce heat and simmer until chicken is no longer pink at the bone (cut to test), 20 to 25 minutes.

3. With a slotted spoon, remove chicken from pan and divide equally among four bowls. Increase heat to high and boil liquid and vegetables to concentrate flavors, about 5 minutes.

4. In a small bowl, blend cornstarch with 2 tablespoons water until smooth. Add to broth mixture and stir until it boils and thickens, about 1 minute. Add salt and pepper to taste. Spoon sauce equally over chicken.

Per serving: 281 cal., 25% (70 cal.) from fat; 40 g protein; 7.8 g fat (1.9 g sat.); 9.8 g carbo (1.7 g fiber); 463 mg sodium; 135 mg chol.

Quick cassoulet is packed with the earthy flavor of its long-cooked counterpart.

Sardine Factory Cioppino

PREP AND COOK TIME: About 40 minutes
NOTES: This is a streamlined version of chef Bert Cutino's cioppino from the Monterey, California, restaurant he cofounded. Have the crabs cleaned and cracked at the seafood market. If desired, ask for the crab butter; press it through a fine strainer and stir it into the broth just before adding the fish in step 2.

MAKES: 6 servings

- 1 tablespoon **olive oil**
- 1 cup chopped **onion** (5 oz.)
- 1 tablespoon minced **garlic**
- 2 cups **dry white wine**
- 1 pound **firm-ripe tomatoes,** rinsed and chopped, or 1 can (14½ oz.) diced tomatoes
- ½ cup **tomato paste**
- 2 tablespoons minced **fresh basil** leaves or 2 teaspoons dried basil
- ½ teaspoon **pepper**
  Salt
- 1 pound **firm, white-fleshed fish** such as halibut
- ½ pound (26 to 30 per lb.) **shelled, deveined shrimp**
- ½ pound **scallops** (1½ in. wide)
- 1 **cooked Dungeness crab** (2 lb.), cleaned and cracked (see notes)
- 1½ pounds **clams in shells** (1 to 1½ in. wide), suitable for steaming
- ¼ cup chopped **parsley**
- 1 loaf (1 lb.) **crusty bread**
  Lemon wedges

Basil-rich fresh tomato broth in seafood cioppino calls for a crusty loaf of bread.

1. Pour olive oil into a 5- to 6-quart pan over medium-high heat; when hot, add onion and garlic and stir often until onion is limp, 3 to 5 minutes. Add wine, tomatoes (with their juice if canned), tomato paste, basil, and pepper; bring mixture to a boil over high heat, then reduce heat and simmer, stirring often, for 10 minutes. Add salt to taste.

2. Meanwhile, rinse and drain fish, shrimp, scallops, and crab; cut fish into 1- to 2-inch pieces. Scrub clams. Gently stir fish, shrimp, scallops, and clams into tomato broth; cover and simmer just until fish, shrimp, and scallops are opaque but still moist-looking in center of thickest part (cut to test) and clams have popped open, 7 to 9 minutes. Discard any clams that don't open. Add crab and press gently to immerse in broth; cover and cook just until hot, 2 to 3 minutes.

3. Ladle cioppino into wide bowls and sprinkle with parsley. Serve with bread and lemon wedges.

Per serving: 532 cal., 15% (79 cal.) from fat; 48 g protein; 8.8 g fat (1.5 g sat.); 51 g carbo (4.9 g fiber); 896 mg sodium; 136 mg chol. ◆

Low-fat diet watch: Good news

■ According to conventional wisdom, the key to weight loss is reducing the amount of fat calories in your diet. Our standard for a low-fat dish at *Sunset* is less than 30 percent of calories from fat, but stringent weight-loss programs may restrict people to as little as 20 percent. Recent research, however, suggests that the more moderate (and much more satisfying) approach is actually more effective: More people are able to lose weight *and keep it off* on a moderate-fat diet than on a very low-fat diet. In a study by Harvard Medical School researchers published in the *International Journal of Obesity,* only one in five participants

stuck with a diet that restricted fat intake to 20 percent of its 1,200 to 1,500 daily calories; more than half stayed with the plan (and maintained a significant weight loss) when 35 percent of those calories came from fat.

Assuming the fats are the right kind (mono- and polyunsaturated, from sources like olive, canola, peanut, corn, and soybean oils; avocados, olives, and nuts; and fish), a moderate-fat diet can actually be healthier for your heart than an extremely low-fat regimen. That's the good news from a study at Pennsylvania State University published in the *American Journal of Clinical Nutrition.*

Two-Tone
Puff Straws

FOOD STYLING: BASIL FRIEDMAN

Cheese straw comeback

A favorite party nibble takes on new shapes and flavors

By Linda Lau Anusasananan • Photographs by Kevin Candland

With the return of the cocktail party comes the rebirth of that old-fashioned appetizer, the cheese straw. Slender, crisp wands of pastry, cheese straws make the perfect companion to a martini or a glass of wine.

But think of classic cheddar—albeit tasty—only for starters. These sticks take well to many flavors, from savory to sweet. We've twisted tomato-basil straws, rolled out curry-seasoned ones, and spritzed blue cheese versions, from homemade pastry, purchased puff pastry, and butter-rich cookie dough. The mildly sweet variations are at home paired with cheeses. The sugar-crusted straws turn ice cream or fruit into a lively dessert.

Two-Tone Puff Straws

PREP AND COOK TIME: About 45 minutes
NOTES: If making up to two days ahead, cool and store airtight at room temperature; freeze to store longer.
MAKES: 14 straws

1 sheet **puff pastry** (half of a 17.3-oz. package), at room temperature

1 **large egg,** beaten to blend
Seasoning mix (see above right)

1½ teaspoons **coarse salt** or 1 tablespoon coarse sugar

1. Unfold pastry sheet; lay flat on a lightly floured board. Roll into a ¹⁄₁₆-inch-thick rectangle (10 by 14 in.); cut in half crosswise. Lightly brush both halves with egg. Sprinkle one evenly with seasoning mix. Set remaining half, egg side down, over seasoned half, aligning edges. Gently roll to seal layers without enlarging rectangle.

2. Cut rectangle lengthwise into ½-inch-wide strips. Brush tops lightly with more egg; save remaining egg for other uses or discard. Sprinkle strips evenly with salt (or sugar if using a sweet seasoning mix); with your hand, press lightly into surface of puff pastry.

3. One at a time, pick up strips by both ends, twist in opposite directions, and transfer to buttered 12- by 15-inch baking sheets (you'll need two), placing strips about 1½ inches apart. Press ends onto sheets. (See photo below.)

4. Bake salt-crusted straws in a 400° regular or convection oven (sugar-crusted ones at 350°) until crisp and lightly browned, 8 to 13 minutes (14 to 20 minutes for sweet), switching pan positions halfway through baking. Let straws cool about 1 minute on sheets, then, with a wide spatula, loosen while still warm and transfer to rack (if straws stick, return pans briefly to oven to reheat). Serve warm or cool.

Pastry Straws

PREP AND COOK TIME: 50 to 60 minutes
NOTES: If making up to 3 days ahead, cool and store airtight at room temperature; freeze to store longer.
MAKES: About 4 dozen straws

> About 1½ cups **all-purpose flour**
> **Seasoning mix** (see right)
> ½ teaspoon **salt**
> ½ cup (¼ lb.) cold **butter** or margarine, cut into ½-inch pieces
> 1 tablespoon **sesame seeds** or coarse sugar
> 1 **large egg**, beaten to blend

1. In a food processor or bowl, combine 1½ cups flour (1¼ cups if using Cornmeal-Parmesan Seasoning Mix), seasoning mix, and salt; whirl or stir to blend. Add butter and pulse or cut in with a pastry blender until mixture forms ¼-inch crumbs.

2. Sprinkle 3 tablespoons cold water (or lemon juice, if using Lemon-Anise Seasoning Mix) over mixture and pulse or mix with a fork until evenly moistened. Gently squeeze about ¼ cup of the dough into a ball; if it won't hold together, crumble lump back into bowl, sprinkle with 1 to 2 more tablespoons cold water, and pulse or mix again until dough is evenly moistened and holds together.

Sweet or savory

puff pastry twists

cookie-press spritz straws

rolled-and-cut strips

3. With lightly floured hands, press dough into a ball; dust lightly with flour and press into a ½-inch-thick rectangle (4½ by 6½ in.). Press edges to make smooth.

4. On a lightly floured board, with a lightly floured rolling pin, roll dough firmly but gently in short strokes from the center outward into a ⅛-inch-thick rectangle (10 by 12 in.). Trim edges to make even. Sprinkle sesame seeds (or coarse sugar, if using Lemon-Anise Seasoning Mix) evenly over dough and roll lightly into surface without enlarging rectangle.

5. With a fluted pastry wheel or a knife, cut rectangle in half crosswise, then cut lengthwise across whole rectangle into ½-inch-wide strips. Brush lightly with beaten egg; save remaining egg for other uses or discard. One at a time, lift strips by both ends and transfer to 12-by 15-inch baking sheets (you'll need two), spacing about 1 inch apart.

6. Bake savory straws in a 375° regular or convection oven (sweet ones at 350°) until lightly browned and crisp, 12 to 20 minutes. Cool on sheets 1 minute, then transfer to racks with a wide spatula. Serve warm or cool.

Golden Spritz Straws

PREP AND COOK TIME: About 45 minutes
NOTES: If making up to 3 days ahead, cool and store airtight at room temperature; freeze to store longer.
MAKES: 20 to 24 straws

> ½ cup (¼ lb.) **butter** or margarine, at room temperature
> ⅓ cup **granulated sugar**
> 1 **large egg**
> 1¼ cups **all-purpose flour**
> 1 tablespoon **coarse sugar**

1. In a bowl, with a mixer on high speed, beat butter and granulated sugar until creamy. Add egg; beat until well blended. Stir in flour, then beat until well blended.

2. Scrape dough into a cookie press fitted with a rosette or star-shaped tip (½ in. across widest dimension). Press dough through tip in straight lines 6 to 8 inches long onto 12- by 15-inch baking sheets (you'll need two), spacing about 1½ inches apart. Sprinkle spritz straws with coarse sugar.

3. Bake in a 350° regular or 325° convection oven until straws are golden brown, 12 to 19 minutes, switching pan positions halfway through baking. With a wide spatula, transfer straws to racks to cool. Serve warm or cool.

CLASSIC CHEDDAR SEASONING MIX. In a small bowl, mix ¾ cup **shredded sharp cheddar cheese** and ¼ teaspoon **cayenne**.
Per straw: 42 cal., 57% (24 cal.) from fat; 1.0 g protein; 2.7 g fat (1.6 g sat.); 3.4 g carbo (0.1 g fiber); 56 mg sodium; 11 mg chol.

CURRY SEASONING MIX. In a small bowl, mix 2 teaspoons **curry powder** and ¼ teaspoon **cayenne**.
Per straw: 36 cal., 53% (19 cal.) from fat; 0.6 g protein; 2.1 g fat (1.2 g sat.); 3.5 g carbo (0.2 g fiber); 45 mg sodium; 8.8 mg chol.

CORNMEAL-PARMESAN SEASONING MIX. In a small bowl, mix ½ cup **grated parmesan cheese**, ¼ cup **yellow cornmeal**, and 2 teaspoons **Italian seasoning** (or 1 teaspoon *each* dried basil and dried oregano).
Per straw: 40 cal., 55% (22 cal.) from fat; 0.9 g protein; 2.4 g fat (1.4 g sat.); 3.5 g carbo (0.1 g fiber); 61 mg sodium; 9.4 mg chol.

LEMON-ANISE SEASONING MIX. In a small bowl, mix ⅓ cup **granulated sugar**, 2 teaspoons grated **lemon** peel, and 1½ teaspoons **anise seeds**.
Per straw: 41 cal., 44% (18 cal.) from fat; 0.6 g protein; 2 g fat (1.2 g sat.); 5.1 g carbo (0.1 g fiber); 45 mg sodium; 8.8 mg chol.

Per straw: 73 cal., 51% (37 cal.) from fat; 1.0 g protein; 4.1 g fat (2.5 g sat.); 8.2 g carbo (0.2 g fiber); 42 mg sodium; 19 mg chol.

Blue Cheese Spritz Straws

Follow recipe for **Golden Spritz Straws** (preceding), but reduce **butter** to ⅓ cup, replace granulated sugar with ½ cup **crumbled blue cheese** (2½ oz.), and replace coarse sugar with 2 tablespoons finely chopped **almonds**.
Per straw: 64 cal., 56% (36 cal.) from fat; 1.7 g protein; 4 g fat (2.2 g sat.); 5.2 g carbo (0.2 g fiber); 70 mg sodium; 18 mg chol.

Gingersnap Spritz Straws

Follow recipe for **Golden Spritz Straws** (preceding), but substitute 1 **large egg** yolk and 3 tablespoons **light molasses** for the egg, and add 2 teaspoons **ground ginger**, ½ teaspoon **ground cinnamon**, and ¼ teaspoon **ground allspice** to the flour. Bake until edges turn slightly darker.
Per straw: 80 cal., 46% (37 cal.) from fat; 0.8 g protein; 4.1 g fat (2.5 g sat.); 10 g carbo (0.2 g fiber); 41 mg sodium; 19 mg chol. ◆

food guide

By Jerry Anne Di Vecchio

Crab salad

Put the citrus squeeze on shellfish

From late fall into very early spring—peaking about now, in fact—the flavor of certain kinds of citrus is at its best, and the fruits' membrane walls are packed to bursting with juice. It's prime time for grapefruit and tangy, vibrant blood oranges.

Dungeness crab has a shorter period of plenty, but the Dungeness harvests along the Pacific Coast are cresting right now, bringing the best-quality, best-priced, meatiest crabs to market.

This serendipitous overlap makes possible a marvelous main-dish salad. You can cook and shell your own crab (my favorite option) for the best value and taste. Or you can purchase shelled cooked crab—in which case you'll appreciate how the rice extends the crab, and therefore the satisfaction factor of the salad, while keeping the cost of ingredients under control.

Dungeness Crab and Winter Citrus Salad

PREP AND COOK TIME: About 1 hour

NOTES: You can cook and season the rice (steps 1 and 2) up to 1 day ahead; when cool, cover and chill. Sliced pickled ginger (the pale pink kind served with sushi) is available canned in many supermarkets and refrigerated in Asian food markets; daikon sprouts are also available in Asian markets, but as an alternative you can use 2 cups rinsed and drained watercress leaves. To economize on the crab, you can replace part with chilled shelled cooked tiny shrimp.

MAKES: 4 to 6 servings

- 1 cup **long-grain white rice**
- 2 cups fat-skimmed **chicken broth**
- 6 tablespoons **rice vinegar**
- 1 tablespoon **sugar**
  About ⅓ cup **sliced pickled ginger**
- 1 **red bell pepper** (8 oz.), rinsed, stemmed, seeded, and finely chopped
- 2 or 3 **ruby grapefruit** (2 to 3 lb. total) or 4 to 6 blood oranges (1½ to 2¼ lb. total)
- 1 pound **shelled cooked Dungeness crab** (about 2¼ cups; see notes)
  Sesame Cream Dressing (recipe follows)
  About 8 ounces **daikon sprouts**, root ends trimmed, rinsed and drained (see notes)

1. In a 1½- to 2-quart pan, combine rice and broth. Bring to a boil over high heat, then reduce heat to very low, cover pan, and cook until liquid is absorbed and rice is just tender to bite, about 20 minutes.

2. Meanwhile, in a wide bowl, mix rice vinegar with sugar. When rice is cooked, spoon it at once into bowl; mix with a fork. Let stand until lukewarm or cooler, about 30 minutes. Sliver ⅓ cup pickled ginger and add, along with bell pepper, to rice mixture. Stir with a fork to loosen rice grains and mix.

3. As rice mixture cools, with a sharp knife, cut peel and outer membrane from grapefruit, then cut between segments and inner membranes to release fruit; drop into a bowl. Discard peel and membranes. Sort through crab and remove and discard any bits of shell.

4. Mound rice mixture equally on dinner plates; top with crab and grapefruit segments. Spoon juice from grapefruit segments and the Sesame Cream Dressing evenly over salads; garnish with daikon sprouts and pickled ginger slices.

Per serving: 415 cal., 30% (126 cal.) from fat; 23 g protein; 14 g fat (2.1 g sat.); 50 g carbo (1.3 g fiber); 1,058 mg sodium; 76 mg chol.

Sesame Cream Dressing. In a bowl, whisk ½ cup **reduced-fat** or regular **mayonnaise**, 6 tablespoons **reduced-sodium soy sauce**, ¼ cup **rice vinegar**, 3 tablespoons **Asian** (toasted) **sesame oil**, and 1 tablespoon firmly packed **brown sugar** until smooth. If making up to 1 day ahead, cover and chill. Makes 1 cup.

Per tablespoon: 49 cal., 73% (36 cal.) from fat; 0.3 g protein; 4 g fat (0.6 g sat.); 2.9 g carbo (0 g fiber); 285 mg sodium; 0 mg chol.

Whip up a dessert

■ Back in June 1956, the closest you could come in this country to France's crème fraîche was a firm, whipped mixture of cream cheese and sweet cream that we introduced as the filling for an incredibly popular recipe called French Cherry Pie. Recently, however, I discovered a way to smooth out what was an admittedly lumpy part of the process—folding the soft whipped cream into the firmer beaten cream cheese: You add the cream as you beat the cheese to soften it; the two whip up together, producing smoother, fluffier results.

Simplified, the French Cream is a classic—and particularly good with blueberries. I spoon it into bowls and top it with fresh Blueberry Pudding (recipe follows) or reverse the process and spoon the cream over the fruit.

French Cream

PREP TIME: **5 to 8 minutes**

NOTES: You can make the cream up to 1 day ahead; cover and chill. If mixture softens, whisk to thicken.

MAKES: **2 cups**

- 1 package (3 oz.) **cream cheese,** chilled
- 1 cup **whipping cream**
- ½ teaspoon grated **lemon** peel
- 1 tablespoon **lemon juice**
- 3 to 4 tablespoons **powdered sugar**

1. Chill a deep bowl and the rotary or whip beater of a mixer for at least 10 minutes.
2. Put cream cheese in bowl and mix on high speed with rotary or whip beater until cheese is spread around base of bowl. With mixer on high speed, pour cream down the side of the bowl (not into beaters) into the cheese, slowly enough that the cheese stays thick and forms ridges like stiffly whipped cream as you beat it;

scrape sides of bowl as necessary.
3. When all the cream is whipped into the cheese, turn off mixer. Add lemon peel, lemon juice, and powdered sugar to taste; mix at medium speed to blend.

Per tablespoon: 34 cal., 85% (29 cal.) from fat; 0.4 g protein; 3.2 g fat (2 g sat.); 1 g carbo (0 g fiber); 11 mg sodium; 11 mg chol.

Blueberry Pudding with French Cream. Sort 2 cups **blueberries** (fresh or partially thawed frozen), discarding any stems and decayed fruit; rinse and drain fresh berries. In a 1½- to 2-quart pan, combine ½ cup of the blueberries, ⅓ cup **sugar,** 1 tablespoon **cornstarch,** ½ teaspoon *each* grated **orange** and **lemon** peel, ½ cup **orange juice,** and 1 tablespoon **lemon juice.** Stir over high heat until boiling, about 3 minutes. Add remaining berries and stir just until mixture boils again. Stir in 1 teaspoon **vanilla.** Pour into bowls. Serve hot, warm, or cool, topped with **French Cream** (recipe precedes). Makes about 2 cups; 4 servings.

Per serving without cream: 134 cal., 24% (32 cal.) from fat; 1.1 g protein; 3.5 g fat (2 g sat.); 33 g carbo (1.8 g fiber); 17 mg sodium; 11 mg chol.

Authenticity in a box

■ Four simple grain mixes from Neera's Spice of Life collection bring the bold, rich flavors of India to your table: Indian urad and channa dal (8.5 oz.; 7 servings), Indian shahi pilau (9.5 oz.; 4 servings), Indian dal with chaunk (7 oz.; 5 servings), and northern Indian biryani (8.5 oz.; 5 servings). They use many ingredients and seasonings that are rarely found in every-day markets. Interestingly, though, the mixes do not include salt (overused in so many packaged products); instead, you add it to your taste. I prepared each of the four as directed; then, on a second round, I cut back on the oil by about half and found the results equally satisfying. Don't ignore the instruction to rinse the grains well, however; it's an important step. While the mixes are slightly more costly than instant risottos and pilafs, they bring you dishes that are still much easier than those prepared from scratch. To order, call (800) 824-4563 or go to www.cinnabarfoods.com.

Little bells

■ At a food show last spring, a colorful display caught my eye. At first glance, I thought I was seeing mounds of fresh chilies. Closer inspection brought a sweet surprise: The shiny, bright red, yellow, and orange vegetables weren't chilies at all—they were bell-type peppers, similar in shape to fresh jalapeño chilies (with very few seeds). From 2 to 4 inches long, they make two or three bites—an ideal size for appetizers and salads. Stuffed with a rice filling and baked, they make a handsome, delectable garnish around a roast.

Master's Touch grows the little peppers in Mexico and Florida, labels them VineSweet Mini-Peppers, and distributes them year-round to chain supermarkets and warehouse stores such as Costco.

Add a little novelty to your table: orange, red, and yellow bite-size sweet peppers.

Stuffed Sweet Mini-Peppers

PREP AND COOK TIME: About 1 hour

NOTES: Assemble through step 2 up to 1 day ahead, cover, and chill; uncover to bake.

MAKES: 4 or 5 appetizer servings

  1 **onion** (about 6 oz.), peeled and diced
     About 3 tablespoons **olive oil**
  ½ cup **long-grain white rice**
  ¼ cup **pine nuts**

     About 1 cup fat-skimmed **chicken broth** or vegetable broth
  1 **dried bay leaf** (3 to 4 in. long)
  ½ teaspoon **dried thyme**
     Salt
 12 to 15 **sweet mini-peppers** (each 3 to 4 in. long; red, yellow, or orange), halved lengthwise and seeded

1. In an 8- to 10-inch frying pan over high heat, stir onion in 1½ tablespoons olive oil often until lightly browned, 5 to 6 minutes. Add rice and pine nuts and stir until some of the rice is opaque and nuts are slightly browned, 2 to 3 minutes. Add broth, bay leaf, and thyme; stir, then cover. When boiling, turn heat to low and simmer, stirring occasionally, until rice is tender to bite, about 15 minutes; add 2 to 4 more tablespoons broth if liquid is absorbed before rice is tender. Remove from heat. Add salt to taste.

2. Lay half the pepper halves side by side, cut side up, in a shallow 8- by 12-inch casserole or pan. Mound rice filling equally in peppers, using it all. Lay remaining pepper halves, cut side down, on rice filling, matching sizes and shapes to bottom halves. Drizzle peppers with 1½ to 2 tablespoons olive oil.

3. Bake in a 375° regular or convection oven until peppers are soft and slightly browned, about 30 minutes. With a wide spatula, transfer filled peppers to a platter or plates. Serve hot, warm, or at room temperature.

Per serving: 208 cal., 52% (108 cal.) from fat; 5.4 g protein; 12 g fat (1.7 g sat.); 22 g carbo (2.2 g fiber); 18 mg sodium; 0 mg chol.

Frieda's finds

■ In 1962, Frieda Caplan launched kiwi fruit into the supermarket and onto our plates. She followed up with a trail of fresh produce, from jicama to lemon grass to spaghetti squash, that had largely been ignored by

major distributors. Thanks to Frieda, shopping for these foods is now a lot easier, and eating is more fun. And like mother, like daughter: Karen Caplan, current president of Frieda's, has just written a handy paperback, *The Purple Kiwi Cookbook* (Frieda's, Los Alamitos, CA, 2001; $16.95; 800/241-1771 or www.purplekiwicookbook.com), that offers more than 120 simple recipes from the company's test kitchens for 58 unusual fruits and vegetables now available.

Armed but not dangerous

■ It would be hard to find a more defensive-looking comestible than rambutan. But the tropical fruit's spiny, leathery shell protects exceptionally juicy, translucent white flesh. A rambutan looks (inside, at least) and tastes much like fragrant litchi fruit and, like a litchi, has a single large seed. What do you do with rambutans? Just peel and eat—they're too special and rare to dilute with fussy recipes.

U.S. agricultural quarantines have prohibited importing fresh rambutans from their native Southeast Asia, but the fruit is now grown in Hawaii. It's available from sources like Melissa's Specialty Produce (800/588-0151 or www.melissas. com) from October through early spring. ◆

Spicy chicken can be made ahead, then baked on chips and topped with cream at the last minute.

Easy entertaining with appetizers

Get a step ahead with these stylish, crowd-pleasing nibbles

By Paula Freschet • Photographs by James Carrier • Food styling by Basil Friedman

One of the friendliest ways to throw a party is to stick with appetizers. Set plates of them around the room, and it will be natural for your guests to circulate and strike up conversations.

Here are some nibbles that will give them something wonderful to talk about. Each has steps built in that you can do ahead—a sauce here, a whole recipe there—to keep the day of the party sane. Choose a couple of the appetizers for a short and sweet occasion; offer all if you want your guests to linger and consider it dinner.

Roast Chicken– Chipotle Nachos with Cilantro-Avocado Crema

PREP AND COOK TIME: About 35 minutes

NOTES: Purchase a roast chicken from a deli; a 2-pound bird produces about 3 cups shredded meat. You can make the chicken-chipotle mixture (step 1) up to 2 days ahead; cool, cover, and chill. Use cold; bake nachos in a 425° oven for 6 to 8 minutes. You can make the crema up to 2 hours ahead; cover and chill.

MAKES: 24 nachos; 8 servings

- ½ cup chopped **onion**
- 1 tablespoon **olive oil**
- ½ teaspoon **cumin seeds**
- ½ teaspoon **dried oregano**
- 1 to 2 **canned chipotle chilies,** chopped
- 2 tablespoons **tomato paste**
- 1 tablespoon **white wine vinegar**
- 2 cups bite-size shreds skinned **cooked chicken** (see notes)
- 24 **corn tortilla chips** (2¾ in. wide)
- 1½ cups **shredded jack cheese** (6 oz.)
  Cilantro-Avocado Crema (recipe follows)
- 24 **fresh cilantro** leaves

1. In a 2½- to 3-quart pan over medium-high heat, frequently stir onion in olive oil until onion begins to brown, 4 to 7 minutes. Add cumin seeds and oregano; stir until fragrant, about 30 seconds. Add chilies, tomato paste, vinegar, and ½ cup water; bring to a boil, then reduce heat and simmer gently, stirring often, to blend flavors, about 5 minutes. Add chicken and stir until hot.

2. Meanwhile, arrange tortilla chips in a single layer in a 12- by 17-inch pan. Sprinkle equal portions of cheese on each chip and spoon about 1 tablespoon chicken mixture on top.

3. Bake in a 450° regular or convection oven until cheese begins to bubble, about 3 minutes. With a spatula, carefully transfer tortilla chips to a platter. Top each with 1 teaspoon Cilantro-Avocado Crema and garnish with a cilantro leaf. Serve warm.

Per serving: 219 cal., 58% (126 cal.) from fat; 16 g protein; 14 g fat (5.6 g sat.); 6.7 g carbo (0.9 g fiber); 227 mg sodium; 55 mg chol.

Cilantro-Avocado Crema. In a small bowl, mix ⅓ cup finely diced **firm-ripe avocado,** 2 tablespoons **sour cream,** 1 tablespoon finely chopped **fresh cilantro** leaves, 2 teaspoons **lime juice,** and 2 teaspoons **milk.** Add **salt** to taste. Makes about ½ cup.

Tomatoes on polenta and mushrooms on crostini can be cooked ahead.

Wild Mushroom–Chèvre Crostini

PREP AND COOK TIME: About 50 minutes

NOTES: You can toast the baguette slices (step 1) and make the mushroom topping (steps 2 and 3) up to 1 day ahead. Allow both to cool before storing. Keep toast airtight at room temperature. Cover and chill mushrooms; reheat in a microwave oven at full power (100%), stirring occasionally, 4 to 5 minutes.

MAKES: 24 crostini; 8 to 12 servings

2 dozen **baguette** slices (cut diagonally ¼ in. thick and 3 in. long; about 8 oz. total)

1 tablespoon **olive oil**

12 ounces **fresh mushrooms** (chanterelle, crimini, morel, oyster, porcini, shiitake, or common; choose about three kinds)

1 tablespoon **butter** or margarine

1 tablespoon minced **garlic**

¼ cup minced **shallots**

1 teaspoon **dried thyme**

¼ cup **dry white wine**

¼ cup fat-skimmed **chicken broth** or vegetable broth

1 tablespoon **balsamic vinegar**

Salt and **pepper**

4 ounces **fresh chèvre** (goat) **cheese**

1 tablespoon chopped **parsley**

1. Arrange baguette slices in a single layer on a 12- by 15-inch baking sheet. Brush tops lightly with oil. Bake on the middle rack in a 350° regular or convection oven until golden, 15 to 20 minutes.

2. Meanwhile, trim and discard discolored stem ends, bits of debris, and bruised spots from mushrooms (for shiitakes, remove entire stem). Rinse mushrooms well and drain. Cut mushrooms larger than ½ inch into ¼- inch-thick slices; leave smaller ones whole.

3. In a 10- to 12-inch frying pan over medium-high heat, melt butter; add garlic and stir often until fragrant, about 1 minute. Add mushrooms, shallots, and thyme; stir often until liquid is evaporated and mushrooms are well browned, about 10 minutes. Add wine, broth, and vinegar and stir to release browned bits; boil until liquid is evaporated, 4 to 6 minutes. Add salt and pepper to taste. Keep warm over low heat, stirring occasionally.

4. Spread chèvre equally on toasted baguette slices. Spoon warm mushroom mixture equally over cheese. Sprinkle evenly with parsley. Serve warm.

Per serving: 111 cal., 37% (41 cal.) from fat; 4.4 g protein; 4.6 g fat (2.2 g sat.); 12 g carbo (0.8 g fiber); 165 mg sodium; 6.9 mg chol.

Panko-crusted Crab Cake Bites with Roasted Pepper–Chive Aioli

PREP AND COOK TIME: 35 to 40 minutes

NOTES: The Japanese-style coarse bread crumbs called panko are available in many well-stocked supermarkets and in Asian grocery stores. You can make the aioli up to 2 days ahead and the crab cakes through step 3 up to 4 hours ahead; in both cases, cover and chill.

MAKES: 24 crab cakes; 8 servings

12 ounces **shelled cooked crab**

¼ cup finely diced **celery**

¼ cup minced **fresh chives**

¼ cup **mayonnaise**

1 **large egg**

2 teaspoons **Dijon mustard**

¼ teaspoon **hot sauce**

1¼ cups **panko** (see notes) or fine dried bread crumbs

Roasted Pepper–Chive Aioli (recipe follows)

Fresh chives, rinsed and cut into 1-inch lengths

1. Sort through crab and discard any bits of shell.

2. In a large bowl, combine celery, minced chives, mayonnaise, egg, mustard, and hot sauce; mix well with a fork. Add crab and ¼ cup panko; stir gently just to mix.

3. Put remaining 1 cup panko in a shallow bowl. Shape crab mixture into 24 cakes, each about 2 inches wide and ½ inch thick. Turn each cake in panko to coat on all sides, pressing gently to make crumbs adhere. Place cakes slightly apart in an oiled 12- by 17-inch baking pan.

4. Bake in a 475° regular or convection oven until golden brown, 15 to 18 minutes. With a spatula, transfer crab cakes to a platter. Spoon a dollop of Roasted Pepper–Chive Aioli onto each cake. Garnish platter with fresh chives. Serve hot.

Per serving: 206 cal., 61% (126 cal.) from fat; 11 g protein; 14 g fat (2.2 g sat.); 7.6 g carbo (0.5 g fiber); 290 mg sodium; 79 mg chol.

Roasted Pepper–Chive Aioli. In a small bowl, mix ⅓ cup **mayonnaise**, ¼ cup chopped drained **canned roasted red peppers**, 1 tablespoon minced **fresh chives**, 2 teaspoons **lemon juice**, and 1 teaspoon minced **garlic**. Makes about ½ cup.

Parmesan Polenta Pizzas with Slow-roasted Pesto Tomatoes

PREP AND COOK TIME: About 2¼ hours

NOTES: For polenta rounds, buy two tubes (about 2 in. diameter; 2 lb. total) prepared polenta; cut into ⅜-inch-thick slices, discarding ends. It's worth spending a little extra for high-quality parmesan cheese (preferably Parmigiano reggiano) for this dish; grate just before using. You can prepare the roasted tomatoes for the pizzas up to 1 day ahead; when cool, cover and chill.

MAKES: 24 pizzas; 8 servings

Crab cakes are baked, not fried—in bite-size rounds for easy nibbling out of hand, aioli and all.

12 **Roma tomatoes** (about 3 oz. each)

Fresh-ground **pepper**

About ¼ cup **purchased** or homemade **pesto**

24 rounds (each about 2 in. wide and ⅜ in. thick) **purchased cooked polenta** (see notes)

1 cup grated **parmesan cheese** (about 3 oz.; see notes)

1. Rinse tomatoes, cut in half lengthwise, and place cut side up in an oiled 10- by 15-inch pan. Sprinkle lightly with pepper. Spread about ½ teaspoon pesto onto cut side of each tomato half.

2. Bake tomatoes in a 350° regular or convection oven until browned on top and slightly shriveled, 1½ to 2 hours (if pan juices begin to scorch, add a few tablespoons water to pan). Let tomatoes cool about 10 minutes.

3. Place polenta rounds slightly apart on an oiled 12- by 17-inch baking sheet. Sprinkle ½ cup parmesan cheese evenly over rounds. Set a tomato half, pesto side up, on each and sprinkle remaining ½ cup cheese on top.

4. Bake polenta pizzas in a 450° regular or convection oven until cheese is melted and beginning to brown, 10 to 13 minutes. Let cool 2 to 3 minutes, then transfer with a spatula to a platter.

Per serving: 188 cal., 36% (68 cal.) from fat; 7.5 g protein; 7.5 g fat (2.5 g sat.); 22 g carbo (3.5 g fiber); 427 mg sodium; 8.5 mg chol. ◆

Close-in counters

Take a front-row seat at these San Francisco restaurants

By Chiori Santiago

Dining at a restaurant counter is not for the timid. Let others huddle around the table, safe in the companionable crowd. At a counter you'll find independent folks who enjoy being close to slinging hash, feeling the heat of the grill, and watching the transformation of ingredients from raw state to dinner plate. At five San Francisco eateries, take a front-row seat to see a riveting choreography of cuisine.

A steamy drama unfolds on the other side of the counter at **Ella's,** where a fast-stepping staff prepares fixings for the evening meal while you're chewing breakfast. Peer over your plate to see the deft hands of prep chef Samuel Ramirez shape cornmeal-molasses dough into fat hamburger buns. Behind him, fellow cooks pull some of the 22 chickens for tonight's pot pie from a boiling vat.

At **Swan Oyster Depot,** the lunch line stretches up the block as seafood fans wait for a coveted seat at the long marble counter. Hulking guys serve up platters of prawns, steamed crabs, and just-shucked oysters glistening in brine. If you have a soft heart, be forewarned: The food's so fresh that your lobster will wave goodbye as it heads to the kettle.

St. Francis Fountain in the Mission District serves a scoop of nostalgia with your banana split. Aside from the prices, hardly anything has changed since it opened in 1918. Your root beer isn't poured from a can; it's mixed individually with a squirt of syrup from the array of silvery dispensers behind the laminated counter. Even the cash register is hand-cranked.

Blue Plate offers classic diner dishes with a nouvelle twist. A six-seat counter puts you inches from the kitchen; you'll feel the same inferno blast that chef-owner Cory Obenour experiences every time he opens the oven for a tray of rosemary flatbread or meatloaf. "You can tell me exactly how you want your food; there's nothing between the cooks and the customer," he says.

Sushi counters are everywhere, but a particularly memorable one is at **Chaya Brasserie.** Most diners opt for a table, so those who walk up can generally find a seat at the sycamore counter. Watch sushi chefs slice rectangles of hamachi into artful bites while you contemplate a view of the Bay Bridge and blue water. ◆

Pull up a chair

You won't need a reservation to sit at these counters, but on busy weekend evenings (or anytime at Swan), you may have to wait for a ringside seat. **Blue Plate.** 6 P.M.–10 P.M. Mon–Sat. 3218 Mission St.; (415) 282-6777. **Chaya Brasserie.** 11:30–2:30 Mon–Fri, 5:30–10 Mon–Wed, 5:30–10:30 Thu–Sat, 5–9 Sun. 132 Embarcadero; (415) 777-8688. **Ella's.** 7 A.M.–9 P.M. Mon–Fri, 8:30–2 Sat–Sun. 500 Presidio Ave.; (415) 441-5669. **St. Francis Fountain.** 7–6 Mon–Fri, 8:30–6 Sat–Sun. 2801 24th St.; (415) 826-4200. **Swan Oyster Depot.** Clam chowder all day. 8–5:30 Mon–Sat. 1517 Polk St.; (415) 673-1101.

Kitchen Cabinet

Readers' recipes tested in *Sunset's* kitchens

By Charity Ferreira

Deconstructing dolmas: This salad has all the flavor of stuffed grape leaves but none of the fuss.

JAMES CARRIER; FOOD STYLING: BASIL FRIEDMAN

Dolmas Salad

Sandra Frankmann, Pueblo West, CO

After making dolmas—stuffed grape leaves—Sandra Frankmann didn't want to discard the grape leaf pieces left over. So she combined them with other dolma ingredients into a salad. It would make a wonderful side dish for roasted lamb. Preserved grape leaves are sold in jars in Middle Eastern markets and in many well-stocked supermarkets.

PREP AND COOK TIME: About 1 hour

MAKES: 4 to 6 servings

- ¼ cup **pine nuts** (1 oz.)
- ½ cup thinly sliced **green onions** (white and pale green parts only)
- 1 tablespoon **olive oil**
- 1½ cups **long-grain white rice**
- 2½ cups fat-skimmed **chicken broth** or vegetable broth
- ½ cup chopped **preserved grape leaves** (reserve ¼ cup brine)
- ¼ cup **lemon juice**
- ¼ cup **raisins**
- ¼ teaspoon **pepper**
- ¼ cup chopped **parsley**
- ¼ cup chopped **fresh dill**
- 1 **lemon** (optional), rinsed and quartered

1. In a 4- to 6-quart pan over medium heat, stir pine nuts and ¼ cup green onions in oil until nuts begin to brown and onions are limp, about 5 minutes.

2. Stir in rice, chicken broth, grape leaves and reserved ¼ cup brine, lemon juice, raisins, and pepper. Bring to a boil, then reduce heat to low, cover, and simmer until liquid is absorbed and rice is tender to bite, 30 to 35 minutes.

3. Fluff rice mixture with a fork; stir in parsley, dill, and remaining ¼ cup green onions. Mound salad on a platter and garnish with lemon quarters if desired. Serve warm or at room temperature.

Per serving: 259 cal., 17% (45 cal.) from fat; 8.3 g protein; 5 g fat (0.7 g sat.); 44 g carbo (1.6 g fiber); 385 mg sodium; 0 mg chol.

Artichoke Frittata

Christie Steiner, Ventura, CA

Christie Steiner got the recipe for this garlicky appetizer from her fifth-grade teacher. She has been making it for parties ever since.

PREP AND COOK TIME: About 1¼ hours

MAKES: 12 appetizer servings

- 2 jars (6 oz. each) **marinated artichoke hearts**
- 1 **onion** (8 oz.), peeled and chopped
- 1 tablespoon minced **garlic**
- 6 **large eggs**
- ¼ cup **fine dried bread crumbs**
- ½ teaspoon **hot sauce**
- ¼ teaspoon **salt**
- ¼ teaspoon **pepper**
- ¼ teaspoon **dried oregano**
- 2 cups shredded **cheddar cheese**
- ¼ cup shredded **parmesan cheese**

1. Drain artichoke hearts, reserving 2 tablespoons marinade; discard remaining marinade. Coarsely chop artichoke hearts. In a 10- to 12-inch nonstick, ovenproof frying pan over medium-high heat, frequently stir onion and garlic in reserved marinade until onion is limp, about 5 minutes.

2. Meanwhile, in a large bowl, whisk together eggs, bread crumbs, hot sauce, salt, pepper, oregano, and cheddar cheese. Stir in artichokes. Pour evenly into pan with onion mixture. Sprinkle parmesan cheese over the top.

3. Transfer pan to a 350° regular or convection oven and bake until center of frittata is set and top is lightly

browned, about 30 minutes.

4. Serve warm or at room temperature; cut into 12 wedges.

Per serving: 165 cal., 65% (108 cal.) from fat; 9.7 g protein; 12 g fat (5.4 g sat.); 6.2 g carbo (1.5 g fiber); 399 mg sodium; 127 mg chol.

Bread Pudding with Caramel Sauce

Martha Rowlands, Santa Rosa, CA

This rich, almond-flavored bread pudding is the only version Martha Rowlands makes. She has served it to many guests over the years, always to rave reviews.

PREP AND COOK TIME: About 1¼ hours, plus 30 minutes to rest

MAKES: About 12 servings

- 1 loaf (1½ lb.) **crusty Italian-style bread**
- 5 **large eggs**
- 2 cups **milk**
- 2 cups **half-and-half**
- 1 cup **sugar**
- ¼ cup **amaretto** or other almond-flavored liqueur or 1 tablespoon almond extract
- 2 teaspoons **vanilla**
- ¾ cup **golden raisins**

   Amaretto Caramel Sauce (recipe follows)

1. Cut bread crosswise into 1-inch-thick slices; trim off and discard crusts (or save for other uses) and cut slices into 1-inch cubes.

2. In a bowl, whisk eggs, milk, half-and-half, sugar, amaretto, and vanilla until well combined. Gently stir in raisins and bread cubes just until evenly moistened; pour mixture into a 9- by 13-inch baking pan. Cover loosely and let stand at room temperature for 30 minutes.

3. Bake pudding in a 350° regular or convection oven until center is set (cut to test), about 1 hour. Scoop out portions or cut and lift out with a wide spatula. Serve warm with Amaretto Caramel Sauce.

Per serving: 447 cal., 24% (108 cal.) from fat; 10 g protein; 12 g fat (6.1 g sat.); 73 g carbo (2.1 g fiber); 365 mg sodium; 116 mg chol.

Amaretto Caramel Sauce. In a 1- to 2-quart pan over low heat, stir 1 cup **sugar** and ¼ cup **water** until sugar is dissolved, about 3 minutes. Increase heat to high and boil, without stirring, until the mixture is amber colored, about 8 minutes; remove pan from heat. Meanwhile, in a 1- to 2-quart pan

over medium-high heat, bring ⅓ cup **whipping cream** to a boil. Off the heat, carefully add hot cream and ¼ cup **amaretto** or other almond-flavored liqueur or 1 tablespoon almond extract to the caramelized sugar; stir until blended (the mixture will bubble up). Serve warm. Makes about 1 cup.

Raisin Sauce

Margery Davis Bennett, Anacortes, WA

This simple, old-fashioned spiced raisin sauce has been a longstanding tradition for Margery Davis Bennett's husband. His family enjoys it with cooked turkey or ham.

PREP AND COOK TIME: About 30 minutes

MAKES: 2¼ cups; 8 to 10 servings

- 1 cup **sugar**
- 1 cup **raisins**
- ⅔ cup **apple jelly**
- 3 tablespoons **white wine vinegar**
- 2 tablespoons **butter** or margarine
- 1 tablespoon **lemon juice**
- ¼ teaspoon **ground cloves**
- ¼ teaspoon **mace**
- ¼ teaspoon **salt**
- ⅛ teaspoon **pepper**

In a 2- to 3-quart pan over medium heat, stir sugar and ½ cup water until the sugar is dissolved, about 2 minutes. Add raisins, jelly, vinegar, butter, lemon juice, cloves, mace, salt, and pepper; reduce heat to low and simmer, stirring often, until raisin sauce is reduced to 2¼ cups, about 15 minutes. Serve warm.

Per ¼ cup: 210 cal., 11% (24 cal.) from fat; 0.6 g protein; 2.7 g fat (1.6 g sat.); 49 g carbo (1 g fiber); 99 mg sodium; 6.9 mg chol.

Spice-rubbed Halibut with Ginger-Orange Glaze

Roxanne Chan, Albany, CA

Roxanne Chan gives extra flavor to fish fillets by rubbing them with a dry spice mixture, then saucing them with a sweet and tangy glaze.

PREP AND COOK TIME: About 30 minutes

MAKES: 2 servings

- ¾ pound **halibut** or tilapia (about 1 in. thick), cut into two equal pieces
- ½ teaspoon **coriander**
- ½ teaspoon **ground cumin**
- ½ teaspoon **curry powder**
- ¼ teaspoon **ground ginger**
- ¼ teaspoon **salt**

- ⅛ teaspoon **cayenne**
- ¼ cup **orange juice**
- 3 tablespoons **rice vinegar**
- 3 tablespoons **honey**
- 1 tablespoon minced **fresh ginger**

1. Rinse fish and pat dry.

2. In a small bowl, mix coriander, cumin, curry powder, ground ginger, salt, and cayenne. Rub mixture all over fish. Set pieces slightly apart in an 8-inch square baking pan.

3. Broil 6 inches from heat for 3 minutes. With a wide spatula, turn fish over and broil until opaque but still moist-looking in center of thickest part (cut to test), 3 to 5 minutes longer.

4. Meanwhile, in a 1- to 1½-quart pan over medium heat, bring orange juice, vinegar, honey, and fresh ginger to a boil; stir often until reduced to about ¼ cup, about 10 minutes.

5. With a spatula, transfer fish to dinner plates. Spoon sauce over fish.

Per serving: 305 cal., 12% (37 cal.) from fat; 36 g protein; 4.1 g fat (0.6 g sat.); 31 g carbo (0.4 g fiber); 381 mg sodium; 54 mg chol.

Cranberry Semolina Tea Bread

Jennifer Kirkgaard, Burbank, CA

Jennifer Kirkgaard makes this Italian-inspired loaf all year long, not just during the holidays as you might expect from the cranberries involved. Semolina flour is available in well-stocked supermarkets; if you can't find it, substitute yellow cornmeal.

PREP AND COOK TIME: About 50 minutes

MAKES: 2 loaves (3½ by 7½ in.); 6 to 8 servings total

   About 1 cup **all-purpose flour**
- 1 cup **semolina flour** (see note above)
- 2 teaspoons **baking powder**
- ½ teaspoon **salt**
- 4 **large eggs**
- ⅔ cup **sugar**
- ½ cup **olive oil**
- 2 teaspoons grated **lemon peel**
- 1 tablespoon **vanilla extract**
- 1 teaspoon **almond extract**
- ¾ cup **dried cranberries**
- ½ cup coarsely chopped **unsalted pistachios**

1. Butter and flour two loaf pans (3½ by 7½ in. each).

2. In a large bowl, mix 1 cup all-purpose flour, semolina flour, baking powder,

Kitchen Cabinet

and salt.

3. In another bowl, beat eggs to blend; whisk in sugar, olive oil, lemon peel, and vanilla and almond extracts.

4. Add egg mixture to dry ingredients and stir just until evenly moistened. Gently stir in cranberries and pistachios. Pour batter equally into prepared pans.

5. Bake in a 350° regular or convection oven until bread is golden brown and a wood skewer inserted in center of loaves comes out clean, 20 to 25 minutes. Cool bread in pans on a rack for 10 minutes. Run a knife between bread and pan sides, then invert pans to release bread; set loaves upright on rack. Serve warm or at room temperature.

Per serving: 442 cal., 43% (189 cal.) from fat; 8.7 g protein; 21 g fat (3.7 g sat.); 54 g carbo (2.6 g fiber); 309 mg sodium; 109 mg chol.

Caldo Verde

Eugene P. Baumann, Gold Beach, OR

Chorizo, cabbage, and kale simmer together for layers of flavor in this hearty, cool-weather soup created by Eugene P. Baumann.

PREP AND COOK TIME: About 1 hour

MAKES: About 4 quarts; 10 to 12 main-dish servings

- 1 pound **firm chorizo** sausage
- 1 **onion** (about 8 oz.), peeled and chopped
- 1 clove **garlic,** peeled and minced
- 10 cups fat-skimmed **chicken broth**
- 2 cups fat-skimmed **beef broth**
- 3½ pounds **thin-skinned potatoes,** peeled and diced (½ in.)

Semolina flour and olive oil give Italian character to tea bread flecked with cranberries and pistachios.

- 1 **carrot** (about 5 oz.), peeled and diced (½ in.)

  About ¼ teaspoon **salt**

  About ¼ teaspoon **pepper**
- ¾ pound **kale**
- 5 cups **shredded cabbage** (about half of a 1-lb. head)

1. Cut chorizo into ¼-inch-thick slices. In a 6- to 8-quart pan over medium-high heat, stir chorizo often until lightly browned, about 10 minutes. With a slotted spoon, transfer to towels to drain. Spoon out and discard all but 1 tablespoon fat in pan.

2. Add onion and garlic to pan and stir often until limp, about 5 minutes. Return chorizo to pan and add chicken and beef broth, potatoes, carrot, ¼ teaspoon salt, and ¼ teaspoon pepper. Cover and bring to a boil over high heat; reduce heat and simmer, uncovered, until potatoes and carrot are tender when pierced, about 15 minutes.

3. Meanwhile, rinse and drain kale. Cut out and discard tough center ribs; chop leaves crosswise into ¼-inch-wide slices. Add kale and cabbage to soup and stir occasionally until tender to bite, 8 to 10 minutes. Add salt and pepper to taste.

Per serving: 326 cal., 41% (135 cal.) from fat; 20 g protein; 15 g fat (5.5 g sat.); 27 g carbo (3.4 g fiber); 613 mg sodium; 33 mg chol. ◆

Tangy tomatillos

They're the main ingredient in *salsa verde*

Tomatillos—those fruits that look like green cherry tomatoes wrapped in parchment—are most often used in Mexican-style salsa verde. Tomatillos can be stored in the refrigerator up to a month; they also freeze well. Don't remove the husks until you're ready to use the fruits.

Spoon the salsa generously over tacos, enchiladas, and huevos rancheros, or try it with grilled chicken or fish.

Roasted Tomatillo Salsa

PREP AND COOK TIME: About 20 minutes

NOTES: This green salsa from Renee Shepherd makes an excellent dip or a topping for grilled chicken or fish.

MAKES: About 1¼ cups

- 1 pound **tomatillos** (about 8, each 2 in. wide)
- 1 **fresh serrano chili** (¼ oz.)
- ¼ teaspoon chopped **garlic**
- 1 or 2 **green onions,** rinsed, ends trimmed, and chopped
- 1 tablespoon **lime juice**
- 1 tablespoon chopped **fresh cilantro**

Salt and **pepper**

1. Remove and discard husks from tomatillos; rinse tomatillos. Rinse chili; remove and discard stem. Place tomatillos and chili in a 9-inch square baking pan and broil 4 inches from heat, turning as needed, until browned well on all sides, 12 to 15 minutes total for tomatillos and 6 to 8 minutes for chili. Remove vegetables as done.

2. In a food processor or blender, whirl tomatillos, chili, garlic, green onions, and lime juice, pulsing just until mixture is coarsely chopped; do not overprocess. Stir in cilantro, then salt and pepper to taste.

Per tablespoon: 7.5 cal., 24% (1.8 cal.) from fat; 0.2 g protein; 0.2 g fat (0 g sat.); 1.4 g carbo (0.4 g fiber); 0.4 mg sodium; 0 mg chol. ◆

—*Linda Lau Anusasananan*

The Wine Guide
Memorable wines on a meat-loaf budget
By Karen MacNeil-Fife

■ This time of year, I'm always a little bothered by that old chestnut "Life's too short to drink bad wine." It's clear that whoever coined the phrase probably hadn't just made a serious dent in the family finances thanks to holiday gift giving and entertaining. January is simply not a good time to be splurging on wine. Not that spending less on wine means you have to drink bad wine. But the fact is, the more austere your budget, the harder it is to drink *very* good wine.

Harder, yes; impossible, no. There does exist a whole universe of moderately priced but delicious wines that are easy to buy and effortless to drink. I call them Wednesday night meat-loaf wines. And, frankly, the world needs them. If every wine were a pricey purchase meant for a special occasion, the historic role of wine as an accompaniment to dinner every night would (sadly) be lost.

From a practical standpoint, then, the question is, How do you get the most bang for your buck? Are there strategies for finding wines with modest price tags that taste like they cost a lot more? Yes. And here are some effective ones.

1. Explore wine regions known for value. Currently, the best place on the globe for this is Australia. Because that country has a relatively sparse population, wine companies there are very savvy about producing good-value wines for export. At the same time, Australian winemakers are some of the most talented in the world, and there are dozens of regions well suited for growing grapes that can be turned into delicious, moderately priced wines. Four other good sources of

JAMES CARRIER

top-notch, reasonable wines are New Zealand, Spain, southern Italy, and, closer to home, Washington State. As for Chile and Argentina, they both produce well-priced, delicious wines, but you may have to sort through a lot of inexpensive, bland-tasting stuff to find them.

2. Within famous wine-growing areas, consider lesser-known regions. A perfect example is the Mâconnais region in Burgundy, France. Mâcons—as some of the wines are known—cost $10 to $14 or so, while the really famous whites from renowned appellations like Puligny-Montrachet can range from $50 to $100. All are made from Chardonnay grapes.

3. Price shop. The best deals aren't necessarily at your local supermarket, the nearest warehouse-type retailer, or your favorite wine shop. On the other hand, the best price *could*

SUNSET'S STEAL OF THE MONTH
McPherson Cabernet Sauvignon 2000 (Southeastern Australia), $8. A soft, mouth-filling wine with tasty black cherry, coffee bean, date, and plum flavors. Pairs well with almost any meat dish.
— KAREN MACNEIL-FIFE

BEST IN THEIR CLASS

WHITES
■ **Geyser Peak Chardonnay 1999 (Russian River Valley, CA),** $16. Juicy and packed with apple fruit and vanilla.

■ **Guenoc Sauvignon Blanc 2000 (North Coast, CA),** $14. A crisp surge of green apple, grapefruit, and lemon.

■ **Jepson Sauvignon Blanc 2000 (Mendocino),** $11. Herbal and melony, with a nice fresh character.

■ **Zaca Mesa Chardonnay 2000 (Santa Barbara County),** $15. Fresh, citrusy, clean, and creamy.

REDS
■ **Barwang "Regional Selection" Merlot 1998 (Coonawarra, Australia),** $14. Richness and spice here, with notes of plum, black currant, and toast.

■ **Bogle Petite Sirah 1999 (California),** $10. Bold and gutsy, this is one big wine for a small price.

■ **Trinchero Family Estates "Proprietor's Series" Zinfandel 1997 (Amador County, CA),** $16. Ripe, rich, and full of berries, this is the kind of wine that ensures Zinfandel its cult following. Available through the winery: (800) 967-4663 or www.sutterhome.com.

---

be at any one of those places. Since most wines move through several middlemen and various distribution channels before they become available to us, wine pricing is complex. So check around before you buy. And if you find a wine you like at a good price, buy a whole case. Virtually every wine shop gives case discounts.

In the end, it's important to have realistic expectations. Wednesday night meat-loaf wines are just that. They're usually not tremendously complex, they probably won't inspire you to write a sonnet, and they're not big on finesse. But when these wines are good, they're very satisfying. They're comfort wines— just what you need in January. ◆

Chocolate truffles for your valentine: You don't have to be a professional to produce these tokens of affection (see page 45).

February

celebrate in
Chinese harmony

Welcome the Year of the Horse with a simple, family-style Cantonese meal

ABOVE: Chinese New Year brings friends and family together for a festive meal. Symbolism plays a strong role: Tangerines with a red envelope of money signify wealth. RIGHT: Rock Sugar Ginger Chicken, a warm yang dish, combats the cold yin season; chicken represents the wholeness of life. Steamed rice, neutral in yin-yang terms, is the ultimate symbol of well-being.

■ Many philosophies strive for balance. Taoism seeks it through a harmonious interaction of opposites, based on the concepts of yin, the feminine, passive force in nature—cold, dark, and wet—and yang, the masculine principle, hot, light, and dry. When yin and yang are in perfect balance, in a meal as in other aspects of life, harmony prevails—to say nothing of good health and happiness.

Yin foods, such as lettuce, crab, cucumber, tofu, and bean sprouts, possess cooling and soothing power. Yang foods—chicken, lamb, chocolate, and butter, for instance—contain warmth and energy. Many foods, however, combine both principles. Furthermore, the nature of any food can be altered by the way it is cooked and seasoned: Steaming, poaching, and boiling are yin methods, while stir-frying, deep-frying, and roasting are yang tech-

niques; ginger, garlic, and chili contribute hot, yang influences. The right combination of yin and yang is believed to restore natural balance to the body.

Chinese New Year, an optimal time to restore one's balance, begins this year on February 12 (dates vary). To celebrate the Year of the Horse, we offer a menu in which ingredients and cooking styles are balanced in yin-yang harmony. The recipes are adapted from *The Wisdom of the Chinese Kitchen: Classic Family Recipes for Celebration and Healing* (Simon & Schuster, New York, 1999; $27.50; www.simonsays.com). Author Grace Young learned about the yin-yang principles of food as she was growing up in a traditional Chinese family in San Francisco. The dishes are straightforward home cooking from her family's own repertoire and are easy to integrate into your own celebration.

By Linda Lau Anusasananan • Photographs by James Carrier • Food styling by Karen Shinto

Yin-Yang New Year's Dinner

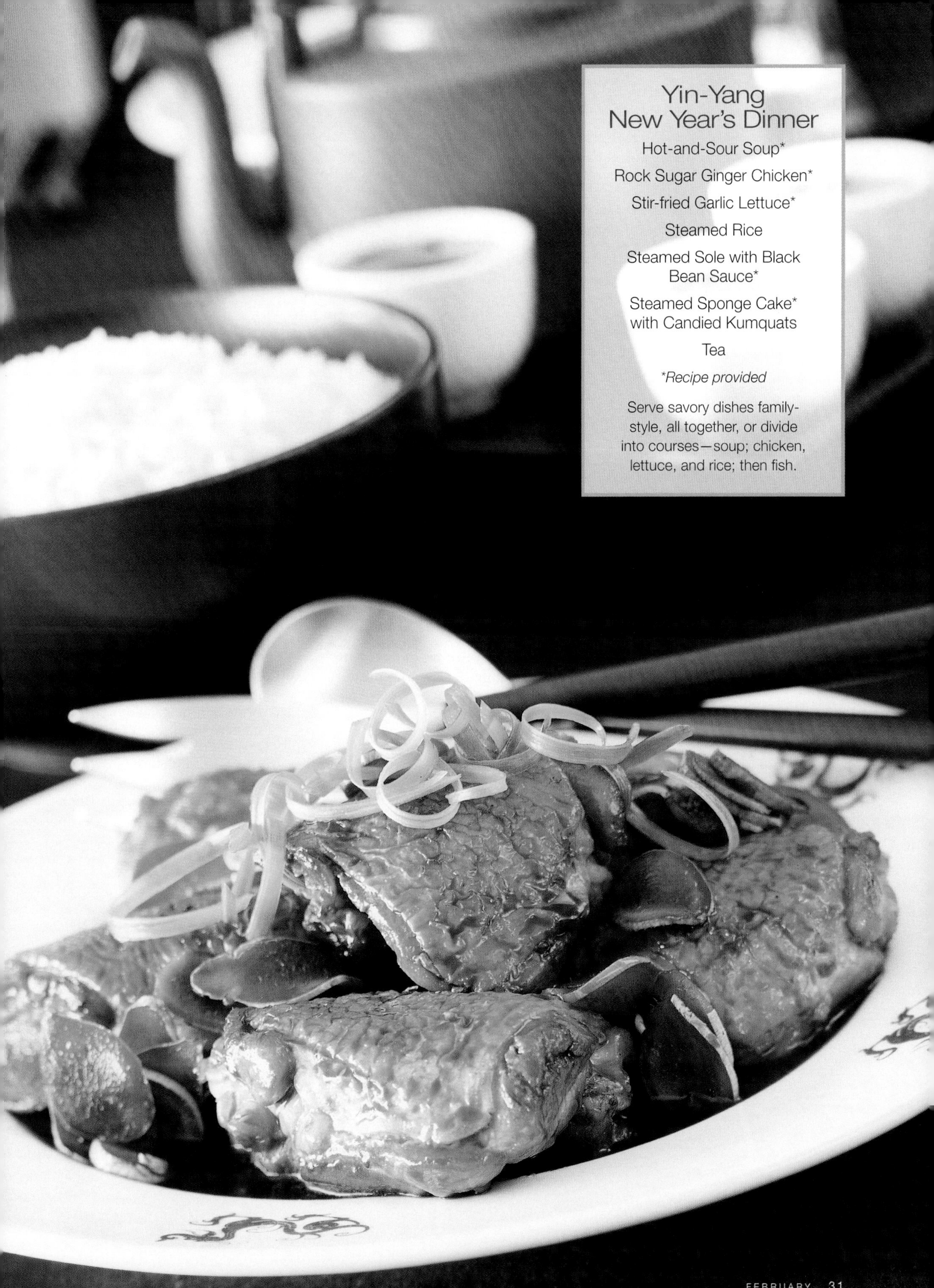

Hot-and-Sour Soup*

Rock Sugar Ginger Chicken*

Stir-fried Garlic Lettuce*

Steamed Rice

Steamed Sole with Black Bean Sauce*

Steamed Sponge Cake* with Candied Kumquats

Tea

**Recipe provided*

Serve savory dishes family-style, all together, or divide into courses—soup; chicken, lettuce, and rice; then fish.

Hot-and-Sour Soup
(Shoon Lat Tong)

PREP AND COOK TIME: About 50 minutes

NOTES: Young's parents make their own broth with chicken, water, and fresh ginger, but canned chicken broth simmered with fresh ginger works well too. If cloud ears and lily buds are unavailable, substitute 1 cup finely shredded cabbage and 1 cup thinly sliced mushrooms and skip step 1; add cabbage and mushrooms to broth in step 4. You can prepare the soup through step 4 up to 1 day ahead; cool, cover, and chill. Reheat, covered, over high heat, then continue with step 5.

MAKES: 6 servings

- ⅓ cup **dried cloud ears** (½ oz.), optional (see notes)
- ⅓ cup **dried lily buds** (¾ oz.), optional (see notes)
- 8 ounces **firm tofu**
- 4 ounces **boned pork butt** or loin, fat trimmed
- ½ cup **canned sliced bamboo shoots**
- 1½ quarts fat-skimmed **chicken broth** (see notes)
- 6 slices (¼ in. thick) **fresh ginger**
- 3 tablespoons **cornstarch**
- 3 tablespoons **cider vinegar**
- 1 **large egg**
- ⅓ cup minced **green onions** (including green tops)
- 1¼ teaspoons **sugar**
- ¾ teaspoon **white pepper**

1. Rinse cloud ears and lily buds under cool running water. Place in a small bowl, cover with cool water, and soak until soft, 15 to 20 minutes; drain. Pinch out and discard any hard spots from cloud ears, then rinse again; tear ears into ½-inch pieces. Remove and discard hard ends from lily buds; tie a knot in the center of each bud.

2. While cloud ears and lily buds are soaking, rinse and drain tofu; cut into ½-inch cubes. Rinse pork and pat dry; cut into ¼-inch-thick matchstick-size pieces about 2 inches long. Rinse and drain bamboo shoots; cut lengthwise into ¼-inch-wide strips.

3. In a 3- to 4-quart pan over high heat, bring broth and ginger to a boil; reduce heat, cover, and simmer to blend flavors, 20 to 25 minutes. Remove and discard ginger.

4. Stir in cloud ears, lily buds, tofu, pork, and bamboo shoots and bring to a boil over high heat. In a small bowl, mix cornstarch and vinegar until smooth; stir into boiling broth mixture and continue stirring until it boils again, 1 to 2 minutes.

5. In a small bowl, beat egg with a fork to blend. Remove soup from heat; immediately stir in egg, green onions, sugar, and pepper. Pour into a large bowl.

Per serving: 157 cal., 32% (51 cal.) from fat; 19 g protein; 5.7 g fat (1.2 g sat.); 7.9 g carbo (0.5 g fiber); 106 mg sodium; 48 mg chol.

Rock Sugar Ginger Chicken
(Bing Tong Gook Geung Gai)

PREP AND COOK TIME: About 45 minute

NOTES: Traditionally, bone-in chicken pieces are chopped up for this dish. We use whole pieces so there will be fewe bone fragments. You can prepare the chicken (through step 2) up to 1 da ahead; cover and chill. Lift off and discard solidified fat, then reheat chicken covered, over medium heat, and continue. Serve with steamed rice and Stir fried Garlic Lettuce.

MAKES: 6 servings

- 6 **bone-in chicken thighs** (2 lb. total)
- 1 tablespoon **salad oil**
- 6 ounces **fresh ginger,** scrubbed and thinly sliced
- ½ cup fat-skimmed **chicken broth**
- 2 ounces **rock sugar** (about ⅓ cup or ¼ cup granulated sugar
- 2 tablespoons **black soy sauce** or 2 tablespoons regular soy sauce plus ½ teaspoon molasses
- ½ teaspoon **salt**

  Thinly sliced **green onions** (optional)

1. Rinse chicken and pat dry. Set a 12 inch frying pan or a 5- to 6-quart pan over high heat. When hot, add oil and ginger; stir often until ginger is lightl browned, 3 to 4 minutes. Reduce hea to medium-high; push ginger to edge

Hot-and-Sour Soup offers a perfect balance of flavors, plus a good omen for a growing family in the new year: The Cantonese word for sour sounds like the word for grandchild. Sweet bean cakes are available in Asian markets.

Steamed Sole with Black Bean Sauce (Dul See Zing Tat Sa Yu)

PREP AND COOK TIME: About 25 minutes

NOTES: In China, a fish must be served with its head and tail intact to properly signify a favorable end of the old year and beginning of the new. Markets that serve a large Asian clientele usually carry small whole fish. You also may be able to order one from your fish market. If all else fails, steam 12 ounces of boned, skinned sole fillets in a single layer until opaque but still moist-looking in the center, about 5 minutes. If desired, serve fish as a separate course after the chicken.

MAKES: 4 to 6 servings as part of a multicourse meal

- 2 teaspoons **salted fermented black beans** or regular soy sauce
- 2 teaspoons minced **garlic**
- ½ teaspoon **sugar**
- ¾ teaspoon **Asian** (toasted) **sesame oil**
- ¾ teaspoon **Shao Xing rice wine** or dry sherry (optional)
- ¼ teaspoon **white pepper**
- ½ teaspoon plus ⅛ teaspoon **salt**
- 1 **whole petrale** or Dover **sole** (1¼ lb.), cleaned, head and tail intact (see notes)
- 4 thin slices **fresh ginger**
- 1 **green onion** (10 in.), rinsed
- 1 tablespoon **regular soy sauce**
- 1 tablespoon **salad oil**

1. Set a rack (cake rack, removable rim of a cake pan, or empty 2-in.-tall cans with both ends cut out) in a 12-inch steamer, 14-inch wok, 12- by 17-inch roasting pan, or 12-inch frying pan (with sides at least 2 in. tall). Pour water into steamer to about ½ inch below top of rack. Cover steamer and bring water to a boil over high heat.

2. Meanwhile, rinse and drain black beans. In a small bowl, with a wooden spoon, mash beans, garlic, and sugar together. Stir in sesame oil, wine, pepper, and ⅛ teaspoon salt.

3. Rinse fish and pat dry. Place in a shallow bowl or on a rimmed plate that will fit inside steamer without touching sides. Sprinkle ½ teaspoon salt inside cavity and over outside of fish. Spread black bean mixture inside and all over outside of fish.

4. Set bowl with fish on rack in steamer and cover. (If cover doesn't fit over fish, tent steamer with a large piece of foil, sealing it around pan edges so steam

ole with Black Bean Sauce cooks in steam, a yin technique. A whole fish ugurs a favorable end to the old year and beginning of the new; indeed, it ncourages a good start and happy end to all aspects of life.

f pan and add chicken pieces, skin ide down, in a single layer. Cook, urning once, until browned on both ides, 7 to 8 minutes total. Drain off nd discard fat from pan.

. Stir broth, ½ cup water, sugar, soy auce, and salt into pan around hicken. Cover and bring to a boil, hen reduce heat to medium and sim-er 8 minutes. Turn chicken pieces ver, cover, and continue cooking until

no longer pink at the bone (cut to test), 7 to 9 minutes longer.

3. With tongs, lift chicken from pan juices and place in a shallow bowl or on a rimmed platter. Skim and discard fat from pan juices; pour juices over chicken. Sprinkle green onions on top of meat if desired.

Per serving: 259 cal., 49% (126 cal.) from fat; 21 g protein; 14 g fat (3.7 g sat.); 11 g carbo (0 g fiber); 705 mg sodium; 72 mg chol.

can't escape.) Steam fish for 5 minutes, then remove from heat and let stand until barely opaque but still moist-looking in center of thickest part (cut to test), about 4 minutes longer. If fish isn't done, return to heat and steam 1 to 2 minutes longer. Remove bowl with fish from steamer; if desired, carefully pour off any liquid in bowl.

5. Meanwhile, stack ginger slices and cut into fine slivers. Trim and discard ends from green onion; cut onion, including green tops, into 2-inch lengths, then cut pieces lengthwise into fine shreds.

6. Sprinkle ginger and green onion over fish. Drizzle soy sauce evenly over all. Pour salad oil into a 6- to 8-inch frying pan over high heat; when hot, in about 30 seconds, drizzle evenly over fish. Serve immediately.

Per serving: 67 cal., 46% (31 cal.) from fat; 7.4 g protein; 3.4 g fat (0.5 g sat.); 1.6 g carbo (0.1 g fiber); 495 mg sodium; 18 mg chol.

Stir-fried Garlic Lettuce is made from a classic yin-yang pair: Lettuce is yin, garlic yang. The bonus: Lettuce signifies money and prosperity.

Ingredient tips

You can cook this entire menu with familiar ingredients from your supermarket, but the authentic Chinese touches are worth seeking out for their interesting tastes and textures. Look for them in Asian markets or order from Uwajimaya (800/889-1928 or www.uwajimaya.com).

■ **Black soy (low zul):** Also called soy superior sauce or dark soy sauce. Aged longer than the more common soy sauce, it's darker, richer, and slightly sweeter. Usually contains a sweetener such as molasses.

■ **Dried cloud ears (wun yee):** Also called tree ears, dried vegetable, and black fungus (pictured at right). These grayish black mushrooms look like small, delicate, paper-thin, crinkled leaves. (Larger, coarser fungus are called wood ears.) Rinse the cloud ears in cold water and then soak until soft. Pinch out the hard, knobby center. Dried cloud ears have little flavor but contribute both crunchy and silky textures to soups and stir-fries. Store airtight in a cool, dry place.

■ **Dried lily buds (gum tzum):** Also called golden needles, lily flowers, tiger lily buds, and lily stems (pictured at lower right). The buds consist of flexible strands, honey-colored to dark brown; the lighter-colored ones are the freshest. Soak the buds in water until soft, then pinch off the knob at the stem end. For aesthetic reasons, the strands are often tied into knots. Dried lily buds contribute an earthy flavor and chewy texture. Store airtight in a cool, dry place.

■ **Rock sugar (bing tong):** Also called rock candy. Rock sugar is crystallized sugar, clear to amber-colored, that comes in chunks. Use a hammer to break large chunks into smaller pieces. Besides sweetness, rock sugar adds a sheen to soups and braised dishes. Store airtight in a cool, dry place.

■ **Salted fermented black beans (dul see):** Also called salted black beans, fermented black beans, preserved beans, or Chinese dried black beans. Fermented with salt and spices, these small black beans add a savory pungency to meat, seafood, and poultry. Store tightly covered in the refrigerator.

■ **Shao Xing rice wine (siu hing zul):** Also known as just rice wine. It's made from fermented glutinous rice. Store tightly capped at room temperature.

■ **Thin soy (sang zul):** Also known as superior soy, premium soy sauce, light soy sauce, or, more commonly, just soy sauce. Most soy sauce sold in Western markets is thin soy; it is not reduced-sodium soy sauce unless specified.

Stir-fried Garlic Lettuce
(Shoon Chow Saang Choy)

PREP AND COOK TIME: About 10 minutes

NOTES: This dish is similar to a wilted salad; the lettuce should retain some crunch. Serve with the ginger chicken.

MAKES: 6 servings

1   head **iceberg lettuce** (1½ lb.)

1½   teaspoons **regular soy sauce**

1½   teaspoons **Asian** (toasted) **sesame oil**

1   teaspoon **Shao Xing rice wine** or dry sherry

¾   teaspoon **sugar**

¼   teaspoon **salt**

¼   teaspoon **white pepper**

1   tablespoon **salad oil**

3   cloves **garlic,** peeled and pressed

1. Rinse and drain lettuce thoroughly. Cut out and discard core. Separate leaves and tear into 3- by 5-inch pieces.

2. In a small bowl, mix soy sauce, sesame oil, wine, sugar, salt, and pepper.

3. Set a 14-inch wok or 12-inch frying pan over high heat. When hot, add oil and garlic; stir-fry until garlic just

Sponge cake, steamed in yin style, rises—hopefully your fortunes will follow in the coming year.

egins to brown, about 30 seconds. dd lettuce and stir just until slightly mp but still bright green and omewhat crisp, about 2 minutes (if l the lettuce doesn't fit, add half, ir until slightly wilted—about 30 conds—then stir in the remaining aves). Stir in soy sauce mixture. Pour nto a platter and serve immediately.

r serving: 56 cal., 59% (33 cal.) from fat; 6 g protein; 3.7 g fat (0.5 g sat.); 5.1 g carbo .1 g fiber); 191 mg sodium; 0 mg chol.

Steamed Sponge Cake (Soy Zing Dan Gow)

REP AND COOK TIME: About 45 minutes

OTES: You can make the cake up to 2 ays ahead; cool and store airtight at oom temperature. Many Chinese pre- r this pale, moist cake plain, but it can e embellished with candied kumquats r a citrus compote if desired.

AKES: 8 or 9 servings

4 **large eggs**

1 **large egg** white

¾ cup **sugar**

1 teaspoon **vanilla**

1 cup sifted **cake flour**

½ teaspoon **baking powder**

1. Line the bottom of an 8-inch round cake pan (with 2- to 3-in.-tall sides) with cooking parchment cut to fit. If pan has a removable rim, wrap outside with foil to prevent water from seeping in.

2. In a large bowl, with a mixer on high speed, beat whole eggs, egg white, and sugar until thick and pale yellow, 4 to 5 minutes. Stir in vanilla. In a small bowl, mix flour and baking powder until blended. With a whisk, fold flour mixture into egg mixture until evenly blended. Scrape batter into pan. Tap pan lightly on work surface to remove air pockets.

3. Set a round rack (cake rack, basket steamer, removable rim from a cake pan, or empty 2-in.-tall cans with both ends cut out) in a 12- to 14-inch steamer, 14-inch wok, or 12-inch frying pan (with at least 2-in.-tall sides; steamer should be wide enough to hold cake pan without sides touching). Pour water into steamer to about ½ inch below top of rack. Cover steamer and bring water to a boil over high heat.

4. Place cake on rack and cover steamer (if cover doesn't fit over cake, tent steamer with a large piece of foil, sealing it around the edges so steam can't escape); reduce heat to medium and steam until a toothpick inserted in center of cake comes out clean, 20 to 25 minutes. If necessary, add more boiling water to maintain level. Remove cover quickly and carefully so condensed steam doesn't drip onto cake. Remove cake from steamer.

5. Run a knife between cake and pan rim to loosen sides. Invert onto a rack, remove pan and parchment, and invert again onto another rack. Let cake cool at least 10 minutes. With a serrated knife, cut cake into diamonds or wedges. Serve warm or cool.

Per serving: 140 cal., 15% (21 cal.) from fat; 4 g protein; 2.3 g fat (0.7 g sat.); 25 g carbo (0.2 g fiber); 61 mg sodium; 94 mg chol. ◆

Steam pushes the batter up and over the top of the pan to form the crusty, craggy crown of a popover.

Foolproof puffs

Easy steps for making classic popovers and cream puffs

Almost like magic, simple mixtures of eggs and flour pouf into expansive, golden mounds—popovers and cream puffs. What's the secret of their silhouette?

Think of these classics as edible hot-air balloons. Both contain eggs, flour, and butter. When the batter is heated quickly, the liquid in it vaporizes; the steam stretches the structure before the proteins in the eggs and flour solidify and form a crisp shell. The oven temperature is critical: It needs to be hot enough to cause the puffs to expand quickly, but not so hot that they set before they have a chance to balloon. Make sure you preheat the oven to just the right temperature, and check its accuracy with an oven thermometer.

That's easy payment for the pleasure of spooning fruity jam into a steaming popover for breakfast or breaking into a cream-filled puff drizzled with chocolate.

Classic Popovers

PREP AND COOK TIME: About 1 hour

NOTES: If using cups that are slightly smaller or larger than ½ cup, adjust the baking time proportionately. You can make the popovers up to 1 day ahead; wrap airtight and store at room temperature. To recrisp, place slightly apart on a baking sheet and bake in a 375° oven until crisp, about 5 minutes.

MAKES: 6 popovers

- 3 **large eggs**
- 1 cup **all-purpose flour**
- 1 cup **milk**
- About 1 tablespoon melted **butter** or margarine
- ¼ teaspoon **salt**

1. In a blender or bowl, whirl or beat eggs, flour, milk, 1 tablespoon butter, and salt until smooth.

2. Generously brush six nonstick popover, custard, soufflé, or muffin cups (½-cup capacity; see notes) with butter; if using pans without a nonstick finish, coat with cooking oil spray instead. Pour batter equally into cups, filling them ¾ to almost full. Set cups about 2 inches apart in a 10- by 15-inch rimmed baking pan.

3. Bake popovers in a 375° regular or convection oven until browned and puffy, 40 to 45 minutes. Pierce each popover in several places with a thin wooden skewer, then continue baking until very well browned and crisp, about 5 minutes longer. Remove from oven and run a thin-bladed knife between edge of each popover and cup to loosen. Lift popovers from cups and serve hot.

Per popover: 172 cal., 41% (71 cal.) from fat; 6.6 g protein; 7.9 g fat (4 g sat.); 18 g carbo (0.6 g fiber); 186 mg sodium; 122 mg chol.

Popover tips

- Beat the batter just until smooth; overbeating it can break up the structure.
- Pour batter into every other cup if your muffin tins have less than 1 inch between cups; popovers need room for their tops to expand.
- Fill cups ¾ to almost full, so batter can pop up over the edges.
- Puncture popovers once they have puffed and the shell has set (to release the steam); return them to oven to firm up.

- Popovers are perfect vehicles for both savory and sweet fillings: Split large ones open and spoon in softly scrambled eggs; top with cheese and salsa or diced tomatoes. Or for dessert, slit popover tops open and fill with a scoop of vanilla or chocolate ice cream; top with peeled orange segments and caramel sauce.

By Linda Lau Anusasananan • Photographs by James Carrier • Food styling by Susan Devaty

Romance your Valentine with a heart-shaped cream puff.

Cream Puff Dough
(Pâte à Choux)

PREP AND COOK TIME: About 15 minutes

NOTES: Use this basic dough to make the Classic Cream Puffs, Berry Hearts with Chocolate-Orange Cream, and Asiago-Pepper Puff Ring that follow.

MAKES: 2½ cups dough; 8 to 10 servings

½ cup (¼ lb.) **butter** or margarine

1 tablespoon **sugar** (optional; for dessert puffs only)

1 cup **all-purpose flour**

4 **large eggs**

1. In a 3- to 4-quart pan, combine 1 cup water, butter, and the sugar if using; bring to a boil over high heat. Add flour all at once and stir quickly until mixture pulls away from pan sides and masses together. Remove from heat and stir until flour is incorporated and mixture is smooth. Let cool about 5 minutes, stirring occasionally.

2. *To mix by hand,* add eggs, one at a time, to warm butter-flour mixture in pan, beating with a wooden spoon after each addition until dough is smooth and satiny.

To mix with an electric mixer or food processor, scrape warm butter-flour mixture into a bowl. Add eggs, one at a time, beating or whirling after each addition just until smooth; do not overmix.

Per serving: 157 cal., 63% (99 cal.) from fat; 3.9 g protein; 11 g fat (6.4 g sat.); 9.8 g carbo (0.3 g fiber); 119 mg sodium; 110 mg chol.

Classic Cream Puffs

PREP AND COOK TIME: About 1¼ hours

NOTES: You can make the puffs (through step 2) up to 12 hours ahead; wrap airtight and store at room temperature. Freeze to store longer. To use, place puffs (thawed, if frozen) slightly apart on a 12- by 15-inch baking sheet. Bake in a 400° oven until crisp, 5 to 8 minutes.

MAKES: 10 servings

1. Spoon **Cream Puff Dough** (recipe precedes) into 10 equal mounds (about ¼ cup each) about 2 inches apart on two lightly **buttered** 12- by 15-inch baking sheets.

2. Bake in a 375° regular or convection oven until puffs are golden, 25 to 35 minutes; if baking the sheets at the same time in one oven, switch their positions halfway through. With a wooden skewer, poke each puff in several places, then continue baking until golden brown, dry, and crisp, 5 to 8 minutes longer. Transfer puffs to racks to cool completely.

3. Slice the top third off each puff. Fill each bottom with ½ cup of one of the following: **ice cream,** Chocolate-Orange Cream (recipe follows), or lightly sweetened whipped cream flavored with vanilla or a liqueur. Cover with tops, and drizzle each puff with 2 to 3 teaspoons **chocolate ice cream topping** or sprinkle lightly with powdered sugar.

Per serving: 332 cal., 54% (180 cal.) from fat; 6.4 g protein; 20 g fat (12 g sat.); 34 g carbo (0.3 g fiber); 196 mg sodium; 142 mg chol.

Berry Hearts with Chocolate-Orange Cream

PREP AND COOK TIME: About 1 hour

NOTES: If you're uncomfortable shaping the hearts freehand, use a felt-tipped pen to draw heart shapes at least 2 inches apart on cooking parchment cut to fit baking sheets. Turn paper over, place on sheets, and spread paste to fill outlines. For the crispest puffs, fill just before serving;

otherwise, fill up to 4 hours ahead, then cover and chill.

MAKES: 10 hearts

1. On two lightly **buttered** 12- by 15-inch baking sheets, using a narrow spatula, shape ¼-cup portions of **Cream Puff Dough** (recipe on page 38) into hearts 3 inches across widest dimension and 3 inches long in the center. Make the V in the top of the hearts deep, since they lose definition as they bake (see notes).

2. Bake and cool as directed for Classic Cream Puffs (recipe precedes), step 2.

3. Slice hearts in half horizontally. Set each base on a dessert plate and fill with **Chocolate-Orange Cream** (recipe follows).

4. Rinse and drain 2 cups **fresh raspberries**; pat dry. Distribute berries evenly over filling (save a few for garnish if desired). Set heart tops over berries. Garnish with **semisweet chocolate** curls and sift **powdered sugar** or unsweetened cocoa lightly over the top.

Per heart: 487 cal., 65% (315 cal.) from fat; 7.7 g protein; 35 g fat (21 g sat.); 38 g carbo (2 g fiber); 235 mg sodium; 182 mg chol.

Chocolate-Orange Cream

PREP TIME: About 20 minutes

NOTES: You can make this filling up to 2 hours ahead; cover and chill.

MAKES: About 1 quart

1. In a bowl, with an electric mixer on high speed, beat 1 package (8 oz.) **neufchâtel** (light cream) **cheese** (at room temperature), 1 teaspoon grated **orange** peel, and 1 teaspoon **vanilla** until smooth. Add 2 cups **whipping cream** and beat on low speed until blended, then on high speed just until mixture resembles stiffly beaten whipped cream (do not overbeat).

2. Sift 1¼ cups **powdered sugar** and fold into cream mixture. Fold in ½ cup finely chopped **semisweet chocolate** until evenly distributed.

Per ½ cup: 373 cal., 68% (252 cal.) from fat; 4.5 g protein; 28 g fat (18 g sat.); 28 g carbo (0.6 g fiber); 135 mg sodium; 88 mg chol.

Chocolate
sauce cascades
over a classic
cream puff.

Asiago-Pepper Puff Ring

PREP AND COOK TIME: About 1 hour

NOTES: Serve as a hot bread with soups and salads. You can make the puff ring up to 1 day ahead; cool on a rack and store airtight at room temperature. To recrisp, place on a baking sheet and bake in a 400° oven until crisp, 5 to 8 minutes.

MAKES: 8 servings

1. Follow recipe for **Cream Puff Dough** (page 38), but in step 1, add ½ teaspoon **pepper** to water and reduce butter to 6 tablespoons. In step 2, after beating in last egg, stir in ¾ cup (3 oz.) **shredded asiago cheese**.

2. On a **buttered** 12- by 15-inch baking sheet, drop eight equal portions (about ⅓ cup each) of asiago-pepper dough, side by side with edges touching, in an 8-inch circle. Sprinkle with another ¼ cup shredded asiago.

3. Bake in a 375° regular or convection oven until browned, 40 to 50 minutes. Pierce each puff in several places with a wooden skewer and return to oven. Bake until well browned and crisp, 5 to 7 minutes longer. With a spatula, slide ring off pan. Serve hot, breaking off puffs to eat.

Per serving: 221 cal., 61% (135 cal.) from fat; 7.9 g protein; 15 g fat (8.7 g sat.); 12 g carbo (0.5 g fiber); 246 mg sodium; 138 mg chol. ◆

By Jerry Anne Di Vecchio

Photographs by James Carrier

Lamb from Down Under

■ I love Australia's vitality, its dynamic food scene, and the crowd of Aussie friends I've accumulated through the years. Take Peter, for instance, and his buddy Bronwyn—culinary enthusiasts both. As house guests one afternoon, they announced they were going to cook lamb shanks, and who knows how to do that better than Australians? As the shanks roasted gently in the oven—untended—their mellow, herbal aroma filled the house, and Peter demonstrated a true virtue of the dish: He took a nap before we shared this cozy winter's-eve meal.

Lamb Shanks with Olives and Capers

PREP AND COOK TIME: About 3½ hours

NOTES: If you can't find pitted olives, you can use those with pits (warn guests to bite with care) or you can cut the olives from their pits (keep the pieces as large as possible).

MAKES: 6 servings

- 6 **lamb shanks** (about 6 lb. total)
- 1 jar (4 oz.) **capers,** drained
- 1½ cups **pitted green olives in brine** such as Picholine (see notes)
- ¼ cup **fresh rosemary** leaves or 3 tablespoons dried rosemary
- 1 bottle (750 ml.) **dry white wine**
- 2 teaspoons fresh-ground **pepper**
- 2 teaspoons grated **lemon** peel
- 3 tablespoons **lemon juice**

  Lemon Couscous (recipe follows)

  About 3 cups **watercress sprigs,** rinsed and crisped

1. Rinse lamb and pat dry; lay shanks side by side in a 12-by-17-inch pan about 2 inches deep. Bake in a 450° regular or convection oven, turning once, until meat is well browned all over, about 25 minutes total. Reduce oven temperature to 325°.

2. Meanwhile, place capers and olives in a fine strainer and rinse with cool water; drain. Mince rosemary or combine with about 1 cup of the wine in a blender and whirl until minced. Scatter capers, olives, and rosemary over lamb (or pour rosemary-wine mixture evenly over lamb) and add the wine (the rest of the wine if whirling some with rosemary); stir around shanks to scrape up browned bits. Sprinkle pepper and lemon peel over meat; add lemon juice to pan. Cover pan tightly with lid or foil.

3. Bake until meat is very tender when pierced and pulls easily from the bone, 3 to 3¼ hours.

4. Spoon equal portions of Lemon Couscous into wide, shallow bowls. With tongs, lift lamb shanks from pan and set one on couscous in each bowl. Skim and discard fat from juices in pan. Ladle juices with olives and capers over meat. Garnish each bowl with about ½ cup watercress sprigs.

Per serving: 676 cal., 24% (162 cal.) from fat; 75 g protein; 18 g fat (5.3 g sat.); 49 g carbo (3.6 g fiber); 1,753 mg sodium; 200 mg chol.

Lemon Couscous. In a 1½- to 2-quart pan over high heat, bring 2 cups fat-skimmed **chicken broth** to a boil. Stir in 1 package (12 oz.) **couscous** and half of a **preserved lemon** (available in gourmet food stores), finely chopped (or use 2 teaspoons grated lemon peel and 3 tablespoons lemon juice). Cover, remove from heat, and let stand 5 minutes. Fluff couscous with a fork and serve. Makes 6 servings.

Per serving: 227 cal., 1.6% (3.6 cal.) from fat; 9.9 g protein; 0.4 g fat (0.1 g sat.); 45 g carbo (1.9 g fiber); 224 mg sodium; 0 mg chol.

Fruit-full balsamics

■ Balsamic vinegar has a natural affinity for fruit. Taking this relationship one step further, Peggy O'Kelly, at the St. Helena Olive Oil Co. in Napa Valley, ages balsamic vinegar with fresh raspberries, strawberries, blueberries, cranberries, or cherries, enriching each batch with a touch of vanilla. The resulting flavors are even more fruit-friendly than plain balsamics. Use them to dress salads, to replace lemon in zippy desserts and beverages, and to complement meat, poultry, and fish; just splash them on the meat or in marinades and sauces. The berry balsamics sell for $4.95 (60 ml) and $11 (250 ml).

If you can't find the berry balsamics at well-stocked supermarkets, gourmet shops, or cookware stores, order them from the company's tasting room at 8576 St. Helena Highway, Rutherford, California (800/939-9880 or www.sholiveoil.com).

Avocado fan

■ If avocados had a fan club like Hollywood stars do, I'd be a member. In the absence of that, I'm a fan of a new tool that quickly and neatly cuts avocados into even slices that you can tip out of the shell and fan dramatically onto a plate—or use any way you choose. Just cut a ripe avocado in half (hard-shell Hass work best), pop out the pit, and glide the avocado slicer (one size fits all) under the flesh against the shell. If there is any pulp left in the shell, scoop it out with a spoon. The slicer, made by Progressive International, is available in cookware stores for about $15.

And now, with avocados at peak quality and tomatoes not worth writing home about, try this seasonal re-do of a BLT—a BLA (no, not *blah*): Layer avocado slices, cooked bacon, and lettuce on whole-grain toast, spreading the bread with any extra avocado scooped from the shell.

Date with a salad

■ Celery is crisp, crunchy— and sometimes stringy. But trim off the long fibers that run the length of the stalks, then shave the stalks paper-thin, and you have a whole new taste and texture: melting snowflakes with a bit of snap. At San Francisco's 42 Degrees restaurant, chef-owner Jim Moffat contrasts the cool, moist celery with intense, sweet dates, topping them with shavings of parmesan cheese for a delightfully simple salad. He seasons the combination with aged balsamic vinegar; the berry balsamics above add a lovely layer of flavor.

Date and Celery Salad

PREP TIME: About 25 minutes

NOTES: You'll need a bunch of celery that weighs about 1¾ pounds; use a vegetable peeler to pare the coarse fibers from the curved back sides of the stalks, then use the peeler or a vegetable slicer to cut them diagonally into paper-thin slices. You can cut the dates, cheese, and celery up to 4 hours ahead; chill them separately airtight. Assemble the salad just before serving.

MAKES: 4 to 6 servings

9 to 12 **Medjool dates**

3 cups paper-thin slices **celery** (see notes)

About ½ teaspoon **kosher** or other coarse **salt**

2 ounces **parmesan cheese,** cut into paper-thin slices

About 2 tablespoons **balsamic** or berry-flavored balsamic **vinegar**

1. With a sharp knife, cut dates from pits lengthwise into ¼-inch-wide strips; discard pits.

2. In a bowl, gently mix the celery with salt to taste (the mixture should taste slightly salty).

3. Mound celery equally on salad plates. Scatter dates, separating pieces, over celery; top equally with parmesan slices. Drizzle about 2 teaspoons vinegar over each salad.

Per serving: 140 cal., 19% (26 cal.) from fat; 5.1 g protein; 2.9 g fat (1.8 g sat.); 26 g carbo (3.2 g fiber); 390 mg sodium; 7.5 mg chol. ◆

The Quick Cook

Presto pasta: Entrées in 30 minutes or less

By Linda Lau Anusasananan • Photographs by James Carrier

A few green onions and fresh herbs add a lively character to linguine with easy-to-use frozen artichoke hearts in a light, lemony sauce.

■ Pasta has countless personalities, and a good share of them come together in the time it takes Tom Brokaw to cover the nightly news. Add salad, hearty bread, and a glass of wine for an ever-so-simple supper that you can vary almost endlessly.

Linguine with Artichokes and Lemon

PREP AND COOK TIME: About 30 minutes
MAKES: 2 or 3 servings

- 9 ounces **fresh linguine**
- 1 cup thinly sliced **green onions**
- ½ teaspoon chopped **fresh** or dried **rosemary** leaves
- 1 tablespoon **olive oil**
- 1 package (8 oz.) **frozen artichoke hearts**, thawed and quartered
- ¾ cup fat-skimmed **chicken broth** or vegetable broth
- ½ cup **dry white wine**
- ¼ cup **whipping cream**
- 1 teaspoon grated **lemon** peel
- 3 tablespoons chopped **parsley**
  Salt and **pepper**
  Lemon wedges

1. In a 5- to 6-quart pan over high heat, bring 3 quarts water to a boil. Add linguine and stir occasionally until barely tender to bite, 2 to 3 minutes.

2. Meanwhile, in a 10- to 12-inch frying pan over medium-high heat, stir onions and rosemary in oil until onions are limp, 1 to 2 minutes. Add artichoke hearts, broth, wine, cream, and lemon peel; stir until boiling, 1 to 2 minutes.

3. Drain pasta and return to pan. Add artichoke sauce, parsley, and salt and pepper to taste. Lift with two spoons to mix. (If pasta has cooled, stir over medium heat until hot.) Pour into a wide serving bowl or distribute among plates. Serve with lemon wedges to squeeze over pasta.

Per serving: 419 cal., 28% (117 cal.) from fat; 15 g protein; 13 g fat (4.8 g sat.); 56 g carbo (7.3 g fiber); 92 mg sodium; 84 mg chol.

Variation: Substitute sliced red and yellow bell peppers for the artichoke hearts, or mushrooms for the artichokes and sherry for the white wine.

Linguine with Sausage and Kale

PREP AND COOK TIME: About 25 minutes
MAKES: 4 servings

- 8 ounces **dried linguine**
- 12 ounces **kale**
- 1 **red bell pepper** (8 oz.)
- 1 **onion** (6 oz.)
- 2 cloves **garlic**
- 8 ounces **linguisa** (Portuguese) or kielbasa (Polish) **sausages**
- 1 tablespoon **olive oil**
- ¼ teaspoon **hot chili flakes**
- 1 cup fat-skimmed **chicken broth**
- ¼ cup **grated parmesan cheese**
  Salt and **pepper**

1. In a 5- to 6-quart pan over high heat, bring 3 quarts water to a boil. Add linguine and stir occasionally until barely tender to bite, 8 to 11 minutes.

2. Meanwhile, rinse kale; trim off and discard tough stems. Cut leaves crosswise into ¼-inch-wide strips. Rinse, stem, and seed bell pepper; cut lengthwise into ¼-inch-wide slivers 2 inches long. Peel and thinly slice onion. Peel garlic and mince. Slice sausages diagonally ¼ inch thick.

3. In a 12-inch nonstick frying pan or 5- to 6-quart pan over high heat, stir sausages in olive oil until lightly browned, 2 to 3 minutes. Add bell pepper, onion, garlic, and chili flakes; stir until onion begins to brown, 2 to 3 minutes. Add kale and stir until wilted, 1 to 2 minutes. Add broth and stir until boiling.

4. Drain pasta and return to pan. Add sausage mixture, cheese, and salt and pepper to taste. (If pasta has cooled down, stir over medium heat until hot.) Pour into a wide serving bowl or distribute evenly among plates.

Per serving: 503 cal., 39% (198 cal.) from fat; 21 g protein; 22 g fat (7.2 g sat.); 56 g carbo (3.8 g fiber); 751 mg sodium; 42 mg chol.

Variation: Substitute chunks of boned, skinned chicken thighs for the sausages and mustard greens, Swiss chard, or spinach for the kale.

Pesto Penne with Green Beans and Potatoes

PREP AND COOK TIME: About 25 minutes

NOTES: This dish was inspired by a menu special from chef-owner Joe Jack at Luna Park in San Francisco. Use homemade or purchased pesto.

MAKES: 3 or 4 servings

- 12 ounces **russet potatoes**
- 12 ounces **green beans**, rinsed
- 12 ounces **dried penne pasta**
- ¾ cup **pesto** (see notes)
  Salt and **pepper**
  Grated parmesan cheese

1. In a 5- to 6-quart pan over high heat, bring 3 quarts water to a boil.
2. Meanwhile, peel potatoes; cut into ¾-inch cubes. Trim and discard ends from beans; remove strings. Cut beans diagonally into 2- to 3-inch lengths.
3. When water is boiling, add potatoes and pasta and cook, uncovered, stirring occasionally, for 8 minutes. Add beans and cook, stirring occasionally, until potatoes are tender when pierced and pasta and beans are barely tender to bite, 4 to 6 minutes longer. Drain, reserving 1 cup cooking liquid.
4. Return pasta mixture to pan and add pesto and ¾ cup cooking liquid; mix gently. If desired, add more reserved cooking liquid to moisten. Gently stir in salt, pepper, and parmesan cheese to taste. Pour into a wide serving bowl or distribute evenly among plates.

Per serving: 633 cal., 34% (216 cal.) from fat; 18 g protein; 24 g fat (4 g sat.); 86 g carbo (4.7 g fiber); 346 mg sodium; 7.5 mg chol.

Farfalle and Shrimp

PREP AND COOK TIME: About 20 minutes

MAKES: 3 or 4 servings

- 8 ounces **dried farfalle pasta** (also called bow-tie or butterfly)
- 1 **onion** (8 oz.), chopped
- 1 tablespoon **olive oil**
- 1 can (14½ oz.) **diced tomatoes**
- ⅓ cup **dry vermouth** or dry white wine
- ⅓ cup fat-skimmed **chicken broth**
- 2 tablespoons drained **capers**
- 1 teaspoon **dried thyme**
- 12 ounces (51 to 60 per lb.) **frozen peeled, deveined shrimp**
- 3 tablespoons chopped **parsley**
  Salt and **pepper**

1. In a 5- to 6-quart pan over high heat, bring 3 quarts water to a boil. Add pasta and stir occasionally until barely tender to bite, 9 to 12 minutes.
2. Meanwhile, in a 10- to 12-inch frying pan over high heat, stir onion in oil until limp, 3 to 5 minutes. Add tomatoes and juice, vermouth, broth, capers, and thyme. Bring to a boil and cook for 3 minutes. Add shrimp, reduce heat, and simmer, stirring occasionally, until barely opaque but still moist-looking in thickest part (cut to test), 3 to 4 minutes.
3. Drain pasta and return to 5- to 6-quart pan. Stir in shrimp mixture, parsley, and salt and pepper to taste. (If pasta has cooled, stir over medium heat until hot.) Pour into a wide serving bowl or distribute evenly among plates.

Per serving: 397 cal., 14% (55 cal.) from fat; 27 g protein; 6.1 g fat (0.9 g sat.); 53 g carbo (3.1 g fiber); 491 mg sodium; 129 mg chol. ◆

A traditional Italian pair—pesto pasta and potatoes—becomes an all-in-one meal with green beans. Garnish the dish with small, fresh basil leaves.

Pasta tips

Quick sauces

Stir bite-size pieces of vegetables and meat on hand in a little olive oil over medium-high heat. Add a flavorful liquid such as broth, wine, or tomato juice and combine with hot cooked pasta.

Fresh or dried?

With a light, thin sauce, both fresh and dried pasta work well. With heavier tomato sauces, use firmer dried pasta. If you like a soft, tender texture, choose fresh. If you prefer "al dente"—very slightly chewy—buy dried.

Domestic or imported?

In a blind tasting of six brands of dried linguine, we preferred the al dente texture of Rustichella d'Abruzzo, De Cecco, and Barilla. The first two come from Italy; Barilla is produced domestically by an Italian company. Our favorite was by far the most expensive, but the runners-up are priced close to many domestic brands.

The Low-Fat Cook

Quick, Light, and Romantic

By Linda Lau Anusasananan • Photograph by James Carrier

A Valentine dinner for two

■ The effort to cook a special dinner just for two people ranks up there with the most romantic gestures of all times. But yikes—Valentine's Day is on a Thursday this year! So here's a simple yet brightly flavored weeknight menu that comes together so quickly an hour leaves you time to light candles all over the house. Better yet, it's not rich: Only 22 percent of the calories in the entire meal comes from fat. Lovers' hearts, after all, should be occupied with warmer thoughts than those of health risks.

FOOD STYLING: BASIL FRIEDMAN

MENU

Arugula and Shrimp Salad

Crusty French Rolls

Maple Mustard–glazed Hens with
Corn and Pea Couscous

Dry Riesling or Sparkling Rosé

Pineapple-Raspberry Brûlée Sundaes

Arugula and Shrimp Salad

In a large bowl, mix ½ teaspoon finely grated **orange** peel and 2 tablespoons *each* fresh **orange juice** and **seasoned rice vinegar.** Add 4 ounces (4 cups) rinsed and crisped **arugula** or baby spinach **leaves** and 4 ounces **shelled cooked tiny shrimp;** mix and add **salt** and **pepper** to taste. Divide between two salad plates and set a **crusty French roll** (2 oz. each) alongside.

Per serving: 245 cal., 9.8% (24 cal.) from fat;
18 g protein; 2.7 g fat (0.6 g sat.); 36 g carbo
(2.5 g fiber); 785 mg sodium; 111 mg chol.

Maple Mustard–glazed Hens with Corn and Pea Couscous

PREP AND COOK TIME: About 40 minutes

NOTES: If you can't find baby carrots, trim larger carrots down to size.

MAKES: 2 servings

1 **Cornish hen** (about 1½ lb.)
6 **carrots** (¾ in. wide; 5 in. long; 6 oz. total; see notes), peeled
2 tablespoons **maple syrup**
2 tablespoons **Dijon mustard**
1 cup **fresh** or frozen **sugar snap peas** (4 oz.)
1 cup fat-skimmed **chicken broth**
1 cup **frozen corn kernels**
2 teaspoons **dried green peppercorns** or drained canned capers
½ cup **couscous**
   Salt and **pepper**

1. Remove neck and giblets from hen; reserve for another use or discard. Pull off and discard any pockets of fat. With poultry shears or kitchen scissors, split bird in half lengthwise through breastbone and backbone. Rinse halves and pat dry; set, skin up and slightly apart, on a lightly oiled rack in a foil-lined 10- by 15-inch baking pan. Arrange carrots slightly apart alongside.

2. Roast in 425° regular or convection oven until hen is lightly browned,

20 to 25 minutes.

3. Meanwhile, in a small bowl, mix maple syrup and mustard. Rinse and string snap peas if using fresh.

4. Remove pan from oven and brush hen halves and carrots with mustard mixture, turning as needed to coat all sides. Set halves skin up on rack and continue roasting with carrots until meat at thigh bone is no longer pink (cut to test), 10 to 14 minutes longer.

5. About 8 minutes before hen is done, in a 1- to 1½-quart pan over high heat, bring broth, corn, snap peas, and peppercorns to a boil. Stir in couscous. Cover pan and remove from heat; let stand until broth is absorbed and couscous is tender to bite, about 5 minutes.

6. Mound couscous equally on plates. Set a hen half on each mound and arrange carrots alongside couscous. Add salt and pepper to taste.

Per serving: 757 cal., 32% (243 cal.) from fat;
46 g protein; 27 g fat (7.4 g sat.); 78 g carbo
(7 g fiber); 625 mg sodium; 187 mg chol.

Pineapple-Raspberry Brûlée Sundaes

PREP AND COOK TIME: About 12 minutes

NOTES: To save time, buy fresh pineapple already peeled and cored.

MAKES: 2 servings

8 ounces **peeled, cored fresh pineapple** (see notes), cut into two rings (each about ¾ in. thick)
1 cup **vanilla nonfat frozen yogurt**
½ cup **raspberries**, rinsed and patted dry
3 tablespoons **sugar**

1. Set each pineapple ring on a plate. Top each with a scoop (½ cup) of frozen yogurt and ¼ cup raspberries.

2. To make the caramel, pour sugar into an 8- to 10-inch frying pan over medium-high heat; shake and tilt pan often until sugar is melted and amber-colored, 2 to 3 minutes. At once, pour slowly, in thin streaks, over desserts.

Per serving: 243 cal., 2.2% (5.4 cal.) from fat;
2.7 g protein; 0.6 g fat (0 g sat.); 58 g carbo
(2.8 g fiber); 46 mg sodium; 0 mg chol. ◆

No mere truffle

You don't have to be a chocolatier to produce or a professional to package these exquisite tokens of affection

By Charity Ferreira and Jil Peters

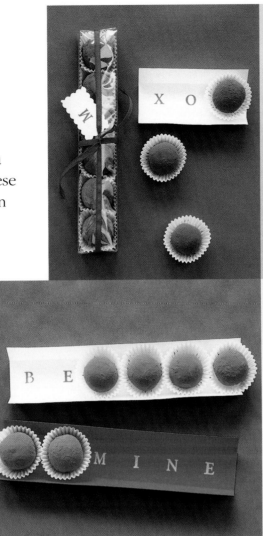

T hat most ubiquitous of Valentine's Day gifts—chocolate—takes on new significance when it comes from your own kitchen. These intense, cocoa-dusted truffles are actually simple to make—so simple, in fact, that their flavor depends entirely on the ingredients you start with. A good-quality chocolate is worth the expense; choose one you would enjoy eating on its own.

MASTER RECIPE

Chocolate Truffles

PREP AND COOK TIME: About 45 minutes, plus at least 3 hours to chill

NOTES: Small paper candy cups are available in the baking section of some well-stocked supermarkets and at stores that sell candy-making supplies. The truffles can be rolled (step 3) up to 3 days ahead.

MAKES: About 2 dozen 1-inch truffles

- ¾ cup **whipping cream**
- 12 ounces **bittersweet** or semisweet **chocolate,** finely chopped
- 1 tablespoon **cognac** or ½ teaspoon **vanilla**

  About ¼ cup **unsweetened cocoa**

1. In a 1- to 2-quart pan over high heat, bring cream to a boil. Meanwhile, place chopped chocolate in a bowl. Pour cream over chocolate and stir gently with a flexible spatula until chocolate is melted and mixture is smooth. (If chocolate does not melt completely, place bowl over a pan of barely simmering water and stir until melted and smooth.) Stir in cognac. Chill mixture until firm, at least 3 hours; if desired, cover and chill up to 1 week.

2. Line a 12- by 15-inch baking sheet with a piece of waxed paper. With a spoon, scoop out 1-tablespoon portions of chocolate mixture; place on waxed paper. If mixture is too firm to scoop, let stand at room temperature about 10 minutes.

3. Place ¼ cup cocoa on a rimmed plate. Dust hands lightly with cocoa. With your hands, roll each scoop of chocolate mixture into a ball, then roll in cocoa to coat. Place each truffle in a small paper candy cup (see notes). To store, place truffles between layers of waxed paper in an airtight container and chill. Advise recipient to chill as well, then bring to room temperature just before serving.

Per truffle: 95 cal., 71% (67 cal.) from fat; 1.3 g protein; 7.4 g fat (4.1 g sat.); 8.6 g carbo (0.6 g fiber); 2.7 mg sodium; 8.3 mg chol. ◆

Flavors to try

Candied Ginger Truffles
Follow recipe for **Chocolate Truffles,** but substitute 1 tablespoon **rum** for cognac and stir ¼ cup minced **candied ginger** into chocolate mixture with rum.

Chocolate-Raspberry Truffles
Follow recipe for **Chocolate Truffles,** but reduce whipping cream to ½ cup, substitute 1 tablespoon **framboise** or other raspberry liqueur for cognac, and stir ¼ cup melted, strained **raspberry jam** into chocolate mixture with the framboise.

Mocha Truffles
Follow recipe for **Chocolate Truffles,** but stir 1 tablespoon **instant espresso powder** into cream until dissolved and substitute 1 tablespoon **Kahlua** for cognac.

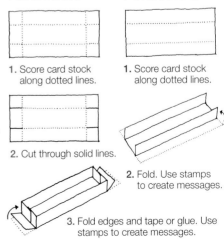

FOR A BOX

1. Score card stock along dotted lines.

2. Cut through solid lines.

3. Fold edges and tape or glue. Use stamps to create messages.

FOR A TRAY

1. Score card stock along dotted lines.

2. Fold. Use stamps to create messages.

Kitchen Cabinet

Readers' recipes tested in *Sunset's* kitchens

By Charity Ferreira

Mayan Chicken

Beverly Smick,
Coulee Dam, WA

This chicken dish, which Beverly Smick serves with rice and beans, was inspired by one she enjoyed on a recent trip to Belize. The chicken gets its red color from a paste made of achiote seeds (from annatto trees), commonly sold in Latin American markets.

PREP AND COOK TIME: About 1¼ hours, plus at least 3 hours to chill

MAKES: 4 servings

- 4 **chicken breast halves** (about 10 oz. each), skinned
- 2 tablespoons **salted red achiote paste** (see note above)
- 1 can (14½ oz.) **crushed tomatoes**
- 2 tablespoons **lemon juice**
- 2 tablespoons minced **fresh ginger**
- 1 tablespoon minced **garlic**
- ½ teaspoon **dried thyme**
- ½ teaspoon **salt**
- ½ teaspoon **ground cumin**
- ½ teaspoon **dried oregano**
- ¼ teaspoon **pepper**
- 1 tablespoon **olive oil**
- 1 **green bell pepper** (8 oz.), rinsed, stemmed, seeded, and chopped
- 1 **onion** (8 oz.), peeled and chopped

1. Rinse chicken and pat dry. Rub achiote paste all over chicken. In a bowl, mix tomatoes, lemon juice, ginger, garlic, thyme, salt, cumin, oregano, and pepper; add chicken and turn to coat. Cover with plastic wrap and chill at least 3 hours or up to 1 day.

2. Pour oil into a 10- to 12-inch frying pan over medium-high heat. When hot, add bell pepper and onion and stir often until limp, about 10 minutes.

3. Add chicken and its marinade to pan and bring to a boil; reduce heat, cover, and simmer until chicken is no longer pink at the bone (cut to test), about 10 minutes. With tongs, transfer chicken to a wide, shallow serving bowl; pour sauce over chicken.

Per serving: 319 cal., 18% (56 cal.) from fat; 45 g protein; 6.2 g fat (1.1 g sat.); 20 g carbo (2.5 g fiber); 762 mg sodium; 107 mg chol.

Achiote paste—sold with Latin American foods—gives this chicken color and flavor.

Salmon Cakes with Cilantro-Ginger Aioli

Jennifer Swezey-Rudnick, Boulder, CO

Jennifer Swezey-Rudnick serves these flavorful cakes over sautéed greens. She bakes the salmon first and makes her own mayonnaise for the aioli; we've simplified by starting with unbaked salmon and prepared mayonnaise.

PREP AND COOK TIME: About 45 minutes

MAKES: 10 cakes; 5 main-dish servings

- 1¾ pounds **boned, skinned salmon fillet,** cut into chunks
- ⅓ cup **cornmeal**
- 3 tablespoons minced **shallots**
- 2 tablespoons **mayonnaise**
- 2 tablespoons **soy sauce**
- 1 tablespoon **Chinese hot mustard**
- 2 teaspoons minced **garlic**
- 2 teaspoons minced **fresh ginger**
- 1 teaspoon **Chinese five spice**
- 2 tablespoons **salad oil**
  Cilantro-Ginger Aioli (recipe follows)

1. In a food processor, working in batches, pulse salmon just until finely chopped. Scrape into a bowl.

2. Add cornmeal, shallots, mayonnaise, soy sauce, mustard, garlic, ginger, and five spice to salmon. Gently shape mixture into 10 equal patties about 3 inches wide and ¾ inch thick; set slightly apart on a sheet of waxed paper or foil.

3. Pour 1 tablespoon oil into a 10- to 12-

inch nonstick frying pan over medium-high heat; when hot, add half the cakes and cook, turning once, until browned on both sides and opaque but still moist-looking in the center (cut to test), 6 to 8 minutes total. As cakes are cooked, transfer to an ovenproof platter and keep warm in a 200° oven. Add remaining tablespoon oil to pan and cook remaining cakes.

4. Serve with Cilantro-Ginger Aioli.

Per serving: 589 cal., 69% (405 cal.) from fat; 36 g protein; 45 g fat (7.4 g sat.); 11 g carbo (0.7 g fiber); 922 mg sodium; 110 mg chol.

Cilantro-Ginger Aioli. In a blender or food processor, whirl ½ cup **mayonnaise,** 2 tablespoons chopped **fresh cilantro** leaves, 1 tablespoon **rice vinegar,** 1 tablespoon **soy sauce,** 1 tablespoon minced **fresh ginger,** 1 teaspoon **Chinese hot mustard,** and 1 peeled clove **garlic** until well blended.

Per tablespoon: 81 cal., 98% (79 cal.) from fat; 0.3 g protein; 8.8 g fat (1.3 g sat.); 0.7 g carbo (0 g fiber); 172 mg sodium; 6.5 mg chol.

Shrimp and Kiwi Fruit Salad

Mickey Strang, McKinleyville, CA

A friend who grows kiwi fruit keeps Mickey Strang's kitchen well supplied. As a result, the fruit turns up in a number of dishes. This salad is a favorite of Strang's husband.

PREP TIME: About 15 minutes

MAKES: 4 servings

- About ¼ teaspoon **hot sauce**
- 2 tablespoons **lemon juice**
- 8 ounces **shelled cooked tiny shrimp,** rinsed and drained
- 4 **kiwi fruit** (12 to 14 oz. total)
- ⅔ cup matchstick-size pieces peeled **jicama**
- ½ cup thinly sliced **celery**
- ½ cup thinly sliced **green onions** (including tops)
- 4 large **butter lettuce** leaves, rinsed and crisped
  Lemon wedges
  Salt

1. In a large bowl, mix ¼ teaspoon hot sauce, lemon juice, and shrimp.

2. Peel kiwi and slice crosswise ¼ inch thick. Add kiwi, jicama, celery, and green onions to bowl; mix gently.

3. Place a lettuce leaf on each plate.

Spoon shrimp mixture equally onto leaves. Place lemon wedges alongside. Add juice from lemon wedges, more hot sauce, and salt to taste.

Per serving: 118 cal., 7.6% (9 cal.) from fat; 13 g protein; 1 g fat (0.2 g sat.); 15 g carbo (4.1 g fiber); 157 mg sodium; 111 mg chol.

Chocolate Truffle Cheesecake

Jane Shapton, Tustin, CA

Three layers of chocolate make Jane Shapton's creamy cheesecake a dessert for serious chocolate lovers. Serve it with whipped cream and raspberries.

PREP AND COOK TIME: About 1½ hours, plus at least 9 hours to cool and chill

MAKES: 12 servings

    9 ounces **chocolate wafer cookies**
    ¼ cup (⅛ lb.) **butter,** melted
    ½ cup **whipping cream**
    6 ounces **semisweet chocolate,** chopped
    3 8-ounce packages **cream cheese**
    1 cup **sugar**
    ⅓ cup **unsweetened cocoa**
    3 **large eggs**
    1 tablespoon **vanilla**

1. In a food processor, whirl cookies into crumbs; you should have 2 cups. Pour into a 9-inch cheesecake pan with removable rim; add butter and mix. Press mixture over bottom and ½ inch up sides of pan. Bake in a 350° oven until crust looks dry, about 10 minutes.

2. In a 1- to 2-quart pan, bring ¼ cup cream to a boil. Remove from heat, add 2 ounces chocolate, and stir until smooth.

3. In a large bowl, with a mixer, beat cream cheese, sugar, and cocoa until smooth. Add eggs, one at a time, beating well after each addition. Add chocolate mixture and vanilla; beat until blended. Scrape into crust; spread level.

4. Bake cheesecake in a 325° regular or 300° convection oven until center jiggles only slightly when pan is gently shaken, about 1 hour. Cool for 1 hour.

5. In a 1- to 2-quart pan, bring remaining ¼ cup cream to a boil. Remove from heat, add remaining 4 ounces chocolate, and stir until smooth. Pour over cake and spread level. Cover and chill at least 8 hours or up to 1 day.

6. Run a knife between cake and pan rim; remove rim. Cut cake into wedges.

Per serving: 514 cal., 63% (324 cal.) from fat; 8.5 g protein; 36 g fat (21 g sat.); 44 g carbo (2.2 g fiber); 353 mg sodium; 138 mg chol. ◆

The Wine Guide
Warming reds for winter meals
By Karen MacNeil-Fife

THOMAS J. STORY

■ In the Napa Valley, where I live, our hot, dry summers and cold, gray winters instill in me the desire—no, the need—to eat and drink seasonally. This time of year, with cold rain whipping around the vines, I'm simply not in the mood for a light salad and a crisp Pinot Grigio. The cold-weather, cozy-wine, comfort-food zeitgeist is upon us, and words like *big, rich,* and *red* make more sense than ever. With that in mind, here are some delicious reds you might consider drinking one night soon.

Zinfandel

Our hometown girl (most of the world's Zin is in California), Zin is a wintertime winner thanks to its hedonistic texture, a fascinating cross between velvet and pancake syrup. The best Zins possess a thick, jammy quality that makes them enormously satisfying with heartwarming dishes like pot roast, pizza, lasagna—even macaroni and cheese. Plus, Zin's extra-fruity quality means it stands up well to spice, making it the perfect wine for, say, a mole dish or enchiladas.

Shiraz

Australian Shiraz is dramatically distinct from its counterpart in France: Syrah. Imagine a wine that's bigger than most Zinfandels and as deeply concentrated as the best Cabernets. Expect tidal waves of menthol, chocolate, blueberry, and licorice flavors. In California and Washington (where the grape is gaining fast in popularity), some Syrahs lean toward the fleshy Australian style; others are leaner, more "French." In Australia, Shiraz is drunk with grilled or broiled meat—often beef or sometimes kangaroo (which leaves you with at least one comforting option).

Cabernet Sauvignon

The king of reds didn't get its reputation by being wishy-washy or bland. Super structured, dense, and full of cassis and dark chocolate flavors, Cabernet is a commanding, compelling wine. It will swamp a delicate entrée, so serve it with something equally powerful: a rib roast, roast leg of lamb, or thick veal chops. ◆

PICKS FOR THE SEASON

■ **Geyser Peak Zinfandel 1998 (Sonoma County),** $17. Jammy and saturated with blueberry and cherry flavors.

■ **Peter Lehmann Shiraz 1999 (Barossa Valley, Australia),** $20. Warm, generous, and mouth-filling, with great density and structure.

■ **McDowell Valley Syrah 1999 (Mendocino),** $12. One of the oldest producers of Syrah in California still makes one of the best bargains, with flavors reminiscent of cherry pie and hints of vanilla. A very satisfying red; a more than satisfying price.

■ **Fetzer Barrel Select Cabernet Sauvignon 1998 (North Coast, CA),** $17. A Cabernet like this—full of simple but delicious boysenberry and cassis flavors—makes a Sunday night roast memorable.

Sample Vietnam's intriguing cuisine, including this spicy grilled catfish on a bed of rice noodles and greens (see page 57).

March

brunch
season

A make-ahead menu that's perfect
for a leisurely spring morning

■ Spring's burgeoning warm weather brings opportunities for entertaining outdoors early in the day: It's the perfect time of year to have friends over for brunch. This menu takes advantage of some of the season's best fresh produce, enlivening it with vibrant flavor—roasted asparagus topped with a caper-studded chopped egg salad, melons marinated with lime juice and mint, strawberries paired with a creamy yogurt panna cotta. The meal's centerpiece is a cinnamon-scented chicken and egg filo pie (rendering moot the question of which came first). Most of the dishes can be prepared ahead of time and just assembled or baked in the morning, to keep brunch a relaxed, easy affair.

By Charity Ferreira • Photographs by James Carrier • Food styling by Jayne Boyle

spring brunch menu

Tangerine Sparklers

Smoked Salmon
and Cream Cheese Roll-ups

Radishes and Olives

Spiced Chicken Filo Pie

Roasted Asparagus with
Chopped Egg Salad

Pistachio Scones

Marinated Melons with
Mint and Feta

Yogurt Panna Cotta

White or Sparkling Wine (see page 54)

Coffee

For the Tangerine
Sparklers (above)—
nonalcoholic mimosas,
if you will—combine
2 parts chilled tangerine
juice with 1 part
chilled club soda or
sparkling water.

Brunch wrap: Smoked salmon and cream cheese roll into an easy appetizer.

Spiced Chicken Filo Pie

PREP AND COOK TIME: About 2½ hours

NOTES: Have the chicken cut up at the meat market. As you work with filo, cover the sheets you're not using with plastic wrap to keep them from drying out. You can prepare through step 4 up to 1 day ahead; wrap nuts airtight and store at room temperature, and chill chicken and egg mixtures separately. The pie can be assembled (step 5) up to 2 hours ahead; wrap airtight and chill.

MAKES: 8 servings

- ½ cup **almonds**
- 1¼ teaspoons **ground cinnamon**
- 1 teaspoon **granulated sugar**
- 1 **chicken** (about 4 lb.), neck and giblets removed, cut into 8 pieces (see notes)
- 6 cups fat-skimmed **chicken broth**
- 1 **onion** (8 oz.), peeled and chopped
- 1 clove **garlic**, peeled and chopped
- 2 teaspoons **ground ginger**
- 1½ teaspoons **turmeric**
- ¼ teaspoon **ground cloves**
  About ¼ teaspoon **salt**
  About ⅛ teaspoon **pepper**
- 6 **large eggs**
- 6 tablespoons **butter**, melted
- 1 package (1 lb.) **filo dough**, thawed (see notes)
- 2 tablespoons **powdered sugar**

1. Place almonds in a 10-inch baking pan. Bake in a 350° regular or convection oven until golden beneath skins, about 10 minutes. Let cool. In a food processor, pulse almonds with ¾ teaspoon cinnamon and the granulated sugar until coarsely chopped (or coarsely chop with a knife).

2. Rinse chicken. In a 5- to 6-quart pot, combine chicken, broth, onion, garlic, ginger, turmeric, and cloves. Bring to a boil over medium-high heat; reduce heat, cover, and simmer until chicken is tender when pierced, about 45 minutes.

3. Pour chicken mixture through a strainer set over a large bowl; return strained broth to pan. With your fingers, remove skin from chicken and pull meat from bones; discard skin and bones. Shred chicken into bite-size pieces. Mix chicken and strained onion in a bowl and moisten with about 2 tablespoons broth. Season to taste with salt and pepper. Let cool; if desired, cover and chill up to 1 day.

4. Bring broth in pan to a simmer over medium-high heat; reduce heat to

Smoked Salmon and Cream Cheese Roll-ups

PREP TIME: About 30 minutes, plus at least 1 hour to chill

NOTES: You can buy soft lahvosh or flatbread in oval or rectangular pieces at many well-stocked supermarkets and in markets that carry Middle Eastern ingredients.

MAKES: 16 roll-ups; about 8 servings

- 2 pieces **soft lahvosh** or flatbread (about 13 by 18 in. each)
- 1 carton (8 oz.) **whipped cream cheese**
- 2 tablespoons chopped **parsley**
  Salt and **pepper**
- 12 ounces **thin-sliced smoked salmon**
- 1 **English cucumber** (about 8 oz.), rinsed and very thinly sliced
- ¾ cup very thinly sliced **red onion** (about 4 oz.)

1. Place one piece of lahvosh on a sheet of plastic wrap. With a flexible spatula or a knife, spread about ½ cup cream cheese in a thin, even layer over entire surface of bread. Sprinkle with 1 tablespoon parsley, then lightly with salt and pepper. Arrange half the smoked salmon slices on top, leaving a 1-inch border along short ends of lahvosh. Arrange half the cucumber and onion slices evenly over salmon.

2. Beginning at a short end, roll lahvosh as tightly as possible, taking care not to push filling forward as you go. Wrap tightly in plastic wrap. Repeat to fill, roll, and wrap second lahvosh. Chill rolls for at least 1 hour or up to 8 hours.

3. Unwrap rolls and trim off about 1 inch from each end (save to eat later). Cut each roll into eight equal pieces and arrange on a platter.

Per roll-up: 208 cal., 48% (99 cal.) from fat; 12 g protein; 11 g fat (7 g sat.); 13 g carbo (1.1 g fiber); 999 mg sodium; 38 mg chol.

Buttered sheets of filo dough enclose a filling of chicken, egg, and almonds spiced with cinnamon. The baked pie can be cut into squares, triangles, or diamonds.

maintain simmer. In a bowl, beat eggs to blend with ¼ teaspoon salt and ⅛ teaspoon pepper. Add eggs to broth; stir gently until set, 1 to 2 minutes. Pour through a strainer into another bowl; reserve broth for other uses. Let eggs cool.

5. Lightly brush the inside of a shallow 3- to 3½-quart casserole or baking dish with melted butter. Place one 13- by 17-inch sheet of filo in dish so that it covers the bottom and sides of casserole and hangs over the edge slightly. Brush sheet lightly with butter. Repeat to layer and butter three more sheets. Sprinkle

half the almond mixture evenly over filo in bottom of casserole; spread chicken mixture over nuts. Cut four sheets of filo in half crosswise to make eight 8½- by 13-inch rectangles. One at a time, brush four half-sheets with butter and layer them over chicken. Sprinkle remaining half of the almond mixture over filo and arrange egg mixture evenly over nuts. Fold in overhanging edges of filo and top with four more buttered half-sheets, tucking any overhanging edges into sides of casserole. Brush top layer with butter.

6. Bake pie in a 375° regular or convection oven until top is well browned, 35 to 40 minutes. Mix powdered sugar with remaining ½ teaspoon cinnamon and sift evenly over top of pie. Cut warm pie into portions; serve warm or at room temperature.

Per serving: 520 cal., 40% (207 cal.) from fat; 39 g protein; 23 g fat (8.1 g sat.); 37 g carbo (1.3 g fiber); 544 mg sodium; 232 mg chol.

Roasted Asparagus with Chopped Egg Salad

PREP AND COOK TIME: About 45 minutes
NOTES: To cook the eggs, place in a 3- to 4-quart pan and cover with cold water. Bring to a boil over high heat, reduce

heat, and boil gently, uncovered, for about 13 minutes. With a slotted spoon, lift eggs from water and immerse in cold water until cool. The asparagus can be roasted (step 1) up to 2 hours ahead; cover loosely and let stand at room temperature. The chopped egg salad can be made (step 2) up to 1 day ahead; wrap airtight and chill. Bring to room temperature, then spoon over asparagus just before serving.
MAKES: 8 servings

- 3 pounds **asparagus**
- ¼ cup **extra-virgin olive oil**
  Salt and **pepper**
- 2 tablespoons **lemon juice**
- 5 hard-cooked **large eggs** (see notes), shelled and coarsely chopped
- 12 **green olives,** pitted and coarsely chopped
- 1 teaspoon drained **capers**
- 2 tablespoons chopped **parsley**
- 4 ounces **arugula** or baby spinach (about 4 cups), rinsed and crisped

1. Rinse asparagus; snap off and discard tough stem ends. In a 12- by 17-inch baking pan, mix asparagus with 2 tablespoons olive oil. Sprinkle generously with salt and pepper. Transfer half the mixture to another 12- by 17-inch baking pan. Bake in a 450° regular or convection oven until asparagus is tender when pierced, 10 to 12 minutes.

2. Meanwhile, in a bowl, mix lemon juice and remaining 2 tablespoons olive oil. Add eggs, olives, capers, and parsley; mix gently to avoid mashing yolks. Season to taste with salt and pepper.

3. Mound arugula on a serving platter. Arrange asparagus on arugula and spoon egg salad over asparagus.

Per serving: 148 cal., 67% (99 cal.) from fat; 8.5 g protein; 11 g fat (2.1 g sat.); 6.3 g carbo (1.7 g fiber); 170 mg sodium; 133 mg chol.

Pistachio Scones

PREP AND COOK TIME: About 1 hour

NOTES: Semolina flour gives these scones a slightly crunchy texture. You can prepare them through step 5 up to 3 days ahead; wrap airtight and freeze. Transfer frozen wedges directly to oven (do not thaw); bake 30 to 35 minutes. Serve scones with apricot jam.

MAKES: 12 scones

About 2¾ cups **all-purpose flour**

2 cups **semolina flour** or cornmeal (see notes)

About ¾ cup **sugar**

¾ cup chopped **unsalted roasted pistachios** or chopped walnuts

1 tablespoon **baking powder**

½ teaspoon **salt**

About ½ cup (¼ lb.) **butter** or margarine

1⅓ cups plus 2 tablespoons **milk**

1 tablespoon grated **lemon** peel

1 **large egg** yolk

1. In a bowl, mix 2¾ cups flour, semolina flour, ¾ cup sugar, pistachios, baking powder, and salt.

2. Cut ½ cup butter into chunks and add to bowl. With your fingers or a pastry blender, rub or cut in butter until mixture forms coarse crumbs.

3. Add 1⅓ cups milk and the lemon peel to flour mixture and stir with a fork just until evenly moistened.

4. Scrape onto a floured board and with lightly floured hands, knead just until dough comes together (it will be sticky). Divide in half and form each half into a ball. Pat each ball into a 7-inch round about 1 inch thick. Cut each round into six equal wedges.

Warm pistachio-studded scones wait for a spoonful of apricot jam.

The Wine Guide

Is noon too soon?

Let's cut right to the chase: Many of us—even the most steadfast wine lovers—never drink wine at brunch. Is noon just too soon for a grown-up beverage? Well, if so, how do you explain that unofficial queen of brunchtime beverages, the Bloody Mary (which, it should be noted, packs a much bigger wallop than the fruit of the vine)?

No, it's probably not our reluctance to indulge a little. But, unlike a Bloody Mary, wine requires a cerebral moment, a delicious question, some advance (if not advanced) thought: Which wine to serve with foods that we haven't imagined drinking wine with before?

The answer is actually easy. Great brunch wines are like great brunches—light and lighthearted. Anything fussy, complicated, very serious, or really expensive is simply out of place. Moreover, a satisfying brunch wine is flexible with food, because everything from scones to smoked salmon might be on the table.

My short list for wines that fit the bill

Muscats. A delicious, exotic wine for daytime sipping. In Italy (where it's known as Moscato), it's the traditional wine drunk on Christmas. All light and fresh, Muscats may be dry or slightly sweet (the label will indicate which). Many are also low in alcohol. Good producers: **Navarro Vineyards** (Anderson Valley, CA) produces a fabulous dry Muscat

Blanc (available by calling the winery; 707/895-3686); **Domaine Zind-Humbrecht** (Alsace, France) makes big, opulent dry Muscats; **Michele Chiarlo** (Italy) has its irresistible Nivole Moscato D'Asti.

Rieslings. Light as a feather on the palate and crisp enough to go with a broad range of dishes. German Rieslings are the lightest (and most aren't sweet—only the very cheap ones are). The dry Rieslings from Alsace and Australia (the new star in this galaxy) have a little more oomph. California and Washington versions are often full bodied, super-fruity, and slightly sweeter than Rieslings made elsewhere. Some top bets: **J. u. H. A. Strub** (Germany), **Domaine Weinbach** (Alsace), **Leeuwin Estate** (Australia), **Chateau St. Jean** (California), and **Chateau Ste. Michelle** (Washington).

Gewürztraminers. Pretty sassy and exotic as wines go, these are the ones for a wild, fun-packed affair. The best are from Alsace, where there are a score of great producers—**Trimbach, Hugel,** and **Domaine Ostertag,** for starters. Great domestic Gewürztraminers are scarcer, but **Navarro Vineyards,** again, does a sensational job; **Thomas Fogarty** (also California) is close on its heels.

Sparklers. Bubbles are a brunchtime no-brainer. Their crisp tingle is a palate-exciting backdrop for dozens of typical dishes—including foods that are traditionally hard on wine, like eggs and smoked salmon. If until now you've considered sparkling wine only an aperitif or a celebration beverage, have one with brunch and prove yourself deliciously wrong. — *Karen MacNeil-Fife*

5. Place wedges 2 inches apart on a buttered 14- by 17-inch baking sheet. Beat egg yolk with remaining 2 tablespoons milk just to blend. Brush tops of wedges with egg mixture and sprinkle lightly with sugar.

6. Bake on the middle rack in a 375° regular or 350° convection oven until scones are richly browned, about 25 minutes. Serve warm.

Per scone: 374 cal., 34% (126 cal.) from fat; 8.8 g protein; 14 g fat (6 g sat.); 55 g carbo (2.5 g fiber); 313 mg sodium; 43 mg chol.

Marinated Melons with Mint and Feta

PREP TIME: About 30 minutes, plus at least 1 hour to chill

MAKES: 3 quarts; about 8 servings

- 1/2 cup **orange juice**
- 1/4 cup **lime juice**
- 1/8 teaspoon **salt**
- 8 pounds **melons** such as cantaloupe, orange-fleshed or regular honeydew, and/or watermelon
- 1/4 cup lightly packed **fresh mint** leaves, rinsed
- 1/2 cup crumbled **feta cheese** (about 2 oz.)

1. In a large bowl, combine orange juice, lime juice, and salt.

2. Cut melons into quarters, discard seeds, and cut off and discard peel. Cut fruit into 1-inch chunks; add to orange juice mixture. Cut mint leaves lengthwise into slivers. Add to bowl and mix gently to coat. Cover airtight and chill at least 1 hour or up to 4 hours.

3. Just before serving, mix marinated melons gently and sprinkle with feta cheese.

Per serving: 109 cal., 20% (22 cal.) from fat; 2.9 g protein; 2.4 g fat (1.8 g sat.); 21 g carbo (1.9 g fiber); 149 mg sodium; 7.5 mg chol.

Yogurt Panna Cotta

PREP AND COOK TIME: About 30 minutes, plus at least 8 hours to chill

NOTES: Use whole-milk yogurt for this dish, not low- or nonfat. Serve panna cotta with fresh strawberries, rinsed, stemmed, and halved or quartered.

MAKES: 6 to 8 servings

- 2 teaspoons **unflavored gelatin** (a 1 1/4-oz. envelope)
- 2 cups **whipping cream**
- 1 **vanilla bean**, split lengthwise, or 1 teaspoon vanilla extract
- 1/2 cup **sugar**
- 3 strips **orange** peel (orange part only; each about 1/2 in. wide and 2 to 3 in. long)
- 1 2/3 cups **plain yogurt** (see notes)
  About 1/2 teaspoon **salad oil**

1. In a small bowl, sprinkle gelatin over 1/4 cup cream. Let stand, without stirring, until gelatin is soft, about 10 minutes.

2. Meanwhile, pour remaining 1 3/4 cups cream into a 1- to 2-quart pan over medium heat. Scrape seeds from vanilla bean into cream, then add the bean (if using vanilla extract, add after yogurt, below), sugar, and orange peel; stir until sugar is dissolved and mixture is simmering. Remove from heat. Add gelatin mixture and stir until gelatin is completely dissolved. Pour into a large bowl. Remove vanilla bean and orange peel and let cool 10 minutes. Add yogurt (and vanilla extract, if using) and stir until well blended.

3. Lightly brush a 4-cup tube mold (or eight 1/2-cup molds) with oil; pour cream mixture into mold. Cover and chill until set, 8 hours or up to 2 days.

4. Just before serving, unmold: Gently run a knife between panna cotta and sides of mold to loosen. Invert a plate over mold and, holding plate and mold together, turn over; lift off mold. If panna cotta doesn't slip out easily, immerse mold to just below rim in warm water for about 2 seconds; lift out, dry bottom of mold, and repeat to invert onto plate.

Per serving: 260 cal., 66% (171 cal.) from fat; 4.5 g protein; 19 g fat (12 g sat.); 18 g carbo (0 g fiber); 55 mg sodium; 69 mg chol. ◆

Yogurt gives this delicate, creamy custard an unexpected tang.

The flavors of
Vietnam

You've tasted this intriguing cuisine in noodle houses and more formal Vietnamese eateries.
Now, widely available ingredients and our simplified techniques make it easy to sample at home

By Linda Lau Anusasananan • Photographs by James Carrier • Food styling by Basil Friedman

Vibrantly seasoned catfish,
on a bed of noodles and
vegetables, is topped with
crisp fried shallots, a
delicious accompaniment
to many dishes.

Political upheaval, ironically, can leave a bright legacy in the kitchen. Out of Vietnam's long history of domination—by the Chinese and, later, the French—emerged an exciting multicultural cuisine. Cooking techniques from those world-class cuisines, applied to the country's tropical bounty, created a vivid palette of flavors and textures unique among Asian traditions.

In the late 1960s and the 1970s, when many of us first became aware of Vietnam during yet another period of upheaval, our country became a beneficiary of that culinary legacy. Many Vietnamese immigrants settled in the West. Restaurants and markets sprang up to serve these communities, and eventually curious Westerners ventured in, drawn by aromas of Chinese five spice, lemon grass, fish sauce, and unusual fresh herbs.

This sampler of Vietnamese classics—which is based on easy techniques—gives you a taste of this intriguing cuisine. Many of the essential ingredients can be found in the Asian section of well-stocked supermarkets. The less familiar fresh herbs are available in Vietnamese grocery stores, but you can also use the supermarket alternatives we give. Either way, the dishes will be a delicious adventure.

Grilled Catfish with Noodles
(Cha Ca)

PREP AND COOK TIME: About 1 hour
NOTES: At the Noodle Ranch in Seattle, head chef Nga Bui sets a hot, spicy fish fillet on a bed of rice noodles and greens for a light, refreshing meal in a bowl. Red curry powder can be found in the spice section of many supermarkets; if it's unavailable, use the more common yellow powder. The grilled fish can also be served with hot cooked rice or in a sandwich.

MAKES: 6 servings

- ⅓ cup minced **shallots**
- 3 tablespoons **Asian fish sauce** (*nuoc mam* or *nam pla*)
- 1 tablespoon **red** or yellow **curry powder** (see notes)
- 1½ teaspoons **ground ginger**
- 1 teaspoon **ground turmeric**
- ½ teaspoon **cayenne**
- 2 cloves **garlic,** peeled and pressed or minced
- 6 **boned, skinned catfish** or tilapia **fillets** (about 6 oz. each)
  About 2 tablespoons **salad oil**
- 4 cups bite-size pieces **iceberg lettuce** (8 oz.), rinsed and crisped
- 3 cups **bean sprouts** (6 to 8 oz.), rinsed
- ½ cup **fresh mint** leaves, rinsed
- ½ cup **fresh cilantro** leaves, rinsed
- 6 to 8 cups cooled **Cooked Rice Noodles** (about ⅛ in. wide; recipe in box at right)

- ½ cup chopped **roasted, salted peanuts**
- ⅓ cup thinly sliced **green onions** (including tops)
- ½ cup chopped **fresh dill**
  About ½ cup **Fried Shallots** (recipe on page 58)
  About 1½ cups **Vietnamese Dipping Sauce** (recipe on page 60)

1. In a small bowl, mix minced shallots, fish sauce, curry powder, ginger, turmeric, cayenne, and garlic. Rinse fish and pat dry. Rub shallot mixture all over fillets and stack in a bowl. Cover and chill 30 minutes or up to 1 day.

2. Brush both sides of fillets lightly with oil. Place fish on a grill 4 to 6 inches above a solid bed of hot coals or over high heat on a gas grill (you can hold your hand at grill level only 2 to 3 seconds); cover gas grill. Cook fish, turning once, until barely opaque but still moist-looking in center of thickest part (cut to test), 4 to 8 minutes total. Serve hot or cool.

3. Meanwhile, divide lettuce, bean sprouts, mint, and cilantro among six deep, wide bowls. Mound noodles equally over vegetables and herbs.

4. Lay a grilled fish fillet on each mound of noodles. Sprinkle peanuts, green onions, dill, and Fried Shallots equally over the top. Serve with Vietnamese Dipping Sauce to drizzle over portions to taste.

Per serving: 705 cal., 38% (270 cal.) from fat; 36 g protein; 30 g fat (5.2 g sat.); 72 g carbo (3.1 g fiber); 1,316 mg sodium; 56 mg chol.

Noodles made from ground rice form the base for many popular Vietnamese dishes. They may be fresh or dried, thick or thin. In the West, they're most commonly available dried and can be found in many supermarkets and in Asian grocery stores.

Throughout Asia, most cooks soak the dried noodles in water until they're pliable. Just before using them, they put the soaked noodles in a wire basket with a long handle and immerse it in boiling water; the noodles cook almost instantly. We skip the soaking step here and boil the noodles just a little longer.

Cooked Rice Noodles (Bun)

PREP AND COOK TIME: About 5 minutes
NOTES: Dried rice noodles range in width from about ¹⁄₁₆ to ¼ inch wide; the cooked yield varies slightly depending on their width (look for width specified in recipe).
MAKES: 6 to 8 cups; 6 to 8 servings

In a 6- to 8-quart pan over high heat, bring 3 to 4 quarts water to a boil. Add 12 to 14 ounces **dried rice noodles** (*mai fun,* rice sticks, or rice vermicelli) and stir to separate; cook until barely tender to bite, 2 to 3 minutes. Drain. If not using immediately, rinse well to keep noodles from sticking together, and drain again.

Per serving: 144 cal., 0% (0 cal.) from fat; 0 g protein; 0 g fat; 36 g carbo (0 g fiber); 75 mg sodium; 0 mg chol.

Hoi An–style Oven-crisped Pork Sandwich
(Banh Mi Thit Hoi An)

PREP AND COOK TIME: About 45 minutes

NOTES: This sandwich is a specialty of Hoi An, a charming old fishing village in central Vietnam. Its interplay of textures—cold cuts (pork loin, ham, or chicken; home-cooked or purchased), ground pork, greens, and cucumbers—is distinctive. Choose a sweet baguette with a light, slightly soft interior and thin, crisp crust. You can assemble the sandwiches through step 2 up to 1 hour ahead; cover loosely and let stand at room temperature.

MAKES: 6 servings

- 1 teaspoon **Chinese five spice** (or ¼ teaspoon *each* ground cinnamon, ground cloves, ground ginger, and anise seeds)
- 1 tablespoon **salad oil**
- ¼ cup chopped **shallots**
- 1 clove **garlic**, peeled and minced
- 12 ounces **ground lean pork**
- 3 tablespoons **soy sauce**
- 1½ teaspoons **sugar**
  Salt
- 3 **baguettes** (8 oz. each; see notes)
  About 2 tablespoons **Asian red chili paste** or sauce
- 8 ounces thinly sliced roast **boned, fat-trimmed pork loin** or cooked ham or chicken (see notes)
- 2 cups thinly sliced **English cucumbers** (about 8 oz.)
- 3 cups **salad mix** (4 oz.), rinsed and crisped
- ½ cup **fresh Thai** or regular **basil** leaves, rinsed and cut into 1-inch pieces
- ½ cup **Fried Shallots** (optional; recipe at right)

1. In an 8- to 10-inch frying pan over medium-high heat, stir five spice until fragrant, about 30 seconds. Stir in oil, shallots, and garlic. Add ground pork and stir often, breaking apart with spoon, until meat is crumbly and no longer pink, about 15 minutes. Add soy sauce, sugar, and salt to taste.

2. Cut baguettes in half crosswise, then split lengthwise almost all the way through, leaving halves attached at one side. Spread about 1 teaspoon chili paste on one cut side of each baguette section. Spoon about ⅙ of the warm ground pork mixture, including juices, over chili paste. Tuck ⅙ of the pork slices evenly into each

Roast pork is layered over five spice–seasoned ground pork for echoes and contrasts in texture and flavor.

sandwich. Set sandwiches slightly apart on a 12- by 15-inch baking sheet.

3. Bake in a 375° regular or convection oven just until filling is warm and crust is crisp, about 5 minutes. Remove sandwiches from oven and fill each with ⅙ of the cucumbers, salad mix, basil, and Fried Shallots. Add more chili paste and salt to taste.

Per serving: 596 cal., 29% (171 cal.) from fat; 35 g protein; 19 g fat (4.2 g sat.); 70 g carbo (4.3 g fiber); 1,290 mg sodium; 64 mg chol.

ASIAN KITCHEN BASICS

Fried shallots make a crisp, flavorful garnish for salads, noodle dishes, and sandwiches.

Fried Shallots (Hahn Phi)

PREP AND COOK TIME: About 15 minutes

MAKES: About ½ cup

In an 8- to 10-inch frying pan over medium heat, stir 1 cup thinly sliced **shallots** in 2 tablespoons **salad oil** until crisp and golden, 6 to 10 minutes (shallots will absorb most of the oil).

Per tablespoon: 45 cal., 69% (31 cal.) from fat; 0.5 g protein; 3.4 g fat (0.4 g sat.); 3.4 g carbo (0.2 g fiber); 2.4 mg sodium; 0 mg chol.

Beef Noodle Soup (Pho Bo)

PREP AND COOK TIME: About 2¼ to 2½ hours

NOTES: The beef broth (steps 1 and 2) can be made up to 1 day ahead; cover beef chuck and broth separately and chill. Bring broth to a boil before serving. For a simpler version of the dish, omit the beef chuck, increase the boned sirloin steak to 2 pounds, and increase the beef broth to 3 quarts; for steps 1 and 2, simmer broth (omit water) with the spice bundle for 30 minutes, then discard bundle and add fish sauce, sugar, and salt to taste. To slice the sirloin as thinly as possible, freeze it flat for 30 to 45 minutes, then cut crosswise into 2- to 3-inch-long strips. You can slice the meat up to 6 hours ahead; cover and chill.

MAKES: 6 servings

½ cup thinly sliced **fresh ginger** (about 3 oz.)

1 cup thinly sliced **shallots** (about 4 oz.)

3 **whole star anise** (or 2 teaspoons pieces) or 1 teaspoon anise seeds

1 **cinnamon stick** (3 in. long)

1½ pounds **boned beef chuck,** rinsed and fat trimmed

2½ quarts fat-skimmed **beef broth** (see notes)

About ¼ cup **Asian fish sauce** *(nuoc mam or nam pla)*

1 tablespoon **sugar**
  Salt

2 cups **bean sprouts** (5 to 6 oz.), rinsed

¼ cup very thinly sliced **fresh hot red** or green **chilies** (about 1 oz.), such as Thai, serrano, or jalapeño

½ cup rinsed **fresh Thai** or small regular **basil** leaves

½ cup rinsed **fresh cilantro** leaves

3 **limes** (3 oz. each), rinsed and cut into wedges

8 ounces **boned beef sirloin steak,** fat trimmed, very thinly sliced (see notes)

6 cups hot **Cooked Rice Noodles** (about ⅛ in. wide; recipe on page 57)

½ cup thinly sliced **yellow onion**

¾ cup thinly sliced **green onions** (including green tops)
  Hoisin sauce (optional)
  Asian red chili paste or sauce (optional)

1. Wrap ginger, shallots, star anise, and cinnamon stick in two layers of cheesecloth (about 17 by 17 in.); tie with heavy cotton string. In an 8- to 10-quart pan, combine beef chuck, broth, 2½ quarts water, ¼ cup fish sauce, sugar, and spice bundle. Cover and bring to a boil over high heat; uncover, reduce heat, and simmer until beef is tender when pierced, 1½ to 1¾ hours.

2. With a slotted spoon, transfer meat to a board. Remove and discard spice bundle. Skim and discard fat from broth. Add salt and more fish sauce to taste. Return broth to a simmer.

3. Meanwhile, arrange bean sprouts, chilies, basil, cilantro, and limes on a platter. When beef chuck is cool enough to handle, thinly slice across the grain.

4. Immerse sliced sirloin in simmering broth (use a wire basket or strainer, if available) and cook just until brown on the outside but still pink in the center, 30 seconds to 1 minute; lift out (with basket or a slotted spoon).

5. Mound hot Cooked Rice Noodles equally in deep bowls (at least 3-cup capacity). Top equally with beef chuck,

sirloin, yellow onion, and green onions. Ladle broth over portions to cover generously.

6. Serve Beef Noodle Soup with platter of condiments, hoisin sauce, and chili paste to add to taste.

Per serving: 592 cal., 17% (99 cal.) from fat; 42 g protein; 11 g fat (4 g sat.); 81 g carbo (1.3 g fiber); 768 mg sodium; 97 mg chol.

Braised Tofu in Caramel Sauce *(Tau Hu Kho)*

PREP AND COOK TIME: About 25 minutes

NOTES: Caramelized sugar infuses the sauce with sweetness and gives it a deep mahogany shine. Serve this great vegetarian dish with hot cooked rice and stir-fried spinach with garlic.

MAKES: 4 servings

1 pound **firm tofu**

3 tablespoons **sugar**

3 tablespoons **soy sauce**

¼ cup minced **shallots**

1 tablespoon minced **fresh ginger**

1 clove **garlic,** peeled and minced

2 tablespoons thinly sliced **green onions** (including tops)

⅛ teaspoon **pepper**

1. Cut tofu into 2- by 3-inch, ½-inch-thick slices and pat dry.

2. Place sugar in a 10- to 12-inch frying pan over medium-high heat; shake pan often until sugar is melted and amber colored, 2 to 3 minutes. Add ½ cup hot water (mixture will bubble vigorously) and stir over medium heat until caramelized sugar is dissolved.

3. Stir in soy sauce, shallots, ginger, and garlic; stir often over high heat until boiling. Lay tofu pieces in a single layer in sauce. Simmer, uncovered, over medium-low heat for about 5 minutes. With a wide spatula, turn pieces over; simmer until hot and coated with sauce, 3 to 4 minutes longer.

4. Transfer tofu and sauce to a serving dish and sprinkle with green onions and pepper.

Per serving: 219 cal., 41% (89 cal.) from fat; 19 g protein; 9.9 g fat (1.4 g sat.); 18 g carbo (0.2 g fiber); 790 mg sodium; 0 mg chol.

Braised Tilapia in Caramel Sauce. Follow the recipe for **Braised Tofu in Caramel Sauce,** preceding, but substitute 1 pound **boned, skinned tilapia** or catfish **fillets** for the tofu and 3 tablespoons **Asian fish sauce** *(nuoc mam or nam pla)* for the soy sauce. In step 1, rinse fish and pat dry; cut fillets crosswise into 2- by 3-inch pieces. In

Braised Tofu in
Caramel Sauce

step 3, lay fish in a single layer in sauce, overlapping edges if necessary to fit. Simmer for about 3 minutes, turn over carefully, and simmer until barely opaque but still moist-looking in center of thickest part (cut to test), 3 to 4 minutes longer. In step 4, transfer fish to serving dish with a slotted spatula. Bring sauce to a boil over high heat and stir often until slightly syrupy and reduced to about ⅔ cup, 2 to 4 minutes; pour over fish, then sprinkle with the green onions and pepper. Makes 4 servings.

Per serving: 187 cal., 19% (36 cal.) from fat; 23 g protein; 4 g fat (0.3 g sat.); 14 g carbo (0.2 g fiber); 508 mg sodium; chol. for tilapia not available.

Chicken with Lemon Grass and Chili (Ga Xao Xa Ot)

PREP AND COOK TIME: About 45 minutes

NOTES: Serve with hot cooked rice, stir-fried green beans, and a light, broth-based soup.

MAKES: 4 servings

1 pound **boned, skinned chicken thighs**

2 stalks **fresh lemon grass** (each 10 to 12 in. long)

About 2 tablespoons **Asian fish sauce** *(nuoc mam* or *nam pla)*

2 teaspoons **sugar**

2 cloves **garlic,** peeled and minced

1 tablespoon **salad oil**

½ cup sliced **shallots**

⅓ cup fat-skimmed **chicken broth**

¾ to 2 teaspoons thinly sliced **fresh hot red** or green **chili,** such as Thai, serrano, jalapeño, or Fresno

Fresh cilantro leaves (optional)

1. Rinse chicken thighs and pat dry. Remove and discard any excess fat. Cut chicken into ¼-inch-thick strips 2 to 3 inches long.

2. Rinse lemon grass. Cut off and discard tough tops and root ends; peel off and discard tough, outer green layers of stalks down to tender white portion of bulbs. Finely chop tender portions; you should have 5 to 7 tablespoons.

3. In a bowl, mix chicken, lemon grass, 2 tablespoons fish sauce, sugar, and garlic.

4. Set a 10- to 12-inch frying pan over high heat; when hot, add oil and shallots and stir until shallots begin to brown, about 1 minute. Add chicken mixture and stir until chicken is no longer pink in the center (cut to test), about 3 minutes.

5. Stir in broth and sliced chili to taste;

bring mixture to a boil. Taste, and add more fish sauce if desired. Spoon into a serving dish and sprinkle with cilantro.

Per serving: 217 cal., 36% (78 cal.) from fat; 25 g protein; 8.7 g fat (1.8 g sat.); 8.7 g carbo (0.2 g fiber); 404 mg sodium; 94 mg chol.

Cabbage and Shrimp Salad (Goi Tom)

PREP TIME: About 45 minutes

NOTES: This salad is traditionally made with finely sliced raw banana blossoms or cabbage; we've gotten excellent results with the cabbage. Spicy *rau ram,* found in Vietnamese markets, adds an aromatic pungency, but fresh mint is a very good alternative. For convenience, use frozen cooked shrimp, thawed, and packaged shredded cabbage (often labeled "angel hair"). Serve the salad for a light lunch or as part of a multi-course meal.

MAKES: 4 main-dish servings

8 ounces (31 to 40 per lb.) **shelled, deveined cooked shrimp** (see notes)

¼ cup **lime juice**

3 tablespoons **Asian fish sauce** *(nuoc mam* or *nam pla)*

2 tablespoons **sugar**

½ to 2 teaspoons minced **fresh hot red** or green **chili,** such as Thai, serrano, jalapeño, or Fresno

1 clove **garlic,** peeled and minced

6 cups **finely shredded cabbage** (10 oz.; see notes)

8 ounces **bean sprouts** (3 to 4 cups), rinsed

¾ cup **fresh *rau ram*** or fresh mint leaves (see notes)

½ cup finely shredded **carrots**

½ cup **Fried Shallots** (recipe on page 58)

½ cup chopped **roasted, salted peanuts**

1. Rinse and drain shrimp; pat dry. Cut each in half lengthwise.

2. In a large bowl, mix lime juice, fish sauce, sugar, ½ teaspoon chili, and garlic. Add shrimp, cabbage, bean sprouts, *rau ram,* carrots, shallots, and ¼ cup peanuts; mix. Taste, and add more chili if desired.

3. Pour the salad onto a platter and sprinkle the remaining ¼ cup peanuts over the top.

Per serving: 348 cal., 47% (162 cal.) from fat; 22 g protein; 18 g fat (2.6 g sat.); 29 g carbo (4.8 g fiber); 681 mg sodium; 111 mg chol. ◆

ASIAN KITCHEN BASICS

In Vietnam, people use this sauce much like we use salt and pepper—drizzled over almost everything.

Based on amber-colored Asian fish sauce, it's lightly sweet, sour, salty, and hot—and very easy to make. Use it as a dip or splash it over noodles, salads, seafood, and meats.

Vietnamese Dipping Sauce (Nuoc Cham)

PREP TIME: About 10 minutes

NOTES: You can make this sauce up to 1 day ahead; cover and chill.

MAKES: About 1½ cups

½ cup **Asian fish sauce** *(nuoc mam* or *nam pla)*

¼ cup **rice vinegar**

¼ cup **lime juice**

2 tablespoons **sugar**

2 cloves **garlic,** peeled and minced

1 to 1½ teaspoons minced **hot red chili,** such as Thai, serrano, jalapeño, or Fresno, or Asian red chili paste

In a bowl, mix ½ cup water, fish sauce, vinegar, lime juice, sugar, and garlic. Add minced chili to taste.

Per tablespoon: 18 cal., 30% (5.4 cal.) from fat; 0.8 g protein; 0.6 g fat (0.1 g sat.); 2.3 g carbo (0 g fiber); 199 mg sodium; 0 mg chol.

The Low-Fat Cook

Lean dishes that show off potatoes in all their versatility

By Charity Ferreira • Photographs by James Carrier

Roasted potatoes soak up the flavor of a tangy mustard vinaigrette.

Off the couch

■ Next time you eat a potato, leave off a little of the butter to find out what the spud really tastes like: It might be sweet, salty, earthy, or even buttery. Its texture might feel creamy, waxy, fluffy, or mealy. Although there's no denying that potatoes taste wonderful prepared with some fat, their various flavors and textures stand out better in a leaner setting. We've taken advantage of these characteristics in dishes that let you appreciate the potato far more than the fat it's served with.

Warm Roasted-Potato Salad with Artichokes

PREP AND COOK TIME: About 35 minutes

NOTES: Rub cut sides of artichokes with half a lemon or drop them into a bowl with 2 cups water and 3 tablespoons lemon juice (drain well before using).

MAKES: 4 to 6 servings

- 2 pounds **thin-skinned potatoes** (1½ in. wide), scrubbed and cut into 1½-inch chunks
- 1 tablespoon **olive oil**
  About ¾ teaspoon **salt**
- 1¼ pounds **baby artichokes** (about 12, each 1½ in. wide; see notes) or 1 package (8 oz.) frozen artichoke hearts, thawed
- 1 tablespoon **lemon juice**
- 2 tablespoons **sherry vinegar** or red wine vinegar
- 1 tablespoon **Dijon mustard**
- 2 cups bite-size pieces rinsed and crisped **frisée** (about 4 oz.) or salad mix, rinsed and crisped
- 1 tablespoon drained **capers**
- 1 tablespoon chopped **fresh tarragon**
  Pepper

1. In a 12- by 15-inch baking pan, mix potatoes with ½ teaspoon olive oil; sprinkle with ½ teaspoon salt and mix to coat. Bake in a 400° regular or convection oven, stirring occasionally, until potatoes are browned and tender when pierced, 25 to 30 minutes.

2. Meanwhile, rinse fresh artichokes; trim off discolored stem ends. Break off and discard coarse outer leaves down to tender, pale green inner ones. Cut off thorny artichoke tips, pare coarse fibers from stems, and cut in

half lengthwise. With a small, sharp knife, trim out fuzzy centers and discard (see notes).

3. In a 10- to 12-inch frying pan over medium-high heat, bring ½ cup water and the lemon juice to a boil. Add artichokes and ¼ teaspoon salt; cover, reduce heat, and simmer until artichokes are tender when pierced, about 10 minutes (if using frozen artichoke hearts, skip step 2 and cook only 3 to 4 minutes). Uncover and boil, stirring often, until most of the liquid has evaporated.

4. In a large bowl, mix remaining 2½ teaspoons olive oil, vinegar, and mustard. Add potatoes, artichokes (with any juices), frisée, capers, and tarragon. Mix gently to coat, and season to taste with salt and pepper. Serve warm.

Per serving: 86 cal., 27% (23 cal.) from fat; 4.1 g protein; 2.5 g fat (0.3 g sat.); 13 g carbo (6.8 g fiber); 351 mg sodium; 0 mg chol.

Curried Potato Pita Sandwiches

PREP AND COOK TIME: About 1 hour

NOTES: The curried potatoes also make a great side dish.

MAKES: 4 to 6 servings

- 1 **onion** (about 8 oz.), peeled, halved lengthwise, and thinly sliced crosswise
- 2 teaspoons minced **garlic**
- 1½ teaspoons **salad oil**
- 2 tablespoons **curry powder**
- 1 teaspoon **cumin**
- ½ teaspoon **cayenne**
  About ½ teaspoon **salt**
- 1½ pounds **Yukon Gold** or other thin-skinned **potatoes**, scrubbed and cut into ½-inch chunks
- ¼ cup chopped **parsley**
- 1 cup **nonfat plain yogurt**
- ½ cup diced peeled **cucumber**
- 1½ tablespoons **lemon juice**
- 3 **pocket breads** (about 6 in. wide), cut in half crosswise to make 6 pockets

1. In a 10- to 12-inch frying pan over medium heat, stir onion and 1½ teaspoons garlic in oil until onion is limp and starting to brown, about 10 minutes. Stir in curry powder, cumin, cayenne, and ½ teaspoon salt.

2. Add potatoes and 1 cup water and bring to a boil over high heat. Reduce

FOOD STYLING: DIANE SCOTT GSELL (2)

heat, cover, and simmer, stirring occasionally, until potatoes are tender when pierced, about 15 minutes; if they start to stick, add 1 to 2 tablespoons water to pan as needed. Stir in parsley and more salt to taste.

3. Meanwhile, in a bowl, mix yogurt, cucumber, lemon juice, and remaining ½ teaspoon garlic. Add salt to taste.

4. Toast pocket breads lightly in a toaster and gently pull open. Spoon potato mixture equally into halves; spoon yogurt sauce over potatoes.

Per serving: 172 cal., 10% (18 cal.) from fat; 7.8 g protein; 2 g fat (0.3 g sat.); 32 g carbo (5.1 g fiber); 394 mg sodium; 0.8 mg chol.

Smoked Trout Brandade

PREP AND COOK TIME: About 1½ hours

NOTES: This garlicky purée makes a good side dish as well as an appetizer. You can prepare through step 4 up to 1 day ahead; chill brandade airtight, and store crumbs airtight at room temperature. Bake chilled brandade 15 to 20 minutes.

MAKES: About 12 appetizer servings

- 12 ounces **boned, skinned smoked trout**
- 3 cloves **garlic**, peeled
- 1⅓ cups **nonfat milk**
- 3 **thyme sprigs** (each about 3 in. long), rinsed
- 1½ pounds **russet potatoes,** peeled and cut into ½-inch chunks
- 2 **baguettes** (8 oz. each), sliced diagonally ¼ inch thick
- 3 tablespoons **olive oil**
  Salt and **pepper**
- 2 tablespoons chopped **parsley**

1. Shred trout with a fork. Thinly slice 2 cloves garlic. In a 2- to 3-quart pan, combine sliced garlic, milk, and thyme sprigs; bring just to a simmer over medium heat. Remove from heat, stir in trout, cover, and let stand about 15 minutes. Remove thyme sprigs.

2. In a 3- to 4-quart pan, combine potatoes and about 1 quart water. Cover and bring to a boil over high heat; reduce heat and simmer until potatoes mash easily, about 20 minutes. Drain potatoes and return to pan.

3. Meanwhile, place four baguette slices in a single layer on a 12- by 15-inch baking sheet. Bake in a 350° regular or convection oven, turning once, until crisp and dry, about 15 minutes total. Let cool. Rub one side of each slice with remaining garlic clove. Whirl slices in a food processor into coarse crumbs, or seal in a plastic bag

and crush with a rolling pin.

4. In a blender or food processor, whirl milk mixture until smooth. Add, with olive oil, to potatoes and beat with an electric mixer, or mash with a potato masher, until smooth. Season to taste with salt and pepper. Scrape into a shallow 1- to 2-quart baking dish.

5. Sprinkle top evenly with bread crumbs, then parsley. Bake in a 400° regular or convection oven until top is browned and center is hot, about 15 minutes. Serve brandade with remaining baguette slices.

Per serving: 240 cal., 28% (68 cal.) from fat; 12 g protein; 7.6 g fat (1.5 g sat.); 30 g carbo (1.9 g fiber); 543 mg sodium; 8 mg chol.

Creamy Potato-Apple Soup

PREP AND COOK TIME: About 1 hour

MAKES: 8 cups; about 4 servings

- 2 slices **turkey bacon** (1 oz. total), chopped
- 1 teaspoon **olive oil**
- 1 **onion** (about 8 oz.), peeled and chopped
- 1 **tart apple** (about 8 oz.), such as Fuji, peeled, cored, and sliced
- 1 teaspoon minced **garlic**
- ¼ cup **dry white wine**
- 2 pounds **thin-skinned potatoes,** peeled and cut into ½-inch chunks
  About ½ teaspoon **salt**
- 1 cup **apple cider** or juice
- ¾ cup **low-fat** (1%) **milk**
- 3 to 4 tablespoons crumbled **blue cheese** (about 1½ oz.)
- ¼ teaspoon **ground nutmeg**
  Pepper
- 2 tablespoons minced **fresh chives**

1. In a 5- to 6-quart nonstick pan over

high heat, stir bacon until browned, 3 to 4 minutes. With a slotted spoon, transfer bacon to paper towels to drain. Add oil to pan; when hot, add onion, apple, and garlic. Stir often over medium heat until onion is very limp and beginning to brown, about 20 minutes. Add wine and stir until evaporated, 3 to 4 minutes.

2. Add potatoes, ½ teaspoon salt, and 3½ cups water; bring to a boil over high heat, then reduce heat, cover, and simmer, stirring occasionally, until potatoes mash easily, 25 to 30 minutes.

3. Meanwhile, in a 1- to 2-quart pan over high heat, boil apple cider until reduced to ¼ cup, 8 to 15 minutes.

4. Add milk to potato mixture and, working in batches, whirl in a blender or food processor until smooth. Return to pan over low heat and stir in apple cider, cheese, nutmeg, and salt and pepper to taste. Stir often just until hot, 2 to 3 minutes. Ladle into bowls and top with chives and bacon.

Per serving: 218 cal., 26% (56 cal.) from fat; 9.2 g protein; 6.2 g fat (2.8 g sat.); 34 g carbo (7.6 g fiber); 571 mg sodium; 15 mg chol. ◆

Apple adds a sweet dimension to velvety potato soup.

choose your potato wisely

Starchy potatoes

High-starch potatoes, such as **russets** (also called Idahos or baking potatoes), have thick, papery brown skin and white flesh. Their dry, fluffy texture makes them good for baking, frying, and mashing.

All-purpose potatoes

Many varieties have textures somewhere between starchy and waxy. Mature thin-skinned white potatoes hold their shape well when cooked and are creamy when mashed. Thin-skinned yellow-fleshed **Yellow Finns** and **Yukon Golds** have a

dense, creamy texture that's great for both roasting and mashing. All of these potatoes are multipurpose choices; they make creamy soups and mashed mixtures without a lot of fat.

Waxy potatoes

Thin-skinned **round red potatoes** and new potatoes (technically any kind that are harvested before maturity) have a smooth, firm texture that makes them well suited to roasting, boiling, and steaming, but they can turn gummy when mashed or puréed.

Aw, shucks

Oyster luxury off the half-shell

Oysters imply luxury, even if only slurped from the shell. But when John D. Rockefeller was setting standards for affluence in the late 19th century, a New Orleans chef created Oysters Rockefeller, a dish that reflected the indulgent era. Butter, greens, herbs, and anise were baked over oysters on the half-shell.

The yen for indulgence is back. At Eastside West in San Francisco, Oysters Decadence is an amplified on-the-half-shell offering. At home, I follow the steps of chef-owner Scott Dammann but use individual ramekins—no shells, no slurping, lots of luxury.

FOOD STYLING: BASIL FRIEDMAN

Roasted Oysters Decadence

PREP AND COOK TIME: About 50 minutes

NOTES: To reserve oyster liquid for the sauce, drain oysters in a strainer over a bowl, then cover oysters and chill. You can use the same frying pan to make and reheat the sauce and to cook the vegetables; rinse between processes.

MAKES: 4 servings

- ¾ cup coarsely chopped **bacon** (about 5 oz.)
- ½ cup finely chopped **red bell pepper**
- ¼ cup finely chopped **onion**
- ½ teaspoon **fresh** or dried **thyme** leaves
- 8 ounces **spinach leaves** (2 qts. lightly packed), rinsed and drained

  Salt and **pepper**
- 1 jar (10 oz.; 1 cup) **refrigerated shucked oysters** or 2 cans (8 oz. each) whole oysters, drained, liquid reserved (see notes)

  Oyster Glazing Sauce (recipe follows)
- 2 tablespoons **lemon juice**
- 2 tablespoons **dry white wine**
- ¼ to ½ cup shredded **gruyère** or Swiss **cheese**

1. In a 10- to 12-inch frying pan over medium-high heat, stir bacon often until browned and crisp, 7 to 9 minutes. Remove from heat and, with a slotted spoon, transfer bacon to paper towels to drain. Reserve 1 tablespoon bacon fat; discard remainder. If making up to 4 hours ahead, wrap bacon in paper towels airtight and let stand at room temperature.

2. Add bell pepper, onion, and thyme to frying pan with the tablespoon bacon fat. Stir over high heat until vegetables are limp, about 3 minutes. Add spinach and stir often until leaves are wilted and liquid is evaporated, about 5 minutes (if all the spinach doesn't fit at once, add half and stir until slightly wilted, then add remaining). Return bacon to pan, mix, and add salt and pepper to taste. Remove from heat.

3. Lift oysters from any remaining liquid and cut large ones into bite-size pieces; divide equally among four shallow ramekins (¾ to 1 cup each). Add liquid to other reserved for sauce. Spoon spinach mixture equally over oysters.

4. Wipe frying pan clean and add Oyster Glazing Sauce, lemon juice, and wine. Whisk over high heat until bubbling, 2 to 3 minutes. Spoon mixture evenly over spinach and oysters to coat. Sprinkle 1 to 2 tablespoons cheese over sauce in each ramekin. Set ramekins on a 12- by 15-inch baking sheet.

5. Bake in a 450° regular or convection oven until tops are lightly browned and juices are bubbling, 7 to 10 minutes.

Per serving: 300 cal., 66% (198 cal.) from fat; 13 g protein; 22 g fat (11 g sat.); 11 g carbo (2.1 g fiber); 389 mg sodium; 91 mg chol.

Oyster Glazing Sauce. Pour up to ½ cup **reserved oyster liquid** (see notes, preceding) into a 1- or 2-cup glass measure; add enough **milk** to make 1 cup total. Discard any remaining oyster liquid. In a 10- to 12-inch frying pan over high heat, stir 2 tablespoons **butter** or margarine and ¼ cup minced **onion** until onion is pale gold, 2 to 3 minutes. Remove from heat and stir in 2 tablespoons **all-purpose flour,** 1 teaspoon **dry mustard,** and ¼ teaspoon **ground nutmeg.** Return pan to high heat and stir until flour is pale gold, 1 to 2 minutes. Remove from heat and add oyster liquid mixture and ¼ cup **whipping cream.** Whisk over high heat until boiling; continue to boil, whisking often, until mixture is reduced to 1 cup, 3 to 5 minutes. Scrape into a bowl. If making up to 1 day ahead, cover and chill. Makes about 1 cup.

Tender roast on a beef chuck budget

■ There's not much challenge in roasting a choice cut of beef to perfection: Rare or well done, it's tender. But it's also pricey—too much so for most of us for everyday meals. An economical, workaday alternative, with excellent beef flavor, is a chuck roast, cut from the shoulder—perhaps hot for dinner one day, cold for sandwiches or salads another. However, to retain its tenderness, this firm-textured meat (favored for long, slow braising) must not be cooked beyond rare; well done, it's just plain chewy. Two more tricks: a brief salt-and-sugar cure to enhance juiciness and flavor, and a final coat of pepper and horseradish that is tempered during roasting.

Salt-and-Pepper Beef Roast

PREP AND COOK TIME: 2½ hours, plus at least 3 hours to chill

NOTES: For a mellow flavor, use the Spice Hunter's white peppercorns, from Sarawak in Malaysia; you'll find them with the spices at most supermarkets. Potatoes, baked alongside the roast, make a perfectly easy accompaniment. The meat, hot or cold, tastes the most tender when sliced very thin; an electric knife does a good job.

MAKES: 12 to 18 servings

  4 to 6 pounds **boned, tied beef cross rib** (chuck) **roast**

  ¼ cup plus 1½ teaspoons **coarse salt**

  ¼ cup **sugar**

  2 tablespoons **coarse-ground pepper** (see notes)

  ½ cup **prepared horseradish**

1. Rinse beef and pat dry. In a small bowl, mix ¼ cup salt and sugar. Rub mixture all over beef, set in a rimmed pan, cover, and chill 3 to 4 hours. Rinse meat and pat dry; if desired, cover and chill up to 1 day.

2. In a small bowl, mix 1½ teaspoons salt, pepper, and horseradish. Set beef on a rack in a 9- by 13-inch pan. Pat horseradish mixture over the top and sides of beef.

3. Roast in a 375° regular or 350° convection oven until a meat thermometer inserted in center of thickest part reaches 120° to 125°, 1½ to 2 hours. Remove from oven and let stand in a warm place at least 20 minutes.

4. Transfer meat to a rimmed platter or board; scrape any pan juices into a small bowl. Cut meat across the grain into very thin slices (see notes). Spoon pan juices onto portions.

Per serving: 267 cal., 64% (171 cal.) from fat; 20 g protein; 19 g fat (7.7 g sat.); 1.3 g carbo (0.4 g fiber); 233 mg sodium; 79 mg chol.

Hearth baking made easy

■ I'm not alone in my passion for the crusty, hearth-baked qualities that stone, brick, or adobe ovens impart to breads and pizzas. But building one of these ovens outdoors—which I have done several times for *Sunset* (most recently with senior home writer Peter Whiteley, for our May 1998 centennial issue)—is no small task, and installing a professional unit in your kitchen is costly and demands a lot of space.

Now, however, you can get stone-oven results at home using an oven insert called the HearthKit. The kit consists of three thick ceramic pieces—one the width and depth of your oven (you order by size) and two that fit vertically alongside the oven walls. Once the ceramic insert is heated as directed, you slide the loaves, pizza, rolls, or containers of foods (casseroles or meats) onto the ceramic floor (misting the oven with water, if you choose, to enhance crust development). The insert effectively re-creates the balanced heat of a hearth oven. The HearthKit oven insert costs about $230 in cookware stores; for more information, call (800) 383-7818 or go to www.hearthkitchen.com.

The kindest cut of all

■ It may be called a pickle slicer, but this sharp little multiple-blade cutter will glide through a variety of foods to create even, narrow strips that you can fan out for decorative purposes. And a few modestly fussy garnishes can make a tray of vegetables for dip appear more sophisticated, a salad look more interesting, a sandwich seem more important, and a slice of purchased pâté look as if it was delivered from a neighborhood bistro. You can use the cutter on pickles,

cucumbers, green onions, celery, and radishes (if they're not too hard). To make the vegetable slices curl apart, after you cut them, immerse them in ice water for 5 to 10 minutes, then drain.

I've seen several kinds of multiple-blade slicers in cookware stores and in markets that sell Asian cooking tools. The one shown here is the very sharp Eminceur (made in France), with eight blades. It sells for about $10 and can be ordered from Bridge Kitchenware (800/274-3435 or www.bridgekitchenware.com). ◆

Glaze of glory

A quick taste of L.A.'s best doughnut shops

By Norman Kolpas

The doughnut. No morning foodstuff has ever been devised that suits itself better to being devoured en route. In fact, it has been a corollary of life in greater Los Angeles that the number of doughnut shops rises in direct proportion to the number of automobiles.

While chains predominate, some independent outlets—including the favorites listed below—have won widespread devotion from doughnut fans through a combination of outstanding goods, unusual settings, and likable owners. ◆

BLINKIE'S DONUT EMPORIUM. This shop in a quiet residential enclave near the San Fernando Valley's southwestern foothills has been a neighborhood gathering spot since the late 1970s. Former owner Mike Butler sold it to Steve and Lisa Lee more than a year ago, and though Butler's film posters and eclectic music are gone, the wide range of raised, cake, and old-fashioned doughnuts remains excellent. *4884 Topanga Canyon Blvd., Woodland Hills; (818) 884-4456.*

BOB'S COFFEE & DOUGHNUTS. One of many food stands that throng the renowned Farmers Market, Bob's makes possible the rare pleasure of enjoying freshly made delectables—including maple cake doughnuts, apple fritters, and kids' treats shaped like dinosaurs and cats—on a shady patio that preserves the leisurely pace of old *Hollywood. 6333 W. Third St., Los Angeles; (323) 933-8929.*

PRIMO'S WESTDALE DONUTS. Celia and Ralph Primo bought this tiny Westside shop in 1956, and the duo is still there almost every morning, serving some 30 varieties of just-fried delights, including buttermilk bars with near-molten centers. "Our success depends on three things," says Ralph. "We use top-of-the-line ingredients, we make

them fresh—and then there's Mrs. Primo and her smile." *Closed Sun. 2918 Sawtelle Blvd., Los Angeles; (310) 478-6930.*

RANDY'S DONUTS. You can't miss the 50-foot-tall concrete doughnut perched atop this drive-through near LAX. Brothers Larry and Ron Weintraub took over the rare survivor of the once mighty Big Donut Drive-In chain 24 years ago. They've kept the walk-up and drive-through queues busy by serving fresh glazed and buttermilk varieties, chocolate old-fashioneds, and a "Texas-sized" glazed as big as a dinner plate. "Here you can eat great doughnuts in front of an L.A. landmark," enthuses Larry. *805 W. Manchester Blvd., Inglewood; (310) 645-4707.*

STAN'S DONUTS. There's no more affable doughnut vendor than Stan Berman. The third-generation baker took over this location in Westwood Village in 1964 and devised some of L.A.'s most imaginative pastries, including a legendary doughnut stuffed with peanut butter and chocolate. "People buy them and take them all over the world," says Stan, who doesn't miss the irony of doctors and nurses from nearby UCLA Medical Center in line each morning. *10948 Weyburn Ave., Los Angeles; (310) 208-8660.*

cooking with herbs

These nine culinary herbs are indispensable for cooks. Here's how to use them in the kitchen

By Lauren Bonar Swezey • Recipes by Linda Lau Anusasananan

Photographs by Thomas J. Story

■ Fresh herbs are simply the best flavorings for many foods and drinks. But there's nothing simple about the complex array of tastes they impart to dishes. "Fresh herbs open up the senses and invite one to cook in a looser, freer way," says Carolyn Dille, author of a book on cooking with herbs and the first chef at Chez Panisse Cafe in Berkeley. "The pleasure they bring to the garden and the kitchen is indispensable."

Dille, who grows her own herbs in her Santa Cruz garden, says that dried herbs are no match for those that are freshly picked. "They're totally different creatures," she emphasizes. "Fresh herbs contain all of their complex volatile oils. Once the herbs have dried, some oils dissipate and flavors change."

Even herbs purchased fresh at the produce market have lost some of their essences by the time they're sold. "From a flavor perspective, it's a real plus to grow your own," says Dille.

Listed at right are nine fresh herbs that cooks won't want to be without.

■ **Basil** *(Ocimum basilicum)*. Some times referred to as the king of herbs, basil has fragrant, bright green leaves on 6-inch- to 2-foot-tall plants.
USES: Eggs, fish, marinades, meats, pastas, pestos, salads, soups, stews, and tomatoes.

■ **Chives** *(Allium)*. Green, grasslike 12- to 24-inch-long spears grow in clumps. Gather chives by snipping the spears to the ground.
USES: Butters, cheeses, eggs, lamb, mayonnaise, potatoes, rice, salads, sauces, seafood, soups, sour cream, stews, and vegetables.

■ **Cilantro** *(Coriandrum sativum)*

Fettuccine with Green Herbs

PREP AND COOK TIME: About 20 minutes
MAKES: 2 or 3 servings

- 8 or 9 ounces **fresh fettuccine**
- 3 tablespoons **extra-virgin olive oil**
- ¼ cup thinly sliced **fresh chives**
- 2 tablespoons coarsely chopped **parsley**
- 2 tablespoons coarsely chopped **fresh oregano, basil, lemon verbena,** or **thyme** leaves (or a combination of two or three)
- 1 teaspoon grated **lemon** peel
- 2 tablespoons **lemon juice**
- ½ teaspoon freshly ground **pepper**

  Salt

1. In a 5- to 6-quart pan over high heat, bring 2 to 3 quarts water to a boil. Add fettuccine and boil, stirring occasionally to separate noodles, until barely tender to bite, 2 to 3 minutes.

2. Meanwhile, in a wide, shallow bowl, combine olive oil, chives, parsley, oregano, lemon peel, lemon juice, and pepper.

3. Drain pasta, reserving ⅓ cup cooking water. Pour hot pasta into bowl with herb mixture. Gently lift with two spoons to mix, adding salt to taste and as much of the reserved pasta cooking water to moisten as desired.

Per serving: 345 cal., 42% (144 cal.) from fat; 8.9 g protein; 16 g fat (2.3 g sat.); 43 g carbo (2 g fiber); 23 mg sodium; 55 mg chol.

Herb Cheese Log

On a 12- by 15-inch piece of plastic wrap, mix 1 tablespoon *each* minced **fresh chives, fresh cilantro,** and **fresh basil** leaves. Roll a 5½- to 6-ounce log of **fresh chèvre (goat) cheese** in herb mixture to coat evenly. Set on a small rimmed plate or serving dish and drizzle with 2 tablespoons **extra-virgin olive oil.** Serve with **baguette** slices.

Bright green leaves grow on foot-tall stems that look similar to flat-leafed parsley. *Cilantro* refers to the leaves; the seeds are called coriander.
USES: Beans, curries, fish, lamb, Mexican dishes, pork, poultry, salads, salsas, sauces, shellfish, and stir-fries.

■ **Oregano** *(Origanum).* Shrubby plant with 1½-inch-long gray green or bright green leaves grows 2 to 3 feet tall.
USES: Beans, cheeses, eggs, meats, pastas, salsas, sauces, soups, stews, and vegetables.

■ **Parsley** *(Petroselinum).* Flat or curly green leaves grow in clumps. Flat-leafed types are best for cooking; the curly type is good as a garnish.
USES: Bouquets garnis, cheese sauces, pestos, soups, stews, stuffings, vegetables, and as a garnish.

■ **Rosemary** *(Rosmarinus).* Short, narrow green leaves with grayish white undersides grow on woody stems ranging from 1 to 6 feet tall.
USES: Beef, breads, cheeses, dressings, eggs, lamb, legumes, marinades, oils, potatoes, poultry, roasted game, seafood, soups, stews, stuffings, and vegetables.

■ **Sage** *(Salvia officinalis).* Shrubby plant from 1 to 3 feet tall with 2- to 3-inch-long leaves.
USES: Apples, beans, breads, butters, cheeses, chowders, fish stock, game stuffings, gravies, lamb, marinades, pork, poultry, soups, stews, and tomatoes.

■ **Sweet marjoram** *(Origanum majorana).* Oval gray green leaves grow on 1- to 2-foot-tall plants. Milder and more floral than oregano. .
USES: Cheeses, eggs, fish, gravies, meats, pastas, poultry, rice, sauces, soups, stews, and vegetables.

■ **Thyme** *(Thymus).* Small, pungent leaves grow on stems up to 1 foot tall.
USES: Bouquets garnis, breads, casseroles, cheeses, eggs, fish, grains, marinades, meats, mushrooms, poultry, soups, stews, tomato-based sauces, and vegetables.

Herbs in a kitchen garden

The best place to grow herbs is near your kitchen, so you can easily duck outside to harvest them. If you don't have a convenient sunny spot in your garden, you can grow herbs in large containers and position them where the light is favorable. For the best flavor and the most growth, herbs need six hours of full midday sun; four hours is minimum for adequate growth.

When you shop for herb plants, keep in mind that within each group—oregano or rosemary, for instance—fragrances differ widely. Some oreganos are mild, almost scentless, and not great for cooking, while others are pungent and flavorful. Rosemaries, on the other hand, can be strong and piney or have a sweet, gingery taste. Since flavor preferences vary, the best way to know if the aroma of a certain herb appeals to you is to give the plant a touch and sniff test. When shopping at the nursery, gently run your fingers over the foliage (don't hurt the plant), then sniff them. If you like the fragrance, buy the plant. ◆

FOOD STYLING: BASIL FRIEDMAN

Flavored vinegars

■ **Lemon Thyme Vinegar** (center, above). With a vegetable peeler, pare a thin spiral strip of peel 6 to 8 inches long from a **lemon.** With a chopstick or wooden skewer, push lemon peel and 6 rinsed sprigs (each 3 in. long) **fresh thyme** into a clean 12- to 16-ounce bottle. Fill bottle with **white wine vinegar** (vinegar should cover herbs completely) and seal. Store in a cool, dark place at least 1 week or up to 4 months.

VARIATIONS

■ **Lemon Verbena Vinegar** (left). Follow recipe for **Lemon Thyme Vinegar** (preceding), except replace the thyme with 2 or 3 sprigs (each 6 to 8 in. long) **lemon verbena;** omit peel, if desired.

■ **Purple Basil Vinegar** (right). Follow recipe for **Lemon Verbena Vinegar** (preceding), but replace verbena with 2 or 3 sprigs (each 4 to 6 in. long) **purple** or **opal basil.** Omit lemon peel.

Kitchen Cabinet

Readers' recipes tested in *Sunset's* kitchens

By Charity Ferreira • Photographs by James Carrier

Feta cheese and bread crumbs top layers of lamb and eggplant baked in a tomato-wine sauce.

FOOD STYLING: BASIL FRIEDMAN

Baked Eggplant and Lamb

Christine Datian, Las Vegas

Christine Datian layers Mediterranean flavors—seasoned ground lamb and slices of eggplant—then tops the works with bread crumbs and feta cheese and bakes it. The result is a simple, hearty dish.

PREP AND COOK TIME: About 1¼ hours

MAKES: 8 to 10 servings

- 2 pounds **eggplant**
  About 3 tablespoons **olive oil**
- 2 slices (½ in. thick and 4 to 5 in. long) **French bread**
- 1 pound **ground lamb**
- 1 **onion** (8 oz.), peeled and chopped
- 8 ounces **sliced mushrooms**
- 1 tablespoon minced **garlic**
- 1½ cups **tomato sauce**
- ½ cup **dry red wine**
- 1 tablespoon **prepared mustard**
- 1 teaspoon **dried basil**
- ½ teaspoon **dried oregano**
- ½ teaspoon **salt**
- ¼ teaspoon **pepper**
- 4 ounces **feta cheese,** crumbled
- ½ cup chopped **parsley**

1. Rinse and dry eggplant; slice crosswise into ¼-inch-thick rounds, discarding ends. Brush both sides of rounds lightly with oil and place in a single layer on two 12- by 15-inch baking sheets. Bake in a 400° regular or convection oven until browned and tender when pierced, 10 to 15 minutes.

2. Meanwhile, cut or tear bread into ½-inch chunks. Put in a food processor or blender and whirl into coarse crumbs; you should have 1 cup. In a 10- to 12-inch nonstick frying pan over medium-high heat, stir crumbs in ½ tablespoon olive oil until lightly browned and crisp, about 5 minutes. Pour from pan.

3. In the same pan over medium-high heat, stir lamb until crumbled and no longer pink, about 5 minutes. With a slotted spoon, transfer lamb to a bowl. Drain all but 1 teaspoon fat from pan. Add onion, mushrooms, and garlic and stir occasionally until onion is limp and mushrooms are browned, about 8 minutes. Add tomato sauce, wine, mustard, basil, oregano, salt, pepper, and the browned lamb. Bring to a simmer and cook, stirring often, to blend flavors, about 10 minutes.

4. Arrange half the eggplant slices in a single layer over the bottom of a shallow 2- to 3-quart baking dish; top with half the lamb mixture. Repeat layers of eggplant and lamb mixture. Sprinkle top with bread crumbs and feta cheese.

5. Bake in a 350° regular or convection oven until browned and bubbling, 20 to 25 minutes. Sprinkle with parsley. Scoop out servings with a large spoon.

Per serving: 228 cal., 55% (126 cal.) from fat; 12 g protein; 14 g fat (5 g sat.); 15 g carbo (2.7 g fiber); 538 mg sodium; 41 mg chol.

Chickpea Soup

Valarie Donnelly, Yuma, AZ

Valarie Donnelly concocted this garbanzo soup primarily from pantry ingredients one night when she was short on time. She was so pleased with the result that she has made it many times since then.

PREP AND COOK TIME: About 30 minutes

MAKES: 8 cups; 4 to 6 main-dish servings

- 1½ teaspoons **olive oil**
- 1 **onion** (about 8 oz.), peeled and chopped
- 2 cloves **garlic,** peeled and minced
- 5½ cups fat-skimmed **chicken broth**
- 1 tablespoon **red wine vinegar**
- 1 can (14½ oz.) **diced tomatoes**
- 1 can (15 oz.) **garbanzos,** rinsed and drained
- 1 tablespoon **dried parsley**
- 1 tablespoon **dried basil**
- ½ tablespoon **dried oregano**
- 1½ cups **dried pasta** (about 5 oz.), such as shells or corkscrews
  Salt and **pepper**

1. Pour oil into a 3- to 4-quart pan over medium-high heat. When hot, add onion and garlic and stir often until onion is limp, about 6 minutes.

2. Add chicken broth, vinegar, tomatoes, garbanzos, parsley, basil, and oregano. Bring to a boil and add pasta; cook, stirring occasionally, until pasta is tender to bite, about 10 minutes. Add salt and pepper to taste.

Per serving: 209 cal., 12% (26 cal.) from fat; 14 g protein; 2.9 g fat (0.3 g sat.); 32 g carbo (3.6 g fiber); 262 mg sodium; 0 mg chol.

Halibut Salad Sandwiches

Sky Natoni, Tacoma

Sky Natoni discovered that halibut—baked, chilled, and shredded—made a good medium for her favorite chicken salad ingredients. She serves the mixture as a sandwich filling on honey whole-wheat rolls.

PREP AND COOK TIME: About 45 minutes, plus at least 1 hour to chill

MAKES: 4 sandwiches

1 pound **boned, skinned halibut** or other firm, white-fleshed fish (³⁄₄ to 1 in. thick)

Salt and **pepper**

½ cup chopped **canned pineapple in juice** (reserve 2 tablespoons juice)

Give your can opener a rest—this halibut salad is a delicious change from that other fish sandwich filling.

¼ cup chopped **cashews**

¼ cup **unsweetened shredded dried coconut**

¼ cup minced **green onions,** white and pale green parts only

¼ cup **mayonnaise**

4 **honey whole-wheat sandwich rolls** (3 oz. each) or 8 slices whole-wheat sandwich bread

2 cups **salad mix,** rinsed and crisped

1. Rinse fish and pat dry. Sprinkle lightly all over with salt and pepper and place on a 12- by 15-inch baking sheet. Bake in a 350° regular or convection oven until opaque but still moist-looking in center of thickest part (cut to test), about 10 minutes. With a wide spatula, transfer fish to a bowl. Chill until cold, at least 1 hour; if desired, cover when cold and chill up to 1 day.

2. Shred fish with fork. Add pineapple

and 2 tablespoons juice, cashews, coconut, green onions, and mayonnaise; mix well.

3. Mound halibut salad equally on bottoms of 4 sandwich rolls. Top with salad mix and roll tops.

Per sandwich: 459 cal., 43% (198 cal.) from fat; 31 g protein; 22 g fat (5.6 g sat.); 36 g carbo (4.8 g fiber); 442 mg sodium; 44 mg chol. ◆

FOOD STYLING: SUSAN DEVATY

Peckish in Seattle

Taste everything from caviar to kangaroo at these food shops

By Heidi A. Scheussler

Do you know gouda from gruyère, or how to cook a bear steak? How about which caviar to serve with raw oysters? Adventurous palates rejoice: At these Seattle food stores, you're allowed—in fact, encouraged—to taste and learn before you buy.

On Saturdays from 11 to 5, Dale and Betsy Sherrow break out the spoons and toast points and set up a tasting bar at their chic **Seattle Caviar Co.** (closed Sun; 2833 Eastlake Ave. E; 206/323-3005). First-timers are welcome: The Sherrows will guide you through the subtleties of flavor, texture, and bead size among Caspian Sea beluga, osetra, and sevruga, as well as a couple of

varieties from the Pacific Northwest.

Shopping at **Seattle's Finest Exotic Meats** (17532 Aurora Ave. N; 206/546-4922) can be daunting to the uninitiated: It's not every day you see coolers full of vacuum-packed snapping turtle meat, kangaroo patties, alligator steaks, and frog legs. Swing by on Saturdays from noon to 6 and taste the weekly special—rattlesnake, anyone?—cooked and served by owner Russell McCurdy, who also shares his recipes and cooking techniques. All the meat is farm raised, without added chemicals or growth hormones, and is USDA approved.

If you're going to spend up to $25 for a pound of cheese, you'd better

like what you're getting. James Cook, owner of **James Cook Cheese Co.** (closed Sun; 2421 Second Ave.; 206/256-0510), makes sure you will. You can taste-test his 100 varieties, which come from small-scale European producers and are flown in fresh every week.

Buying wine doesn't have to be expensive—or intimidating. At **Best Cellars** (2625 N.E. University Village; 206/527-5900), most of the wines cost less than $15 a bottle, and they're separated into categories like fizzy, sweet, and luscious. Every day from 4 to 8, you can taste new varietals, talk to winemakers, or learn what wine to serve with, say, pizza or Thai takeout.

Want to continue your culinary journey? Pick up *The Food Lover's Guide to Seattle,* (Sasquatch Books, Seattle, 2001; $16.95; 800/775-0817), by Katy Calcott, and keep an open palate. ◆

Top off a festive spring feast with Rhubarb-Strawberry Compote, accompanied by Lattice Cookies (recipes on page 75).

April

spring lunch from
garden to table

With cooking-school savvy, transform April bounty into
fresh dishes for a meal with friends

By Linda Lau Anusasananan • Photographs by James Carrier • Food styling by Basil Friedman

Spring in a bowl (left): Artichokes, romaine, peas, and fennel in a rustic vegetable stew. Minced herbs sprinkled over mozzarella crostini (above left and center) make an easy appetizer. Mix Meyer lemon juice with water and sugar for perfect lemonade (right).

■ Contrary to the normal limits of city locations, Mary's garden is growing quite well, thank you. Actually, the land—on San Francisco's Telegraph Hill—belongs to the city, and the garden is tended by students of Mary Risley's Tante Marie's Cooking School. The well-kept plot gives the students—future culinary professionals and avid home cooks—a chance to shepherd foods from ground to plate.

This time of year, the perennial-edged space is lush with herbs, asparagus, lettuces, fava beans, artichokes, rhubarb, and strawberries—provisions for a grand spring feast. Gather a few friends together to cook Mary's complete menu, much as she does in her classroom. Or use the recipes individually for many fresh spring meals.

Fresh Mozzarella and Herb Crostini

PREP AND COOK TIME: About 20 minutes
NOTES: You can toast the bread (step 1) up to 4 hours ahead; cool and store airtight at room temperature.
MAKES: 8 to 12 servings

1 **baguette** (8 oz.)
1¼ pounds **fresh mozzarella cheese**
3 to 4 tablespoons **extra-virgin olive oil**
2 to 3 tablespoons chopped **fresh herb** leaves such as thyme, marjoram, oregano, sage, or rosemary (one kind or a mixture)
Salt and fresh-ground **pepper**

1. Cut baguette diagonally into ⅓-inch-thick slices. Set slices on a rack on a 14- by 17-inch baking sheet. Bake in a 425° regular or convection oven until golden, 6 to 8 minutes.
2. Drain mozzarella and pat dry; cut into ¼-inch-thick slices. Arrange on toast, cutting slices to fit. Drizzle olive oil over cheese. Sprinkle with herbs and salt and pepper to taste.

Per serving: 229 cal., 63% (144 cal.) from fat; 12 g protein; 16 g fat (8.1 g sat.); 9.3 g carbo (0.5 g fiber); 300 mg sodium; 42 mg chol.

Rustic Spring Vegetable Stew

PREP AND COOK TIME: About 1¼ hours
NOTES: Mary Risley adapted this vegetable stew from a recipe in Viana La Place's book *Verdura: Vegetables Italian Style*. You can prepare it through step 3 up to 1 day ahead; cover and chill. Reheat mixture, covered, over medium heat, stirring occasionally, then continue. For a faster version, skip step 1 and replace fresh arti-

Spring Garden Lunch

Fresh Mozzarella and
Herb Crostini

Rustic Spring Vegetable Stew or
Warm Sausage and Potato Salad
with Arugula

Asparagus Salad with Fava Bean
Sauce

Crusty Bread and Butter

*Sauvignon Blanc and
Meyer Lemonade*

Rhubarb-Strawberry Compote
with Lattice Cookies

chokes with 6 cups frozen artichoke hearts (three 8-oz. packages); after adding water in step 3, reduce cooking time to about 6 minutes. You can also replace fresh peas in pods with 2 cups frozen peas (10 oz.).
MAKES: 8 servings

⅓ cup **lemon juice**
8 **artichokes** (6 oz. each; see notes)
2 **onions** (6 oz. each)
2 heads **fresh fennel** (1½ lb. total, untrimmed)
2 pounds **fresh peas in pods** (see notes)
1 head **romaine lettuce** (12 oz.)
¼ cup **olive oil**
Salt and **pepper**
Freshly grated **pecorino romano** or parmesan **cheese**

1. In a large bowl, combine lemon juice and 2 quarts cold water. Slice off top halves of artichokes and discard; break off and discard outer leaves down to tender, pale green inner ones. Trim off and discard stem ends. With a small, sharp knife, pare off dark green fibrous skin from artichoke bottoms and remaining stems. Cut artichokes in half lengthwise; scoop out and discard fuzzy centers and any thorny petals.

Cut each artichoke half in half again lengthwise and drop into lemon water.

2. Peel onions; cut in half lengthwise, then slice lengthwise into ¼-inch-thick slivers. Rinse fennel; trim off and discard stalks and root ends. Reserve a few leafy sprigs for garnish if desired. Cut heads lengthwise into about ¼-inch-thick matchsticks. Shell peas. Rinse lettuce well and trim off and discard core; cut leaves into 3-inch lengths.

3. Drain artichokes. In a 5- to 6-quart

Brown the sausages (above) and combine with arugula, warm potatoes, and a mustard-tarragon vinaigrette (below). Serve with crusty rolls for a simple lunch or light supper.

pan over medium-high heat, frequently stir artichokes, onions, and fennel in olive oil until onions are limp, 7 to 8 minutes. Add 5 cups water and bring to a boil over high heat; cover, reduce heat, and simmer, stirring occasionally, until artichokes are tender when pierced, 12 to 18 minutes.

4. Add peas; bring mixture to a boil over high heat and cook until peas are tender when pierced, 2 to 3 minutes. Stir in lettuce and cook until barely wilted, about 30 seconds. Add salt and pepper to taste. Ladle stew into bowls and garnish with reserved fennel sprigs. Sprinkle with cheese to taste.

Per serving: 169 cal., 39% (66 cal.) from fat; 6.5 g protein; 7.3 g fat (1 g sat.); 23 g carbo (8.6 g fiber); 106 mg sodium; 0 mg chol.

Warm Sausage and Potato Salad with Arugula

PREP AND COOK TIME: About 40 minutes
NOTES: You can prepare the potatoes (steps 1 and 2) up to 2 hours before serving; cover loosely and let stand at room temperature, stirring occasionally. You can cook the sausage (step 3) up to 1 day ahead; cover sausage and cooking liquid separately and chill. Heat liquid in pan before adding to potatoes in step 5.
MAKES: 8 servings

- 2 pounds **thin-skinned potatoes** (1½ in. wide), scrubbed
- ⅓ cup **extra-virgin olive oil**
- 2 tablespoons **red wine vinegar**
- 2 tablespoons **dry white wine** or 1 more tablespoon red wine vinegar
- ¼ cup minced **shallots**
  About 1 teaspoon **salt**
- ¾ teaspoon **white pepper**
- 2 pounds **mild Italian sausages**
  Fat-skimmed **chicken broth** (optional)
- 1 tablespoon **Dijon mustard**
- ⅓ cup chopped **parsley**
- 2 tablespoons thinly sliced **fresh chives** or green onions
- 1 tablespoon minced **fresh tarragon** or oregano leaves
- 6 ounces **arugula leaves** (2 qt.), rinsed and crisped

1. Combine potatoes and 1 to 1½ quarts water in a 5- to 6-quart pan; bring to a boil over high heat, then cover, reduce heat, and simmer just until potatoes are tender when pierced, 15 to 20 minutes. Drain and return to pan. Shake gently over medium heat until liquid is evaporated, about 2

minutes. Remove from heat.

2. Add oil, vinegar, wine, shallots, 1 teaspoon salt, and pepper; mix gently.

3. Meanwhile, combine sausages and ⅓ cup water in a 10- to 12-inch frying pan over medium heat; cover and cook until sausages are firm to touch, about 10 minutes. Pour cooking liquid into a 1-cup glass measure; skim off fat and discard. You need ¼ cup liquid; add chicken broth if necessary or discard remaining. Whisk mustard into measured liquid until smooth.

4. Turn sausages occasionally in pan over medium-high heat until browned, 5 to 7 minutes. Transfer to a board and slice diagonally about ¼ inch thick.

5. Add sausages, warm cooking liquid, parsley, chives, and tarragon to potatoes; mix gently. Add salt to taste. Add arugula and mix gently. Pour into a large bowl. Serve warm.

Per serving: 395 cal., 71% (279 cal.) from fat; 19 g protein; 31 g fat (8.8 g sat.); 10 g carbo (3.7 g fiber); 1,115 mg sodium; 65 mg chol.

Asparagus Salad with Fava Bean Sauce

PREP AND COOK TIME: About 30 minutes
NOTES: This salad was inspired by Loretta Keller of Bizou Restaurant & Bar in San Francisco. If fresh favas aren't available, use 1 cup shelled cooked favas (8 oz.; sold refrigerated in some supermarkets) or frozen baby lima beans. Fresh pecorino cheese, which has a creamy texture similar to that of jack, is available in specialty food stores; don't confuse it with dry pecorino romano. You can make the bean paste (step 3) up to 1 day ahead; cover and chill. Reheat to use.
MAKES: 8 servings

- 2 pounds **asparagus**
- 7 tablespoons **extra-virgin olive oil**
- 1½ teaspoons **white wine vinegar**
- 1 quart bite-size pieces rinsed and crisped **red leaf lettuce** (3½ oz.)
- 1 cup **cherry tomatoes** (optional), rinsed, stemmed, and halved
  Salt and **pepper**
- 2 cloves **garlic,** peeled and chopped
- 1 pound **young fava beans in pods,** shelled (see notes)
- 1 cup shredded **fresh pecorino** (*pecorino fresca;* see notes) or jack **cheese** (4 oz.)

1. In a 5- to 6-quart pan over high heat, bring 2 quarts water to a boil. Meanwhile, rinse asparagus; snap off and discard tough stem ends. Add

asparagus to boiling water and cook until barely tender when pierced, 3 to 4 minutes. Drain and arrange on a platter or plates.

2. In a large bowl, mix 1 tablespoon olive oil and the vinegar. Add lettuce and tomatoes; mix gently to coat. Add salt and pepper to taste. Arrange salad alongside asparagus.

3. In the pan, over medium heat, stir garlic in remaining 6 tablespoons oil until limp, about 30 seconds. Add shelled beans and ⅔ cup water; cover and simmer over low heat until beans are very soft when pressed, 7 to 12 minutes. Mash with a potato masher. Remove from heat and push mixture through a wire strainer; discard skins.

4. Return bean paste to pan over low heat and stir until hot, 2 to 3 minutes. Remove from heat, add cheese, and stir until melted. Sauce should be thin

Bake shortbread in a lattice pattern to decorate rhubarb-strawberry compote. Top with vanilla ice cream.

enough to spoon over asparagus. If necessary, add a little hot water (2 to 4 tablespoons) to thin; do not return sauce to heat or cheese will become grainy. Add salt and pepper to taste.

5. Spoon warm sauce over warm or room-temperature asparagus.

Per serving: 199 cal., 77% (153 cal.) from fat; 9.7 g protein; 17 g fat (4.6 g sat.); 6.3 g carbo (1.8 g fiber); 183 mg sodium; 14 mg chol.

Rhubarb-Strawberry Compote

PREP AND COOK TIME: About 35 minutes
NOTES: This homey dessert was adapted from a recipe by Janet Rikala, former pastry chef at Postrio in San Francisco. You can substitute 2 teaspoons vanilla extract for the vanilla bean if desired; cook with fruit in step 2. You can cook the compote (through step 2) up to 1 day ahead; cool, cover, and chill. Stir gently over low heat until hot.
MAKES: 8 servings

1½ pounds **strawberries**

1½ pounds **fresh rhubarb**

About ¾ cup **sugar**

2 teaspoons **cornstarch**

1 **vanilla bean** (see notes)

1 teaspoon grated **orange** peel

½ teaspoon **ground cinnamon**

1 quart **vanilla ice cream**

Lattice Cookies (recipe follows) or shortbread cookies, optional

1. Rinse and stem strawberries; cut each in half lengthwise. Rinse rhubarb well; trim off and discard ends. Slice stalks crosswise into ¾-inch pieces.

2. In a 3- to 4-quart pan, mix ¾ cup sugar and cornstarch. Add berries and crush with a potato masher. Cut vanilla bean in half lengthwise and scrape seeds into pan. Add vanilla pod, orange peel, cinnamon, and rhubarb. Cover and cook over medium heat, stirring occasionally, until rhubarb is soft when pierced, 15 to 20 minutes. Taste, and add more sugar if desired.

3. Remove vanilla pod. Spoon compote into bowls. Top with scoops (½ cup each) of ice cream and Lattice Cookies.

Per serving: 246 cal., 28% (69 cal.) from fat; 3.4 g protein; 7.7 g fat (4.5 g sat.); 44 g carbo (2.1 g fiber); 56 mg sodium; 29 mg chol.

Lattice Cookies

PREP AND COOK TIME: About 40 minutes, plus 15 to 20 minutes to chill dough
NOTES: You can make these cookies up to 1 day ahead; cover airtight and store at room temperature.
MAKES: 8 servings

1½ cups **all-purpose flour**

About 6 tablespoons **sugar**

⅛ teaspoon **salt**

½ cup (4 oz.) cold **butter** or margarine, cut into chunks

1 **large egg**

1 teaspoon **vanilla**

1. In a food processor or bowl, combine flour, ¼ cup sugar, and salt. Add butter and whirl or cut in with a pastry cutter until fine crumbs form. In a small bowl, beat egg with vanilla to blend. Add to flour mixture and whirl or mix with a fork until dough is evenly moistened and starts to clump together. Press into a ball, then divide in half.

2. On a 12- by 15-inch piece of plastic wrap, using your hands, roll one dough half into a 6-inch-long log; cover with another piece of plastic wrap. With a rolling pin, roll log into an even, ¼-inch-thick rectangle about 6 inches wide and 9 inches long (edges can be ragged). Repeat to roll remaining dough half. Transfer each rectangle to a 14- by 17-inch baking sheet and chill until firm, 15 to 20 minutes.

3. Working with one rectangle at a time (keep other chilled), transfer to a board. Pull off top sheet of plastic wrap and cut dough crosswise into 16 strips about ½ inch wide and 6 inches long. On a 14- by 17-inch baking sheet lined with cooking parchment, or a buttered nonstick baking sheet, arrange four strips in a tic-tac-toe pattern: two parallel, then two over the top, perpendicular to the first, about 1 inch apart. Press lightly where strips cross. Repeat to shape remaining cookies, spacing at least ½ inch apart on baking sheets (you'll need two). Sprinkle with 2 to 3 tablespoons sugar.

4. Bake cookies in a 325° regular or convection oven until lightly browned at edges, 20 to 25 minutes; switch sheet positions halfway through baking. Transfer sheets to racks to cool. With a wide spatula, gently loosen cookies.

Per cookie: 234 cal., 46% (108 cal.) from fat; 3.3 g protein; 12 g fat (7.4 g sat.); 27 g carbo (0.6 g fiber); 162 mg sodium; 58 mg chol. ◆

A taste of Santa Ynez
Some of our favorite dishes from this wine country

By Sara Schneider • Photographs by James Carrier • Food styling by Basil Friedman

■ The historical flavor of California's Santa Ynez Valley has more to do with ranches and cowboys, steak and potatoes, than with up-scale wine country cuisine. But the former tradition and the latter trend are surprisingly compatible, and a handful of chefs are proving it. Their approach—local ingredients in season, often married to wine with a simple sauce—has created a cuisine with a distinctly Santa Ynez style. Here are dishes from several of the valley's talented chefs.

Prosciutto and Poached Egg Sandwiches with Mustard-Wine Sauce
SANTA YNEZ INN

With her beautiful breakfast entrées, executive chef Johanna Trujillo makes dining elsewhere in the valley almost unnecessary for guests of the Santa Ynez Inn.

PREP AND COOK TIME: About 40 minutes
NOTES: The mustard butter and mustard-wine sauce (steps 1 and 2) can be made up to 1 day ahead; cover each and chill. Warm sauce over low heat or reheat in a microwave oven at full power (100%), stirring occasionally, to use. Garnish sandwiches with fresh chive spears.

MAKES: 4 servings

- 3 tablespoons **butter** or margarine, at room temperature
- 2 tablespoons **Dijon mustard**
- ½ cup **dry white wine**
- ¼ cup minced **shallots**
- 1 cup **whipping cream**
  Salt and **pepper**
- 8 **large eggs**
- 4 thick slices (about 2 oz. each) **challah**
- 4 ounces **Appenzell** or gruyère **cheese,** thinly sliced
- 4 ounces **thinly sliced prosciutto**
- 4 ounces **salad mix** (about 2 qts.), rinsed and crisped

1. In a small bowl, with a fork, blend butter and 1 tablespoon mustard.

2. Combine wine and shallots in a 1½- to 2-quart pan; stir often over medium-high heat until liquid is almost evaporated, 5 to 6 minutes. Whisk in cream and remaining 1

tablespoon mustard. Simmer, stirring often, until sauce is reduced to 1 cup and is thick enough to coat spoon in a velvety layer, 8 to 10 minutes. Add salt and pepper to taste.

3. Meanwhile, in a 5- to 6-quart pan over high heat, bring 4 inches of water to a boil. With a slotted spoon, immerse each whole egg in water for 10 seconds. Lift out. Pour out all but 1 inch water; reduce heat so bubbles on pan bottom pop to the surface only occasionally.

4. Spread 1½ teaspoons mustard butter on one side of each slice of bread. Lay, buttered side down, on a griddle or in two 10- to 12-inch frying pans over medium-high heat; spread remaining butter mixture over tops of slices. When bottoms are lightly browned, in about 3 minutes, turn slices over. Top equally with cheese. Reduce heat to medium.

5. One at a time, crack eggs and, holding close to surface of water, break open and let egg slide in. Cook to desired doneness (poke with a spoon to check), 4 minutes for soft yolks.

6. When cheese on sandwiches begins to

melt, in 2 to 3 minutes, top with prosciutto; cook until warm, about 2 minutes.

7. Mound salad mix on plates. Transfer sandwich to each mound. With a slotted spoon, lift poached eggs from water and set two on each sandwich. Ladle mustard-wine sauce over eggs. Serve immediately, adding more salt and pepper to taste.

Per sandwich: 768 cal., 63% (486 cal.) from fat; 36 g protein; 54 g fat (27 g sat.); 33 g carbo (1.7 g fiber); 1,321 mg sodium; 598 mg chol.

Grilled Lamb Loin with Cabernet-Mint Sauce and Garlic Mashed Potatoes
CAFE CHARDONNAY

Just seven years ago, Humberto Huizar was a dishwasher in the kitchen; now he skillfully combines flavors in the compositions that go out on the plates.

plus at least 4 hours to marinate

NOTES: Have the butcher bone a lamb loin (1¾ to 2 lb.; make sure you don't get a tenderloin or the sirloin) and roll and tie it into a roast about 8 inches long and 2½ inches wide. You can marinate the lamb and prepare the sauce through step 3 up to 1 day ahead; bring sauce to a simmer over low heat before serving. Pour Buttonwood Farm Winery's "Trevin" Bordeaux blend to match the Cabernet sauce here.

MAKES: 3 to 4 servings

- 1 **fat-trimmed lamb loin,** boned, rolled, and tied (about 1 lb. total; see notes)
- 30 cloves **garlic,** peeled
- ½ cup plus ½ tablespoon **extra-virgin olive oil**
- ½ cup **balsamic vinegar**
- ½ cup chopped **shallots** (about 4 oz.)
- 2 tablespoons **fresh thyme** leaves or 1 tablespoon dried thyme
- 1 tablespoon chopped **Italian parsley**
   About ½ teaspoon **salt**
   About ¼ teaspoon **pepper**
- 2 cups **Cabernet Sauvignon** or other dry red wine
- 3 cups fat-skimmed **low-sodium beef broth**
- ½ cup (¼ lb.) plus 1 tablespoon **butter** or margarine
- ¼ cup chopped **fresh mint** leaves
- 1¾ pounds **Yukon Gold** or russet potatoes, peeled and cut into 1½-inch chunks
- ½ cup **whipping cream**
   Milk (optional)

1. Rinse lamb and pat dry. Chop 10 cloves of garlic. In an 8- by 10-inch baking dish, mix half the chopped garlic, ½ cup olive oil, vinegar, shallots, thyme, parsley, ½ teaspoon salt, and ¼ teaspoon pepper. Add lamb and turn to coat. Cover and chill at least 4 hours or up to 1 day, turning occasionally.

2. On a 12- by 12-inch sheet of foil, mix remaining 20 cloves garlic with ½ tablespoon olive oil to coat; seal foil around garlic. Bake in a 350° regular or convection oven until cloves are soft when pressed, about 45 minutes, turning packet over halfway through baking.

3. While garlic is baking, in a 10- to 12-inch frying pan over high heat, boil wine until reduced to 1 cup, about 10 minutes. Add broth and boil, stirring occasionally, until mixture is reduced to about 1½ cups, about 20 minutes. Whisk in 1 tablespoon butter, then stir in mint and the roasted garlic. Keep warm over low heat.

4. In a 5- to 6-quart pan, combine potatoes and remaining chopped garlic; add water to cover. Bring to a boil over high heat; cover, reduce heat, and simmer until potatoes mash easily when pressed, 20 to 25 minutes.

5. Meanwhile, heat cream with the remaining ½ cup butter in a microwave-safe container in a microwave oven at full power (100%), stirring at 20-second intervals, until butter is melted and mixture is steaming (do not boil), about 1½ minutes total.

6. Drain potatoes and garlic. Mash with a potato masher or a mixer until almost smooth. Add cream mixture and mash to desired consistency; if potatoes are thicker than desired, add a little milk. Add salt and pepper to taste. Keep warm over low heat if necessary.

7. While potatoes cook, lift lamb from marinade and drain well (discard marinade). Lay on a barbecue grill over a solid bed of medium-hot coals or medium-high heat on a gas grill (you can hold your hand at grill level only 3 to 4 seconds); close lid on gas grill. Turn occasionally until lamb is browned on all sides and a thermometer inserted in center of thickest part reaches 135° for medium-rare (pink in the center), 20 to 25 minutes, or until done to your liking. Transfer lamb to a board and let rest in a warm place at least 5 minutes.

8. Mound mashed potatoes equally on plates. Cut and remove string from lamb; slice loin crosswise and fan slices over potatoes. Spoon sauce with garlic around meat and mashed potatoes.

Per serving: 738 cal., 62% (459 cal.) from fat; 33 g protein; 51 g fat (26 g sat.); 39 g carbo (3.4 g fiber); 500 mg sodium; 178 mg chol.

Rollino Veneto (Pizza Rolls from Venice) with Tomato-Basil Salad
TRATTORIA GRAPPOLO

Ingredients and tradition get as much respect as wine at this lively, four-year-old Italian eatery. Wine, in fact, *is* the traditional ingredient in the excellent risottos and seafood specialties from owners Leonardo Curti and Daniele Serra. If Leonardo's brother, Alfonso—a former baker in the family's hometown of Cariati in the Calabria region of Italy—is cooking, it might even find its way into the pizza dough for crispy creations from the wood-burning oven.

PREP AND COOK TIME: About 2 hours
NOTES: Sangiovese is a great match for this appetizer; try the Vandale 1999.

MAKES: 2 rolls; about 8 appetizer servings

- 1 package **active dry yeast**
- 2½ to 3 cups **all-purpose flour**
- 2 teaspoons **salt**
- 1 **onion** (6 oz.), peeled and thinly sliced
- 3 tablespoons **extra-virgin olive oil**
- 1 head **radicchio** (about 8 oz.), rinsed, cored, and thinly sliced
- ¾ cup **Sangiovese** or other dry red wine
   Salt and **pepper**
- 8 ounces **smoked** or regular **mozzarella cheese,** shredded (about 2 cups)
- 6 cups diced (½ in.) **firm-ripe tomatoes** (about 3 lb. total)
- 1 cup slivered **fresh basil** leaves
- 2 tablespoons minced **garlic**

1. *To make the dough,* in a large bowl, sprinkle yeast over 1 cup warm (about 110°) water. Let stand until yeast is softened, about 5 minutes. Add 2½ cups flour and the salt; beat with a mixer on low speed until incorporated, then on medium-high speed until dough is stretchy, about 3 minutes.

2. *If using a dough hook,* beat on high speed until dough is smooth and elastic, about 5 minutes. If dough is still sticky, beat in more flour, 1 tablespoon at a time.

If kneading by hand, scrape dough onto a lightly floured board. Knead until smooth, springy, and no longer sticky, about 10 minutes. Add flour as necessary to prevent sticking.

3. Divide dough in half and shape each half into a ball. Set balls on a lightly floured surface in a warm place and cover loosely with plastic wrap. Let rise until doubled in size, 45 minutes to 1 hour.

4. *Meanwhile, make filling:* In a 10- to 12-inch frying pan over medium-high heat, stir onion in 1 tablespoon olive oil often until limp and beginning to brown, 3 to 5 minutes. Add radicchio and stir often until limp and beginning to brown, 5 to 7 minutes. Stir in wine and cook, stirring occasionally, until evaporated, 10 to 12 minutes. Add salt and pepper to taste. Let cool at least 20 minutes.

5. Punch each ball of dough down and knead lightly to expel air. On a lightly floured surface, with a lightly floured rolling pin, roll each ball into a 10- to 11-inch round. Sprinkle half the mozzarella over half of each round, to within 1 inch of edge; top cheese equally with radicchio mixture. Fold the bare

Stellar wines from a maverick region

By Karen MacNeil-Fife

■ Santa Ynez winemakers aren't afraid to go out on the edge to give us delicious wines. I could almost taste the excitement recently, as I worked my way through some 120—an effort that revealed some stellar bottles (and there are many more I didn't have the chance to try): sensational Syrahs and Pinot Noirs, as well as exciting unusual wines, such as Albariño, Cortese, and Tempranillo, all of which, while new here, are classics in Europe.

However, as with all relatively new (and creatively inclined) wine regions, Santa Barbara County is still on the front end of the learning curve, so the wines occasionally play out that nursery rhyme "When they're good they're very, very good, but when they're bad…." Many of the Chardonnays, especially, are over-oaked and too sweet for my taste.

This quality range makes it hard to characterize the wines in 200 words or so. But if Dustin Hoffman had been a young Santa Barbara County winemaker in *The Graduate,* Mr. Robinson surely would have whispered these two in his ear: "Syrah" and "Pinot Noir."

Whites

Brander "au Naturel" Sauvignon Blanc 2000 (Santa Ynez Valley), $30. This Sauvignon Blanc is not exactly a steal, but it's one of the most interesting and exotic Sauvignon Blancs in California. The wine is an explosion of green things: pea shoots, green tea, arugula, lime, green figs, green pepper—you name it. Sassy and sensational.

Byron "Sierra Madre Vineyard" Chardonnay 1998 (Santa Maria Valley), $35. In trying to make a rich, dense Chardonnay, it's easy to go overboard and end up with something that tastes like sugary candy topped with oak sauce. Not this one, however—an elegant, opulent Chardonnay with a beautiful streak of limey acidity running up through the middle.

Lafond "Northside" 2000 (Santa Ynez Valley), $12. Here's the steal of the group— a fascinating, refreshing blend of Sauvignon Blanc and Riesling. Historically, these two varieties have rarely been blended, but this wine's a charmer, with Riesling's peachy, floral crispness and Sauvignon Blanc's fresh, herbal edge. Got crab cakes?

Mosby Cortese 2000 (Santa Barbara County), $14. Cortese is the highly regarded grape behind the well-known Italian wine Gavi. Mosby specializes in fascinating Italian varieties and does an amazingly good job with them. This wine is gorgeously aromatic, fresh, and clean—just the ticket for salads and other light dishes. (For a great steak wine, try Mosby's powerfully tannic Teroldego.)

Verdad "Ibarra-Young Vineyard" White Wine 2000 (Santa Ynez Valley), $16. *Verdad* means "truth" in Spanish, but maybe it ought to mean "excitement," because this wine promises to usher in more white wines based on Spanish varieties (a completely new trend in California). Made from Albariño, it's modeled on the fresh, zingy Albariños of northwestern Spain—and it's a success, with a wonderful light nuttiness and a splash of ginger.

Reds

Buttonwood Cabernet Franc 1998 (Santa Ynez Valley), $18. This sleek wine is a great bet at a great price, with all the classic Cabernet Franc flavors and aromas—violets, leather, blackberry, and cassis. Perfect for a roast or grilled steak.

Hartley Ostini Hitching Post "Highliner" Pinot Noir 1998 (Santa Barbara County), $50. My favorite Santa Barbara Pinot Noir; burgundy lovers will go mad over it. The very complex nose (earth, damp moss, licorice) leads to ravishingly rich, sweet, spicy flavors.

LinCourt Syrah 2000 (Santa Barbara County), $20. In a word: dramatic. Luscious dark flavors of bitter chocolate, espresso, licorice, and blackberry are swirled together with hints of spice and vanilla. Try this with lamb or duck.

Melville Estate "Clone 115 Indigene" Pinot Noir 2000 (Santa Ynez Valley), $35. Don't look for subtlety (or burgundian resemblance) here. This is a pedal-to-the-floor, juicy Pinot Noir with loads of ripe fruit draped in vanilla and oak flavors.

Qupé "Los Olivos Cuvée" Rhône Blend 1999 (Santa Barbara County), $20. This delicious blend of Syrah, Mourvèdre, and Grenache shows off Qupé's expertise with Rhône varietals. The wine is evocative of southern France (all those earthy, gamy flavors), with a lip-smacking core of berry flavors.

Santa Barbara Winery Syrah 1999 (Santa Ynez Valley), $22. Imagine an enchanted forest that smells like rich, damp earth, lavender, and herbs, and you come close to this Syrah's enticing aroma. The blackberry pie flavors are irresistible too.

Zaca Mesa "B³ (Black Bear Block)" Syrah 1998 (Santa Barbara County), $45. A sip conjures visions of chocolate-espresso cake topped with whipped cream—hedonism in a bottle. Love thick, syrupy wines? This one's for you.

---

half of each dough round over filling, aligning edges; pinch edges to seal. Starting at fold, roll each pizza into a tight log; pinch log ends together to seal. Transfer logs, seam down, to a 12- by 15-inch baking sheet, shaping into equal-size half-rings and spacing at least 3 inches apart.

6. Bake in a 425° regular or convection oven until golden brown, 25 to 30 minutes.

7. *Meanwhile, make salad:* In a bowl, mix tomatoes, basil, garlic, and remaining 2 tablespoons olive oil; add salt and pepper to taste.

8. With two wide spatulas, transfer each half-ring to a rimmed board or platter, fitting ends together to form a complete ring. Using a slotted spoon, mound about 2 cups tomato-basil salad in the center of the ring set bowl with the remaining salad alongside board or platter. Cut the pizza ring into 1½- to 2-inch sections and serve with salad.

Per serving: 344 cal., 34% (117 cal.) from fat; 13 g protein; 13 g fat (5.4 g sat.); 45 g carbo (4.5 g fiber); 737 mg sodium; 30 mg chol. ◆

The Quick Cook

A Spanish tapas-bar staple makes a satisfying weeknight meal

By Charity Ferreira

Save a slice of this Spanish tortilla from supper for breakfast the next morning.

JAMES CARRIER; FOOD STYLING: BASIL FRIEDMAN

■ A Spanish tortilla is nothing like the flat flour or corn wrap most of us know best. A favorite bar snack in Spain, the tortilla is a stack of potatoes and onions, anointed with a fragrant dose of olive oil and lightly bound with egg—a tasty, simple entrée. Put together the tangy salad while the tortilla is finishing in the oven. And drizzle honey over creamy ricotta cheese for a practically instant dessert.

Spanish Tortilla

PREP AND COOK TIME: **About 30 minutes**

MAKES: **4 servings**

- 2 tablespoons **olive oil**
- 1 **onion** (about 8 oz.), peeled, halved, and thinly sliced crosswise
- 2 pounds **thin-skinned potatoes,** peeled and sliced into ⅛-inch-thick rounds
- ¾ teaspoon **salt**
- ½ teaspoon **pepper**
- 5 **large eggs**

1. Pour olive oil into a 10- to 12-inch nonstick ovenproof frying pan over medium-high heat; when hot, add onion and stir often until limp, about 5 minutes. Add potatoes, ½ teaspoon salt, and ¼ teaspoon pepper; mix to coat. Add ⅓ cup water and bring to a boil; reduce heat to medium, cover, and cook until potatoes are tender when pierced, about 10 minutes. If any liquid remains in pan, boil, uncovered, until evaporated, 1 to 2 minutes.

2. Meanwhile, in a large bowl, beat eggs with ¼ teaspoon salt and ¼ teaspoon pepper to blend. Add potato mixture and mix gently. Place unwashed frying pan over medium-high heat; when hot, pour in egg mixture. Reduce heat to medium-low and cook until eggs begin to set and bottom is lightly browned, 5 to 8 minutes.

3. Transfer pan to oven and broil tortilla about 6 inches from heat until top is set, 3 to 5 minutes. Run a spatula between tortilla and pan to loosen; invert tortilla onto a plate. Cut into wedges and serve warm or at room temperature.

Per serving: 338 cal., 35% (117 cal.) from fat; 12 g protein; 13 g fat (2.9 g sat.); 42 g carbo (4.3 g fiber); 532 mg sodium; 266 mg chol.

Salad with Marinated Peppers and Pine Nuts

PREP AND COOK TIME: **About 15 minutes**

MAKES: **4 servings**

- ⅓ cup **pine nuts**
- 3 tablespoons **sherry vinegar** or cider vinegar
- 3 tablespoons **extra-virgin olive oil**
- 1 cup **canned peeled roasted red peppers**
- ¼ cup chopped **pitted Spanish-style green olives**
- 2 quarts **salad mix** (8 oz.), rinsed and crisped

  Salt and **pepper**

1. In a 6- to 8-inch frying pan over medium heat, stir pine nuts often until golden, 5 to 8 minutes.

2. In a large bowl, whisk vinegar and olive oil to blend. Cut peppers lengthwise into ½-inch-wide strips. Drop into bowl and mix to coat with dressing. Add olives, salad mix, and toasted nuts and mix gently. Add salt and pepper to taste.

Per serving: 190 cal., 81% (153 cal.) from fat; 3.6 g protein; 17 g fat (2.4 g sat.); 8.5 g carbo (2.4 g fiber); 283 mg sodium; 0 mg chol.

Ricotta with Strawberries and Honey

Mound 1 cup **whole-milk ricotta cheese** on a plate. Arrange about 2 cups sliced **fresh strawberries** around cheese. Drizzle cheese and strawberries with 2 to 3 tablespoons **honey.** Serve with **wheat biscuits** or cookies if desired. Makes 4 servings.

Per serving: 162 cal., 46% (75 cal.) from fat; 7.4 g protein; 8.3 g fat (5.1 g sat.); 16 g carbo (2 g fiber); 53 mg sodium; 31 mg chol. ◆

Hawaiian ways with fish

Banana leaves, coconut milk, and pineapple give seafood a touch of the Islands

By Linda Lau Anusasananan

Photographs by James Carrier

FOOD STYLING: BASIL FRIEDMAN (2)

I n Hawaii, fish flaunts a sassy attitude. Local ingredients, colorful presentations, and unique species, such as opakapaka, onaga, and opah, give dishes unmistakable regional identity.

To bring this beguiling Islands style to fish on the mainland, we watched local chefs cook at renowned culinary seminars such as the Mauna Kea Resort's Winter Wine Escape (808/ 880-3023) and the Kapalua Wine and Food Festival (800/527-2582). They proved that it's deceptively easy to give any fish a little tropical flair.

Of course, Hawaiian anglers reel in fish we don't often see on the mainland. Although some of their unique species can be ordered (check with your local fish market if you're interested), we've built our recipes around types readily available throughout the West. Hawaiian flavors can turn any fish into flamboyant fare.

Pan-steamed Sole with Shrimp and Pork Hash

PREP AND COOK TIME: About 1 hour

NOTES: Alan Wong, chef-owner of Alan Wong's Restaurant in Honolulu, demonstrated this richly flavored combination of fish and pork at the Winter Wine Escape. Wong uses moi, a pond-raised, delicate, white-fleshed fish once reserved for Hawaiian royalty; sole, flounder, and tilapia are all good substitutes. Serve with hot cooked rice.

MAKES: 4 servings

8 thin slices (quarter-size) peeled **fresh ginger**

2 **green onions** (each 10 in. long)

6 ounces **baby bok choy**

¾ to 1 pound **boned, skinned sole**, flounder, or tilapia **fillets**

1 cup fat-skimmed **chicken broth**
   Shrimp and Pork Hash (recipe follows)

4 teaspoons **soy sauce**

2 tablespoons **peanut** or salad **oil**
   Fresh cilantro sprigs, rinsed
   Salt

1. Cut ginger into thin slivers. Rinse green onions and trim and discard ends; cut onions (including tops) into 3-inch lengths, then cut lengthwise into shreds. Rinse bok choy and trim and discard stem ends; cut bok choy diagonally into ½-inch-thick slices.

2. Rinse fish and pat dry. Cut into four equal pieces, 3 to 4 inches square.

3. In a 12-inch frying pan or 5- to 6-quart pan over high heat, bring broth to a simmer. Form Shrimp and Pork Hash into four equal patties about 3 inches wide; set in simmering broth as formed. Cover, adjust heat to maintain simmer, and cook until

patties are no longer pink on top, 3 to 4 minutes.

4. With a wide spatula, turn patties over; drape a piece of fish on each. Cover and simmer just until fish is barely opaque but still moist-looking in center of thickest part and patties are no longer pink in the center (cut both to test), 4 to 5 minutes longer.

5. Meanwhile, in an 8- to 10-inch frying pan over high heat, bring ¼ cup water to a boil; add bok choy, cover, and cook just until bright green and tender-crisp to bite, about 2 minutes. Drain bok choy in a colander. Rinse and dry pan.

6. When fish and hash are done, with spatula, transfer one patty with fish to each of four wide, shallow bowls or rimmed plates. Top portions equally with bok choy and green onions. Drizzle evenly with soy sauce. Spoon hot broth equally around fish.

7. In frying pan, heat oil and ginger over high heat until oil ripples over pan bottom, about 30 seconds. Spoon hot oil and ginger equally over servings. Garnish with cilantro sprigs. Add salt to taste.

Per serving: 300 cal., 45% (135 cal.) from fat; 31 g protein; 15 g fat (3.7 g sat.); 9.5 g carbo (1.3 g fiber); 857 mg sodium; 104 mg chol.

Shrimp and Pork Hash

PREP TIME: About 15 minutes

NOTES: Traditionally this mixture is steamed in a shallow dish and eaten with rice.

MAKES: About 1 1/4 cups

Mince 4 ounces **peeled, deveined shrimp** until it forms a coarse paste. In a bowl, mix shrimp; 4 ounces **ground lean pork**; 1 **large egg** white; 2 tablespoons *each* **cornstarch**, chopped peeled **fresh** or canned **water chestnuts**, and thinly sliced **green onion**; 1 tablespoon **prepared oyster sauce**; 1 teaspoon minced **garlic**; 1/4 teaspoon *each* **Asian** (toasted) **sesame oil** and **salt**; and 1/8 teaspoon **pepper**.

Per serving: 140 cal., 44% (61 cal.) from fat; 12 g protein; 6.8 g fat (2.4 g sat.); 6.8 g carbo (0.6 g fiber); 396 mg sodium; 64 mg chol.

LEFT: This bok choy–garnished fish fillet rests atop a shrimp and pork patty. ABOVE: A banana leaf cradles a whole salmon fillet.

Salmon with Crab and Vegetables in a Foil Packet

PREP AND COOK TIME: About 45 minutes

NOTES: For the Kapalua Wine and Food Festival, chef Christian Hugo Jorgensen of the Westin Maui framed a party-size salmon fillet with tropical leaves. He used fresh ti leaves, which are readily available in Hawaii and sometimes at mainland florist shops. But frozen banana leaves, sold in Asian markets, are a good substitute; you can also omit the leaves altogether. If assembling through step 4 up to 4 hours before baking, chill packet.

MAKES: 6 to 8 servings

- 1 piece (12 by 18 in.) **frozen banana leaf** (optional; see notes)
- 1 **whole salmon fillet** (2 1/2 lb.)
- 3 tablespoons chopped **fresh cilantro**
- 2 teaspoons minced **fresh thyme** leaves or 3/4 teaspoon dried thyme
- 2 teaspoons minced **fresh oregano** leaves or 3/4 teaspoon dried oregano
- 6 ounces **shelled cooked crab**
- 1/3 cup **mayonnaise**
- 2 tablespoons **Dijon mustard**
- 2 **yellow crookneck squash** (8 oz. total)
- 1 **red bell pepper** (8 oz.)
- 3 tablespoons **dry white wine** or water
- 1 tablespoon **olive oil**
  About 1/4 teaspoon **salt**
  Pepper

1. Center an 18- by 28-inch piece of foil (or overlap two 12-inch-wide pieces) in a 14- by 17-inch baking pan. Rinse banana leaf and pat dry; center lengthwise on foil. Rinse fish and pat dry; rub your fingers over the flesh to find any bones, pull out with tweezers, and discard. Center fillet lengthwise, skin down, on leaf.

2. Mix the cilantro, thyme, and oregano. In a bowl, mix half the herb mixture with crab, mayonnaise, and mustard. Spread evenly over salmon. Rinse and dry bowl.

3. Rinse squash and bell pepper. Trim and discard stems from squash; stem and seed pepper. Cut vegetables into matchstick-size strips (about 3 in. long). Put vegetables, wine, olive oil, 1/4 teaspoon salt, and rest of herbs in bowl and mix to coat.

4. Spread vegetable mixture over crab layer. Bring long sides of foil together over fish, wrapping banana leaf partially around fish, then fold in ends to seal.

5. Bake in a 450° regular or convection oven until fish reaches 140° in center of thickest part (insert thermometer through foil and vegetable and crab layers to test), 20 to 25 minutes. Transfer packet to a platter and unwrap to serve; or, if desired, with two wide spatulas, carefully transfer leaf and fish from foil to platter. Add salt and pepper to taste. Cut fish into portions; slip a spatula between skin and fillet and lift off portions, leaving skin behind.

Per serving: 352 cal., 59% (207 cal.) from fat; 30 g protein; 23 g fat (4.1 g sat.); 3 g carbo (0.7 g fiber); 349 mg sodium; 102 mg chol.

Hawaiian Ceviche with Pineapple Salsa

PREP AND COOK TIME: About 25 minutes, plus at least 40 minutes to chill

NOTES: Stephen Marshall, executive chef at the Ritz-Carlton Kapalua, created this ceviche for the Kapalua Wine and Food Festival. He used onaga; halibut is a good substitute. Taro chips are available at some supermarkets and in specialty food shops.

MAKES: 6 to 8 first-course servings

- 1 pound **boned, skinned halibut**
- 1/2 cup **lime juice**
- 1 cup **pineapple juice**
- 1/2 cup **coconut milk**
- 1 cup minced **red onion**
- 1 tablespoon minced **garlic**
- 1/4 cup chopped **fresh cilantro**
- 1 to 1 1/2 teaspoons **hot sauce**
  Salt
  Pineapple Salsa (recipe follows)
  Taro chips (optional)

1. Rinse fish and pat dry; cut lengthwise into 1/4-inch-thick strips, then stack two or three at a time and cut into pieces 1 to 1 1/2 inches long. Place in a bowl. Pour lime juice over fish and mix.

2. In a 1 1/2- to 2-quart pan over high heat, bring pineapple juice, coconut milk, onion, and garlic to a boil; cook 2 minutes. Stir in fish mixture and remove from heat. Let cool about 5 minutes, stirring occasionally, then chill until cold, at least 40 minutes, or up to 4 hours, stirring occasionally.

3. Stir in cilantro and add hot sauce and salt to taste. Spoon equal portions into martini or wine glasses or small bowls. Garnish with a generous spoonful of Pineapple Salsa. Serve with taro chips if desired.

Per serving without salsa: 120 cal., 33% (40 cal.) from fat; 13 g protein; 4.4 g fat (2.9 g sat.); 7.7 g carbo (0.4 g fiber); 54 mg sodium; 18 mg chol.

Pineapple Salsa

PREP TIME: About 15 minutes

MAKES: About 1 1/4 cups

In a bowl, mix 1 cup 1/2-inch chunks peeled **fresh pineapple**, 1/2 cup 1/2-inch chunks **firm-ripe tomato**, and 1/4 cup chopped **fresh cilantro**. Add 1 to 1 1/2 teaspoons minced **fresh jalapeño chili** and **salt** to taste.

Per tablespoon: 4.8 cal., 0% from fat; 0.1 g protein; 0 g fat; 1.2 g carbo (0.1 g fiber); 0.5 mg sodium; 0 mg chol. ◆

By Jerry Anne Di Vecchio

Photographs by James Carrier

Sandwich special

Egg salad savoir faire

The egg—a pillar in many cuisines—embodies simplicity and sophistication. Its form has no wasted line. Its taste is delicate yet satisfying. And in a sandwich, it's a chameleon—capable of pleasing one and all.

At home, David and I are prone to impromptu gatherings, with menus that necessarily grow from staples on hand, including the incredible egg. When we use it for open-faced sandwiches, with whatever bread and toppings are available, and put a small green salad alongside, we have a rather significant meal—without significant effort.

Toppings we use on many occasions are smoked salmon or trout, marinated red peppers, or marinated mushrooms (all from the larder). We've even been known to do as chef Anne Gingrass does at Desiree Cafe in San Francisco's Presidio: Sizzle tender oyster mushrooms in butter until faintly browned, drizzle them with a little white truffle oil, and spoon them over the egg salad. Short of wild mushrooms and truffle oil, our favorite embellishments are these made-in-minutes pickled onions and marinated cucumbers.

Sumptuous Egg Salad Sandwiches

PREP AND COOK TIME: About 1 hour

NOTES: The texture of the salad depends on how you mash the eggs: For a fluffier quality, separate the whites and yolks and mash with a fork or whirl separately in a food processor to desired consistency; for a creamier texture, mash or whirl whites and yolks together. As flavor alternatives, substitute 1 teaspoon curry powder and/or 1 tablespoon chopped fresh dill for the tarragon. You can make the egg salad (step 1), Pickled Onion Salad, and Melted Cucumbers up to 1 day ahead; cover separately and chill.

MAKES: 4 servings

- 8 hard-cooked **large eggs**, shelled and mashed (see notes)
  About ½ cup **mayonnaise** (regular or reduced fat) or sour cream (or equal portions of each)
- 1½ tablespoons **Dijon mustard**
- 1½ teaspoons minced **fresh tarragon** or ½ teaspoon dried tarragon (see notes)
- ½ teaspoon minced **fresh thyme** leaves or dried thyme
  Salt and **pepper**
- 6 cups **baby salad mix,** rinsed and crisped

- 2 tablespoons **extra-virgin olive oil**
- 2 tablespoons **balsamic vinegar**
- 8 slices **dense-textured pumpernickel bread** or toasted firm-textured white bread or 4 English muffins, split and toasted

  Pickled Onion Salad (recipe follows)

  Melted Cucumbers (recipe follows)

1. In a bowl, mix eggs with enough mayonnaise for desired consistency. Stir in mustard, tarragon, and thyme. Add salt and pepper to taste.

2. Put salad mix in another bowl; mix with olive oil and vinegar, and salt and pepper to taste.

3. Place two slices of bread on each plate. Spread egg salad equally on slices. Top equally with Pickled Onion Salad and Melted Cucumbers. Mound salad mix alongside.

Per serving: 637 cal., 59% (378 cal.) from fat; 21 g protein; 42 g fat (7.8 g sat.); 43 g carbo (6.6 g fiber); 1,105 mg sodium; 441 mg chol.

Pickled Onion Salad. Peel and thinly slice 1 **red onion** (about 6 oz.; 1½ cups sliced). In a 4- to 5-quart pan over high heat, bring 4 cups **water,** ¼ cup **white wine vinegar,** 1 tablespoon **mustard seeds,** 1 teaspoon **cumin seeds,** and 1 teaspoon **coriander seeds** to a boil. Add onion, stir, and cook for 2 minutes. Pour into a fine strainer, discarding liquid. In a bowl, combine onion and spice seeds with 2 tablespoons **lemon juice; salt** to taste. Let cool at least 20 minutes, stirring occasionally. Makes about 1 cup; 4 servings.

Per serving: 33 cal., 27% (9 cal.) from fat; 1.5 g protein; 1 g fat (0 g sat.); 5.4 g carbo (1.2 g fiber); 6.6 mg sodium; 0 mg chol.

Melted Cucumbers. In a bowl, combine 1½ cups thinly sliced **English cucumbers,** 1 tablespoon **kosher** or coarse **salt,** 2 tablespoons **sugar,** and 2 tablespoons **white wine vinegar.** With your hands, gently crush cucumbers until limp; let stand at least 10 minutes. Add 3 cups **water,** mix, and pour into a strainer, pressing gently to remove excess liquid; discard liquid. Makes about ¾ cup; 4 servings.

Per serving: 9.8 cal., 0% (0 cal.) from fat; 0.6 g protein; 0 g fat; 2.2 g carbo (0.6 g fiber); 243 mg sodium; 0 mg chol.

Local spice route

■ The port city of Malacca in Malaysia has faded from its 16th-century spice trade glory. But as I wandered its streets recently with Lucia Cleveland, a modern-day spice hunter (and founder of the company by that name), we came across many seasonings still to be discovered by adventurous cooks, and others—such as tangy tamarind—that are already in Western markets. At lunch that day in the Seri Nyonya Peranakan Restaurant, Florence Tan served shrimp in a very easy, glossy brown sauce based on tamarind. It makes as delectable a dish for this century as for any in the past.

Malaysian Tamarind Shrimp

PREP AND COOK TIME: About 35 minutes

NOTES: Like dates, fresh tamarinds, with their sticky, dense flesh and dry exterior pods, last indefinitely stored at room temperature. You'll find the pods in many supermarkets as well as in Mexican, Asian, and Indian food markets. To use them, pull off and discard the hull; pack the fruit and seeds to measure. Tamarind pulp (with seeds, and often some shell) is sold in solid blocks in the same ethnic markets as the fresh fruit. You'll also find liquid tamarind concentrate from Southeast Asia and Mexico; substitute ½ cup concentrate for ¼ cup pulp. Serve shrimp on hot cooked basmati rice.

MAKES: 4 servings

- ¼ cup packed **tamarind pulp** (see notes)
- ½ cup **sugar**
- ¼ cup **rice vinegar**
- 3 tablespoons **soy sauce**
- 1 teaspoon **hot sauce**
- 1 tablespoon **salad oil**
- 1½ pounds **shelled, deveined shrimp** (15 to 24 per lb.), rinsed and well drained
- 2 **green onions,** ends trimmed, cut into thin slivers

1. In a small bowl, mix tamarind pulp and ¾ cup boiling water. Let stand until lukewarm, 8 to 10 minutes; rub pulp with your fingers to mix well and release from seeds. Rub mixture through a strainer into a 10- to 12-inch frying pan; discard residue.

2. Add sugar, vinegar, soy sauce, and hot sauce to frying pan. Bring mixture to a boil over high heat and stir often until reduced to about ¾ cup, about 5 minutes. Scrape the reduced sauce back into a bowl (or, if making up to 1 week ahead, into a jar or refrigerator container; cover and chill).

3. Rinse the frying pan and wipe dry. Place over high heat and add the oil; when hot, add shrimp and stir until they begin to turn pink, about 2 minutes. Pour into a bowl. Add the tamarind sauce to pan and stir until it's boiling vigorously; return shrimp to pan and stir until opaque but still moist-looking in center of thickest part (cut to test), 3 to 6 minutes longer.

4. Spoon shrimp and sauce onto plates or into a bowl. Garnish with green onions.

Per serving: 353 cal., 17% (59 cal.) from fat; 36 g protein; 6.5 g fat (1 g sat.); 38 g carbo (0.2 g fiber); 1,062 mg sodium; 259 mg chol.

View from the top

■ The rule for accurately determining the level of the ingredients in a transparent measuring cup is to bend down and look through at eye level—effective but awkward. Now OXO Good Grips (800/545-4411 or www.oxo.com) has taken the bending out of measuring with its new 2-cup angled measure. An ingeniously positioned scale, with markings for cup and milliliter units, spirals up the interior of the container, to be read just by looking down. The measuring cup is available for about $7 in most cookware and hardware stores. One caution, though: The unit is made of plastic that can't take the heat of chores like melting butter in a microwave oven.

Go with the (old) grain

■ A wheatlike grain popular during the golden days of old Rome has enjoyed a revival in Italy and now is popping up in Italian delicatessens and natural-food stores here. In Italy it's called *farro* or *farro intero;* in botanical Latin, *Triticum dicoccom.*

By any name, the grain has an appealing earthy, wholesome flavor and a texture that's at once chewy and creamy. It makes a delicious alternative to cracked wheat, rice, and similar side-dish carbs with meats, poultry, and fish. Cooked with sausage, then mixed with diced apples for a sweet crunch, farro makes a savory side dish for roast chicken.

Italian Farro with Sausage and Apples

PREP AND COOK TIME: About 40 minutes
MAKES: About 6 cups; 4 to 6 side-dish servings

- 1 cup **hulled whole-grain farro**
- ¾ cup **bulk pork sausage** (about 3 oz.) or pork sausages, casings removed
  Butter or olive oil (if needed)
- 2½ cups fat-skimmed **chicken broth**
- 1 cup finely chopped **parsley**
- 1 **Fuji apple** (8 oz.)
- 2 tablespoons **lemon juice**
  Salt and **pepper**

1. Sort farro, discarding strawlike bits of hulls and other debris. Pour farro into a bowl, cover completely with cool water, stir, and skim off and discard any additional hulls that float to the surface. Drain farro.

2. In a 5- to 6-quart pan over high heat, crumble sausage with a spoon and stir often until browned, about 5 minutes. Spoon out and discard all but 1 tablespoon fat or, if necessary, add butter to equal 1 tablespoon fat in pan. Add farro to sausage in pan and stir until grains are dried, about 2 minutes.

3. Add broth and bring to a boil, then reduce heat, cover pan, and simmer (mixture foams, so check and stir occasionally to keep it from boiling over) until farro is tender to bite and no longer tastes starchy, about 25 minutes. Stir in parsley, cover, remove from heat, and let stand 10 minutes.

4. Meanwhile, peel and core apple; cut into about ¼-inch dice and mix with lemon juice. Stir into farro, season to taste with salt and pepper, and pour into a bowl.

Per serving: 181 cal., 19% (35 cal.) from fat; 9.4 g protein; 3.9 g fat (1.3 g sat.); 27 g carbo (2.7 g fiber); 150 mg sodium; 7.1 mg chol. ◆

Farro cooking tips

My experience in cooking farro contradicts the instructions I've come across. In Italy, I was told to soak the grain overnight, then cook it for an hour or more. The results were mushy to my taste. In reality, farro requires no soaking and cooks to tenderness as quickly as rice. Here are some basic tips.

- 500 grams (1.1 lb.) of farro is about 2¾ cups; each cup yields about 2 cups cooked.
- Before cooking, sort through farro and discard debris, then rinse and drain the grain.
- Use 1 part farro to 3 parts seasoned liquid, such as chicken broth.
- As it cooks, the mixture foams, so 1 cup farro needs at least a 4- to 5-quart pan.
- Simmer farro, covered, until tender to bite, about 25 minutes.
- If you want a creamy texture, let stand off the heat for about 10 minutes.
- If cooking farro ahead of time, drain while still hot; save liquid to add when reheating or—since the grain makes a good salad—to use as part of a dressing. Let farro cool, then cover and chill up to 2 days. Reheat in a microwave oven or use cold.

The Low-Fat Cook

A savory sandwich for a simple meal, Middle Eastern–style

By Linda Lau Anusasananan

■ In restaurants around the Middle East, thin slices of meat, impaled on long skewers, turn on vertical rotisseries. As the edges of the meat cook, they're sliced off and enclosed in soft flatbread—*lahvosh*. The sandwich is called *shawarma*. Hilda and Ray Marangosian of San Mateo, California, devised this fast, light version, which requires no special equipment or shopping. Just stir strips of beef in a frying pan, stuff them into pocket bread, and add broiled tomatoes and a simple yogurt sauce.

Spiced Beef Pockets

PREP AND COOK TIME: About 45 minutes

MAKES: 6 servings

- 2 pounds **boned beef sirloin steak,** fat trimmed
- ¼ cup **lemon juice**
- 1 teaspoon **ground allspice**
  About ¼ teaspoon **pepper**
- 12 **Roma tomatoes** (2 lb. total)
- 6 **pocket breads** (6 to 7 in. wide), cut in half crosswise
  Salt
- ½ cup thinly slivered **red onion**
- ¼ cup **chopped parsley**
- 1 cup diced **dill pickles** or cucumber
- 1 cup **Sesame Yogurt Sauce** (recipe follows)

1. Rinse beef and pat dry; slice crosswise into ⅛-inch-thick strips 2½ inches long. In a bowl, mix beef, lemon juice, allspice, and ¼ teaspoon pepper; let stand 10 minutes.

2. Meanwhile, rinse and core tomatoes; cut each in half lengthwise. Set halves, skin up, in a 10- by 15-inch baking pan. Broil about 4 inches from heat until richly browned, 6 to 9 minutes. Reduce oven temperature to 200°. Stack pocket breads and wrap in foil. Warm in oven with tomatoes until ready to serve, 5 to 10 minutes.

3. Set a 10- to 12-inch nonstick frying pan over high heat. When hot, add beef mixture; stir until meat is no longer pink, 4 to 5 minutes. With a slotted spoon, transfer beef to a wide bowl or platter. Boil juices until reduced to ¼ cup, 2 to 4 minutes; pour over meat. Stir in salt to taste.

4. Arrange tomatoes beside beef. Sprinkle onion and parsley over meat. Serve pocket breads, pickles, and Sesame Yogurt Sauce alongside. To eat, spoon beef mixture, tomatoes, onion, and pickles into pocket bread halves. Add yogurt sauce to taste.

Per serving: 438 cal., 18% (79 cal.) from fat; 42 g protein; 8.8 g fat (2.7 g sat.); 47 g carbo (3.8 g fiber); 788 mg sodium; 93 mg chol.

Sesame Yogurt Sauce

PREP AND COOK TIME: About 5 minutes

MAKES: About 1 cup

- 1 tablespoon **sesame seeds**
- 1 cup **plain nonfat yogurt**
- 1 clove **garlic,** peeled and minced
  Salt and **pepper**

1. In a 6- to 8-inch frying pan over medium heat, stir sesame seeds until golden, 2 to 3 minutes.

2. In a small bowl, mix yogurt, garlic, and toasted sesame seeds. Add salt and pepper to taste.

Per tablespoon: 11 cal., 25% (2.7 cal.) from fat; 0.9 g protein; 0.3 g fat (0.1 g sat.); 1.3 g carbo (0.1 g fiber); 11 mg sodium; 0.3 mg chol. ◆

JAMES CARRIER; FOOD STYLING: BASIL FRIEDMAN

Kitchen Cabinet

Readers' recipes tested in *Sunset's* kitchens

By Charity Ferreira • Photographs by James Carrier

Strips of chicken and seared shiitake mushrooms nestle in a tangle of pasta.

Garlic Chicken Noodles

Kim Chan, Sunnyvale, CA

Kim Chan's family loves to be greeted by the pungent smell of this garlicky dish when they walk in the door at the end of the day.

PREP AND COOK TIME: About 1 hour
MAKES: 4 to 6 servings

- 4 **boned, skinned chicken breast halves** (5 to 6 oz. each)
- 1 pound **fresh Asian-style noodles**
- 2 tablespoons **salad oil**
- 1 **onion** (about 8 oz.), peeled and thinly sliced
- 6 ounces **fresh shiitake mushrooms,** rinsed, stems removed, and sliced
- ¼ cup chopped **green onions** (including tops)
- ¼ cup minced **garlic**
- ½ cup **rice wine**
- ¼ cup **rice vinegar**
- 3 tablespoons **soy sauce**

1. Rinse chicken and pat dry. Cut breast halves crosswise into ⅛-inch-wide strips.

2. In a 5- to 6-quart pan over high heat, bring about 4 quarts water to a boil; add noodles and cook, stirring occasionally, until tender to bite, about 3 minutes. Drain noodles and return to pan.

3. Meanwhile, pour oil into a 10- to 12-inch frying pan over medium-high heat. When hot, add onion, mushrooms, green onions, and garlic; stir often until onion and mushrooms begin to brown, about 8 minutes. Add chicken and stir often until no longer pink in the center (cut to test), about 3 minutes. Add rice wine, vinegar, and soy sauce; cook to blend flavors, 1 to 2 minutes longer.

4. Add chicken mixture to noodles in pan and stir over medium-high heat until hot, 2 to 3 minutes. Divide equally among four wide bowls.

Per serving: 481 cal., 17% (81 cal.) from fat; 34 g protein; 9 g fat (1.6 g sat.); 61 g carbo (3.2 g fiber); 595 mg sodium; 127 mg chol.

Mediterranean Couscous

Susan Brown, Puyallup, WA

Looking for something to serve with baked chicken one night, Susan Brown improvised this nearly instant side dish from ingredients in her pantry.

PREP AND COOK TIME: About 15 minutes
MAKES: 2 to 3 side-dish servings

- 1 cup **couscous**
- 1 tablespoon **dried basil**
- 1 tablespoon **extra-virgin olive oil**
- 1 tablespoon **balsamic vinegar**
- ½ teaspoon minced **garlic**
- ⅓ cup **canned peeled roasted red peppers,** drained and cut into thin strips
- ¼ cup chopped **pitted calamata olives**

1. In a 2- to 3-quart pan over high heat, bring 1¼ cups water to a boil. Stir in couscous and basil. Remove from heat, cover, and let stand 5 minutes.

2. Meanwhile, in a small bowl, whisk together olive oil, vinegar, and garlic. Fluff couscous with a fork and stir in peppers and olives. Add oil mixture and mix well.

Per serving: 315 cal., 23% (73 cal.) from fat; 8.1 g protein; 8.1 g fat (1.1 g sat.); 52 g carbo (2.4 g fiber); 239 mg sodium; 0 mg chol.

Sesame Water Crackers

Gemma Sanita Sciabica, Modesto, CA

Gemma Sanita Sciabica pairs these crisp homemade water crackers—which she sometimes flavors with chopped fresh herbs or cracked black pepper—with cheeses, spreads, salads, and soups.

PREP AND COOK TIME: About 45 minutes, plus 20 minutes to rest
MAKES: About 4 dozen crackers

- About 2 cups **all-purpose flour**
- 1 teaspoon **baking powder**
- 1 teaspoon **salt**
- ⅓ cup **olive oil**
- 1 **large egg white,** lightly beaten
- 2 tablespoons **sesame seeds**

1. In a large bowl, mix 2 cups flour, baking powder, and ½ teaspoon salt. Add ⅔ cup water and the oil and mix

just until dough comes together. Scrape onto a lightly floured board and knead two or three turns. Divide dough into thirds; shape each portion into a ball, flatten slightly, and cover loosely with plastic wrap. Let rest 20 minutes.

2. One at a time, with a lightly floured rolling pin, roll each portion into a rectangle about $1/16$ inch thick. Using a lightly floured knife, cut rectangle into 2-inch squares (discard uneven edge pieces if desired). With a wide spatula, transfer squares to buttered or cooking parchment–lined 12- by 15-inch baking sheets, spacing squares slightly apart.

3. Brush tops lightly with egg white (discard any remaining) and sprinkle evenly with sesame seeds and remaining $1/2$ teaspoon salt. Pierce each square with the tines of a fork to make several rows of indentations.

4. Bake in a 300° regular or convection oven until light golden brown, 20 to 25 minutes; if baking more than one sheet at a time in one oven, switch their positions halfway through baking. Transfer crackers to a rack to cool completely.

Per cracker: 37 cal., 41% (15 cal.) from fat; 0.7 g protein; 1.7 g fat (0.2 g sat.); 4.6 g carbo (0.2 g fiber); 60 mg sodium; 0 mg chol.

Cream Cheese Hummus

Pam McGee, University Place, WA

Pam McGee shared with us this pungent dip for vegetables, crackers, and chips. We thought it made a great sandwich spread too.

PREP TIME: About 10 minutes
MAKES: About $1^1/2$ cups

- 1 can (15$1/2$ oz.) **garbanzos,** drained (reserve liquid) and rinsed
- 1 package (3 oz.) **regular** or reduced-fat **cream cheese,** at room temperature
- 1 tablespoon **lemon juice**
- $1/4$ cup minced **green onions** (white and pale green parts only)
- 1 to 2 teaspoons **prepared horseradish**
  About $1/2$ teaspoon **salt**

In a food processor or blender, whirl garbanzos, $1/4$ cup reserved liquid, cream cheese, lemon juice, green onions, 1 teaspoon horseradish, and salt until smooth. Taste, and add more horseradish and salt if desired.

Per tablespoon: 22 cal., 41% (9 cal.) from fat; 1 g protein; 1 g fat (0.5 g sat.); 2 g carbo (0.5 g fiber); 84 mg sodium; 2.5 mg chol.

Burger and spice: Plum sauce, ginger, and Chinese five spice make a unique, flavorful beef patty.

Chinese Five Spice Burgers

Linda Lum, Steilacoom, WA

Asian seasonings make Linda Lum's hamburgers aromatic and tangy. You can now find Chinese five spice blends in the spice section of most supermarkets, where you'll also find prepared plum sauce and Asian sesame oil. If you can't find five spice, substitute this mixture: $1/8$ teaspoon *each* ground cinnamon, ground cloves, ground ginger, and anise seeds.

PREP AND COOK TIME: About 30 minutes
MAKES: 4 servings

- About 1 teaspoon **olive** or salad **oil**
- 1 cup thinly sliced **mushrooms** (3$1/2$ oz.)
- $1/3$ cup thinly sliced **green onions** (including tops)
- 6 tablespoons **prepared Chinese plum sauce**
- 1 pound **ground lean beef**
- 2 tablespoons **soy sauce**
- 1 teaspoon **Asian** (toasted) **sesame oil**
- 1 teaspoon minced **garlic**
- $1/2$ teaspoon **Chinese five spice** (see notes)
- $1/4$ teaspoon **ground ginger**
- 4 **sesame seed–topped hamburger buns** (about 3 oz. each), cut in half horizontally
  Lettuce leaves, rinsed and crisped
  Salt

1. Pour oil into an 8- to 10-inch nonstick frying pan over high heat; when hot, add mushrooms and stir until lightly browned, about 4 minutes. Stir in the green onions and plum sauce and remove from heat.

2. In a bowl, gently mix ground beef with soy sauce, sesame oil, garlic, Chinese five spice, and ginger. Shape beef mixture into four equal patties, each about $1/2$ inch thick.

3. Lay patties on a lightly oiled barbecue grill over a solid bed of medium-hot coals or medium-high heat on a gas grill (you can hold your hand at grill level only 3 to 4 seconds); close lid on gas grill. Cook patties until no longer pink in the center (cut to test) or a thermometer inserted in center reaches 160°, 6 to 8 minutes total, turning once to brown evenly. After 5 minutes, lay bun halves, cut side down, on grill and toast lightly, 1 to 2 minutes.

4. Lay a lettuce leaf on each toasted bun base, top with a beef patty, and spoon mushroom mixture equally over burgers. Add salt to taste and cover with bun tops.

Per serving: 608 cal., 46% (279 cal.) from fat; 31 g protein; 31 g fat (12 g sat.); 52 g carbo (2.5 g fiber); 1,119 mg sodium; 85 mg chol.

Southwestern Spoon Bread with Avocado Salsa

Mickey Strang, McKinleyville, CA

Mickey Strang likes to serve this custardy casserole as an entrée for brunch or a light lunch or as a side dish for her husband's *chili con carne.*

PREP AND COOK TIME: About 1 hour
MAKES: 4 to 6 side-dish servings

- 2 teaspoons **salt**
- 1 cup **yellow cornmeal**

4 **large eggs**

1 cup **buttermilk**

1 can (4 oz.) **diced green chilies**

1½ teaspoons **chili powder**

Avocado Salsa (recipe follows)

1. In a 2- to 3-quart pan over high heat, bring 2½ cups water and the salt to a boil. Gradually whisk in cornmeal and stir until mixture is thick and smooth, about 1 minute. Remove from heat.

2. In a bowl, beat eggs and buttermilk just to blend. Whisk into cornmeal mixture until completely incorporated. Stir in chilies and chili powder. Scrape mixture into a buttered 8-inch square baking dish.

3. Bake in a 400° regular or convection oven until top is browned and a wooden skewer inserted in the center comes out clean, about 35 minutes. Let stand 10 minutes. Scoop out portions with a spoon and serve with Avocado Salsa.

Per serving: 231 cal., 39% (90 cal.) from fat; 8.9 g protein; 10 g fat (2.2 g sat.); 27 g carbo (3.1 g fiber); 1,146 mg sodium; 143 mg chol.

Avocado Salsa

PREP TIME: About 15 minutes
MAKES: About 2⅓ cups

1¼ cups chopped **firm-ripe tomatoes** (8 oz.)

1 cup diced **firm-ripe avocado** (about 8 oz.)

⅓ cup minced **red onion**

2 tablespoons minced **fresh jalapeño chilies**

2 tablespoons **lime juice**

2 tablespoons chopped **fresh cilantro**

Salt

In a bowl, combine tomatoes, avocado, onion, chilies, lime juice, and cilantro. Mix gently and add salt to taste. ◆

Dig in!

From Washington to Pismo Beach, clammers find a bounty of bivalves

By Karl Samson
and Ann Marie Brown

Although you aren't likely to find any pirate gold, there's buried treasure on the beaches of many inland coastal waterways. From Bellingham to Pismo Beach, scratch the surface of the right beaches at low tide and you're likely to unearth handfuls of clams. Depending on where you dig, tidal flats can yield a mix of clam species. Northwestern clammers unearth native littlenecks, Manila littlenecks, butter clams, geoduck, and cockles. Along the California coastline you'll find gaper, Washington, littleneck, and Pismo clams.

They are yours for the taking with a few key tools: a state fishing license, a clamming shovel (or fork or rake), and the ability to dig when you spot the telltale squirting hole that reveals a clam's location.

Timing is key. If you want to find clams instead of sand, you must head for the beach during an ultralow minus tide, when a clam's hideout is exposed by the ebbing Pacific. Location is also critical. Check with the state Department of Fish and Wildlife (or Game) to find out which beaches are open when you want to go out.

So where are these tasty bivalves hiding? Most bury themselves in sandy gravel, leaving only hints of their existence: siphon holes in the sand. Once you find the right mix of sand and gravel, just dig down a few inches and you should find clams—especially if you go out during low tide.

You can't hunt for Pismo clams by strolling on the tidal flats as you can for their cousins to the north. Pismo clams are found in knee-high water at low tide, burrowed about 6 inches below the sand. Locating them requires probing the sand with a clamming fork while waging an ongoing battle with the incoming surf. (Always face the breaking surf so you're aware of approaching waves; never try to clam in water deeper than your waist.)

Planning on clamming?

Wear rubber boots or prepare to get wet and muddy. Take along a valid shellfish license, a tide table (or check www.saltwatertides.com), and a clam gauge. This latter item, often just a simple plastic ring, allows you to measure your clams to make sure they are of legal size. You'll also need a shovel or other digging tool (such as a three-pronged garden cultivator) and a bucket or ice chest to hold your clams. Fill the container with enough saltwater to cover your hand several inches deep.

Before clamming, check regulations for your destination on the state Department of Fish and Wildlife (or Game) website or at any sporting goods store that sells fishing licenses. (Rules and limits vary according to state, clam species and location). Because clams are occasionally affected by biotoxins such as paralytic shellfish poisoning, check the state DFW or DFG hotline and the local health department before heading out. Also, when cleaning clams, strip away and discard all the dark parts and the gills—a must from May to October.

And now, the payoff—a pan of your very own hard-earned roasted clams.

1 tablespoon **olive oil**

6 ounces **fresh chanterelle** or common **mushrooms,** rinsed, tough stem ends trimmed, and cut into ¾-inch chunks (see notes)

2 cloves **garlic,** peeled and thinly sliced

6 tablespoons **unsalted butter** or margarine

3 tablespoons **dry white wine**

1 cup **cherry tomatoes,** rinsed, stemmed, and cut in half, or 3 firm-ripe Roma tomatoes (about 10 oz. total), rinsed, cored, seeded, and diced

½ cup **pitted calamata** or oil-cured black **olives** (see notes)

4 sprigs (about 4 in. long) **fresh thyme,** rinsed

2 pounds **clams in shells,** suitable for steaming, well scrubbed under cool running water

1 **lemon** (about 4 oz.), rinsed and cut lengthwise into 6 wedges

1. In a 10- to 12-inch ovenproof frying pan (with at least 2½-in. sides) over medium-high heat, stir bacon often until browned and crisp, 3 to 5 minutes. Add olive oil, mushrooms, and garlic and stir often until mushrooms are slightly limp, 2 to 3 minutes.

2. Add butter, wine, tomatoes, olives, and thyme sprigs; stir often over high heat until butter is melted and liquid is boiling. Add clams and squeeze 2 lemon wedges over clams, discarding seeds and peels. Cover pan.

3. Transfer pan to a 500° regular or convection oven and bake until clams pop open, 12 to 15 minutes.

4. Ladle clam mixture and juices equally into four wide, shallow bowls; discard any clams that didn't open. Garnish each serving with a lemon wedge.

Per serving: 404 cal., 85% (342 cal.) from fat; 7.6 g protein; 38 g fat (16 g sat.); 7.6 g carbo (1.4 g fiber); 476 mg sodium; 72 mg chol. — *Sara Schneider* ◆

Oven-roasted Clams with Chanterelles, Bacon, and Tomatoes

PREP AND COOK TIME: 35 to 40 minutes

NOTES: This robust combination of flavors comes from Seattle chef Tom Douglas of Etta's Seafood, the Palace Kitchen, Dahlia Lounge, and now the Dahlia Bakery. If chanterelles are unavailable, you can substitute fresh crimini or shiitake mushrooms (for the shiitakes, trim off and discard the entire tough stem). Douglas leaves the olive pits in but warns diners before they dig in. Serve the clams with toasted slices of hearty bread rubbed with garlic, to sop up the juices, and a Chardonnay that's light on oak: Try the 2000 Frog's Leap, Clos du Val, or Savannah-Chanelle.

MAKES: 4 appetizer servings

½ cup diced **bacon** (about 3 slices; 3 oz. total)

Spicy Chicken Tagine, a traditional North African stew, is updated to make a quick weeknight meal (recipe on page 106).

May

morning glory

Pancakes from breakfast spots
around the West
bring a weekend ritual closer to home

By Charity Ferreira • Photographs by James Carrier
Food styling by Susan Devaty

Pancakes inspire a special kind of ardor, as do the places we go to eat them. Weekend mornings are for sticking close to home: We tend not to stray farther than our favorite neighborhood breakfast spot, where steaming cups of coffee, tiny glasses of orange juice, and stacks of pancakes dripping with butter and syrup help us make the ritual transition from the sanctuary of sleep to the relaxed pace of a weekend day.

We collected pancake recipes from breakfast spots with passionate local followings around the West to make your trip from bed to breakfast even shorter.

JOHN GRANEN

ASADENA

Marston's
Restaurant

On weekends, Pasadenans begin gathering outside half an hour before this homey restaurant opens its doors. No doubt some in line sustain themselves with thoughts of the hearty omelets and home fries with peppers and cheese, but I imagine most rose early for the sweeter offerings—macadamia nut, blueberry, seven-grain pancakes and crispy, cornflake-coated French toast. The thick slabs of sourdough take a while to cook, but, as owner Jim McCardy points out with a grin that is equal parts pleasure and surprise, nobody seems to mind waiting.

MARSTON'S RESTAURANT, *151 Walnut St.; (626) 796-2459. — C.F.*

CLOCKWISE FROM LEFT: Our take on Marston's blueberry buttermilk pancakes; doors open for breakfast at 8 at La Note in Berkeley; an order is up at Seattle's Coastal Kitchen.

Blueberry Buttermilk Pancakes

PREP AND COOK TIME: About 30 minutes

NOTES: For consistency, cooks at Marston's prefer canned Maine blueberries in syrup; we like fresh blueberries in their batter too. Serve these pancakes with butter and warm maple syrup.

MAKES: About 20 pancakes; 5 to 6 servings

- 2 cups **all-purpose flour**
- 1½ teaspoons **baking soda**
- 1½ teaspoons **baking powder**
- ½ teaspoon **salt**
- 2 **large eggs**
- 2½ cups **buttermilk**
- ¼ cup (⅛ lb.) **butter** or margarine, melted
- 1 cup **fresh blueberries**, rinsed and drained, or canned blueberries, drained (see notes)
- **Salad oil**

1. In a bowl, mix flour, baking soda, baking powder, and salt. In a small bowl, whisk eggs, buttermilk, and butter until blended. Stir egg mixture into flour mixture, then gently stir in blueberries.

2. Place a nonstick griddle or a 12-inch nonstick frying pan over medium heat (350°). When hot, coat griddle lightly with oil and adjust heat to maintain temperature (see "The perfect pancake," page 97). Spoon batter in ⅓-cup portions onto griddle and cook until pancakes are browned on the bottom and edges begin to look dry, about 2 minutes; turn with a wide spatula and brown other sides, 1½ to 2 minutes longer. Coat pan with more oil as necessary to cook remaining pancakes.

3. Serve pancakes as cooked, or keep warm in a single layer on baking sheets in a 200° oven for up to 15 minutes.

Per serving: 322 cal., 36% (117 cal.) from fat; 10 g protein; 13 g fat (6.4 g sat.); 41 g carbo (1.7 g fiber); 841 mg sodium; 96 mg chol.

BERKELEY
La Note Restaurant Provençal

This southern French restaurant is known for rustic bistro fare at lunch and dinner, but at breakfast rumpled locals come in droves to relax over inspired egg dishes, toasted brioche with lavender honey, and oatmeal-raspberry or crème fraîche pancakes accompanied by café au lait served in bowls so big it's almost hard to find room for them on the little wooden tables. Charming details—the chunky Provençal pottery, French-country table linens, bowls of jam and brown sugar cubes—make this the next best thing to being in France.

LA NOTE RESTAURANT PROVENÇAL, *2377 Shattuck Ave.; (510) 843-1535. — C.F.*

Add fresh berries and butter to the mixed-berry coulis over oatmeal-raspberry pancakes. RIGHT: La Note is a little bit of Provence in Berkeley.

Oatmeal-Raspberry Pancakes with Berry Coulis

PREP AND COOK TIME: About 1 hour

NOTES: Cooks at La Note swirl a little of the jamlike coulis on top of the pancakes. You can make the coulis up to 1 week ahead; chill airtight. Also offer butter and syrup with the pancakes.

MAKES: About 12 pancakes; 5 to 6 servings

1½ cups **rolled oats**

1 cup **buttermilk**

1½ cups **all-purpose flour**

¼ cup **sugar**

1 teaspoon **baking soda**

1 teaspoon **baking powder**

½ teaspoon **salt**

4 **large eggs**

1½ cups **milk**

1 teaspoon **vanilla**

1 cup **fresh raspberries**, rinsed

Salad oil

Berry coulis (recipe follows)

1. In a bowl, mix oats and buttermilk; let stand at least 15 minutes or up to 30 minutes.

2. Meanwhile, in a small bowl, mix flour, sugar, baking soda, baking powder, and salt.

3. In a large bowl, beat eggs, milk, and vanilla to blend. Stir in flour and oat mixtures just until evenly moistened, then gently stir in raspberries.

4. Place a nonstick griddle or a 12-inch nonstick frying pan over medium heat (350°); when hot, coat lightly with oil and adjust heat to maintain temperature (see "The perfect pancake," page 97). Pour batter in ½-cup portions onto griddle and cook until pancakes are browned on the bottom and edges begin to look dry, about 2 minutes; turn with a wide spatula and brown other sides, 1½ to 2 minutes longer. Coat pan with more oil as necessary to cook remaining pancakes.

5. Serve the pancakes as cooked, or keep them warm in a single layer on baking sheets in a 200° oven for up to 15 minutes. Stack pancakes on plates and serve with berry coulis (see notes).

Per serving: 341 cal., 22% (74 cal.) from fat; 13 g protein; 8.2 g fat (2.6 g sat.); 53 g carbo (3.9 g fiber); 591 mg sodium; 149 mg chol.

Berry Coulis

In a 3- to 4-quart pan, combine 2 cups rinsed **fresh blueberries**, 2 cups rinsed **fresh raspberries**, 1½ cups **sugar**, and ¼ cup **lemon juice**. Bring to a boil over medium-high heat, then reduce heat and simmer, stirring occasionally, until berries begin to disintegrate and mixture starts to thicken, about 15 minutes. Press through a fine strainer into a bowl, extracting as much liquid as possible with the back of a spoon or a spatula; discard seeds and skins. Serve coulis warm; if mixture cools before you're ready to serve, reheat in a microwave oven. If it's too thick, stir in a little warm water. Makes about 2 cups.

Per ¼ cup: 91 cal., 2% (1.8 cal.) from fat; 0.3 g protein; 0.2 g fat (0 g sat.); 23 g carbo (0 g fiber); 2.1 mg sodium; 0 mg chol.

TUCSON

Arizona Inn

There's just no beating the right pancake in the right place. No offense to the other versions on the menu at Tucson's Arizona Inn (they're terrific too), but the blue corn pancakes with prickly pear syrup—the rich, dense cornmeal setting off the fruity hints of the syrup—deliver the perfect desert breakfast experience.

ARIZONA INN, 2200 E. Elm St.; (520) 325-1541 or www.arizonainn.com. Pancakes available in the dining room and through room service 7–10 A.M. — Matthew Jaffe

Blue Corn Pancakes

PREP AND COOK TIME: About 25 minutes

NOTES: Though the Arizona Inn serves these thin, slightly crunchy pancakes with butter and prickly pear syrup, they taste great with regular maple syrup too.

MAKES: 10 pancakes; 4 to 5 servings

1 cup **blue** or yellow **cornmeal**

1 cup **all-purpose flour**

1 tablespoon **baking powder**

½ teaspoon **salt**

1½ cups **milk**

2 **large eggs**, beaten to blend

6 tablespoons **butter** or margarine, melted

Salad oil

1. In a bowl, mix cornmeal, flour, baking powder, and salt. Whisk in milk and eggs until blended, then whisk in butter.

2. Place a nonstick griddle or a 12-inch nonstick frying pan over medium heat (350°); when hot, coat lightly with oil and adjust heat to maintain temperature (see "The perfect pancake," page 97). Spoon batter in ⅓-cup portions onto griddle and cook until pancakes are browned on the bottom and edges begin to look dry, about 2 minutes; turn with a wide spatula and brown other sides, 1½ to 2 minutes longer. Coat pan with more oil as necessary to cook remaining pancakes.

3. Serve pancakes as cooked or keep warm in a single layer on baking sheets in a 200° oven for up to 15 minutes.

Per serving: 410 cal., 46% (189 cal.) from fat; 10 g protein; 21 g fat (11 g sat.); 45 g carbo (2.1 g fiber); 727 mg sodium; 132 mg chol.

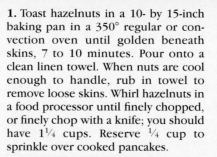

Nuts, spices, and a touch of whole wheat start the morning right.

Coastal Kitchen

Coastal Kitchen knows where to draw the line at too much of a good thing. The regional lunch and dinner menus at this Capitol Hill cafe change often, shifting from foods of Gascony one quarter to Indian or Patagonian cuisine the next, and the eclectic art on the walls changes as often as the menu. But happily the pancakes remain un-touched—cinnamon-hazelnut, but-termilk, fruit-of-the-day, and corn pancakes every day, with the occa-sional regional specialty. All come with real maple syrup; add a side of ham or sausage—the best you'll ever eat.

COASTAL KITCHEN, *429 15th Ave. E; (206) 322-1145.*

— *Jim McCausland*

Cinnamon-Hazelnut Pancakes

PREP AND COOK TIME: About 1 hour

NOTES: Chefs at the Coastal Kitchen serve these chunky pancakes simply, with butter and maple syrup.

MAKES: 20 pancakes; 6 to 8 servings

- 1¼ cups **hazelnuts** (about 6 oz.)
- 1¾ cups **all-purpose flour**
- ¾ cup **whole-wheat flour**
- 2 tablespoons **sugar**
- 2 teaspoons **ground cinnamon**
- 1½ teaspoons **baking powder**
- ½ teaspoon **baking soda**
- ½ teaspoon **salt**
- 2 **large eggs**
- 3 cups **buttermilk**
- 3 tablespoons **butter** or margarine, melted
- **Salad oil**

1. Toast hazelnuts in a 10- by 15-inch baking pan in a 350° regular or con-vection oven until golden beneath skins, 7 to 10 minutes. Pour onto a clean linen towel. When nuts are cool enough to handle, rub in towel to remove loose skins. Whirl hazelnuts in a food processor until finely chopped, or finely chop with a knife; you should have 1¼ cups. Reserve ¼ cup to sprinkle over cooked pancakes.

2. In a bowl, mix all-purpose flour, whole-wheat flour, sugar, cinnamon, baking powder, baking soda, and salt. In a small bowl, whisk eggs, butter-milk, and butter until blended. Stir egg mixture into flour mixture until evenly moistened, then gently stir in remaining 1 cup hazelnuts.

3. Place a nonstick griddle or a 12- inch nonstick frying pan over medium heat (350°). When hot, coat lightly with oil and adjust heat to maintain temperature (see "The perfect pan-cake," page 97). Spoon batter in ⅓-cup portions onto griddle and cook until pancakes are browned on the bottom and edges begin to look dry, about 2 minutes; turn with a wide spatula and brown other sides, 1½ to 2 minutes longer. Coat pan with more oil as necessary to cook remaining pancakes.

4. Serve pancakes as cooked or keep warm in a single layer on baking sheets in a 200° oven for up to 15 min-utes. Sprinkle with reserved hazelnuts.

Per serving: 395 cal., 50% (198 cal.) from fat; 12 g protein; 22 g fat (4.8 g sat.); 41 g carbo (3.9 g fiber); 473 mg sodium; 68 mg chol.

Crest Cafe

With hip, comfortable food and a retro diner look made slightly prim and proper by church pews enjoying their second life as cafe seating, Crest Cafe has been packing in Hillcrest-area habitués since 1982. Favorite menu items include a famous "onion loaf" (a deep-fried tangle of battered rings), grilled sandwiches, and honey-glazed pork chops. On weekends, breakfast specials such as the divine lemon- or orange-ricotta buttermilk pancakes and blackberry-topped whole wheat–cottage cheese "power pancakes" raise pancake expertise to an art form.

CREST CAFE, *425 Robinson Ave.; (619) 295-2510.* — *Peter Jensen*

Try these light and fluffy lemon-ricotta pancakes with the berry coulis on page 95.

Lemon-Ricotta Pancakes

PREP AND COOK TIME: About 30 minutes

NOTES: This is our adaptation of Crest Cafe's lemon-ricotta pancakes, which are served with fresh strawberries and bananas. Top the bananas with a sprinkling of grated lemon peel and offer warm maple syrup to drizzle over the fruit and cakes.

MAKES: About 8 pancakes; 4 servings

1 1/2 cups **all-purpose flour**

2 tablespoons **sugar**

1 teaspoon **baking soda**

1/2 teaspoon **salt**

1 1/2 cups **buttermilk**

2 **large eggs,** separated

1 tablespoon grated **lemon** peel

1/3 cup **part-skim ricotta cheese**

Salad oil

1. In a large bowl, mix flour, sugar, baking soda, and salt. In a medium bowl, whisk buttermilk, egg yolks, and lemon peel to blend. Stir buttermilk mixture into flour mixture just until evenly moistened. Gently stir in ricotta cheese.

2. In a bowl, with a mixer on high speed, beat the egg whites until soft peaks form. With a flexible spatula, gently fold the whites into the batter just until they are incorporated.

3. Place a nonstick griddle or a 12-inch nonstick frying pan over medium heat (350°); when hot, coat lightly with oil and adjust heat to maintain temperature (see "The perfect pancake," at right). Drop batter in 1/2-cup portions onto the griddle and cook until pancakes are browned on the bottom and edges begin to look dry, about 2 minutes; turn cakes with a wide spatula and brown other sides, 1 1/2 to 2 minutes longer. Coat pan with more oil as necessary to cook remaining pancakes.

4. Serve pancakes as cooked, or keep warm in a single layer on baking sheets in a 200° oven for up to 15 minutes.

Per serving: 318 cal., 21% (68 cal.) from fat; 13 g protein; 7.6 g fat (2.6 g sat.); 48 g carbo (1.4 g fiber); 759 mg sodium; 116 mg chol.

the perfect pancake

In many ways, making pancakes couldn't be simpler—at their most basic level, they consist only of flour, leavening, eggs, liquid (most often in the form of milk or buttermilk), and sometimes melted butter or oil. But there are a few simple techniques that ensure turning out a perfect pancake every time.

• **Combine** the dry ingredients first, then mix the liquid ingredients with the dry ingredients gently with a flexible spatula, just until evenly moistened. Avoid overmixing the batter, which can result in tough, rubbery pancakes.

• **Use** the right pan and amount of oil. The outside texture of the pancake depends on the surface of the griddle or pan and how much oil you use. While some people prefer the dark rings produced by a cast-iron surface, we like the results of a nonstick surface that has been coated with oil, then quickly wiped nearly clean with a paper towel.

• **Heat** the pan over medium-high heat until a small dollop of batter dropped in makes a sizzling noise. Lower the heat, add the first pancake, and observe how it cooks: By the time the edges of the pancake start to look dry and bubbles are forming and popping on top, the underside should be golden brown. Lower the heat if the pancake darkens too fast and raise it if the pancake is still too light when bubbles form.

WHITEFISH, MONTANA

Buffalo Cafe

Although located just *off* Central Avenue, Buffalo Cafe is breakfast central in Whitefish. Ranchers and skiers gather in the morning at the lunch counter or in comfortable booths, surrounded by walls adorned with snowshoes, wooden skis, and a bulletin board posting notices for craft bazaars and sea-kayaking lessons. It's the kind of place, says Linda Maetzold, who owns the cafe with her husband, Charlie, "where people talk from table to table, because everybody knows everybody."

BUFFALO CAFE, *514 Third St. E; (406) 862-2833.*

— *Caroline Patterson*

Strawberry Pancake Roll-ups

PREP AND COOK TIME: About 1 hour

NOTES: This is our version of a popular spring breakfast special at the Buffalo Cafe. Thin and tender, the pancakes are rolled around a strawberry pink filling. You can make the strawberry sauce and cream cheese mixture (steps 1 and 2) up to 2 days ahead; cover separately and chill.

MAKES: About 8 roll-ups; 4 servings

1½ quarts **fresh strawberries,** rinsed and hulled

6 tablespoons **sugar**

2 tablespoons **lemon juice**

8 ounces **cream cheese,** at room temperature

1½ cups **all-purpose flour**

1 teaspoon **baking soda**

½ teaspoon **salt**

2 **large eggs**

1½ cups **buttermilk**

1 cup **milk**

Salad oil

Sweet and lively breakfast for the season at the Buffalo Cafe—buttermilk pancakes filled with tangy strawberry cream cheese.

1. Thinly slice 2 cups strawberries. In a blender or food processor, whirl remaining 1 quart strawberries until smooth. Press through a fine strainer into a bowl, extracting as much liquid as possible with the back of a spoon or a spatula; discard residue. Whisk ¼ cup sugar and the lemon juice into strawberry purée.

2. In the blender or food processor (no need to rinse), whirl cream cheese and ½ cup of the strawberry purée until blended and smooth.

3. In a bowl, mix flour, baking soda, salt, and remaining 2 tablespoons sugar. In another bowl, whisk eggs, buttermilk, and milk just to blend. Whisk milk mixture into flour mixture just until evenly moistened.

4. Place a nonstick griddle or a 12-inch nonstick frying pan over medium heat (350°); when hot, coat lightly with oil and adjust heat to maintain temperature (see "The perfect pancake," page 97). Spoon batter in ½-cup portions onto griddle and cook until pancakes are browned on the bottom and edges begin to look dry, about 2 minutes; turn with a wide spatula and brown other sides, 1½ to 2 minutes longer. As pancakes are cooked, transfer to baking sheets and keep warm in a 200° oven. Coat pan with more oil as necessary to pan to cook remaining pancakes.

5. Spread each pancake with about 2 tablespoons cream cheese mixture and roll up. Set two roll-ups on each plate, top evenly with sliced strawberries, and drizzle with a little strawberry purée; serve with remaining purée to add to taste.

Per serving: 646 cal., 40% (261 cal.) from fat; 19 g protein; 29 g fat (15 g sat.); 81 g carbo (7.5 g fiber); 936 mg sodium; 181 mg chol. ◆

Chile that's over the top

Share New Mexico's love affair with the great Frito pie

By Sharon Niederman
Photographs by Douglas Merriam

Elmer Doolin of San Antonio, Texas, made a bid for culinary immortality when he founded the Frito Company in 1932, originally manufacturing his crunchy corn chips in the family kitchen.

But mom did him one better. Sometime during the early 1930s, Daisy Dean Doolin gave in to a curious impulse: She dumped her chile over a bunch of Fritos. It was the invention of the Frito pie, and since Mrs. Doolin's time, generations of Cub Scouts, rodeo attendees, and county fair–goers have accumulated fond memories of this down-home dish. In fact, the state of New Mexico has adopted it as its own, with several eateries churning out some of the best Frito pies you'll find anywhere.

The formula of pie

The most authentic Frito pie, many say, is created when red chile is ladled directly into a small bag of Fritos. That's the way Teresa Hernandez makes the "world famous" Frito pies she serves at the Five and Dime General Store in Santa Fe. Hernandez began working at Woolworth's (now the Five and Dime) on the plaza in 1953, introducing the Frito pie there in the 1960s. Today, the establishment serves more than 56,000 tasty Frito pies a year made with her mother's secret recipe for tangy red chile. She refuses to add any garnishes, maintaining that "the original didn't have lettuce or tomato!" Says Hernandez: "The trick is to get the chile in the bag."

The Diner's Frito Pie with Barbara Cozart's Red Chile

Here's a down-home version of the Southwest classic that's easy and unpretentious and hits the spot—perfect for a meal that's often eaten out of a Frito bag.

PREP AND COOK TIME: About 30 minutes

MAKES: 6 servings

- 2 pounds **ground lean** (7% fat) **beef**
- 1 tablespoon **garlic powder**
  About 1 teaspoon **salt**
- 2 tablespoons **all-purpose flour**
- 1 can (15 oz.) **black beans** (optional), rinsed and drained
- 3 tablespoons **ground dried New Mexico chilies** or chili powder
  About 4½ cups **Fritos corn chips** (15-oz. bag)
- 6 tablespoons finely chopped **onion**
- 1½ cups shredded **longhorn** cheddar **cheese**
- 2 cups finely shredded **iceberg lettuce**
- ¾ cup chopped **tomato**

1. In a 5- to 6-quart pan over medium-high heat, stir ground beef, garlic powder, and 1 teaspoon salt until beef is crumbly and well browned, 6 to 8 minutes.

2. With a large slotted spoon, push beef mixture to one side of pan and tilt pan so liquid runs to opposite side. Stir flour into liquid until well blended, then mix with beef mixture. Add 2 cups water, black beans if using, and dried chilies; stir until mixture boils and thickens, about 8 minutes.

3. Spread about ¾ cup Fritos in each of six wide, shallow bowls and sprinkle chopped onion equally on top. Divide chili equally among bowls and top with cheese, lettuce, and tomato. Add more salt to taste.

Per serving: 776 cal., 53% (414 cal.) from fat; 44 g protein; 46 g fat (14 g sat.); 45 g carbo (3.9 g fiber); 1,088 mg sodium; 117 mg chol. — *Sara Schneider*

Next to nostalgia, the quality of the red chile is probably the most important ingredient in the Frito pie. At the Diner, a popular stop in Tres Piedras, 30 miles northwest of Taos on U.S. 285, the chile is irresistible.

Owner Barbara Cozart prepares her chile from her own recipe, using only locally grown red chilies from the Espanola Valley. Her version is rich, crimson, and satisfying, with the meat-and-bean-filled chile saturating the crispy Fritos to just the right level of pliability. Built in the early 1940s, the Diner has its original red stools and mirrored stainless steel counter.

A slightly updated version of the Frito pie is found at Orlando's New Mexican Cafe in El Prado, a couple of miles north of the Taos plaza via Paseo del Pueblo Norte (State 68). Orlando's Frito pie is a deep-dish wonder consisting of your choice of beef or chicken, beans, savory red or green chile, and plenty of shredded lettuce, tomatoes, and cheese.

This family business is among the area's favorite New Mexican restaurants. San Pasqual, the patron saint of the kitchen, presides over an interior reminiscent of Mexican folk art. Umbrellas shade a patio packed with diners until the stars come out.

Bag New Mexico's Frito pie

Five and Dime General Store. 58 E. San Francisco St., Santa Fe; (505) 992-1800.

The Diner. U.S. 64 and U.S. 285, Tres Piedras; (505) 758-3441.

Orlando's New Mexican Cafe. Closed Sun. 1114 Don Juan Lane, El Prado; (505) 751-1450. ◆

Cinco de Mayo mixed grill

Cheese Quesadillas and Radishes

Mexican Mixed Grill

Fresh Salsa (Chop Sauce)

Roasted-Poblano Cream

Pot Beans

Warm Corn Tortillas

Cinnamon-Scented Rice Milk *(Horchata)* and Beer

Three-Milk Cake *(Pastel Tres Leches)*

Guests can build
their meal from the grill:
orange-achiote chicken and green Anaheim
chilies with fresh salsa, beans, and tortillas.

Cinco de Mayo fiesta!

Celebrate Mexico—past and present—with a delicious mixed grill and all the fixings

By Linda Lau Anusasananan • Photographs by James Carrier • Food styling by Basil Friedman and Susan Devaty

In our enthusiasm for all things Mexican, we've made Cinco de Mayo an exuberant north-of-the-border holiday, with parades, festivals, and food. Often mislabeled Mexican Independence Day, May 5 is in fact the anniversary of the Battle of Puebla, the Mexican army's (temporarily) successful stand against the French in 1862 and a rather minor holiday in Mexico today. Regardless, it's a wonderful time to celebrate our lively Mexican heritage here in the West with a fiesta.

Ruben and Leticia Salinas, owners of Los Caporales Restaurant in Ojai, California, provide the perfect menu, from Leticia's home state of Sonora, for a mixed grill party *(parrillada)*. Guests fill warm tortillas with grilled meats and chilies, add chop sauce (a fresh salsa that doubles as a salad) and roasted-poblano cream, and wrap the bundle like a burrito or fold it taco-style. Pot beans (pinto beans) are the simple side dish, and another classic, *pastel tres leches* (three-milk cake), makes a rich, sweet ending.

Mexican Mixed Grill

PREP AND COOK TIME: About 1 hour, plus at least 30 minutes to marinate

NOTES: Latino markets often sell wide pieces of boned pork shoulder or butt thinly sliced, and skirt steak butterflied open in large, thin slabs called *arrachera*. If they're unavailable, ask your butcher to cut wide, thin slices off a boned pork shoulder or butt roast, and use regular skirt steak. Buy firm chorizo sausages with the texture of pepperoni; they maybe labeled *longaniza*. For a simpler grill, choose one kind of meat and marinade, and multiply quantities proportionally.

MAKES: 10 to 12 servings

1 pound **boned, skinned chicken thighs**

1 pound **boned pork shoulder** or butt, fat trimmed, cut into ¼-inch-thick slabs (see notes)

1 pound **beef skirt steak,** fat trimmed (see notes)

About ⅓ cup **orange-achiote marinade** (recipe follows)

About ½ cup **red chili sauce** (recipe follows)

About 1 teaspoon **seasoned salt**

About 1 teaspoon **pepper**

10 to 12 **green onions** (6 to 8 oz. total), rinsed

10 to 12 **fresh Anaheim** (California or New Mexico) **chilies** (about 1¼ lb. total), rinsed

1 tablespoon **salad oil**

1 pound **firm chorizo sausages** (see notes)

1. Rinse chicken, pork, and beef; pat dry. Cut skirt steak crosswise into 6- to 8-inch lengths. If chicken, pork, or beef

is thicker than ¼ inch, place between sheets of plastic wrap and, with a flat mallet, gently and evenly pound to about ¼ inch thick.

2. On a rimmed plate, coat chicken completely with orange-achiote marinade and layer thighs; on another rimmed plate, coat pork completely with red chili sauce and layer slices. Cover and chill at least 30 minutes or up to 1 day (if marinating chicken and pork a day ahead, wrap beef airtight and chill). Shortly before grilling, lightly sprinkle both sides of beef with seasoned salt and pepper; set on a plate.

3. In a wide bowl, mix green onions and chilies with oil to coat. Set onions, chilies, and sausages on a barbecue grill over a solid bed of hot coals or high heat on a gas grill (you can hold your hand at grill level for only 2 to 3 seconds); close lid on gas grill. Cook, turning occasionally, until onions and chilies are well browned and sausages are browned on the outside and cooked through, 2 to 3 minutes for onions, 5 to 8 minutes for chilies and sausages. As done, transfer to a large board or platter.

4. Lay chicken, pork, and beef on grill; close lid on gas grill. Cook, turning once, until chicken and pork are no longer pink in the center and beef is done to your liking (cut to test), 5

Grilled cheese quesadillas (above), with salsa or roasted-poblano cream, make a great starter. Anaheim or poblano chilies (below) carry mild heat.

to 8 minutes total. Transfer meat to board or platter with vegetables and sausages. Add more seasoned salt and pepper to taste.

Per serving: 396 cal., 57% (225 cal.) from fat; 33 g protein; 25 g fat (9 g sat.); 8 g carbo (1.1 g fiber); 901 mg sodium; 113 mg chol.

Orange-Achiote Marinade

PREP TIME: About 5 minutes

NOTES: Achiote paste is sold in reddish orange blocks in Latino markets; if it's unavailable, use 1 more tablespoon paprika (1 tablespoon and 2 teaspoons total). The recipe for this marinade can be doubled. It's also delicious on pork. You can make the marinade up to 2 days before using; cover and chill.

MAKES: About 1/3 cup, enough to marinate 1 to 2 pounds meat

In a bowl, mix 1/3 cup **orange juice**, 1 tablespoon **salted red achiote paste** (see notes), 1 tablespoon **soy sauce**, 2 teaspoons **paprika**, 1 teaspoon **instant chicken bouillon**, 1 teaspoon minced **garlic**, and 1/4 teaspoon **pepper**.

easy fundamentals

- **Cheese quesadillas.** Spread about 1/2 cup **shredded jack cheese** over half of each of 5 or 6 flour tortillas (8 in. wide); fold bare halves over cheese. Grill over a solid bed of hot coals or high heat on a gas grill (you can hold your hand at grill level for only 2 to 3 seconds), turning once, for 2 minutes total. Cut into wedges.

- **Pot beans.** Heat 6 or 7 cans (15 oz. each) drained **pinto beans** and 1 1/2 cups water over medium heat, stirring occasionally, until hot; or cook 4 to 5 cups dried pinto beans according to package directions. Add salt to taste.

- **Warm tortillas.** Divide 30 to 40 **corn tortillas** (6 in. wide) into stacks of 10; wrap each stack in plastic wrap. Heat one packet at a time in a microwave oven on full power (100%) until hot and steamy, 30 to 45 seconds. Wrap packets in clean linen towels to serve.

Per tablespoon: 15 cal., 6% (0.9 cal.) from fat; 0.3 g protein; 0.1 g fat (0 g sat.); 3.4 g carbo (0 g fiber); 304 mg sodium; 0 mg chol.

Red Chili Sauce

PREP AND COOK TIME: About 20 minutes, plus at least 15 minutes to cool

NOTES: The recipe for this sauce can be doubled. It can also be used to marinate beef or chicken. You can make the sauce up to 2 days before using; cover and chill.

MAKES: About 1/2 cup, enough to marinate 1 to 2 pounds meat

1. Rinse 2 **dried guajillo** or ancho (sometimes mislabeled pasilla) **chilies** (about 1/2 oz. total). Snap off and discard stems; shake out most of the seeds. With scissors, working over a 1- to 2-quart pan, cut chilies into 1-inch pieces; drop into pan.
2. Add 1/2 cup **water**, 1 peeled clove **garlic**, 1/2 teaspoon *each* **ground cumin** and **dried oregano**, and 1/8 teaspoon *each* **ground cinnamon** and **ground cloves**. Bring to a boil; cover, reduce heat, and simmer, stirring occasionally, until chilies are soft, 10 to 15 minutes.
3. Pour chili mixture into a blender and whirl until smooth. If you have less than 1/2 cup, add water to make that amount. Add **salt** to taste. Let cool at least 15 minutes.

Per tablespoon: 5.2 cal., 35% (1.8 cal.) from fat; 0.2 g protein; 0.2 g fat (0 g sat.); 0.9 g carbo (0.3 g fiber); 0.7 mg sodium; 0 mg chol.

Roasted-Poblano Cream

PREP AND COOK TIME: About 30 minutes

NOTES: Poblano chilies are big, triangular dark green chilies, often mislabeled pasilla; if they're not available, substitute fresh Anaheim (California or New Mexico) chilies. You can prepare the vegetables through step 2 up to 1 day ahead; wrap the grilled or roasted vegetables airtight and chill.

MAKES: 1 quart; 10 to 12 servings

1. Rinse 12 ounces **fresh poblano** chilies (see notes) and 8 ounces **Roma tomatoes**. Peel 1 **onion** (8 oz.) and cut into 3/4-inch-thick slices; rub 1 teaspoon **salad oil** over onion slices. Place chilies, whole tomatoes, and onion slices on a barbecue grill 4 inches above a solid bed of hot coals or over high heat on a gas grill (you can hold your hand at grill level for only 2 to 3 seconds); close lid on gas grill. (Or arrange vegetables in a 10- by 15-inch baking pan and broil 4 inches from heat.) Cook vegetables, turning as needed, until well browned on all sides, 8 to 12 minutes; as done, transfer to a board.
2. When cool enough to handle, peel stem, and seed chilies; core and peel tomatoes. Chop chilies, tomatoes, and onions.
3. In a 10- to 12-inch frying pan over medium heat, stir chopped vegetables until hot, about 2 minutes. Add 2 cups **sour cream** and stir just until hot but not boiling, about 2 minutes. Add **salt** and **pepper** to taste. Scrape into a bowl.

Per 1/4 cup: 78 cal., 73% (57 cal.) from fat; 1.4 g protein; 6.3 g fat (3.7 g sat.); 4.4 g carbo (0.6 g fiber); 18 mg sodium; 13 mg chol.

Cinnamon-scented Rice Milk

PREP TIME: About 10 minutes, plus at least 24 hours to soak

NOTES: *Horchata* is a traditional Latin beverage made from rice softened in water, with cinnamon and sugar. To finely grind the soaked rice, use a blender with sharp blades; it may take several minutes to blend each batch until smooth. You can prepare the drink through step 2 up to 1 day ahead; cover and chill.

MAKES: 3 quarts; 10 to 12 servings.

1. In a bowl, combine 2 cups **long grain white rice** and 10 cups **water**; cover and chill until grains break easily when squeezed, about 24 hours, or up to 2 days.
2. In a blender, whirl about 2 cups o

the rice mixture with 1 cup **sugar**, 4 teaspoons **vanilla**, and 1½ teaspoons **ground cinnamon** until sugar is dissolved and mixture is smooth; pour into a large bowl or pitcher (at least 3½ qt.). Whirl remaining rice mixture without seasonings, in batches if necessary; add to bowl and stir until well blended with flavored batch. Taste, and add more sugar if desired.

5. Just before serving, stir mixture (ground rice will have settled to bottom). Fill glasses with **ice cubes,** then horchata.

Per serving: 182 cal., 1% (1.8 cal.) from fat; 2.2 g protein; 0.2 g fat (0.1 g sat.); 42 g carbo (0.3 g fiber); 1.9 mg sodium; 0 mg chol.

Chop Sauce

PREP TIME: About 25 minutes

NOTES: You can make this salsa-salad up to 2 hours ahead; cover and chill.

MAKES: About 5 cups; 10 to 12 servings

Remove and discard husks from 12 ounces **fresh tomatillos;** rinse tomatillos. Rinse and core 12 ounces **firm-ripe tomatoes.** Chop tomatillos and tomatoes and put in a bowl. Add ¾ cup chopped **onion,** ½ cup chopped **fresh cilantro,** 3 tablespoons **lime juice,** 2 teaspoons minced **garlic,** 1½ to 2 tablespoons chopped **fresh jalapeño chilies** (remove seeds, if desired, for less heat), and **salt** to taste.

Per ¼ cup: 12 cal., 15% (1.8 cal.) from fat; 0.3 g protein; 0.2 g fat (0 g sat.); 2.4 g carbo (0.6 g fiber); 2.2 mg sodium; 0 mg chol.

Three-Milk Cake

PREP AND COOK TIME: About 1 hour, plus at least 3 hours to soak

MAKES: About 12 servings

    8 **large eggs**
 1½ cups **sugar**
    2 cups **all-purpose flour**
    1 tablespoon **baking powder**

Dairy products effectively neutralize the heat of chilies. Cool off after this mixed grill with a three-milk cake.

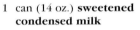

The chop sauce (fresh salsa) and roasted-poblano cream are savory embellishments for all of the meats in this mixed grill.

    1 can (14 oz.) **sweetened condensed milk**
    1 can (12 oz.) **evaporated milk**
    1 cup **milk**
  ¼ cup **Kahlua** (or strong coffee)
    1 teaspoon **vanilla**
        Lightly sweetened softly **whipped cream**
        Sliced **strawberries**

1. In a large bowl, with a mixer on high speed (use whip attachment if available), beat eggs and sugar until thick and pale yellow, 5 to 6 minutes. In a small bowl, mix flour and baking powder. With mixer on medium speed, gradually add flour mixture in small increments and beat until smooth. Scrape batter into a buttered 9- by 13-inch baking pan.

2. Bake in a 325° regular or convection oven until a toothpick inserted in the center comes out clean, 30 to 40 minutes.

3. Meanwhile, in a blender, whirl condensed milk, evaporated milk, regular milk, Kahlua, and vanilla until well blended. Pour evenly over hot cake; let cool about 15 minutes, then cover and chill until cake has absorbed all the milk mixture, at least 3 hours, or up to 1 day.

4. Cut cake into squares or rectangles, lift out with a wide spatula, and set on plates. Top each piece of cake with a spoonful of whipped cream and garnish with strawberries.

Per serving: 401 cal., 22% (88 cal.) from fat; 12 g protein; 9.8 g fat (5 g sat.); 65 g carbo (0.6 g fiber); 253 mg sodium; 166 mg chol. ◆

mixed-grill logistics

☐ **Up to 3 days ahead**
Soak rice for rice milk.

☐ **Up to 2 days ahead**
Make marinades for mixed grill.

☐ **Up to 1 day ahead**
Marinate meats, grill vegetables for poblano cream, purée rice mixture for horchata, and make cake.

☐ **About 2 hours ahead**
Make chop sauce.

☐ **About 40 minutes ahead**
If using a charcoal grill, ignite briquets.

☐ **About 30 minutes ahead**
If using a gas grill, preheat.

☐ **About 20 minutes ahead**
Grill chilies and green onions for mixed grill. Heat beans.

☐ **About 10 minutes ahead**
Assemble and grill quesadillas. Finish poblano cream.

☐ **Just before serving**
Grill meats and warm tortillas.

☐ **About 5 minutes before dessert**
Whip cream; cut and garnish cake.

By Jerry Anne Di Vecchio

JAMES CARRIER; FOOD STYLING: KAREN SHINTO

Salad adventures

A Malaysian dish echoes an old French favorite

■ The siren song of travel for me is discovering new foods. However, the more I roam, the more I'm amazed by the similarity of specialties that have emerged with seeming spontaneity continents apart. Take salad niçoise, for instance, which hails from the Côte d'Azur in southern France: It has tuna at its heart, surrounded by cold potatoes, green beans, and hard-cooked eggs, all drenched with olive oil and vinegar. In Malaysia recently, as I munched through various local *gado gado* salads, it dawned on me that, despite the fact that the protein core was usually chicken or shrimp instead of tuna, and the dressing was a thick, spicy peanut-based sauce, many of the other ingredients on the plate were the same as for salad niçoise. Granted, gado gado (dressing and salad go by the same name) sounds more exotic and exciting, but the adventure of this dish is in tweaking familiar ingredients for a refreshing change.

Gado Gado Salad

PREP AND COOK TIME: About 1 hour and 20 minutes

NOTES: Buy a roast chicken from a deli, chill, and tear into strips. Cooking the potatoes slowly preserves their texture and keeps them from splitting; you can prepare the remaining ingredients and the dressing while they cook. Or, if time is short, sprinkle all the crisp shallots over salads and use a purchased Asian-style peanut sauce instead of the gado gado dressing; thin, if desired, with chicken broth or coconut milk.

MAKES: 4 main-course, 8 first-course servings

- 4 **thin-skinned potatoes** (4 oz. each), scrubbed
- 8 ounces **green beans**, rinsed and ends trimmed
- 1 cup sliced (¼ in. thick) **English cucumber**
- 2 cups matchstick slivers **jicama** or 2 cups bean sprouts, rinsed
- 1 cup long, thin **carrot** shreds
- 2 hard-cooked **large eggs**, shelled and quartered lengthwise
- 2 cups thin strips **cooked boned, skinned chicken** (see notes)
- 2 cups **watercress sprigs,** rinsed and crisped

  Crisp shallots and **gado gado dressing** (recipes follow)
- 2 **limes** (about 3 oz. each), rinsed and halved or quartered

  Salt

1. Put potatoes in a 2- to 3-quart pan and cover with about 1 inch of water. Bring just to a simmer over high heat, then cover, reduce heat to low, and cook, without letting water bubble, until potatoes are tender when pierced, about 50 minutes. Drain and immerse in cold water until lukewarm, about 5 minutes, or let stand at room temperature until warm, about 20 minutes. Cut crosswise into ¼- to ½-inch-thick slices.

2. Meanwhile, in another 2- to 3-quart pan over high heat, bring about 1 quart water to a boil. Add green beans and cook until tender to bite, 3 to 6 minutes. Drain and immerse immediately in ice water until cool, about 2 minutes; drain again.

3. On dinner plates, arrange equal portions of potato slices, green beans, cucumber, jicama, carrot, eggs, chicken, watercress, and limes. Scatter crisp shallots equally over salads. Spoon gado

gado dressing over salads and add salt and juice from limes to taste.

Per serving: 555 cal., 45% (252 cal.) from fat; 33 g protein; 28 g fat (9.3 g sat.); 49 g carbo (8.7 g fiber); 1,000 mg sodium; 200 mg chol.

Crisp Shallots and Gado Gado Dressing. In an 8- to 10-inch frying pan, combine 3 tablespoons **salad oil** and ¾ cup thinly sliced **shallots**. Stir frequently over high heat until shallots are well browned, 6 to 8 minutes; lift from pan with a slotted spoon and drain on paper towels. Add about ⅓ cup chopped **fresh jalapeño chilies** (with seeds for maximum heat), ½ teaspoon **coriander seeds**, and ½ teaspoon **cumin seeds** to pan; stir often until chilies are lightly browned, about 5 minutes. Scrape mixture into a food processor. Add about 2 tablespoons crisp shallots, 1 teaspoon grated **lemon** peel, 1 teaspoon **anchovy paste**, 1 tablespoon minced **fresh ginger**, 2 tablespoons **soy sauce**, 2 tablespoons packed **brown sugar**, ⅓ cup **lime juice**, and ⅔ cup **chunky-style peanut butter**; whirl until ingredients are well mixed. Add 1 cup **canned coconut milk** (reduced fat or regular; stir before using) and whirl until well blended. Use, or cover and chill up to 1 week. Makes 2½ cups; allow ¼ to ½ cup per serving.

Just loafing around

■ If meat loaf means winter to you, think again, especially if you fancy meat loaf sandwiches. This time of year, start with ground turkey instead of beef, then add tropical jerk flavors from the Caribbean, and finally, swathe the loaf in thin slices of prosciutto. Enhanced like this, with very little effort, meat loaf becomes a classy terrine. And even though it's easy enough for a family supper, it also suits a party picnic or garden brunch.

Jerk-spiced Turkey Picnic Loaf

PREP AND COOK TIME: About 1½ hours

NOTES: Serve the loaf hot, at room temperature, or chilled: After inverting, lay a few bay leaves on top and sprinkle with peppercorns; surround with marinated mild red peppers. Serve slices of the loaf with a sweet-hot mustard and crusty bread. You can make the loaf up to 3 days ahead; after unmolding, cover and chill.

MAKES: 8 servings

- 8 ounces **mushrooms**, rinsed, drained, and finely chopped
- 1 **onion** (8 oz.), peeled and finely chopped
  About 2 tablespoons **salad oil**
- ½ teaspoon **salt**
- ½ teaspoon **ground nutmeg**
- ½ teaspoon **ground allspice**
- ¼ teaspoon **ground cinnamon**
- ¼ teaspoon **cayenne**
- 3 tablespoons **cider** or distilled white **vinegar**
- 2 tablespoons **molasses**
- ½ cup **all-purpose flour**
- 1½ pounds **ground turkey** (breast or a combination of breast and dark meat)
- ½ cup fat-skimmed **chicken broth**
- 1 **large egg**
- ¾ cup drained **pickled cocktail onions**, each cut in half
  About 6 ounces **paper-thin slices prosciutto**

1. In a 10- to 12-inch frying pan over high heat, stir mushrooms and onion in 2 tablespoons oil until they begin to brown, 7 to 8 minutes.

2. Add salt, nutmeg, allspice, cinnamon, and cayenne; stir until fragrant, about 2 minutes. Add vinegar and molasses; stir often until liquid is evaporated. Scrape into a large bowl. Add flour and mix to blend, then stir often until lukewarm, about 5 minutes.

3. Add turkey, broth, and egg to bowl; mix well. Gently stir in pickled onions.

4. Oil a 5- by 9-inch nonstick loaf pan (2 qt.). Line pan neatly with a single layer of prosciutto slices, overlapping edges slightly; press ends of prosciutto against pan sides up to, but not over, rim. Scrape meat mixture into pan and gently pat or spread level. Fold ends of prosciutto slices neatly over meat.

5. Bake turkey loaf in a 350° regular or convection oven until a thermometer inserted in center of thickest part reaches 160° and meat is no longer pink (cut to test), about 55 minutes; loaf will begin to shrink from pan sides.

6. Let stand at room temperature for at least 10 minutes. Invert a slightly larger, rimmed platter over pan; hold pan and platter together and invert. Lift pan off to release loaf.

Per serving made with turkey breast: 253 cal., 28% (71 cal.) from fat; 30 g protein; 7.9 g fat (1.6 g sat.); 15 g carbo (1 g fiber); 971 mg sodium; 97 mg chol. ◆

The Quick Cook

An old tradition makes a great new weeknight meal

By Sara Schneider

Turn chicken breasts into an exotic stew in minutes.

JAMES CARRIER; FOOD STYLING: BASIL FRIEDMAN

1. Rinse chicken and pat dry; cut into 1½- to 2-inch pieces. Pour olive oil into a 10- to 12-inch frying pan over medium-high heat; when hot, add chicken and turn pieces often to brown on all sides, 5 to 8 minutes total. With a slotted spoon, transfer chicken to a bowl.

2. Add butter to pan; when melted add onions and garlic and stir often until onions are limp and beginning to brown, 5 to 7 minutes. Return chicken to pan and spread level. Sprinkle cumin, ginger, cinnamon, turmeric, paprika, ½ teaspoon salt, dark and golden raisins, and pistachios over chicken. Add preserved lemons if using. Pour 1 cup broth evenly over all. Cover and bring to a boil, then reduce heat and simmer, stirring occasionally, until chicken is no longer pink in the center (cut to test), 5 to 6 minutes.

3. Meanwhile, in a 3- to 4-quart pan over high heat, bring 1½ cups water to a boil; stir in couscous and return to a boil. Cover pan, remove from heat, and let stand until water is absorbed, about 5 minutes. Fluff couscous with a fork and stir in mint.

4. Scoop couscous equally onto dinner plates or into wide bowls. If chicken tagine is drier than desired, thin with more broth. Spoon over couscous and sprinkle with cilantro. Add salt and pepper to taste.

Per serving: 668 cal., 19% (126 cal.) from fat; 54 g protein; 14 g fat (3.5 g sat.); 82 g carbo (6.3 g fiber); 527 mg sodium; 107 mg chol.

■ Old food traditions rarely bring to mind quick meals. Foreign-sounding dishes, especially, look like hard work. Tagines, however, make a good case that things aren't always what they seem. An interestingly spiced North African stew—named for the dish it's braised in—the tagine has traveled north to France and settled into the culinary fabric there. We found this delicious version in Bordeaux at Château de Reignac, where the Vatelots—committed to great food but more interested in spending time making good wine and playing with their children than laboring in the kitchen—have streamlined tradition.

Chicken Tagine with Raisins and Pistachios

PREP AND COOK TIME: About 40 minutes

NOTES: Tangy, salty preserved lemons are available in some upscale supermarkets and specialty food stores.

MAKES: 4 servings

- 4 **boned, skinned chicken breast halves** (about 1½ lb. total)
- 1 tablespoon **olive oil**
- 1 tablespoon **butter** or margarine
- 2 **onions** (about 1 lb. total), peeled and slivered lengthwise
- 1 tablespoon minced **garlic**
- 2 teaspoons **ground cumin**
- 2 teaspoons **ground ginger**
- ½ teaspoon **ground cinnamon**
- ½ teaspoon **ground dried turmeric**
- ½ teaspoon **paprika**

  About ½ teaspoon **salt**
- ¼ cup **dark raisins**
- ¼ cup **golden raisins**
- ¼ cup **shelled roasted, salted pistachios**
- 2 **preserved lemons** (optional; see notes), drained and quartered

  About 1 cup fat-skimmed **chicken broth**
- 1½ cups **couscous**
- ¼ cup finely chopped **fresh mint leaves**
- ¼ cup finely chopped **fresh cilantro**

  Pepper

BELL PEPPER AND OLIVE SALAD WITH ORANGE-CUMIN VINAIGRETTE. In a large bowl, whisk together ½ cup **orange juice**, 2 tablespoons **sherry vinegar** or white wine vinegar, 2 tablespoons **extra-virgin olive oil**, 1 tablespoon **Dijon mustard**, ½ teaspoon **ground cumin**, ½ teaspoon **salt**, and ¼ teaspoon **pepper**. Add 2 quarts rinsed and crisped **salad mix** (about 7 oz.), 1 cup drained **pitted calamata** or other black **olives**, 1 cup finely slivered **red onion** (about 5 oz.), and 1 cup slivered **yellow** or red **bell pepper** (about 7 oz.). Mix gently to coat. Add more salt and pepper to taste. Makes 4 servings.

Per serving: 223 cal., 65% (144 cal.) from fat; 1.8 g protein; 16 g fat (2.1 g sat.); 17 g carbo (2.9 g fiber); 1,004 mg sodium; 0 mg chol. ◆

The Wine Guide

Why can't I find that wine?

By Karen MacNeil-Fife

We've all been there—standing in a shop holding a piece of paper on which we've scrawled the name of a wine we've read is fantastic. But no one in the shop has ever heard of the wine, or worse, the salesperson scoffs when we ask for it—no mere mortal would ever be able to put his or her hands on *that* wine.

What's going on here? Why does it often seem that the higher the praise (or the score) a wine receives, the less likely it is we'll ever find it? And are there any insider techniques for getting ahold of wines that everyone says are impossible to find?

First, the harsh reality: Unlike cars, stereos, or even most foods, wine is a finite entity, the production of which cannot be increased at will. Let's say that one night at a restaurant you sprung for a bottle of Shafer's special Hillside Select Cabernet Sauvignon and loved it. The next day you tried to find it, but no luck. Here's why: Shafer Vineyards is one of about 280 wineries in the relatively small Napa Valley, located in an even smaller section known as the Stags Leap District, just 3 miles long and barely 1 mile wide. And the wine called Hillside Select comes from only certain sites on the estate. The upshot of it is, every year Shafer can make only 1,800 to 2,200 cases of Hillside Select for the entire world. (And while that isn't

JAMES CARRIER

very much, many desirable wines are made in even smaller quantities.)

And who gets that wine? First of all, top restaurants. A winery always prefers to sell its wine to restaurants because of the exposure it will get. Thousands of people will see the wine on the list, and over time, hundreds of people will try it. Even a single bottle might be shared by, say, four diners. By contrast, in a retail shop, one individual can snap up every case the shop has.

Of course, most fine wines are made in enough quantity that some will be available through wine shops. But, even then, you may not see it because wine shops often hold aside rare and hard-to-find wines for frequent, loyal customers. For an outsider, it can be practically impossible to break into this loop.

SUNSET'S STEAL OF THE MONTH

■ **Meridian Sauvignon Blanc 2000 (California)**, $8. Fresh, crisp, and melony. A great price for a very tasty wine that's a cinch to find.

What to do

1. While there are great wines that are hard to find, there are also great wines that aren't. Don't be too obsessed with your search.

2. Read carefully. If a wine magazine carries a glowing review, but then notes that only 200 cases of the wine were made, your chances of securing it are slim. Forget about it and move on to something else.

3. Be a good customer. Develop a rapport with a wine shop, especially with the person who actually buys the wine; let him or her know that you're interested in trying special wines. Every now and then, ask what the shop might have "in the back room." Just because you don't see the wine on the shelves doesn't mean the shop doesn't have a few bottles stashed away somewhere.

4. Make special requests. Even if a shop doesn't carry a wine, it can often order it. This won't cost you any more—in fact, most wine shops are happy to do this as a way of making loyal customers.

5. Check the winery's website. Although we don't have space here to go into the complex legalities that govern wine distribution and sales in the United States, you may live in one of those states that allows you to buy wine directly from the winery. If you do, get on the winery's mailing list.

6. If all else fails, call the winery and ask for a list of shops and restaurants near you where its wine is sold. ◆

DELICIOUS WINES YOU PROBABLY CAN FIND

■ **Geyser Peak Sauvignon Blanc 2000 (Sonoma County)**, $10. Easy to drink, easy to pair with food, and easy to afford. Lots of fresh green flavors.

■ **Grgich Hills Chardonnay 1999 (Napa Valley)**, $33. Grgich Hills is always dependable and always available. If you like big, rich, round, well-balanced Chardon-

nays, you'll love this one.

■ **Trefethen Dry Riesling 2000 (Napa Valley)**, $15. Snappy, sassy, bone-dry, and sleek, Trefethen's dry Riesling is one of the best in California.

■ **Black Opal Cabernet/Merlot 1999 (Barossa Valley, Australia)**, $11. Supple, dense, and mouth-filling, this combo

from Oz is packed with irresistible cherry flavors and just the right bite of menthol.

■ **Rosemount Estate Diamond Shiraz 1998 (Southeast Australia)**, $12. This is the best-selling Australian red wine in the United States, and no wonder—soft and thick on the palate and packed with plummy fruit flavors.

The Low-Fat Cook

Get inspiration for big flavor with little fat from this Hawaiian menu

By Linda Lau Anusasananan • Photographs by James Carrier

Pan-roasted fish on a soybean and mushroom stew tastes light but meaty.

Easy spa supper

■ A visit to a luxurious spa is like a sojourn in a cocoon: You emerge relaxed, refreshed, and a little hungry. After a green tea wrap, an aromatherapy massage, or a caviar facial, your putty-limp muscles can barely hold you up. You need a light meal to pamper your body, just as the treatment nourished your soul.

At JW Marriott Ihilani Resort and Spa at Ko Olina, on the western shore of Oahu in Hawaii, executive chef Randal Ishizu serves up bright-tasting dishes that restore guests' energy. Feasts like the one that follows have flavors so intense that no blissed-out spagoer would ever miss the fat. With the make-ahead steps in these recipes, it's easy to put together your own spa dinner. Now all you need is an on-call massage therapist to create your own resort at home.

Roasted Fish with Kabocha Coulis

PREP AND COOK TIME: About 1 hour

NOTES: If you don't have a nonstick frying pan with an ovenproof handle, skip the browning step for the fish and simply bake it in a baking pan for about 10 minutes. In Hawaii, the fish would be onaga; halibut is a good alternative. Make Kabocha coulis before preparing fish; cover and let stand. While soybeans cook (step 4), reheat coulis in a 3- to 4-quart pan over low heat, stirring occasionally, or in a microwave oven at full power (100%), stirring occasionally.

MAKES: 4 servings

- 4 pieces (about 1 in. thick, 4 to 5 oz. each) **boned, skinned halibut** or other firm white-fleshed fish (see notes)
- About 1 tablespoon **olive oil**
- **Salt** and **pepper**
- 6 ounces **fresh shiitake** or portabella **mushrooms** (or 3 oz. of each)
- 1 tablespoon minced **garlic**
- ½ cup fat-skimmed **chicken broth**
- ½ cup **tomato sauce**
- 1 cup **frozen shelled soybeans**
- 2 tablespoons thinly sliced **fresh chives** or green onions
  Kabocha coulis (recipe follows; see notes)
- 2 tablespoons chopped **fresh basil** leaves (optional)

1. Rinse fish and pat dry; coat pieces with about 2 teaspoons olive oil. Sprinkle lightly all over with salt and pepper. Set a 10- to 12-inch nonstick frying pan with ovenproof handle over high heat; when hot, set fish in pan and cook until lightly browned on the bottom, 2 to 3 minutes.

2. Transfer pan with fish to a 350° regular or convection oven and bake until fish is barely opaque but still moist-looking in center of thickest part (cut to test), 7 to 9 minutes.

3. Meanwhile, rinse and drain mushrooms; trim off and discard stems for shiitakes (tough stem ends only for portabellas). Cut mushrooms into ½-inch chunks.

4. In an 8- to 10-inch nonstick frying pan over medium-high heat, stir mushrooms and garlic in 1 teaspoon oil until mushrooms are limp, about 5 minutes.

FOOD STYLING: KAREN SHINTO

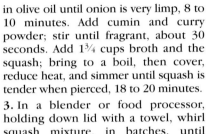

Thinly sliced raw beets resemble beef carpaccio; drizzled with a miso dressing and topped with a puff of baby salad greens, they're refreshingly low in fat.

Add broth, tomato sauce, and soybeans; simmer, uncovered, stirring occasionally, until soybeans are tender to bite, about 5 minutes. Stir in 1 tablespoon chives. Add salt and pepper to taste.

5. Mound a fourth of the soybean mixture in the center of each of four dinner plates. Top each mound with a piece of fish, pan-browned side up, and spoon Kabocha coulis equally around soybean mixture. Gently shake each plate to level coulis. Garnish fish with remaining tablespoon chives and scatter chopped basil over coulis if desired. Add more salt and pepper to taste.

Per serving: 471 cal., 29% (135 cal.) from fat; 46 g protein; 15 g fat (2 g sat.); 44 g carbo (10 g fiber); 296 mg sodium; 36 mg chol.

Kabocha Coulis

PREP AND COOK TIME: About 45 minutes

NOTES: You can make the coulis up to 1 day ahead; cover and chill. Thinned with chicken or vegetable broth, it makes a delicious soup.

MAKES: About 3 cups; 4 servings

1½ pounds **Kabocha** or butternut **squash**

1 **onion** (8 oz.), peeled and chopped

1 tablespoon chopped **fresh ginger**

1 teaspoon **olive oil**

¾ teaspoon **ground cumin**

¾ teaspoon **curry powder**

1¾ to 2 cups **vegetable** or fat-skimmed chicken **broth**

Salt and **pepper**

1. Rinse squash and cut in half lengthwise (if necessary, use a mallet to gently pound knife through squash). Scoop out seeds and discard; with a small, sharp knife, pare peel and discard. Cut squash into 1-inch chunks; you should have about 4 cups.

2. In a 3- to 4-quart nonstick pan over medium-high heat, stir onion and ginger in olive oil until onion is very limp, 8 to 10 minutes. Add cumin and curry powder; stir until fragrant, about 30 seconds. Add 1¾ cups broth and the squash; bring to a boil, then cover, reduce heat, and simmer until squash is tender when pierced, 18 to 20 minutes.

3. In a blender or food processor, holding down lid with a towel, whirl squash mixture, in batches, until smooth. If sauce is thicker than desired, whirl in a little more broth. Add salt and pepper to taste.

Per serving: 112 cal., 13% (14 cal.) from fat; 2.5 g protein; 1.6 g fat (0.2 g sat.); 25 g carbo (3.6 g fiber); 40 mg sodium; 0 mg chol.

Beet Carpaccio with Ginger-Miso Vinaigrette

PREP TIME: About 35 minutes

NOTES: To avoid staining your hands when preparing beets, wear rubber gloves. Gold-colored *shiro miso* (the same used for Japanese miso soup; also called light or white soybean paste) is available with ethnic foods in some supermarkets and in Asian grocery stores. You can make the vinaigrette and prepare the beets (steps 1 and 2) up to 1 day ahead; cover separately airtight and chill.

MAKES: 4 first-course servings

¾ teaspoon **dry mustard**

4 teaspoons **lemon juice**

4 teaspoons **honey**

4 teaspoons **shiro miso** (see notes) or soy sauce

2 teaspoons **salad oil**

¾ teaspoon minced **fresh ginger**

2 **beets** (2 in. diameter, about 6 oz. each)

3 cups **salad mix** (1½ oz. total), rinsed and crisped

Salt and **pepper**

1. In a small bowl, mix mustard with 4 teaspoons water until smooth; let stand

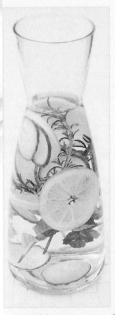

Herb-infused Spa Water

In a 2- to 2½-quart pitcher, combine 6 cups chilled **still spring** or mineral **water**; 12 thin slices **cucumber**; 4 thin slices **lemon**; 4 sprigs (each 2 in. long) **fresh mint**, slightly crushed; and 2 sprigs (each 2 in. long) **fresh rosemary**, slightly crushed. Serve, or cover and chill at least 2 hours or up to 8 hours. Add **ice cubes** just before serving. Makes about 1½ quarts; about 4 servings.

Mango Sorbet with Litchis and Raspberries

PREP TIME: About 7 minutes

MAKES: 4 servings

Place 1 or 2 scoops (about ½ cup total) of **mango** or pineapple **sorbet** in each of four bowls or wineglasses. Garnish each serving with 3 or 4 drained chilled **canned litchis** and 3 or 4 rinsed **fresh raspberries**.

Per serving: 221 cal., 0% (0 cal.) from fat; 0.1 g protein; 0 g fat; 56 g carbo (2 g fiber); 23 mg sodium; 0 mg chol.

5 minutes. Whisk in lemon juice, honey, miso, oil, and ginger.

2. Trim and discard tops and root ends from beets. Scrub beets well, then pare peel with a vegetable peeler and discard. Using the vegetable peeler or a mandoline, slice beets paper thin. Arrange slices equally, slightly overlapping, in a ring on each of four salad plates.

3. In a bowl, mix 2 tablespoons ginger-miso vinaigrette with salad mix. Arrange greens equally in the center of beets. Drizzle remaining dressing over beets. Add salt and pepper to taste.

Per serving: 84 cal., 30% (25 cal.) from fat; 1.7 g protein; 2.8 g fat (0.3 g sat.); 14 g carbo (1 g fiber); 254 mg sodium; 0 mg chol. ◆

Kitchen Cabinet

Readers' recipes tested in *Sunset's* kitchens

By Charity Ferreira • Photographs by James Carrier

A fresh tomato vinaigrette turns grilled salmon into a dressy summer salad.

FOOD STYLING: KAREN SHINTO (2)

Per serving: 600 cal., 59% (351 cal.) from fat; 44 g protein; 39 g fat (11 g sat.); 20 g carbo (3 g fiber); 1,151 mg sodium; 123 mg chol.

TOMATO VINAIGRETTE. In a bowl, combine 1 cup diced **firm-ripe tomatoes** (about 8 oz.), ¼ cup **red wine vinegar,** 2 tablespoons **extra-virgin olive oil,** 1 tablespoon minced **shallot,** ½ teaspoon **dry mustard,** ½ teaspoon **salt,** and ¼ teaspoon **black pepper.** Mix well. Makes about 1 cup.

Per ¼ cup: 77 cal., 82% (63 cal.) from fat; 0.6 g protein; 7 g fat (0.9 g sat.); 3.7 g carbo (0.8 g fiber); 295 mg sodium; 0 mg chol.

Spicy Chicken and Vegetables

Tim Rosefield, Fair Oaks, CA

Tim Rosefield's love for Thai and Vietnamese food inspired him to put together this spicy stir-fry, which he serves over basmati or long-grain white rice. Hot bean paste is available in jars at some well-stocked supermarkets and in Asian markets. If you can't find it, you can substitute 1 teaspoon hot sauce and 2 additional teaspoons soy sauce for the bean paste.

PREP AND COOK TIME: About 35 minutes

MAKES: 3 to 4 servings

- 1 pound **boned, skinned chicken breasts**
- 2 teaspoons **chili powder**
- 1 teaspoon **ground cumin**
- ½ teaspoon **ground dried turmeric**
- 1 tablespoon **salad oil**
- 1 cup thinly sliced **onion** (4 oz.)
- 1½ tablespoons minced **garlic**
- ½ tablespoon minced **fresh ginger**
- ⅔ cup fat-skimmed **chicken broth**
- 2 tablespoons **rice vinegar**
- 1 tablespoon **hot bean paste** (see notes)
- 1 teaspoon **soy sauce**
- 1 teaspoon **sugar**
- 1 **zucchini** (about 8 oz.), rinsed, halved lengthwise, and cut into ⅛- to ¼-inch-thick slices
- 8 ounces **green beans,** rinsed, ends and strings removed, and cut into 1-inch lengths

1. Rinse chicken and pat dry; cut into 1-inch chunks. In a bowl, combine chili powder, cumin, and turmeric. Add chicken and mix to coat.

2. Pour oil into a 12-inch frying pan or 14-inch wok over high heat; when hot, add onion, garlic, and ginger. Stir until

Grilled-Salmon Salad

Kathy Mickey, Reno

Kathy Mickey gets many compliments on this salad's great flavor. You can make the tomato vinaigrette up to 3 hours ahead; cover and chill.

PREP AND COOK TIME: About 30 minutes, plus at least 30 minutes to chill

MAKES: 4 servings

- 1½ pounds **boned, skinned salmon fillet,** cut into 4 equal pieces
- 3 tablespoons **light brown sugar**
- 1 tablespoon **ground cumin**
- 1 teaspoon **chili powder**
  About 1 teaspoon **salt**
  About 1 teaspoon **black pepper**
- 8 ounces **salad mix,** rinsed and crisped
  Tomato vinaigrette (recipe follows)
- 4 ounces **fresh chèvre** (goat) **cheese,** crumbled
- ¼ cup minced **green onions** (white and pale green parts only)
- ¼ cup **pine nuts**

1. Rinse salmon and pat dry. In a bowl, mix brown sugar, cumin, chili powder, and 1 teaspoon *each* salt and pepper. Place salmon in bowl and rub pieces all over with spice mixture. Cover and chill at least 30 minutes or up to 4 hours.

2. Lay salmon on a barbecue grill over a solid bed of hot coals or high heat on a gas grill (you can hold your hand at grill level only 2 to 3 seconds); close lid on gas grill. Cook, turning once, until a thermometer inserted in center of thickest part reads 140°, 6 to 8 minutes total.

3. Meanwhile, divide salad mix equally among four plates. Place a piece of salmon on each mound of greens. Drizzle salads equally with tomato vinaigrette and sprinkle evenly with goat cheese, green onions, and pine nuts. Add salt and pepper to taste.

onion is limp, about 2 minutes. Add chicken and stir until white on the outside but still slightly pink in the middle (cut to test), about 3 minutes.

3. Meanwhile, in a 2-cup glass measure, mix chicken broth, vinegar, bean paste, soy sauce, and sugar. Add to pan along with zucchini and green beans. Bring to a boil and cook, stirring occasionally, until vegetables are barely tender to bite and chicken is no longer pink in the center (cut to test), about 5 minutes. Pour into a serving dish.

Per serving: 218 cal., 23% (50 cal.) from fat; 30 g protein; 5.5 g fat (0.8 g sat.); 12 g carbo (2.2 g fiber); 219 mg sodium; 66 mg chol.

Chard Lasagna

Dorothy Pinson, Borrego Springs, CA

Dorothy Pinson created this recipe to use the chard growing abundantly in her vegetable garden. You can make the lasagna through step 4 up to 1 day ahead; cover and chill.

PREP AND COOK TIME: About 1½ hours
MAKES: 10 to 12 servings

  1 package (8 oz.) **dried lasagna**
  1 pound **red** or **green chard**
  1 cup **ricotta cheese**
    Salt and **pepper**
  1 **onion** (about 8 oz.), peeled and chopped
  1 clove **garlic,** peeled and pressed or minced
  1 tablespoon **olive oil**
  3 cans (14½ oz. each) **crushed tomatoes**
  1½ teaspoons **dried basil**
  1½ teaspoons **dried oregano**
  1 cup **shredded parmesan cheese**

1. In a 5- to 6-quart pan over high heat, bring 3 quarts water to a boil. Add lasagna and cook, stirring occasionally to separate noodles, until barely tender to bite, about 10 minutes. Drain pasta, immerse in cold water until cool, and drain again. Cover loosely.

2. Meanwhile, rinse and drain chard. Trim and discard discolored stem ends. Thinly slice stems crosswise and coarsely chop leaves. In a 4- to 6-quart pan over high heat, bring about 1 cup water to a boil. Add chard, reduce heat, and simmer, stirring occasionally, until stems are tender-crisp to bite, 4 to 6 minutes. Drain, extracting as much water as possible with the back of a spoon. In a bowl, mix chard with ricotta; add salt

and pepper to taste.

3. In the same pan over medium-high heat, stir onion and garlic in oil until limp, about 10 minutes. Add tomatoes, basil, and oregano; cover and simmer to blend flavors, about 15 minutes. Add salt and pepper to taste.

4. Cover bottom of a 9- by 13-inch baking dish with a third of the noodles, then half the chard mixture, spreading it level to edges of dish. Spoon a third of the tomato sauce over chard mixture and sprinkle with a third of the parmesan. Repeat layers of noodles, chard mixture, sauce, and cheese. Cover with remaining noodles, then remaining tomato sauce and cheese.

5. Bake in a 350° regular or convection oven until hot in the center and bubbling at edges, 25 to 30 minutes. Let stand 10 minutes before serving.

Per serving: 194 cal., 34% (65 cal.) from fat; 10 g protein; 7.2 g fat (3.7 g sat.); 23 g carbo (2.1 g fiber); 437 mg sodium; 18 mg chol.

Lemon Poppy Seed Muffins

Karen Fukui, Olympia, WA

Karen Fukui improved on a recipe to come up with this tender, cake-like muffin with a tangy glaze.

PREP AND COOK TIME: About 1 hour
MAKES: 12 muffins

  3 cups **all-purpose flour**
  ⅓ cup **poppy seeds**
  1 tablespoon **baking soda**
  ½ teaspoon **salt**
  ½ cup **butter** or margarine, melted
  1 cup **sugar**
  2 **large eggs**
  2 tablespoons grated **lemon** peel
  ⅓ cup **lemon juice**
  ⅔ cup **milk**
    Lemon glaze (recipe follows)

1. In a bowl, mix flour, poppy seeds, baking soda, and salt.

2. In another bowl, beat butter and sugar until well blended. Add eggs and beat until incorporated. Beat in lemon peel and lemon juice. Add half the flour mixture and stir just until evenly moistened, then stir in milk and remaining flour mixture. Spoon batter equally into 12 paper-lined muffin cups.

3. Bake in a 350° regular or convection oven until tops are browned and a wooden skewer inserted in the center comes out clean, 15 to 18 minutes. Let stand on a rack 5 minutes, then remove muffins and let cool completely.

4. Dip top of each muffin in lemon glaze; allow excess to drip off. Return to rack until glaze is set, about 15 minutes.

Per muffin: 310 cal., 32% (99 cal.) from fat; 5.5 g protein; 11 g fat (5.5 g sat.); 48 g carbo (1.3 g fiber); 510 mg sodium; 58 mg chol.

LEMON GLAZE. In a bowl, mix ½ cup **powdered sugar,** 2 tablespoons **lemon juice,** and ½ teaspoon **vanilla** until smooth. Use immediately. ◆

Sweet lemon glaze makes distinguished muffins.

Red and Green Melange Salad is a refreshing, colorful, and crunchy addition to a summer buffet (recipe on page 122).

June

A dessert destined to
become a new favorite for
summer entertaining

shortcake
surprise

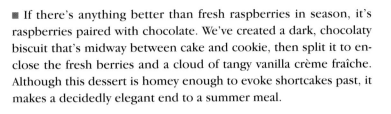

By Charity Ferreira

Photograph by James Carrier

Food styling by Basil Friedman

■ If there's anything better than fresh raspberries in season, it's raspberries paired with chocolate. We've created a dark, chocolaty biscuit that's midway between cake and cookie, then split it to enclose the fresh berries and a cloud of tangy vanilla crème fraîche. Although this dessert is homey enough to evoke shortcakes past, it makes a decidedly elegant end to a summer meal.

Chocolate Raspberry Shortcakes

PREP AND COOK TIME: About 1 hour

MAKES: 6 servings

> About 2 cups **all-purpose flour**
>
> $2/3$ cup plus 2 tablespoons **granulated sugar**
>
> $2/3$ cup **unsweetened cocoa**
>
> 2 teaspoons **baking powder**
>
> $1/2$ teaspoon **baking soda**
>
> $1/2$ teaspoon **salt**
>
> $1/2$ cup ($1/4$ lb.) cold **butter**
>
> 2 **large egg** yolks
>
> $3/4$ cup **buttermilk**
>
> 4 cups **fresh raspberries**
>
> **Vanilla crème fraîche** (recipe follows) or lightly sweetened whipped cream
>
> **Powdered sugar**

1. In a food processor or bowl, combine 2 cups flour, $2/3$ cup granulated sugar, cocoa, baking powder, baking soda, and salt; whirl or mix until blended.

2. Cut butter into $1/2$-inch chunks and add to flour mixture. Whirl, cut in with a pastry blender, or rub in with your fingers until mixture forms fine crumbs; pour into a bowl if using processor.

3. In a small bowl, whisk egg yolks with buttermilk to blend; add to flour mixture and stir just until evenly moistened.

4. Turn dough out onto a floured board and, with lightly floured hands, knead just until it comes together. Pat out to about $1 1/4$ inches thick. With a 3-inch round cutter, cut out shortcakes; gather dough scraps and pat out again as necessary to make all six shortcakes. Set 2 inches apart on a 14- by 17-inch baking sheet.

5. Bake on the middle rack in a 375° regular or 350° convection oven until tops look dry and feel firm when pressed, about 25 minutes. Transfer shortcakes to a rack and let cool completely.

6. Meanwhile, rinse raspberries. In a blender or food processor, whirl half the berries with the remaining 2 tablespoons granulated sugar until smooth. Press through a fine strainer into a bowl; discard residue.

7. To assemble shortcakes, slice each in half horizontally; set bottoms on plates. Spoon vanilla crème fraîche over bottoms, top with remaining berries, and drizzle with raspberry sauce. Place shortcake tops over berries and sprinkle with powdered sugar.

Per serving: 713 cal., 50% (360 cal.) from fat; 11 g protein; 40 g fat (24 g sat.); 83 g carbo (7.9 g fiber); 663 mg sodium; 164 mg chol.

VANILLA CRÈME FRAÎCHE. In a bowl, combine 1 cup **crème fraîche** (8 oz.), $1/4$ cup **whipping cream,** and 2 tablespoons **granulated sugar.** Cut a 3-inch length of **vanilla bean** in half lengthwise and scrape seeds into crème fraîche mixture (reserve vanilla pod for another use or discard). With a mixer at medium speed, beat mixture until soft peaks form, 2 to 3 minutes. Use at once or cover and chill up to 1 week. Makes about $1 1/3$ cup.

Per $1/4$ cup: 219 cal., 82% (180 cal.) from fat; 1.8 g protein; 20 g fat (13 g sat.); 6.6 g carbo (0 g fiber); 34 mg sodium; 51 mg chol. ◆

small plates, big flavors

Make a summer party sizzle with spicy Caribbean dishes

By Charity Ferreira • Photographs by James Carrier
Styling by Philippine Scali • Food styling by Susan Devaty

■ Call them tapas, appetizers, small plates—what you will. The important thing is that, when you eat little servings of foods, you can sample a wider variety. And it's more fun than a skimpy-course meal.

The small-plate trend has evolved to include cuisines from all over the world. We've put together a collection of lively dishes from the Caribbean and Latin America—and a manageable make-ahead plan—for a casual summer party.

Follow the countdown on page 118 and assemble the entire menu for 8 to 10 people, or choose a few of the dishes for a smaller gathering. Set out a stack of bright little plates to encourage small helpings and a pitcher of mojitos to ensure great fun.

shrimp and scallop ceviche

small-plate party
for 8 to 10

- *Mojitos and Beer*
- Shrimp and Scallop Ceviche
- Mahimahi Escabeche
- Papaya and Avocado Salad with Sour Orange Dressing
- Black Bean Cakes with Mango Salsa and Roasted Plantains
- Spiced Pulled Pork Sandwiches
- Tortilla Chips
- Cuban Coffee Ice Cream with Dulce de Leche

Mojitos

PREP AND COOK TIME: About 40 minutes

NOTES: Double the recipe for the mint syrup if you're planning to make more than one batch of mojitos.

MAKES: 4 cups; 6 to 8 servings

- 2 cups **light rum**
- 1 cup **mint syrup** (recipe follows)
- 1 cup **lime juice**
- **Ice cubes**
- **Fresh mint leaves**, rinsed (optional)

In a pitcher (at least 2 qt.), combine rum, mint syrup, and lime juice; add about 2 cups ice cubes. Pour into ice-filled glasses and garnish with mint leaves if desired.

Per serving: 136 cal., 0% (1 cal.) from fat; 0.2 g protein; 0.1 g fat (0 g sat.); 15 g carbo (0.4 g fiber); 5.9 mg sodium; 0 mg chol.

Mint Syrup. In a 1- to 2-quart pan, combine 1¼ cups lightly packed rinsed **fresh mint** leaves, 1 cup **water,** and ½ cup **sugar.** Stir over medium heat until sugar is dissolved and mixture is simmering. Remove pan from heat, cover, and let stand 30 minutes. Pour mixture through a fine strainer into a small pitcher or bowl; discard mint leaves. Use syrup or cover and chill up to 1 week. Makes about 1 cup.

Shrimp and Scallop Ceviche

PREP AND COOK TIME: About 25 minutes, plus 6 hours to chill

NOTES: Chill coconut milk before opening can; before measuring the milk, scrape off the layer of cream that forms on top and save it for other uses such as in soups or curries.

MAKES: 4 cups; 8 to 10 servings

- 1 pound **shelled, deveined shrimp** (31 to 40 per lb.)
- 1 pound **bay scallops**
- 1 cup **coconut milk** (see notes)
- ½ cup **lime juice**
- ¼ cup minced **red bell pepper**
- 2 **fresh serrano chilies**, rinsed, stemmed, seeded, and minced
- 3 tablespoons chopped **fresh cilantro**
- 2 tablespoons minced **fresh ginger**
- 1 teaspoon **salt**

1. Rinse shrimp and scallops. Fill a bowl with ice water.

2. In a 3- to 4-quart pan over high heat, bring about 2 quarts water to a boil. Add the shrimp, reduce heat to maintain a simmer, and cook until shrimp are opaque but still moist-looking in center of thickest part (cut to test), 1 to 2 minutes. Remove with a strainer or a slotted spoon and immerse in ice water until cool. Add scallops to simmering water and cook until opaque but still moist-looking in the center (cut to test), 1 to 2 minutes; lift out and immerse in ice water until cool. Drain shrimp and scallops. Cut each shrimp crosswise into thirds.

3. Meanwhile, in a glass or ceramic bowl, mix coconut milk, lime juice, bell pepper, chilies, cilantro, ginger, and salt. Stir in shrimp and scallops. Cover and chill at least 6 hours or up to 1 day.

4. Spoon into a large serving bowl or onto a rimmed platter.

Per serving: 137 cal., 39% (54 cal.) from fat; 17 g protein; 6 g fat (4.5 g sat.); 3.4 g carbo (0.1 g fiber); 379 mg sodium; 84 mg chol.

mahimahi
escabeche

mango
salsa

mojito

Mahimahi Escabeche

PREP AND COOK TIME: About 30 minutes, plus at least 8 hours to chill

MAKES: 8 to 10 servings

- 1 pound **mahimahi** or opah, cut into 4 or 5 equal pieces
- 1½ tablespoons **olive oil**
- 1 **red onion** (about 8 oz.), peeled, halved, and slivered lengthwise
- 1 cup **cider vinegar**
- 1 tablespoon **whole allspice**
- 1 teaspoon **black peppercorns**
- 1 **dried bay leaf**
- 1 clove **garlic,** peeled and slightly crushed with the side of a large knife
- ½ teaspoon **salt**
- ½ teaspoon **sugar**

1. Rinse mahimahi and pat dry. Heat ½ tablespoon oil in a 10- to 12-inch nonstick frying pan over medium-high heat; when hot, add fish and cook, turning once, until browned on both sides and opaque but still moist-looking in the center (cut to test), 8 to 10 minutes total. Transfer to a shallow 2- to 3-quart glass or ceramic dish.

2. In the same pan, heat remaining tablespoon oil over medium-high heat; add onion and stir until limp and browned, about 8 minutes. Spoon onion over fish.

3. In pan, combine vinegar, allspice, peppercorns, bay leaf, garlic, salt, sugar, and 1¼ cups water; bring to a boil over high heat. Remove from heat and pour over fish and onion. Let stand until cooled to room temperature, about 15 minutes, then cover and chill at least 8 hours or up to 1 day.

4. Let come to room temperature. To serve, lift fish from liquid and arrange on a platter. Arrange onion slices on fish. Discard liquid.

Per serving: 67 cal., 33% (22 cal.) from fat; 8.7 g protein; 2.4 g fat (0.4 g sat.); 2.4 g carbo (0.3 g fiber); 72 mg sodium; 33 mg chol.

Mango Salsa

PREP TIME: 30 minutes

NOTES: This salsa is great alongside the pork sandwiches and for scooping onto chips. You can make it up to 4 hours ahead; cover and chill.

MAKES: About 4 cups

- 2 **firm-ripe mangoes** (about 1 lb. each)
- ¾ cup diced **red onion**
- 1 **fresh hot red chili,** rinsed, stemmed, seeded, and minced
- 2 tablespoons chopped **fresh cilantro**
- 1 tablespoon **lime juice**
- ¼ teaspoon **salt**

1. Peel mangoes. Slice fruit off pits and cut into ¼-inch chunks; discard pits.

2. In a bowl, combine mangoes, onion, chili, cilantro, lime juice, and salt; mix gently.

Per serving: 54 cal., 3% (1.8 cal.) from fat; 0.6 g protein; 0.2 g fat (0.1 g sat.); 14 g carbo (1 g fiber); 76 mg sodium; 0 mg chol.

spiced pulled
pork sandwich

COUNTDOWN

☐ **Up to 1 week ahead:** Purchase plantains. Make mint syrup, ice cream, and dulce de leche.

☐ **Up to 3 days ahead:** Marinate pork.

☐ **Up to 2 days ahead:** Prepare pulled pork.

☐ **Up to 1 day ahead:** Make ceviche, escabeche, and sour orange dressing.

☐ **Up to 4 hours ahead:** Make mango salsa. Roast plantains.

☐ **Up to 2 hours ahead:** Slice papayas and jicama. Make batter for black bean cakes.

☐ **Up to 1 hour ahead:** Remove escabeche from refrigerator. Cook black bean cakes.

☐ **About 15 minutes ahead:** Reheat plantains. Set out ceviche and escabeche.

☐ **Just before serving:** Slice avocados. Assemble salad and sandwiches. Mix mojitos.

papaya and avocado salad

Crunchy jicama makes a lively contrast to silky avocado and juicy papaya in this easy salad.

Papaya and Avocado Salad with Sour Orange Dressing

PREP TIME: About 25 minutes
MAKES: 8 to 10 servings

- 2 **firm-ripe papayas** (about 1 lb. each)
- 8 ounces **jicama**
- 2 **firm-ripe avocados** (about 8 oz. each)
- 1/2 cup **orange juice**
- 1/4 cup **lime juice**
- 1 teaspoon **rice vinegar**
- 1/4 teaspoon **salt**

1. Peel and seed papayas; cut lengthwise into 1/2-inch-thick slices. Peel and rinse jicama; cut into matchstick-size strips about 1/8 inch thick and 3 inches long. Pit and peel avocados; cut lengthwise into thin slices.

2. In a small pitcher or bowl, mix orange juice, lime juice, rice vinegar, and salt.

3. Arrange papaya and avocado slices on a rimmed platter. Top with jicama and drizzle with sour orange dressing.

Per serving: 92 cal., 51% (47 cal.) from fat; 1.3 g protein; 5.2 g fat (0.8 g sat.); 12 g carbo (2.2 g fiber); 64 mg sodium; 0 mg chol.

Black Bean Cakes

PREP AND COOK TIME: About 1 hour
NOTES: *Queso fresco,* a mild white Mexican cheese, is available in well-stocked supermarkets and Latino grocery stores. The black bean batter can be made through step 2 up to 2 hours ahead; cover and chill until you're ready to cook the cakes. Serve the black bean cakes with additional queso fresco crumbled over the top, with the roasted plantains and mango salsa on the side.
MAKES: About 18 cakes; 8 to 10 servings

- 3 cans (15 oz. each) **black beans,** rinsed and drained
- 2 **large egg** yolks
- 1/4 cup **all-purpose flour**
- 1/2 teaspoon **baking powder**
- 1/3 cup minced **green onions** (including green tops)
- 2 **fresh serrano chilies,** rinsed, stemmed, seeded, and minced
- 1 1/2 teaspoons **ground cumin**
- 1 teaspoon **rice vinegar**
- 1/2 teaspoon **salt**
- 4 **large egg** whites
- 1 cup crumbled **queso fresco** (about 4 oz.; see notes) or shredded jack cheese

About 2 tablespoons **salad oil**

1. In a food processor, whirl black beans just until slightly chunky. Scrape into a bowl and stir in egg yolks, flour, baking powder, green onions, chilies, cumin, vinegar, and salt.

2. In another bowl, with a mixer on high speed, beat egg whites until they form soft peaks. Fold whites into black bean mixture just until incorporated. Gently stir in queso fresco.

3. Pour 1 teaspoon oil into a 10- to 12-inch nonstick frying pan over medium-high heat; when hot, drop batter in 1/4-cup portions into pan and spread into 2-inch-wide cakes with the bottom of measuring cup. Cook, turning once with a wide spatula, until cakes are browned on both sides and firm to touch in the center, about 6 minutes total. As cakes are cooked, arrange in a single layer on 12- by 15-inch baking sheets in a 200° oven; cover loosely with foil and keep warm up to 30 minutes. Repeat to cook remaining cakes, adding more oil to pan as necessary.

Per serving: 191 cal., 36% (69 cal.) from fat; 11 g protein; 7.7 g fat (2.7 g sat.); 20 g carbo (7.1 g fiber); 521 mg sodium; 51 mg chol.

Roasted Plantains

PREP AND COOK TIME: About 30 minutes
NOTES: Fully ripe plantains have black peels; buy the plantains a week in advance and let them ripen at room temperature. They can be roasted up to 4 hours ahead; cover and let stand at room temperature. Reheat in a 350° oven for about 15 minutes before serving.
MAKES: 8 to 10 servings

- 3 pounds **ripe plantains** (about 5; see notes)

2 tablespoons **salad** or peanut **oil**

About ½ teaspoon **salt**

1. Peel plantains and slice diagonally ¼ inch thick. Pour oil into a 12- by 15-inch baking pan; add plantains and ½ teaspoon salt and mix to coat. Transfer half the plantains to a second 12- by 15-inch baking pan and spread slices in both pans into a single layer.

2. Bake in a 400° regular or convection oven, turning plantains occasionally with a wide spatula, until browned on the outside and tender when pierced, 15 to 20 minutes; switch pan positions halfway through baking. Serve plantains warm. Add more salt to taste.

Per serving: 132 cal., 21% (28 cal.) from fat; 1.2 g protein; 3.1 g fat (0.4 g sat.); 28 g carbo (2 g fiber); 119 mg sodium; 0 mg chol.

Spiced Pulled Pork Sandwiches

PREP AND COOK TIME: About 3 hours, plus at least 2 hours to chill

NOTES: The spiced pulled pork filling for these sandwiches can be made (through step 4) up to 2 days ahead; cover and chill. Bring to room temperature (or warm slightly in a microwave oven) before filling sandwiches. Serve sandwiches piled on a large platter.

MAKES: 8 to 10 sandwiches

1½ pounds **boned pork shoulder** or butt, fat trimmed

4 ounces **green onions**, rinsed, ends trimmed, and coarsely chopped

2 cloves **garlic**, peeled

2 **fresh Fresno** or other hot green **chilies** (about 1 oz. total), rinsed, stemmed, and seeded

2 tablespoons **tomato paste**

2 tablespoons **brown sugar**

2 teaspoons **ground allspice**

1 teaspoon **ground dried thyme**

About 1 teaspoon **salt**

About ½ teaspoon **pepper**

¼ cup **cider vinegar**

8 to 10 **soft dinner rolls** (about 1 oz. each), sliced in half horizontally

1. Rinse pork and pat dry.

2. In a blender or food processor, whirl green onions, garlic, chilies, tomato paste, brown sugar, allspice, thyme, 1 teaspoon salt, and ½ teaspoon pepper until finely chopped. Add vinegar and whirl until smooth. Scrape mixture into a heavy 5- to 6-quart pan. Add pork and turn to coat completely. Cover and chill at least 2 hours or up to 1 day.

3. Add 1 cup water to pan, cover, and bring to a simmer over medium-high heat; reduce heat to very low and simmer pork, turning once, until meat is very tender when pierced and shreds easily with a fork, 2 to 2½ hours.

4. Remove from heat and let cool about 15 minutes. Transfer meat to a bowl. Skim and discard fat from surface of cooking liquid. Measure liquid; if there's more than 1½ cups, boil over high heat until reduced to 1½ cups. With a fork or your fingers, pull meat into thin shreds; remove and discard fat. Mix meat with cooking liquid. Add more salt and pepper to taste.

5. Spoon about ¼ cup pulled pork onto each roll bottom; set tops in place.

Per serving: 262 cal., 30% (78 cal.) from fat; 17 g protein; 8.7 g fat (2.7 g sat.); 28 g carbo (1.3 g fiber); 550 mg sodium; 46 mg chol.

Cuban Coffee Ice Cream with Dulce de Leche

PREP AND COOK TIME: About 1 hour and 15 minutes, plus at least 2 hours to cool

NOTES: *Dulce de leche* is a caramel made by cooking milk with sugar until the mixture is reduced to a thick amber syrup. You can make the sauce up to 1 week ahead; cover and chill. Bring to room temperature before serving. If time is short, buy prepared dulce de leche at a Latino market.

MAKES: 6 to 8 servings

6 **large egg** yolks

2 cups **whole milk**

2 cups **whipping cream**

¾ cup **sugar**

1 cup **dark-roasted coffee beans**, coarsely chopped

2 tablespoons **rum**

1 teaspoon **vanilla**

About 1 cup **dulce de leche** (recipe follows; see notes) or purchased caramel sauce

1. In a bowl, beat egg yolks to blend.

2. In a 3- to 4-quart pan over medium-high heat, combine milk, cream, sugar, and coffee beans; stir until sugar is dissolved and mixture is simmering. Remove from heat, cover, and let stand 30 minutes. Pour through a fine strainer into a bowl; discard coffee beans. Rinse pan, return milk mixture to it, and bring to a simmer over low heat.

3. Whisk ½ cup of the warm milk mixture into egg yolks; pour yolk mixture into pan. Stir constantly over low heat until mixture is thick enough to coat the back of a spoon, 4 to 6 minutes; do not boil.

4. Pour into a clean bowl and chill, stirring occasionally, until cold, about 2 hours; if desired, cover and chill up to 1 day.

5. Stir rum and vanilla into custard. Freeze mixture in a 1-quart or larger ice cream maker according to manufacturer's directions. Serve, or transfer ice cream to an airtight container and freeze until firm, at least 6 hours, or up to 1 week. Scoop into bowls and top with dulce de leche.

Per serving: 453 cal., 54% (243 cal.) from fat; 7.9 g protein; 27 g fat (16 g sat.); 45 g carbo (0 g fiber); 141 mg sodium; 245 mg chol.

Dulce de Leche. In a heavy 5- to 6-quart pan over medium-high heat, stir 4 cups **whole milk** and 1¼ cups **sugar** until sugar is dissolved and mixture is boiling. Stir in ½ teaspoon **baking soda**. Reduce heat to low and simmer, stirring occasionally with a flexible spatula, until mixture is golden brown and reduced to about 2 cups, about 1½ hours. Pour through a fine strainer into a bowl; discard residue. Makes 2 cups. ◆

Cuban coffee ice cream with dulce de leche

Rum gives this intense ice cream an extra tropical kick.

Great ideas in food and wine

WINES

White mischief

Chardonnay is a comforting old standby, but sometimes you need more than comfort in your glass. Here—just in time for summer—are some of the West's most wonderful and avant-garde white wines.

Bonny Doon Ca' del Solo Moscato del Solo 2000 (Monterey), $15. Refreshingly fizzy and low in alcohol, with lip-smacking mandarin orange, jasmine, and litchi flavors. **Bottom line:** A fabulous summer afternoon quencher.

Havens Albariño 2001 (Napa Valley, Carneros), $24. Albariño is the great white grape of Spain, and this sensational California wine proves why. **Bottom line:** An irresistible crisp, citrusy, spicy explosion of freshness.

Thomas Fogarty Gewürztraminer 2001 (Monterey), $15. Scrumptious, racy peach and ginger flavors. **Bottom line:** Planning something spicy for dinner?

Trefethen Dry Riesling 2000 (Napa Valley), $15. Dry Riesling from the West Coast is surging into the limelight. Bone-dry, snappy, and utterly fresh. **Bottom line:** This one's just waiting for a hot night and a cool summer salad. — *Karen MacNeil-Fife*

RESTAURANT

Dip into Nonya

AN ADVENTURE IN ASIAN COOKING—IN PASADENA

■ London restaurateur Simon Tong has introduced Southern California to Nonya—a spicy amalgam of Chinese, Malaysian, and Indonesian cuisines. Bright flavors characterize dishes like *mangga ikan,* a halibut and mango salad, and there are rewards for the adventurous—like ice *gajat,* an ice cream parfait with layers of shaved ice, red beans, and cubes of herbal jelly. *Nonya, 61 N. Raymond Ave.; (626) 583-8398.*

RECIPE: **Sambal Sauce.** Executive chef Tony Pat suggests using this chili sauce with shrimp satay or grilled fish and vegetables. **1** Soak ¼ cup seeded **dried hot red chilies** in ¼ cup hot **water** until soft, about 10 minutes. Whirl mixture in blender until smooth. **2** In a 10-inch frying pan over medium-high heat, stir ½ cup minced **red bell pepper,** ⅓ cup minced **onion,** 3 tablespoons minced **garlic,** 2 tablespoons minced **dried shrimp** (or 1 teaspoon anchovy paste), and ¼ cup minced seeded **fresh hot red chilies** in 2 teaspoons **salad oil** until vegetables are limp, about 3 minutes. **3** Stir in dried chili mixture, 3 tablespoons **liquid tamarind concentrate** (or lime juice), ⅓ cup firmly packed **brown sugar,** and ½ teaspoon **salt;** cook 2 to 3 more minutes. Makes 1 cup. — *Charity Ferreira*

Chef To[...] Pat tops off *har knay teon*—rice noodles with beef and shrimp.

INGREDIENT

Sake gets hot

NOW THAT YOU'RE SIPPING SAKE, TRY COOKING WITH IT ■ Roy Yamaguchi serves a line of Oregon-produced sakes, the Y Saké collection, at his international chain of Roy's restaurants. To make this easy, fusion-style scampi appetizer, he simmers shrimp and garlic in Sky, a semidry, medium-bodied sake (other sakes work well too). The perfect companion to this dish? A glass of the same sake—chilled, of course.

RECIPE: **Shrimp in Sake-Garlic Sauce. 1** In an 8- to 10-inch frying pan over medium heat, stir 1 teaspoon minced **garlic** and 1 teaspoon minced **onion** or shallot in 1 teaspoon **olive oil** until golden brown, about 2 minutes. **2** Add 8 ounces rinsed deveined peeled medium **shrimp** (41 to 50 per lb.) and ½ cup **sake.** Stir often until shrimp are opaque but still moist-looking in center of thickest part (cut to test), 2 to 3 minutes. **3** Add 3 tablespoons **butter,** 1 tablespoon **soy sauce,** and 1 teaspoon chopped **parsley;** stir until butter is melted and blended into sauce. **4** Spoon into 4 small shallow bowls. Serve with crusty bread or hot cooked rice. Makes 4 appetizer servings. — *Linda Lau Anusasananan*

Spice under wraps

By Jerry Anne Di Vecchio

Nutmeg is a spice that conjures cozy, comfy thoughts. Mace, on the other hand, puzzles. It sounds familiar—you might even have a little tin of it if you set up your spice rack with one of everything from the supermarket. But do you use mace? Do you even know what it tastes like? Or do you suspect it's the essence of the spray designed to repel muggers?

Nutmeg and mace come from the same plant, yet nutmeg gets all the press. In fact, it's a multilayered story. Traveling through spice-rich India and Malaysia last year, I finally saw and understood. Nutmeg is the inner seed of a fruit about the size of a baseball. The exterior of the fruit is leathery and brown, with a layer of firm white flesh just beneath. The flesh smells and tastes like nutmeg— Malaysians like to candy it. Underneath that is a beautiful red, lacy layer of *aril*—also called mace blades—that cling to the thin, hard shell surrounding the nutmeg. This is the source of mace as we know it.

The relationship of nutmeg and mace makes it easy to use them interchangeably. Mace, available dried and ground, is as intensely aromatic as nutmeg but also has distinctive floral and fruity overtones, making it well suited to cakes and pastries. I love it in those made with apricots and peaches, both of which blossom when mingled with this spice. One of the easiest and most delectable ways to appreciate mace is in a cobbler—apricot or peach. And because cobbler crust can be manhandled without serious consequences, my grandsons, Henry (5) and Jackie (3), often join me in assembling this homey dessert. They pat out the dough by the handfuls, lay the lumps over the fruit, then seal them with a final "patty-cake." Child's play.

Great match for mace: baked apricots.

peaches, peeled and sliced, with ½ cup sugar. Serve the cobbler warm, with sweetened whipped cream or vanilla ice cream. You can make it up to 1 day ahead; cover airtight when cool and let stand at room temperature. Reheat in a 350° oven for about 10 minutes.

MAKES: 6 servings

¾ to 1¼ cups packed **powdered sugar** (see notes)

¼ to ½ teaspoon **ground mace** (see notes)

¾ teaspoon **almond extract**

½ teaspoon grated **orange** peel

6 cups **apricot** quarters (about 2 lb. whole fruit)

Patty-cake crust (recipe follows)

1. In a large bowl, with a flexible spatula, combine sugar, mace, almond extract, and orange peel. Add apricots and mix. Scrape mixture into a buttered shallow 1½- to 2-quart casserole and spread level.

2. With lightly floured hands, tear off lumps (3- to 4-tablespoon size) of the patty cake crust and pat into cakes about ¼ inch thick; lay them as shaped over fruit, covering fairly evenly (a few gaps are fine). When all the dough is in place, press down lightly to join portions.

3. Bake cobbler in a 375° regular or convection oven (if using a 1½-qt. casserole, set on a large sheet of foil in case mixture boils over) until fruit is bubbling and crust is well browned, 50 to 60 minutes. Let stand at least 10 minutes or until cool. Scoop fruit and crust into bowls, adding more sugar to taste.

Per serving: 349 cal., 41% (144 cal.) from fat; 5.4 g protein; 16 g fat (9.6 g sat.); 47 g carbo (2.4 g fiber); 148 mg sodium; 77 mg chol.

Patty-cake Crust. In a food processor or bowl, combine 1 cup **all-purpose flour**; 6 tablespoons **butter** cut into thin slices; ¼ cup **cream cheese** (2 oz.), cut into small pieces; ½ teaspoon grated **orange** peel; and ¼ teaspoon **ground mace.** Whirl or rub with your fingers until mixture forms fine crumbs. Add 1 **large egg** yolk and whirl or stir until dough holds together. Press into a ball. ◆

Vertical credit: JAMES CARRIER; FOOD STYLING: BASIL FRIEDMAN

Apricot Patty-cake Cobbler

PREP AND COOK TIME: About 1½ hours, plus at least 10 minutes to cool

NOTES: As the apricots cook, their tartness comes forward. If the fruit is firm and underripe, it will require the maximum amount of sugar. If the apricots are ripe and sweeter, start with ¾ cup sugar. For a strong mace flavor, use the larger amount. Instead of ground mace, you can use the same amount of fresh-grated or ground nutmeg. Instead of apricots, you can use ripe

Fly the tricolor standard

Simple salad is a match for the season

A summer salad has high standards to meet under tough conditions. It needs to be crisp, green, and refreshing just when the weather is warmest. This one—bright, fresh, colorful, and full of crunchy textures—is also sturdy: It holds up well on a summer buffet, staunchly resisting the wilt factor.

JAMES CARRIER (4); FOOD STYLING: BASIL FRIEDMAN

Red and Green Mélange Salad

PREP TIME: About 15 minutes

NOTES: If you're concerned about bacteria on raw bean sprouts, immerse them in boiling water, drain immediately, immerse in ice water, and drain when cold.

MAKES: 4 to 6 servings

- 2 cups thinly sliced **English cucumber**
- 2 teaspoons **salt**
- 1 **red bell pepper** (8 oz.), rinsed, stemmed, and seeded
- 3 cups **bean sprouts** (about 8 oz.), rinsed and drained (see notes)
- 2 cups lightly packed **arugula** (about 4 oz.), rinsed and drained
- 3 tablespoons **rice vinegar**
- 1½ tablespoons **Asian fish sauce** (*nuoc mam* or *nam pla*) or reduced-sodium soy sauce
- 2 teaspoons **sugar**
- 2 teaspoons minced **fresh ginger**

1. In a bowl, mix cucumber and salt; gently crush slices with your hand until they feel limp. Let mixture stand for 5 to 10 minutes.

2. Meanwhile, dice bell pepper into ⅛-inch pieces. Sort through bean sprouts and pinch off and discard any discolored tips. Chop the arugula very coarsely.

3. In a wide serving bowl (3 to 4 qt.), mix vinegar, fish sauce, sugar, and ginger.

4. Rinse cucumber slices well in cold water, then squeeze slices gently to remove excess moisture. Add cucumbers, bell peppers, bean sprouts, and arugula to bowl with dressing and mix to coat. Spoon onto plates.

Per serving: 45 cal., 14% (6.3 cal.) from fat; 3 g protein; 0.7 g fat (0.1 g sat.); 8.1 g carbo (1.7 g fiber); 252 mg sodium; 0 mg chol.

— Jerry Anne Di Vecchio

Tight squeeze for freshness

■ A common commercial trick for keeping foods fresh is now possible at home: Pull the air away from foods, then seal them with a vacuum sealer. Frozen foods resist freezer burn better, and marinades penetrate meats more effectively. My friend vacuum-packs and freezes stews and pastas, then later heats the foods right in the plastic bags in boiling water. The FoodSaver by Tilia is available in cookware departments and stores in a number of models, including the 300 ($99), the 550 (at right; $149), or more expensive units that also vacuum-seal jars and bottles. *(800) 777-5452. — J.D.V.*

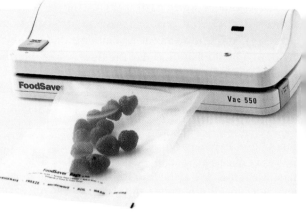

Rhubarb in the raw

■ I've never granted any aura of exotica to rhubarb because, as I was growing up, it was a staple in the garden and ended up in pies I didn't really like. But on a recent tour in Turkey, while nibbling through a momentous spread of *meze* (individually an appetizer, but collectively an entire meal), I came upon a real surprise—a platter of thin, crisp pink-green slices of what looked like celery to dip in salt; on the tongue, it was downright zingy. To my amazement, it was rhubarb. With rhubarb now in season, consider this scintillatingly simple offering as an appetizer: Just rinse the stalks and slice them diagonally; either sprinkle the slices at the last minute with coarse sea salt or serve the salt alongside to dip into. — *J.D.V.*

The Wine Guide

With this issue, Karen MacNeil-Fife begins a series on how to enjoy wine every day.

Discover Sauvignon Blanc

By Karen MacNeil-Fife

Maybe it's freshness or food friendliness. But after decades of being something of a downtrodden stepsister to Chardonnay, Sauvignon Blanc has emerged as the Cinderella of white wines. It has never been more exciting, more dynamic, and more delicious. I recently tasted some 60 Sauvignon Blancs, and wine after wine was crisp, sassy, fresh-tasting, and packed with flavor. A bonus: Sauvignon Blancs are among the best-priced wines in the West right now.

The name

Sauvignon comes from the French word *sauvage*, which means "wild." It's a reference to how the vine grows, but also an apt description of the wine's flavor. Don't be confused by the term *Fumé Blanc;* wines made from Sauvignon Blanc grapes can, by law, be called either Sauvignon Blanc or Fumé Blanc. But even though *fumé* is French for "smoked," it's not true that those labeled Fumé Blanc have a smoky flavor.

That flavor

There's nothing shy about this wine. An avalanche of green herbal notes (which is one of the reasons it works well with food— herbs being an asset to most dishes) gives way to all sorts of fascinating permutations, from green tea to green figs to melons and limes, with a streak of refreshing acidity that makes it feel crisp and snappy on your palate.

The top regions

In the West, delicious Sauvignon Blanc is made primarily in California, Washington, and Texas. Some of the wildest Sauvignons of all, however, come from New Zealand—don't miss them. In France, it's the grape behind Sancerre and Pouilly-Fumé. And in Bordeaux, it is blended with Sémillon to make white Graves.

Our top picks

Benziger Fumé Blanc 2000 (Sonoma County), $13. Crisp, with lime and ginger flavors and just a hint of vanilla at the end.

Brancott Vineyards Sauvignon Blanc 2000 (Marlborough, New Zealand), $10. Outrageous green lime flavors. Think grilled shrimp.

Buttonwood Farm Sauvignon Blanc 2000 (Santa Ynez Valley), $12. Herbs, green olives, and a note of green figs. Perfect with a salade niçoise.

Davis Bynum "Shone Farm" Fumé Blanc 2001 (Russian River Valley), $16. Sassy grapefruit and melon flavors, with penetrating acidity but a rich core. Try with crab cakes.

Handley "Ferrington Vineyard" Sauvignon Blanc 2000 (Anderson Valley), $15. Exotic—if limes could be crossed with pear sorbet …

Hogue Fumé Blanc 2000 (Columbia Valley, WA), $10. Lively—as refreshing as limeade. ◆

New take on tofu

This popular protein is showing up in unusual places

By Linda Lau Anusasananan • Photographs by James Carrier

Fill tortillas with chili-seasoned tofu, cabbage, and salsa for lively vegetarian tacos.

FOOD STYLING: BASIL FRIEDMAN (2)

Tofu—or bean curd—long a staple in the Asian diet, has become mainstream in the West. Recently, it has earned even more converts due to its widely touted health benefits as a cholesterol- and lactose-free complete protein that is low in saturated fat and sodium. But it's tofu's versatility—a chameleon-like ability to take on the flavors of the foods it's cooked with—that keeps people coming back for more.

Last year, 30,000 attendees of the Los Angeles Tofu Festival tasted this protein in myriad forms, from savory to sweet. Its meaty texture made it a natural as an entrée, but its creaminess was a particular asset in salad dressings and frozen desserts. Our recipes for sesame tofu dressing and banana-strawberry tofu sherbet on page 125 were adapted from the festival cookbook, *The Four Seasons of Tofu*.

Tofu Tacos

PREP AND COOK TIME: About 25 minutes

NOTES: If your wooden skewers are too long to fit in the pan, cut them to size with scissors.

MAKES: 3 or 4 servings

- 12 ounces **water-** or vacuum-**packed extra-firm tofu** (see box at right)
- 2 tablespoons **soy sauce**
- 1 tablespoon **lime juice**
- 1 tablespoon **chili powder**
- 1 teaspoon **ground cumin**
- 1 teaspoon **garlic powder**
- ¼ teaspoon **cayenne**
- 3 cups finely shredded **cabbage**
- 2 tablespoons **seasoned rice vinegar**
- 8 **corn tortillas** (6 in. diameter)
      About 1 cup **tomato salsa**
      About ½ cup **reduced-fat sour cream** (optional)

1. Rinse tofu, drain in a colander for about 5 minutes, then pat dry with paper towels. Cut into 1-inch cubes and lightly blot with more paper towels.

2. In a bowl, mix soy sauce, lime juice, chili powder, cumin, garlic powder, and cayenne. Add tofu and mix gently to coat cubes completely. Let stand 5 to 10 minutes, stirring occasionally.

3. Meanwhile, in another bowl, mix cabbage with vinegar. Stack tortillas and enclose in plastic wrap.

4. Thread tofu cubes equally onto four 8-inch wooden skewers (see notes). Set a 12-inch nonstick frying pan over medium-high heat. When pan is hot, lay skewers in pan and turn as needed to brown tofu on all sides, 5 to 6 minutes total. Transfer to a serving platter. Mound cabbage mixture alongside.

5. Heat tortillas in a microwave oven at full power (100%) until hot and steamy, 30 to 45 seconds. Wrap in a towel. Serve with tofu and cabbage, salsa, and sour cream. Eat taco style, filling tortillas as desired.

Per serving: 246 cal., 12% (30 cal.) from fat; 16 g protein; 3.3 g fat (0.2 g sat.); 39 g carbo (7.6 g fiber); 1,198 mg sodium; 0 mg chol.

Spicy Lemon Grass Tofu

PREP AND COOK TIME: About 40 minutes

NOTES: This Vietnamese dish was adapted from *Pleasures of the Vietnamese Table*, by Mai Pham (HarperCollins, NY, 2001; $27.50).

MAKES: 3 or 4 servings

- 1 package (12 to 16 oz.) **water-packed firm tofu** (see box at right)
- 2 stalks **fresh lemon grass** (each 10 to 12 in. long)
- 1½ tablespoons **soy sauce**
- 1½ to 2 teaspoons minced **fresh hot chili** such as Thai bird or serrano
- 2 teaspoons **sugar**
- 1 teaspoon **ground turmeric**
      About ½ teaspoon **salt**
- ½ cup thinly sliced **onion**
- 2 tablespoons minced **shallots**
- 1 teaspoon minced **garlic**
- 1 teaspoon **salad oil**
- ⅔ cup **fresh Thai** or regular **basil** leaves
- 3 tablespoons chopped **unsalted roasted peanuts**
- 4 cups hot cooked **rice**

1. Rinse tofu, drain in a colander for about 5 minutes, then pat dry with paper towels. Cut into ¾-inch cubes and lightly blot with more towels.

2. Rinse lemon grass. Cut off and discard tough tops and root ends; peel off and discard tough, green outer layers of stalks down to tender white portion of bulbs. Finely chop tender portions; you should have 4 to 7 tablespoons.

3. In a bowl, mix lemon grass, soy sauce, chili, sugar, turmeric, and ½ teaspoon salt. Gently stir in tofu. Let marinate for 5 to 10 minutes, stirring occasionally.

4. In a 10- to 12-inch nonstick frying pan over high heat, stir onion, shallots, and garlic in oil until fragrant, about 1 minute; push to one side of pan. Add tofu mixture. Gently turn cubes occasionally and stir onion mixture until tofu is browned around the edges and onion is soft, 5 to 7 minutes.

5. Stir in basil leaves and half the peanuts. Add salt to taste. Pour into a serving dish. Garnish with remaining peanuts. Serve with hot cooked rice.

Per serving: 413 cal., 26% (108 cal.) from fat; 21 g protein; 12 g fat (1.8 g sat.); 57 g carbo (2.2 g fiber); 692 mg sodium; 0 mg chol.

Sesame Tofu Dressing

PREP TIME: About 10 minutes

NOTES: This creamy dressing tastes as smooth and rich as one made with mayonnaise, but it is far leaner and higher in protein. Serve it as a dip for raw vegetables or as a salad dressing. Chill airtight up to 1 week.

MAKES: 2½ to 3 cups

1 package (12 to 16 oz.) **water-packed soft** or aseptic-packed silken **tofu** (see box below)

1 cup **seasoned rice vinegar**

2 cloves **garlic**, peeled

⅓ cup coarsely chopped **fresh cilantro**

¼ cup thinly sliced **green onions** (including tops)

3 tablespoons **honey**

2 teaspoons **Asian** (toasted) **sesame oil**

2 teaspoons **low-sodium soy sauce**

½ teaspoon **hot chili flakes**

1. Drain tofu in a colander for about

Tofu is the creamy base for a cilantro-rich dressing on butter lettuce.

5 minutes, then pat dry with paper towels.

2. In a food processor or blender, combine tofu, vinegar, garlic, cilantro, green onions, honey, sesame oil, soy sauce, and chili flakes. Whirl until very smooth.

Per tablespoon: 14 cal., 26% (3.6 cal.) from fat; 0.3 g protein; 0.4 g fat (0 g sat.); 2.4 g carbo (0 g fiber); 108 mg sodium; 0 mg chol.

Banana-Strawberry Tofu Sherbet

PREP TIME: About 40 minutes if quick-chilling, 1½ hours otherwise

NOTES: Store airtight in the freezer up to 2 weeks.

MAKES: About 3½ cups; 5 to 6 servings

1 package (12 to 16 oz.) **water-packed soft** or aseptic-packed silken **tofu** (see box below)

2 **ripe bananas** (12 oz. total), peeled and cut into 1-inch chunks

3 tablespoons thawed **frozen orange juice concentrate**

1 tablespoon **vanilla**

2 cups **strawberries,** rinsed and hulled

About 4 tablespoons **honey**

1. Drain tofu in a colander for about 5 minutes, then pat dry with paper towels.

2. In a blender or food processor, combine tofu, bananas, orange juice concentrate, vanilla, strawberries, and 4 tablespoons honey; whirl until very smooth. Taste, and add more honey if desired.

3. To quick-chill, pour tofu mixture into a bowl and nest in ice water; stir often until cold, about 5 minutes. Otherwise, cover and chill until cold, about 1 hour.

4. Pour tofu mixture into an ice cream maker (1 qt. or larger). Freeze according to manufacturer's directions until dasher is hard to turn or machine stops. Serve, or cover and freeze until firm, at least 3 hours. If sherbet gets too hard, soften in a microwave oven at half power (50%), checking at 15-second intervals, until it can be scooped, 30 to 60 seconds total.

Per serving: 143 cal., 12% (17 cal.) from fat; 3.6 g protein; 1.9 g fat (0.1 g sat.); 29 g carbo (2 g fiber); 5.7 mg sodium; 0 mg chol. ◆

How tofu is made

Turning soybeans into tofu requires soaking, crushing, cooking, and filtering to create a soy milk. Coagulants are added to the milk to solidify it, then the tofu is molded into blocks and packaged in water or vacuum-packed without (for a longer shelf life) and refrigerated. These traditional forms of tofu may be fairly coarse and firm to quite soft, depending on how much whey was pressed out.

In a newer method, the soy milk is poured into an aseptic package. Coagulants are added, and the package is sealed and heated. The resulting tofu is smooth and custardlike—what manufacturers call *silken.*

There are no industry standards for describing the firmness of tofu; labels vary widely among brands. In general, however, use soft tofu, such as aseptic-packed silken styles, when you want a smooth, creamy texture but don't need the substance to hold its shape. Choose firm, medium-dense tofu for all-purpose uses, such as in purées or cut into chunks (perfect tidbits for toddlers). Use extra-firm tofu (sometimes labeled *nigari*), which holds its shape well, in sautés and stir-fries and on the grill.

International tastes

Great reader contributions, tested in *Sunset's* kitchens

By Charity Ferreira • Photographs by James Carrier

This is a simple, delicious picnic salad—just assemble it when you arrive.

Greek Tortellini Salad

Marilou Robinson, Portland

Marilou Robinson combined some of her favorite flavors in this main-dish salad. As a shortcut, use a purchased salad dressing instead of the lemon-herb vinaigrette.

PREP AND COOK TIME: About 30 minutes, plus at least 2 hours to chill

MAKES: 8 servings

- 1 package (20 oz.) **fresh cheese-filled tortellini**
- ½ cup **extra-virgin olive oil**
- ¼ cup **lemon juice**
- ¼ cup **red wine vinegar**
- 2 tablespoons chopped **parsley**
- 1 teaspoon **dried oregano**
- ½ teaspoon **salt**
- 1 pound **baby spinach leaves,** rinsed and crisped
- 1 cup crumbled **feta cheese** (about 6 oz.)
- ½ cup slivered **red onion**
- 6 hard-cooked **large eggs,** peeled and quartered

1. In a 5- to 6-quart pan over high heat, bring 2 quarts water to a boil. Add tortellini and cook, stirring occasionally, until tender to bite, 3 to 5 minutes. Drain.

2. Meanwhile, in a large bowl, combine olive oil, lemon juice, red wine vinegar, parsley, oregano, and salt. Add cooked tortellini and mix to coat. Cover and chill at least 2 hours or up to 1 day.

3. Add spinach, feta cheese, and onion to tortellini and mix gently. Mound salad on a platter and arrange egg quarters around the edge.

Per serving: 485 cal., 50% (243 cal.) from fat; 18 g protein; 27 g fat (8.3 g sat.); 44 g carbo (4.4 g fiber); 780 mg sodium; 207 mg chol.

Spaghetti with Black Beans and Clams

Theresa Liu, Alameda, CA

Theresa Liu combines salty Chinese fermented black beans with clams and pasta in a simple, innovative take on spaghetti with clam sauce. Fermented black beans can be found in Asian markets and many well-stocked supermarkets.

PREP AND COOK TIME: About 30 minutes

MAKES: 4 servings

- 2 tablespoons **fermented black beans** (see note above)
- 3 cans (6 oz. each) **chopped clams**
- 8 ounces **dried spaghetti** or soba noodles
- 2 teaspoons **salad oil**
- 2 tablespoons minced **garlic**
- ½ teaspoon **hot red chili flakes** (optional)
- ¼ cup **dry white wine**
- ¼ cup chopped **fresh cilantro**

1. Rinse and drain black beans; mince. Drain clams, reserving ¾ cup juice.

2. In a 5- to 6-quart pan over high heat, bring 3 quarts water to a boil. Add spaghetti and cook, stirring occasionally, until tender to bite, 7 to 9 minutes; drain. Rinse in cold water.

3. In the same pan, heat oil over medium-high heat. Add black beans, garlic, and, if desired, chili flakes; stir until fragrant, 1 to 2 minutes. Add clams, reserved clam juice, and wine. Bring to a boil and cook for 1 minute. Stir in spaghetti and cook until heated through, 1 to 2 minutes. Pour into a serving bowl and sprinkle with cilantro.

Per serving: 355 cal., 12% (44 cal.) from fat; 25 g protein; 4.9 g fat (0.5 g sat.); 48 g carbo (1.5 g fiber); 298 mg sodium; 44 mg chol.

Eggplant Salad

Cindy Wu, Sunnyvale, CA

This garlicky eggplant salad was a favorite recipe of Cindy Wu's mother. Asian eggplants are long and thin; use either the deep purple Japanese variety or the sweeter, amethyst-colored Chinese eggplant. You can make the salad up to 4 hours ahead; cover and chill. Serve as an appetizer, with toasted baguette slices or sesame crackers.

PREP AND COOK TIME: About 1 hour, plus at least 30 minutes to chill

MAKES: 4 servings

8 **Asian eggplants** (about 1¾ lbs. total; see note above)

2 tablespoons **Asian** (toasted) **sesame oil**

2 tablespoons **soy sauce**

2 tablespoons **rice vinegar**

1 tablespoon minced **garlic**

¼ cup minced **green onions** (including green tops)

. Place eggplants in a 12- by 15-inch aking pan; pierce each several times ith a sharp knife. Bake in a 400° regular r convection oven until very soft when ressed, 40 to 50 minutes. Let stand ntil cool enough to handle, about 15 ninutes. Cut off and discard stems; slice ggplants in half lengthwise. With a fork r your fingers, remove flesh in long hreds. Discard peels.

. Meanwhile, in a bowl, mix sesame il, soy sauce, rice vinegar, and garlic. dd eggplant and mix gently to coat. over and chill at least 30 minutes or p to 4 hours.

. Sprinkle eggplant salad with green nions just before serving.

er serving: 113 cal., 56% (63 cal.) from fat; 5 g protein; 7 g fat (1 g sat.); 12 g carbo 2.6 g fiber); 522 mg sodium; 0 mg chol.

Tomatoes with Sicilian White Bean Purée

Roxanne E. Chan, Albany, CA

For a casual first course, Roxanne Chan tops fresh tomatoes with a savory bean mixture. Mash the beans into a chunky purée with a potato masher or pulse a few times in a food processor.

PREP TIME: About 20 minutes

MAKES: 6 to 8 appetizer servings

2 tablespoons **pine nuts**

1 can (15 oz.) **cannellini** (white) **beans,** rinsed, drained, and mashed (see note above)

3 tablespoons chopped **fresh basil** leaves

2 tablespoons **mayonnaise**

2 tablespoons **grated parmesan cheese**

1 tablespoon **lemon juice**

1 tablespoon drained **capers**

1 tablespoon **dried currants**

1 tablespoon minced **green onion** (including green top)

1 clove **garlic,** peeled and minced

Salt and **pepper**

Tangy white bean purée is flavored with pine nuts, capers, and currants.

3 **firm-ripe tomatoes** (about 1¾ lbs. total), rinsed, cored, and sliced crosswise ¼ inch thick

1. In a 6- to 8-inch frying pan over medium heat, stir pine nuts often until golden, 5 to 10 minutes.

2. In a bowl, mix mashed beans, basil, mayonnaise, parmesan, lemon juice, capers, currants, green onion, and garlic until well blended. Add salt and pepper to taste.

3. Arrange tomato slices, overlapping, on a platter. Spoon bean mixture down the center of tomatoes. Sprinkle with pine nuts.

Per serving: 104 cal., 41% (43 cal.) from fat; 4.7 g protein; 4.8 g fat (0.9 g sat.); 12 g carbo (3.7 g fiber); 165 mg sodium; 3 mg chol. ◆

Picnic time

cenic nosh spots in ortland and Seattle

By Karl Samson

Dig out the picnic basket and treat yourself to an early-summer alfresco meal in one f these idyllic outdoor areas.

ortland

Kelley Point Park. At the conflu-nce of the Willamette and Columbia ivers, this park has beaches, forest, nd a meadow ideal for picnicking. WHERE: From I-5, take N. Marine Dr. est. CONTACT: (503) 823-7529.

Oak Island on Sauvie Island. Best nown for its fruit stands, beaches, nd biking, Sauvie Island also offers reat picnic areas. One of the best is)ak Island, where a trail leads to an xpansive meadow with views of Mt.

Adams and Mt. St. Helens. WHERE: From U.S. 30, cross Sauvie Island Bridge, drive 2½ miles north, turn right on Reeder Rd. In 1¼ miles, turn left on Oak Island Rd. and con-tinue 3 miles. FYI: Get your parking permit ($3.50) at the Cracker Barrel, a minimart just over the bridge. CON-TACT: (503) 621-3488.

■ Powell Butte Nature Park. Well known to area mountain bikers, this park on the east side of Portland, near Gresham, has acres of rolling meadows with plenty of secluded spots. Take Mountain View Trail, which heads south from the parking area to the top of the hill. WHERE: S.E. Powell Blvd. and S.E. 162nd Ave. CONTACT: (503) 823-2223.

Seattle

■ Discovery Park. You can spread your blanket on the blufftop or head down to the beach, where the views stretch from Mt. Rainier to Mt. Baker.

WHERE: 3801 W. Government Way. CONTACT: (206) 386-4236.

■ St. Edward State Park. This Ken-more park was once a seminary, and the Romanesque revival building provides a fascinating backdrop for a picnic on the wide lawns. Trails wind through the park and down to the shore of Lake Washington. There's also a bit of lawn down by the lake. WHERE: Juanita Dr. NE at N.E. 143rd St. (Take exit 20A off northbound I-405 and drive west on 116th St., which becomes Juanita Dr.) CON-TACT: (425) 823-2992.

■ Washington Park Arboretum. With acres of trees, flowers in bloom, and secluded glades, Seattle's arboretum is the city's best bet for an early-sum-mer picnic. Allow 30 minutes or so to search for the perfect spot. WHERE: From State 520, take Lake Washington Blvd. exit, then turn left into the arboretum. CONTACT: (206) 543-8800. ◆

Move your summer party outdoors with a collection of delicious dishes, including Garlic Shrimp (recipe on page 139).

July

cobblers crisps & grunts are

easier than pie

They are far from elegant, with the relaxed aspect of old friends, and names that express what many of us want to do when faced with making a piecrust: Buckle. Slump. Grunt. • "People want to bake with fruit, but they have the impression that pies and cakes are hard to make—that they have to look good," says Carolyn Weil, a San Francisco Bay Area baker, writer, and cooking teacher. "But these desserts are comfortable and approachable. Anyone can make them, and they're at home on the kitchen table." • Weil's recipes for unfussy summer desserts like easy blackberry cobbler, juicy peach pandowdy, and warm blueberry grunt leave no excuse for not taking advantage of summer fruit at its peak.

Raspberry-Rhubarb Crisp

PREP AND COOK TIME: About 1 hour
NOTES: Serve this crisp with lightly sweetened softly whipped cream or vanilla ice cream.
MAKES: 6 to 8 servings

- 1 cup **rolled oats**
- ½ cup **all-purpose flour**
- ½ cup finely chopped **walnuts** (2½ oz.)
- ½ cup **brown sugar**
- ½ teaspoon **ground cinnamon**
- ½ teaspoon **ground ginger**
- ⅛ teaspoon **salt**
- ½ cup (¼ lb.) cold **butter,** cut into chunks
- 12 ounces **rhubarb** (about 3 stalks)
- ¾ cup **granulated sugar**
- 2 tablespoons **cornstarch**
- 4 cups **raspberries,** rinsed and drained

1. In a large bowl, mix oats, flour, walnuts, brown sugar, cinnamon, ginger, and salt. With your fingers or a pastry blender, rub or cut butter into oat mixture until coarse crumbs form. Cover and chill.

2. Rinse rhubarb; trim off and discard green parts of stalks. Cut red parts into ½-inch-thick slices; you need 2 cups. In a large bowl, combine granulated sugar, cornstarch, raspberries, and rhubarb and mix gently to coat. Pour into a shallow 2- to 3-quart baking dish and sprinkle evenly with topping.

3. Bake in a 350° regular or convection oven until topping is golden brown and fruit is bubbling, about 45 minutes. Serve warm or at room temperature.

Per serving: 398 cal., 41% (162 cal.) from fat; 4.7 g protein; 18 g fat (7.8 g sat.); 58 g carbo (4.6 g fiber); 163 mg sodium; 31 mg chol.

Blackberry Cobbler

PREP AND COOK TIME: About 1 hour
NOTES: Serve with vanilla ice cream.
MAKES: 6 to 8 servings

- 1¼ cups **sugar**
- 2 tablespoons **cornstarch**
- 2 tablespoons **quick-cooking tapioca**
- 6 cups **blackberries,** rinsed and drained
- 1 teaspoon grated **lemon** peel
- 1 tablespoon **lemon juice**
- 2 cups **all-purpose flour**
- 1 tablespoon **baking powder**
- 1 teaspoon **salt**
- ½ cup (¼ lb.) cold **butter,** cut in chunks
- 1 cup **whipping cream**

1. In a large bowl, combine 1 cup sugar, cornstarch, tapioca, blackberries, lemon peel, and lemon juice. Mix gently to coat. Pour into a shallow 3- to 4-quart baking dish.

2. In another bowl, mix flour, baking powder, salt, and remaining ¼ cup sugar. With your fingers or a pastry blender, rub or cut butter into flour mixture until coarse crumbs form. Add cream and stir just until mixture forms a soft, crumbly dough.

3. Pat ¼-cup portions of dough into flat disks ½ inch thick and arrange evenly over fruit.

4. Bake in a 350° oven until topping is golden brown and fruit is bubbling, 45 to 55 minutes. Serve warm or at room temperature.

Per serving: 498 cal., 38% (189 cal.) from fat; 4.8 g protein; 21 g fat (13 g sat.); 74 g carbo (5.8 g fiber); 614 mg sodium; 64 mg chol.

By Charity Ferreira • Photographs by James Carrier • Food styling by Dan Becker

Blueberry Grunt

PREP AND COOK TIME: About 45 minutes

NOTES: This old-fashioned dessert, which is a close cousin to a slump, is made by simmering barely sweetened dumplings in spiced blueberries. Be careful not to let the mixture come to a full boil or it may overflow the sides of the pan.

MAKES: 4 servings

- 4 cups **blueberries,** rinsed and drained
- ⅓ cup plus 1 tablespoon **sugar**
- ¼ cup **light molasses**
- 2 teaspoons grated **lemon** peel
- 3 tablespoons **lemon juice**
- ¼ teaspoon **ground nutmeg**
- ⅛ teaspoon **ground cloves**
- 1½ cups **all-purpose flour**
- 2 teaspoons **baking powder**
- ¼ teaspoon **salt**
- 3 tablespoons cold **butter,** cut into chunks
- ¾ cup **milk**

  About ½ cup **whipping cream** (optional)

1. In a 10- to 12-inch frying pan over medium heat, frequently stir blueberries, ⅓ cup sugar, molasses, lemon peel, lemon juice, nutmeg, cloves, and ½ cup water until the mixture comes to a boil. Reduce heat and simmer gently until the berries have released their juices and the flavors are blended, about 10 minutes.

2. Meanwhile, in a large bowl, mix flour, baking powder, salt, and the remaining 1 tablespoon sugar. With your fingers or a pastry blender, rub or cut the butter into the flour mixture until coarse crumbs form. Add the milk and stir just until mixture forms a soft dough (do not overmix).

3. Drop ¼-cup portions of the dough into the simmering fruit mixture. Cover the frying pan and simmer until a wooden skewer inserted in the center of the dumplings comes out clean, about 15 minutes. Spoon the warm dumplings and fruit equally into four bowls and drizzle the portions with cream if desired.

Per serving: 492 cal., 20% (99 cal.) from fat; 7.5 g protein; 11 g fat (6.4 g sat.); 94 g carbo (4.7 g fiber); 518 mg sodium; 30 mg chol.

Spiced Peach Pandowdy

PREP AND COOK TIME: About 1¾ hours

NOTES: To peel peaches, cut a ½-inch X through peel on the bottom of each. Immerse in boiling water until peels pull off easily, 1 to 2 minutes. Transfer peaches to a strainer and rinse under cold running water until cool. Starting at the cut end, slip off and discard peels.

MAKES: About 6 servings

- 1½ cups **all-purpose flour**
- 3½ tablespoons **granulated sugar**
- ¼ teaspoon **salt**
- 7 tablespoons cold **butter**
- 5 cups sliced peeled **firm-ripe peaches** (about 2⅔ lb.; see notes)
- 2½ tablespoons **lemon juice**
- 1 cup **brown sugar**
- 2 tablespoons **cornstarch**
- 1½ teaspoons **ground cinnamon**
- ½ teaspoon **ground nutmeg**

1. In a large bowl, mix flour, 1½ tablespoons granulated sugar, and salt. Cut 6 tablespoons butter into chunks and, with your fingers or a pastry blender, rub or cut it into flour mixture until coarse crumbs form. Sprinkle 4 tablespoons water evenly over mixture and stir until dough comes together; if necessary, add 1 to 2 more tablespoons water.

2. Turn dough out onto a lightly floured sheet of waxed paper and pat into a flat disk. With a lightly floured rolling pin, roll into an 11-inch round about ¼ inch thick. Slide waxed paper onto a 12- by 15-inch baking sheet and chill pastry.

3. In a large bowl, mix peaches, lemon juice, brown sugar, cornstarch, cinnamon, and nutmeg. Pour into a 9-inch pie pan. Cut remaining tablespoon butter into ¼-inch chunks and distribute evenly over fruit. Remove pastry round from refrigerator and let stand at room temperature 5 minutes. Slide off waxed paper and center over filling. With a small, sharp knife, trim dough ½ inch beyond pan rim. Tuck edges inside rim.

4. Place pie pan on a 12- by 15-inch baking sheet and bake in a 375° regular or convection oven until pastry is golden, about 30 minutes. Remove from oven and, with a sharp knife, cut crust into 1-inch squares. With the back of a spoon, gently press crust into filling so juice flows over edges of squares. Sprinkle remaining 2 tablespoons granulated sugar over the top, return to oven, and bake until peaches are tender when pierced and juices are thickened, 25 to 30 minutes longer. Serve warm or at room temperature.

Per serving: 488 cal., 26% (126 cal.) from fat; 4.7 g protein; 14 g fat (8.5 g sat.); 89 g carbo (3.4 g fiber); 249 mg sodium; 36 mg chol.

Plum Buckle

PREP AND COOK TIME: About 1¼ hours

NOTES: A buckle is a simple butter cake that bakes up around sliced fresh fruit.

MAKES: About 9 servings

- 1 cup (½ lb.) **butter,** at room temperature
- 1 cup plus 2 tablespoons **sugar**
- 2 **large eggs**
- 1 teaspoon grated **lemon** peel
- 1½ cups **all-purpose flour**
- 1 teaspoon **baking powder**
- ¼ teaspoon **salt**
- ¼ teaspoon **ground nutmeg**
- ⅓ cup **milk**
- 4 cups sliced unpeeled **firm-ripe plums** (about 1¼ lb.)
- ½ teaspoon **ground cinnamon**

1. In a large bowl, with a mixer on high speed, beat butter and 1 cup sugar until smooth. Add eggs one at a time, beating well after each addition. Beat in lemon peel.

2. In a small bowl, mix flour, baking powder, salt, and nutmeg. Stir half the flour mixture into the butter mixture, then add the milk, followed by the remaining flour mixture; stir just until incorporated. Scrape batter into a buttered and floured 8-inch square glass or ceramic baking pan and spread level. Overlap plum slices in rows or concentric circles over batter. In a small bowl, mix remaining 2 tablespoons sugar and the cinnamon; sprinkle evenly over plums.

3. Bake in a 325° regular or convection oven until a wooden skewer inserted in the center comes out clean, 45 to 50 minutes. Serve warm or at room temperature.

Per serving: 416 cal., 50% (207 cal.) from fat; 4.6 g protein; 23 g fat (14 g sat.); 50 g carbo (1.9 g fiber); 350 mg sodium; 105 mg chol. ◆

Bubbling summer fruit, sweet pastry, and—best of all—no bottom crust

Great ideas in food and wine

WINE

Hammock wines

There are wines for special celebrations, wines for dinner parties, wines that make great gifts. And then there are hammock wines—delicious, uncomplicated treats to sip when you're doing nothing more than lounging with a favorite novel.

Bonny Doon Ca' del Solo Freisa Frizzante 2001 (Monterey County), $15. My favorite hammock wine in all the world—shockingly magenta, low in alcohol, and slightly fizzy, with the deepest essence of strawberries.
Bottom line: Imagine a Shirley Temple for adults.

Chateau St. Jean Johannisberg Riesling 2001 (Sonoma County), $15. Peachy, uncomplicated, and just a tad sweet.
Bottom line: Perfect if you're reading a romance novel.

Jade Mountain "La Provençale" 1999 (California), $16. This irresistible blend of Mourvèdre, Grenache, and Syrah has supple licorice, lavender, and blackberry flavors and a rich, soft texture.
Bottom line: Guaranteed to mentally transport you to the south of France.

Navarro Chardonnay 1999 (Mendocino County), $13.50. Expect light tropical and orange marmalade notes.
Bottom line: For diehard Chardonnay lovers, here's one that's fresh-tasting rather than oaky. Available only from the winery: (800) 537-9463.
— *Karen MacNeil-Fife*

RECIPE

Tarragon Pesto and Pear Melt

1 In a food processor, whirl 1½ cups lightly packed rinsed **parsley**, ½ cup shredded **parmesan cheese**, ¼ cup **olive oil**, 3 tablespoons coarsely chopped fresh **tarragon** or 4 teaspoons dried, and 2 peeled cloves **garlic** until finely chopped.

2 Rinse, peel, core, and slice 3 firm-ripe **pears** (8 to 9 oz. each); in a bowl, mix with 2 tablespoons **lemon juice.**

3 Slice 1 **baguette** (about 10 oz.) in half crosswise, then lengthwise. Arrange pieces cut side up on a 10- by 15-inch baking sheet and broil 4 to 6 inches from heat until lightly browned, 1½ to 2 minutes.

4 Spread tarragon pesto on toasted bread. Overlap pear slices on top. Sprinkle 1¾ cups shredded **gruyère cheese** evenly over pears, then generously grind **pepper** over cheese.

5 Return to broiler until cheese is melted, about 2 minutes. Slice diagonally into 1½- to 2-inch-wide pieces. Makes 5 to 8 appetizer servings.

— *Lisl Hampton*

INGREDIENT

Tarragon américain

A NATIVE OF FRANCE MOVES TO CALIFORNIA. Hilary Rinaldi, who runs Cherry Creek Herbs in Atascadero, California, has a degree in horticulture and 15 years of experience working with plants, so the thought of growing certified organic tarragon in the United States—offering a source outside of France—was just the thing that would appeal to her. Plus, Rinaldi loves tarragon: "We never get tired of it. You can put it in anything." Try tarragon warmed in a little butter and poured over chicken or fish. You can also use it instead of basil in pesto, as in this recipe we adapted from Rinaldi. *Order fresh or dried tarragon from www.tarragoncentral.com.*

INGREDIENT

Cool cubes

FROZEN WATERMELON IS THE PERFECT ADDITION TO A SUMMER COOLER. Watermelons contain up to 92 percent water, so they freeze beautifully into ice cubes. Pop them into a drink to nibble on as they thaw. While red-fleshed watermelon will do fine, jazz it up with yellow or orange varieties.

RECIPES

Watermelon Ice Cubes. Cut peeled **seedless watermelon** into 1½-inch cubes. Set on a baking sheet, cover, and freeze until hard, about 3 hours, or up to 1 week (cover airtight when solid).

Margarita Cooler. Rub the rim of a glass (12 oz.) with a cut **lime** and dip rim in **coarse salt.** Pour 2 tablespoons **tequila**, 2

tablespoons **lime juice**, and 1 tablespoon **orange-flavored liqueur** into glass. Place **watermelon ice cubes** in glass and fill with about ½ cup chilled **sparkling water.** Makes 1 serving.

— *Linda Lau Anusasananan*

OUTDOOR ENTERTAINING

Delicious ideas for great patio parties all summer long

A cozy dining-room dinner party on a cold winter night is a wonderful thing. But the scenery's always the same—all you can change are the linens. Come summer, though, you can move the party outdoors, where the setting is in constant flux—delicate yellow green and leafy one day, dark green and sultry the next. Blooms appear here, then there, changing the mood from week to week. • There's a spirit of newness and change out in the yard in summer that fosters the liveliest parties of the year. We've collected menus, dishes, and how-to guides to make it easy to move the party outside—and experiment with flavors foreign (an authentic paella from Valencia) or familiar (seasoned salmon on the grill), with friends new and old.

— *Sara Schneider*

MENUS, DISHES, AND TIPS

JAMES CARRIER; STYLING: PHILIPPINE SCALI; FOOD STYLING: BASIL FRIEDMAN

Paella party

Make an authentic Valencian paella on the barbecue or a quick version on the stove.
Take your pick for a lively midsummer meal

By Linda Lau Anusasananan • Photographs by James Carrier • Food styling by Basil Friedman • Styling by Philippine Scali

■ Paella has transcended Spanish borders and earned international fame primarily as an extravagant, saffron-scented rice and seafood dish cooked in a wide, flat pan. But in its native home of Valencia, paella comes in many forms, from rustic versions based on products from the land to showy variations using the bounty of the sea.

David Llodrá grew up eating paella in Alboraya, a small town north of Valencia in a rice-growing region near Albu-fera Lake. His grandmother made a traditional country-style version, with chicken, rabbit, and beans, over a fire fueled with wood from orange trees. One day, however, having broken her arm, she was unable to cook. Llodrá's craving prompted initiative: "Just tell me what to do, and I'll make it," he pleaded. And a new paella master was born.

Llodrá himself has emigrated from Spain and now lives in Sonoma, California, with his wife, Katherine, and 1-year-old daughter, Eden. Here, he has adapted his authentic paella to American ingredients and equipment—charcoal briquets instead of felled and split orange trees, for instance. The natural cycle of a charcoal fire in a kettle barbecue matches the stages of cooking paella: browning the chicken, simmering the broth, and cooking the rice. The even heat also produces a delicious brown crust on the bottom, called *socarrat*, a highly prized delicacy in a well-made paella. The pans themselves are now easy to find here (see page 139). California medium-grain rice works just as well as more expensive imported Spanish rice. And, in what also seems like a departure but really isn't, Llodrá rarely uses expensive saffron. Most Spaniards, he says, actually use a product called *colorante*, which gives the rice a yellow tinge; we find turmeric a suitable alternative.

Paella cooked as Llodrá does it, on the barbecue, makes for a leisurely outdoor party. Prepare all the ingredients beforehand, then cook the paella while guests nibble on tapas and watch the proceedings. If you are uncomfortable with an audience in the yard, however, or want a lighter, contemporary seafood paella, choose our simplified stovetop version on page 139. Either dish makes a great party centerpiece.

Menu: Paella choices

The barbecued paella below and the seafood version on page 139 feed five or six people as a main course. If you have a few more guests, offer more substantial tapas (appetizers) and smaller paella servings.

Tapas: Choose three to five Olives • Roasted, salted almonds • Spanish cheeses such as Cabrales, Manchego, Mahon, and Iberico • Sliced baguettes • Thinly sliced serrano ham or prosciutto • Garlic Shrimp* • Roasted red peppers drizzled with extra-virgin olive oil and sherry vinegar

Green Salad with sliced onions and tomatoes in vinaigrette

Chicken Paella Valenciana from the Barbecue* or Simple Seafood and Sausage Paella*

Cava (Spanish Sparkling Wine), Red Rioja (see page 151), or Clarita (equal parts light lager beer and sparkling lemonade)

Watermelon or honeydew melon

Flan

Espresso

*Recipe provided

Family-style dining

In Valencia, it's common for everyone to eat right out of the paella pan. The Llodrás do that for casual parties with close friends and family. They set the pan on a stack of newspapers, on a newspaper-covered square or round table, and each diner gets a large spoon. First they mark out their territory—a wedge-shaped portion directly in front of them (dividing the paella like a pizza)—and move all the chicken to the center so everyone can choose the pieces they want. Then they dig in, starting at the edge and scooping the rice toward them, eating their way to the center. Chicken bones go onto the newspaper. Salad and melon—whacked into wedges—are served in the same communal style, on large platters, while the flan is served on individual plates. Cleanup is easy—they just roll up the newspapers and throw them away.

Chicken Paella Valenciana from the Barbecue

PREP AND COOK TIME: About 2 hours on gas, 2½ hours on charcoal

NOTES: If using a whole chicken, you can have it cut into pieces (step 2) at the meat counter. If using a gas barbecue, make sure the paella pan will fit. Temperatures vary among barbecue models; you may need to adjust the heat and cooking times. If using charcoal, make sure the ingredients are ready before you start the fire, so you don't miss the peak heat. Follow the steps carefully, and the heat should cool down gradually as needed.

MAKES: 5 or 6 main-dish servings or 7 to 8 smaller servings supplemented with more substantial tapas

- 1 cup **dried large lima beans** (6 oz.)
- 3 pounds **bone-in chicken thighs** or 1 chicken (about 3 lb.)
- 1 pound **fresh Italian** (Romano) or regular **green beans** or thawed frozen Italian green beans
- 3 tablespoons **olive oil**
- 1 cup **canned diced tomatoes** About 1½ teaspoons **salt**
- ½ teaspoon **paprika**
- ½ teaspoon **ground dried turmeric**
- 2½ cups **medium-grain white rice**
- 2 **lemons** (5 oz. each), cut in half

1. Pour lima beans into a colander; sort and remove debris, then rinse and drain beans. In a 4- to 5-quart pan over high heat, bring 2½ to 3 quarts water and beans to a boil; cook for 2 minutes. Cover tightly, remove from heat, and let stand for 1 hour. Drain beans, reserving 2 quarts cooking liquid.

2. Rinse chicken and pat dry. Cut each thigh in half lengthwise along one side of bone; or with a cleaver, cut whole chicken through bones into 2- by 3-inch pieces (see notes). Pull off and discard any lumps of fat. Rinse green beans and remove and discard stem ends and any tough strings; cut beans into 3-inch lengths.

3. *If using a charcoal barbecue* (at least 22 in. wide), ignite 160 briquets (about 9½ lb.) on the firegrate; open dampers. When coals are dotted with ash, in 15 to 20 minutes, spread into an even double layer about 2 inches wider than base of paella pan. Set grill 4 to 6 inches above charcoal. Let coals burn down until they're hot (you can hold your hand at grill level only 2 to 3 seconds), 5 to 10 minutes.

If using a gas barbecue (at least 19 in. wide), turn temperature to high, close lid, and let heat for 10 minutes.

4. Set a 17-inch paella pan on grill over hot coals or high heat on a gas grill. Add 2 tablespoons oil; with a wide spatula, spread to coat bottom of pan. When oil is hot, add chicken pieces *(close lid on gas barbecue);* cook, turning once, until lightly browned on both sides, 6 to 12 minutes total.

5. Add tomatoes and stir until most of the juices have evaporated, 1 to 2 minutes. Stir in remaining 1 tablespoon oil, green beans, 1½ teaspoons salt, paprika, and turmeric. Add soaked lima beans and the reserved 2 quarts cooking liquid (if it's cold, heat in a microwave oven or pan until hot before adding). Note level of liquid in pan: Measure distance from pan rim or handle rivets to level of liquid. *(Close lid on gas barbecue.)* Bring to a gentle boil.

6. Boil gently to flavor broth, 25 to 30 minutes *(on gas barbecue, regulate heat as needed to maintain gentle boil).* Remove about 1 cup broth from pan. Add enough water to match original level of liquid, 3 to 5 cups. Taste broth in pan, and season to taste with more salt; also taste reserved broth and season with salt.

7. Pour rice in a band down center of pan (see photo, page 137 top left). Draw a wooden spoon or spatula in a wide zigzag pattern through rice and across pan to distribute rice evenly. Push any grains floating above broth back under. Simmer, without stirring, until rice is tender to bite, 25 to 30 minutes. If rice begins to scorch before it's tender, remove pan from heat and let coals burn down to a lower temperature before continuing. *(On gas barbecue, close lid and regulate heat so liquid simmers briskly in the beginning, then lower heat when most of the liquid has evaporated; rotate pan occasionally so bottom cooks evenly.)* If rice is still firm, drizzle about ½ cup of the reserved broth evenly over the top and cook for a few more minutes; repeat if necessary. (If reserved broth isn't needed, save for another use.)

8. With spoon, push aside a little of the top layer of rice to see if there is a brown crust on the bottom; if one hasn't formed yet, cook a few more minutes *(adjust gas heat as necessary to brown, but not burn, rice).* Remove from heat and let stand for about 5 minutes. Squeeze juice from lemons over rice. Add salt to taste.

Per serving: 859 cal., 37% (315 cal.) from fat; 44 g protein; 35 g fat (8.9 g sat.); 90 g carbo (8.1 g fiber); 793 mg sodium; 151 mg chol.

Garlic Shrimp

PHOTO ON PAGE 128

PREP AND COOK TIME: About 20 minutes

MAKES: 6 to 8 appetizer servings

- 3 tablespoons minced **garlic**
- ⅓ cup **olive oil**
- 1 pound **peeled, deveined shrimp** (26 to 30 per lb.), rinsed
- ⅓ cup **dry sherry** or dry white wine
- 2 tablespoons chopped **parsley**
- ½ teaspoon **hot chili flakes**
  Salt

1. In a 10- to 12-inch frying pan over medium-high heat, stir garlic in olive oil just until it begins to turn gold, 2 to 3 minutes. Add shrimp and stir until almost completely pink, about 2 minutes.

2. Add sherry, parsley, and hot chili flakes and stir often until shrimp are barely opaque but still moist-looking in center of thickest part (cut to test), about 1 minute. Add salt to taste. Pour into a serving dish or individual bowls.

Per serving: 158 cal., 56% (89 cal.) from fat; 12 g protein; 9.9 g fat (1.4 g sat.); 2.3 g carbo (0.1 g fiber); 86 mg sodium; 86 mg chol.

Pan for it

Paella pans—wide, shallow, two-handled affairs—are becoming more widely available in the United States. Use them as you would a large, wide frying pan. Prices start at about $25 for a 15-inch pan and $30 for a 17-inch pan, but they vary widely. Check specialty cookware or import stores or these sources:

The Spanish Table in Berkeley, California, and Seattle: (510) 548-1383, (206) 682-2827, or www.tablespan.com.

Tienda.com in Williamsburg, Virginia: (888) 472-1022 or www.tienda.com.

Simple Seafood and Sausage Paella

PREP AND COOK TIME: About 1 hour

MAKES: About 6 servings

- 12 ounces **linguisa** (Portuguese), firm chorizo, or other cooked **sausages**
- 1 tablespoon **olive oil**
- 1 **onion** (8 oz.), peeled and chopped
- 1 **red bell pepper** (8 oz.), rinsed, stemmed, seeded, and diced (¼ in.)
- 2 tablespoons minced **garlic**
- 2 cups **arborio** or other short-grain white **rice**
- 1 cup **dry white wine**
- 1 quart fat-skimmed **chicken broth**
- ½ teaspoon **paprika**
- ¼ teaspoon **ground dried turmeric**
- ¼ teaspoon **saffron threads,** crumbled
  Salt and **pepper**
- 8 ounces **boned, skinned firm white-fleshed fish,** such as halibut
- 1 pound **shelled, deveined shrimp** (26 to 30 per lb.), tails left on
- 8 ounces **mussels** in shells
- ¼ cup slivered **green onions** (including green tops)
  Lemon wedges

1. In a 15-inch paella pan or 12-inch frying pan (with at least 2¼-in.-tall sides) over high heat, turn sausages occasionally until browned on both sides, 3 to 5 minutes total. With tongs, transfer to a board.

2. Reduce heat to medium-high and add olive oil to pan; when hot, add onion, bell pepper, and garlic and stir often until onion is limp, 4 to 5 minutes. Add rice and stir until it begins to turn opaque, 2 to 3 minutes. Stir in wine, chicken broth, paprika, turmeric, and saffron. Bring to a boil over high heat, then reduce heat and simmer, uncovered, stirring once or twice, until rice is almost tender to bite, 15 to 18 minutes. Add salt and pepper to taste.

3. Meanwhile, rinse and drain fish and shrimp; cut fish into 1-inch pieces. Pull beards off mussels and scrub mussels; discard any gaping ones that don't close when you tap their shells. Cut sausages diagonally into ½-inch-thick slices.

4. Gently stir fish, shrimp, and sausages into rice mixture; arrange mussels on top. Cover pan with foil or lid and cook until rice is tender to bite, fish and shrimp are opaque but still moist-looking in center of thickest part (cut to test), and mussel shells have popped open, 7 to 8 minutes.

5. Sprinkle evenly with green onions. Garnish with lemon wedges. Serve from pan, adding juice from lemon wedges and more salt and pepper to taste.

Per serving: 663 cal., 37% (243 cal.) from fat; 49 g protein; 27 g fat (8.9 g sat.); 53 g carbo (5.2 g fiber); 921 mg sodium; 180 mg chol.

— *Sara Schneider* ◆

A great steak or chop, a savory marinade, and the right heat on the grill yield the perfect summer meal.

FOOD STYLING: BASIL FRIEDMAN

Where there's smoke

Tools and rules to guarantee grilling success

By Linda Lau Anusasananan • Photographs by James Carrier

■ Charcoal grilling is cooking at its most elemental: Put a piece of meat on a hot fire, and you've got a great dinner, not to mention a cool kitchen. But, as anyone who's faced down a paper plate of charred or half-raw meat knows, a little know-how is crucial for a good barbecue. We've uncovered the techniques for building the best fire, the marinades that make for the most flavorful meat, and the cuts of meat that grill best over direct heat.

As you get the fire going, you can marinate the meats fast: Our marinades rely on salt (or salty soy sauce and Worcestershire), sugar or other sweeteners, and acid (vinegar, wine, or citrus juice) to tenderize and carry flavor into protein fibers quickly—no need to plan days ahead for a simple summer barbecue. Just study our master recipe, make the marinades, and stoke the fire, and within an hour you'll look—and, more important, cook—like a natural.

Grilled Marinated Meat

PREP AND COOK TIME: Varies; at least 1 hour, including 30 minutes to marinate.

NOTES: Marinating the meat in a heavy zip-lock bag is efficient, but you can also use a large bowl or baking dish; turn pieces in marinade to coat, then cover and chill, turning pieces occasionally. If the marinade includes a little oil, sticking during grilling is not usually a problem. However, if the meat is very lean or has no marinade, or if your marinade contains a lot of sugar, brush the food or grill lightly with oil to prevent sticking. If you use cuts of meat that are slightly thinner than 1 inch, check for doneness sooner; if meat is thicker—1¼ to 1½ inches—use medium-hot coals (see our heat guide on page 141) and allow a few more minutes for cooking.

MAKES: 4 to 6 servings

1 to 1½ pounds **tender beef steak; pork or lamb chops; boned, skinned chicken pieces; or fish fillets or steaks** (for specific cuts, see page 141), about 1 inch thick

½ to ¾ cup **marinade** (choices follow)

1. Trim and discard excess fat from meat (dripping fat can cause flare-ups). Rinse pieces and pat dry; if necessary, cut into serving-size pieces.

2. Place meat in a heavy zip-lock bag (1-gal. size; see notes). Seal bag and turn to coat pieces in marinade. Chill, turning occasionally, at least 30 minutes or up to 1 day for meats and poultry, 20 to 30 minutes for fish.

3. With tongs, lift pieces from bag and lay on a barbecue grill 4 to 6 inches above a single, solid layer of hot coals or high heat on a heated gas grill (you can hold your hand at grill level only 2 to 3 seconds; see notes); close lid on gas barbecue. Discard marinade.

4. With a wide spatula or tongs, turn pieces over halfway through cooking. (For fish fillets with skin, grill skin side down first; to turn, slip spatula under flesh and flip onto another place on grill. Remove and discard skin.) Cook beef or lamb until done to your liking (cut to test), 8 to 10 minutes total for medium-rare; pork and chicken until no longer pink in center of thickest part (cut to test), 9 to 12 minutes total; or fish until barely opaque but still moist-looking in center of thickest part (cut to test), 9 to 12 minutes total. Transfer meat to a board or platter and let rest 2 to 3 minutes before serving.

Spiced Cider and Maple Marinade

PREP TIME: About 5 minutes

NOTES: This slightly sweet, aromatic marinade is delicious on all kinds of fish and meats, especially pork and chicken. Multiply the recipe for larger batches; cover and chill up to 2 weeks.

MAKES: About ⅔ cup, enough for 1 to 1½ pounds meat, poultry, or fish

In a blender, whirl ⅓ cup **cider vinegar,** 2 tablespoons **maple syrup,** 2 tablespoons chopped **fresh ginger,** 1 tablespoon **Worcestershire,** 1 tablespoon **salad oil,** 1 teaspoon **fennel seeds,** and ¼ teaspoon **ground allspice** until ginger is finely ground.

Lemon-Pepper Marinade

PREP TIME: About 10 minutes

NOTES: This zesty, versatile marinade works well on all kinds of meats but is especially good on fish and poultry. The recipe can be multiplied for larger batches; cover and chill up to 1 week.

MAKES: About ½ cup, enough for 1 to 1½ pounds meat, poultry, or fish

In a small container, mix 1 teaspoon grated **lemon** peel, ¼ cup **lemon juice,** 2 tablespoons **white wine vinegar,** 2 tablespoons **Asian fish sauce** (nuoc mam or nam pla) or soy sauce, 2 tablespoons minced **green onion**, 1 tablespoon **sugar**, 1 tablespoon **olive oil**, 1 teaspoon minced **garlic**, and ¹⁄₂ teaspoon **coarse-ground pepper**.

Soy-Balsamic Marinade

PREP TIME: About 5 minutes

NOTES: This marinade imparts a rich mahogany sheen and spicy bite to red meats and salmon. The recipe can be multiplied for larger batches; cover and chill up to 2 weeks.

MAKES: About ¹⁄₂ cup, enough for 1 to 1¹⁄₂ pounds meat, poultry, or fish

In a small container, mix ¹⁄₄ cup **soy sauce**, 3 tablespoons **balsamic vinegar**, 1 tablespoon **honey**, 1 tablespoon **Asian** (toasted) **sesame oil**, ¹⁄₄ to ¹⁄₂ teaspoon **hot chili flakes**, and 1 clove **garlic**, peeled and minced.

Wine and Herb Marinade

PREP TIME: About 5 minutes

NOTES: If marinating fish, poultry, or pork, use white wine and white wine vinegar; for beef or lamb, use red. The recipe can be multiplied for larger batches; cover and chill up to 1 week.

MAKES: About ²⁄₃ cup, enough for 1 to 1¹⁄₂ pounds meat, poultry, or fish

In a small container, mix ¹⁄₃ cup **dry white** or red **wine** (see notes), 3 tablespoons **white** or red **wine vinegar**, 2 tablespoons minced **shallots**, 1 tablespoon **olive oil**, 1 tablespoon **sugar**, 1 tablespoon minced **garlic**, 1 tablespoon **dry mustard**, 1 teaspoon **dried oregano**, 1 teaspoon **dried basil**, 1 teaspoon **dried marjoram**, ³⁄₄ teaspoon **salt**, and ¹⁄₄ teaspoon **pepper**.

Our four easy marinades add great flavor to meat, fish, or poultry.

The best cuts

Grilling over direct heat works best with tender cuts up to 1 inch thick, trimmed of excess surface fat or very fatty skin. These are our favorites.

• **Beef.** Bone-in or boned steaks from the loin (top loin, tenderloin, T-bone, porterhouse), rib (rib eye, rib), flank and short plate (skirt, flank), and sirloin.

• **Pork.** Bone-in or boned chops or steaks from the loin (blade, rib, loin, top loin, sirloin, sirloin cutlet, tenderloin fillet) and shoulder (blade).

• **Lamb.** Bone-in or boned chops from the loin (top loin, loin), rib, shoulder (blade, arm), and leg (center slice, sirloin, top steak).

• **Chicken.** Boned and skinned or bone-in and skin-on chicken breast halves and thighs.

• **Fish.** Boned fillets, skinned or with skin on, of moderately firm– to firm-fleshed fish (salmon, Pacific halibut, mahimahi).

Charcoal 101

Timing is everything when you work with charcoal. It takes 20 to 30 minutes after the briquets are ignited to reach the hot coals stage. Make sure your food is ready to grill when the coals are. If you wait too long and the coals have cooled, fuel the fire by adding more briquets.

• **To grill by direct heat with charcoal.** Clean out any accumulated ash under the firegrate. Open the bottom dampers if your barbecue has them. On the grate, spread briquets in a single layer at least 2 inches wider than the grill area required for the food; the edges of the briquets should touch to form a solid layer. You'll need 65 to 75 briquets (4¹⁄₂ lb.) to cover a 19-inch firegrate. Mound the briquets in the center and ignite (see below).

When all the briquets are dotted with ash, in 15 to 25 minutes, spread into a single solid layer. Set the grill in place. Let the briquets burn down to desired temperature (see "How hot is hot?").

Light your fire

Compressed charcoal briquets, with rounded rectangular edges, don't catch on fire easily. But tools or starters help ignite briquets quickly. Don't expect flames, though—they'll just be dotted or coated with gray ash. These are our favorite ways to get the coals lit.

• **Fire chimney.** Set this metal cylinder with a handle on the firegrate of the barbecue. Stuff a few wadded sheets of newspaper in the base under the chimney (directly on the firegrate), then fill the chimney with briquets. Light the newspaper with a match. The draft of the chimney draws the flames up to the briquets long enough to get them started. When the briquets are spotted with gray ash, in 15 to 25 minutes, lift the chimney off or tip it and pour the hot coals onto the firegrate.

• **Electric starter.** You'll need an electric outlet near your grill or an extension cord to reach the nearest outlet. Set the heating element of an electric starter on a few briquets on the firegrate, then mound remaining briquets on top. Plug in the starter and wait until about half of the briquets are dotted with gray, 10 to 15 minutes. Remove starter and mound unlit briquets on those with gray spots.

• **Solid fire starters.** Made from environmentally friendly compounds such as sawdust, wood chips, newsprint, and paraffin, solid fire starters are safe, portable, and easy to ignite. They come in different shapes; one is even designed to light like a match when struck. Follow directions on package.

How hot is hot?

To determine the temperature of your barbecue—for both charcoal and gas—place your hand, palm down, at grill level, and time how long you can hold it there comfortably. No second hand on your watch? Just count: one-thousand-one, one-thousand-two, one-thousand-three….

• **Hot.** You can hold your hand at grill level only 2 to 3 seconds; the charcoal is barely covered with gray ash and may have some low flames.

• **Medium-hot.** You can hold your hand at grill level only 3 to 4 seconds.

• **Medium.** You can hold your hand at grill level only 4 to 5 seconds; the charcoal is ash-covered and may have a red glow.

• **Medium-low.** You can hold your hand at grill level only 5 to 6 seconds.

• **Low.** You can hold your hand at grill level only 6 to 7 seconds; the charcoal is covered with a thick layer of gray ash. ◆

Stir fresh pesto into a simple risotto for intense basil flavor.

Basil summer

Guess who's coming to dinner—and lunch? Versatile basil adds a delicious bite to both meals

By Lisl Hampton • Photographs by James Carrier

■ There's a saying among gardeners that if you curse basil when planting it, you'll get bunch after bunch of the delicious, sweet herb. And it must work: My garden is a pungent sea of green. When I think about summer, I'm not plotting an exotic vacation; I'm planning what I'm going to eat—specifically, what I'm going to do with all that basil.

It's pretty straightforward, really. Basil's best friend is the tomato. I use them together in every way possible—in salads, bruschetta, sauces, or as a plain pair. Basil also goes into some of my favorite dishes: pesto (see year-round strategy below), risotto, shrimp scampi, potato pancakes, and icy lemon granita—an exotic touch to make up for that vacation I won't be taking.

Even if you don't have basil plants burgeoning in your backyard, the aromatic bouquets available in practically every farmers' market and grocery store, and the recipes here, are reason enough to make this a basil summer.

Preserving pesto

An all-time favorite home for basil is in pesto. Those in the know make up a large batch and freeze it in ice cube trays. When it's firm, you can pop out the cubes and store them in heavy zip-lock plastic bags. They'll melt into a summery sauce months after your shorts have gone into storage.

Basil Risotto

PREP AND COOK TIME: **About 50 minutes**

NOTES: Roasted red peppers are wonderful with this dish; serve them whole, on the side, or minced, on top.

MAKES: **6 servings**

About 6½ cups fat-skimmed **reduced-sodium chicken broth**

1   cup lightly packed **fresh basil** leaves

2   cloves **garlic**, peeled

1   tablespoon **olive oil**

1   cup **shredded parmesan cheese**

3   tablespoons **butter**

3   **shallots** (about 2½ oz. total), peeled and finely chopped

1½ cups **arborio** or other short- or medium-grain white **rice**

¾   cup **dry white wine**

1. In a 2- to 3-quart pan over high heat, bring 6½ cups broth to a simmer; cover and reduce heat to maintain simmer.

2. Meanwhile, in a food processor, whirl basil, garlic, and 1 teaspoon olive oil until coarsely chopped. Add cheese and whirl until finely ground.

3. Add remaining 2 teaspoons oil and the butter to a 5- to 6-quart pan over medium-high heat; when hot (mixture will be foamy), add shallots and stir often until limp, 1 to 2 minutes. Add rice and stir often until beginning to turn opaque, 1 to 2 minutes.

4. Add wine and stir until absorbed, about 1 minute. Add 6 cups broth, 1 cup at a time, stirring after each addition until almost absorbed, 25 to 30 minutes total. Stir in basil mixture and cook, stirring often, until rice is barely tender to bite and mixture is creamy, about 2 minutes longer. If risotto is thicker than desired, stir in a little more broth.

5. Ladle risotto into wide, shallow bowls, and serve immediately.

Per serving: 316 cal., 37% (117 cal.) from fat; 13 g protein; 13 g fat (6.4 g sat.); 38 g carbo (4.5 g fiber); 932 mg sodium; 26 mg chol.

Basil Shrimp Scampi

PREP AND COOK TIME: **About 40 minutes**

NOTES: To sliver the basil, stack about six leaves at a time; starting at tip ends, roll up tightly, then thinly slice rolls crosswise. If desired, serve scampi with grated parmesan cheese to add to taste.

MAKES: **4 servings**

1 pound **dried linguine**

¼ cup (⅛ lb.) **butter**

2 tablespoons **olive oil**

1½ pounds **shrimp** (35 to 40 per lb.), peeled (tails left on), deveined, and rinsed

2 tablespoons minced **garlic**

¾ teaspoon **hot chili flakes**

¼ teaspoon fresh-ground **pepper**

About ¼ teaspoon **salt**

1 cup **dry white wine**

2 cups lightly packed **fresh basil** leaves, slivered (see notes)

1. In a 6- to 8-quart pan over high heat, bring about 4 quarts water to a boil; add linguine and cook, stirring occasionally, just until tender to bite, 6 to 8 minutes. Drain pasta, reserving about ⅓ cup cooking liquid; return pasta to pan.

2. Meanwhile, in a 10- to 12-inch frying pan over medium-high heat, melt butter with olive oil. Add shrimp, garlic, chili flakes, pepper, and ¼ teaspoon salt; stir for 2 minutes. Add wine; stir often until shrimp are opaque but still moist-looking in center of thickest part (cut to test), 3 to 4 minutes longer. Stir in basil.

3. Pour shrimp mixture into pan with cooked pasta; mix gently. If mixture is too dry, add reserved pasta-cooking liquid. Divide evenly among four wide, shallow bowls. Add salt to taste.

Per serving: 795 cal., 26% (207 cal.) from fat; 45 g protein; 23 g fat (8.8 g sat.); 91 g carbo (5.4 g fiber); 479 mg sodium; 242 mg chol.

Savory Summer Pancakes

PREP AND COOK TIME: **40 minutes**

NOTES: Instead of sour cream, serve the pancakes with a mixture of ¼ cup rice vinegar and 2 tablespoons soy sauce.

MAKES: 12 pancakes (2 inch); 4 to 6 servings

1 **large egg**

½ teaspoon **salt**

¼ teaspoon **pepper**

2 **zucchini** (about 6 oz. total), rinsed and ends trimmed

1 **carrot** (3 oz.), peeled

1 **russet potato** (8 oz.), peeled

½ cup plus 2 tablespoons chopped **fresh basil** leaves

1 tablespoon **all-purpose flour**

About 3 tablespoons **olive oil**

About ½ cup **sour cream**

1. In a large bowl, beat egg, salt, and pepper to blend. Using a food processor or the large holes on a hand

A new twist: Basil balances the tart lemon flavors in this refreshing granita.

grater, coarsely shred zucchini, carrot, and potato. Add shredded vegetables, ½ cup basil, and flour to egg mixture; stir just to combine.

2. Pour 1 tablespoon oil into a 10- to 12-inch nonstick frying pan over medium-high heat; when hot, drop batter in ¼-cup portions into pan, three or four at a time, and flatten with bottom of measuring cup or the back of a spoon into about 3½-inch rounds. Cook, turning as needed, until browned and crisp on both sides, 6 to 8 minutes total. Transfer pancakes as cooked to an ovenproof platter and keep warm in a 200° oven. Repeat to cook remaining pancakes, adding more oil to pan as necessary.

3. In a small bowl, mix sour cream with remaining 2 tablespoons basil. Serve pancakes warm, topped with sour cream mixture (see notes).

Per serving: 152 cal., 71% (108 cal.) from fat; 3 g protein; 12 g fat (3.7 g sat.); 9.5 g carbo (1.4 g fiber); 221 mg sodium; 44 mg chol.

Basil-Lemon Granita

PREP TIME: **20 minutes, plus about 6 hours to freeze**

NOTES: Lemon basil makes a nice alter-

native to regular basil in this granita. You can make the granita (through step 3) up to 1 week ahead; freeze airtight.

MAKES: About 3 cups; 6 servings

4 to 5 **lemons** (1⅓ lb. total), rinsed

⅔ cup **sugar**

⅓ cup minced **fresh basil** leaves (see notes)

1. Grate 1 tablespoon peel (yellow part only) from about three lemons. Ream juice from enough lemons to make ¾ cup. In an 8- or 9-inch square baking pan, mix peel, juice, and 1½ cups water.

2. In a food processor or blender, whirl sugar until very fine. Add basil and whirl until very finely minced. Stir sugar mixture into lemon mixture until sugar is dissolved.

3. Cover and freeze mixture until firm, about 6 hours.

4. Scrape the tines of a fork quickly across frozen mixture to break into fluffy granules. Scoop granita into chilled bowls or wine or sherbet glasses and serve immediately.

Per serving: 96 cal., 0% (0 cal.) from fat; 0.2 g protein; 0 g fat; 25 g carbo (0.4 g fiber); 0.8 mg sodium; 0 mg chol. ◆

Cherry tomatoes rival corn for sweetness in this bright salad.

FOOD STYLING: BASIL FRIEDMAN

King corn

Celebrate the sweet kernel of summer

By Charity Ferreira • Photographs by James Carrier

■ Corn—enshrined in childhood memories of nibbling rows of kernels from the cob, typewriter-fashion—is surely one of the most eagerly anticipated tastes of summer.

In Olathe, Colorado, where the population more than doubles on the day of the Olathe Sweet Corn Festival (August 3 this year), revelers come in droves to celebrate the town's eponymous variety of corn. It's a blowout affair that includes an unlimited number of roasted ears for every participant.

With its mellow nature, fresh corn is equally at home in a spicy grilled salsa, such as the one at right from a festival goer, or our Asian-inspired chowder (see page 145). So even if you're celebrating corn season on a smaller-than-Olathe scale, you will find recipes here to help you pay homage to a very sweet vegetable.

Cutting kernels

An average ear of corn weighs from 10 to 14 ounces and yields about 1 cup of kernels. To remove them, with a large, sharp knife, cut off and discard the stem end of each ear down to the beginning of the kernels. Pull off and discard the husks and silks; rinse ears. Holding each ear upright, shear off the kernels close to the cob.

Corn and Tomato Salad

NOTES: You can make this salad (through step 2) up to 4 hours ahead; cover and chill. Bring to room temperature to serve. Sprinkle with cheese just before serving.

PREP AND COOK TIME: About 30 minutes

MAKES: 4 to 6 servings

- ½ cup chopped **red onion**
- 1 tablespoon **olive oil**
- 4 cups **fresh corn** kernels (see "Cutting kernels," below left)
- 2 cups **cherry tomatoes** such as Sweet 100s (about 10 oz.), rinsed, stemmed, and halved if larger than ¾ inch
- ¼ cup slivered **fresh basil** leaves
- 3 tablespoons **sherry vinegar** or red wine vinegar
  Salt and **pepper**
- 2 ounces **fresh chèvre** (goat) **cheese**, crumbled

1. In a 10- to 12-inch frying pan over medium-high heat, stir onion in olive oil until limp, 5 to 7 minutes. Add corn and stir often just until tender to bite, 5 to 6 minutes.

2. Pour mixture into a wide serving bowl and stir in tomatoes, basil, and vinegar. Add salt and pepper to taste.

3. Sprinkle goat cheese over salad; serve warm or at room temperature.

Per serving: 159 cal., 37% (59 cal.) from fat; 6 g protein; 6.5 g fat (2.5 g sat.); 24 g carbo (4.2 g fiber); 70 mg sodium; 7.5 mg chol.

Grilled-Corn Salsa

PREP AND COOK TIME: About 55 minutes

NOTES: This salsa, created by Susan Woody, of Montrose, Colorado, is from the Olathe festival cookbook. Besides tasting great with chips, it's perfect alongside barbecued burgers, ribs, or other meats.

MAKES: 7 cups

- 4 ears **fresh corn** (about 1¾ lb. total), husked, silks removed
- 1 **onion** (8 oz.), peeled and cut crosswise into ½-inch-thick slices
- 1 **red bell pepper** (8 oz.), rinsed, stemmed, seeded, and halved
- 6 ounces **fresh jalapeño chilies** (about 8), rinsed, stemmed, seeded, and halved
  About 1 tablespoon **olive oil**
- 2 **firm-ripe tomatoes** (about 1 lb. total), rinsed, cored, and chopped
- 2 cloves **garlic**, peeled and minced
- ¼ cup chopped **fresh cilantro**

¼ cup **lime juice**

½ teaspoon **ground cumin**
 Salt

1. Rub corn, onion, bell pepper, and jalapeños lightly all over with olive oil. Place on a barbecue grill over a solid bed of hot coals or high heat on a gas grill (you can hold your hand at grill level only 2 to 3 seconds); close lid on gas grill. Cook, turning corn occasionally and other vegetables once, until slightly charred all over, about 5 minutes total for jalapeños, 8 to 10 minutes for other vegetables. Remove to a board as done; let cool. Cut corn kernels from cobs (see page 144), chop onion and bell pepper, and mince jalapeños.

2. Meanwhile, in a bowl, combine tomatoes, garlic, cilantro, lime juice, and cumin. Stir in grilled vegetables and add salt to taste.

Per ¼ cup: 23 cal., 27% (6.3 cal.) from fat; 0.7 g protein; 0.7 g fat (0.1 g sat.); 4.3 g carbo (0.8 g fiber); 4 mg sodium; 0 mg chol.

Pasta Shells with Corn and Bacon

PREP AND COOK TIME: **About 35 minutes**

MAKES: **6 servings**

 1 pound **dried pasta shells** (about 1 in. long)

 4 ounces **bacon,** chopped

 About 2 tablespoons **butter**

 ½ cup minced **shallots**

 4 cups **fresh corn** kernels (see page 144)

 1 cup **dry white wine**

 ½ cup **whipping cream**

 ¼ cup chopped **fresh tarragon**

1. In a 6- to 8-quart pan over high heat, bring about 4 quarts water to a boil; add shells and cook, stirring occasionally, until barely tender to bite, 8 to 10 minutes.

2. Meanwhile, in a 10- to 12-inch nonstick frying pan over medium-high heat, stir bacon until browned, 4 to 5 minutes. With a slotted spoon, transfer bacon to paper towels to drain.

3. Add enough butter to pan to equal about 3 tablespoons fat; when melted, add shallots and stir until limp, 3 to 5 minutes. Add corn, wine, and cream; boil, stirring often, for 5 minutes.

4. Drain shells and return to pan. Stir in corn mixture, bacon, and tarragon. Pour into a wide serving bowl.

Per serving: 605 cal., 34% (207 cal.) from fat; 16 g protein; 23 g fat (11 g sat.); 80 g carbo (5.2 g fiber); 200 mg sodium; 45 mg chol.

Bacon and corn make a smoky-sweet team in this creamy pasta dish.

FOOD STYLING: BASIL FRIEDMAN

Coconut Corn Chowder

PREP AND COOK TIME: **35 to 40 minutes**

NOTES: Stir the coconut milk before measuring. To sliver basil, stack leaves; starting at tip end, roll up, then thinly slice rolls crosswise.

MAKES: **About 7 cups; about 4 servings**

 1 **red onion** (8 oz.), peeled and chopped

 1 tablespoon **olive oil**

 5 cups **fresh corn** kernels (see page 144)

 2 cups **milk**

 1 cup **canned coconut milk** (see notes)

 ½ cup fat-skimmed **chicken broth** or water

 1 **fresh serrano chili**, rinsed, stemmed, seeded, and minced

 2 tablespoons **lime juice**

 5 **fresh basil** leaves, slivered (see notes)

 Salt and **pepper**

 Lime wedges

1. In a 4- to 5-quart pan over medium-high heat, stir onion in olive oil until limp, 3 to 5 minutes.

2. Stir in corn, milk, coconut milk, broth, and chili; bring to a simmer, reduce heat, and cook, stirring occasionally, until corn is tender to bite, 10 to 15 minutes.

3. With a slotted spoon, remove about 2 cups corn kernels from pan and reserve. In a blender or food processor, working in batches and holding down lid with a towel, whirl remaining corn mixture until smooth. Return to pan.

4. Add lime juice, basil, and reserved corn. Stir soup over medium heat until hot, 2 to 3 minutes. Add salt and pepper to taste. Ladle into bowls and garnish with lime wedges.

Per serving: 409 cal., 48% (198 cal.) from fat; 13 g protein; 22 g fat (14 g sat.); 49 g carbo (7.1 g fiber); 113 mg sodium; 17 mg chol. ◆

A crisp filo wrapping makes warm, savory brie seem like a present.

FOOD STYLING: BASIL FRIEDMAN

A Feast at Starvation Peak

Filo-wrapped Brie*

Creamy Tomato and Roasted Pepper Soup*

Shrimp Salad with Ceviche Dressing*

Hogue Cellars Fumé Blanc

Car Dogs' Sweet Cured and Smoked Salmon*

Rice Pilaf • Green Beans

Henry Estate Pinot Noir or Fetzer Sundial Chardonnay

Blackberry Meringues*

*Recipe provided

Sample the bounty

An alfresco party showcases Northwest flavors

By Linda Lau Anusasananan • Photographs by James Carrier

■ No one goes hungry at Joan and George Cathey's parties, even though their home—a 100-acre ranch, farm, and vineyard in southwest Washington—is named Starvation Peak. Every summer, with their friends Mike and Judy Williams, the Catheys host a down-home bash, dubbed Taste of the Hill, for about 120 friends. Guests wander among appetizer, salad, soup, main-dish, and dessert stations, sampling the bounty, then head over to the bar to fill their glasses with the house wine.

The party is packed with the flavors of the season and the region, from succulent cured salmon to sweet, dead-ripe blackberries. To pull their lavish spread together, the Catheys and their crew of relatives and friends start cooking weeks in advance. We adapted a smaller menu that serves eight and figured out some do-ahead possibilities (see "Countdown," page 148). Call it a taste of the Taste of the Hill or just a relaxed get-together for a few good friends: Either way, it's a delicious meal for a warm summer evening.

Filo-wrapped Brie

PREP AND COOK TIME: 30 to 40 minutes

NOTES: Thaw frozen filo dough in the refrigerator for at least 8 hours. You can prepare cheese through step 5 up to 1 day ahead; cover and chill. Serve with thin baguette slices or crackers.

MAKES: 8 servings

¼ cup **pine nuts**

¼ cup **oil-packed dried tomatoes,** drained, with 1 tablespoon oil reserved

2 tablespoons melted **butter**

4 sheets (12 by 18 in.) **filo dough,** thawed if frozen (see notes)

¼ cup chopped **fresh basil** leaves

1 round (8 oz.) **firm-ripe brie cheese**

1. Place nuts in a 9-inch pie pan and bake in a 350° regular or convection oven until golden, 5 to 7 minutes.

2. Meanwhile, chop tomatoes. In a small bowl, mix oil and butter.

3. Cut filo sheets into 12-inch squares. One at a time, brush squares lightly with butter mixture and stack.

4. Spread chopped tomatoes, basil, and toasted nuts in center of filo stack in a round that matches the size of the cheese. Place cheese on top of tomato mixture. Fold corners of filo stack, one at a time, over cheese and brush lightly with butter mixture. Press filo against cheese to make a smooth package.

5. Place wrapped cheese, smooth side up, in 9-inch pie pan. Brush top of filo with remaining butter mixture.

6. Bake in a 350° regular or convection oven until filo is golden, 25 to 30 minutes. Cool about 10 minutes.

7. With a wide spatula, transfer filo-wrapped brie to a plate. To serve, cut a big X in center or cut off a corner so guests can scoop out cheese mixture.

Per serving: 205 cal., 70% (144 cal.) from fat; 8.2 g protein; 16 g fat (2.4 g sat.); 7.8 g carbo (1.1 g fiber); 284 mg sodium; 36 mg chol.

Creamy Tomato and Roasted Pepper Soup

PREP AND COOK TIME: **About 40 minutes**

MAKES: **8 servings**

- 2 tablespoons **butter**
- 2 tablespoons **all-purpose flour**
- 1 can (11.5 oz.) **tomato juice**
- 1 cup **whipping cream**
- 42 ounces (one 28-oz. can and one 14-oz. can) **canned diced tomatoes**
- 1 cup drained **canned roasted red peppers,** chopped
- 1 clove **garlic,** peeled and pressed
- 1 teaspoon **sugar**
- 1 teaspoon **dried tarragon**
- 1/8 teaspoon **cayenne**
  Salt and **pepper**
- 1/2 cup **sour cream**
- 1 **firm-ripe tomato** (6 oz.), rinsed, cored, and finely chopped
- 2 tablespoons chopped **parsley**

1. In a 3- to 4-quart pan over medium heat, melt butter. Add flour and stir for about 30 seconds. Whisk in tomato juice and cream until smooth.

2. Add canned tomatoes (including juice), roasted peppers, garlic, sugar, tarragon, and cayenne. Stir often until soup just begins to simmer, about 10 minutes. Add salt and pepper to taste.

3. Ladle into bowls. Garnish each with a spoonful of sour cream, chopped fresh tomato, and parsley.

Per serving: 202 cal., 71% (144 cal.) from fat; 3.3 g protein; 16 g fat (9.5 g sat.); 15 g carbo (1.9 g fiber); 483 mg sodium; 47 mg chol.

Shrimp Salad with Ceviche Dressing

PREP AND COOK TIME: **About 30 minutes, plus 20 minutes to cool**

NOTES: You can prepare the shrimp mixture (step 1) up to 4 hours ahead; when cool, cover and chill.

MAKES: **8 servings**

- 1/2 teaspoon **cumin seeds**
- 3 tablespoons **olive oil**
- 3 cloves **garlic,** peeled and pressed
- 1 cup chopped **onion**

The smoky, slightly sweet richness of Car Dogs' salmon pairs well with Chardonnay.

- 1 cup chopped **red bell pepper**
- 1 cup **fresh** or thawed frozen **corn** kernels
- 1 tablespoon minced **fresh jalapeño chili**
- 1/2 cup **lime juice**
- 1/4 cup **lemon juice**
- 3/4 pound **peeled, deveined cooked shrimp** (41 to 50 per lb.), thawed if frozen
- 1 cup diced (1/2 in.) **firm-ripe tomato**
- 1/4 cup chopped **cilantro**
- 4 quarts **salad mix** (8 oz.), rinsed and crisped
  Salt and **pepper**

1. In a 10- to 12-inch frying pan over medium-high heat, stir cumin seeds until fragrant, about 1 minute. Add oil, garlic, onion, and bell pepper; stir often until onion is limp, about 3 minutes. Add corn, jalapeño, lime juice, and lemon juice; bring to a boil. Remove from heat; stir in shrimp. Chill, stirring occasionally, until cool, 15 to 20 minutes.

2. Stir in tomato and cilantro.

3. Place salad greens in a large bowl. Spoon shrimp mixture over greens; mix to serve. Add salt and pepper to taste.

Per serving: 134 cal., 40% (53 cal.) from fat; 11 g protein; 5.9 g fat (0.8 g sat.); 11 g carbo (1.8 g fiber); 112 mg sodium; 83 mg chol.

Car Dogs' Sweet Cured and Smoked Salmon

PREP AND COOK TIME: **About 1 hour, plus about 3 hours to cure**

NOTES: Joan Cathey's sister, Marcia Tabery, and Tabery's partner, Jack Rogers, own a catering company called Car Dogs; they contribute their lightly smoked salmon to the festivities.

MAKES: **8 servings**

- 1 cup **salt**
- 1 cup plus 2 tablespoons firmly packed **light brown sugar**
- 3 1/2 tablespoons **garlic powder**
- 3 1/2 tablespoons **onion powder**
- 3 1/2 teaspoons **dried savory**
- 2 1/2 teaspoons **dried tarragon**
- 1 tablespoon **dried dill weed**
- 1 **whole salmon fillet** (3 lb.)
- 1 cup **alder,** apple, or mesquite **wood chips**

1. In a bowl, mix salt, 1 cup brown sugar, 3 tablespoons garlic powder, 3 tablespoons onion powder, 1 tablespoon savory, 2 teaspoons dried tarragon, and all of the dill weed.

2. Rinse salmon and pat dry. Set salmon, skin down, in an 11- by 17-

inch roasting pan lined with plastic wrap. Spread salt mixture evenly over flesh of salmon. Cover and chill 3 hours.

3. Rinse fish under cool water and pat dry. Set fillet, skin down, on a large sheet of foil; cut foil to fit outline of fish. Let fish stand until flesh is tacky to touch, 20 to 30 minutes.

4. Meanwhile, in a small bowl, mix remaining 2 tablespoons brown sugar, remaining 1½ teaspoons *each* garlic powder and onion powder and remaining ½ teaspoon *each* savory and tarragon.

5. *If using charcoal,* mound 50 briquets on the firegrate of a barbecue with a lid and ignite; *if using a gas grill,* turn heat to high and close lid. Pour enough warm water over wood chips in a bowl to make them float; let soak at least 15 minutes.

6. When coals are dotted with gray ash, in about 20 minutes, push half to each side of firegrate. Drain wood chips and scatter half on each mound of coals. If using a gas grill, adjust for indirect heat; put drained chips in a foil pan and set directly on heat.

7. Cover barbecue and heat until chips start to smolder, about 10 minutes. Set grill 4 to 6 inches above the firegrate.

8. Place salmon on foil in center of grill (not directly over heat). Sprinkle sugar mixture evenly over fish.

9. Cover barbecue and cook salmon until a thermometer inserted in center of thickest part reaches 140°, 20 to 25 minutes.

10. Using two wide spatulas, slide fillet with foil onto a rimless baking sheet, then transfer from sheet to a platter. Tuck edges of foil under fillet. Serve hot or cool.

Per serving: 310 cal., 49% (153 cal.) from fat; 31 g protein; 17 g fat (3.4 g sat.); 6.1 g carbo (0 g fiber); 531 mg sodium; 92 mg chol.

Blackberry Meringues

PREP AND COOK TIME: About 1½ hours, plus at least 2 hours to cool

NOTES: If using frozen berries, thaw in a colander over a bowl for about 1½ hours. In step 5, stir the cornstarch mixture into the berry juice to thicken, then fold in thawed berries. You can make meringues up to 1 day ahead

(steps 1 through 4); cool completely and store airtight. You can prepare berry mixture (step 5) up to 4 hours ahead; cover and chill.

MAKES: 8 servings

- 4 **large egg** whites (½ cup)
- ½ teaspoon **cream of tartar**
  About 1⅓ cups **sugar**
- 6 cups **fresh** or frozen **blackberries** (see notes)
- 2 teaspoons **cornstarch**
- 1 cup **whipping cream**
  Fresh mint sprigs

1. Line two 14- by 17-inch baking sheets with cooking parchment or buttered and floured foil. Draw eight 4-inch circles on the parchment, spaced at least 3 inches apart.

2. In a bowl, with a mixer on high speed, beat egg whites with cream of tartar until foamy. Gradually add 1 cup sugar, beating until stiff peaks form.

3. Mound mixture equally on circles and form a slight depression in the center of each with the back of a spoon, or spoon the meringue into a pastry bag fitted with a ½-inch-diameter plain or star tip and pipe mixture to fill in circles completely.

4. Bake in a 250° oven (or 225° convection oven) until meringues begin to turn pale gold and feel firm to

COUNTDOWN

- ☐ **Up to 1 day ahead:** Prepare brie appetizer. Bake meringues.
- ☐ **Up to 4 hours ahead:** Cure salmon. Make shrimp mixture for salad. Make berry mixture.
- ☐ **1 hour ahead:** Rinse salmon and place on foil. Bake appetizer.
- ☐ **50 minutes ahead:** Prepare sugar mixture for fish. Soak wood chips. Ignite charcoal or turn on gas grill.
- ☐ **40 minutes ahead:** Make soup.
- ☐ **35 minutes ahead:** Set wood chips on gas grill. Cook rice.
- ☐ **25 minutes ahead:** Cook salmon.
- ☐ **10 minutes ahead:** Cook green beans.
- ☐ **Just before serving:** Assemble salad.
- ☐ **Just before serving dessert:** Whip cream and assemble meringues.

touch, about 1¼ hours (1½ hours in convection oven); switch pan positions halfway through baking. Turn oven off and leave meringues in oven until cool, 2 to 2½ hours.

5. Meanwhile, in a 2- to 3-quart pan, mash 1 cup berries. Mix cornstarch and ⅓ cup sugar; stir into mashed berries. Stir berry mixture over high heat until boiling. Remove from heat and let stand, stirring occasionally, until cool to touch, 5 to 10 minutes. Fold in remaining 5 cups berries. Taste, and add more sugar if desired.

6. Just before serving, in another bowl with a mixer on high speed, beat cream until soft peaks form. Add sugar to taste and beat until blended.

7. Set meringues on plates. Top equally with berry mixture and whipped cream. Garnish with mint.

Per serving: 283 cal., 31% (87 cal.) from fat; 3.2 g protein; 9.7 g fat (5.8 g sat.); 49 g carbo (4.9 g fiber); 38 mg sodium; 33 mg chol. ◆

Juicy blackberries and soft whipped cream contrast deliciously with crunchy, featherlight meringues.

Epicurean tuna

By Jerry Anne Di Vecchio

The first time I had lunch with James Beard in New York, he took me to his favorite place—very French and very fine—the latter quality no doubt influenced by the regular presence of this culinary giant in the restaurant.

Where we ate the second time, however, became *my* favorite place. Delayed by errands, I missed our meeting time and arrived at his home on West 12th Street just as lunch preparations were underway. Ever hospitable, James invited me to stay, put me to work, and threw an impromptu lesson into the conversation.

His first tip: Keep a well-stocked pantry, including humble goods. Among the boxes and bags of cereals, flours, and sugars; tins of tomatoes; and bottles of vinegars and oils was a stack of canned tuna—large, firm chunks.

His second tip: A well-stocked refrigerator includes a generous selection of long-lasting condiments. His own sheltered a dizzying trove of staples—mayonnaise, mustards, olives, and capers, not to mention pickled this and pickled that, tubes of pastes (anchovy, tomato, chestnut, and perhaps even some fish roe), all kinds of jams and jellies, as well as a multitude of interesting-looking little pots and jars whose contents I couldn't readily identify.

Tuna salad can be garnished with tomatoes and olives or grapes and almonds.

These stores made it a cinch to expand his original plan for simple tuna sandwiches into a more elaborate salad. A recent trip to the market provided celery for the crunch he preferred, hard-cooked eggs to add another nourishing layer, crisp lettuce leaves, and a few cherry tomatoes. There was coarse, country-style bread to slice thickly, toast, and butter. And a cool, dry white wine to uncork. Dessert? It was a creamy tapioca pudding he'd been testing that morning. What started as a snack in the kitchen became a feast in the garden (the house dog—a pug, as I recall—scouted hopefully for stray tidbits as we carted our meal outside).

So what did I really learn that day? Utter simplicity does not make a dish less interesting; it's the setting and company you keep that flavor meal memories most richly. Our lunch at that swanky French restaurant was elegant, but in my mind, tuna salad with James Beard in his own garden paints a sweeter image.

Garden Tuna Salad

PREP AND COOK TIME: About 25 minutes

NOTES: As an alternative, omit the tomatoes and olives and mix about ¾ cup rinsed and drained green seedless grapes with the tuna salad; garnish with more grapes and sprinkle with chopped salted almonds.

MAKES: 4 servings

2 cans (6 oz. each) **oil-** or **water-packed albacore** or chunk-style **tuna,** drained well

4 hard-cooked **large eggs,** shelled

1 cup finely chopped inner **celery** stalks, tender leaves reserved

¼ cup drained **capers**

3 tablespoons finely chopped **red onion** or shallots

About ¾ cup **mayonnaise** (regular, or half reduced-fat and half sour cream)

About ½ teaspoon fresh-ground **pepper**

Salt

About 4 cups inner **romaine** or butter **lettuce** leaves, rinsed and crisped

1 to 2 tablespoons minced **parsley**

Paprika (optional)

About 1 cup **small cherry tomatoes,** stemmed, rinsed, and drained (see notes)

About ½ cup drained **niçoise** or black ripe **olives** (see notes)

1 **lemon,** rinsed and cut into 8 wedges

1. Put tuna in a bowl. Coarsely chop 2 eggs; add to tuna. Cut remaining eggs in half lengthwise and set aside.

2. Add celery, capers, and onion to bowl; mix well with a fork, breaking tuna into small pieces. Add ¾ cup mayonnaise and ½ teaspoon pepper and mix. Add more mayonnaise, if desired. Season to taste with salt (be cautious—capers are salty).

3. Arrange lettuce and celery leaves equally in four wide, shallow bowls. Mound tuna salad on greens, sprinkle with parsley, and dust with paprika if desired. Set an egg half alongside each salad and garnish with tomatoes, olives, and lemon wedges. Season salads to taste with juice from wedges and more salt and pepper.

Per serving: 611 cal., 75% (459 cal.) from fat; 31 g protein; 51 g fat (8.4 g sat.); 8.3 g carbo (3.1 g fiber); 1,240 mg sodium; 262 mg chol. ◆

Cream rises to the top

Local producers bring crème fraîche—French-style sour cream—to the market

■ Crème fraîche seems ubiquitous in restaurants these days: dolloped on berries, swirled into soups, and even whisked into salad dressings. Until recently, crème fraîche was available only in pricey little cartons imported from France. Now, several California companies are making high-quality crème fraîche, and it's turning up in more grocers' cases.

What's all the fuss about? Slightly misnamed, crème fraîche is not in fact fresh but rather cultured, like sour cream. It's silky smooth and, because of its higher fat content, doesn't break or curdle when heated, making it a perfect base for sauces. Its gentle tang also complements sweets beautifully; use it instead of cream in dark chocolate ganache or whip it and spoon it over cake. Crème fraîche is best displayed simply, as in this rich but refreshing cucumber soup.

— *Kate Washington*

Chilled soup is flavored with vegetables cooked well ahead of time.

Creamy Cucumber Soup

PREP AND COOK TIME: About 45 minutes, plus at least 2 hours to chill

NOTES: This elegant soup comes from chef Kurt Alldredge of the Vintage Room at Fess Parker's Wine Country Inn & Spa in Los Olivos, California.

MAKES: 4 first-course servings

About 2½ cups fat-skimmed **chicken broth** or vegetable broth

1 pound **White Rose** or Yukon Gold **potatoes,** peeled and cut into 1-inch chunks

1 cup thinly sliced **onion** (4 oz.)

1 cup thickly sliced **celery** (about 2 stalks; 5 oz.)

¼ cup coarsely chopped **parsley**

1 **green onion,** rinsed, ends trimmed, coarsely chopped

½ teaspoon **fresh thyme** leaves or 1 teaspoon dried thyme

1 tablespoon **butter**

1 **English cucumber** (about 12 oz.), rinsed, or regular cucumber, peeled and seeded

About ¾ cup **crème fraîche** or sour cream

About ½ teaspoon **salt**

About ⅛ teaspoon **hot sauce**

1. Combine 2½ cups broth, potatoes, onion, celery, parsley, green onion, thyme, and butter in a 5- to 6-quart pan; cover and bring to a boil over high heat, stirring occasionally. Reduce heat and simmer, stirring occasionally, until potatoes mash easily with a fork, 20 to 25 minutes.

Remove from heat and let cool to room temperature, about 1 hour.

2. Meanwhile, thinly slice a fourth of the cucumber; wrap airtight and chill. Coarsely chop remaining.

3. Working in batches, whirl potato mixture and chopped cucumber in a blender until smooth; pour into a large bowl. Stir in ¾ cup crème fraîche, ½ teaspoon salt, and ⅛ teaspoon hot sauce. Cover and chill until cold, at least 1 hour, or up to 1 day.

4. Thin soup with more broth. If desired, add more salt and hot sauce to taste. Ladle into bowls and garnish with sliced cucumber and more crème fraîche.

Per serving: 322 cal., 56% (180 cal.) from fat; 10 g protein; 20 g fat (12 g sat.); 26 g carbo (3.9 g fiber); 440 mg sodium; 45 mg chol.

— *Sara Schneider*

Put a good spin on it

■ Herbs have a water problem: Thyme sprigs need a bath before you season your sauce with them, but those tiny leaves are a bear to pluck from their twiggy stems when they're dripping. Tarragon or cilantro or basil needs a rinse too, before you whirl it with olive oil and nuts into pesto, but then—well, it's wet. And everyone knows water and oil don't mix. Enter the spin doctor—OXO's new little salad and herb spinner. Expertly propelled with a toplike mechanism, the spinner even has a brake to terminate activity when delicate herbs have had enough. And as for the little salad spinner's other intended use (implied by the name)—drying small amounts of greens—the durable gadget puts the best spin on salad for one. It's available in cookware departments and stores or directly from OXO (800/545-4411) for about $18. — S.S.

The Wine Guide
Spanish finds

By Karen MacNeil-Fife

By the age of 30, I had visited every major wine-producing region in Spain and had, in general, fallen completely in love with Spanish flavors—vinous and culinary. One whiff of the savory aroma of paella cooking on the stove and there I am again, a young American in Spain, on a mission to find the greatest paella and the greatest Spanish wines to go with it. Spain had been (and continues to be) the best-kept secret in Europe.

Taking paella as my inspiration again this month (see page 136), I've given some thought to what a wine lover should know about the wines of Spain now:

First, that the best reds have some of the softest, most sublime and earthy flavors of any wines anywhere. That gentleness is due in large part to the fact that Spanish wines are aged for comparatively long periods of time in oak barrels—especially reds from the two top regions, Rioja and Ribera del Duero. In both places, wines are made mainly from the red grape Tempranillo (called Tinto Fino in Ribera del Duero).

Among the dozens of Spanish white wines, the two to know about are cava and Albariño. Cava, Spanish sparkling wine, is fresh, crisp, and wonderfully inexpensive. Spaniards don't wait for special occasions; they drink it at the drop of a hat. Albariño is quickly gaining a cult following in the United States. Snappy, sassy, citrusy, and gingery, it's an enchanting white wine,

sensational with seafood.

So what would a Spaniard drink with paella? Depending on the season and what's in the paella, any of the above. In Spain, rules are less important than discoveries.

Iberian stars
Morgadio Albariño 2000 (Rias Baixas), $17. Pure and citrusy, with hints of almonds, apricots, and ginger.
Bodegas Bretón "Loriñón" Reserva 1997 (Rioja), $17. Nuanced and earthy, with coffee, vanilla, and leather notes.
Hacienda Monasterio 1998 (Ribera del Duero), $30. Scrumptious chocolate and wild blackberry flavors, with a plush texture.

Muga Rioja Reserva 1997 (Rioja), $17. Supple, with hints of blackberry and mocha.

A sip of tradition
In Valencia, paella might be matched with either of two hauntingly dry, breathtakingly crisp styles of sherry—manzanilla (light and elegant) or fino (powerful). Try **Vinícola Hidalgo "La Gitana" Manzanilla** (about $12) or **Tio Pepe Palomino Fino** (about $13). ◆

Tastes of summer

Readers' recipes tested in *Sunset's* kitchens

By Charity Ferreira

Photographs by James Carrier

Caprese Melts

Dominique Ng, Los Altos Hills, CA

When their parents were away for the weekend, 19-year-old Dominique Ng and her sisters Madeline, 16, and Gabby, 12, survived nicely on these easy toasted sandwiches.

PREP AND COOK TIME: About 15 minutes

MAKES: 3 sandwiches

- 6 slices **buttermilk** or sourdough **sandwich bread**

  About 1 tablespoon **olive oil**

- 15 **fresh basil** leaves, rinsed

- 2 **firm-ripe tomatoes** (about 8 oz. total), sliced ¼ inch thick

- 4 ounces **fresh mozzarella cheese,** sliced ¼ inch thick

  Salt and **pepper**

1. Brush one side of each bread slice with olive oil. Place 3 slices, oil side down, on a 10- by 15-inch baking sheet and layer evenly with basil leaves, tomato slices, and mozzarella slices. Sprinkle lightly with salt and pepper and top with remaining bread slices, oil side up.

2. Broil sandwiches 6 inches from heat, turning once, until bread is golden brown and cheese is melted, 2 to 3 minutes total. Serve immediately.

Per sandwich: 314 cal., 46% (144 cal.) from fat; 13 g protein; 16 g fat (6.9 g sat.); 30 g carbo (2.5 g fiber); 465 mg sodium; 33 mg chol.

Chicken and Bread Salad

Debbie Rueben, Lebanon, OR

Debbie Rueben developed this main-dish salad for her daughter's wedding reception. Use leftover cooked chicken or roast chicken from a deli (buy about 1½ lb. chicken on the bone to get 12 oz. meat). You can make the dressing up to 2 days ahead; cover and chill.

PREP AND COOK TIME: About 1 hour

FOOD STYLING: BASIL FRIEDMAN

The classic combination of basil, tomato, and fresh mozzarella is delicious as a toasted sandwich.

MAKES: 3 to 4 main-dish servings

- ½ cup **olive oil**
- ¼ cup **lemon juice**
- ⅓ cup crumbled **feta cheese** (about 3 oz.)
- 3 cloves **garlic,** peeled
- 2 tablespoons packed **fresh basil** leaves, rinsed
- ½ teaspoon **dried oregano**
- ½ teaspoon **salt**
- ¼ teaspoon **pepper**
- 12 ounces **cooked chicken,** shredded or cut into 1-inch chunks
- 1 **baguette** (8 oz.), cut into 1-inch cubes
- 1 cup **cherry tomatoes** (about 8 oz.), rinsed, stemmed, and halved
- ½ **red bell pepper** (about 4 oz.), rinsed, stemmed, seeded, and cut into 1-inch chunks
- ½ **yellow bell pepper** (about 4 oz.), rinsed, stemmed, seeded, and cut into 1-inch chunks
- ⅓ cup thinly sliced **red onion**
- ¼ cup chopped **pitted calamata olives**
- 4 ounces **salad mix,** rinsed and crisped

1. In a blender, whirl olive oil, lemon juice, feta, garlic, basil, oregano, salt, and pepper until smooth.

2. In a large bowl, combine chicken, bread cubes, tomatoes, red and yellow bell pepper, onion, and olives. Add dressing and mix gently to coat.

3. Divide salad mix evenly among four plates. Mound bread mixture over greens.

Per serving: 685 cal., 55% (378 cal.) from fat; 34 g protein; 42 g fat (9.2 g sat.); 42 g carbo (4 g fiber); 1,115 mg sodium; 95 mg chol.

Peanut Cucumber Salad

Eva Shaw, Carlsbad, CA

Although this tangy, simply dressed cucumber salad was inspired by a dish the Shaw family enjoyed in a Chinese restaurant, Eva Shaw has found that it complements almost any meal.

PREP TIME: About 15 minutes

MAKES: 6 to 8 servings

- ¼ cup **rice vinegar**
- 1 teaspoon **sugar**

  About ½ teaspoon **salt**

- 3 **English cucumbers** (about 1½ lb. total)
- ½ cup **unsalted roasted peanuts,** coarsely chopped

1. In a large bowl, combine vinegar, sugar, and ½ teaspoon salt.

2. Peel cucumbers, if desired, and slice very thin. Add to dressing and mix to coat. Add more salt to taste and sprinkle with peanuts.

Per serving: 64 cal., 63% (40 cal.) from fat; 3.4 g protein; 4.4 g fat (0.6 g sat.); 4.2 g carbo (1.8 g fiber); 145 mg sodium; 0 mg chol.

Thai Chili Shrimp with Rice

Susan Banks, Seattle

Susan Banks serves this spicy broiled shrimp dish with a green salad and cold beer. Red chili paste is sold in Asian markets and in many well-stocked grocery stores.

PREP AND COOK TIME: About 45 minutes

MAKES: 4 servings

- 2 tablespoons **salad oil**
- 2 tablespoons **Asian red chili paste**
- 1 tablespoon **soy sauce**
- 2 teaspoons **lemon juice**
- 1 teaspoon **sugar**
- 2 cloves **garlic**, peeled and chopped
- 2 teaspoons minced **fresh ginger**
- 12 ounces (30 to 35 per lb.) **shelled, deveined shrimp**, rinsed
- 1 cup **long-grain white rice**
- ½ teaspoon **salt**
- 3 tablespoons chopped **fresh cilantro**

1. In a blender or food processor, whirl oil, chili paste, soy sauce, lemon juice, sugar, garlic, and ginger until well blended. In a shallow 2- to 3-quart baking dish, mix shrimp and chili paste mixture; cover with plastic wrap and chill at least 30 minutes or up to 1 day.
2. Meanwhile, in a 2- to 3-quart pan over high heat, bring 1½ cups water to a boil. Stir in rice and salt. Reduce heat to low, cover, and simmer until liquid is absorbed and rice is tender to bite, about 20 minutes.
3. Spread shrimp into a single layer in baking dish. Broil 5 to 6 inches from heat until bright pink and opaque but still moist-looking in center of thickest part (cut to test), 4 to 5 minutes.
4. Mound rice equally on four dinner plates; spoon shrimp and juices equally over rice. Sprinkle with cilantro.

Per serving: 357 cal., 28% (99 cal.) from fat; 21 g protein; 11 g fat (1.5 g sat.); 42 g carbo (0.5 g fiber); 716 mg sodium; 129 mg chol.

Chocolate Chip Blondies

Catherine Renno, Fairfax, CA

One of Catherine Renno's favorite chocolate chip cookie recipes has evolved over the years into this tender, buttery bar studded with chips and nuts.

PREP AND COOK TIME: About 1¼ hours

MAKES: 24 blondies

- ¾ cup **butter,** at room temperature
- ¾ cup **granulated sugar**
- ¾ cup **brown sugar**
- 1½ teaspoons **vanilla**
- 3 **large eggs**
- 2¼ cups **all-purpose flour**
- 1 teaspoon **salt**
- 1 teaspoon **baking soda**
- ¾ cup **butterscotch chips**

Cookie meets brownie in this butterscotch-flavored blondie.

- ¾ cup **chocolate chips**
- ¾ cup **chopped walnuts** (about 3 oz.)

1. In a bowl, with a mixer on medium speed, beat butter, granulated sugar, and brown sugar until smooth. Add vanilla and eggs and beat until well blended.
2. Stir in flour, salt, and baking soda until well combined. Stir in butterscotch chips, chocolate chips, and walnuts. Butter a 9- by 13-inch baking pan and spread dough level in pan.
3. Bake in a 350° regular or convection oven until top is browned and a wooden skewer inserted in center comes out with moist crumbs attached, about 30 minutes. Cool on a rack for 15 minutes, then cut into 24 rectangles. Serve warm or cool.

Per bar: 243 cal., 44% (108 cal.) from fat; 2.8 g protein; 12 g fat (7 g sat.); 31 g carbo (0.8 g fiber); 229 mg sodium; 43 mg chol. ◆

Star-studded Coolers

For the colored sugar rims. Put red, white, and blue sparkling sugar crystals in three plastic bags and crush with a rolling pin. Rub a lemon wedge around the rim of a glass and dip the rim in the crushed sugar.

To make the star. Use a small star-shaped cookie cutter on a slice of apple, sprinkled with lemon juice to prevent browning, or a piece of fruit leather. Pierce the fruit star with a skewer and use it as a swizzle stick.

Raspberry Lemonade. In a small bowl, with a potato masher or spoon, mash 1 cup rinsed **fresh raspberries** (6 oz.) with ⅔ cup **sugar.** Let stand 10 minutes. Press through a fine strainer into a pitcher (at least 1½ qt.); discard seeds. Stir in 1 cup **lemon juice** and 2 cups **water.** Taste and add more sugar if desired. Pour into tall, ice-filled glasses. Makes about 1 quart; 4 servings.

Per cup: 157 cal., 1.9% (3 cal.) from fat; 0.5 g protein; 0.3 g fat (0 g sat.); 41 g carbo (0 g fiber); 13 mg sodium; 0 mg chol.

— *Kate Washington*

Simple and refreshing, seafood salads make satisfying light meals for hot summer days (recipes begin on page 159).

August

cool comfort

Shake, blend, and pour your way to soda-fountain contentment

■ The feeling that comes from sipping something cold, sweet, and thick enough to stand a straw in is one of summer's meltingly ephemeral pleasures, meant to be seized whenever inspiration strikes. These creamy frozen drinks—from a frothy raspberry soda to a grown-up grasshopper milkshake spiked with crème de menthe— will transport you back to an old-fashioned soda fountain. Guileless and utterly soothing, these drinks are a snap to make whenever you want an instant fix of childhood memories.

By Charity Ferreira
Photograph by James Carrier
Food styling by Basil Friedman

Raspberry Cream Soda

Pour ¼ cup **raspberry syrup** (such as Torani) into a chilled tall glass (at least 16 oz.). Add 2 scoops **vanilla ice cream** and slowly pour in 8 ounces **club soda.** Makes about 1½ cups; 1 serving.

Per serving: 333 cal., 20% (66 cal.) from fat; 2.3 g protein; 7.3 g fat (4.5 g sat.); 68 g carbo (0 g fiber); 103 mg sodium; 29 mg chol.

Grasshopper Milkshake

In a blender, combine 2 cups **mint–chocolate chip ice cream,** ½ cup **milk,** and 2 tablespoons **crème de menthe.** Whirl until smooth and pour into a chilled tall glass. Garnish with 1 miniature or broken **cream-filled chocolate sandwich cookie.** Makes 2½ cups; 1 to 2 servings.

Per serving: 445 cal., 42% (189 cal.) from fat; 8.3 g protein; 21 g fat (14 g sat.); 47 g carbo (0.2 g fiber); 137 mg sodium; 59 mg chol.

Frozen Mango Lassi

In a blender, combine 1 cup **mango sorbet** and 1 cup **plain yogurt.** Whirl until smooth and pour into a chilled tall glass. If desired, garnish with a fresh **mint leaf.** Makes 2 cups; 1 to 2 servings.

Per serving: 189 cal., 17% (33 cal.) from fat; 3.9 g protein; 3.7 g fat (2.4 g sat.); 36 g carbo (1 g fiber); 52 mg sodium; 15 mg chol. ◆

A cilantro, chili
and cumin
seed dressing
gives zest to
halibut and
finely shredded
cabbage in
this Mexican-
inspired salad

Sea of greens

Seafood salads make refreshing meals for sizzling summer days

By Linda Lau Anusasananan

Photographs by James Carrier

Food styling by Dan Becker

On hot summer nights, salad seems just the right solution for supper, especially when it's made more substantial with a generous dose of seafood. Leafy greens, sweet ripe tomatoes, or crisp shredded cabbage are perfect counterpoints to cool, sweet shrimp, scallops, crab, fish, or calamari. To keep the seafood tender and flavorful—and the house cool—we use simple techniques like gentle steeping for shellfish or quick grilling for fish fillets. Sophisticated touches such as lively homemade dressings, fresh herbs, or even a little fresh fruit elevate these simple salads to sensational light meals. With a basket of bread and a cold drink, they're the perfect meals for beating the heat.

Grilled Fish on Cilantro-Chili Slaw

PREP AND COOK TIME: About 25 minutes

NOTES: Serve this salad with warm corn tortillas and a cold beer. For a shortcut, you may substitute 6 cups (14 oz.) purchased coleslaw mix for the shredded cabbage.

MAKES: 4 servings

⅔ cup **cider vinegar**

⅓ cup **extra-virgin olive oil**

⅓ cup chopped **fresh cilantro**

1 clove **garlic,** peeled and pressed or minced

1 teaspoon **cumin seed**

About ¾ teaspoon **salt**

5 to 6 teaspoons minced **fresh jalapeño chilies**

4 pieces (6 oz. each) **boned, skinned halibut** or mahimahi **fillet**

About 1 pound **red cabbage** (see notes)

½ cup thinly slivered **red onion,** rinsed

1. In a small bowl, mix vinegar, olive oil, cilantro, garlic, cumin seed, ¾ teaspoon salt, and chilies to taste.

2. Rinse fish and pat dry. In a heavy zip-lock plastic bag (1-gal. size), combine fish and ⅓ cup of the vinegar mixture. Let stand, turning occasionally, for about 15 minutes.

3. Meanwhile, rinse and drain cabbage. Cut through core into quarters; cut out and discard core sections. Slice each quarter lengthwise into thin shreds to make about 6 cups. In a large bowl, mix shredded cabbage, onion, and ½ cup of the vinegar mixture. Add salt to taste.

4. Lift fish from marinade (discard marinade) and place on an oiled grill over a solid bed of hot coals or high heat on a gas grill (you can hold your hand at grill level only 2 to 3 seconds); close lid on gas grill. Cook fish, turning once, until barely opaque but still moist-looking in center of thickest part (cut to test), 6 to 8 minutes.

5. Mound cilantro-chili slaw equally on four dinner plates. Top each mound with a piece of hot or warm grilled fish. Drizzle remaining dressing equally over fish. Add salt to taste.

Per serving: 389 cal., 53% (207 cal.) from fat; 37 g protein; 23 g fat (3.2 g sat.); 11 g carbo (2.3 g fiber); 542 mg sodium; 54 mg chol.

Kung Pao Shrimp and Spinach Salad

PREP AND COOK TIME: About 15 minutes

NOTES: This salad was inspired by one created by Catherine Allswang at Le Sept Quinze in Paris. Its flavor echoes the popular Chinese dish kung pao shrimp.

MAKES: 4 servings

1 pound **peeled, deveined shrimp** (31 to 40 per lb.)

1 tablespoon **peanut** or salad **oil**

⅓ cup **unsalted roasted peanuts**

½ teaspoon **hot chili flakes**

¼ cup **rice vinegar**

2 tablespoons **soy sauce**

1 tablespoon **Asian** (toasted) **sesame oil**

2 teaspoons **sugar**

2½ quarts **baby spinach leaves** (10 oz.), rinsed and crisped

½ cup shredded **carrot**

1. Rinse and drain shrimp. Set a 10- to 12-inch nonstick frying pan over high heat; when hot, add 1 teaspoon peanut oil and the shrimp. Stir until shrimp are barely opaque but still moist-looking in center of thickest part (cut to test), 2 to 4 minutes. Pour into a large bowl.

2. Return pan to heat; when hot, add remaining 2 teaspoons peanut oil and the peanuts. Stir until peanuts are lightly browned, 1 to 2 minutes. Stir in chili flakes and remove from heat. Add vinegar, soy sauce, sesame oil, and sugar, and stir until sugar is dissolved. Pour over shrimp.

3. Add spinach and carrot to shrimp and mix gently. Mound salad equally on plates.

Per serving: 302 cal., 45% (135 cal.) from fat; 28 g protein; 15 g fat (2.2 g sat.); 16 g carbo (5.7 g fiber); 821 mg sodium; 173 mg chol.

Spicy mango dressing, avocado slices, and taro chips put a tropical spin on shrimp, scallops, and greens.

Caribbean Seafood Salad

PREP AND COOK TIME: **About 30 minutes**

NOTES: This is a simplified version of a recipe from Bob Hurley, chef-owner of a soon-to-open restaurant in Yountville, California. Taro and other root vegetable chips are available in gourmet markets and specialty food stores. You can prepare the salad through step 2 up to 1 day ahead; cover and chill seafood, mango, and dressing separately.

MAKES: **4 servings**

    8   ounces **shelled, deveined shrimp** (31 to 40 per lb.), rinsed

    8   ounces **bay scallops**, rinsed

    1   **firm-ripe mango** (1¼ lb.)

    ½   cup **salad oil**

    ¼   cup **lime juice**

    ½   teaspoon **ground cumin**

    ½   teaspoon **ground ginger**

    ¼   teaspoon **ground cinnamon**

    1   clove **garlic**, peeled

        About ½ teaspoon **hot sauce**

        About ½ teaspoon **salt**

    1   **firm-ripe avocado** (8 oz.)

    3½ quarts **baby lettuce salad mix** (12 oz.), rinsed and crisped

    1   to 2 dozen **taro** or sweet potato **chips** (optional)

1. In a 5- to 6-quart pan over high heat, bring 2½ to 3 quarts water to a boil. Add shrimp and cook for 1 minute. Add scallops, cover tightly, and remove pan from heat. Let stand until shrimp and scallops are barely opaque but still moist-looking in center of thickest part (cut to test), 2 to 3 minutes. Drain and rinse in cold water until cool.

2. Meanwhile, peel and pit mango. Slice fruit lengthwise about ½ inch thick. Coarsely chop enough of the scraps to make ½ cup. In a blender or food processor, whirl chopped mango, oil, lime juice, cumin, ginger, cinnamon, and garlic until smooth. Add ½ teaspoon hot sauce and ½ teaspoon salt; taste, and add more hot sauce and salt if desired.

3. Peel and pit avocado. Slice lengthwise about ½ inch thick.

4. In a large bowl, gently mix shrimp and scallops, mango dressing, salad mix, and mango slices. Mound equal portions on four dinner plates. Garnish with avocado slices and taro chips. Add salt to taste.

Per serving: 504 cal., 64% (324 cal.) from fat; 24 g protein; 36 g fat (4.8 g sat.); 26 g carbo (2.8 g fiber); 498 mg sodium; 105 mg chol.

Orange-Ginger Calamari Salad

PREP AND COOK TIME: **About 1 hour**

NOTES: This salad is adapted from on served by executive chef Mark Dom men of Julia's Kitchen at Copia i Napa, California. Small squid (als called calamari) are frequently sol cleaned as tubes (mantles), tubes an tentacles, or rings (sliced tubes Sometimes a few pieces slip throug without thorough cleaning. Chec whole tubes and pull out and discar any long, clear quills; squeeze ou and discard material in tubes. You ca prepare salad through step 4 up t 1 day ahead; cover and chill ingred ents separately.

MAKES: **4 servings**

Pair this tarragon-scented crab and pea salad with a crisp Sancerre or white Burgundy.

1 pound **cleaned squid** (calamari; see notes) or bay scallops

3 **oranges** (10 oz. each)

3 tablespoons **grape seed** or salad **oil**

3 tablespoons **lime juice**

2 tablespoons minced **shallots**

1 tablespoon minced **fresh ginger**

2 teaspoons **sugar**

About ½ teaspoon **salt**

Pepper

3 quarts (15 oz.) bite-size pieces rinsed and crisped **butter lettuce** leaves

1 cup matchstick-size pieces (3 in. long) **jicama**

⅓ cup finely shredded **fresh mint** leaves

1. In a 5- to 6-quart pan over high heat, bring 2½ to 3 quarts water to a boil. Meanwhile, if necessary, cut squid tubes crosswise into ¼-inch-thick rings; leave tentacles whole. Rinse and drain squid or scallops.

2. Stir squid or scallops into boiling water; cover tightly and remove from heat. Let stand just until squid feels firm when pressed, about 1 minute (do not overcook or squid may turn rubbery), or scallops are barely opaque but still moist-looking in the center (cut to test), about 2 minutes. Drain, rinse in cold water, and drain again thoroughly. Pour the seafood into a large bowl.

3. Cut and discard peel and white membrane from oranges. One at a time, hold oranges over a bowl and cut between membranes and fruit to release segments into the bowl. Squeeze juice from membranes into the bowl; discard membranes.

4. Pour orange segments and juice into a wire strainer set over a 1- to 1½-quart pan. Reserve segments. Bring juice to a boil over high heat and boil, stirring occasionally, until reduced to 2 tablespoons, 2 to 6 minutes. Remove from heat. Stir in oil, lime juice, shallots, ginger, sugar, and salt and pepper to taste.

5. Add orange dressing, orange segments, lettuce, jicama, and mint to squid; mix gently. Add more salt and pepper to taste. Divide mixture evenly among four dinner plates.

Per serving: 311 cal., 35% (108 cal.) from fat; 21 g protein; 12 g fat (1.5 g sat.); 31 g carbo (6.9 g fiber); 351 mg sodium; 265 mg chol.

Tarragon Crab Salad in Tomato Cups

PREP TIME: **About 15 minutes**

NOTES: Serve this salad with sourdough bread.

MAKES: 2 servings

2 **firm-ripe tomatoes** (3½ to 4 in. wide, 12 oz. each)

⅓ cup **mayonnaise**

1 tablespoon **white wine vinegar**

1 tablespoon minced **fresh tarragon** or 2 teaspoons dried tarragon

8 ounces **shelled cooked crab** or shelled cooked tiny shrimp

½ cup **frozen petite peas**, thawed

½ cup chopped **celery**

2 tablespoons minced **shallots**, rinsed

Salt and **pepper**

2 **butter** or leaf **lettuce** leaves, rinsed and crisped

Fresh tarragon sprigs (optional)

1. Rinse tomatoes. Cut ½ inch off the top of each and reserve. With a spoon, carefully scoop out seeds and inner flesh, leaving a shell ¼ to ½ inch thick; reserve interiors for another use. Set tomato shells and lids, cut side down, on a paper towel.

2. In a large bowl, mix mayonnaise, vinegar, and minced tarragon until smooth. Add crab, peas, celery, and shallots; mix gently to coat. Add salt and pepper to taste.

3. Line each of two salad plates with a lettuce leaf. If tomatoes do not sit flat, trim bottoms slightly, as needed. Mound tarragon crab salad in tomato cups and set on lettuce leaves. Garnish with tomato lids and tarragon sprigs if desired.

Per serving: 462 cal., 62% (288 cal.) from fat; 28 g protein; 32 g fat (4.7 g sat.); 19 g carbo (5.6 g fiber); 629 mg sodium; 135 mg chol. ◆

Great ideas in food and wine

WINE

Sparkling personality

The best way to beat the heat on a hot night? With a chilled glass of snappy, refreshing sparkling wine. Here are a few of our summertime favorites.

Mirabelle Brut nv (North Coast), $16. Light and fresh with just a hint of creaminess. **Bottom line:** Delicious bubbly at a steal of a price. Who needs Chardonnay?

Gloria Ferrer Sonoma Brut nv (Sonoma), $18. A real thirst-quencher. Crisp and appley with a delicious light creaminess. **Bottom line:** There's no better way to cool off in summer.

Domaine Chandon Brut Classic nv (California), $17. Light, fresh, and easy to drink. **Bottom line:** An ever-so-slightly softer style for those summer backyard parties.

Mumm Cuvée Napa Valley Brut Prestige nv (Napa Valley), $18. Light caramel and fresh apple flavors with a good streak of crispness. **Bottom line:** Had a hard day? This will fix things.

Iron Horse Wedding Cuvée 1998 (Green Valley, Sonoma County), $28. Exotic, yeasty, and creamy. **Bottom line:** You don't need to be getting married to sip this.
— *Karen MacNeil-Fife*

INGREDIENT

Wild berry scoop

A COOL WAY TO BRING WILD BERRIES TO YOUR TABLE. Come August, it seems that every creek bottom and hillside in the West is covered with brambles of blackberries, fat and gleaming in the dust. A simple sherbet is just the thing for bringing their special, dusky sweetness to the table.

RECIPE: **Blackberry Sherbet. 1** In a blender or food processor, whirl 3 cups (about 1 lb.) rinsed **blackberries,** 1¼ cups **sugar,** 1 tablespoon **lemon juice,** and ⅛ teaspoon **salt** until smooth. **2** Press through a fine strainer into a bowl; discard seeds. Taste, and add more sugar (up to ¼ cup) if desired. **3** Stir in 1½ cups **half-and-half** (light cream). Cover and chill until cold, about 1 hour. **4** Pour into an ice cream maker (1½-qt. or larger capacity); freeze according to manufacturer's directions until mixture is softly frozen. Serve soft, or freeze airtight until firm, about 3 hours, or up to 3 days. Makes about 1 quart; 6 to 8 servings. — *Kate. Washington.*

DINING

Football eats in Tempe

TWO NEW RESTAURANTS AND A BAR OFFER A TIME-OUT FROM TAILGATING. At Arizona State University's home games, take a break from tailgating in Sun Devil Stadium's blistering parking lot and sample more exotic cuisine before or after a game.

Bamboo Club. Opened last November, the pan-Asian restaurant has a sophisticated Brits-in-the-tropics ambience. **The scene:** Guests like to sit out on the balcony of the second-floor restaurant or indoors in the "champagne room," with its slinky sheer curtains and cushy booths. **What to try:** Flash-fried spinach or the crackling calamari salad, accompanied by sake or a martini. *699 S. Mill Ave.; (480) 967-1286.*

Harry's Place. The bar at Tempe Mission Palms Hotel is named for Harry Mitchell, Tempe's gregarious former mayor. **The scene:** Convivial atmosphere, with outdoor patio and fireplace. **What to try:** Single-malt scotches, specialty drinks tied in to visiting football teams, elegant bar food. *60 E. Fifth St.; (480) 894-1400.*

Iguana Lounge. Longtime restaurateur Spyros Scocos's most recent venture. **The scene:** Intimate indoor-outdoor restaurant serving a Latino- and Cuban-influenced menu against a modernist backdrop of concrete, steel, and glass. **What to try:** Sip a mojito (rum, mint, and soda) and snack on lamb empanadas. *502 S. College Ave.; (480) 829-7707.*
— *Nora Burba Trulsson*

Surf snack

TAKE SOME FOCACCIA TO THE BEACH. A simple topped bread will stand up to coastal conditions, especially when cut into squares and individually wrapped in waxed paper. Our easy version is conveniently made from purchased bread dough; you can top it with items from an Italian deli counter or supermarket, from artichokes to olives. We especially like silvery little marinated anchovies plus a sprinkling of coarse sea salt—both of which add appealing flavors from the briny deep.

Beach Focaccia

1 Thaw 2 pounds **frozen bread dough** at room temperature. **2** Pour 3 tablespoons **extra-virgin olive oil** into a 10-by 15-inch nonstick baking pan. **3** If you are using two 1-pound loaves, pinch dough together firmly. Spread dough flat in pan, pushing to cover bottom of pan (if dough pulls back and will not spread, let it rest 5 minutes and try again). Let rise until surface is bubbled, 45 to 60 minutes. **4** With your fingers, poke dough at 1-inch intervals until entire surface is dimpled (do not pierce dough). **5** Drizzle surface evenly with ¼ cup extra-virgin olive oil and top as desired with any of the following: **marinated anchovies,** sliced **marinated artichoke hearts,** pitted **oil-cured black olives, cherry tomatoes,** thinly sliced **red onions,** and/or **roasted red peppers.** Drizzle with additional olive oil and sprinkle with **fresh rosemary** leaves and **coarse sea salt. 6** Bake in a 400° regular oven until top and bottom surfaces are golden, 20 to 25 minutes. **7** Remove from pan and let cool on a wire rack at least 10 minutes before serving; to serve, cut into squares. — *K. W.*

JAMES CARRIER; FOOD STYLING: KAREN SHINTO

Must-try pies

From Seattle to Seaview, your guide to Washington's most irresistible homemade pies

By Jim Gullo

We pie lovers demand to know why so many family restaurants no longer have cases full of fresh homemade pies. Sadly, it's getting harder to find pie that isn't commercially made, or frozen and served up limp and stale. To that end, we've been scouring Washington for first-rate pies and have found the following gems.

Who makes the best pie? Said one baker, a trifle sheepishly, "The thing about pie is that you're never going to make it as good as Mama does." But these places come pretty close, and we would go (and have gone) out of our way to tuck into thick wedges of their specialties.

Chimacum Cafe, Chimacum
Rhubarb

Why do Olympic Peninsula locals flock to this friendly, family-style restaurant in little Chimacum? Because of the long list of homemade pies, all available daily. Try the rhubarb—it's refreshingly tart, with a flaky crust—then think about working your way through the other two dozen or so pies on the menu. *9253 Rhody Dr.; (360) 732-4631.*

Dahlia Bakery, Seattle
Triple-coconut cream

The pies at Tom Douglas's restaurants (Etta's Seafood, Dahlia Lounge, Palace Kitchen) are so good, so rich, creamy, and utterly satisfying that Douglas opened a bakery last year in large part to meet his customers' demand for slice after slice. "Everybody loves it," said executive pastry chef Toby Matasar. "It's a huge comfort food." She starts with an all-butter crust that's flecked with coconut and holds up a delicious custard of co-conut, vanilla beans, heavy cream, eggs, and just the right amount of sugar. On top she adds more toasted coconut, hefty dollops of whipped cream, and shavings of white chocolate. Heavenly. *Closed Sun. 2001 Fourth Ave.; (206) 441-4540.*

The Shoalwater Restaurant, Seaview
Blackberry and apple

In late summer, when local wild berries are at their peak, Ann Kischner turns out these exquisite pies at her Long Beach Peninsula restaurant from a recipe passed down from her mother's Pennsylvania childhood. She tops them with a Dutch crumb topping for the perfect combination of crust and fruit. Great, but possibly bested by the pies she produces in the fall, combining pear, ginger, and locally harvested cranberries. *4415 Pacific Hwy.; (360) 642-4142.*

Twede's Cafe, North Bend
Cherry

This is the pie that launched a tourism industry when, in 1990, a character on the popular *Twin Peaks* television show raved about the cafe's cherry pie and "a damn fine cup of coffee." A North Bend staple since 1941, the cafe has been newly renovated with that slogan slapped on its side. Owner Kyle Twede says to make his crust ultraflaky, he adds a little vinegar and egg to the flour, sugar, shortening, and butter; sure enough, it makes a fine slice of pie. "We mostly sell it with about a half a pound of vanilla ice cream on top," said Twede. Any way you slice it—with or without the ice cream—the pie here is worth all the hype. *137 W. North Bend Way; (425) 831-5511.* ◆

Hot cheese

Halloumi, a firm cheese from Cyprus, makes a great quick meal

Halloumi cheese holds its shape when warm. It's usually made from sheep's milk and folded into a rectangle, but you'll find it shaped into half-moons as well.

JAMES CARRIER (4); FOOD STYLING: JOANNA CANTRALL

■ A friend recently mentioned to me that she had been cooking halloumi; I thought either she had a cold or she had found some kind of unusual fish. It turned out neither was the case: Halloumi is a cheese from Cyprus and is now becoming easier to find in American markets. It's a stretched-curd cheese, like mozzarella, but what sets this cheese apart is that it doesn't melt, so it can be baked, broiled, fried, and even grilled, making it a quick option for lunch or dinner on the run. Halloumi is salty, with a flavor somewhere between that of mozzarella and feta (plus a touch of mint, which many producers add) and an unusual texture: Cooked and then cooled, it squeaks between your teeth, but when hot and soft, it's pliant and delicious. Its browned crust is perfect for those of us whose favorite part of a grilled cheese sandwich is the crisp bit that has escaped from between the bread slices. I use halloumi to top baked potatoes, with steamed broccoli and lemon wedges on the side; cubed and browned in a dry skillet, as croutons on a salad of roasted beets and arugula; or on this quick dish of couscous and greens.

— *Kate Washington*

Halloumi with Couscous and Greens

PREP AND COOK TIME: About 20 minutes

MAKES: 4 servings

> 5 tablespoons **extra-virgin olive oil**
>
> About ½ teaspoon **salt**
>
> ¼ teaspoon **cayenne**
>
> 1½ cups **couscous**
>
> 1 cup **sugar snap peas,** rinsed and any strings pulled off
>
> 1 package (8 to 9 oz.; 250 g.) **halloumi cheese,** sliced crosswise ¼ inch thick
>
> ¼ cup **lemon juice**
>
> **Pepper**
>
> 6 ounces **salad mix,** rinsed and crisped
>
> 1 cup **cherry tomatoes,** rinsed and stemmed
>
> 2 tablespoons chopped **parsley**
>
> 2 tablespoons chopped **fresh mint** leaves
>
> **Lemon** wedges

1. In a 3- to 4-quart pan over high heat, bring 2¼ cups water, 1 tablespoon olive oil, ½ teaspoon salt, and cayenne to a boil. Remove from heat; add couscous and sugar snap peas; cover, and let stand until couscous is tender to bite, about 5 minutes. Fluff with a fork.

2. Meanwhile, place halloumi slices in a single layer in a 10- to 12-inch nonstick frying pan over medium-high heat. Cook, turning once, until browned on both sides, 5 to 7 minutes total. Remove pan from heat, but leave cheese in pan to keep warm.

3. In a 1-cup glass measure, mix lemon juice, remaining ¼ cup olive oil, and salt and pepper to taste. In a large bowl, mix salad greens with ¼ cup of the dressing. Mound equally on four plates. Stir cherry tomatoes, parsley, and mint into couscous and mound over greens. Top portions equally with halloumi slices, then dressing. Garnish with lemon wedges.

Per serving: 631 cal., 46% (288 cal.) from fat; 23 g protein; 32 g fat (13 g sat.); 62 g carbo (4 g fiber); 1,166 mg sodium; 38 mg chol.

The Wine Guide
The lightest of them all

By Karen MacNeil-Fife

If the wines you drink are mainly from the western United States, you're drinking some of the world's most powerfully alcoholic wines. These big-bodied wines—wonderful, to be sure—are the result of nature. Compared to the rest of the wine-producing world, the West is drenched in sun, which soon loads the grapes with sugar. And when yeast begins gobbling up all that sugar, a lot of alcohol is created—often more than 14 percent. In the heat of August, that can feel a little heavy.

So while our grapes are absorbing all that sun, it's nice to know about a place where the wines commonly have only 8 to 10 percent alcohol and as a result, taste gracefully light, elegantly fresh, and almost sheer on the palate. Best of all, like a great sorbet, even while light, they can have rivetingly intense flavors.

Where is this magical place? The Mosel region of Germany. I know—many people think of German wines as, first, sweet and, second, confusing. But the vast majority of fine German wines are not sweet (except intentional dessert wines), and here's a game plan to avoid confusion.

1. If you want an ultra-light wine, of all the German wine regions (and there are many), just remember the Mosel. Wines from the Mosel are not only light, they're also precise and fresh, with a streak of bright, thirst-quenching acidity.

2. Opt for the *kabinett* category. You will see *spätlese, auslese,* and so on, on German labels, but kabinett is the lightest of the bunch. Happily, it's also the least expensive— a good kabinett usually costs from $12 to $16.

3. Don't worry about the terms under the producer's name, like Urziger Würztgarten or Zeltingener Sonnenuhr. These are the names of the village and the vineyard—the sort of detail Germans love, but not necessary to know in order to pick a good wine.

4. Choose Riesling. Other varieties are made in the Mosel, but Riesling is the most filigreed and featherlight.

5. Be adventurous: Choose any producer. I mean it. Fine German estates are small, so you may not find the wines in Tucson that you saw in Tacoma. What's important is to get to know the kabinetts at your local wine shop. And speaking of which, shop around. Some retailers are up on the exciting Rieslings coming out of the Mosel; others are less so.

6. Pour the wine for dinner this month and notice: A Riesling kabinett from the Mosel is a magnificent refreshment with almost any summer food.

My favorite Mosel Riesling producers
Selbach-Oster, Fritz Haag, Dr. Loosen, Willi Schaefer, Joh. Jos. Prüm, and Merkelbach.

Native roots

What were the foods to the south of us like before Columbus's voyage? Much more interesting, complex, and varied than popular history has led us to believe. And those culinary roots linger in the lands of the Aztecs, Mayans, and Incas with more fidelity than you might expect. This is the focus of *Spirit of the Earth: Native Cooking from Latin America,* by Beverly Cox and Martin Jacobs (Stewart, Tabori & Chang, New York, 2001; $40; 800/345-1359, ext. 874). The book's authority is reinforced by text contributed by well-credentialed anthropologists Michael D. Coe and Jack Weatherford.

— *Jerry Anne Di Vecchio* ◆

Lemon, garlic, and chilies make a bright marinade for chicken and a flavorful sauce.

Chicken piri-piri

Put a popular Portuguese dish on the grill for a simple meal

By Sara Schneider

Africa is the source of the heat, but it was the Portuguese spirit of adventure that brought us chicken piri-piri, a spicy grilled dish common in southern Portugal and in Portuguese-style restaurants in Africa (where *piri-piri* is a small hot chili). It was a yen for wealth more than culinary creativity that propelled 15th- and 16th-century Portuguese explorers like Vasco da Gama along the spice route around the Cape of Good Hope to India and back to Europe. But the flavors they collected along the way—layered on the heat of chilies that later came to the Old World from the New—make an exciting sauce for seafood and meats.

Traditionally, piri-piri includes a splash of lemon and a hint of garlic with its roundup of herbs and spices; we're more generous with both in our version. As a marinade for chicken and an all-purpose sauce, rub, and dip for the rest of the meal, it's the foundation for a very lively party menu.

Chicken Piri-Piri

PREP AND COOK TIME: About 1 hour, plus at least 4 hours to marinate

NOTES: Buy the chicken already cut into pieces or have your butcher cut it. It's important to bring the marinade to a simmer in step 3 to ensure that you have killed any bacteria from the raw chicken. Brush the piri-piri sauce over hot corn on the cob, drizzle it over the grilled chicken, and use it as a dunking sauce for the bread.

MAKES: 6 to 8 servings

2 **chickens** (each 3½ to 4 lb.), each cut into 8 pieces (see notes)
Piri-piri marinade (recipe follows)
½ cup (¼ lb.) **butter**
Lemon wedges

1. Rinse chicken and pat dry; trim off and discard excess fat. Put chicken in a large bowl. Stir piri-piri marinade, pour over chicken, and turn pieces to coat. Cover and chill at least 4 hours or up to 1 day, turning chicken occasionally.

2. With tongs, lift chicken from marinade, drain well, and lay on a barbecue grill over a solid bed of medium coals or medium heat on a gas grill (you can hold your hand at grill level only 4 to 5 seconds; keep a spray bottle of water handy to douse any flare-ups); close lid on gas grill. Cook, turning occasionally, until skin is well browned and meat at bone is no longer pink (cut to test), 35 to 40 minutes total; brush occasionally with marinade until about 10 minutes before chicken is done. As pieces are done, transfer to a platter and cover loosely with foil to keep warm.

3. Pour remaining marinade into a 1½- to 2-quart pan over medium-low heat. Stirring occasionally, bring mixture to a simmer; adjust heat to maintain simmer. Add butter and stir until melted and incorporated; turn heat to low and stir occasionally until ready to serve. Pour sauce into a small bowl or pitcher.

4. Garnish chicken with lemon wedges and serve with sauce.

Per serving: 719 cal., 70% (504 cal.) from fat; 48 g protein; 56 g fat (17 g sat.); 4.7 g carbo (0.4 g fiber); 560 mg sodium; 185 mg chol.

Piri-Piri Marinade

PREP TIME: About 15 minutes
NOTES: The marinade can be made 2 to 3 days before using; chill airtight.
MAKES: About 2 cups

1 cup **lemon juice**
¾ cup **olive oil**
¼ cup minced **garlic**
2 tablespoons **hot chili flakes**
2 teaspoons **dried oregano**
1 teaspoon **dried thyme**
1 teaspoon **ground cumin**
1 teaspoon **salt**

In a 1-quart glass measure or a bowl, mix lemon juice, olive oil, garlic, chili flakes, oregano, thyme, cumin, and salt.

Per tablespoon: 50 cal., 92% (46 cal.) from fat; 0.2 g protein; 5.1 g fat (0.7 g sat.); 1.2 g carbo (0.1 g fiber); 75 mg sodium; 0 mg chol. ◆

Sweet relief

Vintage soda fountains put some fizz into summer's dog days

When the thermometer heads into the triple digits, some of the sweetest places to cool off are the old-fashioned ice cream parlors that dot the Mountain West, many situated along well-traveled routes. Some have a Victorian feeling; others are more '50s retro. But all of them have authentic, original fountains. If you know where to look, your next chocolate ice cream soda, made with real carbonated water from a vintage soda fountain, could be waiting for you in that little town just down the road.

Colorado

DENVER: Soda Rock Cafe. The marble soda fountain from Weiss's Drugstore now graces the city's last old-time soda fountain. Owners David Renne and Teresa Faliskie, who grew up around the corner, scoop up fabulous homemade ice cream—heaping cones, rich sundaes, bubbly sodas, thick shakes, and more. Try one of the specials like Crème Brûlée, Chocolate Oreo Cheesecake, or Cinnamon Cream. *9–9 Mon–Fri, 11–9 Sat, 12–9 Sun. 2217 E. Mississippi Ave.; (303) 777-0414. — Claire Walter*

IDAHO SPRINGS: Skippers Ice Cream Parlor. This corner store is filled with Skip and Brenda Gorman's collection of kids' pedal cars, posters, and vintage bikes; jukebox melodies from the '50s and '60s fill the air. Custom flavors—the reigning fave being Colorado Gold Nugget, a mix of vanilla ice cream, toffee, chocolate, caramel, and Skip's secret sauce—fill out old standby fountain treats. *10–6 daily. 1501 Miner St.; (303) 567-4544. — C. W.*

LAKE CITY: San Juan Soda Company. Belly up to this 1890s marble-topped bar and you may meet with an Avalanche—a vanilla sundae crested with hot fudge, marshmallow, and whipped cream. Titanic scoops of 35 flavors, thick powder malts mixed in a 1940s blender, and sodas crafted by hand from original fountain pumps are three reasons this 125-year-old pharmacy–turned–gift store is always packed. *10–5 Mon–Sat, 2–5 Sun. 227 Silver St.; (970) 944-0500. — Sharon Niederman*

LYONS: Lyons Soda Fountain & Bakery. Firefighters saved the mirrored soda fountain, circa 1921, when the old drugstore burned in 1967. Sip an old-fashioned phosphate, a New York–style egg cream, or the signature Chai Delight, a trendy combo of vanilla ice cream and chai tea concentrate. Or bring a bunch of gluttons to share the humongous Lyons Roar: three bananas, 10 scoops of ice cream, nuts and toppings, whipped cream, and cherries. *7–7 daily. 400 Main St.; (303) 823-5393. — C. W.*

Idaho

TWIN FALLS: Crowley's Soda Fountain & General Store. A giant mural of Norman Rockwell's *Soda Jerk*, a 1953 *Saturday Evening Post* cover, welcomes sweet-toothed visitors. This downtown emporium has been a local favorite since 1918 and in the same family since 1942. Thirty-two kinds of soda syrup include wild huckleberry pie, toasted marshmallow, and, of course, chocolate. *7:30–7:30 Mon–Fri, 10–6 Sat. 144 Main Ave. S; (208) 733-1041. — Julie Fanselow*

Montana

HELENA: The Parrot Confectionery. Since 1922, schoolchildren have run pell-mell through Last Chance Gulch to press their noses against the glass cases of more than 80 homemade candies, including mints, chocolate, and pecan parrots. These days, they also gather in mahogany booths for homemade sodas, phosphates, and the Parrot sundae: three ice cream scoops and caramel, fudge, and marshmallow sauces. *9–6 Mon–Sat. 42 N. Main St.; (406) 442-1470.— Caroline Patterson*

Nevada

BOULDER CITY: Happy Days Diner. Since it was built in 1931, the Green Hut has had several incarnations; it's now the Happy Days Diner. The milkshakes and malts come from turquoise 1930s mixers, the jukebox plays vintage 45s, and the Double Decker Chubby Checker burger recalls the days of Elvis and the Platters. Cozy up with a banana split or a root beer float. *7–8 daily. 512 Nevada Hwy.; (702) 293-4637. — Brian Beffort*

Utah

LOGAN: Bluebird Restaurant. In a state known for its collective sweet tooth, it's surprising that the Bluebird—the oldest restaurant in the state—is one of the few remaining vintage soda fountains. Dating from 1914, the fountain is the focal point of a long marble counter fronting 22 stools; a large mural shows vignettes of Logan history, starting with Native Americans in 1856. The cafe is known for its iron port and cherry soda; fountain regulars return for a lime freeze—a shake made with a scoop of vanilla ice cream, soda, and lime. *11–9:30 Mon–Thu, 11–10 Fri–Sat. 19 N. Main St.; (435) 752-3155. — Jeff Phillips*

Wyoming

CHUGWATER: Chugwater Soda Fountain. Originally, the establishment was a pharmacy and soda fountain. The draw here is a soda, malt, or shake, and the community's icon food: Chugwater Chili. You can also order a deli sandwich. *9–8 daily. 314 First St.; (307) 422-3222. — Candy Moulton*

SHOSHONI: Yellowstone Drug. Last year soda jerks poured 65,016 malts and shakes, serving them to folks seated at the long counter or one of the round tables with wire-backed chairs. *10–8 daily. 127 Main St.; (307) 876-2539. — C. M.* ◆

This gazpacho-like soup was inspired by the spicy, juicy salads—called *chaat*—sold as street food in India.

Super cool

Take the heat off with light, flavorful cold soups

By Kate Washington

Photograph by James Carrier

■ When the mercury rises, appetites fall. Suddenly, it seems far too warm to cook, eat, or do anything more strenuous than lounge in the shade sipping iced tea. But you have to keep your strength up somehow, to combat that heat—it's just that the last thing you want is to eat something warm or heavy. Healthy cold soups can range in flavor from subtle and elegant to bold and spicy. Make them in the morning or the night before you plan to serve them, and chill them during the day to keep both you and your kitchen cool. When dinnertime rolls around, slice a crusty loaf of bread, pour yourself a tall iced tea or glass of cold white wine, and relax on a shady patio with a bowl of soup.

Indian-spiced Tomato Soup

PREP AND COOK TIME: About 40 minutes, plus 1 hour to chill

NOTES: Nigella seeds (also called *kalonji*) add an oniony flavor. Look for them and for tamarind concentrate at Indian markets and some specialty food stores. If you can't find tamarind concentrate, substitute ¼ cup lime juice mixed with 2 teaspoons molasses.

MAKES: 4 to 6 servings

- 2 cloves **garlic**, peeled
- 1 **fresh green serrano chili,** rinsed, stemmed, and seeded
- 1 **sweet onion** (8 oz.), peeled and coarsely chopped
- 1 **English cucumber** (12 oz.), rinsed and diced (⅛ in.)
- 2 teaspoons **salt**
- 3 pounds **firm-ripe tomatoes**
- 1 tablespoon **tamarind concentrate** (see notes)
- 1 cup chopped **fresh cilantro**
- ½ cup chopped **fresh mint** leaves
- 2 tablespoons grated **fresh ginger**
- 1 teaspoon **ground cumin**
  About 1 cup **nonfat plain yogurt**
- 1 teaspoon **salad oil**
- 2 teaspoons **cumin seeds**
- 1 teaspoon *each* **yellow** and **black** or brown **mustard seeds**
- 1 teaspoon **nigella seeds** (see notes; optional)

1. In 5- to 6-quart pan over high heat, bring 3 quarts water to a boil. In a food processor, whirl garlic and chili until minced. Add onion and pulse until minced. Scrape into a large bowl and stir in cucumber and salt.

2. Cut an X in the bottom of each tomato and immerse in boiling water until peel begins curling back, about 30 seconds. Rinse under cold running wa-

Three easy pieces

It's easy to cool off healthy hot soups for the summer months.

- **Purée and chill** a favorite meatless black bean soup, then top with spicy salsa and chopped fresh cilantro.
- **Add cooked vegetables** such as asparagus or broccoli to leek and potato soup; purée and chill.
- **Make cold borscht** by grating roasted beets and adding chicken broth and sherry vinegar; top with plain yogurt and a pinch of caraway seeds.

ter until cool. Set a strainer over bowl with onion mixture. Working over strainer, pull peels off tomatoes and cut out and discard cores. Gently squeeze juice and seeds out of tomatoes. Press seeds to extract juice; discard seeds. On a cutting board with a juice well, mince tomatoes; pour any juice that collects into strainer. Add minced tomatoes to bowl with onion mixture.

3. In a small bowl, mix tamarind concentrate with ¼ cup warm water. Stir into tomato mixture, along with cilantro, mint, and ginger. In a 6- to 8-inch nonstick frying pan over medium heat, stir ground cumin until fragrant, 2 minutes; add to soup. Cover and chill until cold, at least 1 hour, or up to 1 day.

4. Ladle soup into bowls; top each serving with about ¼ cup yogurt. In a 1- to 2-quart nonstick pan that has a tight-fitting lid, combine oil, cumin seeds, mustard seeds, and nigella seeds. Set over high heat and stir until spices begin to pop, 30 seconds to 1 minute. Cover and shake vigorously until popping begins to subside, 1 to 2 minutes. Spoon hot seeds equally over soup.

Per serving: 106 cal., 17% (18 cal.) from fat; 5.7 g protein; 2 g fat (0.3 g sat.); 19 g carbo (4.8 g fiber); 835 mg sodium; 0.8 mg chol.

Arugula-Herb Soup with Shrimp

PREP TIME: 10 to 15 minutes, plus 1 hour to chill

MAKES: 4 first-course servings

- 3 cups **low-fat buttermilk**
- 1 cup **nonfat plain yogurt**
- 2 cups **arugula** leaves, rinsed
  About ½ cup chopped **fresh chives**
- ½ cup chopped **parsley**
- ¼ cup chopped **shallots**
- 1 tablespoon **lemon juice**
  Salt and **pepper**
- 8 ounces **shelled cooked tiny shrimp**, rinsed

1. In a blender, whirl 1 cup buttermilk, yogurt, arugula, ½ cup chives, parsley, and shallots until almost smooth. Pour into a bowl; stir in remaining buttermilk and the lemon juice. Season to taste with salt and pepper. Cover and chill until cold, at least 1 hour, or up to 1 day.

2. Reserve about ¼ cup shrimp; mound remainder equally in four wide, shallow bowls. Pour soup around shrimp; top servings equally with reserved shrimp and more pepper and chives.

Per serving: 192 cal., 13% (24 cal.) from fat; 23 g protein; 2.7 g fat (1.4 g sat.); 18 g carbo (0.8 g fiber); 441 mg sodium; 123 mg chol. ◆

FOOD STYLING: DAN BECKER

Tiny tarts hold several bites of berries. Served unfilled, upside down, they resemble packed and stacked sand castles at the beach.

Swedish sand

By Jerry Anne Di Vecchio

Swedish sand pastries convey summer celebrations for me. My introduction to them came in the form of cookies made by a Swedish friend who wanted to mark a midsummer's day with her California neighbors. Years later, I was actually in the right place at the right time—Sweden, on the longest day of the year, which, to be properly observed, must be feted through the pale gray of night until early dawn of the next day. Sand pastries—this time little tarts with summer berries—were part of the grand buffet that went on through the hours of merrymaking. They're tasty enough to deserve a place in your jolly times throughout the months of summer.

What makes sand tarts taste so pleasant is their crumbly, silky texture and toasty flavor from browned butter and ground roasted almonds. You can, in fact, control the flavor and texture by how you make the tarts: If baked just until golden brown, they're tender; if richly browned—which is how I love them—they take on a crunchy bite when cool, with a melt-away texture on the palate.

Most cookware stores will carry various shapes and at least a couple of sizes of the tiny tart pans. You can use tiny ones for pretty pick-up treats or larger ones for a full-size dessert.

Sand Tarts

PREP AND COOK TIME: About 1 hour

NOTES: Served plain, sand tarts are like cookies; invert them on the plate so the impression of the mold shows. If you serve the pudgy little pastries right side up, spoon a small puff of sweetened whipped cream in the slightly depressed center and top with several fresh berries—strawberries, raspberries, or blueberries—or fresh currants. You can make the dough (steps 1 and 2) up to 3 days ahead; wrap airtight and chill. Bring to room temperature before continuing. You can make the tarts up to 3 days ahead; wrap airtight when cool and let stand at room temperature. Freeze to store longer.

MAKES: 14 tarts 2½ inches wide or 7 tarts 3 inches wide

- ½ cup (¼ lb.) **butter**
- ⅓ cup **roasted salted almonds**
- ⅓ cup **sugar**
- 1 **large egg** white
- 1 teaspoon **vanilla**
- ¼ teaspoon **almond extract**
- ¾ cup **all-purpose flour**

1. In a 1- to 1½-quart pan over medium heat, cook butter until particles on pan bottom and foam that floats on melted butter turn amber-colored and smell toasted (mixture may bubble up), 5 to 6 minutes. Let cool at least 10 minutes.

2. In a food processor or blender, whirl almonds and sugar to a fine powder (if using a blender, transfer to a bowl). Scrape browned butter into container with nuts and sugar; add egg white, vanilla, almond extract, and flour. Whirl or stir with a fork until blended (dough will be sticky).

3. *For petite tarts,* use 2½-inch round tart pans (about ¾ in. deep; 2-tablespoon capacity), lining each with about 1½ tablespoons dough.

For cookie-size tarts, use 3-inch round tart pans (about 1¼ in. deep; 5-tablespoon capacity), lining each with about 3 tablespoons dough.

With your fingertips, press dough evenly over bottom and up sides of pans (nonstick or regular), flush with rims. Set slightly apart in a shallow, rimmed pan (10 by 15 in.).

4. Bake in a 300° regular or convection oven until tarts are richly browned at the edges and slightly paler in the center, 25 to 35 minutes; small tarts brown faster, so start checking them early. (If you prefer slightly softer tarts, bake only until edges are golden brown, 20 to 30 minutes.) The tarts puff up in the center as they cook, leaving only a small depression.

5. Transfer pans to a rack and let stand until tarts are warm but comfortable to touch, 5 to 8 minutes. Then invert one pan at a time onto a flat surface and gently squeeze, tapping very gently. If tart doesn't fall out, ease free with the tip of a sharp knife. Serve warm or cool.

Per 2½-inch tart: 126 cal., 63% (79 cal.) from fat; 1.8 g protein; 8.8 g fat (4.3 g sat.); 10 g carbo (0.6 g fiber); 100 mg sodium; 18 mg chol. ◆

JAMES CARRIER; FOOD STYLING: DAN BECKER

Spice-rubbed ribs are sized for party nibbling.

Spice up summer meals

Readers' recipes tested in *Sunset's* kitchens

By Charity Ferreira • Photographs by James Carrier

Terry's Barbecued Ribs

Theresa Liu, Alameda, CA

Theresa Liu knows a barbecue party has been a success when she sees lots of bare rib bones on each guest's plate. Ask the butcher to cut the rack in half lengthwise for appetizer-size portions. The ribs can be rubbed with the spice mixture up to one day ahead; wrap airtight and chill. Liu uses equal parts chipotle and pasilla chili powders, both available in the spice section of well-stocked supermarkets or Latino markets.

PREP AND COOK TIME: About 1 hour, plus at least 8 hours to chill

MAKES: About 8 appetizer servings

¼ cup **chili powder**

1 tablespoon **garlic powder**

2 teaspoons **ground cumin**

1½ teaspoons **dried oregano**

1½ teaspoons **dried thyme**

¾ teaspoon **hot dry mustard**

¾ teaspoon **salt**

¼ teaspoon **black pepper**

⅛ teaspoon **ground cloves**

1 rack **pork back ribs** (2¼ to 2½ lb.; see note at left), fat trimmed, cut in half lengthwise

2 **limes**, quartered

1. In a bowl, mix chili powder, garlic powder, cumin, oregano, thyme, mustard, salt, pepper, and cloves. Rinse ribs and pat dry. Rub ribs all over with spice mixture. Wrap airtight and chill 8 hours or overnight.

2. If using charcoal briquets, mound and ignite 50 briquets on the firegrate of a barbecue with a lid. When briquets are dotted with gray ash, in 15 to 20 minutes, push equal amounts to opposite sides of firegrate. Set a drip pan on firegrate between coals. If using a gas barbecue, turn all burners to high and close lid for 10 minutes. Adjust burners for indirect cooking (no heat down center) and lower side burners to medium heat. Lay ribs along center of the grill (not directly over heat). Cover the barbecue (if using charcoal, open vents) and cook, turning once midway through cooking time, until meat is browned, about 15 minutes. Wrap ribs in foil and return to grill. Cook until meat is tender when pierced, about 30 minutes longer.

3. Transfer ribs to a platter and cut apart between bones. Garnish with lime wedges to squeeze over portions to taste.

Per serving: 247 cal., 69% (171 cal.) from fat; 16 g protein; 19 g fat (6.8 g sat.); 3.3 g carbo (1.3 g fiber); 319 mg sodium; 73 mg chol.

Plum Pork Wraps

Mickey Strang, McKinleyville, CA

Mickey Strang combined leftover cooked pork tenderloin, fresh plums, and dressed cabbage to devise this simple and tasty wrap. When we tested these sandwiches, we also liked them with mustard instead of hoisin sauce. If you have leftover pork on hand, you may use it here; slice pork ¼ inch thick and begin recipe with step 2.

PREP AND COOK TIME: About 40 minutes

MAKES: 4 wraps

1 pound **pork tenderloin**, fat trimmed

½ teaspoon **salad oil**

¼ cup **rice vinegar**

2 teaspoons **soy sauce**

2 cups shredded **napa cabbage**

⅓ cup chopped **green onions**

4 **flour tortillas** (10-inch)

About 2 tablespoons prepared **hoisin sauce** (see notes)

2 firm-ripe **plums** (10 oz. total), rinsed, pitted, and thinly sliced

1. Rinse pork tenderloin and pat dry. Pour oil into an ovenproof frying pan over high heat. When hot, add pork and cook, turning to brown all sides, until well browned, about 5 minutes. Transfer pan with pork to a 400° regular or convection oven; bake until a thermometer inserted in center of thickest part of meat reaches 155°, 15 to 18 minutes. Let cool. Slice ¼ inch thick.

2. In a bowl, mix vinegar and soy sauce. Add cabbage and green onions and mix to coat.

3. Heat tortillas in microwave at full power (100%) until warm and pliable, 15 to 20 seconds. Spread each tortilla with about ½ tablespoon hoisin sauce. Arrange a fourth of the pork and plum slices down the center of each tortilla; top with a fourth of the cabbage mixture. Roll tortillas up around filling and slice in half crosswise.

Per wrap: 384 cal., 20% (75 cal.) from fat; 30 g protein; 8.3 g fat (2 g sat.); 46 g carbo (3.7 g fiber); 654 mg sodium; 74 mg chol.

Lemon-Mustard Potato Salad

Ellen Burr, Los Angeles

Ellen Burr's love of experimenting with bright seasonings resulted in this aromatic salad, which she garnishes with fresh mustard flowers.

PREP AND COOK TIME: About 35 minutes

MAKES: 6 to 8 servings

3 pounds **Yukon Gold** or thin-skinned **potatoes**, scrubbed and cut into 1-inch chunks

¼ cup **lemon juice**

¼ cup **extra-virgin olive oil**

1 tablespoon **prepared hot mustard**

1 teaspoon **salt**

1 cup chopped **onion**

2 tablespoons chopped **fresh dill**

1. In a 6- to 8-quart pan, combine potatoes and 4 quarts water. Cover and bring to a boil over high heat. Reduce heat and simmer until potatoes are tender when pierced, about 20 minutes. Drain.

2. Meanwhile, in a large bowl, mix lemon juice, olive oil, mustard, and salt. Add potatoes, chopped onion, and dill and mix gently to coat. Serve warm, at room temperature, or chilled.

Per serving: 206 cal., 32% (65 cal.) from fat; 3.8 g protein; 7.2 g fat (1.1 g sat.); 33 g carbo (3 g fiber); 326 mg sodium; 0 mg chol.

Portabella Penne

Michelle Mortenson, Portland

As a vegetarian married to a meat lover, Michelle Mortenson appreciates the meaty flavor of portabella mushrooms in this pasta sauce.

PREP AND COOK TIME: About 30 minutes

MAKES: 3 to 4 servings

12 ounces **dried penne pasta**

1 tablespoon **olive oil**

½ cup chopped **onion**

3 cloves **garlic**, peeled and minced or pressed

12 ounces **portabella mushroom caps**, rinsed and cut into ½-inch chunks

⅓ cup **dry red wine**

1 can (28 oz.) **diced tomatoes**
Salt and **pepper**

2 tablespoons chopped **parsley**

½ cup grated **asiago** or parmesan **cheese** (about 1½ oz.)

1. In a 5- to 6-quart pan over high heat, bring 4 quarts water to a boil. Add penne and stir occasionally until tender to bite, 7 to 9 minutes. Drain and return to pan.

2. Meanwhile, pour oil into a 10- to 12-inch frying pan over medium-high heat; when hot, add onion, garlic, and mushrooms. Stir frequently until onion and mushrooms are limp, about 8 minutes. Add wine and cook until most of the liquid has evaporated, 1 to 2 minutes.

3. Add tomatoes and bring to a boil; reduce heat and simmer to blend flavors, about 10 minutes. Add salt and pepper to taste. Pour over hot pasta and mix to coat with sauce. Spoon into four wide, shallow bowls and top evenly with parsley and cheese.

Per serving: 478 cal., 16% (76 cal.) from fat; 18 g protein; 8.4 g fat (3 g sat.); 79 g carbo (5.3 g fiber); 459 mg sodium; 7.6 mg chol.

Tuna Tortas with Pico de Gallo

Jennifer Lira, Pleasant Hill, CA

We loved the way the fresh tastes of cilantro and lime brightened the flavor of canned tuna in this Mexican-style sandwich created by Jennifer Lira. To seed tomatoes, cut in half crosswise; squeeze out and discard seeds and juice. If desired, garnish sandwiches with lettuce leaves.

PREP TIME: About 10 minutes

MAKES: 2 sandwiches

1 can (6 oz.) **solid white tuna** packed in water

4 ounces **Roma tomatoes**, rinsed, seeded, cored, and chopped (see notes)

¼ cup chopped **fresh cilantro** leaves

3 tablespoons **lime juice**

⅓ cup minced **red onion**

2 **fresh serrano chilies** or other small hot chilies, rinsed, stemmed, seeded, and minced

½ teaspoon **salt**

2 **sandwich rolls** (3 oz. each), split in half horizontally

1. Drain tuna well; flake into a bowl with a fork. Stir in tomatoes, cilantro, lime juice, onion, chilies, and salt.

2. Mound tuna equally on sandwich roll bottoms and set tops in place.

Per sandwich: 402 cal., 18% (71 cal.) from fat; 33 g protein; 7.9 g fat (2.4 g sat.); 54 g carbo (4.2 g fiber); 1,314 mg sodium; 33 mg chol. ◆

Fresh, spicy salsa mixed with tuna makes a great sandwich filling.

Inspired by the flavors of a Tuscan summer, zucchini timbales show off the season's fresh vegetables (recipe on page 176).

September

A juicy rare steak, served over peppery greens, shows off the earthy elegance of Tuscan cuisine. ABOVE RIGHT: Friends share laughter and wine at the table; wrap breadsticks in prosciutto for a delicious, simple starter.

Bring Tuscany home

A simple late-summer supper with friends makes the most of Italian flavors

By Linda Lau Anusasananan • Photographs by James Carrier • Food styling by Karen Shinto

■ Italy's charms—its people, its art, and especially its food—tend to cast a spell on visitors, and San Franciscans Donald Frediani and Renata Gasperi are no exception. They've been captivated by this seductive land, which they've visited 14 times in the past 25 years. They go to spend time with family and tend a small inherited house, but most of all for the cuisine of their Italian heritage.

Frediani, the cook of the pair, records each meal in his travel diary. Back in California, he recreates dishes for enthusiastic guests. This Tuscan menu draws inspiration from a meal Frediani and Gasperi had at La Grotta in Montepulciano. It shows off fresh ingredients naturally and simply.

This summer supper for 6 to 8 comes together easily—each course can be made ahead (see "Time Plan," page 177) or finished while guests relax around the table. Offer breadsticks wrapped with thinly sliced prosciutto as an hors d'oeuvre, then unmold zucchini timbales and grill a big steak, rare and juicy, the way the Tuscans like it. Harvest vegetables, roasted until sweet, go alongside. The meal comes to a leisurely close with wedges of custard-filled *torta* or purchased almond biscotti served with *vin santo*, a sweet golden dessert wine, or espresso. From start to finish, this simple menu brings the enchanting flavors of the Tuscan countryside into your own home: *Mangia bene!*

Grilled Steak on Arugula

PREP AND COOK TIME: About 1 hour

NOTES: You can slice the artichokes up to 1 hour before serving; if you can't find baby artichokes, omit them. Buy a block of parmesan cheese larger than needed (at least 4 oz.) so you can shave curls from it. Drizzle the steak with a Tuscan or other peppery olive oil.

MAKES: 6 to 8 servings

- 2 tablespoons **lemon juice**
- 12 ounces **baby artichokes** (each about 2 in. wide; see notes), optional
- 2 **boned beef top loin steaks** or 1 sirloin steak (2 in. thick; 2½ to 3 lb. total)

About 5 tablespoons **extra-virgin olive oil**

- 2 tablespoons **balsamic vinegar**
- 8 ounces (2 qt.) **baby** or bite-size pieces rinsed and crisped **arugula** leaves or tender watercress sprigs

Salt and fresh-ground **pepper**

About 2 ounces **parmesan cheese** (see notes)

1. In a large bowl, combine 1 quart water and the lemon juice. Rinse artichokes. Starting with lower, outer petals, snap off and discard leaves near bases, down to those that are half green and half yellow. Slice green tops off cones. Cut stems flush with bases

and trim off any remaining dark green. Cut artichokes in half lengthwise and, if the center is fuzzy or prickly, scrape out. Drop artichokes in lemon water as trimmed. Lift artichokes out and slice paper-thin in food processor, with a hand guard on a box slicer or mandoline, or with a sharp knife. Return slices to lemon water.

2. Rinse beef and pat dry; trim off excess surface fat. Rub 1 tablespoon olive oil all over steak.

3. Set steak on a barbecue grill over a solid bed of medium coals or medium heat on a gas grill (you can hold your hand at grill level only 5 to 6 seconds); close lid on gas grill. Cook, turning once, until rare (red to pinkish red

BELOW: A carafe of vin santo makes a sweet ending.
RIGHT: Zucchini timbales offer the flavor of fresh herbs.

in the center and pale pink near the surface; cut to test or insert a thermometer in center of thickest part—it should register about 125°), 12 to 16 minutes total, or medium-rare (pinkish red in center, gray near surface, 135° in center), 16 to 20 minutes total. Let rest in a warm place for about 5 minutes.

4. Meanwhile, in a large bowl, mix 1 tablespoon *each* olive oil and balsamic vinegar. Add arugula and mix gently to coat. Arrange arugula on a large platter. To the bowl, add 1 more tablespoon *each* olive oil and balsamic vinegar. Drain artichoke slices well and add to bowl; mix gently. Add salt and pepper to taste. Spread artichokes and dressing evenly over arugula.

5. Cut steak crosswise into ¼-inch-thick slices and arrange, slightly overlapping, on arugula. Sprinkle lightly with salt and pepper. With a vegetable peeler, shave curls of cheese onto steak. Drizzle with 2 tablespoons olive oil; offer more oil to add to taste.

Per serving: 283 cal., 60% (171 cal.) from fat; 26 g protein; 19 g fat (5.4 g sat.); 1.6 g carbo (0.5 g fiber); 177 mg sodium; 66 mg chol.

Zucchini Timbales

PREP AND COOK TIME: About 1 hour
NOTES: If making up to 1 day ahead, prepare through step 5; cover and chill. Let warm to room temperature and unmold.
MAKES: 6 to 8 servings

> About 1½ ounces **crusty Italian** or French **bread**
>
> 3 pounds **zucchini**
>
> ¼ to ½ cup **olive oil**
>
> 3 cloves **garlic,** peeled and minced
>
> 1½ tablespoons chopped **fresh** or 1½ teaspoons dried **oregano** leaves
>
> About ½ teaspoon **salt**
>
> About ¼ teaspoon **pepper**
>
> ½ cup **grated parmesan cheese**
>
> 4 **firm-ripe tomatoes** (6 oz. each)
> **Fresh oregano** sprigs (optional), rinsed

1. Cut bread into ½-inch chunks. In a food processor or blender, whirl into coarse crumbs; you should have ⅔ cup.
2. Rinse zucchini and trim and discard ends. Cut into ⅛-inch-thick rounds.
3. In a 5- to 6-quart pan over medium heat, stir bread crumbs often until golden and crisp, about 5 minutes. Pour into a bowl.
4. Add 3 tablespoons olive oil to pan and increase heat to medium-high. Stir in zucchini, garlic, chopped oregano, ½ teaspoon salt, and ¼ teaspoon pepper. Cover and cook, stirring occasionally, until zucchini begins to soften, about 5 minutes. Uncover and stir often until zucchini is browned and soft when pressed, 7 to 10 minutes longer. Remove from heat and stir in toasted crumbs, the parmesan cheese,

and more salt and pepper to taste.
5. Generously oil six to eight ramekins (½- to ¾-cup size) with 1 tablespoon olive oil. Divide zucchini mixture evenly among ramekins and press in firmly. Let stand at room temperature at least 5 minutes or up to 4 hours (see notes).
6. Rinse and core tomatoes; cut crosswise into ¼-inch-thick slices. Arrange 3 tomato slices on each of 6 to 8 salad or dinner plates. Run a knife around inside edge of ramekins and invert zucchini timbales onto tomatoes; if necessary, hold each ramekin and plate together and shake gently to release. If desired, garnish with oregano sprigs. Add more salt and pepper to taste. If desired, drizzle a little olive oil over tomatoes to taste.

Per serving: 153 cal., 65% (99 cal.) from fat; 5.2 g protein; 11 g fat (2.2 g sat.); 12 g carbo (2 g fiber); 281 mg sodium; 4 mg chol.

Roasted Vegetables

PREP AND COOK TIME: About 1 hour and 20 minutes
MAKES: 6 to 8 servings

> 1 **eggplant** (1 lb.)
>
> 2 pounds **crookneck** or pattypan **squash**
>
> 3 **red bell peppers** (8 oz. each)
>
> 2 **fresh rosemary** sprigs (5 in. each) or 1 teaspoon dried rosemary
>
> 2 pounds **red thin-skinned potatoes** (2 in. wide)
>
> ⅓ cup **olive oil**
>
> About ½ teaspoon **salt**
>
> About ¼ teaspoon **pepper**

1. Rinse eggplant, squash, bell peppers, and rosemary sprigs. Scrub potatoes. Trim and discard ends of eggplant and squash. Stem and seed bell peppers. Cut eggplant, squash, and bell peppers into 1½-inch chunks and potatoes into halves. Combine vegetables, rosemary, olive oil, ½ teaspoon salt, and ¼ teaspoon pepper in an 11-by 17-inch roasting pan (2 to 2½ in. deep); mix well.
2. Bake in a 400° regular or convection oven, stirring occasionally, until potatoes are browned and tender when pierced, about 1 hour. Mound on a large platter. Add more salt and

BELOW: Serve roasted vegetables family style. RIGHT: A custard torte pairs well with ripe fruit.

pepper to taste. Serve warm or at room temperature.

Per serving: 223 cal., 39% (86 cal.) from fat; 4.3 g protein; 9.6 g fat (1.3 g sat.); 32 g carbo (5 g fiber); 159 mg sodium; 0 mg chol.

Grandmother's Custard Torte

PREP AND COOK TIME: About 1¼ hours, plus 1½ hours to cool

NOTES: You can make this torte up to 1 day ahead. Serve it with raspberries or sliced ripe peaches or strawberries.

MAKES: 6 to 8 servings

- ⅓ cup **granulated sugar**
- ⅓ cup **all-purpose flour**
- 2 cups **milk**
- 1 teaspoon grated **lemon** peel
- 1 **large egg**, separated
- 1 **large egg** yolk
- **Butter pastry** (recipe follows)
- ¼ cup **pine nuts**
- ¼ cup **slivered almonds**
- **Powdered sugar**

1. In a 1½- to 2-quart pan, mix granulated sugar and flour. Whisk in milk and lemon peel. Stir over medium-high heat until mixture boils and is thickened and smooth, 4 to 7 minutes. Remove from heat. In a small bowl, beat the 2 egg yolks lightly to blend. Whisk about ¼ cup of the hot milk mixture into the yolks, then whisk egg mixture into milk mixture in pan. Nest pan in a bowl of ice water and stir occasionally

until cool, about 10 minutes.

2. Coat a 9-inch pie pan, including rim, with cooking oil spray or butter. Divide butter pastry into two portions, one ⅔ of the total and the other ⅓. Press the larger portion into a flat disk and place between two sheets of plastic wrap (about 15 by 15 in.; overlap sheets, if necessary, to make wide enough). Roll into a 13-inch round about ⅛ inch thick. Peel plastic wrap off one side of dough; invert and center pastry over prepared pie pan and gently ease into pan. Peel off remaining plastic wrap. Trim pastry edges flush with rim. If there are any tears in pastry, press dough together to repair. Spread the cooled custard evenly in pastry.

3. Gather pastry scraps and add to remaining portion. Press into a disk and place between two sheets of plastic wrap (about 12 by 15 in.). Roll into a 10-inch round about ⅛ inch thick. Peel plastic wrap off one side of pastry, invert, and center over pie pan. Peel off plastic wrap. Trim off excess dough flush with rim. With the tines of a fork, lightly press pastry edges together on rim.

4. Beat egg white lightly to blend and brush pastry just to coat. Sprinkle evenly with almonds and pine nuts; press nuts lightly into surface.

5. Bake in a 350° regular or convection oven until golden brown, 30 to 40 minutes. Cool on a rack at least 1½ hours before serving. When completely cool, cover and chill. Serve cool or cold. Shortly before serving, sift powdered sugar over the top.

Butter pastry. In a food processor or a bowl, whirl or mix 2 cups **all-purpose flour**, 6 tablespoons **sugar**, and 1½ tea-

spoons **baking powder** to blend. Add ½ cup (4 oz.) cold **butter**, cut into ½-inch chunks. Whirl or, with a pastry blender, cut butter into flour mixture until cornmeal-size pieces form. Add 1 **large egg** and 1 **large egg** yolk; whirl or mix with your hands until dough comes together. Shape into a ball.

Per serving: 423 cal., 45% (189 cal.) from fat; 10 g protein; 21 g fat (9.8 g sat.); 50 g carbo (1.7 g fiber); 257 mg sodium; 146 mg chol. ◆

Time plan

Since the zucchini timbales and roasted vegetables can be served at room temperature, the timing on this meal is relaxed.

☐ **Up to 1 day ahead:** Make custard torte and zucchini timbales.

☐ **About 1½ hours ahead:** Roast vegetables and let zucchini timbales warm to room temperature.

☐ **About 1 hour ahead:** Prepare artichokes. Wrap thinly sliced prosciutto around breadsticks; wrap airtight.

☐ **About 45 minutes ahead:** If using a charcoal barbecue, ignite briquets. Unmold timbales and arrange on tomatoes.

☐ **About 30 minutes ahead:** If using a gas barbecue, preheat grill.

☐ **About 20 minutes ahead:** Grill steak.

☐ **About 5 minutes ahead:** Dress arugula and artichokes; slice steak.

☐ **Shortly before dessert:** Dust torte with powdered sugar; prepare fruit.

the lure of the harbor

PORT ANGELES, TRINIDAD, NEWPORT
Brave and beautiful, three classic fishing ports
invite you to share
their passion for the sea

town

BY MATTHEW JAFFE • PHOTOGRAPHS BY MAREN CARUSO • RECIPES BY SARA SCHNEIDER

I t's low tide on Yaquina Bay, Oregon, on the afternoon before the annual blessing of the fleet. Great blue herons fish the shallow channels that flow through the mudflats, where clam diggers in knee-high rubber boots poke at the liquid earth. An osprey wheels overhead as a fishing boat glides under the 1936 Yaquina Bay Bridge, passes an 1871 lighthouse, and heads out into the open ocean trailed by the low moan of a foghorn. ■ Down the waterfront, crews scrub down decks and mend nets on a fleet of boats with names straight out of John Steinbeck's Cannery Row: *Anona Kay, Miss Yvonne,* and *Pacific Hooker.* Sea lions haul out beneath the Abbey Street Pier; crab traps, still redolent of the depths where they were deployed, sit in head-high stacks in front of a mural depicting Moby Dick wreaking mayhem on a whaling boat. ■ Watching all the activity are Newport's tourists, who, after gazing their fill at the harbor, window-shop along Bay Boulevard, then make a lunchtime stop at Mo's, famous for its clam chowder. These visitors are part of a tourist tradition that dates back to the 19th century. But the coverall-clad fishermen grabbing a late cup of coffee or picking up supplies at marine supply stores are a reminder that, above all else, this is a working community, forever connected to the sea. ■ Newport is one of the West's classic harbor towns. These are places where life plays out according to a set of rhythms dictated by the tides, the seasons, and the ebb and flow of commerce. In Newport and in such other Pacific harbor towns as Port Angeles, Washington, and Trinidad, California, the heart-stopping beauty of the coast and the grittier realities of industry coexist. Salmon, halibut, and Dungeness crabs still are caught by local boats, but many harbor towns are places in transition. The depletion of the bounty on which they have long depended along with more stringent regulations have forced sometimes difficult economic and social changes.

In Port Angeles, on Washington's Olympic Peninsula, the Victoria ferry emerges from the mists like some modern-day ghost ship, then fires off a couple blasts of its horn as it eases into the harbor after making the passage across the Strait of Juan de Fuca. Down the waterfront at High Tide Seafoods, workers busily assemble 1,000 boxes and scrub down

floors and tables in anticipation of the arrival of several tons of halibut.

The company is now the last fish processing facility in town. Strict limits on commercial fishing takes combined with low prices for salmon decimated the local fleet and its support businesses. While there's still plenty of sportfishing, most of Port Angeles's commercial fishing boats are gone, and the longtime annual Salmon Derby festival tradition has gone with them. And yet some Port Angeles residents refuse to give up.

Oyster stew achieves legendary
status at Mo's in Newport.

A TASTE OF PORT ANGELES:
C'EST SI BON

Paupiette de Saumon au Crabe

With wit and good will, Michele and Norbert Juhasz of **C'est Si Bon** bring French country classics, like chicken in mustard sauce and salmon in parchment, to diners in Port Angeles. But in keeping with the fluctuations of the local wild salmon catch and the need to diversify, they offer this truly local pairing: wild salmon stuffed with Dungeness crab. Whim in the kitchen dictates the nature of the sauce on any given day; it might be spiked with Scotch and flambéed. But this version is an evergreen favorite—poached in vermouth with leeks.

PREP AND COOK TIME: 35 to 40 minutes
NOTES: To save time, you can have the salmon thinly sliced off the skin at your seafood market. Serve the stuffed rolls with simple parsleyed potatoes to share the flavorful sauce.

MAKES: 4 servings

- 1 **leek** (about 6 oz.)
- 3 tablespoons **butter**
- 6 ounces **shelled cooked crab** (¾ cup)
- 1 pound **boned salmon fillet with skin** (7 to 8 in. wide)
- 2 cups **dry vermouth**
- ½ cup **whipping cream**
   Salt and **pepper**
- 2 tablespoons thinly sliced **fresh chives** (optional)
   Lemon wedges (optional)

1. Trim and discard stem end and tough green top from leek; cut leek in half lengthwise and hold each half under cold running water, separating layers to rinse well, then thinly slice. In a 10- to 12-inch ovenproof nonstick frying pan over medium heat, melt 1 tablespoon butter. Add leek and stir often until limp, about 5 minutes. Transfer to a bowl.

2. Sort through crab and discard any bits of shell. Add remaining 2 tablespoons butter to pan; when melted, add crab and stir often just until hot, 1 to 2 minutes. Push to one side of pan.

3. Meanwhile, rinse salmon and pat dry. Holding a sharp knife at a 45° angle, cut flesh crosswise off the skin into ⅛- to ¼-inch-thick slices; you should have about 12 (see notes). One at a time, lay slices flat and spoon about 1 tablespoon warm crab onto wide end. Starting at that end, roll salmon tightly around crab and place, seam down, in frying pan. Pour vermouth around rolls.

4. Transfer pan with salmon rolls to a 450° regular or convection oven and bake until fish is opaque but still moist-looking in center of thickest part (cut to test), 12 to 15 min-

utes. With a slotted spoon, transfer salmon rolls to plates, cover loosely with foil or plastic wrap, and let stand in a warm place.

5. Add cream and reserved leek to pan and boil over high heat until liquid is slightly thickened and reduced to about 1⅓ cups, 8 to 9 minutes. Season to taste with salt and pepper. Spoon sauce equally around salmon rolls and garnish with chives and lemon wedges if desired.

Per serving: 426 cal., 63% (270 cal.) from fat; 30 g protein; 30 g fat (13 g sat.); 8.4 g carbo (0.2 g fiber); 291 mg sodium; 159 mg chol.

PORT OF CALL
PORT ANGELES, WASHINGTON

WHERE: About 2½ hours west of Seattle on the Olympic Peninsula.

ON THE WATERFRONT: The Port Angeles Waterfront Trail runs about 5 miles from near the city center to the end of Ediz Hook and passes a variety of waterfront businesses.

The **Arthur D. Feiro Marine Life Center** on the city pier offers a good introduction to local marine life.

(360) 417-6254.

OTHER ATTRACTIONS: Port Angeles is the gateway to **Olympic National Park** and the embarkation point for the ferry to Victoria, British Columbia. East of Port Angeles, **Dungeness National Wildlife Refuge** has great beach hiking to a historic lighthouse.

DINING: Bella Italia. Locally grown organic produce, a huge wine selection, and an inventive menu in the heart of town. *118 E. First St.; (360) 457-5442.*

C'est Si Bon. Owners Michele and Norbert Juhasz have created a unique French country dining experience. *Closed Mon. 23 Cedar Park Dr.; (360) 452-8888.*

LODGING: Red Lion Hotel Port Angeles. Offers waterfront lodging and dining. *186 rooms from $89. 221 N. Lincoln St.; (360) 452-9215.*

CONTACT: Port Angeles Chamber of Commerce: (360) 452-2363 or www. portangeles.org.

"Salmon hit rock bottom in 1995–96. But I guess I was just too stubborn to quit," says High Tide's co-owner Jim Shefler, who works with Native American commercial fishers. "When I started in the mid-1970s, wild coho went for $1 a pound. But with farmed salmon, the price is now 25 cents a pound, so we have had to diversify with crab and black cod. If we tried to do what we did 15 years ago, we would have gone out of business."

Port Angeles has always depended on its harbor. Ediz Hook, a curving 2½-mile-long sand spit where logging trucks once lined up almost bumper-to-bumper, creates the deepest natural harbor on the West Coast. During the Civil War, the harbor was considered such an important national resource that in 1862 President Abraham Lincoln established a military and naval reserve on the site. High hopes for a grand future led city fathers to base the town's original layout on that of Cincinnati.

But the grandest ambitions of Port Angeles never came to pass. With major shifts in timber and commercial fishing, the city of 19,000 is turning its waterfront into a recreational asset. The Port Angeles Waterfront Trail includes a path for walking and bicycling that passes restored wetlands areas and an observation tower with views of the city's incomparable Olympic Mountains backdrop. Eventually it will become part of the planned Olympic Discovery Trail, which will allow visitors to bicycle from Port Townsend to the Pacific Ocean.

"The waterfront is becoming our front door, rather than the place where people work," says community development director Brad Collins. "But people can come here and still see the old working harbor town. With the exception of one mill, everything that was here is

PORT OF CALL
NEWPORT, OREGON

WHERE: About 2½ hours southwest of Portland.

ON THE WATERFRONT: The **Oregon Coast Aquarium** is one of the best in the West. *10–5 daily; $10.75. 2820 S.E. Ferry Slip Rd.; (541) 867-3474.* Newport's historic waterfront blends a still-active fishing industry and an assortment of shops and attractions.

OTHER ATTRACTIONS: There are two 19th-century **lighthouses in the area**, at Yaquina Bay and at Yaquina Head north of town.

DINING: Blackfish Cafe. Worth the 30-minute drive north of town to Lincoln City: Well-executed flavors, from a Vietnamese salad to steamed clams in an herby wine broth. *Closed Tue. 2733 N.W. U.S. 101, Lincoln City; (541) 996-1007.* **Canyon Way Restaurant & Bookstore.** The best of beach funk—in a 1910 building. Crispy fried oysters and cornmeal-coated local fish with peel-on fries. *1216 S.W. Canyon Way; (541) 265-8319.* **Kam Meng Chinese Restaurant.** Tiny restaurant offers great crab and clay pot specialties. *Closed Wed. 837 S.W. Bay Blvd.; (541) 574-9450.* **Mo's Restaurant.** A seafood institution. *622 S.W. Bay; (541) 265-2979.* **Whale's Tale.** Excellent local seafood in a circa 1976 spot. *452 S.W. Bay; (541) 265-8660.*

LODGING: Elizabeth Street Inn. All rooms have ocean views and fireplaces. *From $109. 232 S.W. Elizabeth St.; (877) 265-9400 or www.elizabethstreetinn.com.* **Sylvia Beach Hotel.** A literary-themed inn, with rooms named for writers from Herman Melville to Dr. Seuss. *From $83. 267 N.W. Cliff St.; (888) 795-8422, (541) 265-5428or www.sylviabeachhotel.com.*

CONTACT: Greater Newport Chamber of Commerce: (800) 262-7844 or www.newportchamber.org.

A TASTE OF NEWPORT: MO'S RESTAURANT
Mo's Oyster Stew

Mohava Niemi—erstwhile innkeeper, radio announcer, and generous, chain-smoking host—is the stuff of legend in Newport. Mo's clam chowder, now served in the restaurant's six locations, might have put the institution on the map, but its oyster stew connects it concretely to the place—the oyster beds just around the point inside Yaquina Bay Bridge, in one of the cleanest estuaries on the coast. According to Cindy McEntee, Mo's granddaughter and caretaker of the legend (to say nothing of the business), only medium Pacifics from these beds go into the stew.

PREP AND COOK TIME: 12 to 14 minutes
NOTES: Mo's uses whole milk in this stew, which makes the wonderful, briny flavor of the oysters stand out. For a richer texture but milder oyster flavor, you can substitute half-and-half (light cream) for 1 to 2 cups of the milk. Serve the stew with dense, fresh sourdough bread.
MAKES: 5½ cups; 4 servings

- 1 quart **whole milk** (see notes)
- 1 pound **shucked oysters** in their liquor
-   **Salt** and **pepper**
- 2 tablespoons **butter**

1. In a 2½- to 3-quart pan over medium heat, stir milk often just until steaming, about 6 minutes; do not boil.

2. Meanwhile, drain oysters (reserve liquor) and cut into bite-size pieces. Add oysters and liquor to milk and occasionally stir gently just until heated through, 3 to 4 minutes. Add salt and pepper to taste.

3. Ladle stew evenly into four wide, shallow bowls and top each with ½ tablespoon butter.

Per serving: 278 cal., 55% (153 cal.) from fat; 16 g protein; 17 g fat (9.4 g sat.); 16 g carbo (0 g fiber); 305 mg sodium; 112 mg chol.

still here. It's hardly changed. This will be one of the last bastions of what the Pacific Northwest used to be."

The romance of harbor-town life is balanced by not only the economic realities but also the inherent danger of small vessels heading out into the Pacific. Almost every harbor town has its indelibly poignant memorial, a marker to its sons and daughters who have died at sea.

In Newport, the Fishermen's Memorial Sanctuary is an octagonal structure on a bluff in Yaquina Bay State Park. A black granite podium shows a fishing boat heading out to a sunset sea. Inscribed into the stone are the names of locals who went out into the Pacific and never returned.

On this afternoon, the top of the podium is crowded with offerings: bouquets of flowers, a 24-ounce can of malt liquor, a candle wrapped with a photo of a smiling young bearded man, and a card offering wishes to one fisherman on what would have been his 22nd birthday.

As an outsider it's difficult to fully appreciate the risks of living here—but equally difficult to understand the rewards. For many people in Newport, this is a life they could never give up. Over the last years, the city has worked very hard to ensure that it remains both a visitor destination and a working port.

Says Newport poet and businessman John Baker, "I like seeing the lumber ships come in. And whenever I drive over the bridge, I always look out to see how many fishing boats are coming in or going out. The town has a life of its own, and the life around it supports the community."

The next afternoon, the boats line up on Newport's Yaquina Bay: trollers and crabbers, long-liners and shrimpers, draggers, charters, and pleasure craft. From a staging area off Idaho Point, they sail toward the bridge, where they receive blessings from ministers standing on a coast guard lifeboat. In this way the Newport fleet connects to an ancient maritime tradition of asking for safe passage and a bountiful catch. A glass float by local artist Toni Kuchar is then dropped into the ocean to drift with the flow, its tricolored swirls symbolizing the currents of this day: black for mourning, green for life, and blue for the sea itself.

A t Trinidad on the Northern California coast, a boat out of Fortuna ties up to the pier, where a crew unloads a stack of crab traps. It's been a bad year for Dungeness, and everyone is hoping that things will pick up once the salmon run begins.

The town's tiny fishing fleet rolls in languid swells that lap up against the tree-topped sea stacks along its shore. Trinidad feels peacefully timeless: a town of 300 or so residents with a barely-there commercial district, its nearby redwood forests and empty, driftwood-strewn beaches like something out of another century.

But in the mid-1800s, Trinidad was a bustling port town. During the Gold Rush on the Klamath and Trinity Rivers, Trinidad's population swelled with eager gold-seekers who had made the trip by boat from San Francisco. Then, with the decline in mining and whaling, Trinidad was quickly overshadowed by the nearby lumber center of Eureka.

PORT OF CALL
TRINIDAD, CALIFORNIA

WHERE: About six hours north of San Francisco.

ON THE WATERFRONT: Trinidad's waterfront is more natural than working, though there is a pier with fishing boats. You can do the short hike to the top of **Trinidad Head** to see a replica of a cross left by Spanish explorers. There is plenty of beach exploring near town at **Luffenholtz County Park** and **Trinidad State Beach.**

OTHER ATTRACTIONS: Patrick's **Point State Park** just north of town has an excellent blufftop trail and a driftwood-filled beach. **Redwood National Park** is about 20 minutes away.

DINING: Katy's Smokehouse. Some of the best smoked fish you'll ever eat. *740 Edwards St.; (707) 677-0151.* **Larrupin Cafe.** Filled with weavings and art, the restaurant has a soulful atmos-

phere that complements beautifully prepared local seafood and grilled items. *1658 Patrick's Point Dr.; (707) 677-0230.* **Seascape Restaurant.** Casual waterfront dining at the base of Trinidad Pier. *(707) 677-3762.*

LODGING: Lost Whale Bed & Breakfast Inn. A child-friendly spot with a New England ambience, it sits high above a rocky cove north of Trinidad. *From $170. 3452 Patrick's Point; (800) 677-7859 or www.lostwhaleinn.com.* **Turtle Rocks Oceanfront Inn.** Private decks and panoramic views from each of its spacious rooms. *From $165. 3392 Patrick's Point; (707) 677-3707 or www.turtlerocksinn.com.*

CONTACT: Trinidad Chamber of Commerce: (707) 677-1610 or www. trinidadcalifchamber.org.

Larrupin Cornish Hens with Orange-Brandy Glaze

Trinidad's whimsical **Larrupin Cafe** is the 19-year-old creation of Dixie Gorrell, inspired by memories of her aunt's ultimate praise: "That's larrupin' good food, honey!" Diners lured in for dinner more than one night running (a common phenomenon) have "larrupin'" options for changing the pace from seafood—ribs, the local favorite, and these hearty hens among them. The birds are marinated in a brew of beer, soy sauce, and brown sugar, then finished with an orange-brandy glaze.

PREP AND COOK TIME: About 1½ hours, plus at least 4 hours to marinate

NOTES: You can make the glaze (step 2) up to 1 day ahead; cover and chill.

MAKES: 4 servings

- 4 **Cornish hens** (about 1 lb. each)
- 4½ cups **beer** such as pale ale (three 12-oz. bottles)
- 2 cups **soy sauce**
- ¾ cup firmly packed **brown sugar**
- ¼ cup **molasses**
- 2 tablespoons minced **garlic**
- 2 tablespoons minced **fresh ginger**
- 1 tablespoon **dry mustard**
- 1 tablespoon **black pepper**
- ¾ cup **frozen orange juice concentrate** (half of a 12-oz. container)
- ½ cup **brandy**
- ½ cup fat-skimmed **chicken broth**
- ½ cup **whipping cream**
  Orange slices (optional)

1. Remove necks and giblets from hens; reserve for another use or discard. Rinse hens. In a large bowl, whisk beer, soy sauce, ½ cup brown sugar, molasses, garlic, ginger, dry mustard, and black pepper until well blended. Immerse hens in marinade; cover and chill at least 4 hours or up to 1 day, turning hens occasionally and submerging in liquid.

2. Meanwhile, in a 2½- to 3-quart pan, combine orange juice concentrate, remaining ¼ cup brown sugar, and the brandy. Bring mixture to a boil over medium-high heat and stir until sugar is dissolved, 2 to 4 minutes. Use warm or cool.

3. Lift hens from marinade (discard marinade) and set breast up in a 10- by 15-inch pan. Brush generously with orange-brandy glaze.

4. Bake in a 400° regular or convection oven, brushing every 10 minutes with glaze, until hens are richly browned and meat at breast and thigh bones is no longer pink (cut to test), 30 to 40 minutes. Transfer hens to a platter or plates and let stand in a warm place.

5. Meanwhile, skim and discard fat from pan juices. Add broth, cream, and remaining orange-brandy glaze to pan and stir often over medium-high heat, scraping up browned bits, until liquid is slightly thickened, 10 to 12 minutes. Pour into a small pitcher or bowl. Garnish hens with orange slices, if desired, and serve with pan juices.

Per serving: 716 cal., 55% (396 cal.) from fat; 46 g protein; 44 g fat (15 g sat.); 31 g carbo (0.5 g fiber); 1,177 mg sodium; 283 mg chol.

Destiny had passed Trinidad by.

The kind of economic shifts occurring in Port Angeles happened here long ago. Yet even with all the changes, there are locals who still count on Trinidad's most basic elements—a safe harbor and a steady food supply from the sea—just as the Tsurai Indians did for hundreds of years before the arrival of Spanish explorers, Russian fur traders, and, finally, American miners. In harbor towns, some things change and some things don't. ◆

Great ideas in food and wine

WINE
The next big red

SEPTEMBER SEEMS THE RIGHT TIME TO LEARN ABOUT SOMETHING NEW. Like Syrah. At the moment, Syrah isn't as well known as Cabernet Sauvignon, Merlot, or Zinfandel, but just wait: Winemakers say Syrah is poised to become the West's next major red wine.

JADE MOUNTAIN Syrah 1999 (Napa Valley), $28. Classic gamey, earthy, cherry flavors with touches of licorice and chocolate. **Bottom line:** Grilled duck breast would be just the ticket.

BONTERRA Syrah 1999 (Mendocino), $24. Juicy flavors reminiscent of bing cherries and boysenberries. **Bottom line:** Satisfying and supple on the palate.

QUPÉ Los Olivos Cuvée 1999 (Santa Barbara County), $20. Syrah blended with a little Mourvedre and Grenache. Rugged yet lush with dark berry and earth flavors. **Bottom line:** Think Saturday night and slowly braised lamb shanks.

ALBAN "Reva" Syrah 2000 (Edna Valley), $44. Dark rich brooding fruit and beautiful structure. **Bottom line:** Made for romance.

— *Karen MacNeil-Fife*

RESTAURANT
Charlie's Angels

YOUNG WOMEN POWER AN OLD-WORLD RESTAURANT. Enter the quiet, dark, clubby atmosphere of **Charles Nob Hill** in San Francisco and you might not guess that the power in the kitchen lies in the hands of executive chef Melissa Perello. Just 26 years old, she produces intensely flavored dishes with great sophistication. Together with sommelier Jane Rate and pastry chef Shelly Kaldunski—collectively nicknamed Charlie's Angels—they produce dinners that belie their youth. "We have an energetic staff that fills the restaurant with youthful energy. It's conveyed through the whole dining experience—you really feel it," says Perello. *1250 Jones St.; (415) 771-5400.*

RECIPE: **Fried Green Tomatoes**

1 Rinse 2 **green** (unripe) **tomatoes** (8 oz. each); cut crosswise into ½-inch-thick slices, discarding tops and bottoms. Lightly sprinkle both sides of slices with **salt** and **pepper**. Lay in a single layer on paper towels. Let stand 5 to 10 minutes. **2** Meanwhile, cut 2 **ripe red tomatoes** (8 oz. each) in half and squeeze juice and flesh into a fine strainer set over a bowl; press enough tomato solids through strainer to make about ⅓ cup liquid. **3** Coat green tomato slices in **semolina flour** or yellow cornmeal. Pour 2 tablespoons **olive oil** into a 10- to 12-inch nonstick frying pan over medium heat. Cook tomato slices in a single layer until golden brown on both sides, 8 to 10 minutes total. Stack slices on two dinner plates. **4** Add the ⅓ cup tomato juice and solids, 2 tablespoons **sherry vinegar** or red wine vinegar, and 2 tablespoons **butter** to pan; stir constantly over medium-high heat until butter is melted and incorporated into juices, 1 to 2 minutes. Add 1 tablespoon chopped **parsley** and **salt** and **pepper** to taste. Spoon sauce over tomato stacks. **5** Mix 1 cup rinsed and crisped **frisée** or baby salad mix with 1 teaspoon **olive oil;** mound equally on tomato stacks. Makes 2 servings. — *Linda Lau Anusasananan*

Power trio (l to r): Kaldunski, Rate, and Perello of Charles Nob Hill.

INGREDIENT
Hawaii gold

A BITE OF THIS NEW PINEAPPLE IS A QUICK TRIP TO PARADISE. Del Monte Fresh Produce's Hawaii Gold is the first new Hawaiian variety to hit the market in more than 20 years; we think it was worth the wait. Grown in Hawaii, it comes packed with extra sweetness and vitamin C. While eating it plain is wonderful, sprinkling it with tingly Southeast Asian chili salt is a zippy change of pace. Cut the fruit decoratively in pretty notched slices, or simply cut the rind deep enough to remove the eyes, then slice it into rounds.

RECIPE: **Thai Sweet-Hot Pineapple Blossoms.**
Cut ½ inch off the top and bottom of 1 **pineapple** (4 to 5 lb.). Slice off rind about ¼ inch deep, from top to bottom. To remove eyes and make decorative notched edges, use a small knife to cut continuous, parallel, wedge-shaped rows (½ in. deep) into the sides of pineapple, following the spiral pattern of the eyes and working from top to bottom. Cut fruit crosswise into ¼- to ½-inch-thick slices; arrange on a platter or plates. Cut 2 **limes** (3 to 4 oz. each) into halves or wedges. Mix 1 tablespoon **salt** with ¼ teaspoon **hot chili flakes** and ¼ teaspoon **cayenne**. Squeeze lime over fruit and offer chili salt to add to taste. Makes 8 to 10 appetizer servings.
— *Linda Lau Anusasananan*

Go-go boba

AN ICED DRINK THAT GIVES YOU SOMETHING TO CHEW ON. Boba (or bubble) tea, a Taiwanese version of the ubiquitous iced drink, trickled into tea-houses in the West several years ago after taking hold in Taiwan in the 1980s as the beverage of choice for young professionals. In recent months, however, the chewable drink—it features sweetly flavored tapioca balls at the bottom of the glass—has spread beyond the Taiwanese and Chinese communities in Los Angeles to major cities across the country. *For make- your-own boba tea instructions or to order tapioca balls and other supplies, go to www. tenren.com.*

WHERE TO GO FOR BOBA

Boba Bar Bubble Tea Lounge. Coffee-house vibe, with rotating art exhibits. *12044¹/₂ Ventura Blvd., Studio City; (818) 763-4790.*

One cool drink: Boba tea is advancing across the West.

Sweet Delite. Owner Bianca Yao prepares boba in the traditional Tai-wanese fashion but with some untraditional flavors: mango, watermelon, and taro, which tastes like cookies 'n cream. *519 Clement St., San Francisco; (415) 386-8222.*

Sweetheart Café. Bustling cafe serves burgers, ice cream, and more than 100 different kinds of bubble tea, including sesame and almond. *2523 Durant Ave., Berkeley; (510) 540-0707.*

Tea Station. Dim sum, Chinese board games, and imported silk screens. *158 W. Valley Blvd., San Gabriel; (626) 288-3785.*

Hong Kong Garden Deli. Owner Wai Chu Ip offers more than a dozen standard boba flavors, but he delights in brewing up custom concoctions such as fresh strawberries, pineapple, and cream. *Closed Tue. 1044 S. Federal Blvd., Denver; (303) 937-8882.*

— *Laura Randall, Kris Carber, James Boone*

An easy turkey enchilada casserole makes a hearty autumn dinner.

JAMES CARRIER; FOOD STYLING: JOANNA CANTRALL

Hot turkey

Quick weeknight way to spice up lean ground turkey

By Tiffany Armstrong

■ Ground turkey is almost a cliché of low-fat cooking—for good reason: It's a great way to serve a meaty dish with a lot of protein but little saturated fat. It's also inexpensive and widely avail-able. Best of all, though, turkey does a great job of absorbing and carrying seasonings, making it a natural for spicy preparations where you want the flavor—not the fat—to be the star.

Turkey Enchilada Casserole

PREP AND COOK TIME: About 45 minutes
NOTES: If desired, serve with reduced-fat sour cream.
MAKES: 8 to 10 servings

- 1¹/₂ pounds **ground turkey breast**
- ¹/₂ cup chopped **onion**
- 1 tablespoon minced **garlic**
- 2 tablespoons minced **fresh oregano** leaves or 1 tablespoon dried
- ¹/₂ teaspoon **ground cumin**
- 1 teaspoon **salad oil**
- 1 can (29 oz.) **red enchilada sauce**
  Salt
- 12 **corn tortillas** (6 in. wide)
- 2 cups **shredded reduced-fat jack cheese** (8 oz.)
  Chopped **fresh cilantro**

1. In a 5- to 6-quart pan over high heat, stir turkey, onion, garlic, oregano, and cumin in oil until turkey is crumbly and no longer pink, about 4 minutes. Stir in 1 cup enchilada sauce. Add salt to taste.

2. Meanwhile, cut tortillas in half. Arrange a fourth of the halves evenly over the bottom of a shallow 3-quart casserole, overlapping to fit. Sprinkle a fourth of the cheese evenly over the tortillas, then top with a third of the turkey mixture and a fourth of the remaining enchilada sauce, spreading each level. Repeat to make two more layers of tortillas, cheese, turkey mixture, and sauce; top with another layer of tortillas and sauce, then cheese.

3. Bake in a 425° regular or convection oven until cheese is melted and casserole is hot in the center, 18 to 20 minutes. Sprinkle with chopped cilantro.

Per serving: 249 cal., 20% (51 cal.) from fat; 27 g protein; 5.7 g fat (3.1 g sat.); 23 g carbo (1.7 g fiber); 1,048 mg sodium; 58 mg chol. ◆

JOHN GRANEN

Farmers' market special

Posy and porcini pasta makes a beautiful autumn meal

JAMES CARRIER; FOOD STYLING: BASIL FRIEDMAN

Porcini–Zucchini Blossom Orecchiette

PREP AND COOK TIME: About 30 minutes

NOTES: Zucchini blossoms are sold in some specialty produce stores as well as in farmers' markets (often attached to the squash), and can sometimes be ordered there. But if you don't have access to the blossoms, don't shy away from this dish; it's almost as tasty—if not as beautiful—without the flowers.

MAKES: 4 servings

- 1 pound **dried orecchiette pasta**
- 1½ cups **zucchini blossoms** (see notes)
- 6 tablespoons **extra-virgin olive oil**
- 2 tablespoons minced **garlic**
- 8 ounces **fresh porcini** or common **mushrooms**, rinsed briefly, tough stem ends removed, and thinly sliced
- ¼ cup chopped **fresh herbs** such as mint and basil leaves and/or Italian parsley (choose one or a mixture)
- 2 cups **cherry tomatoes** such as Sweet 100s (about 12 oz.), rinsed, stemmed, and halved if larger than ¾ inch

  Salt and fresh-ground **pepper**

  Parmesan cheese curls (optional)

Short of a roadside produce stand, farmers' markets are about the most direct route fruits and vegetables can take from field to kitchen. And occasionally, two or three items appear in markets at the same time that together capture the beauty and earthiness of the harvest.

In early fall, porcini mushrooms and zucchini blossoms are just such a pair. Porcinis have two seasons a year—spring and fall—and zucchini squash, of course, are available in spades (and therefore the blossoms too) all summer long in the West. But in the fall, they overlap.

Chef Matt Lyman of One Pico, at Santa Monica's Shutters on the Beach hotel, takes full advantage of produce timing, shopping at the farmers' market for the restaurant's seasonal menu. When I trailed him through the market, he bagged delicate young zucchini blossoms and fresh porcinis, then later stirred the blossoms into pasta and shaved the mushrooms over the top. Since the porcinis and the squash blossoms available aren't always quite so delicate, I sauté the mushrooms and quarter the petals of the flowers.

1. In a 5- to 6-quart pan over high heat, bring 3 to 4 quarts water to a boil. Add orecchiette and cook, stirring occasionally, until barely tender to bite, 15 to 18 minutes.

2. Meanwhile, rinse and drain zucchini blossoms; reserve about four blossoms for garnish. Pull petals from remaining blossoms and cut lengthwise into quarters; discard tough stem ends and other parts.

3. Pour 2 tablespoons olive oil into a 10- to 12-inch frying pan over medium-high heat; when hot, add garlic and porcini and stir just until mushrooms are limp and liquid is evaporated, 5 to 6 minutes. Stir in herbs and remove from heat.

4. Drain pasta, reserving 1 cup cooking liquid, and return to pan. Add mushroom mixture, along with tomatoes, quartered zucchini blossoms, remaining ¼ cup olive oil, and salt and pepper to taste. Mix gently over medium-low heat until warmed through, 5 to 7 minutes. If pasta is too dry, add reserved cooking liquid as desired. Spoon into wide, shallow bowls and garnish portions with reserved whole zucchini blossoms. Top with parmesan curls if desired.

Per serving: 643 cal., 32% (207 cal.) from fat; 17 g protein; 23 g fat (3.3 g sat.); 94 g carbo (5 g fiber); 20 mg sodium; 0 mg chol.

— *Sara Schneider*

Culinary calculations

If you find a simple calculator valuable in the kitchen, then you'll find the Kitchen Calc Pro *in*valuable. It not only adds, subtracts, multiplies, and divides, but it also converts cups to tablespoons and ounces to grams, as well as performing all manner of other calculations. In addition, the Kitchen Calc Pro has a digital timer that can run while you adjust recipe proportions or serving sizes or calculate anything else. The numbers are large, and the calculator fits into a plastic sleeve that keeps it clean in food-prep battle zones. Produced by aptly named Calculated Industries in Carson City, Nevada, and available in specialty cookware stores, the countertop Kitchen Calc Pro (model 8304) sells for about $40; a smaller handheld model costs about $25. *(800) 854-8075 or www.calculated.com. — Jerry Anne Di Vecchio*

The Wine Guide
Daring pairing

By Karen MacNeil-Fife

This is a wine story, but it starts with a fig—and with a woman named Sondra Bernstein, one of California Wine Country's dynamic chef-restaurateurs. Bernstein owns the Girl & the Fig restaurant in Sonoma as well as the Girl & the Gaucho in the nearby hamlet of Glen Ellen. Bernstein (the "girl") is a passionate wine lover and isn't afraid to admit she loves to eat. Her approach to creating satisfying meals accompanied by delicious wines is a lesson for those of us faced with choosing wines to serve with our food.

In 1997, when Bernstein opened the Girl & the Fig (then located in a small bungalow in Glen Ellen) on the barest shoestring budget, she "only had enough money for a small wine list," as she puts it. It had just 14 wines, and every one of them was a Rhône variety (one traditionally grown in France's Rhône Valley). "I wanted food-friendly wines that were relaxed, comfortable, reasonably priced, and that felt right with our simple country dishes," Bernstein explains. "But I also knew that in opening my own restaurant, I was being daring. I looked around me at all the great wine-makers who were being daring too, and they were making Rhône-style wines. It all fit perfectly."

In the beginning, customers looked at the list, furrowed their brows, and asked Bernstein if she had any Chardonnay. She smiled and brought them a taste of Viognier instead (see "Bernstein's advice" below left). She still gives guests a complimentary taste of any opened wine.

Maybe it's that gesture of generosity, but sitting in the Girl & the Fig's sun-filled dining room eating a grilled-fig salad and drinking a glass of Viognier feels like you're in Bernstein's home. Which is perhaps why her choice of reasonably priced, comforting Rhône wines makes sense for anyone who entertains. Wines that don't break the bank, that are extremely food-friendly, and that embody a relaxed lifestyle are, well, wines for our times. "We're so busy as a culture," says Bernstein, "that a simple delicious dish and a great glass of wine have become something more than themselves—they've become the ultimate escape." ◆

Bernstein's advice

Three great food matches—and the best Rhônes for your taste

■ **Fig salad** (arugula, toasted pecans, grilled figs, pancetta, and crumbled goat cheese) with Roussanne. Favorite choice: Sobon Estate.

■ **Grilled lamb chops** in a Syrah wine reduction sauce with Syrah or Carignane. Favorite choice: Ballentine Syrah.

■ **Grilled pork chops** with apple cider sauce and an apple–sweet potato gratin with a red Rhône blend. Favorite choice: Joseph Phelps Le Mistral (Grenache, Syrah, Mourvèdre, Alicante Bouchet, Carignane, and Petite Syrah).

JAMES CARRIER; ABOVE: E. SPENCER TOY

If you're a ...	and you like ...	try ...
Sauvignon Blanc drinker	melon, fig, floral, and herbal flavors	Roussanne
Chardonnay drinker	big, buttery whites	Viognier
Merlot drinker	soft, super-fruity reds	Mourvèdre
Cabernet Sauvignon drinker	intense, rich reds	Syrah (also called Shiraz)

Fresh figs

New ways with an ancient fruit, from sandwich to dessert

By Charity Ferreira

Photographs by James Carrier

There is no better emblem of the double-edged pleasure of seasonality than a backyard fig tree. On one hand, you have uncommon access to an extraordinary fruit that has been revered for centuries, the subject of legends and lore from the Bible to Homer—a fruit whose grassy sweetness evokes sunny and exotic climates.

On the other hand, you're likely to tread on ripe figs when they drop onto the ground and melt into a puddle of sticky syrup. The more prolific the tree, the greater the sweet urgency to appreciate as many of them as you can—now. Fig season (actually seasons—see "At the market" at right) is short; once they're gone, they're gone. Make the most of this season's crop, whether from that backyard tree or the market, in tempting dishes such as flatbread, grilled salmon, or fruit-topped cakes.

At the market

Most varieties of fig trees bear fruit twice a year, giving us two seasons. Look for them in the market in early summer and then again in late summer to early fall. Choose figs that are soft and unblemished, wrap them loosely in a plastic bag, and refrigerate. They'll last between a few days and a week, depending on how ripe they are when you buy them.

Grilled Chicken Sandwich with Fig Relish

PREP AND COOK TIME: About 30 minutes
NOTES: Use soft-ripe figs for the relish, which is also good with crackers or toasted baguette slices as an appetizer or alongside roast chicken.
MAKES: 3 sandwiches

- 3 **boned, skinned chicken breast halves** (about 6 oz. each)

  About ¼ cup **olive oil**

  Salt and **pepper**

- 6 slices (about 5 by 3 in. and ½ in. thick) **sourdough bread**

- ¾ cup **arugula leaves** or salad mix, rinsed and crisped

  Fig relish (recipe follows)

1. Place each chicken breast half between two sheets of plastic wrap; with a flat mallet or rolling pin, gently pound to ½ inch thick. Brush both sides of chicken lightly with olive oil and sprinkle with salt and pepper.

2. Lay chicken on an oiled grill over a solid bed of hot coals or high heat on a gas grill (you can hold your hand at grill level only 2 to 3 seconds); close lid on gas grill. Cook, turning once, until chicken is no longer pink in the center (cut to test), 6 to 8 minutes total. Meanwhile, brush both sides of bread lightly with oil. When you turn chicken, lay bread slices on grill and cook, turning once, until lightly toasted, about 4 minutes total.

3. To assemble each sandwich, top one slice of bread with about ¼ cup arugula leaves. Place chicken on arugula and top with about ⅓ cup fig relish. Top with second slice of grilled bread. Serve warm.

Per sandwich: 546 cal., 36% (198 cal.) from fat; 45 g protein; 22 g fat (3.4 g sat.); 42 g carbo (4.1 g fiber); 517 mg sodium; 99 mg chol.

Fig relish. In a bowl, combine 1½ tablespoons **balsamic vinegar**, 1 tablespoon minced **shallot,** and ⅛ teaspoon **salt.** Let stand 10 minutes. Rinse 8 ounces ripe **Mission figs**; pat dry and trim off and discard stem ends. Cut figs into ½-inch chunks; add to vinegar mixture. Stir in 2 teaspoons chopped **fresh mint** leaves and ¼ teaspoon minced **fresh rosemary** leaves, breaking figs up slightly with spoon. Makes about 1 cup.

Per ¼ cup: 45 cal., 4% (1.8 cal.) from fat; 0.5 g protein; 0.2 g fat (0 g sat.); 12 g carbo (2 g fiber); 75 mg sodium; 0 mg chol.

Fig and Ricotta Cheese Flatbread

PREP AND COOK TIME: About 1½ hours, plus 35 to 45 minutes to rise

NOTES: You can make the dough through step 2 up to 1 day ahead; punch it down, cover bowl with plastic wrap, and chill. Let stand at room temperature about 1 hour before proceeding with shaping (step 4).

MAKES: 4 flatbreads; about 12 appetizer or 6 main-course servings

1 package (2¼ teaspoons) **active dry yeast**

About 1 teaspoon **salt**

2 tablespoons **olive oil**

About 3½ cups **all-purpose flour**

3 **red onions** (about 1¾ lb. total), peeled, halved, and thinly sliced

2 tablespoons **balsamic vinegar**

About ¼ teaspoon **pepper**

About ¼ cup **yellow cornmeal**

About 2 cups (1 carton, 15 oz.) **ricotta cheese**

1 pound **firm-ripe figs**, rinsed, stem ends trimmed, and halved lengthwise

½ cup **chopped walnuts**

½ cup crumbled **blue cheese** (about 3 oz.), optional

3 ounces **arugula leaves** (about 2 cups), rinsed and crisped

1. In a large bowl, sprinkle yeast over 1½ cups warm (110°) water. Let stand until softened, about 5 minutes. Stir in ½ teaspoon salt and 1 tablespoon olive oil. Gradually mix in 3½ cups flour until a soft dough forms.

2. *If using a mixer,* beat with a dough hook on high speed until dough no longer feels sticky and pulls cleanly from sides of bowl, 5 to 7 minutes. If dough is still sticky, beat in more flour, 1 tablespoon at a time.

If kneading by hand, scrape dough onto a lightly floured board. Knead until smooth, springy, and no longer sticky, 15 to 20 minutes; add flour as needed to prevent sticking. Place dough in an oiled bowl and turn to coat.

Cover and let rise in a warm place until doubled, 35 to 45 minutes.

3. Meanwhile, in a 10- to 12-inch frying pan over medium-high heat, stir onions in remaining 1 tablespoon olive oil until very limp, 25 to 30 minutes. If onions start to burn or stick, reduce heat and stir in 1 tablespoon water. Add balsamic vinegar, ¼ teaspoon pepper, and ½ teaspoon salt and stir until liquid is evaporated, 1 to 2 minutes longer.

4. Scrape dough onto a lightly floured board; press gently to expel air. Divide into four equal pieces. Place pieces on floured board and cover with plastic wrap; let rest 10 minutes. Roll or stretch one piece at a time into a 13- by 7-inch oval about ¹⁄₁₆ inch thick. Place each oval on a cornmeal-dusted 12- by 15-inch rimless baking sheet; stretch dough, if needed, to reshape.

5. Arrange about ½ cup red onions evenly over each oval. Drop ricotta in ½-tablespoon portions over onions (about 12 on each oval); arrange figs, cut side up, around cheese. Sprinkle about 2 tablespoons walnuts and 2 tablespoons blue cheese (if desired) evenly over each oval.

6. Bake in a 450° regular or convection oven until crust is well browned on top and bottom, 15 to 20 minutes (10 to 15 minutes in a convection oven). If baking two sheets in one oven, switch their positions halfway through baking. Slide each flatbread onto a cutting board or plate. Mound arugula leaves equally on top; cut each oval in half lengthwise, then crosswise into eight slices. Add salt and pepper to taste.

Per appetizer serving: 347 cal., 34% (117 cal.) from fat; 12 g protein; 13 g fat (4.9 g sat.); 47 g carbo (3.9 g fiber); 333 mg sodium; 23 mg chol.

Pork Tenderloin with Figs and Blue Cheese Polenta

PREP AND COOK TIME: About 40 minutes
MAKES: 4 servings

1 **pork tenderloin** (about 1 lb.)

About ½ teaspoon **salt**

Pepper

½ teaspoon **olive oil**

12 **firm-ripe figs**, rinsed, stem ends trimmed, and halved lengthwise

3 **thyme sprigs** (each about 3 in. long), rinsed

1 cup **coarse polenta**

About ⅓ cup crumbled **blue cheese** (about 1½ oz.)

1 cup **dry red wine**

1 tablespoon **honey**

1 teaspoon grated **orange** peel

1. Rinse pork and pat dry; trim and discard fat and any silvery membrane from tenderloin. Sprinkle meat lightly with salt and pepper. Pour oil into a 10- to 12-inch nonstick, ovenproof frying pan over high heat, tilting pan to coat bottom; when oil is hot, add tenderloin and turn as needed to brown on all sides, about 4 minutes total. Remove from heat; arrange figs and thyme sprigs around pork.

2. Transfer pan with pork to a 400° regular or convection oven; bake until a thermometer inserted in center of thickest part of meat reaches 155°, 18 to 25 minutes.

3. Meanwhile, in a 4- to 6-quart pan, combine polenta, ½ teaspoon salt, and 4½ cups water. Stir over high heat until mixture boils; reduce heat to medium-low and simmer, stirring occasionally, until polenta is smooth to taste, 25 to 30 minutes. Remove from heat and stir in ⅓ cup blue cheese; add salt and

Warm figs, cheese, and nuts contrast deliciously on crisp flatbread.

pepper to taste. Cover and keep warm.

4. Transfer tenderloin and figs to a rimmed platter and let stand in a warm place for 5 minutes. Add wine, honey, and orange peel to unwashed frying pan. Boil over high heat, stirring to release browned bits, until mixture is reduced to about $\frac{1}{2}$ cup, 4 to 5 minutes. Remove and discard thyme sprigs.

5. Slice pork diagonally across the grain $\frac{1}{2}$ inch thick. Spoon polenta mixture equally onto four dinner plates. Arrange pork and figs over polenta; spoon sauce equally over pork and figs. Top with more blue cheese if desired.

Per serving: 457 cal., 22% (99 cal.) from fat; 30 g protein; 11 g fat (4.4 g sat.); 62 g carbo (6.7 g fiber); 500 mg sodium; 83 mg chol.

Grilled Salmon in Fig Leaves with Fig Skewers

PREP AND COOK TIME: About 50 minutes
NOTES: The bundles can be assembled through step 4 up to 4 hours ahead; wrap airtight and chill. Let stand at room temperature for 15 minutes before grilling. If you can't find fresh fig leaves, omit; brush fish with reduced vinegar and place directly on the grill.
MAKES: 4 servings

$\frac{2}{3}$ cup **balsamic vinegar**

$1\frac{1}{2}$ pounds **boned, skinned salmon fillet,** cut into 4 equal pieces

Salt and **pepper**

About 6 **fig leaves** (about 8 by 8 in.; see notes)

About $\frac{1}{3}$ cup **olive oil**

Fig skewers (recipe follows)

1. In a 1- to 2-quart pan over medium-high heat, boil vinegar until slightly syrupy and reduced to about $\frac{1}{3}$ cup, about 6 minutes. Let cool to room temperature, 5 to 10 minutes.

2. Meanwhile, rinse salmon and pat dry. Sprinkle with salt and pepper.

3. Rinse fig leaves and pat dry. Lay dark side down, stem end pointing toward you. Break center vein of leaf close to stem so leaf will fold easily. Generously brush top of leaf with reduced vinegar.

4. Place one piece of salmon horizontally across middle of leaf. If salmon has a thin end, tuck under so the piece is evenly thick. Brush salmon with reduced vinegar. Fold stem end of leaf over salmon. Fold in sides, then roll up to enclose fish (if leaf is not large enough to wrap around fish, unfold and lay a second leaf slightly overlapping the first; use both leaves to wrap fish). Dampen a 12-inch length of heavy cotton string and wrap around center of bundle, then turn 90° and wrap in the other direction; tie securely, then trim string ends $\frac{1}{2}$ inch from knot. Repeat to wrap remaining salmon. Brush outsides of bundles with olive oil.

5. Lay bundles on an oiled grill over a solid bed of hot coals or high heat on a gas grill (you can hold your hand at grill level only 2 to 3 seconds); close lid on gas grill. Cook, turning once, until a thermometer inserted through leaf into center of fish reaches 140°, 8 to 10 minutes total. With a wide spatula, transfer each bundle to a dinner plate. Cut string and serve with fig skewers; unwrap bundles and discard fig leaves before eating.

Per serving: 626 cal., 53% (333 cal.) from fat; 35 g protein; 37 g fat (6.2 g sat.); 41 g carbo (6.6 g fiber); 250 mg sodium; 100 mg chol.

Fig skewers. Soak 8 wood skewers (at least 8 in. long) in cold water for about 10 minutes. Rinse 16 **firm-ripe figs** and pat dry. Trim away stem ends; cut figs in half lengthwise. Thread 4 fig halves onto each skewer. Drizzle cut sides with a total of 2 tablespoons **lime juice** and sprinkle with about $\frac{1}{4}$ teaspoon **salt**. Grill figs cut side down over high heat until warm and slightly charred, about 2 minutes. Makes 4 servings.

Hazelnut-Brown Butter Cakes with Figs

PREP AND COOK TIME: About $1\frac{1}{4}$ hours
MAKES: 6 servings

$\frac{1}{2}$ cup ($\frac{1}{4}$ lb.) **butter**

$\frac{3}{4}$ cup **hazelnuts** (about 4 oz.)

$\frac{1}{2}$ cup **all-purpose flour**

$\frac{3}{4}$ cup **granulated sugar**

1 teaspoon grated **lemon** peel

$\frac{1}{2}$ teaspoon **salt**

$\frac{1}{2}$ teaspoon **ground cinnamon**

6 **large egg** whites, at room temperature

12 **firm-ripe figs,** rinsed, stem ends trimmed, and sliced lengthwise

About $\frac{1}{3}$ cup **powdered sugar**

1. Butter and flour six ramekins or muffin cups (1-cup size). In a 5- to 6-quart pan over high heat, melt $\frac{1}{2}$ cup butter; stir often until butter is golden brown with dark brown flecks, 3 to 5 minutes. Remove at once from heat and let stand until just warm, 15 to 20 minutes.

2. Meanwhile, place hazelnuts in an 8- or 9-inch-wide pan and bake in a 350° regular or convection oven until golden beneath skins, about 10 minutes. Pour onto a clean linen towel and let stand until cool enough to handle, then rub nuts in towel to remove loose skins.

3. In a food processor, whirl nuts with flour, $\frac{1}{2}$ cup granulated sugar, lemon peel, salt, and cinnamon until finely ground.

4. In a large bowl, with a mixer on high speed, whip egg whites until frothy. Gradually add remaining $\frac{1}{4}$ cup granulated sugar and continue to whip until mixture holds soft peaks. Gently stir in nut mixture. Gradually add brown butter, stirring until well blended. Spoon batter equally into ramekins. Overlap fig slices on tops in a circular pattern.

5. Bake in a 350° regular or convection oven until cakes are lightly browned and a toothpick inserted in the center comes out clean, about 30 minutes (25 minutes in convection oven). Set cakes on a rack to cool for 10 to 15 minutes.

6. To remove cakes from ramekins, run a thin-bladed knife between each cake and ramekin to loosen; invert to unmold, then set upright. Serve warm or at room temperature. Sprinkle with powdered sugar just before serving.

Per serving: 531 cal., 51% (270 cal.) from fat; 8.2 g protein; 30 g fat (12 g sat.); 64 g carbo (5.2 g fiber); 426 mg sodium; 47 mg chol. ◆

Fiesta stacks

Put savory seafood fillings
between tortillas for layers of fun

By Sara Schneider

JAMES CARRIER; FOOD STYLING: DAN BECKER

Halibut, tomatoes, and cheese make a tempting meal when layered with the freshest corn tortillas available.

Tortillas are folded and rolled around countless mixtures in Mexican entrées. But in Mexico City recently, I learned a simple lesson: You don't have to bend tortillas to create a festive dish. They make a big impression just stacked with seafood and melty cheeses. Carmen Titita Ramirez Degollado, who has introduced true *cocina mexicana* to many foreigners—and reintroduced it to numerous locals—at her El Bajio restaurant, suggests serving fish with oregano and tomatoes. Chef Felix Arias at Villa Maria restaurant, where the menu is based on foods from his native state of Tabasco, creates layers with an easy shrimp sauté. We've adapted their ideas for stacks that make great centerpieces for a family fiesta or small dinner party.

Fish Stacks with Mexican Crema

PREP AND COOK TIME: About 30 minutes
NOTES: Cotija cheese and Mexican crema are available in many supermarkets and in Latino grocery stores.
MAKES: 4 servings

- 1 cup finely chopped **onion**
- 1 tablespoon **olive oil**
- 1½ pounds **firm, white-fleshed fish,** such as halibut, rinsed, dried, and cut into ½-inch chunks
- ¼ cup **lemon juice**
- 3 tablespoons chopped **fresh oregano** leaves or 1 tablespoon dried oregano
- 1 cup chopped **firm-ripe tomatoes**
  Salt and **pepper**
- 12 **corn tortillas** (6 in.)
- 2 cups crumbled **cotija** or feta **cheese** (8 oz.)
- ½ cup **Mexican crema** or sour cream
- 1 **firm-ripe avocado** (8 oz.), pitted, peeled, and thinly sliced
  Lemon wedges

1. In a 10- to 12-inch nonstick frying pan over medium-high heat, stir onion in olive oil until limp, about 1 minute. Add fish and gently stir until opaque on outside, 2 to 3 minutes. Add lemon juice and 2 tablespoons oregano (2 teaspoons if using dried) and cook, gently stirring occasionally, until most of the liquid has evaporated and fish is opaque but still moist-looking in center (cut to test), 1 to 2 minutes. Gently stir in tomatoes and add salt and pepper to taste.

2. Lay 4 tortillas flat on a 14- by 17-inch nonstick baking sheet (if you don't have a nonstick sheet, coat a regular one lightly with cooking oil spray). Divide half the fish mixture among tortillas and spread level to within ½ inch of edges. Sprinkle a third of the cheese evenly over fish. Lay another tortilla on each stack and top equally with remaining fish mixture and another third of the cheese. Cover with remaining tortillas and sprinkle remaining cheese over the top.

3. Bake in a 400° regular or convection oven until cheese on top is beginning to brown, 10 to 12 minutes.

4. Meanwhile, in a small bowl, mix crema with remaining tablespoon oregano (1 teaspoon if using dried). With a wide spatula, transfer fish stacks to plates. Top equally with avocado slices and crema mixture. Garnish with lemon wedges to squeeze over stacks to taste.

Per serving: 747 cal., 46% (342 cal.) from fat; 57 g protein; 38 g fat (17 g sat.); 47 g carbo (6 g fiber); 1,228 mg sodium; 129 mg chol.

Garlic Shrimp Stacks

PREP AND COOK TIME: About 30 minutes
NOTES: At Villa Maria, Felix Arias makes one of the restaurant's delicious *antojitos* (regional snacks) by layering garlic shrimp with soft masa dough; we've used soft flour tortillas instead.
MAKES: 2 to 4 servings

- 2 tablespoons minced **garlic**
- 1 tablespoon **olive oil**
- 1½ pounds (51 to 60 per lb.) **shelled, deveined shrimp** (tails removed), rinsed
- ¼ cup **lime juice**
- ½ cup chopped **green onions**
- ¼ cup chopped **fresh cilantro**
  Salt and **pepper**
- 6 **flour tortillas** (8 to 10 in.)
- 2 cups shredded **jack cheese**
  Tomato salsa
  Lime wedges

1. In a 10- to 12-inch nonstick frying pan over medium-high heat, stir garlic in olive oil often until limp, about 1 minute. Add shrimp and stir often until pink on the outside, 2 to 3 minutes. Add lime juice and stir occasionally until most of the liquid has evaporated and shrimp are opaque but still moist-looking in center of thickest part (cut to test), about 3 to 5 minutes. Stir in all but 2 tablespoons green onions and the cilantro and add salt and pepper to taste.

2. Lay 2 tortillas flat on a 14- by 17-inch nonstick baking sheet. Divide half the shrimp mixture between tortillas and spread to within ½ inch of edges. Sprinkle a third of the cheese over shrimp. Lay another tortilla on each stack and top equally with remaining shrimp mixture and another third of the cheese. Cover with remaining tortillas and sprinkle remaining cheese over the top.

3. Bake in a 400° regular or convection oven until cheese is melted around edges of stacks and beginning to brown on top, 10 to 12 minutes. With a wide spatula, transfer stacks to plates. Sprinkle with reserved green onions. Serve with salsa and lime wedges.

Per serving: 607 cal., 40% (243 cal.) from fat; 54 g protein; 27 g fat (12 g sat.); 35 g carbo (2.1 g fiber); 812 mg sodium; 319 mg chol. ◆

Serve braised broccoli and sausage on its own or with soft polenta.

FOOD STYLING: BASIL FRIEDMAN (2)

Fall flavors

Readers' recipes for great weeknight meals and snacks, tested in *Sunset's* kitchens

By Charity Ferreira • Photographs by James Carrier

Braised Broccoli with Turkey Sausage

Tina Williams, Pasadena

Tina Williams came up with this savory dish one morning for breakfast, but we thought it made a great lunch or dinner entrée too, especially when served over soft polenta.

PREP AND COOK TIME: About 30 minutes

MAKES: 4 servings

- 8 **turkey sausage patties** (about 8 oz. total)
- 1 tablespoon **olive oil**
- 1 **onion** (8 oz.), peeled, halved, and thinly sliced
- 2 teaspoons minced **garlic**
- 3 cups **broccoli florets** (about 8 oz.), rinsed and drained
- ½ cup **dry white wine**
- **Salt** and **pepper**

- 8 **cherry tomatoes**, rinsed, stemmed, and halved
- ¼ cup shredded **parmesan cheese** (about 1 oz.)

1. In a 10- to 12-inch nonstick frying pan over medium-high heat, cook sausage patties in a single layer, turning once, until well browned on both sides and no longer pink in the center, about 8 minutes total. Transfer to paper towels to drain.

2. Return pan to medium heat. Add oil, onion, and garlic and cook until onion is limp and starting to brown, 5 to 8 minutes. Add broccoli; cook 2 to 3 minutes. Add wine and sprinkle with salt and pepper. Cover and simmer, stirring occasionally, until broccoli is tender when pierced, 4 to 6 minutes.

3. Gently stir in sausage and tomatoes and cook just until hot, about 1 minute. Sprinkle with parmesan cheese.

Per serving: 220 cal., 49% (108 cal.) from fat; 14 g protein; 12 g fat (3.7 g sat.); 8.9 g carbo (2.6 g fiber); 591 mg sodium; 50 mg chol.

Mahimahi Fajitas

Rachael Pashkowski, Orondo, WA

Rachael Pashkowski's sweet and spicy fish dish is a great filling for warm flour tortillas.

PREP AND COOK TIME: About 40 minutes

MAKES: 4 to 6 servings

- 1 pound **mahimahi fillets**
- 1 tablespoon **ground cumin**
- 1 tablespoon **chili powder**
- 1 teaspoon **garlic powder**
- ½ teaspoon **salt**
- 1 **red bell pepper** (about 8 oz.)
- 1 **green bell pepper** (about 8 oz.)
- 1 **yellow bell pepper** (about 8 oz.)
- 1½ tablespoons **salad oil**
- 1 **onion** (about 8 oz.), slivered lengthwise
- ½ cup **mango** or mango-blend **juice**
- 2 tablespoons **lime juice**
- 8 **flour tortillas** (8 in.)

1. Rinse fish and pat dry; cut fillets crosswise into 1-inch-wide strips. In a small bowl, mix cumin, chili powder, garlic powder, and salt. Rub fish all over with spice mixture. Rinse, core, and seed bell peppers; cut lengthwise into ¼-inch-wide slices.

2. Pour 1 tablespoon oil into a 10- to 12-inch nonstick frying pan over medium-high heat. When hot, add onion and bell peppers and stir frequently until limp, 5 to 6 minutes. Transfer to a plate. In the same pan, heat remaining ½ tablespoon oil; add fish and cook, turning once, until fish is browned on both sides, about 4 minutes total.

3. Add mango juice and bring to a boil. Cook until fish is opaque but still moist-looking in the center of the thickest part (cut to test), 2 to 3 more minutes. Add bell pepper mixture and lime juice to fish and stir just until heated through. Serve with warm flour tortillas.

Per serving: 307 cal., 23% (71 cal.) from fat; 20 g protein; 7.9 g fat (1.1 g sat.); 40 g carbo (4 g fiber); 501 mg sodium; 55 mg chol.

Orange Tea Cakes

Helen Knowlton, Eugene, OR

Helen Knowlton writes that these simple, moist, slightly sweet cakes make a delicious accompaniment to a cup of tea.

PREP AND COOK TIME: About 1 hour
MAKES: 24 1¾-inch cakes

½ cup (¼ lb.) **butter**, at room temperature

⅔ cup **sugar**

1 **large egg**

½ cup **orange juice**

2 cups **all-purpose flour**

2 tablespoons grated **orange** peel

1 teaspoon **baking powder**

½ teaspoon **salt**

¼ teaspoon **baking soda**

⅔ cup **buttermilk**

1. In a bowl, with a mixer on high speed, beat butter and sugar until smooth. Add egg and beat well. Beat in orange juice.

2. In another bowl, mix flour, orange peel, baking powder, salt, and baking soda. Stir half the flour mixture into the butter mixture, then the buttermilk, followed by the rest of the flour mixture, until just incorporated. Spoon batter equally into 24 buttered miniature muffin cups or 12 regular muffin cups (⅓ cup).

3. Bake in a 350° regular or convection oven until tops are lightly browned and a wooden skewer inserted into the center of one muffin comes out with moist crumbs attached, 20 to 25 minutes. Invert pan to remove cakes. Serve warm, or let cool to room temperature.

Per tea cake: 106 cal., 40% (42 cal.) from fat; 1.6 g protein; 4.7 g fat (2.8 g sat.); 15 g carbo (0.3 g fiber); 136 mg sodium; 21 mg chol. ◆

Miniature orange cakes are just the right size for an afternoon snack.

Salad days

Rice chills out for an easy weeknight meal

By Linda Lau Anusasananan
Photograph by James Carrier

■ Fried rice, a savory meal in a bowl, is a wonderful guilty pleasure of Chinese takeout. Richard Wong, the Sausalito, California, creator of China-blue sauces, put together this version of the classic, taking out all the guilt and leaving the pleasure. He doesn't actually fry the rice; instead, he tosses it with vegetables and his own Sesame Soy Sauce to create a fast main-dish salad, perfect for a summer supper.

Unfried Rice Salad

PREP AND COOK TIME: About 35 minutes

NOTES: This salad is a simplified, lightened version of Richard Wong's original. Make your own seasoning sauce as directed here or, for a shortcut, use a purchased sauce such as his China-blue Sesame Soy Sauce.

MAKES: 4 servings

2 cups fat-skimmed **chicken broth**

2 cups **long-grain white rice**

8 ounces **fat-trimmed boned pork loin** or sirloin

¼ cup **sesame-soy sauce** (recipe follows; see notes)

2 **Roma tomatoes** (8 oz. total)

4 **green onions** (each 10 in. long)

2 cups **frozen petite peas**

1 **large egg**

½ teaspoon **salad oil**

1 quart **finely shredded cabbage** (6 oz.; also called angel hair coleslaw mix)

Soy sauce or salt (optional)

1. In a 2½- to 3-quart pan over high heat, bring broth, 1⅓ cups water, and rice to a boil. Reduce heat to medium-high and cook, uncovered, until most of the liquid is absorbed, 7 to 10 minutes. Turn heat to low, cover, and cook until rice is tender to bite, 10 to 15 minutes longer.

This delicious main-dish salad tastes like fried rice but is far healthier.

2. Meanwhile, rinse pork and pat dry; cut into ½-inch chunks. In a small bowl, mix pork and 2 tablespoons sesame-soy sauce. Rinse and core tomatoes and cut into ½-inch cubes. Rinse green onions, trim and discard ends, and thinly slice (including green tops).

3. When rice is done, scoop into a large bowl. Add frozen peas and mix gently. Let cool slightly, about 5 minutes.

4. In a small bowl, with a fork, beat egg lightly. Pour oil into a 10- to 12-inch nonstick frying pan over high heat; tilt pan to coat. Add egg; tilt pan to spread thinly. When egg appears almost set, in 20 to 30 seconds, slide it onto rice; return pan to high heat. With a wide spatula, break egg into ½-inch pieces.

5. Add pork mixture to pan; stir until meat is no longer pink in the center (cut to test), 2 to 3 minutes; add to rice. Add tomatoes, onions, and remaining 2 tablespoons sesame-soy sauce to rice; mix gently.

6. Spread cabbage over the bottom of a large, shallow serving bowl; mound rice mixture on top. Add soy sauce to taste.

Per serving: 589 cal., 13% (77 cal.) from fat; 31 g protein; 8.6 g fat (2.1 g sat.); 94 g carbo (8.5 g fiber); 1,000 mg sodium; 87 mg chol.

Sesame-Soy Sauce. In a small bowl, mix 3 tablespoons **soy sauce**, 1 tablespoon **sherry**, 2 teaspoons **Asian** (toasted) **sesame oil**, 1 teaspoon **sugar**, and 1 teaspoon minced **fresh ginger**. Makes ¼ cup. ◆

FOOD STYLING: BASIL FRIEDMAN

Speedy supper: Shrimp cooked cacciatore-style in tomato sauce make a quick topping for pasta (recipe on page 212).

October

Smart main dish tarts

Combine savory fillings with shortcut crusts to craft stylish entrées

By Charity Ferreira • Photographs by James Carrier • Food styling by Basil Friedman

■ Baking a beautiful main-dish tart tends to be too time-consuming to do on a regular basis, but the elegant simplicity of a hearty tart is hard to resist for an autumn lunch or dinner. With a little ingenuity, the wide variety of prepared doughs available in the refrigerator and freezer cases of the grocery store can quickly turn into tasty crusts for all kinds of savory pastries. Once you're free to concentrate your efforts on flavorful fillings—like chard and ricotta, golden squash custard with sage, sautéed mushrooms, or thinly sliced potatoes topped with capers and smoked salmon—assembling an impressive one-dish meal becomes a much simpler proposition.

Smoked Salmon and Potato Galette

PREP AND COOK TIME: About 1 hour

NOTES: Accompany slices of this tart with dressed salad greens for a light lunch entrée.

MAKES: 3 to 4 servings

- 2 teaspoons **olive oil**
- 1 cup rinsed and thinly sliced **leeks** (white and pale green parts only)
- 8 ounces **Yukon Gold** or thin-skinned white **potatoes**
- 1 9- by 9-in. sheet **frozen puff pastry dough** (half of a 17.3-oz. package), thawed
  Salt and **pepper**
- 2 tablespoons **whipping cream**
- 1 tablespoon drained **capers**
- 4 ounces thinly sliced **smoked salmon**

1. Pour oil into a 10- to 12-inch frying pan over medium-high heat; when hot, add leeks and cook, stirring occasionally, until very limp, about 10 minutes. Let cool to room temperature, about 15 minutes.

2. Meanwhile, peel potatoes and slice crosswise very thinly ($^1/_{16}$ in.). Lay puff pastry dough flat on a lightly floured board. Trim off corners to form a circle and, with a lightly floured rolling pin, roll out slightly to make an 11-inch round. Transfer to a 12- by 15-inch baking sheet.

3. Spread leeks in the center of dough, leaving a 2-inch border around the edge; sprinkle lightly with salt and pepper. Arrange potato slices in slightly overlapping layers over leeks, sprinkling each layer lightly with salt and pepper. Fold in edges of dough over potatoes. Drizzle cream over potatoes.

4. Bake in a 375° regular or convection oven, rotating baking sheet midway through baking time, until crust is brown and potatoes are tender when pierced, about 35 minutes (if crust is brown before potatoes are tender, cover tart loosely with foil).

5. Top tart with capers and smoked salmon slices while warm. Cut into wedges and serve warm.

Per serving: 470 cal., 56% (261 cal.) from fat; 11 g protein; 29 g fat (5.3 g sat.); 41 g carbo (2.1 g fiber); 825 mg sodium; 15 mg chol.

Frozen puff pastry makes an easy and elegant tart crust.

Refrigerated pie dough doubles as a crust for a squash custard tart.

Kabocha-Leek Tart

PREP AND COOK TIME: About 1 hour 45 minutes

NOTES: You can cook and purée the squash and cook the leeks (steps 1 and 2) up to 1 day ahead; cover separately and chill. If you have leftover squash purée, freeze it for stirring into soup or risotto.

MAKES: 6 to 8 servings

- 2 pounds **kabocha** or butternut **squash**
- 1 tablespoon **olive oil**
- 1½ cups rinsed and thinly sliced **leeks** (white and pale green parts only)
- 3 **large eggs**
- ¾ cup **milk**
- ⅓ cup **whipping cream**
- 1 tablespoon chopped **fresh sage** leaves
- ¾ teaspoon **salt**
- ¼ teaspoon **pepper**
- 1 11-inch-round **refrigerated pie dough** (half of a 15-oz. package)
- ¾ cup (about 3 oz.) shredded **gruyère** or parmesan **cheese**

1. Cut squash in half crosswise and scoop out seeds. Place cut side down on a 12- by 15-inch baking pan or sheet, cover with foil, and bake in a 425° regular or convection oven until soft when pierced, 25 to 40 minutes. When cool enough to handle, scoop out flesh and whirl in a blender or food processor until smooth. You will need 1½ cups purée (see notes).

2. Meanwhile, pour oil into a 10- to 12-inch frying pan over medium-high heat. When hot, add leeks and cook, stirring occasionally, until soft, about 10 minutes. Let cool to room temperature, about 10 minutes.

3. In a bowl, whisk eggs, milk, and cream to blend. Whisk in squash purée, sage, salt, and pepper.

4. Unfold pie dough and ease gently into a 9-inch tart pan with removable rim, pressing against sides of pan; trim off overhanging dough flush with rim. Place tart pan on an uninsulated baking sheet. Scatter leeks, then cheese evenly over bottom of crust; pour in squash mixture (discard any filling that does not fit in shell).

5. Bake on the bottom rack of a 425° regular or 375° convection oven for 20 minutes; reduce heat to 375° (350° for convection oven) and bake until custard is puffed up and browned, 10 to 15 more minutes. Let cool 10 minutes, then remove pan rim. Serve warm or at room temperature, cut into wedges.

Per serving: 301 cal., 54% (162 cal.) from fat; 7.8 g protein; 18 g fat (8 g sat.); 29 g carbo (2 g fiber); 395 mg sodium; 110 mg chol.

Chard and Ricotta Torta

PREP AND COOK TIME: About 1½ hours

NOTES: You can cook the chard (steps 2 and 3) up to 1 day ahead; cover and chill. Frozen bread dough is usually sold in packages containing two or three 1-pound portions. To thaw, remove one portion, place on a lightly floured surface, cover with plastic wrap, and let stand at room temperature for about 45 minutes.

MAKES: 6 to 8 servings

- 1 pound **frozen bread dough,** thawed (see notes)
- 3 pounds **red** or green **chard** (about 3 bunches)
- 1 tablespoon **olive oil**
- 1 tablespoon minced **garlic**
- 2 **large eggs**
- ¾ cup **part-skim ricotta cheese**
- 6 tablespoons **whipping cream**
- ¼ cup chopped pitted **calamata olives**
- 2 teaspoons grated **lemon** peel
- ¼ teaspoon **ground nutmeg**
- ¼ teaspoon **salt**
- ⅛ teaspoon **pepper**

1. Cut off a third of the bread dough. With lightly floured hands, flatten both portions into disks. Cover with plastic wrap and let stand while preparing filling, about 30 minutes.

2. Rinse chard and tear leaves from center ribs; discard center ribs and stems or save for another use.

3. Pour oil into a 12-inch frying pan or a 14-inch wok over medium-high heat; when hot, add garlic and stir until fragrant, about 1 minute. Add chard and stir frequently until evenly wilted, 12 to 15 minutes. Transfer mixture to a strainer and let drain until cool enough to handle. Squeeze chard to remove all liquid, then coarsely chop.

4. In a bowl, mix chard, 1 egg, ricotta, ¼ cup cream, olives, lemon peel, nutmeg, salt, and pepper.

5. With a lightly floured rolling pin, on a lightly floured surface, roll the larger portion of dough into a 12-inch round about ¼ inch thick. Brush off excess flour. Fit into a 10-inch cheesecake pan with removable rim and fold excess dough down so that edges come about halfway up sides of pan; press dough gently against sides of pan. Add chard mixture and spread level. Roll remaining dough into a 10-inch round. Center over filling and pinch with the sides to

Chopped calamata olives flavor a savory filling of greens and cheese in this torta.

seal. In a small bowl, beat remaining egg with remaining 2 tablespoons cream to blend. Brush top crust with egg mixture; discard remainder.

6. Bake in a 375° regular or convection oven until top is richly browned, 35 to 40 minutes. Let cool about 10 minutes, then run a small sharp knife between tart and pan rim to loosen; remove rim. Use a serrated knife to slice into wedges. Serve warm or cool.

Per serving: 314 cal., 37% (117 cal.) from fat; 13 g protein; 13 g fat (4.5 g sat.); 41 g carbo (3.8 g fiber); 820 mg sodium; 73 mg chol.

Mushroom Strudel

PREP AND COOK TIME: About 1¼ hours

NOTES: Thaw frozen filo overnight in the refrigerator.

MAKES: 6 to 8 servings

2 tablespoons **olive oil**

¼ cup minced **shallots**

2 cloves **garlic,** peeled and minced

2 pounds **fresh mushrooms,** (cremini, shiitake, porcini, or common, or a mixture), rinsed, tough stem ends trimmed, and sliced

2 tablespoons **sherry** or red wine **vinegar**

2 teaspoons **fresh thyme** leaves

1 cup shredded **manchego** or parmesan **cheese** (4 oz.)

3 tablespoons chopped **parsley**

About ¼ teaspoon **salt**

About ⅛ teaspoon **pepper**

6 sheets (about 12 by 18 in.) **filo dough,** thawed (see notes)

About ¼ cup (⅛ lb.) **butter,** melted

1. Pour 1 tablespoon olive oil into a 12-inch nonstick frying pan over medium heat; when hot, add half of the shallots and garlic and stir until shallots are limp, 3 to 5 minutes. Add half of the mushrooms and stir until mushrooms begin to brown and any liquid is evaporated, 5 to 8 minutes. Add half of the vinegar and thyme; cook, stirring often, to blend flavors, 1 to 2 minutes longer. Pour into a bowl, repeat to cook remaining mushrooms, and pour into the bowl. Let cool to room temperature, about 25 minutes. Stir cheese and parsley into mushroom mixture; add salt and pepper to taste.

2. On a 12- by 24-inch piece of plastic wrap, lay one filo sheet flat (cover the remaining filo with plastic wrap to prevent drying) and brush lightly with melted butter. Top with another filo sheet and brush lightly with more butter. Repeat this process to stack all six sheets.

3. Spread mushroom mixture in a 3-inch band along one long side of dough, 2 inches in from the edge and the sides. Fold long edge and the ends of dough over filling. Gently lift plastic wrap under filled side of dough and guide it forward to form a compact roll, ending with seam down.

4. Gently transfer roll, seam down, to a buttered 14- by 17-inch baking sheet. Brush top with more melted butter; save any remaining for other uses.

5. Bake on the center rack in a 375° regular or convection oven until golden brown all over, 45 to 55 minutes. Serve warm, cut into 1½-inch slices.

Per serving: 217 cal., 62% (135 cal.) from fat; 7.3 g protein; 15 g fat (7.7 g sat.); 14 g carbo (1.5 g fiber); 287 mg sodium; 31 mg chol. ◆

Homemade cupcakes in Halloween flavors— Devil's food and pumpkin (left).

Sweet treats

Throw a Halloween party full of not-so-scary surprises

By Charity Ferreira and
Kate Washington

Photographs by James Carrier

From the tiniest goblin to the kid at heart in grown-up disguise, everyone ringing the doorbell on Halloween has the same question: "Trick or treat?" But there's really no need to choose; sometimes a little trick can conceal a bona fide treat.

For a Halloween party, sweets with a twist delight fairy princesses and Spider-Men alike. We've devised cupcakes that, like the partygoers themselves, are all dressed up: Devil's food cupcakes have a gooey marshmallow filling, and what looks like plain vanilla is actually orange cream cheese frosting on spiced pumpkin cakes.

But candy is the real point of Halloween as far as kids are concerned. Make it even more of a treat by tucking it into clever paper cones, for partygoers and trick-or-treaters alike. Both know the treats are that much more special when they're also tricks.

Devil's Food Cupcakes with Marshmallow Filling

PREP AND COOK TIME: About 1½ hours, plus at least 35 minutes to cool
MAKES: 16 cupcakes

- ¾ cup (⅜ lb.) **butter,** at room temperature
- 1½ cups **sugar**
- 2 **large eggs**
- 2 cups **all-purpose flour**
- ½ cup **Dutch-process unsweetened cocoa**
- 2 teaspoons **baking powder**
- ½ teaspoon **salt**
- 1 cup **milk**
- 1 jar (7 oz.) **marshmallow cream**
  Chocolate cream cheese frosting (recipe follows)

1. In a bowl, with a mixer on medium speed, beat butter and sugar until smooth. Add eggs, one at a time, beating well after each addition and scraping down sides of bowl as needed.
2. In another bowl, mix flour, cocoa,

baking powder, and salt. Stir half the flour mixture into butter mixture. Stir in milk just until blended. Add remaining flour mixture and stir just until incorporated. Spoon batter equally into 16 muffin cups (⅓-cup capacity; cups should be almost full) lined with paper baking cups.
3. Bake in a 350° regular or convection oven until tops spring back when lightly pressed in the center and a wooden skewer inserted into the center comes out clean, about 20 minutes. Let cool in pans on racks for 5 minutes; remove cupcakes from pans and set on racks to cool completely, at least 30 minutes.
4. With a small, sharp knife, cut a cylinder about ¾ inch wide and 1 inch deep from the center of the top of each cupcake. Trim off and discard about ½ inch from the bottom of each cylinder. With tip of knife, hollow out a small cavity inside each cupcake.
5. Spoon marshmallow cream into a pastry bag fitted with a ½-inch plain tip. Twist end of bag tightly to secure. Place tip in cavity of one cupcake; without moving tip, squeeze filling into cavity, to ¼ inch from top. Repeat to fill remaining cupcakes. Insert cake cylinders into holes.

Surprise trick-or-treaters with decorative, candy-filled paper cones.

6. Spoon chocolate cream cheese frosting into another pastry bag, fitted with a ³⁄₄-inch star tip, and pipe onto tops of cupcakes, or spread on cupcakes with a knife.

Per cupcake: 421 cal., 47% (198 cal.) from fat; 5.1 g protein; 22 g fat (13 g sat.); 55 g carbo (0.4 g fiber); 378 mg sodium; 83 mg chol.

Chocolate cream cheese frosting. In a bowl, with a mixer on low speed, beat 8 ounces **cream cheese** and ¹⁄₂ cup (¹⁄₄ lb.) **butter,** both at room temperature, until well blended. In another bowl, sift together 1¹⁄₂ cups **powdered sugar** and 6 tablespoons **unsweetened cocoa.** Beat into cream cheese mixture until frosting is smooth.

Pumpkin Cupcakes with Orange Cream Cheese Frosting

PREP AND COOK TIME: About 1¹⁄₂ hours, plus at least 35 minutes to cool

MAKES: 12 cupcakes

- ¹⁄₂ cup (¹⁄₄ lb.) **butter,** at room temperature
- 1 cup **sugar**
- 2 **large eggs**
- 1 cup **canned pumpkin**
- 1 tablespoon **vanilla**
- 1¹⁄₂ cups **all-purpose flour**
- 2 teaspoons **baking powder**
- ¹⁄₂ teaspoon **ground cinnamon**
- ¹⁄₄ teaspoon **ground nutmeg**
- ¹⁄₄ teaspoon **ground cloves**
- ¹⁄₄ teaspoon **salt**
- ¹⁄₄ cup **milk**
  Orange cream cheese frosting (recipe follows)
  Candy sprinkles (optional)

1. In a bowl, with a mixer on medium speed, beat butter and sugar until smooth. Add eggs, one at a time, beating well after each addition and scraping down sides of bowl as needed. Add pumpkin and vanilla and beat until well blended (mixture will look separated at this point).

2. In another bowl, mix flour, baking powder, cinnamon, nutmeg, cloves, and salt. Stir half the flour mixture into pumpkin mixture. Stir in milk just until blended. Add remaining flour mixture and stir just until incorporated. Spoon batter equally into 12 muffin cups (¹⁄₃-cup capacity; cups should be about ³⁄₄ full) lined with paper baking cups.

3. Bake in a 350° regular or convection oven until tops spring back when

Dandified candy

Small, holiday-themed boxes were used to hold candy for trick-or-treaters around the turn of the last century. They are valued by collectors today, but you can make a modern version for a fraction of the cost. Designer John McRae of San Francisco's Every Day's A Holiday, an expert on the containers, shares the secret of making candy cones:

1. Cut out a circle of **construction paper**—ours measures 12 inches in diameter. Cut the circle into quarters.

2. Use a **small paintbrush** dipped in **glue** to draw a Halloween motif in the center of one quarter-circle. Sprinkle **fine-grain glitter** over it and allow it to dry.

3. Roll the quarter-circle into a cone, using glue or **transfer tape** to secure the end.

4. Next, cut out a slightly larger circle of **tissue paper** and quarter it. Roll one quarter-circle into a loose cone, drop it into the construction-paper cone, and secure with glue.

5. Fill the cone with **candy.** Tie the tissue paper closed with **raffia** or string.

— *Mary Jo Bowling*

lightly pressed in the center and a wooden skewer inserted into center comes out clean, about 20 minutes. Let cool in pans on racks for 5 minutes; remove cupcakes from pans and set on racks to cool completely, at least 30 minutes.

4. Spoon orange cream cheese frosting into a pastry bag fitted with a ³⁄₄-inch star tip and pipe onto tops of cupcakes, or spread on cupcakes with a knife. Decorate with candy sprinkles, if desired.

Per cupcake: 376 cal., 48% (180 cal.) from fat; 4.2 g protein; 20 g fat (12 g sat.); 46 g carbo (0.8 g fiber); 323 mg sodium; 88 mg chol.

Orange cream cheese frosting. In a bowl, with a mixer on low speed, beat 6 ounces **cream cheese** and 6 tablespoons **butter,** both at room temperature, until well blended. Beat in 1¹⁄₂ cups **powdered sugar,** 1 tablespoon finely minced **orange** peel, and ¹⁄₄ to ¹⁄₂ teaspoon **orange extract** until smooth. ◆

Native Southwest

Authentic pueblo flavors on the Santa Fe Trail

By Jerry Anne Di Vecchio

■ When the Spanish marched into the Southwest more than four centuries ago, pueblo dwellers expanded their culinary repertoire to include ingredients that many of us assume are indigenous. Chilies, for example—the Spanish brought them up from Mexico along with Old World foods such as wheat, rice, lamb, and chicken. The tale of these foods' integration into pueblo culture was shared with me long ago by Helen Cordero and was later confirmed by Juanita Tiger Kavena, two fine Native American cooks.

In the Cochiti Pueblo of New Mexico, I lent a hand as the now-late Cordero, fabled potter, cooked for a feast day. Among the dishes was chicken and rice *(arroz con pollo)*, which had a pleasant, subtle flavor that puzzled me. The chicken was seasoned with onions, mild chilies (fresh green and powdered red), and a wild herb (the mystery taste).

From Kavena, who married into the Hopi Pueblo and has studied and written about native and cultivated plants, I learned that the mysterious nuance was likely from a wild mint *(Mentha arvensis)*. She also taught me that wild onions *(Allium cernuum)* abound in the region and that wild greens are often added to chicken and rice for a one-pan meal. Lamb's quarter *(Chenopodium album,* also

called wild spinach) is the probable choice—I've seen it at the farmers' market in Santa Fe—but regular spinach substitutes nicely. Native *piñones (Pinus edulis),* or any market variety of pine nuts, make a dressy finish.

Cordero used a whole chicken that had scratched in the earth for its living and required a fair amount of cooking. I've adapted the recipe to modern time constraints by using just thighs or breasts—a reasonable compromise in the interest of getting a traditional dish on the table quickly.

Cochiti Arroz con Pollo

PREP AND COOK TIME: About 1 hour

NOTES: Instead of bone-in chicken thighs, you can use 6 boned, skinned chicken breast halves (about 2¼ lb. total): Lightly brown them in oil as directed for skinned thighs in step 2, for 5 to 8 minutes. But instead of adding chicken in step 4, add breasts after rice has simmered for 10 minutes in step 5, pushing them down into liquid; turn over after 5 minutes and continue to cook, stirring occasionally, until rice is tender to bite and breasts are no longer pink in center of thickest part (cut to test), 5 to 8 minutes longer. Then complete step 6.

Instead of the canned green chilies, you can use fresh: Rinse and dry 6 green Anaheim chilies (about 1 lb. total); lay slightly apart on a baking sheet and broil about 3 inches from heat, turning as necessary, until charred on all sides, 10 to 15 minutes total. Let stand until cool enough to touch, then pull off and discard tough skin, discard seeds, and trim and discard stem ends. Cut chilies in half lengthwise.

MAKES: 6 servings

- ¼ cup **pine nuts**
- 2 tablespoons **salad oil** (if using skinned chicken; otherwise omit)
- 6 **chicken thighs,** with or without skin (about 2 lb. total), rinsed and patted dry (see notes)
- 1 **onion** (about 8 oz.), peeled and chopped
- 2 tablespoons **chili powder**
- 7 cups fat-skimmed **chicken broth**
- 2 cans (7 oz. each) **whole green chilies** (see notes)
- 1¼ cups **long-grain white rice**
- 8 cups lightly packed rinsed **spinach leaves** (about 8 oz.)
- 5 tablespoons chopped **fresh mint** leaves
  Salt and **pepper**

1. In a 6- to 8-quart pan over medium heat, stir pine nuts until lightly toasted, 2 to 3 minutes; pour from pan.

2. If using skinned chicken, pour oil into pan and turn heat to medium-high. When pan is hot, add thighs, skin side down, in a single layer (brown in batches if they don't all fit); turn occasionally until lightly browned, 10 to 12 minutes. Transfer to a plate.

3. Add onion to pan and stir often until limp, about 5 minutes; add chili powder and stir for about 10 seconds.

4. Add broth to pan and increase heat to high. Cut green chilies in half lengthwise. When broth is boiling, return chicken and any drippings to pan; add green chilies. Reduce heat, cover, and simmer for 15 minutes.

5. Stir rice into pan, making sure all grains are submerged. Cover and simmer, stirring occasionally, until rice is tender to bite, 20 to 25 minutes.

6. Uncover pan and turn heat to high; add spinach and ¼ cup mint, pushing down into liquid, and stir gently until wilted, 1 to 2 minutes. Season to taste with salt and pepper. Ladle mixture into wide bowls, then sprinkle with remaining tablespoon mint and the toasted pine nuts.

Per serving: 511 cal., 39% (198 cal.) from fat; 36 g protein; 22 g fat (5.7 g sat.); 41 g carbo (4.4 g fiber); 501 mg sodium; 100 mg chol. ◆

At the risk of telling you something you already know, the steakhouse is back.

Or did it ever leave? Almost everybody secretly loves a good steak. It stands to reason that the West, with its legacy of the open range, would have some of the very best in the land where beef is still king. We've sought out prime steakhouse choices, from the truly old-school (one was founded around the time of the Civil War) to the new. What they all have in common is great atmosphere and, above all, fantastic steaks—thick, juicy, and prepared exactly as you like them. In case you can't get to one of our picks soon, we've also included recipes for making a great steak—and the sauces to enhance it—at home. — *Kate Washington*

Great steakhouses of the West

Our picks for the places that offer the sizzle *and* the steak

■ Acme Chophouse, San Francisco

Here's a steakhouse that ties America's past to a healthy future in a way that's pure San Francisco. Acme Chophouse, a new venture by executive chef and partner Traci Des Jardins and director of operations Larry Bain, at the corner of the Giants' Pacific Bell Park, combines a warm, sleek dining room and a build-your-own menu with a conscience. Most of the ingredients are organic, and the steaks are described in terms of their green credentials—grass-fed or grain-finished. But the bone-in rib eye is the standard by which all rib eyes should be judged. The béarnaise is textbook-perfect (see page 205); the red wine–shallot sauce and chimichurri are close seconds. And the scalloped potatoes, creamed spinach, and macaroni and cheese almost make you forget you came for steak. Acme is worth a trip south of Market even when the Giants aren't in town. *24 Willie Mays Plaza (at Third and King Streets); (415) 644-0240 or www.acmechophouse.com. — Sara Schneider*

■ Balboa Restaurant & Lounge, West Hollywood, CA

Los Angeles's steakhouses have long been the stomping grounds of big-shot entertainment types. But times have changed. "The classic joints were our parents' hangouts," says Lee Maen, one of Balboa's partners. "We needed one of our own." Balboa delivers the flash and sizzle Sunset Boulevard used to be famous for, as Hollywood's hippest meat eaters clink glasses of Shiraz over bass-thumping acid jazz. But the real attraction is the meat. The 40-day dry-aged New York strip steak is quite simply one of the best in America, the 28-day bone-in filet runs a close second, and Caesar salads are spun to order tableside. *8462 W. Sunset Blvd. (at the Grafton Hotel); (323) 650-8383. — Brad A. Johnson*

■ The Buckhorn Saloon & Opera House, Pinos Altos, NM

The Buckhorn Saloon in the mining ghost town of Pinos Altos, 7 miles north of Silver City on State 15, serves up hefty portions of history along with its steak. A thick-walled adobe structure with hand-hewn timbers and converted gaslights, the Buckhorn first swung open its doors 140 years ago, give or take a decade. Try the Buckhorn Specialty, a tender New York strip with green chili and cheese, or the old-time favorite rib eye or the succulent 3-inch-thick filet (served butterflied) with all the fixings. *32 Main St.; (505) 538-9911. — Sharon Niederman*

■ El Gaucho, Seattle

Longtime Seattleites recall the original El Gaucho, which stood at Seventh and Olive for decades, famed for elaborate service and flaming shish kebabs. That tradition lives on in Belltown, where the restaurant came back to life in 1996. It's reminiscent of an elegant dinner club of yesteryear, with midnight blue walls, subtle lighting, and live piano. Prime steaks star on the menu, grilled to perfection over charcoal. The downstairs Pampas Room (open Friday–Saturday) serves much of the same menu in a nightclub setting, but upstairs offers the flourishes of grand tableside service. *2505 First Ave.; (206) 728-1337. — Cynthia Nims*

■ Maddox Ranch House, Perry, UT

The Sputnik-like sign ringed with glittery letters spelling out *Maddox Fine Food* stands out like an exclamation point on U.S. 89 in the tiny northern Utah town of Perry. Operating since 1949, this family-owned landmark is a casual, down-home place. Think knotty pine decor and a menu that offers "Deluxe Dinner Plates," with baskets of soft dinner rolls and corn pone. Some of Maddox's beef is homegrown and hormone-free; all of it is aged on site. There are endless pitchers of icy well water, but no alcohol. *1900 S. U.S. 89; (435) 723-8545.* — *Virginia Rainey*

■ Emil-Lene's Sirloin House, Aurora, CO

Located on a dusty road out near Denver International Airport, Emil-Lene's Sirloin House is more Western than the stock show. There is no menu here. Instead, the no-nonsense waitresses—and you don't want to mess with them—rattle off the evening's choices: steak, steak, and more steak, with a few fin, fur, and fowl dishes thrown in. All of the beef is prime, and your slab arrives with abundant sides—fresh vegetables, spaghetti, soup or salad, and a baked potato with all the fixings. *16000 Smith Rd.; (303) 366-6674.* — *Lori Midson*

■ The Hitching Post, Casmalia, CA
The Hitching Post II, Buellton, CA

Frank Ostini didn't want to run the family steakhouse, the Hitching Post, in the little Santa Barbara County town of Casmalia. "My dad and mother worked too hard," he recalls. So off he went to study environmental planning. As it turned out, Ostini liked cooking steaks so much he opened a second Hitching Post in nearby Buellton. Now brother Bill runs the original, which adheres to a traditional steakhouse menu, while at Hitching Post II, Frank has branched out to quail and steamed mussels. Still, steak—simply seasoned and grilled over a red oak fire—remains king at both. Toast yo[ur] T-bone with a glass of Hartley-Ostini Hitching Post Pinot Noir, as good [a] steak wine as you'll find anywhere. *The Hitching Post: 3325 Point Sal R[d.] (805) 937-6151 or www.hitchingpost1.com. The Hitching Post II: 406* State 246; (805) 688-0676 or www.hitchingpost2.com.* — *Peter Fish*

■ The Mint Bar & Cafe, Belgrade, MT

Step into the Mint and you're thrust into Belgrade's agricultural pas[t,] large sepia photographs of local ranchers along with Hereford an[d] Longhorn cattle mounts. The six-year-old restaurant was built on th[e] site of the 1904 Mint Bar and is now where ranchers and young pro[-] fessionals mingle in this bedroom community of Bozeman. Besides [a] 28-ounce T-bone, you can get barbecued shrimp or salmon with [a] blueberry beurre blanc, and one of the best Caesar salads in Montan[a.] *27 E. Main St.; (406) 388-1100.* — *Caroline Patterson*

■ Pinnacle Peak Patio, Scottsdale, AZ

This vast steakhouse is as touristy as it gets, with a Wild West façad[e,] red-checkered tablecloths, and cowboy hat–wearing waiters arme[d] with giant scissors to lop off the necktie of any man who defies th[e] casual dress code. But since 1957, the restaurant has been equal[ly] well known for its simple menu of tender, hand-cut beef, grilled over [a] mesquite fire outdoors. If you're starving, try a "Cowboy," a pound and [a]

JAMES CARRIER

Same steak— your house

To take the steakhouse experience home, you need a few essentials: great meat, a ho[t] fire, and some stellar sauces. We provide the recipes, and you can supply the heat. It[']s the meat that is hardest to come by; the flavorful, dry-aged, prime steak that restaurant[s] offer is just not sold in the average supermarket in the West. (Most butcher-counter meat i[s] choice, a step below prime on the USDA's grading scale.) That doesn't mean it's unavailable[,] though. Ask around at specialty butcher stores, or try mail-order services. We especially lik[e] Lobel's, a venerable New York butcher that offers a full array of thick, never-frozen prime steak[s;] next-day shipping is now available to the West. *(877) 783-4512 or www.lobels.co[m]*
— *Kate Washingto[n]*

Grilled Steak

PREP AND COOK TIME: About 40 minutes
NOTES: Choose well-marbled cuts such as porterhouse, rib eye, T-bone, tenderloin (filet mignon), or top loin (New York or strip) about 1 inch thick. If meat is thicker—up to 2 inches—use medium heat (you can hold your hand at grill level only 3 to 4 seconds) and allow extra time—up to 20 minutes for a medium-rare 2-inch-thick steak, 25 for medium.
MAKES: 4 servings

4 **tender bone-in** or boned **beef steaks** (1 to 1½ in. thick and 8 to 16 oz. each; see notes)

Salt and **pepper**

1. *If using charcoal briquets,* ignite 65 to 75 briquets (about 4½ lb.) on the firegrate; open dampers. When coals are dotted with ash, in 15 to 20 minutes, spread into an even, solid layer and allow to burn down until they are hot (you can hold your hand at grill level only 2 to 3 seconds), 5 to 10 minutes.

If using a gas barbecue, turn all burners to high and close lid for at least 10 minutes, the[n] adjust to desired heat.

2. Trim and discard excess fat from steak[s] (dripping fat can cause flare-ups). Rins[e] steaks and pat dry. Sprinkle lightly all ove[r] with salt and pepper.

3. Lay steaks on grill 4 to 6 inches abov[e] heat; close lid on gas barbecue. Cook unt[il] done to your liking, 6 to 8 minutes for medium[-] rare (cut to test; see notes), turning once with [a] wide spatula or tongs halfway through cookin[g.] Transfer to a board or platter and let rest abou[t] 5 minutes before serving.

Per 8-ounce steak (uncooked): 387 cal., 65% (252 cal.) from fat; 31 g protein; 28 g fat (11 g sat.) 0 g carbo (0 g fiber); 77 mg sodium; 105 mg chol.

Balboa "J-1" Sauce

PREP AND COOK TIME: About 2¼ hours
NOTES: This twist on the classic A-1 sauc[e] comes from executive chef Joni Fay Hill a[t] Balboa Restaurant & Lounge, who note[s] that it is much tangier than the usual stea[k] sauce. Look for tamarind concentrate i[n]

half of porterhouse, or a half-pound steak burger. Just don't order anything well done: You'll be served a charred cowboy boot. *10426 E. Jomax Rd.; (480) 585-1599 or www.pppatio. com.* — Nora Burba Trulsson

■ **Saddles Steakhouse, Sonoma, CA**
California wine country's answer to the steakhouse is located in MacArthur Place, an upscale hotel. At Saddles, you can sit inside the pleasantly appointed "barn" or on the garden patio. Choose from selections cut to order or a list of steaks and chops, then prepare yourself for serious toppings—caramelized onions, peppercorn sauce, and Cabernet demi-glace—all in huge amounts. Sides include potatoes prepared five ways and traditional creamed spinach. For lighter fare, order the market vegetables; they taste Sonoma-grown. *29 E. MacArthur St.; (707) 933-3191.*— Katie Tamony

■ **Tumalo Feed Company Steakhouse and Saloon, Bend, OR**
The Tumalo Feed Company lies about as far as you can toss a steer off U.S. 20, minutes north of Bend and well into high-desert frontier territory. Folks feel right at home with its down-at-the-heels Victorian parlor furniture, checkered tablecloths, and enormous steer's head on the wall. Head straight for the choice steaks, seasoned perfectly and grilled on the rare side. Pile your plate with fried potatoes and soupy red beans, but skip the onion rings and garlic bread to save room for the marionberry cobbler. *64619 W. U.S. 20; (541) 382-2202.* — Stacey Philipps ◆

quintessential newcomers

Two of the newest kids on the block show the range of today's steakhouses, from haute to historic.

• **CraftSteak,** a Vegas spin-off of Tom Colicchio's Craft in New York, is a foodie temple where every delicious slice of house-cured duck ham and grass-fed New York strip is treated like a gem. CraftSteak's ultrasimple preparations may contrast with its flashy location in the MGM Grand, but the exorbitant prices are pure Vegas. *3799 Las Vegas Blvd. S; (702) 891-7318.*
• At Carmel Valley's **Will's Fargo,** Cal Stamenov combines California's obsession over high-quality ingredients with its old love of steak. Having raised the culinary bar at Bernardus and Quail Lodges, Stamenov has also revived the village's 43-year-old roadhouse and is turning out stellar rib eyes against the backdrop of its historic decor. *17 E. Carmel Valley Rd., Carmel Valley, CA; (831) 659-2774.* — K. W. and S. S.

Indian markets and specialty food stores; if you cannot find it, substitute 1 teaspoon molasses and 1 tablespoon lime juice.

MAKES: About 3 cups

In a 3- to 4-quart pan, combine 1¾ cups **ketchup,** 1½ cups **orange juice,** ¾ cup **raisins,** ¼ cup firmly packed **brown sugar,** ¼ cup **Worcestershire,** 3 tablespoons **rice wine vinegar,** 2 tablespoons **soy sauce,** 2 tablespoons minced peeled **fresh ginger,** 2 tablespoons minced **garlic,** 1 tablespoon **onion powder,** 1 tablespoon **tamarind concentrate** (see notes), and 2 teaspoons **Asian red chili sauce** (such as Sriracha). Bring to a simmer over medium-low heat, then reduce heat and barely simmer (a few bubbles breaking on surface), stirring occasionally, until sauce is thick, glossy, and dark brown, about 2 hours. In a blender or with a handheld blender, pulse until almost smooth. If sauce is too thick, thin with a little more orange juice. Let cool; serve or chill airtight up to 1 month.

Per ¼ cup: 109 cal., 1.7% (1.8 cal.) from fat; 1.6 g protein; 0.2 g fat (0 g sat.); 27 g carbo (1.2 g fiber); 653 mg sodium; 0 mg chol.

Acme Béarnaise Sauce

PREP AND COOK TIME: About 45 minutes

NOTES: The egg yolks in this sauce are not fully cooked; if you are concerned about egg safety, use yolks from eggs pasteurized in the shell (available at some grocery stores). It's crucial to whisk constantly to create a stable emulsion in this sauce. If it curdles or breaks, stop adding butter and whisk vigorously.

MAKES: About 1½ cups

6 sprigs **fresh tarragon,** rinsed
½ cup **dry white wine**
½ cup **white wine vinegar**
½ cup chopped **shallots**
2 teaspoons cracked **black peppercorns**
¾ cup (⅜ lb.) **butter**
3 **large egg** yolks (see notes)
About ⅛ teaspoon **hot sauce**
Salt

1. Chop enough tarragon leaves to measure 1 tablespoon. In a 2- to 3-quart pan over medium-high heat, bring white wine, vinegar, shallots, peppercorns, and remaining tarragon sprigs to a boil. Cook, stirring often, until liquid is reduced to about ⅓ cup, about 10 minutes. Pour through a fine strainer into a bowl, pressing on solids to extract liquid (discard solids).

2. Meanwhile, in a 1- to 1½-quart pan over low heat, melt all but 2 tablespoons butter; keep warm. In a nonreactive bowl, with a whisk or handheld mixer on high speed, vigorously whisk or beat egg yolks until pale yellow and thick, about 5 minutes by hand. Add 3 tablespoons white-wine mixture; whisk or beat to combine. Add remaining 2 tablespoons solid butter. Nest bowl over a 3- to 4-quart pan of barely simmering water (bottom of bowl shouldn't touch water). Whisk vigorously or beat until butter has melted and mixture has emulsified and thickened, about 3 minutes. Remove from over water.

3. Whisking or beating constantly, pour in warm melted butter in a very thin, even stream; sauce should become smooth and emulsified (see notes). Continue whisking or beating until all butter is incorporated and sauce is creamy, 5 to 7 minutes. Add chopped tarragon and hot sauce; taste and add more wine mixture, more hot sauce, and salt if desired. If sauce is too cool for your liking, set bowl back over hot water and whisk just until warm to touch, no longer than 2 minutes. Serve at once.

Per tablespoon: 63 cal., 94% (59 cal.) from fat; 0.5 g protein; 6.5 g fat (3.8 g sat.); 0.9 g carbo (0 g fiber); 62 mg sodium; 42 mg chol.

Chimichurri

PREP TIME: 15 minutes

NOTES: This spicy, fresh-tasting sauce is a popular condiment in Argentina. Our version is moderately hot; adjust the spiciness by using more or less jalapeño.

MAKES: About ½ cup

In a blender or food processor, combine 1 rinsed and stemmed **jalapeño chili** (see notes), 1 peeled clove **garlic,** 2 tablespoons chopped **fresh cilantro,** 2 tablespoons chopped **parsley,** 1 tablespoon **fresh oregano** leaves, 1 teaspoon **ground dried ancho chilies** or chili powder, ¼ cup **olive oil,** 3 tablespoons **lime juice,** and 1 teaspoon **salt.** Whirl until thick and almost smooth. Use, or cover and chill up to 2 days; shake or stir before using.

Per tablespoon: 64 cal., 95% (61 cal.) from fat; 0.1 g protein; 6.8 g fat (0.9 g sat.); 1 g carbo (0.2 g fiber); 296 mg sodium; 0 mg chol. ◆

Great ideas in food and wine

WINE

Tricky treats

ELEGANT AND SUB-LIME TO SWEET AND SEXY. Compared to other grape varieties, Pinot Noir is finicky, erratic, difficult to work with, and painfully sensitive to conditions that range from where it's planted to when it's bottled (which, by the way, is why it's expensive). Despite these challenges, the West continues to produce Pinots that are treats.

Cristom "Jessie Vineyard" Pinot Noir 1999 (Willam-ette Valley, OR), $39. Elegant and sublime. Lightly spiced cherries and rose petals. **Bottom line:** Understated and refined.

Sanford Pinot Noir 2000 (Santa Barbara County), $26. A knockout of delicious cocoa, raspberry, vanilla, licorice, and tea flavors. Supple texture; long finish. **Bottom line:** Irresistible.

Williams Selyem Pinot Noir 2000 (Russian River Valley, CA), $39. Can be tricky to get a hold of, but worth the hunt. Silky texture. Flavors that are evocative of rhubarb pie, pomegranates, cherries, and spiced tea. **Bottom line:** Satisfying and soulful.

A STEAL: Echelon Pinot Noir 2000 (Central Coast), $12. Juicy flavor is all about cherries (pie, jam, cola) with some pomegranate and vanilla notes for good measure. **Bottom line:** Unbeatable with simple meat dishes. — *Karen MacNeil-Fife*

PROJECT
Quick bread in a bottle

Friendship bread: give a gift of home cooking that's also fun to make.

COOL WEATHER PUTS US IN THE MOOD TO BAKE. So why not give a friend a head start? Layer the dry ingredients from step 1 for this easy quick bread into a milk bottle. The mix will keep for up to 18 months—then all that's left is to add the wet ingredients and bake. We used craft paper adhered with double-stick tape to cover the original milk bottle graphics and the lid. A label on the back of the bottle contains the recipe instructions.

RECIPE: Chocolate Chip Oatmeal Quick Bread
1 In a large bowl, mix the contents of this bottle: 2 cups **all-purpose flour**, 1 cup **rolled oats**, ½ cup **granulated sugar**, ½ cup **brown sugar**, 2 teaspoons **baking powder**, 1 teaspoon **baking soda**, ½ teaspoon **cinnamon**, ½ teaspoon **salt**, ½ cup chopped **walnuts**, and ½ cup **miniature chocolate chips**. 2 In a small bowl, beat 1½ cups **buttermilk**, 2 large **eggs**, and ¼ cup melted **butter**. 3 Stir wet mixture into dry ingredients just until evenly moistened (batter will be lumpy). 4 Scrape into a buttered and floured 9- by 5-inch loaf pan, and bake in a 350° oven until a wooden skewer inserted in the center comes out clean, about 50 minutes. — *Charity Ferreira and Jil Peters*

RESTAURANTS

No pressure cooker

TWO STAR CHEFS IN DENVER THINK SMALL AND SCORE BIG. After becoming the father of twins, Sean Kelly closed his restaurant, Aubergine, took almost a year off, and re-emerged with the smaller but equally divine **Clair de Lune.** Kelly now cooks for a maximum of 40 diners a night, offering a small but perfectly balanced menu with something for every palate. Meanwhile, Hugh O'Neill pulled the plug on Hugh's American Bistro and opened **St. Kilian's Cheese Shop.** Compared to the pressures on a top chef, cheese-selling is mild, says O'Neill. "Cheese is so simple. It's peasant food. The biggest pressure is from people who hold up a bottle of wine and ask what cheese to eat with it, like they're afraid to try it unless they get my advice. I tell them, 'Close your eyes and point to a cheese, and then just eat it.' Anyone can become an expert with open curiosity and experimentation." *Clair de Lune: 1313 E. Sixth Ave.; (303) 831-1992. St. Kilian's Cheese Shop: 3211 Lowell Blvd.; (303) 477-0374. — Claire Walter*

E. SPENCER TOY; RIGHT: JAMES CARRIER (3)

Salad days for Latin food

NUEVO LATINO HEATS UP THE WEST.
An emerging cuisine is appearing on menus at restaurants like **Destino, La Luna Restaurant,** and **Asia de Cuba** in San Francisco; **Xiomara** in Pasadena; **Miramonte Restaurant and Café** in the Napa Valley; and **Fandango** in Seattle. The inspiration for Nuevo Latino often comes from blending (or trying to blend) Latin foods with European or Asian elements. Taste a deliciously successful merger in this lively salad from Johnny Alamilla at **Alma** in San Francisco's Mission District (415/401-8959).

RECIPE: **Cuban Bread Salad 1** In a 1- to 1½-quart pan over high heat, boil ½ cup **orange juice** until reduced to ¼ cup, 4 to 5 minutes. Let cool. Add 3 tablespoons minced **shallots,** 2 tablespoons *each* **lime juice** and **lemon juice,** and ½ teaspoon **ground cumin.** Whisk in ½ cup **salad oil.** Add 1 to 1½ tablespoons minced **fresh jalapeño chilies,** plus **salt** and **pepper** to taste. **2** Remove and discard husks from 12 ounces **tomatillos** (2 in. wide); rinse and cut into quarters. In a bowl, mix tomatillos with 1 tablespoon **extra-virgin olive oil.** Cut 6 ounces **potato-garlic** or French **bread** into 1-inch-thick slices. Set tomatillo quarters and bread slices on a grill over a solid bed of hot coals or a gas grill on high heat and turn as needed until browned on all sides, 1 to 2 minutes total for bread, 5 to 7 minutes for tomatillos. Let cool. Cut bread into 1-inch cubes. **3** In a large bowl, mix tomatillos, bread, 12 cups (8 oz.) rinsed and crisped **baby arugula,** and dressing. With a vegetable peeler, shave about ½ cup thin slices (2 oz.) off a wedge of **Manchego cheese.** Mix cheese and **salt** and **pepper** to taste into salad. Makes 6 servings. — *Linda Lau Anusasananan*

Your freshest Caesar

Romaine lettuce tastes best when you grow your own

By Lauren Bonar Swezey
Recipe by Sara Schneider

Determined chefs go out of their way to find the freshest, most tender heads of romaine lettuce available in the produce market. Grocery shoppers, on the other hand, are often limited to big heads with tough, strong-tasting leaves.

Luckily, lettuce is one of the easiest crops to grow. Seeds germinate quickly and plants grow with little fuss. In most areas of the West, you can grow successive crops in fall and spring; in mild coastal areas, you can grow lettuce year-round. So get going and soon you'll be able to try the salad below.

Garden Caesar Salad

PREP AND COOK TIME: About 30 minutes

NOTES: If you are concerned about bacteria in the uncooked egg yolks, or if there is a risk of salmonella in your area, use eggs pasteurized in the shell (available in some supermarkets). Marinated fresh anchovies have silver skin and a more delicate flavor than the standard anchovies canned in olive oil. They are available at some Italian markets and in specialty food stores.

MAKES: 4 to 6 servings

12 diagonal slices (¼ in. thick) **baguette** (about ¼ of an 8-oz. loaf)
   About 6 tablespoons **extra-virgin olive oil**
1 large clove **garlic,** peeled
2 tablespoons **lemon juice**
2 **canned anchovy fillets,** drained and minced (optional)
⅛ teaspoon **Worcestershire**
3 **large egg** yolks (see notes)

1 pound **romaine lettuce** (1 large or 2 small heads), rinsed, crisped, and large leaves torn into large pieces (leave small inner leaves whole)
½ cup freshly shredded **parmesan cheese**
   Fresh-ground **pepper**
4 **radishes,** stemmed and rinsed
8 **marinated fresh anchovies** (optional; see notes)

1. Brush one side of each baguette slice with olive oil. Cut garlic clove in half and rub a cut side lightly over oiled side of each slice. Place slices oiled side up on a 10- by 15-inch baking sheet. Bake in a 350° regular or convection oven until crisp and golden, 8 to 10 minutes. Let croutons cool.

2. Meanwhile, mince or press 1 teaspoon garlic from remainder of garlic clove. In a 1- to 2-cup glass measure, combine 5 tablespoons olive oil, lemon juice, minced anchovies, Worcestershire, and minced garlic. In a large salad bowl, whisk egg yolks to blend. Whisking constantly, pour olive oil mixture slowly into egg yolks, pausing to whisk occasionally so that mixture forms a smooth emulsion.

3. Add romaine and parmesan to bowl and mix gently to coat. Grind pepper into salad to taste. Mound equally on plates. Very thinly slice 4 radishes and sprinkle over salads. Arrange croutons alongside; if desired, drape marinated anchovies, skin side up, over croutons.

Per serving: 231 cal., 78% (180 cal.) from fat; 7 g protein; 20 g fat (4.4 g sat.); 8.6 g carbo (2.1 g fiber); 227 mg sodium; 113 mg chol. ◆

Reduced-fat sour cream and fresh tomato salsa make a cooling garnish for black bean chili.

Red hot chili peppers

Smoky puréed chipotles are an easy way to add earthy spice

By Charity Ferreira

■ Chipotle chilies are smoked jalapeños that are sold dried or canned in adobo sauce. The canned variety in particular is packed with a lot of flavor but very little fat, so the chilies are perfect for healthy cooking. Purée a can and keep it in the refrigerator to have on hand for adding smoky, pickled heat to beans, soups, and meat stews; for stirring into mayonnaise to spread on sandwiches; or for adding spice and depth to any fresh or jarred salsa. A few tablespoons of this complex chili purée go a long way toward seasoning dishes like meatless black bean chili or shredded chicken in red sauce, folded into soft corn tortillas.

Black Bean Chili

PREP AND COOK TIME: About 30 minutes
MAKES: 6 cups; about 4 servings

- 1 **onion** (8 oz.), peeled and chopped
- 2 teaspoons pressed or minced **garlic**
- 2 teaspoons **olive oil**
- 3 cans (14½ oz. each) **black beans**, rinsed and drained
- 1 can (14½ oz.) **crushed tomatoes**
- 1½ teaspoons **ground cumin**
- ¼ cup chopped **fresh cilantro**
- 1 tablespoon **canned chipotle chili** purée (see "Chili whiz," at right)
- 1 tablespoon **rice vinegar**
  Salt
- ¼ cup **reduced-fat sour cream**
  Tomato salsa (optional)

1. In a 3- to 4-quart pan over medium-high heat, cook onion and garlic in olive oil, stirring often, until onion is limp and starting to brown, 6 to 8 minutes.

2. Add beans, tomatoes and their juice, cumin, and ½ cup water; bring to a boil, then reduce heat and simmer, stirring occasionally, to blend flavors, about 15 minutes.

3. Stir in cilantro, chipotle purée, and rice vinegar. Add salt to taste. Spoon chili equally into four bowls and top each with 1 tablespoon sour cream and, if desired, with tomato salsa to taste.

Per serving: 265 cal., 21% (56 cal.) from fat; 14 g protein; 6.2 g fat (1.5 g sat.); 40 g carbo (10 g fiber); 709 mg sodium; 5 mg chol.

Chili whiz

To make chipotle purée, whirl a 7-ounce can of chipotle chilies, including the adobo sauce, in a blender or food processor until smooth. Scrape into a plastic container and store airtight in the refrigerator up to 1 week or in the freezer for several months.

Chicken Soft Tacos

PREP AND COOK TIME: About 45 minutes
NOTES: You can make the filling for these tacos (through step 2) up to 2 days ahead; chill airtight, then reheat in a pan on the stove or in the microwave before serving.
MAKES: 2 or 3 servings

- 1 pound **boned, skinned chicken breasts**
- 1 can (14½ oz.) **chicken broth**
- 3 tablespoons **lime juice**
- 1½ tablespoons **canned chipotle chili** purée (see "Chili whiz," below)
- 1 tablespoon **salad oil**
- 1¼ cups minced **sweet onion**
- 1 clove **garlic**, minced
- 1 can (8 oz.) **tomato sauce**
- ¼ cup chopped **fresh cilantro** leaves
  Salt
- 2 cans (15 oz. each) **pinto beans**, rinsed and drained
- 6 **corn tortillas** (4 to 6 in.)

1. Rinse chicken. In a 3- to 4-quart pan over medium-high heat, bring chicken broth, 2 tablespoons lime juice, and chipotle purée to a simmer. Add chicken breasts, adjust heat to maintain simmer, and cook until chicken is no longer pink in the center of the thickest part (cut to test), 10 to 15 minutes. With tongs, transfer chicken to a bowl; reserve broth. When chicken is cool enough to handle, tear or cut into bite-size shreds.

2. Meanwhile, heat oil in an 8- to 10-inch frying pan over medium heat. When hot, add ¼ cup onion and the garlic and stir frequently until onions are limp, about 5 minutes. Add reserved chicken broth and tomato sauce and bring to a boil; reduce heat and simmer to blend flavors, about 5 minutes. Pour sauce over chicken and mix to coat.

3. In a small bowl, mix remaining 1 cup minced onion, remaining 1 tablespoon lime juice, cilantro, and salt to taste.

4. In a 3- to 4-quart pan over medium-high heat, warm pinto beans until hot. Stack tortillas and wrap in microwave-safe plastic wrap. Heat in a microwave oven at 50 percent power until steaming, about 1½ minutes. Remove plastic and wrap tortillas in a towel to keep warm. Serve tortillas, beans, chicken mixture, and onion relish separately, letting each person fill tacos as desired.

Per serving: 556 cal., 15% (85 cal.) from fat; 53 g protein; 9.4 g fat (1.4 g sat.); 67 g carbo (13 g fiber); 1,858 mg sodium; 88 mg chol. ◆

A stirring issue

A little do-ahead secret makes risotto a great party dish

Soothing yet sophisticated, risotto seems perfect for entertaining—but few would dream of cooking it for a party. All that last-minute stirring may make for great risotto, but it hardly makes for a composed host. That's why we were delighted to learn of an easy way to make risotto ahead of time: just pull the pan off the heat before adding the last bit of broth; then, just before serving, put it back on to finish the process.

This idea came to us from Inspired Chef, a company that offers in-home cooking lessons from professional chefs. It was demonstrated by Rebecca Ets-Hokin, one of their certified culinary professionals, who hit upon the trick by accident as a new mother. "I was about 75 percent done making wild-mushroom risotto when my baby woke up," she says. "I turned off the heat but left the risotto on the stove. About an hour later, I came back to finish it. The risotto was perfect." Our testing confirmed Ets-Hokin's results: firm but creamy risotto that rivals constantly stirred versions. (One caveat: made this way, risottos with high ratios of liquid to rice may become slightly mushy.) This innovative, fusion-style risotto from Inspired Chef is great started ahead. *Inspired Chef: (800) 528-1030 or www.inspiredchef.com.*

Thai Red Curry Risotto

PREP AND COOK TIME: About 1 hour

NOTES: Thai red curry paste is available in many supermarkets. It's hot—add more or less to suit your taste. This risotto also works well without interruption; just leave it on the heat after step 3 and continue with step 4.

MAKES: 6 servings

JAMES CARRIER; FOOD STYLING: SUSAN DEVATY

1 **onion** (about 6 oz.), peeled and chopped

3 tablespoons grated peeled **fresh ginger**

2 cloves **garlic,** peeled and chopped

¼ cup **grape seed** or other salad **oil**

2 teaspoons **paprika**

¾ teaspoon **Thai red curry paste** (see notes)

1½ cups **arborio** or other short-grain white **rice**

½ cup **dry sherry**

About 4 cups fat-skimmed **chicken broth**

4 ounces **fresh shiitake mushrooms,** rinsed, stems removed, and sliced; or common mushrooms, rinsed, tough stem ends trimmed, and sliced

1 cup **coconut milk** (regular or low-fat; stir before measuring)

1½ cups **frozen petite peas**

3 tablespoons chopped **fresh cilantro**

Salt

1 **lime** (about 3 oz.), rinsed and cut into 6 wedges

1. In a 12-inch frying pan or 14-inch wok over medium heat, stir onion, ginger, and garlic in oil until onion is barely limp, about 2 minutes.

2. Stir in paprika, curry paste, and rice, mixing well to coat rice. Pour in sherry and cook, stirring to scrape up any browned bits, until sherry is absorbed, about 2 minutes.

3. Pour in 1 cup chicken broth and stir until broth is mostly absorbed, 3 to 4 minutes. Add mushrooms and coconut milk; stir gently until liquid is mostly absorbed, about 1 minute. Add 2 more cups broth, 1 cup at a time, stirring after each addition until almost absorbed, about 15 minutes total. Rice should be almost tender but still slightly firm to bite. Remove from heat and let stand, uncovered, up to 4 hours.

4. Return pan to medium-high heat, add 1 more cup broth, and stir until liquid is absorbed and rice is creamy and tender to bite, about 9 minutes. If risotto is too dry or rice isn't quite tender, add a little more broth and cook until risotto reaches desired consistency. Stir in peas, cilantro, and salt to taste. Spoon risotto into serving bowls and garnish each serving with a lime wedge.

Per serving: 393 cal., 41% (162 cal.) from fat; 12 g protein; 18 g fat (8.1 g sat.); 47 g carbo (6.5 g fiber); 563 mg sodium; 0 mg chol.

— *Kate Washington*

Green laws

E. SPENCER TOY

■ If your jar of salsa is labeled "Made with organic ingredients," what does that mean? Until now, a lack of nationally consistent standards for growing, processing, and labeling organic foods has made it hard to know for sure. But as of October 21, that changes: products labeled organic will have to be certified by a USDA-accredited agency and comply with national organic standards—or their producers will face penalties (fines and/or jail time).

Here are the phrases you'll see on labels, and what they mean:

• **100 percent organic.** Contains only organic ingredients.

• **Organic.** Contains at least 95 percent organic ingredients.

• **Made with organic ingredients.** Contains at least 70 percent organic ingredients.

For products made with less than 70 percent organic ingredients, the organic ones may be identified only in the ingredient list—and only if all of one qualifies (the tomatoes in that salsa, for instance). Note: Water and salt are excluded in the content calculations.

Only the first two categories can sport the "USDA Organic" seal (at left), and now it really means something. For more information: USDA website, www.ams.usda.gov/nop; and *The Organic Foods Sourcebook,* by Elaine Marie Lipson (McGraw-Hill, New York, 2001; $15.95; www.books.mcgraw-hill.com). — *Sara Schneider*

The Wine Guide
What's at steak

By Karen MacNeil-Fife

In the history of compelling wine-and-food marriages, there have always been Champagne and caviar, Sauternes and foie gras, Port and Stilton, and a slew of other European classics. Isn't it about time we added a few pairings that are uniquely, unabashedly American? My first vote would be for steak and … what? Westerners have been grilling steaks and pulling corks for more than a century, and during that time, we've discovered that many wines work—at least pretty well. That's because grilling imparts charred and caramelized flavors that are great counterpoints to the light toasty and sweet flavors wines take on when they're made and/or aged in oak barrels.

Still, experience suggests that some wines are better matches for steak than others. With apologies to Webster, here's my definition of a steak wine: a red wine with enough grip, texture, and structure to stand up to the density and meaty flavor of a thick, juicy slice of grilled, broiled, or pan-fried beef. *Synonym:*

JAMES CARRIER; FOOD STYLING: KAREN SHINTO

Cabernet Sauvignon, especially from countries in the New World whose cuisines were historically built on grilling, such as the western United States and Australia. (Middle English *steke* might derive from Old Norse *steik,* but Scandinavian wines are out of the question.) *Usage note:* If Cabernet Sauvignon is not available, secondary synonyms may serve as intriguing substitutes: Syrah (Shiraz), Petite Syrah, Rhône-style blends, substantial Merlots,

and powerful Zinfandels.

What do all of these wines have in common? Serious structure: the sense of an imposing form, or architecture. A wine like this often reminds me of a Gothic cathedral with flying buttresses. The French, on the other hand, often describe a wine's structure as its "bones" or "skeleton."

Most red wines get their structure from tannin—the compound in grape skins and seeds that also acts as a preservative, allowing the wine to age well. A great Cabernet Sauvignon, for example, has a lot of tannin, and, as a result, a lot of structure and aging potential. (To compare a wine that has a lot of tannin and structure to one without much of either, try a Cabernet Sauvignon next to a Beaujolais.)

Steak calls for tannin and structure. The density of the meat, the concentration of flavor, the combination of protein and fat—all add up to a substantial foil for a big wine. For me, there is no more classic (or delicious) match than steak and Cabernet. Think of it as America's power marriage.

Cabs to match

Hess Collection, Jordan, Silverado, and **Chimney Rock "Elevage,"** all from California. And a steal: **Black Opal Cabernet-Merlot** from Australia, about $11. ◆

Mash notes

Pair sausages with mashed potatoes for an easy dinner

By Kate Washington

■ The British call it "bangers and mash": savory sausages served over mashed potatoes. We just call it a delicious weeknight meal (perfect for fall) and pull it together quickly through strategic use of both kitchen equipment and personnel (see "Efficiency rules" at right). The best thing, though, is that your whole family will like it; we tested the dish on several kids, and not a single nose turned up. They'll like it even better if you tell them the funny name.

JAMES CARRIER; FOOD STYLING: KAREN SHINTO

Roasted Sausages with Beer-braised Onions

PREP AND COOK TIME: 30 minutes

NOTES: Choose fully cooked sausages for this dish; we prefer pork such as smoked bratwurst, or mild poultry such as chicken-apple, but any flavor (or mixture) will work.

MAKES: 4 servings

- 3 **onions** (1½ lb. total), peeled and slivered lengthwise
- 1 tablespoon **salad oil**
- 1 cup **stout** or dark beer (such as Guinness)
- 1 teaspoon **fresh thyme** leaves
  Salt and **pepper**
- 8 **sausages** (1½ to 2 lb. total; see notes)
- 2 tablespoons chopped **parsley**

1. In a 10- to 12-inch ovenproof frying pan over high heat, frequently stir onions in oil until somewhat limp and beginning to brown, about 4 minutes. Stir in stout and thyme; cook until liquid is reduced by about half, 3 to 5 minutes. Stir in salt and pepper to taste.

2. Prick sausages all over with the tip of a sharp knife and arrange in a single layer on onion mixture.

3. Bake in a 375° regular or convection oven until sausages are heated through (cut to test), about 20 minutes. Sprinkle with parsley.

Per serving: 439 cal., 62% (270 cal.) from fat; 28 g protein; 30 g fat (8 g sat.); 17 g carbo (2.6 g fiber); 1,200 mg sodium; 151 mg chol.

Mashed Potatoes

PREP AND COOK TIME: 20 minutes

MAKES: 4 servings

About 1 teaspoon **salt**

- 2½ pounds **russet potatoes,** peeled and cut into 1-inch chunks
  About ¾ cup **milk**
  About 2 tablespoons **butter**
  Pepper

1. In a 4- to 5-quart pan over high heat, bring 2 quarts water and 1 teaspoon salt to a boil. Add potatoes. Cover and return to a boil, then reduce heat to medium and simmer until potatoes mash easily, 8 to 10 minutes. Drain potatoes and return to pan.

2. Meanwhile, in 1- to 1½-quart pan over low heat, warm ¾ cup milk until steaming (do not boil), about 5 minutes; or heat in a microwave-safe container in a microwave oven on full power (100%), stirring occasionally, about 1 minute.

3. Add 2 tablespoons butter and ½ cup of the hot milk to potatoes and mash with a potato masher or an electric mixer on medium speed until mixture is as lumpy or smooth as you like, gradually beating in up to ¼ cup additional milk and more butter, if desired, until potatoes reach desired consistency. Add salt and pepper to taste.

Per serving: 285 cal., 24% (69 cal.) from fat; 6.5 g protein; 7.7 g fat (4.5 g sat.); 48 g carbo (4.3 g fiber); 537 mg sodium; 22 mg chol.

Gingersnap Baked Apples

PREP AND COOK TIME: About 1 hour

MAKES: 4 servings

- 3 ounces **gingersnap cookies** (about a dozen 2-in. cookies), broken into pieces
- 2 tablespoons firmly packed **brown sugar**

Efficiency rules

Timely moves get the main course of this menu on the table in about 30 minutes. First, heat the water for the mashed potatoes and turn on the oven for the sausages. Then slice and sauté the onions. While they cook, peel and cube the potatoes (take a few quick breaks to stir, and to add the beer to the onions). Top onions with sausages and pop them into the oven, then drop the potatoes into the boiling water. Use the 10 minutes while the potatoes cook to core and stuff the apples; they bake at the same temperature as the sausages, so slide them into the oven as well. When the potatoes are drained and mashed, the sausages should be heated through. Chop a little parsley, sprinkle it on top, and serve up dinner. By the time you're ready for dessert, the apples will be too.

- 4 **sweet apples,** such as Fuji (about 2 lb. total), rinsed
- ¼ cup (⅛ lb.) **butter**
- ½ cup **whipping cream** (optional)

1. In a blender or food processor, whirl gingersnaps and brown sugar to fine crumbs.

2. With a small, sharp knife, starting from stem ends, cut around cores to about ¾ of the way through apples; scoop out cores with a spoon, making a 1½-inch-wide cavity and leaving bases intact. Set apples slightly apart in a shallow 2- to 3-quart baking dish.

3. Spoon 1 tablespoon gingersnap mixture into each cavity and top with ½ tablespoon butter. Sprinkle apples evenly with remaining gingersnap mixture.

4. Bake in a 375° regular or convection oven until apples are tender when pierced, about 45 minutes. Transfer to individual bowls and pour 2 tablespoons cream around each if desired.

Per serving: 346 cal., 39% (135 cal.) from fat; 1.3 g protein; 15 g fat (7.9 g sat.); 55 g carbo (5 g fiber); 297 mg sodium; 32 mg chol. ◆

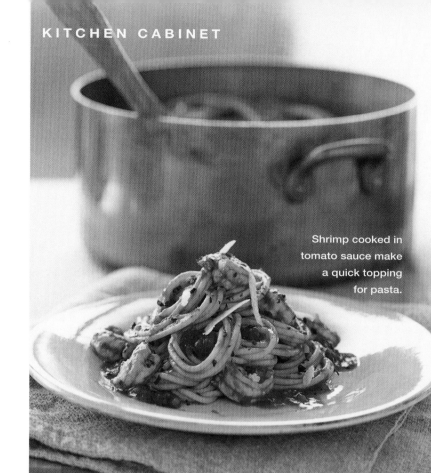

Shrimp cooked in tomato sauce make a quick topping for pasta.

FOOD STYLING: BASIL FRIEDMAN

House specialties

Readers' recipes tested in *Sunset's* kitchens

By Charity Ferreira • Photographs by James Carrier

Italian-style Shrimp with Spaghetti

Lynne Schaefer, Novato, CA

Lynne Schaefer found that a favorite recipe for cacciatore-style chicken was also a great way to prepare shrimp.

PREP AND COOK TIME: About 25 minutes

MAKES: 4 servings

- 8 ounces **dried spaghetti**
- ½ cup finely chopped **shallots** (about 3 oz.)
- 1 teaspoon minced **garlic**
- 2 teaspoons **olive oil**
- 1 can (14½ oz.) **Italian-style diced tomatoes**
- 1 can (6 oz.) **tomato paste**
- ½ cup **dry white wine**
- 1 teaspoon **dried oregano**
- 1 teaspoon **dried basil**
- 1 pound (40 to 50 per lb.) **frozen shelled deveined shrimp**, thawed
- 2 tablespoons chopped **parsley**
  Salt and **pepper**
  Shredded romano or parmesan cheese

1. In a 4- to 5-quart pan over high heat, bring 2 quarts water to a boil. Add pasta and cook, stirring occasionally, until tender to bite, about 10 minutes. Drain and return to pan.

2. Meanwhile, in a 10- to 12-inch frying pan over high heat, stir shallots and garlic in olive oil until shallots are limp, about 5 minutes. Stir in tomatoes (with juice), tomato paste, wine, oregano, and basil. Bring to a boil, then reduce heat and simmer, stirring occasionally, about 5 minutes.

3. Rinse and drain shrimp; add to sauce. Stir often just until opaque but still moist-looking in center of thickest part (cut to test), 5 to 6 minutes.

4. Stir sauce into cooked pasta. Divide mixture equally among four bowls.

Sprinkle with parsley; add salt, pepper, and cheese to taste.

Per serving: 447 cal., 11% (50 cal.) from fat; 33 g protein; 5.5 g fat (0.9 g sat.); 59 g carbo (4.3 g fiber); 675 mg sodium; 173 mg chol.

Cajun Fried Rice

Betsy Malloy, San Jose

Betsy Malloy keeps her freezer stocked with sausage and okra so that she can assemble this spicy rice dish whenever she has leftover cooked rice. Use a prepared Cajun spice blend or mix ¾ to 1 teaspoon cayenne, 1 teaspoon paprika, and ½ teaspoon salt.

PREP AND COOK TIME: About 45 minutes

MAKES: 4 servings

- 1 tablespoon **vegetable oil**
- 8 ounces **andouille** or other cooked spicy **sausage**, diced (about ¼ in.)
- 1 **onion** (8 oz.), peeled and chopped
- 1 teaspoon minced **garlic**
- 10 ounces **frozen sliced okra,** thawed
- 4 cups cooked **long-grain white rice**
- 1 tablespoon **Cajun spice blend** (see notes)

1. Pour oil into a 12-inch frying pan or a 14-inch wok over medium-high heat. When hot, add sausage and stir often until slightly browned, 1 to 2 minutes. Add onion, garlic, and okra; stir often until onion is limp, about 5 minutes.

2. Gently mix in rice and Cajun spice blend; stir occasionally until the rice is hot and golden and the okra is tender, about 5 minutes. Pour into a serving bowl.

Per serving: 462 cal., 39% (180 cal.) from fat; 14 g protein; 20 g fat (6.2 g sat.); 57 g carbo (3.7 g fiber); 1,247 mg sodium; 38 mg chol.

Pumpkin Flapjacks

Jane Shapton, Tustin, CA

Jane Shapton serves these fluffy pancakes with warm cranberry sauce; they're also great with maple syrup.

PREP AND COOK TIME: About 45 minutes

MAKES: About 14 pancakes

- 2 cups **all-purpose flour**
- ¼ cup firmly packed **brown sugar**
- 1 tablespoon **baking powder**
- 1 tablespoon **cinnamon**
- ¼ teaspoon **salt**
- 2 cups **milk**
- 1 cup **canned pumpkin**
- 4 **large eggs**, separated
- ¼ cup (⅛ lb.) **butter**, melted
  Salad oil

1. In a bowl, mix flour, sugar, baking powder, cinnamon, and salt. In another bowl, beat milk, pumpkin, egg yolks, and butter to blend. Stir into flour mixture until evenly moistened.

2. In another bowl, with a mixer on high speed, beat egg whites until soft peaks form. Gently fold egg whites into batter just until incorporated.

3. Place a nonstick griddle or a 12-inch nonstick frying pan over medium heat (350°); when hot, coat lightly with oil and wipe dry with a paper towel. Pour batter in ½-cup portions onto griddle, spreading slightly with the back of a spoon, and cook until pancakes are browned on the bottom and edges begin to look dry, about 3 minutes; turn with a wide spatula and brown other sides, 2 to 3 minutes longer. Adjust heat as needed to maintain an even temperature.

4. Serve pancakes as cooked, or keep warm in a single layer on baking sheets in a 200° oven up to 15 minutes.

Per pancake: 169 cal., 38% (65 cal.) from fat; 5 g protein; 7.2 g fat (3.4 g sat.); 21 g carbo (0.8 g fiber); 218 mg sodium; 75 mg chol.

Cotija Cheese Potatoes

Anne Callison, Denver

Anne Callison found a way to incorporate cotija, a flavorful Mexican cheese that she discovered in a specialty cheese shop, into a warm potato side dish. Cotija is available in some well-stocked supermarkets and in Latino markets. If you can't find it, substitute a shredded firm white cheese such as white cheddar or jack.

PREP AND COOK TIME: About 1¾ hours

MAKES: 8 to 10 servings

- 1 tablespoon **olive oil**
- 1 **onion** (8 oz.), peeled, halved, and thinly slivered lengthwise
- 2 cloves **garlic**, peeled and minced
- 1¾ pounds **firm-ripe Roma tomatoes**, rinsed, cored, and chopped
- ½ to 1 tablespoon **hot sauce**
- ½ teaspoon **dried basil**
- ½ teaspoon **dried thyme**
- ½ teaspoon **salt**
- ½ teaspoon **pepper**
- 3 pounds **russet potatoes**
- 2 cups crumbled **cotija cheese** (8 oz.; see notes)

1. Pour oil into a 10- to 12-inch frying pan over medium heat. When oil is hot, add onion and garlic and stir frequently until onion is limp, about 5 minutes. Add tomatoes, hot sauce,

basil, thyme, salt, and pepper. Stir occasionally until tomatoes are soft, about 5 minutes.

2. Meanwhile, peel potatoes and slice ⅛ inch thick. In a 9- by 13-inch baking pan, layer about a third of the tomato mixture, followed by half the potatoes and half the cheese. Repeat layers, ending with tomatoes. Cover tightly with foil.

3. Bake in a 400° regular or convection oven until potatoes are tender when pierced, 40 to 50 minutes. Uncover and bake until browned on top and bubbling around the edges, 20 to 25 minutes longer.

Per serving: 214 cal., 33% (70 cal.) from fat; 8.9 g protein; 7.8 g fat (4.1 g sat.); 28 g carbo (3.3 g fiber); 567 mg sodium; 18 mg chol.

Shortbread Caramel Brownie Bars

Linda Tebben, Menlo Park, CA

This three-layer bar cookie created by Linda Tebben has a flaky shortbread crust, a band of caramel, and a brownielike chocolate top.

PREP AND COOK TIME: About 2 hours

MAKES: 24 bars

- 1½ cups (¾ lb.) **butter**
- 2½ cups **all-purpose flour**
- 1¼ cups **sugar**
- 2 tablespoons **cornstarch**
- 12 ounces individually wrapped **soft caramels,** such as Kraft
- ¼ cup **whole milk**
- 10 ounces **bittersweet** or semisweet **chocolate,** finely chopped
- 3 **large eggs**
- 1 tablespoon **vanilla**
- ½ teaspoon **baking powder**
- ¼ teaspoon **salt**

Good things come in small squares, like these triple-layer brownie bars.

1. Cut 1 cup butter into chunks. In the bowl of a food processor, combine 2 cups flour, ½ cup sugar, cornstarch, and the butter chunks. Whirl until dough comes together. Press evenly over the bottom of a buttered 9- by 13-inch baking pan. Bake in a 325° regular or convection oven until top feels dry and is just beginning to brown, about 25 minutes. Let cool completely.

2. Meanwhile, unwrap caramels and place in a microwave-safe bowl with milk. Cook in a microwave oven on full power (100%) for 1 minute. Stir mixture, then cook and stir at 30-second intervals until melted and smooth, about 3 minutes longer. Spread caramel mixture evenly over cooled crust and chill until firm, about 20 minutes.

3. In a large bowl set over a pan of barely simmering water (bottom of bowl should not touch water), stir chocolate and remaining ½ cup butter often until melted and smooth. Remove bowl from over water and, with a whisk or a mixer on medium speed, beat in remaining ¾ cup sugar, eggs, and vanilla until well blended. Stir in remaining ½ cup flour, baking powder, and salt until well blended.

4. Pour chocolate mixture over caramel layer and use a knife or spatula to spread level, completely covering caramel.

5. Bake in a 350° regular or convection oven until a wooden skewer inserted into the chocolate layer comes out clean, 35 to 40 minutes. Let cool completely, then cut into 24 bars.

Per bar: 322 cal., 50% (162 cal.) from fat; 3.8 g protein; 18 g fat (10 g sat.); 39 g carbo (0.6 g fiber); 200 mg sodium; 58 mg chol. ◆

Sweet pears and tart cranberries baked under a buttery crisp topping make a delicious ending (recipe on page 226).

November

Thanksgiving with friends in Ojai

When everyone cooks together, the meal tastes even better

By Linda Lau Anusasananan • Photographs by James Carrier • Food styling by Christine Masterson • Prop styling by Robin Turk

Cooperative Thanksgiving

Ode-to-Chèvre Bruschetta

Wild and Mild Stuffed Mushrooms

Squash Soup with Chili Purée

Green Salad*

Ojai Roast Turkey with Rosemary, Lemon,
and Garlic

Classic Gravy (recipe on page 231)

Lemon-Rosemary Roasted Onions and Garlic

Apricot, Wild Rice, and Bread Dressing

Anise Pear-Cranberry Sauce

Cumin-braised Brussels Sprouts

Mashed Potato Cloud

*Sauvignon Blanc, Pinot Gris, Dry Rosé,
or Pinot Noir*

Tarte Tatin • *Coffee*

*Recipe not provided

■ "Our Thanksgiving certainly involves a big dinner," says Sheila Schmitz of Los Gatos, California, "but the celebration is actually in the kitchen." Over time, Schmitz and a group of her friends have created a modern, convivial, and distinctly Western Thanksgiving tradition. Marty Bonvechio hosts the party in her roomy kitchen in Ojai, California, where everyone works together to produce a lavish but casual meal. "I come from a large family," Bonvechio says. "We always had huge holiday feasts. But I work for a newspaper. They don't believe in holidays! So the only way to do it is to create your own family where you live." Schmitz, Bonvechio, and their friends—including Philippe Berger, a chef; Jeff Hanley, whom Bonvechio calls "the king of appetizers"; and Lisa McKinnon—work and eat together all day long, so that the cooking is as much a part of the event as the serving. Together, they've developed a menu that's a delicious fusion of tradition and innovation, from spicy stuffed mushrooms to brussels sprouts flavored with cumin. The relaxed spirit of a cooking and eating party can work with almost any group in almost any home (see "An Easy Schedule," page 218). Use this menu from the Ojai group, or plan your own. If space and equipment are limited, ask people to bring the ingredients for their dishes prepped for minimal last-minute assembly. Although at first the kitchen might seem crowded, by the day's end it will just seem full—of laughter, friendship, and a perfect Thanksgiving feast.

THIS PAGE, CLOCKWISE FROM LEFT: Arrange flowers loosely for a look that's easygoing but sophisticated; the guests—and cooks—arrive, ingredients in hand; the Thanksgiving meal combines traditional elements with updated flavors.

LEFT: **Chèvre bruschetta** are the perfect size for snacking on throughout the preparations. RIGHT: **Dry rosé,** a great food wine, fits the meal's varied flavors.

An easy schedule

Sheila Schmitz describes the day: *Things start around noon or 1 P.M., when Marty throws open the kitchen and pops open a bottle of red wine. She has usually started the prep work the day before, but she's now getting the turkey into the oven and pressing one of her vintage tablecloths. As we work, we begin the feast. Appetizers become our lunch; there's always something great to munch on.*

Each person makes a dish or two. *As we go, we load the dishwasher and clean up, making room for others to work on their food. Everyone keeps an eye on the oven and stove, watching for an opening but making sure they're not interfering at a critical moment in someone else's dish.*

When the turkey is ready, *Marty takes it out of the oven, and Philippe begins to carve it; others take advantage of the new oven space to finish their side dishes. Dinner is usually served around 4 or 5, and we always declare it the best yet.*

After we're suitably stuffed, *we wander into the yard or the living room and rest a while before Lisa brings out a pie or two.*

Ode-to-Chèvre Bruschetta

PREP AND COOK TIME: About 40 minutes

NOTES: The day starts with a light lunch in the form of these bruschetta, contributed by Schmitz. In Ojai, vine-ripened tomatoes are available even in November. If you have trouble finding them, look for Roma or cherry tomatoes; they tend to be better quality than other types during cool-weather months.

MAKES: About 30 appetizers

  1 **baguette** (8 oz.; about 2½ in. wide and 24 in. long)

  5 tablespoons **extra-virgin olive oil**

  2 pounds **firm-ripe tomatoes** (see notes)

1½ tablespoons **lemon juice**

1½ teaspoons **Dijon mustard**

 ¼ cup chopped **pitted calamata olives**

  3 tablespoons chopped **fresh basil** leaves or 1 tablespoon dried basil

  2 cloves **garlic,** peeled and minced

     Salt and **pepper**

  6 ounces **fresh chèvre** (goat cheese)

1. Slice baguette on a slight diagonal about ⅓ inch thick; reserve ends for another use. Arrange slices on racks on two baking sheets (each 12 by 15 in.). Brush tops lightly with 2 tablespoons olive oil. Bake in a 425° regular or convection oven until lightly browned, 5 to 8 minutes.

2. Meanwhile, rinse, stem, and core tomatoes. Cut in half crosswise and squeeze out and discard seeds; chop tomatoes. (If not serving immediately, put tomatoes in a strainer or colander to drain.)

3. In a bowl, mix remaining 3 tablespoons olive oil, the lemon juice, and mustard. Stir in tomatoes, olives, basil, and garlic. Add salt and pepper to taste.

4. Spread cheese over one side of each slice of toast. Mound tomato mixture equally on top. Serve at once.

Per piece: 71 cal., 58% (41 cal.) from fat; 2.2 g protein; 4.6 g fat (1.6 g sat.); 5.7 g carbo (0.6 g fiber); 104 mg sodium; 4.5 mg chol.

Wild and Mild Stuffed Mushrooms

PREP AND COOK TIME: About 2 hours

NOTES: Jeff Hanley of Los Gatos makes two varieties of stuffed mushrooms—habanero for asbestos palates and blue cheese for those with milder tastes. For the former, he uses two of the fiery chilies and has been known to clear a room while chopping them. We've reduced the chili to one for a moderate heat level. If you want to sweat, though, add another one or don't remove the seeds and veins, which is where the heat is concentrated. You can prepare the mushrooms through step 7 up to 1 day ahead; cover and chill. Uncover and bake as directed in step 8.

MAKES: About 4 dozen

  4 dozen **mushrooms** (about 2-in.-wide caps; 3 lb. total)

  5 tablespoons **butter**

 ½ cup chopped **shallots**

  1 fresh **habanero chili** (¼ to ⅓ oz.)

  4 ounces **crumbled blue cheese** (⅔ cup)

  3 ounces **hard sourdough pretzels** (about 4 large)

  1 package (8 oz.) **cream cheese,** at room temperature

     Salt and **pepper**

1. Rinse and drain mushrooms and trim off tough stem ends. Gently snap off stems; finely chop stems.

2. In a 10- to 12-inch frying pan over high heat, frequently stir half the mushroom caps in 1 tablespoon butter until browned on both sides, about 7 minutes. Pour into a bowl and repeat to brown remaining mushrooms in 1 more tablespoon butter; pour into same bowl.

3. To unwashed pan, add another tablespoon butter, chopped mushroom stems, and shallots; stir often over high

Creamy squash soup gets a little bite from chili powder.
BELOW RIGHT: Cooks assemble as Berger brings out the turkey.

Squash Soup with Chili Purée

PREP AND COOK TIME: About 1¹⁄₂ hours

NOTES: Lisa McKinnon of Ventura, CA, adds a dollop of chili purée to this rustic squash soup. The soup can be made through step 4 up to 2 days ahead; cover and chill. Reheat, covered, over medium heat, stirring occasionally.

MAKES: 10 to 12 servings

- 5 pounds **kabocha** or butternut **squash**

  About 2 tablespoons **olive oil**
- 1¹⁄₄ pounds **leeks** (about 4)
- 2 cloves **garlic**, peeled and chopped
- 1 tablespoon chopped **fresh ginger**
- 2 tablespoons **butter**
- 1 teaspoon **ground coriander**
- 6 to 9 cups **vegetable** or fat-skimmed chicken **broth**

  Salt and **pepper**

  Sour cream

  Chili purée (recipe follows) or chili powder

1. Rinse squash. With a large, heavy knife, cut in half lengthwise, using a mallet or hammer gently, if necessary, to force knife through squash. Scoop out and discard seeds. Brush cut surfaces with olive oil. Set squash cut side down in a 10- by 15-inch baking pan.

2. Bake in a 375° regular or convection oven until squash is soft when pressed, 45 to 60 minutes. Reserve pan juices. Scoop flesh from peels (you should have about 5 cups) and discard peels.

3. Meanwhile, trim and discard root

heat until lightly browned, about 6 minutes. Divide mixture equally between two small bowls.

4. Rinse chili. Wearing rubber gloves, cut chili in half lengthwise and remove stem; scrape out and discard seeds and veins (see notes). Finely chop chili. Add chili to unwashed pan and stir often over high heat until limp, 1 to 2 minutes. Scrape into one portion of shallot mixture. Add blue cheese to other portion.

5. Meanwhile, place pretzels in a heavy zip-lock plastic bag and, with a rolling pin, coarsely crush; you should have about 1 cup.

6. Add ¹⁄₃ cup pretzel crumbs and half the cream cheese to each portion of the shallot mixture. Beat with a wooden spoon or an electric mixer on medium speed until blended. Add salt and pepper to taste.

7. With your hands or a spoon, mound 1 to 1¹⁄₂ teaspoons chili–cream cheese mixture in the cavity of each of half the mushroom caps; mound blue cheese–cream cheese mixture in remaining caps. Arrange each flavor of mushrooms in a 9- by 13-inch baking dish or pan. In a small microwave-safe bowl, melt remaining 2 tablespoons butter in a microwave oven; mix with remaining ¹⁄₃ cup pretzel crumbs. Sprinkle over mushrooms, gently pressing into filling.

8. Bake in a 350° regular or convection oven until mushrooms are well browned, 15 to 20 minutes. With a wide spatula, transfer to a platter. Serve warm.

Per mushroom: 50 cal., 66% (33 cal.) from fat; 1.7 g protein; 3.7 g fat (2.2 g sat.); 3.2 g carbo (0.4 g fiber); 91 mg sodium; 10 mg chol.

ends and tough dark green tops from leeks. Cut leeks in half lengthwise and rinse thoroughly under cold running water, flipping layers to release grit. Chop leeks.

4. In a 5- to 6-quart pan over medium-high heat, stir leeks, garlic, and ginger in butter until leeks begin to brown, 6 to 7 minutes. Add coriander, squash, reserved pan juices, and 5 cups broth. With a potato masher, mash squash. (Soup will be chunky; for a smoother texture, pour it into a large bowl, then purée in a blender, a portion at a time, and return to pan.) If soup is thicker than you like, thin with 1 to 4 more cups broth.

5. Cover and heat soup until steaming. Add salt and pepper to taste. Ladle into bowls and garnish with a dollop of sour cream and a teaspoon or two of chili purée (or a sprinkling of chili powder).

Per serving: 147 cal., 28% (41 cal.) from fat; 2.6 g protein; 4.6 g fat (1.5 g sat.); 27 g carbo (3.1 g fiber); 84 mg sodium; 5.2 mg chol.

Chili Purée

PREP AND COOK TIME: About 15 minutes

NOTES: You can make this purée up to 3 days ahead; cover and chill.

MAKES: ³⁄₄ to 1 cup

Rinse 3 ounces **dried New Mexico** or California **chilies** (9 to 12; each about 4 in. long). Break off and discard stems and shake out as many seeds as you can. With scissors, cut chilies into ¹⁄₂-inch pieces and drop into a 1- to 2-quart pan. Add 1¹⁄₂ cups **water**, ¹⁄₃ cup chopped **shallots,** and ¹⁄₂ teaspoon **ground cinnamon.** Bring to a boil over high heat, then reduce heat, cover, and simmer until chilies are soft, 5 to 10 minutes. In a blender, whirl mixture until smooth. Press purée through a strainer set over a bowl. Stir in **salt** and **pepper** to taste.

Per teaspoon: 6 cal., 45% (2.7 cal.) from fat; 0.2 g protein; 0.3 g fat (0.1 g sat.); 1.1 g carbo (0.4 g fiber); 0.6 mg sodium; 0 mg chol.

Ojai Roast Turkey with Rosemary, Lemon, and Garlic

PREP AND COOK TIME: 2¹⁄₂ to 3¹⁄₂ hours, plus at least 15 minutes for turkey to rest; for cooking times for other turkey sizes, see chart on page 231.

NOTES: As the host, Marty Bonvechio prepares the turkey. Since rosemary grows rampant in her garden, she uses it liberally in her cooking. The rosemary and vegetables she stuffs the turkey with aren't usually eaten at this meal—she uses then to add aroma and flavor to the bird—but the onions taste great in a next-day turkey soup.

MAKES: Allow ³⁄₄ pound uncooked turkey per person, or 1 pound if you want leftovers

    1 **turkey** (14 to 23 lb.)
       Salt and **pepper**

    8 **fresh rosemary** sprigs (each 6 to 8 in. long), rinsed, or 1 tablespoon dried rosemary

    6 cloves **garlic,** peeled

    1 **onion** (about 8 oz.), peeled and cut into 1-inch chunks

    2 **lemons** (about 5 oz. each), rinsed and cut into 1-inch chunks

1. Follow recipe for classic roast turkey (page 230), except sprinkle body and neck cavities with salt and pepper. Fill body cavity loosely with rosemary, garlic, onion, and lemons; if they don't all fit, tuck remaining into neck cavity. Fold skin flap under to hold in place.

2. Roast as directed in chart, 2 to 3 hours. Remove herbs and vegetables from cavities and save for other uses (see notes) or discard.

Per ¹⁄₄ pound boned cooked turkey with skin, based on percentages of white and dark meat in an average bird: 229 cal., 39% (90 cal.) from fat; 32 g protein; 10 g fat (3 g sat.); 0 g carbo; 82 mg sodium; 93 mg chol.

Lemon–Rosemary Roasted Onions and Garlic

PREP AND COOK TIME: About 1 hour

NOTES: If you have only one oven, roast the vegetables up to 1 day ahead; cover and chill. Let warm to room temperature to serve, or return the roasted vegetables to a 400° oven after the turkey is done; bake cold onions, uncovered, until warm, about 5 minutes. Squeeze the roasted garlic from peels onto potatoes or turkey.

MAKES: 10 to 12 servings

    5 or 6 **onions** (about 8 oz. each), unpeeled, rinsed

    1 **lemon** (about 6 oz.), rinsed

 ¹⁄₄ cup **olive oil**

    2 dozen large cloves **garlic,** unpeeled, rinsed

    6 **fresh rosemary** sprigs (each 6 to 8 in. long), rinsed, or 2 teaspoons dried rosemary

       About ¹⁄₄ teaspoon *each* **salt** and **pepper**

1. Cut onions in half lengthwise. Cut lemon in half lengthwise, then cut each half crosswise into ¹⁄₄-inch-thick slices; discard seeds and ends.

2. In a 12- by 17-inch baking pan, mix lemon, ¹⁄₄ cup water, olive oil, garlic, rosemary, and ¹⁄₄ teaspoon *each* salt and pepper. Spread level in pan. Lay onions, cut side down, in pan, on and around lemons and herbs.

3. Bake in a 400° regular or convection oven until onions are soft when squeezed, 50 to 60 minutes. Check occasionally; if pan juices evaporate before onions are tender, add a few tablespoons of water. Arrange onions, cut side up, on a platter; distribute lemon, garlic, and rosemary over onions. Serve hot or at room temperature. Add more salt and pepper to taste.

Per serving: 87 cal., 48% (42 cal.) from fat; 1.6 g protein; 4.7 g fat (0.6 g sat.); 12 g carbo (2.3 g fiber); 52 mg sodium; 0 mg chol.

Apricot, Wild Rice, and Bread Dressing

PREP AND COOK TIME: About 2¹⁄₄ hours

NOTES: You can prepare through step 3 up to 1 day ahead; cover and chill. Bake chilled dressing 20 to 30 minutes longer.

MAKES: About 10 cups; 10 to 12 servings

 ¹⁄₂ cup **wild rice**

    2 cups chopped **walnuts** or pecans

 1¹⁄₂ cups chopped **celery**

    1 cup chopped **onion**

 ¹⁄₃ cup **butter**

    1 cup **long-grain white rice**

    3 cups **vegetable** or fat-skimmed chicken **broth**

    1 cup **apricot nectar**

 ¹⁄₂ cup **brandy** (or more broth)

    2 teaspoons **dried thyme**

    1 teaspoon **dried rubbed sage**

 ¹⁄₂ teaspoon **ground nutmeg**
       About ¹⁄₂ teaspoon **pepper**

    6 cups **herbed bread-cube stuffing** (8 oz.)

    1 cup chopped **dried apricots**
       Salt

    2 tablespoons chopped **parsley** (optional)

1. In a 2¹⁄₂- to 3-quart pan over high heat, bring 1¹⁄₂ quarts water to a boil. Rinse and drain wild rice and add to water. Return to a boil, cover, reduce heat, and simmer until rice begins to split, 40 to 45 minutes. Drain.

2. Meanwhile, put nuts in a 10- by 15-inch baking pan. Bake in a 325° (if roasting turkey at that temperature) or 350° (if using a different oven than one for turkey) regular or convection oven until lightly browned, 15 to 20 minutes.

3. In a 5- to 6-quart pan over medium-high heat, stir celery and onion in butter until onion is limp, 7 to 10 minutes. Add white rice and stir until edges turn opaque, 3 to 4 minutes. Add broth, apricot nectar, brandy, thyme, sage, nutmeg, and pepper. Bring to a boil, cover, reduce heat, and simmer until rice is tender to bite, 15 to 20 minutes. Stir in bread-cube stuffing, apricots, wild rice, and toasted nuts. Add salt and more pepper to taste. Cover and cook over low heat, stirring occasionally, until bread cubes are evenly moist, 7 to 12 minutes. Pour into a 3-quart casserole and cover tightly.

4. Bake in a 325° (if roasting turkey at that temperature) or 350° (if using a different oven than one for turkey) regular or convection oven until dressing is hot in the center, 30 to 40 minutes. For a crustier top, uncover casserole for the last 15 to 20 minutes. Sprinkle with parsley, if desired.

Per serving: 380 cal., 45% (171 cal.) from fat; 8.4 g protein; 19 g fat (4.3 g sat.); 48 g carbo (4 g fiber); 282 mg sodium; 14 mg chol.

Anise Pear–Cranberry Sauce

PREP AND COOK TIME: About 30 minutes

NOTES: "When we took our California Thanksgiving to the French countryside last year, our French hosts were fascinated by this traditional American side dish," says Bonvechio. "Leftovers were a prized item." The sauce can be made up to 3 days ahead; cover and chill.

MAKES: 4 cups

  2 **Bosc pears**
     (about 1 lb. total)

  1 **orange** (about 8 oz.)

 ¾ cup **sugar**

  1 **star anise** or ¾ teaspoon
     anise seeds

  1 **cinnamon stick** (3 in. long)

 ½ cup **honey**

  3 cups **fresh** or frozen
     cranberries (12 oz.)

1. Rinse, peel, and core pears; cut into about ½-inch cubes. Grate enough peel (orange part only) from orange to make 1½ teaspoons. Ream juice from orange; measure, and add enough water to make ½ cup.

2. In a 3- to 4-quart pan over high heat, stir orange juice mixture, grated peel, sugar, star anise, and cinnamon stick until sugar is dissolved, 1 to 2 minutes. Stir in honey and pears and bring to a boil; reduce heat to medium and stir occasionally until edges of pears are barely tender to bite, about 3 minutes.

3. Stir in cranberries. Cook, stirring occasionally, until cranberries begin to pop and pears are tender when pierced, 6 to 8 minutes. Let cool. Pour into a bowl. Serve cool or cold.

Per ¼ cup: 99 cal., 2% (1.8 cal.) from fat; 0.3 g protein; 0.2 g fat (0 g sat.); 26 g carbo (1.4 g fiber); 0.8 mg sodium; 0 mg chol.

Cumin-braised Brussels Sprouts

PREP AND COOK TIME: About 25 minutes

NOTES: Schmitz claims this recipe has been known to convert brussels sprouts skeptics.

MAKES: 10 to 12 servings

 2½ pounds **brussels sprouts**

  1 tablespoon **olive oil**

  1 teaspoon **cumin seeds**

 ⅓ cup chopped **fresh basil** leaves or
     2 tablespoons dried basil

  2 tablespoons **butter**

     Salt and **pepper**

1. Trim and discard stem ends from brussels sprouts; rinse sprouts. Cut each in half, through stem end.

2. Add olive oil, brussels sprouts, and

Pears and star anise add new taste to jewel-like cranberry sauce.

cumin seeds to a 5- to 6-quart pan over high heat; stir often until sprouts are slightly browned, about 5 minutes. Add 1 cup water (and the basil if using dried); cover, reduce heat to medium-high, and cook, stirring occasionally, until sprouts are tender when pierced, 6 to 8 minutes. If liquid evaporates before sprouts are tender, add a little more water to prevent scorching.

3. Uncover and add butter; stir often until butter is melted. Stir in fresh basil, if using, and salt and pepper to taste. Pour into a serving bowl.

Per serving: 65 cal., 46% (30 cal.) from fat; 3 g protein; 3.3 g fat (1.4 g sat.); 7.8 g carbo (5 g fiber); 41 mg sodium; 5.1 mg chol.

Mashed Potato Cloud

PREP AND COOK TIME: About 1 hour

NOTES: In Berger's first Thanksgiving with the group, he won everyone over with his magical whipped potatoes. He always moved too fast for anyone to learn the secret, but we got him to share it. If the potatoes are done a few minutes early, cover them and keep warm in a 200° oven.

MAKES: 10 to 12 servings

  7 pounds **russet potatoes**

  6 cloves **garlic**, peeled

  6 tablespoons **butter**, cut
     into small chunks

 ¾ to 1 cup **whipping cream**,
     heated until steaming

     Salt and **white pepper**

1. In an 8- to 10-quart pan over high heat, bring 1½ quarts water to a boil. Peel potatoes and cut into 1-inch chunks. Add potatoes and garlic to boiling water; cover and return to a boil, then reduce heat to medium and simmer until potatoes mash easily, 12 to 15 minutes. Drain and pour into the bowl of a heavy-duty electric mixer fitted with a wire whisk, or return to pan.

2. Add butter and ½ cup cream. Beat with electric mixer on medium speed, or by hand with a heavy-duty whisk, just until smooth. If mixture is stiffer than you like, beat in more cream until potatoes reach desired consistency. Add salt and pepper to taste. Scrape into a serving bowl.

Per serving: 156 cal., 58% (90 cal.) from fat; 5.7 g protein; 10 g fat (6.5 g sat.); 12 g carbo (5.5 g fiber); 81 mg sodium; 32 mg chol.

the top) ovenproof frying pan (2½-to 3-qt. capacity); set over high heat and stir often until mixture is blended and bubbly, 1 to 2 minutes. Remove from heat.

4. Arrange a single layer of apples, rounded side down, in a circle around edge of pan, then fill in center to cover bottom; fit remaining apples evenly over the top. Cook over medium-high heat, gently shaking pan occasionally (do not stir), until sugar mixture turns deep gold (juices should bubble up through slices; if they bubble out of pan, reduce heat slightly), 25 to 35 minutes.

5. Peel one piece of plastic wrap from pastry and invert pastry over apple mixture in pan; peel off remaining plastic wrap. Trim off excess pastry flush with pan rim. Cut 1-inch slits through pastry in 10 to 12 places to let steam escape. Set pan in an 11- by 17-inch baking pan.

6. Bake in the middle of a 375° regular or convection oven until crust is golden brown and juices are bubbling, 35 to 45 minutes. Let cool 5 to 10 minutes.

7. Invert a serving plate over tarte; holding pan and plate together, invert again. Lift off pan and fit any apples that are stuck to pan back onto dessert. Cut tarte into wedges and serve hot or warm with vanilla ice cream.

Per serving: 322 cal., 34% (108 cal.) from fat; 2.4 g protein; 12 g fat (7.3 g sat.); 53 g carbo (2.4 g fiber); 120 mg sodium; 31 mg chol. ◆

Tarte Tatin

PREP AND COOK TIME: About 2 hours

NOTES: You can prepare the tarte through step 4 up to 6 hours ahead; reheat apples over medium heat, then continue.

MAKES: 10 to 12 servings

- 2 cups **all-purpose flour**
- 1⅓ cups **sugar**
- ¾ cup (⅜ lb.) **butter**
- 2 teaspoons **vanilla**
- 3 pounds **Golden Delicious apples** (about 6 oz. each)
- 2 tablespoons **lemon juice**

  Vanilla ice cream, crème fraîche, or softly whipped cream

1. In a food processor or bowl, mix flour and ⅓ cup sugar until blended. Cut ½ cup butter into ½-inch chunks and add to flour mixture. Whirl or rub with your fingers until mixture forms fine crumbs. Mix 1 teaspoon vanilla with ¼ cup cold water. Add to flour mixture and whirl or stir with a fork just until evenly moistened. If mixture is too dry to hold together when pressed, gently mix in 1 more tablespoon water at a time. With your hands, press dough into a ball. Place between two sheets of plastic wrap (each 15 by 15 in.) and roll into an even ¼-inch-thick round. Chill until firm, about 30 minutes, or up to 1 day.

2. Meanwhile, rinse and peel apples; quarter lengthwise and cut out and discard cores. Cut quarters in half lengthwise; you should have 8 cups.

3. Combine remaining 1 cup sugar, ¼ cup butter, 1 teaspoon vanilla, and lemon juice in a 10- to 11-inch (across

Slices of tarte tatin, rich with the flavor of caramel, make a perfect ending to the meal. ABOVE LEFT: Schmitz and friends toast their efforts.

Legendary salmon

Feasting in the firelight with M. F. K. Fisher

By Jerry Anne Di Vecchio

JAMES CARRIER; FOOD STYLING: KAREN SHINTO

When Mary Frances Kennedy Fisher was still living in her yellow Victorian on Oak Street in St. Helena, California, we planned a picnic. I was to bring the main course, wine, a few friends who were dying to meet this literary legend (whose culinary wit they had consumed in *The Art of Eating* and other tomes), and my daughter, Angela. More impressed at that time by Peter Rabbit stories than great food writing, Angela was looking forward to the special candies from Provence that Mary Frances had saved for her. The legend herself was providing appetizers, dessert, and more wine; we were to pick her up, along with her provisions, on our way to the picnic site.

All went well but the weather. By the time we arrived in the Napa Valley, the sky had faded from blue to gray, and the wind had whipped up a cold, biting edge. As Mary Frances opened the door, I could see the dance of firelight in the room beyond. "No park!" she said. But the

Cured salmon makes a beautiful first course for dinner as well as a light entrée for a picnic.

picnic was still on. Our destination: the fireside in the living room. As my friends tried to engage Mary Frances in literary conversation (she demurred with disarming smiles), we spread out the meal: mellow olives; curry-spiced salmon cured with sugar and salt, sliced into rosy ribbons and draped over dense bread for open-faced sandwiches; fruit; and, of course, the Provençal candies. It was a lovely picnic—cozy, comfortable, full of laughter, and absolutely without ants.

Spice-cured Salmon

PREP TIME: About 35 minutes if starting with thawed frozen fish, plus 24 to 36 hours to cure

NOTES: If using fresh salmon, freeze uncured fish airtight at −4° for at least 7 days to destroy any parasites. If you purchase salmon that has been frozen, this step can be omitted. Salmon can be prepared through step 5 up to 3 days before serving. Garnish servings with fresh dill sprigs.

MAKES: 8 light entrée servings

¼ cup **sugar**

3 tablespoons **kosher** or coarse **salt**

1 tablespoon **curry powder**

1 tablespoon **peppercorns** (white or black)

1 teaspoon **dry mustard**

1 teaspoon **cumin** (ground or seeds)

1 teaspoon **coriander** (ground or seeds)

1 **salmon fillet with skin** (about 1½ lb., cut from center section, 1 to 1½ in. thick at thickest part), thawed if frozen (see notes)

1 cup lightly packed **fresh dill**, rinsed and coarse stems removed

8 slices (about 3 by 6 in.) **dense, dark bread** such as pumpernickel, or crust-trimmed, toasted firm white or rye bread

About 1 cup **sour cream**

Curried mustard sauce (recipe follows)

Lemon wedges

1. In a blender or mini food processor, combine sugar, salt, curry powder, peppercorns, dry mustard, cumin, and coriander. Pulse until whole spices are coarsely ground. (Or coarsely crush whole spices in a mortar with a pestle or with the flat bottom of a glass, and mix with remaining ingredients.)

2. Rinse salmon and pat dry.

3. In a shallow glass or ceramic casserole in which fish will lie flat (the dish can be a few inches wider and longer than fish), sprinkle about 1 tablespoon of the spice mixture. Lay fish, skin side down, in casserole. Rub spice mixture up onto sides of salmon, then pat remainder evenly over the top of the fish. Lay dill sprigs on fish, pressing down lightly.

4. Cover fish airtight and chill for 24 (for 1-in.-thick fillet) to 36 hours (for 1½-in.-thick fillet).

5. Discard dill. Hold fish over a fine strainer (to catch whole spices) under cold running water for 1 to 2 minutes,

rubbing gently to remove some of the salt. Scrape any spices from casserole into strainer and rinse and drain; also rinse and dry casserole. Pat fish dry, lay skin side down in casserole, and scatter reserved spices on top.

6. To serve, lay salmon, skin side down, on a board. With a sharp knife held at an angle, thinly slice fish crosswise from skin (use the skin as an anchor to hang onto as you slice fish from opposite edge).

7. Lay a slice of bread on each plate. Mound 2 tablespoons sour cream on the center of each slice. Drape salmon equally over bread and sour cream to cover. Spoon curried mustard sauce onto salmon and accompany with lemon wedges to squeeze over portions to taste.

Per serving (not including curried mustard sauce): 288 cal., 47% (135 cal.) from fat; 19 g protein; 15 g fat (5.5 g sat.); 18 g carbo (2 g fiber); 984 mg sodium; 58 mg chol.

Curried mustard sauce. In a bowl, mix ½ cup **Dijon mustard** with ¼ cup **salad oil**, ¼ cup chopped **fresh dill**, 2 tablespoons **white wine vinegar** or rice vinegar, 2 to 3 teaspoons **sugar** (to taste), and ½ teaspoon **curry powder**. Serve or cover and chill up to 3 days. Makes about 1 cup.

Per tablespoon: 46 cal., 76% (35 cal.) from fat; 0 g protein; 3.9 g fat (0.5 g sat.); 0.7 g carbo (0 g fiber); 206 mg sodium; 0 mg chol. ◆

Fall vegetables over soft polenta make a bountiful main course.

Green Thanksgiving

A vegetarian holiday menu that everyone can love, from the chef at San Francisco's Greens Restaurant

By Charity Ferreira • Photographs by James Carrier

As executive chef at Greens, San Francisco's landmark vegetarian restaurant, Annie Somerville's tastes run to the refined but unfussy. Equally straightforward is her advice on planning a meatless holiday menu.

"It's not about finding a substitute for meat or fish," she says. "It's about combining beautiful produce and high-quality ingredients to make great food." In her upcoming book, *Everyday Greens* (Scribner, New York, scheduled for spring 2003), Somerville hopes to convey that flavorful vegetarian food doesn't have to be complicated. This Thanksgiving menu is a good example: autumn root vegetables, leafy greens, hearty beans and grains, and seasonal fruit

are deftly coaxed into simple dishes that are distinctive enough for the holiday table.

Start the meal by offering a casually assembled variety of flavors—marinated vegetable salads, olives, a few special cheeses, and slices of artisan bread. Follow the selection of room-temperature appetizers with a warm spinach salad tossed with goat cheese, crisp Fuji apple slices, pumpkin seeds, and roasted sweet onions. The centerpiece of the meal, a juicy autumn vegetable ragout with white beans, butternut squash, and kale, is served over a mound of soft polenta. Sweet pears and tart cranberries baked under a buttery crisp topping make a delicious ending to a meal from which nothing is missing.

Holiday menu

Relish Plate:
Roasted Beets with Orange Vinaigrette
Celery Root Salad
Olives
Assorted Cheeses
Artisan Bread

Warm Spinach Salad with
Goat Cheese and Apples

Autumn Vegetable Ragout with
Soft Polenta

Cranberry-Pear Crisp

For wine recommendations, see "Paired vegetables" on page 226

Autumn Vegetable Ragout with Soft Polenta

PREP AND COOK TIME: About $1^{3}/_{4}$ hours, plus at least 2 hours to soak beans

NOTES: If using dried beans, save 4 cups cooking liquid to use in the ragout; if using canned beans, reserve and measure the liquid when draining and add water to equal 4 cups. You can roast the vegetables and blanch the kale up to 4 hours ahead; wrap separately and chill, then proceed from step 4. Prepare the polenta while the ragout cooks.

MAKES: 6 to 8 servings

$1^{1}/_{2}$ cups **dried small white beans,** rinsed, or 2 cans (15 oz. each) white beans (see notes)

3 tablespoons **olive oil**

2 tablespoons minced **garlic**

1 **onion** (about 8 oz.), peeled and cut into 1-inch chunks

1 pound **parsnips,** peeled, ends trimmed, and cut into 1-inch chunks

$2^{1}/_{2}$ pounds **butternut squash,** peeled, seeded, and cut into 1-inch chunks

About $^{1}/_{2}$ teaspoon **salt**

About $^{1}/_{4}$ teaspoon **pepper**

1 pound **kale**

1 can (28 oz.) **diced** or crushed **tomatoes**

$^{1}/_{2}$ cup pitted **calamata olives,** chopped

Soft polenta (recipe follows)

1. Sort beans for debris, then rinse. In a 5- to 6-quart pan over high heat, bring beans and about 2 quarts water to a boil. Cover, boil for 2 minutes, and re move from heat. Let stand at least 2 and up to 4 hours. Drain beans, rinse, return to pan, and add 2 quarts water. Bring to a simmer over high heat, cover, reduce heat to maintain a simmer, and cook until beans are tender to bite, about 40 minutes. Drain beans, reserving 4 cups cooking liquid (see notes).

2. Meanwhile, in a large bowl, mix olive oil and garlic. Add onion, parsnips, squash, ½ teaspoon salt, and ¼ teaspoon pepper; mix to coat evenly. Spread mixture in single layers in two 12- by 15-inch baking pans. Bake in a 400° regular or convection oven for 15 minutes. Stir with a wide spatula and bake until vegetables are tender when pierced, 10 to 15 minutes longer.

3. Rinse kale and tear leaves from center ribs; discard ribs and stems. In a 6- to 8-quart pan over high heat, bring about 2 quarts water to a boil. Add kale leaves and cook, uncovered, until tender to bite, 2 to 3 minutes. Lift out with a slotted spoon and immerse in cold water until cool. Drain and coarsely chop.

4. In a 6- to 8-quart pan over high heat, combine beans, the 4 cups reserved bean cooking liquid (see notes), roasted vegetables, tomatoes with their juices, and olives. Adjust heat to maintain a simmer and cook for 15 minutes to blend flavors. Add kale and cook to heat, 1 to 2 minutes. Add additional salt and pepper to taste. Mound polenta on dinner plates or in shallow bowls and ladle vegetable ragout over polenta.

Per serving: 348 cal., 22% (77 cal.) from fat; 13 g protein; 8.6 g fat (1.2 g sat.); 60 g carbo (11 g fiber); 489 mg sodium; 0 mg chol.

Soft polenta. In a 4- to 6-quart pan over medium-high heat, bring 9 cups water to a boil. Whisk in 1 teaspoon **salt** and 2 cups **coarse polenta.** Reduce heat and simmer, stirring occasionally, until polenta is smooth to taste, 25 to 30 minutes. Remove from heat and stir in ¼ cup (⅛ lb.) **butter** and ¾ cup shredded **parmesan cheese;** add **pepper** to taste. Cover and keep warm over low heat.

Per serving: 213 cal., 37% (79 cal.) from fat; 6.1 g protein, 8.8 g fat (5.2 g sat.); 27 g carbo (1.8 g fiber); 493 mg sodium; 22 mg chol.

Roasted Beets with Orange Vinaigrette

PREP AND COOK TIME: About 1¼ hours

NOTES: You can make this salad up to 1 day ahead; cover and chill. Bring to room temperature before serving, and season to taste with additional vinegar, salt, and pepper. If you combine red beets with yellow or pink, the red will discolor the others; toss each separately with a portion of the vinaigrette, then combine just before serving.

MAKES: About 7 cups; 6 to 8 servings

2½ pounds (including tops) **golden, pink,** or red **beets** (each 2 to 3 in. wide; see notes), rinsed and greens trimmed and discarded or reserved for another use

6 tablespoons **orange juice**

3 tablespoons **champagne vinegar** or white wine vinegar

2 tablespoons minced **shallots**

1 teaspoon **salt**

Pepper

1. Place beets in a 9- by 13-inch baking pan. Add ½ inch water. Cover tightly with foil and bake in a 375° regular or convection oven until tender when pierced, 45 to 60 minutes. When cool enough to handle, peel and cut into ½-inch wedges.

2. Meanwhile, in a bowl, combine orange juice, vinegar, shallots, salt, and pepper to taste. Add the warm beets and stir to coat. Serve warm or at room temperature.

Per serving: 33 cal., 2.7% (0.9 cal.) from fat; 1 g protein; 0.1 g fat (0 g sat.); 7.5 g carbo (0.6 g fiber); 333 mg sodium; 0 mg chol.

Celery Root Salad

PREP AND COOK TIME: About 25 minutes

NOTES: You can make this salad up to 1 day ahead; cover and chill. Bring to room temperature before serving, and season to taste with additional vinegar, salt, and pepper.

MAKES: 8 cups; 6 to 8 servings

¼ cup **extra-virgin olive oil**

2 tablespoons **whole-grain mustard**

2 tablespoons **champagne vinegar** or white wine vinegar

About ¼ teaspoon **salt**

1½ pounds **celery root**

½ cup **Italian parsley** sprigs, rinsed and long stems trimmed

Pepper

1. In a bowl, whisk olive oil, mustard, vinegar, and ¼ teaspoon salt to blend.

2. In a 4- to 6-quart pan, bring 3 to 4 quarts water to a boil. Meanwhile, peel celery root and cut into 2-inch-long matchstick-size strips. Add celery root to water and cook until tender-crisp, 2 to 3 minutes. Drain and immediately add to dressing, along with parsley. Mix

A celery root salad dressed with a mustard vinaigrette is part of a relish plate of Thanksgiving appetizers.

to coat. Add salt and pepper to taste. Serve warm or at room temperature.

Per serving: 94 cal., 69% (65 cal.) from fat; 1.2 g protein; 7.2 g fat (1 g sat.); 7.1 g carbo (0.2 g fiber); 191 mg sodium; 0 mg chol.

Warm Spinach Salad with Goat Cheese and Apples

PREP AND COOK TIME: About 40 minutes

NOTES: Look for green, hulled pumpkin seeds (sometimes labeled *pepitas*) for this recipe. To toast pumpkin seeds, stir in a 6- to 8-inch frying pan over medium heat until they begin to brown, about 5 minutes.

MAKES: 6 to 8 servings

1½ pounds **sweet onions,** such as Vidalia or Oso, peeled and sliced into ¼-inch-thick rings

5 tablespoons **olive oil**

1 teaspoon minced **garlic**

About ½ teaspoon **salt**

¼ cup **apple cider vinegar**

3 tablespoons **apple juice**

1 pound **baby spinach leaves,** rinsed and drained

3 **sweet apples** such as Fuji (about 1½ lbs. total), rinsed, cored, and cut into ¼-inch slices

4 ounces **fresh chèvre** (goat cheese), crumbled

Bake cranberry-pear crisp in ramekins for elegance or in a larger pan for ease.

Paired vegetables

If you're used to choosing wines based on the meat, fish, or fowl you're serving, a vegetarian menu may seem confounding. The old rules about red with red meat and white with chicken or fish clearly don't apply, but an even older rule does: think about the flavors of the dish and choose a wine with complementary flavors. Our picks for each course of this special-occasion menu:

For the starters, Sauvignon Blanc's crisp, green flavors are a natural. For a fairly delicate wine, try Meridian Sauvignon Blanc 2000 from California (a real deal at $8). Or, for a wilder pick, look for Kim Crawford Sauvignon Blanc 2001 from Marlborough, New Zealand (about $17).

With the main course, go with either Chardonnay or Pinot Noir. A refined, not-too-oaky Chardonnay pairs beautifully with the polenta. Try the Brancott Chardonnay 2000 from Gisborne, New Zealand (a steal at $10), or the richer Chalone Chardonnay 2000 from Monterey County (about $28). If you prefer red, serve Pinot Noir to match the earthy roasted vegetables. Consider Saintsbury Pinot Noir 2000 from Carneros (about $24) with its beautiful cherry compote, licorice, tea, earth, and spice flavors.

To end the evening on a celebratory note, pair the cranberry-pear crisp with muscat or sparkling wine. Robert Pecota Moscato d'Andrea 2000 Muscat Canelli from the Napa Valley (about $12 for the 375 ml. half-bottle) is light, super-fresh, and not a bit sugary. Another great choice: a lightly sweet sparkler like Schramsberg Crémant from California (about $33).

— *Karen MacNeil-Fife*

½ cup **pumpkin seeds,** toasted (see notes)

Pepper

1. In a 12- by 17-inch baking pan, mix onions with 1 tablespoon olive oil, the garlic, and ¼ teaspoon salt. Bake in a 375° regular or convection oven, stirring halfway through baking time, until onions are soft and browned, 25 to 35 minutes.

2. Meanwhile, in a large bowl, mix vinegar, apple juice, and remaining ¼ teaspoon salt. Add onions, spinach, apples, goat cheese, and pumpkin seeds. Heat remaining 4 tablespoons oil in a small frying pan over high heat. When hot, pour over salad and mix to coat and wilt evenly. Season with more salt and pepper to taste. Serve immediately.

Per serving: 239 cal., 49% (117 cal.) from fat; 6.1 g protein; 13 g fat (3.4 g sat.); 29 g carbo (6.5 g fiber); 313 mg sodium; 6.5 mg chol.

Cranberry-Pear Crisp

PREP AND COOK TIME: About 1 hour

MAKES: **8 servings**

1 cup **all-purpose flour**

½ cup **granulated sugar**

¼ cup **light brown sugar**

½ teaspoon **cinnamon**

¼ teaspoon **nutmeg**

¼ teaspoon **salt**

½ cup (¼ lb.) cold **butter,** cut into chunks

¼ cup chopped **walnuts**

3 pounds **firm-ripe pears,** peeled, cored, and cut into 1-inch chunks

1 cup **fresh cranberries,** rinsed and sorted

1. In a bowl, mix flour, ¼ cup granulated sugar, the brown sugar, cinnamon, nutmeg, and salt. With a mixer fitted with a paddle attachment on low speed, or your fingers, mix or rub in butter until mixture forms coarse crumbs and begins to come together. Stir in walnuts.

2. In a large bowl, mix pears, cranberries, and remaining ¼ cup granulated sugar. Divide fruit among eight 8-ounce ramekins or pour into a 9-inch square or round baking dish and spread level. Sprinkle evenly with flour mixture.

3. Bake in a 375° regular or convection oven until juices are bubbly, pears are tender when pierced, and topping is golden brown, 30 to 35 minutes for ramekins, 40 to 50 minutes for large crisp.

Per serving: 357 cal., 38% (135 cal.) from fat; 2.9 g protein; 15 g fat (7.4 g sat.); 57 g carbo (4.9 g fiber); 192 mg sodium; 31 mg chol. ◆

Grand new roasts

Flavorful sidekicks make holiday main dishes memorable

By Jerry Anne Di Vecchio
Photographs by James Carrier

Creamy fennel and endive turn roast pork into a holiday special.

FOOD STYLING: DAN BECKER (2)

Feasting, to be done well, requires scale. A magnificent roast is the traditional entrée for establishing grandeur on special occasions. Although modern households are rarely big enough to consume a saddle of this or a baron of that, a pork roast made of two loins bound together and a playful crown of chicken drumsticks are delicious smaller-but-impressive choices.

They get even better with the perfect companion dish: with the pork, a lavish fennel and Belgian endive casserole, and to fill the ring of chicken drumsticks, bacon-laced cornbread dressing with tangy glazed pecans and a homey cream gravy. The very best news is that these side dishes can be prepared, for the most part, a day ahead of time, leaving you time to think about that final festive touch: the perfect wine to pour with your grand roast (see page 229).

Double Pork Loin Roast with Fennel and Sage

PREP AND COOK TIME: About 2½ hours, plus about 15 minutes to rest

NOTES: Two boned pork loins tied together create an impressive-looking roast. This shape is found in many markets; you can also ask your butcher to assemble one for you. Garnish with some of the extra fennel greens from the accompanying fennel and Belgian endive casserole.

MAKES: 10 to 12 servings

1 **fat-trimmed, boned, tied double pork loin roast** (4¾ to 5 lb.; see notes)

1 tablespoon **fennel seeds**

2 teaspoons **dried rubbed sage**

2 teaspoons **whole black peppercorns**

About 1½ teaspoons **kosher** or coarse **salt**

1 cup fat-skimmed **chicken broth**

Fennel and Belgian endive casserole (recipe follows)

1. Rinse pork and pat dry.

2. In a food processor (a mini model works best), blender, or mortar with pestle, coarsely crush fennel seeds with sage, peppercorns, and 1½ teaspoons salt. Rub all the fennel-seed mixture evenly over pork, tucking some into crevice where roasts join.

3. Set meat on a rack in a 9- to 10-inch by 13- to 15-inch rimmed pan. Bake in a 375° regular or convection oven until a thermometer inserted in center of roast reaches 150°, about 2¼ hours.

4. Transfer roast to a platter; let rest in a warm place for at least 10 and up to 30 minutes.

5. Meanwhile, skim and discard fat from pan drippings. Add chicken broth

to pan; scrape bottom to release browned bits. Set pan over high heat and stir until boiling. Pour any juices accumulated on platter into pan. Pour mixture through a fine strainer into a small pitcher.

6. Slice meat and serve with pan juices, salt to add to taste, and fennel and Belgian endive casserole.

Per serving: 291 cal., 40% (117 cal.) from fat; 40 g protein; 13 g fat (4.8 g sat.); 0.5 g carbo (0.3 g fiber); 322 mg sodium; 111 mg chol.

Fennel and Belgian Endive Casserole

PREP AND COOK TIME: 1¾ hours

NOTES: The vegetables cook in a plentiful cheese and cream sauce; spoon the sauce over the sliced pork. You can prepare the casserole through step 8 up to 1 day ahead; cool after baking, cover with plastic wrap, and chill. To reheat, remove plastic wrap; cover casserole tightly with foil and bake in a 375° regular or convection oven until bubbling and hot in the center, about 30 minutes, then continue with step 9.

MAKES: 12 servings

The prince and the pauper: make a royal crown from ordinary chicken drumsticks.

6 heads **fennel with stalks** (each 3 to 3½ in. wide)

3 heads **Belgian endive** (about 4 oz. each)

¼ cup (⅛ lb.) **butter** or olive oil

3 ounces **thinly sliced prosciutto**

3 tablespoons **all-purpose flour**

2 cups fat-skimmed **chicken broth**

1 cup **whipping cream**

8 ounces **gorgonzola** or dolce gorgonzola **cheese**, crumbled (about ¾ cup)

1. Pinch off tender green fennel leaves; rinse, drain, wrap in a towel, place in a plastic bag, and chill up to 1 day.

2. Trim off and discard stalks, root ends, and any bruised areas from fennel heads. Rinse heads and cut in half lengthwise across widest dimension.

3. Trim off and discard discolored root ends and any discolored leaves from endive. Cut heads in half lengthwise.

4. Melt 2 tablespoons butter in a 10- to 12-inch frying pan over medium-high heat. Lay as much fennel as will fit, cut side down, in pan and brown lightly, 3 to 4 minutes; turn and brown curved sides, 3 to 4 minutes longer. If butter starts to scorch, add water, 1 to 2 tablespoons at a time. As it is browned, transfer fennel, cut side up, to a shallow 3-quart casserole or 9- by 13-inch bak-

ing dish, and brown remaining pieces.

5. When all fennel is browned, lay endive cut side down in frying pan and brown, 3 to 4 minutes, adding 1 to 2 tablespoons water if it begins to scorch. Turn over and brown top sides, 3 to 4 minutes longer.

6. Remove pan from heat and transfer endive to a cutting board. Cut halves in half lengthwise. Tear prosciutto slices into long, narrow strips. Wrap endive sections equally with prosciutto. Fit endive pieces evenly among fennel pieces in casserole.

7. In the unwashed frying pan over high heat, melt remaining 2 tablespoons butter; add flour and stir until lightly browned, about 2 minutes. Remove from heat and gradually whisk in broth and cream. Return pan to high heat and whisk until boiling; boil and stir 2 minutes longer. Add ⅓ cup cheese and whisk until melted. Pour sauce evenly over fennel and endive, coating all surfaces. Cover tightly with foil.

8. Bake in a 375° regular or convection oven until fennel is just tender when pierced, about 40 minutes.

9. Uncover, dot with remaining cheese, and bake until browned, about 20 minutes. Chop ½ cup reserved fennel leaves and sprinkle over casserole. Serve hot.

Per serving: 246 cal., 66% (162 cal.) from fat; 10 g protein; 18 g fat (11 g sat.); 15 g carbo (5.9 g fiber); 541 mg sodium; 55 mg chol.

Drumstick Crown Roast

PREP AND COOK TIME: About 1 hour and 20 minutes

NOTES: Use white cotton string and a large-eye needle (the kind used for yarn stitching, found in craft and hobby shops and fabric stores) to lace the roast together. For the form, use a soufflé dish; a straight-sided, ovenproof bowl; a cheesecake pan; or plain tart rings (stack and wrap smoothly with foil for adequate height).

MAKES: 8 servings

16 **chicken drumsticks** (equal size, about 4 lb. total)

2 tablespoons **all-purpose flour**

1 tablespoon **paprika**

About 1½ teaspoons **salt**

About ½ teaspoon **pepper**

Cornbread and candied pecan dressing (recipe follows)

Country cream gravy (recipe follows)

Parsley sprigs

1. Rinse drumsticks and pat dry.

2. Thread white cotton string (about 48 in. long; see notes) through a needle. About ½ inch from large end of one drumstick, push needle through flesh, perpendicular to and against the bone; pull string through (if needle is too slippery to grasp, use pliers). Repeat to thread the remaining drumsticks together, keeping larger, curved sides aligned in the same direction. Leave equal lengths of string loose at both ends of drumstick chain.

3. Thread needle with another 48-inch length of string. About 1 inch from narrow end of drumsticks, on the same side of bones where first string is threaded, push needle through flesh perpendicular to and against bones; pull string through, leaving equal lengths of string loose at ends.

4. In a small bowl, mix flour, paprika, 1½ teaspoons salt, and ½ teaspoon pepper. Rub evenly over drumsticks.

5. Set a 6- to 7-inch-wide round, straight-sided, ovenproof dish or pan, 2½ to 3 inches tall (see notes for options), in the center of a 12- to 14-inch nonstick pizza pan. Lean drumsticks, narrow ends up, against and around the dish (a second set of hands helps); tie bottom string ends snugly to hold drumsticks close to dish, then tie top string ends together to keep drumsticks stable. Gently adjust drumsticks so they are equally spaced.

6. Set pan on a rack in the lower half

of a 375° regular or convection oven. Bake until drumsticks are well browned, **55 to 60 minutes**. Protecting your hands with oven mitts, firmly hold drumsticks against dish and transfer to a platter at least 12 inches wide.

7. Mound cornbread and candied pecan dressing in the dish; reserve drippings in pizza pan for country cream gravy. Sprinkle dressing and platter rim with reserved candied pecans. (Keep crown warm in oven with door ajar while making gravy.) Garnish with sprigs of parsley to conceal center dish.

8. To serve, snip string and pull off drumsticks; arrange on plates with dressing and pecans. Spoon gravy over dressing; add salt and pepper to taste.

Per serving, chicken only: 242 cal., 45% (108 cal.) from fat; 29 g protein; 12 g fat (3.3 g sat.); 2.1 g carbo (0.1 g fiber); 533 mg sodium; 98 mg chol.

Cornbread and Candied Pecan Dressing

PREP AND COOK TIME: About 50 minutes

NOTES: For the cornbread, use your own favorite recipe or a mix. You can toast cornbread cubes 1 day ahead; let cool in pan, wrap airtight, and store at room temperature. You can bake dressing (step 6) in same oven with chicken, on a rack below.

MAKES: 8 servings

8 cups **cornbread** cubes (½ in.; see notes)

About 2 tablespoons **butter**

1½ cups **pecan halves**

2 tablespoons **sugar**

¼ cup **white wine vinegar**

6 **bacon slices** (about 6 oz.), diced

1 **onion** (about 8 oz.), peeled and chopped

½ teaspoon **dried thyme**

½ teaspoon **ground nutmeg**

1 cup minced **parsley**

About 2 cups fat-skimmed **chicken broth**

Salt

1. Spread cornbread cubes level in a 10- by 15-inch rimmed pan. Bake in a 375° regular or convection oven until lightly toasted, **20 to 25 minutes**, turning cubes occasionally with a wide spatula.

2. Meanwhile, lightly butter one side of a 12-inch-long sheet of foil. Lay foil flat on a counter, buttered side up.

3. In a 10- to 12-inch frying pan over high heat, stir 2 tablespoons butter, pecans, sugar, and 2 tablespoons vinegar just until liquid is evaporated and sugar mixture is dark brown, **4 to 5 minutes**. Scrape nuts onto foil and push apart.

4. Rinse frying pan and wipe dry. Return to medium-high heat and add bacon; stir often until well browned, **5 to 8 minutes**. With a slotted spoon, transfer bacon to paper towels. Discard all but 2 tablespoons fat from pan. Add onion and stir often until limp and lightly browned, **5 to 8 minutes**. Add remaining 2 tablespoons vinegar and stir until liquid is evaporated, about 1 minute. Add thyme and nutmeg and mix; add parsley and stir until wilted, about 1 minute. Remove from heat.

5. Pour toasted cornbread into a large bowl. Add onion mixture and mix well; add 2 cups broth and mix well. Mix in ½ cup candied pecans and salt to taste.

6. Return cornbread mixture to 10- by 15-inch pan; spread level. Bake in a 375° oven until hot, about 10 minutes. If you prefer a more moist dressing, stir in more broth.

7. Spoon hot dressing into center of drumstick crown roast; garnish with remaining pecans.

Per serving of dressing: 502 cal., 54% (270 cal.) from fat; 11 g protein; 30 g fat (7.2 g sat.); 47 g carbo (3.9 g fiber); 775 mg sodium; 64 mg chol.

Country Cream Gravy

PREP AND COOK TIME: About 20 minutes

NOTES: You can prepare through step 2 up to 1 day ahead; cool, cover, and chill. Return to high heat and continue with step 3.

MAKES: 8 servings

½ cup minced **onion**

2 tablespoons **butter**

⅛ teaspoon **ground nutmeg**

2 tablespoons **all-purpose flour**

1½ cups fat-skimmed **chicken broth**

½ cup **whipping cream**

¼ cup **dry white wine**

Drumstick crown roast drippings (preceding)

1. In a 10- to 12-inch frying pan over medium-high heat, frequently stir onion in butter until onion is limp and pale gold, about 5 minutes. Add nutmeg and flour and stir until golden, about 2 minutes.

2. Remove pan from heat. Gradually whisk in broth, cream, and wine until smooth. Return to high heat and stir until boiling. Reduce heat; simmer gently, stirring often, until mixture is reduced to about 2 cups, about 10 minutes.

3. Skim fat from drumstick crown roast drippings and discard. Scrape juices and any browned bits into gravy; turn heat to high and stir until boiling vigorously. Pour into a gravy boat or small serving bowl.

Per serving of gravy (not including drippings): 87 cal., 78% (68 cal.) from fat; 2.2 g protein; 7.5 g fat (4.7 g sat.); 2.9 g carbo (0.2 g fiber); 49 mg sodium; 24 mg chol. ◆

Grand wine pairings

The right wine can create a delightful union with a roast and companion dish. Here are the types—and a few specific bottles—that complement each menu. If these labels aren't available to you, ask the salesperson at your wine shop to suggest wines with a similar profile.

• For the fennel- and sage-seasoned pork with gorgonzola-sauced fennel and Belgian endive casserole. A lighter dry red wine, well balanced and smooth, with cherry, plum, and berry overtones that can handle the bite of the cheese. From the biggest to the most subtle:

Le Clos du Caillou Vieilles Vignes, Sylvie et Jean-Denis Vacheron-Pouizin 2000 (Côtes du Rhône, France), about $14.

Muga Reserva 1995 (Rioja, Spain), about $25.

Joseph Phelps Vineyards Le Mistral 1999 (California), $25.

• For the chicken, cornbread dressing with sweet glazed pecans, and gravy. A crisp, fresh, clean dry white wine with gentle fruitiness and good acid balance. From the crispest and freshest to the faintly herbal:

Bonny Doon Pacific Rim Dry Riesling 2000 (America); the name is hard to spot on this uniquely labeled bottle, $10.

Swanson Vineyards Napa Valley Pinot Grigio 2000 (Napa Valley), $18.

Matanzas Creek Winery Sauvignon Blanc 2000 (Sonoma County), $22.

Secrets of holiday success

Tips for perfect roast turkey and gravy

By Linda Lau Anusasananan
Photographs by James Carrier

To stuff or not to stuff

A stuffed turkey may be traditional, but it carries a slightly higher risk of incubating harmful bacteria than an unstuffed one; moist dressing in a warm cavity is bacteria's ideal growth environment. You can avoid the problem by cooking the bird and the dressing separately. Another advantage of this is that both cook more evenly and quickly. But if the traditionalists in your crowd insist on a stuffed turkey, follow these guidelines for safety:

- Do not stuff the turkey the night before. Fill body and neck cavities lightly (don't pack stuffing in) just before you put the bird in the oven. You can make the dressing a day ahead; just cover and chill until ready to use.
- Make sure the dressing gets hot enough during roasting. Since it heats more slowly inside the turkey than in a separate container, harmful bacteria have a greater chance to grow. They're killed after 3 minutes at 140° and instantly at 160°. Check the temperature in the center of the dressing; if the stuffing hasn't met either of these guidelines, scoop it from the bird into a casserole and bake, covered, until it has.
- Do not let stuffing sit in the roasted bird for very long, especially at temperatures between 60° and 120°. Scoop dressing into a separate bowl to serve.

To many first-timers—and plenty of repeat performers—the most intimidating aspects of Thanksgiving center on the turkey: roasting it, stuffing it (or not), concocting a decent gravy to ladle over it, and carving it. And yet, these are the elements that define the traditional meal.

Relax. Living up to expectations is easier than you think. Cooking a turkey is not much different than roasting a chicken; it's just bigger. Today's turkeys, more tender than those of our grandmothers' era, cook much faster (no need to rise at 5 A.M. to get the turkey in the oven). Follow our recipes and tips for success.

Classic Roast Turkey

PREP AND COOK TIME: About 10 minutes to prep (20 if stuffing the bird), plus roasting time (see chart, page 231) and 15 to 30 minutes to rest

NOTES: If using a frozen turkey, start thawing it in a pan in the refrigerator 3 to 4 days before roasting, depending on its size. If turkey overlaps pan rim, tuck a strip of heavy-duty foil along pan sides during roasting to keep fat from dripping over.

MAKES: Allow ¾ pound uncooked turkey per serving, at least 1 pound if you want leftovers

1 **turkey** (10 to 30 lb.; see notes)

Melted **butter** or olive oil

1. Remove and discard leg truss from turkey. Pull off and discard any lumps of fat. Remove giblets and neck (they're often packed in neck or body cavity) and save for gravy (recipe follows). Rinse turkey inside and out; pat dry. Rub turkey all over with butter.

2. Place turkey, breast up, on a V-shaped rack in a 12- by 17-inch roasting pan (or one that is at least 2 in. longer and wider than the bird). Insert a meat thermometer straight down through thickest part of breast to the bone. (If using an instant-read thermometer, insert when checking temperature.)

3. Roast in a 325° or 350° (temperature depends on size of bird; see chart, page 231) regular or convection oven

until thermometer registers 160°.

4. If turkey is unstuffed, tip slightly to drain juices from body cavity into pan. Transfer turkey to a platter. Let stand in a warm place, uncovered, for 20 to 30 minutes, then carve (see page 231). If thigh joints are still pink (common in an oven-roasted bird), cut drumsticks from thighs, place thighs in a baking pan, and bake in a 450° oven until no longer pink, 10 to 15 minutes, or put on a microwave-safe plate and cook in a microwave oven at full power (100%) for 1 to 3 minutes.

Per ¼ pound boned cooked turkey with skin, based on percentages of white and dark meat in an average bird: 229 cal., 39% (90 cal.) from fat; 32 g protein; 10 g fat (3 g sat.); 0 g carbo; 82 mg sodium; 93 mg chol.

The right tools

STURDY ROASTING PAN: Choose one at least 2 inches longer and wider than the bird. A good all-purpose size is about 12 by 17 inches with sides 2 to 3 inches tall.

V-SHAPED RACK: This shape supports the bird while allowing heat to circulate underneath for better browning.

THERMOMETER: Choose either a meat thermometer that remains in the bird during the entire roasting time or an instant-read version that you insert when you want to check the temperature (do not leave it in the oven).

Classic Gravy

PREP AND COOK TIME: About 1¾ hours

NOTES: You can prepare through step 4 up to 1 day ahead; cover and chill. After turkey is done, continue with step 5.

MAKES: 7 to 8 cups without giblets; 10 to 12 servings

Giblets, neck, and **liver** from a 10- to 30-pound turkey

2 **onions** (about 12 oz. total), peeled and quartered

2 **carrots** (about 8 oz. total), peeled and cut into 1-inch chunks

¾ cup sliced **celery**

About 2 quarts fat-skimmed **chicken broth**

½ teaspoon **pepper**

Classic roast turkey (recipe precedes) or rosemary-lemon turkey (page 220)

½ cup **cornstarch**

Salt

1. Rinse giblets and neck; chill liver airtight to add later, or save for other uses. In a 5- to 6-quart pan, combine giblets, neck, onions, carrots, celery, and 1 cup water. Cover and bring to a boil over high heat, then reduce heat and simmer for 15 minutes. Uncover and stir often over high heat until liquid is evaporated and giblets and vegetables are browned and begin to stick to pan, 15 to 20 minutes longer.

2. Add 1 quart broth and the pepper to pan; stir to scrape browned bits free. Cover, reduce heat, and simmer, stirring occasionally, until gizzard is tender when pierced, 1 to 1½ hours. If desired, add liver and cook 10 minutes longer.

3. Pour mixture through a fine strainer into a bowl. If desired, reserve neck, giblets, and liver for gravy; pull meat off neck and finely chop neck meat, giblets, and liver. Discard bones and vegetables. Measure turkey stock; if necessary, add more chicken broth to make 1 quart.

4. In the unwashed 5- to 6-quart pan, combine the 1 quart turkey stock and chopped neck meat, giblets, and liver, if using.

5. When turkey is done, remove rack and bird from roasting pan. Skim off and discard fat from pan juices. Add 2 more cups chicken broth to roasting pan and stir over low heat to scrape browned bits free. Pour mixture, through a fine strainer if desired, into turkey stock and bring to a boil over high heat.

6. In a small bowl, blend cornstarch with ½ cup water until smooth. Add to stock mixture and whisk until boiling, 3 to 5 minutes. Add salt to taste.

Per serving: 64 cal., 7% (4.5 cal.) from fat; 7.4 g protein; 0.5 g fat (0.1 g sat.); 6.7 g carbo (0.4 g fiber); 65 mg sodium; 21 mg chol.

Carving the bird

There is no *one* way to cut a turkey down to size, but here are our tips.

TOOLS. Use **two sharp knives:** a short-bladed one (4 to 6 in. long) for poking into joints and a long, thin one for slicing. Use a **carving fork** to hold the bird, or grip the bird with your hand using a **clean pot holder** or napkin.

TURKEY. Let the cooked bird rest at least 20 minutes before carving.

1. Roll bird to one side; pull top wing away from body to reveal wing-body joint. Poke short knife into joint; cut between connecting bones. Cut elbow joint; set parts on a platter.

2. Pull the top leg (thigh and drumstick) down and away from body until you see the hip joint. Poke short knife into the joint; cut between the bones, then cut thigh meat away from breast. Lay leg on platter; cut through the joint between drumstick and thigh. Slice meat off thigh, parallel to bone.

3. With the long knife, make a deep horizontal cut along bottom of breast, starting at the wing joint. Then angle blade upward, following bone, until you reach the base of the vertical breastbone. Insert carving fork into top of breast and, starting at outside edge, cut thin slices parallel to breastbone down to the base cut (so slices separate neatly).

4. To carve other side, repeat steps.

Oven-roasted turkey: temperatures and times

See our classic roast turkey recipe (preceding) for directions on preparing and roasting the bird, then follow this chart for oven temperatures and cooking times.

Turkey weight with giblets	Oven temp.	Internal temp.*	Cooking time**
10–13 lb.	350°	160°	1½–2¼ hr.
14–23 lb.	325°	160°	2–3 hr.
24–27 lb.	325°	160°	3–3¾ hr.
28–30 lb.	325°	160°	3½–4½ hr.

*To measure the internal temperature of the turkey, insert a thermometer through the thickest part of the breast to the bone.

**Times are for unstuffed birds. A stuffed bird may cook at the same rate as an unstuffed one; however, be prepared to allow 30 to 50 minutes longer. While turkeys take about the same time to roast in regular and convection heat, a convection oven does a better job of browning the bird all over. ◆

Serve this steamed pumpkin pudding with rum-flavored whipped cream.

The sweetest endings

Bend tradition with unusual desserts this holiday season

By Charity Ferreira • Photographs by James Carrier

Even for die-hard traditionalists among us who look forward to sitting down to the same dishes every Thanksgiving, there always seems to be room to try something a little different at the end of the meal. This year, our Thanksgiving sweets bend tradition while staying true to the best dessert flavors of the season. A shortbread tart is filled with a thick layer of tangy cranberry jam; steaming gives a rum-flavored pumpkin pudding its moist texture; and ground espresso beans imbue a creamy cheesecake with dark flecks and rich coffee flavor. Whichever ones you try, don't be surprised if next year it just doesn't feel like Thanksgiving without them.

Steamed Pumpkin-Cornmeal Pudding

PREP AND COOK TIME: About 1½ hours

NOTES: Serve this moist steamed pudding with sweetened whipped cream flavored to taste with rum.

MAKES: 6 to 8 servings

- 1 cup **all-purpose flour**
- ½ cup **yellow cornmeal**
- 1½ teaspoons **baking powder**
- ½ teaspoon **ground nutmeg**
- ¼ teaspoon **salt**
- ¾ cup (⅜ lb.) **butter,** at room temperature
- 1¾ cups **sugar**
- 2 **large eggs**
- 1½ cups **canned pumpkin**

- ¼ cup **rum**
- 1 tablespoon grated **lemon** peel
- 1 teaspoon **vanilla**

1. In a bowl, mix flour with cornmeal, baking powder, nutmeg, and salt.

2. In another bowl, with a mixer on high speed, beat butter and sugar until well blended. Add eggs one at a time, beating well after each addition. Beat in pumpkin, rum, lemon peel, and vanilla. Stir in flour mixture until well incorporated.

3. Scrape batter into a buttered 8- to 9-cup bundt pan and set in a 12- by 17-inch baking pan. Place on bottom rack of a 350° regular or convection oven. Carefully pour boiling water around bundt pan almost to the level of pudding. Cover entire baking pan tightly with foil.

4. Bake until the pudding feels firm to the touch and a wooden skewer inserted into the center comes out clean, 1 hour to 1 hour 10 minutes. Let cool 10 minutes, then invert over a plate to unmold. Serve warm, or let cool completely and cover loosely until serving. Reheat in a 350° regular or convection oven until warm, about 10 minutes. To serve, slice into wedges.

Per serving: 458 cal., 39% (180 cal.) from fat; 4.6 g protein; 20 g fat (12 g sat.); 67 g carbo (1.8 g fiber); 370 mg sodium; 103 mg chol.

Espresso Bean Cheesecake

PREP AND COOK TIME: About 1½ hours, plus 1 hour to steep and at least 3 hours to cool

NOTES: Buy coffee ground for a French press coffeemaker (a slightly coarser grind), or whirl whole beans in a coffee grinder or food processor. You can bake this cheesecake up to 2 days ahead; chill until cool, then cover loosely with plastic wrap and chill until ready to serve.

MAKES: 10 to 12 servings

- 6 ounces **chocolate wafer cookies**
- 3 tablespoons **butter,** melted
- ½ cup **whipping cream**
- ⅓ cup coarsely ground **dark-roasted coffee beans** (see notes)
- 3 packages (8 oz. each) **cream cheese,** at room temperature
- 1¼ cups **sugar**
- 4 **large eggs**
- 2 teaspoons **vanilla**

FOOD STYLING: SUSAN DEVATY (2)

1. In a food processor, whirl cookies into fine crumbs; you should have 1½ cups. Pour into a 9-inch cheesecake pan with removable rim; add butter and mix. Press mixture over bottom and ½ inch up sides of pan.

2. In a 1- to 2-quart pan over medium-high heat, combine cream and coffee beans. Bring to a simmer, remove from heat, cover, and let stand 1 hour. Pour mixture through a fine strainer, pressing to extract as much of the liquid as possible (the finer grounds will pass through the strainer); discard residue.

3. In a bowl, with a mixer on medium speed, beat cream cheese and sugar until smooth. Add eggs one at a time, beating well after each addition and scraping down sides of bowl, if necessary. Beat in cream mixture and vanilla. Pour into crust-lined pan.

4. Bake in a 300° regular or convection oven until center barely jiggles when cake is gently shaken, about 1 hour.

5. Run a thin-bladed knife between cake and pan rim. Refrigerate cake until cool, at least 3 hours, or up to 2 days (see notes).

6. To serve, remove pan rim and cut cake into wedges.

Per serving: 422 cal., 62% (261 cal.) from fat; 7.6 g protein; 29 g fat (17 g sat.); 33 g carbo (0.4 g fiber); 305 mg sodium; 152 mg chol.

Cranberry Jam Tart

PREP AND COOK TIME: About 1½ hours, plus at least 1 hour to chill

NOTES: You can make the jam mixture (step 1) and the dough (step 2) for this tart up to 3 days ahead; cover separately and chill.

MAKES: 8 servings

12 ounces **fresh** or thawed frozen **cranberries**

About 1¾ cups **sugar**

½ cup **apple juice**

2 tablespoons **lemon juice**

¾ cup **raspberry jam** (about 6 oz.)

1 cup (½ lb.) **butter,** at room temperature

2 **large egg** yolks

2⅓ cups **all-purpose flour**

1 teaspoon **baking powder**

¼ teaspoon **salt**

1. Sort cranberries, discarding any stems and bruised or decayed fruit; rinse and drain berries. In a 3- to 4-

A cookielike crust holds a tangy cranberry jam filling.

quart pan over medium heat, stir cranberries, 1 cup sugar, apple juice, and lemon juice occasionally until berries have broken down and released their juices and mixture is bubbly, 10 to 15 minutes. Stir in jam and cook 1 minute longer. Whirl mixture in a blender or food processor until smooth. Press through a fine strainer into a bowl, extracting as much liquid as possible with the back of a spoon or a spatula; discard seeds and skins. Cover and chill until cold, at least 1 hour, or up to 3 days (see notes).

2. With a mixer, beat butter with ¾ cup sugar until smooth; beat in egg yolks. Stir in flour, baking powder, and salt until well blended. Divide dough into two slightly unequal portions. Wrap the larger portion in plastic and flatten into a rectangular shape. Press the smaller portion over bottom and up sides, to rim, of a 9-inch fluted tart pan with removable rim. Chill wrapped dough and tart shell until firm, at least 1 hour, or up to 3 days (see notes).

3. Spoon jam mixture into tart shell and spread level.

4. Unwrap the second portion of dough and place on a lightly floured surface. With a lightly floured rolling pin, roll out dough into a shape that closely approximates an 8- by 10-inch rectangle. With a knife or fluted cutter, cut dough into eight 1- by 10-inch strips. Arrange four strips over filling about 1 inch apart. Place remaining strips over tart at a 45° angle to the first set of strips. Trim edges flush with dough in pan. Sprinkle top of tart lightly with sugar.

5. Place tart on an uninsulated baking sheet and bake on the lower rack of a 350° regular or convection oven, rotating tart halfway through baking time, until top is golden brown, 35 to 40 minutes. Serve warm or at room temperature.

Per serving: 604 cal., 37% (225 cal.) from fat; 5.1 g protein; 25 g fat (15 g sat.); 94 g carbo (2.8 g fiber); 380 mg sodium; 115 mg chol. ◆

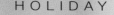

1. Rinse lemon, orange, and kumquats and thinly slice them, discarding seeds; quarter the orange slices. Put fruit in a 4- to 5-quart pan. Add honey, sugar (use the smaller amount if you prefer drinks on the tart side, the larger if you want a sweeter flavor), cloves, and all-spice. With a knife, cut the cinnamon sticks lengthwise into thinner strips. Add cinnamon and 2 cups water to pan; bring to a boil over high heat, then reduce heat and boil gently for 5 minutes.

2. Pour wine into hot citrus base (see notes) and heat until steaming, about 8 minutes. Keep warm over low heat. Ladle into heatproof cups or wineglasses.

Per serving: 125 cal., 0% (0 cal.) from fat; 0.3 g protein; 0 g fat; 12 g carbo (0.3 g fiber); 7.4 mg sodium; 0 mg chol.

Clockwise from top: hot mojito tea, Christmas kir, mocha nog, and mulled white wine.

JAMES CARRIER; FOOD STYLING: KAREN SHINTO

Christmas Kir

PREP AND COOK TIME: About 10 minutes, plus at least 1 hour to chill

NOTES: You can make the cranberry-kir base (steps 1 and 2) up to 1 week ahead. Keep it on hand for quick refreshment; use just the amount you need and keep the rest chilled airtight.

MAKES: 1 1/2 cups cranberry-kir base, enough for 32 servings

- 1 **lemon** (about 2 in. wide), rinsed
- 1 **orange** (about 2 1/2 in. wide), rinsed
- 1/3 cup **sugar**
- 1 can (11.5 oz.) **cranberry-raspberry fruit juice concentrate**
- 1/2 cup **dried cranberries**
- 6 quarts **sparkling apple juice**, chilled

1. Slice lemon crosswise, discarding seeds and ends. With a vegetable peeler, pare peel from orange (colored part only); reserve orange for another use. In a food processor, whirl lemon and orange peel until finely chopped.

2. In a 3- to 4-quart pan, combine citrus mixture, sugar, fruit juice concentrate, and dried cranberries. Boil over high heat, stirring often, until reduced to 1 1/2 cups, 3 to 4 minutes. Cover and chill until cold, at least 1 hour.

3. Stir cranberry base. Spoon 1 tablespoon of the mixture, including fruit, into each glass (at least 1-cup size), add 3/4 cup sparkling apple juice, stir, and serve.

Per serving: 140 cal., 0.6% (0.9 cal.) from fat; 0.1 g protein; 0.1 g fat (0 g sat.); 34 g carbo (0.3 g fiber); 6.5 mg sodium; 0 mg chol.

Bring on the cheer

Season's greetings by the glass

By Jerry Anne Di Vecchio

Mulling over holiday party refreshments—of the liquid variety? Try these merry twists on tradition: If mulled wine appeals to you, but red-wine stains don't, mull white wine instead. For kir without alcohol, add sparkling apple juice to a lively cranberry base. Give chocolate lovers a seasonal surprise with mocha nog. And for a wintry version of the popular mojito rum cocktail, pour steaming mojito tea into a martini glass.

Mulled White Wine

PREP AND COOK TIME: About 20 minutes

NOTES: A lean white wine that hasn't been aged in oak works best for this drink. You can make the citrus base (step 1) up to 1 day ahead; cover and chill. Reheat to continue. For a clearer mulled wine, in step 2, pour the citrus base through a fine strainer into the wine, then add the whole spices. Add a few fresh lemon, orange, and kumquat slices for decoration as well, if you like.

MAKES: 12 servings

- 1/2 **lemon** (about 2 in. wide)
- 1/2 **orange** (about 2 1/2 in. wide)
- 4 **kumquats** (each about 1 in. long)
- 2 tablespoons **honey**
- 1/3 to 1/2 cup **sugar**
- 6 **whole cloves**
- 6 **whole allspice**
- 2 **cinnamon sticks** (each 3 in. long)
- 2 bottles (750 ml. each) **dry white wine** such as Pinot Grigio, Soave, or Sauvignon Blanc (see notes)

Hot Mojito Tea

PREP AND COOK TIME: **5 to 10 minutes**

NOTES: To warm glasses, fill with hot water, then drain. Garnish each glass with a mint sprig and a lime slice.

MAKES: **2 servings**

- 2 tablespoons lightly packed rinsed **fresh mint** leaves
- 2 teaspoons firmly packed **brown sugar**
- 1 **tea bag** (English Breakfast, Earl Grey, or black tea)
- ¼ cup **rum** (dark or light)
- 1 tablespoon **lime juice**

1. Rinse a small teapot with hot water, then drain. Add mint leaves, brown sugar, tea bag, and 1 cup boiling water; cover and let stand for 2 minutes, jiggling tea bag several times. Lift tea bag out and add rum and lime juice.

2. Pour mojito tea through a fine strainer into warmed heatproof martini or wineglasses (at least 1-cup size).

Per serving: 87 cal., 1% (0.9 cal.) from fat; 0.2 g protein; 0.1 g fat (0 g sat.); 5.8 g carbo (0.4 g fiber); 8.6 mg sodium; 0 mg chol.

Mocha Nog

PREP TIME: **5 to 10 minutes**

NOTES: For a shortcut, you can use pressurized whipping cream; squirt 1 cup of it into the mocha nog, then squirt more onto servings.

MAKES: **4 servings**

- ¾ cup **whipping cream**
- 1½ cups **chocolate milk** (regular or low-fat)
- ¼ cup **dark rum**
- ¼ cup **Kahlua** or other coffee-flavored liqueur
- ¼ cup **Frangelico** or other hazelnut-flavored liqueur
- 1 cup finely crushed **ice**
- ¼ cup **semisweet chocolate** curls

1. In a bowl, with a mixer at high speed, whip cream until it holds soft peaks (see notes).

2. In another bowl, whisk chocolate milk, rum, Kahlua, Frangelico, ice, and about ⅔ of the whipped cream until blended. Pour into tall glasses.

3. Spoon remaining cream in puffs onto drinks and sprinkle with chocolate curls.

Per serving: 374 cal., 48% (180 cal.) from fat; 4.4 g protein; 20 g fat (12 g sat.); 27 g carbo (2 g fiber); 73 mg sodium; 61 mg chol. ◆

Weeknight spice

A healthy stir-fry solves the school-night dinner dilemma

By Kate Washington

■ After work, school, and errands, the whole family may be exhausted; they're also likely to be ravenous—and tired of takeout. This aromatic Thai stir-fry will perk everyone up. A savory, balanced meal-in-a-bowl, it's easy to put together, easy to adapt, and especially easy to like.

Thai Basil–Turkey Stir-Fry

PREP AND COOK TIME: **About 30 minutes**

NOTES: This Thai dish is often made with minced chicken; ground turkey speeds preparation. Add or subtract chilies to suit your heat tolerance.

MAKES: **4 to 6 servings**

- 8 ounces **green beans**, rinsed, ends trimmed, and any strings removed
- 2 teaspoons **salad oil**
- 2 cloves **garlic,** peeled and minced
- 2 **green onions** (including green tops), rinsed and thinly sliced
- 2 **serrano** or other hot red or green **chilies,** rinsed, stemmed, and thinly sliced crosswise into rings (see notes)
- 1 pound **ground turkey** breast
- ⅔ cup fat-skimmed **chicken broth**
- 2 tablespoons firmly packed **brown sugar**
- 2 tablespoons **Asian fish sauce** (*nam pla* or *nuoc mam*)
- 1 tablespoon **soy sauce**
- 2 teaspoons **pepper**
- 1 cup chopped **fresh Thai** or sweet **basil** leaves
- ¼ cup **roasted cashews**
- 4 cups hot cooked **jasmine rice**

1. In a 3- to 4-quart pan over high heat, bring 2 quarts water to a boil. Add green beans and cook just until they turn bright green and are tender-crisp, 30 seconds. Drain and immediately rinse under cold running water until cool to touch. Cut beans diagonally into 1-inch lengths.

2. Pour oil into a 12-inch nonstick frying pan or 14-inch wok over high heat. When hot, add garlic, half the green onions, and half the chilies. Stir until fragrant, 1 minute. Add ground turkey and stir frequently until very little pink remains and turkey is crumbly, about 5 minutes.

3. Meanwhile, in a 2-cup glass measure, mix chicken broth, brown sugar, fish sauce, soy sauce, and pepper. Pour over turkey mixture and stir until liquid is partly evaporated and turkey is no longer pink in center of thickest pieces (cut to test), about 4 minutes. Stir in green beans and ¾ cup chopped basil.

4. Pour into a serving bowl and sprinkle with the remaining basil, green onions, and sliced chilies. Top with the cashews. Serve alongside hot cooked jasmine rice.

Per serving: 410 cal., 12% (48 cal.) from fat; 27 g protein; 5.3 g fat (1 g sat.); 64 g carbo (1.8 g fiber); 435 mg sodium; 47 mg chol. ◆

Golden puff pastry dome conceals rich and creamy mushroom soup.

JAMES CARRIER; FOOD STYLING: SUSAN DEVATY

Hat trick

Make an elegant soup for the holidays—but take a shortcut

Executive chef George Morrone of Redwood Park in San Francisco takes laborious steps to ensure dining in the luxurious restaurant will be special. He caps rich soups, for instance, with flaky, golden domes. It's a showy technique, with a simple shortcut: purchased puff pastry. You can prepare this mushroom bisque, inspired by his—or make your own favorite bisque—and top the portions with dough, then bake them for easy flair. When your guests break through the crisp crust and stir a nugget of sherry-shallot butter into the pungent soup, they'll swear you're hiding a cadre of chefs in the kitchen.

Mushroom Bisque with Pastry Top Hats

PREP AND COOK TIME: About 2 hours
NOTES: Morrone uses fresh chanterelles in this soup, but it's also delicious with common button mushrooms. You can prepare the soup through step 6 up to 1 day ahead; let stand uncovered until egg coating on crusts is dry, about 15 minutes, then cover and chill. Bake chilled portions 10 to 15 minutes

longer in step 7. For a slightly less rich soup, replace ¾ cup of the whipping cream with chicken broth.
MAKES: 6 servings

- 1¼ pounds **common mushrooms** or chanterelles (see notes)
- 1 slice **bacon** (1 oz.), chopped
- ¾ cup chopped **onion**
- ½ cup chopped **celery**
- 2 cloves **garlic,** peeled and chopped
- ¼ cup **cognac** or brandy
- ⅓ cup **dry white wine**
- 3 cups fat-skimmed **chicken broth**
- 1½ cups **whipping cream**
  Salt and **white pepper**
- 1 package (10 oz.) **frozen puff pastry shells,** thawed
- 1 **large egg,** lightly beaten
  Sherry-shallot butter (recipe follows), optional

1. Trim and discard tough or discolored stem ends and any bruised spots from mushrooms. Rinse common mushrooms and drain well. (If using chanterelles, submerge in cool water and gently agitate with your hands to loosen dirt. Drain, rinse under running water, and gently pat dry with a towel.) Coarsely chop mushrooms.

2. In a 5- to 6-quart pan over high heat, stir bacon until fat begins to render, about 1 minute. Add onion, celery, and garlic; stir until onion is limp, about 3 minutes. Add mushrooms and stir often until their liquid is evaporated and mushrooms begin to brown, 15 to 20 minutes.

3. Add cognac and stir to scrape up browned bits from pan bottom and sides. Add wine and boil until most of the liquid has evaporated, 1 to 2 minutes. Add broth and return to a boil, then cover, reduce heat, and simmer, stirring occasionally, to blend flavors, 20 to 30 minutes. Remove from heat.

4. In a blender, holding down lid with a towel, whirl mixture, a portion at a time, until smooth. Pour into a bowl. Stir in cream, then salt and pepper to taste. Chill, stirring occasionally, until soup is at room temperature, 10 to 15 minutes.

5. Spoon soup into six round soufflé dishes or ovenproof bowls (1¼- to 1½-cup size; 3½ to 4½ in. wide) to within ½ inch of rim.

6. On a lightly floured board, roll each puff pastry shell into a round 1 to 1½ inches wider than top of soufflé dishes. Brush egg in a ½-inch border around the bottom edge (unscored side) of each pastry round. Carefully drape each round, egg side down, over a dish so that it doesn't touch soup; press edges firmly around sides of dish. Brush more egg lightly over pastry tops and sides (discard remaining egg or save for another use). Set dishes at least 1 inch apart in a 12- by 17-inch baking pan.

7. Bake in a 375° regular or convection oven until pastry is richly browned, 15 to 20 minutes. Serve at once, with sherry-shallot butter to stir into portions at the table.

Per serving: 533 cal., 69% (369 cal.) from fat; 10 g protein; 41 g fat (16 g sat.); 33 g carbo (2.5 g fiber); 247 mg sodium; 107 mg chol.

Sherry-shallot butter. In an 8- to 10-inch frying pan over high heat, stir ⅓ cup minced **shallots** and ⅓ cup **dry sherry** often until liquid is evaporated and shallots begin to brown, 5 to 8 minutes. Pour into a small bowl and let cool. Add 3 tablespoons **butter** (at room temperature) to shallots and mix. Divide into six equal portions and, with your hands, roll each into a ball. Arrange on a small plate. Cover and chill until firm, at least 15 minutes. Makes 6 servings.
— *Linda Lau Anusasananan*

Weighing in

Weight is often a vital measurement for cooking, but one of the tools most absent from home kitchens is a scale. One reason: old-fashioned, accurate balance scales take up a lot of space. Another: bouncy, spring-loaded alternatives aren't always trustworthy. Soehnle electronic scales provide a solution, with computer-calibrated measurements, easy-to-decipher digital readouts (in grams or kilograms and pounds or ounces), and sleek lines designed for easy cleaning. Battery operated, they shut off automatically and have overload protection to avoid damage. The Soehnle scales, priced from about $50 to $195, depending on model and capacity, are available in cookware stores and catalogs and online; (800) 827-2582 or www.frieling.com. — *Jerry Anne Di Vecchio*

SCOTT PETERSON; ABOVE: THOMAS J. STORY

The Wine Guide

Western Zins

By Karen MacNeil-Fife

When I lived in New York, I knew about Zinfandel; I occasionally even drank Zinfandel. But for me—as, I suspect, for most New Yorkers—it was just another wine, no more special than Italian Chianti or Chilean Merlot. That all changed when I moved to the West.

I think Westerners have a passion for Zinfandel not found anywhere else in the country. (Our gain.) For Zinfandel, more than any other grape variety, is tied to the history of the American West. It first gained prominence here after the Gold Rush, as legions of men who didn't get rich turned to agriculture and viticulture. Then, the leading variety was the so-called Mission grape, first brought by the Spanish colonists to Mexico and later by Catholic priests and missionaries (hence its name) to California. But Mission made merely tolerable wine, and as the West boomed, so did its thirst for something more lively, more satisfying, more delicious. Zinfandel was one of the answers.

And in many ways, it has remained the West's "answer" for more than a century. Today, it's the third leading red wine grape in planted acreage (49,700), after Cabernet Sauvignon and Merlot.

Ironically, it turns out that Zinfandel's native home is, in fact, in Europe—Croatia to be exact. Last December, researchers at the University of California at Davis determined that Zinfandel is the same as the Croatian grape Crljenak kastelanski. (It's a pretty safe bet we'll continue calling it Zinfandel.)

Whatever its origin, Zinfandel has a twofold appeal: First, the grape is all about immediate gratification. Zinfandel is juicy, jammy, lip-smacking, mouth-filling, and packed with dark berry flavors. What's not to like? Second, Zinfandel spans the seasons like no other red. On the one hand, it's warming and dense—a true comfort wine for fall and winter evenings (like tonight) when you're cooking a roast or a stew. But the wine is also great in the summer, when it becomes a magic match for grilled meats.

To be honest, Zinfandel also has an ugly side. The grape is notoriously good at producing high levels of sugar the longer it's left to ripen. Since all that sugar eventually turns into alcohol, Zinfandel can become a huge oaf of a wine, so full of alcohol that it smells like a nurses' station in a hospital. The best winemakers balance that power with underlying elegance. Powerful elegance? Elegant power? If these are oxymorons, then, with Zinfandel at least, oxymorons taste best.

SOME TOP ZINS

Many producers make a number of different Zinfandels, so experiment with several from a single winery to decide which you like best. Here are some of my favorites. Prices are for the current vintage and may vary according to location.

A. Rafanelli Zinfandel (Dry Creek Valley, CA), $28. **BV Beaulieu Vineyard Zinfandel** (Napa Valley), $14. **D-Cubed Zinfandel** (Napa Valley), $25. **Dry Creek Vineyard "Heritage Clone" Zinfandel** (Sonoma County), $15. **Lolonis Zinfandel** (Redwood Valley, Mendocino), $18. **Ridge "Geyserville" Zinfandel** (Geyserville, CA), $30. **Terra d'Oro by Montevina SHR Field Blend** (Zinfandel, Petite Syrah, and Barbera; Amador County, CA), $24. **Trinchero Family Estates Montevina Zinfandel** (Amador County), $10. ◆

Corn, cilantro, and jalapeños put a Southwestern spin on potato cakes.

FOOD STYLING: KAREN SHINTO (2)

1. In a 5- to 6-quart pan over high heat, bring about 4 quarts water to a boil. Add whole potatoes and cook until tender when pierced, 20 to 30 minutes. Drain and rinse in cold water until cool enough to handle; peel and grate (or press through a food mill or ricer).

2. In a large bowl, mix potatoes, corn, cheddar cheese, cottage cheese, eggs, onions, cilantro, jalapeños, cornmeal, cumin, salt, and pepper until well blended.

3. Pour 1 teaspoon oil into a 10- to 12-inch nonstick frying pan over medium-high heat; when hot, drop batter into pan in about ⅓-cup portions, and use a spoon to spread slightly into 3- to 4-inch cakes. Cook, turning once with a spatula, until cakes are browned on both sides and firm to the touch in the center, about 6 minutes total. Transfer to an ovenproof plate and keep warm in a 200° oven while you cook remaining cakes, adding more oil to pan as necessary.

Per serving: 263 cal., 41% (108 cal.) from fat; 16 g protein; 12 g fat (4.9 g sat.); 27 g carbo (5.2 g fiber); 1,565 mg sodium; 125 mg chol.

Sweet Braised Winter Greens

J'nene Wade, Sandpoint, ID

J'nene Wade makes two versions of this cool-weather side dish—one with Swiss chard, dried sour cherries, and pecans and this one, with collard greens, raisins, and pine nuts.

PREP AND COOK TIME: About 30 minutes

MAKES: 6 side-dish servings

- 2 pounds **collard greens**
- 3 tablespoons **olive oil**
- 1 **red onion** (about 8 oz.), peeled, halved, and thinly slivered lengthwise
- 2 cloves **garlic,** peeled and thinly sliced
- 3 tablespoons **balsamic vinegar**
- 2 tablespoons **brown sugar**
- 2 tablespoons **golden raisins**
- 2 tablespoons **pine nuts**

  Salt and **pepper**

1. Rinse collard greens and tear leaves from center ribs; discard center ribs and stems.

2. Pour oil into a 12- to 14-inch frying pan over medium-high heat; when hot, add onion and garlic and stir frequently until onion is limp, 5 to 8 minutes. Stir in vinegar, brown sugar, raisins, pine nuts, and collard greens.

Tastes of home

Readers' recipes tested in *Sunset's* kitchens

By Charity Ferreira • Photographs by James Carrier

Potato-Corn Cakes

Annette Leonard, Eugene, OR

When making potato pancakes one night, Annette Leonard experimented with some new flavors. The result has become a favorite main dish, which she serves with salsa and sour cream.

PREP AND COOK TIME: About 1 hour

MAKES: About 12 cakes; 3 or 4 servings

- 1¼ pounds **russet potatoes,** scrubbed
- 1 can (15½ oz.) **corn,** drained
- ⅔ cup shredded **cheddar cheese** (2 oz.)
- ½ cup **small-curd cottage cheese**
- 2 **large eggs,** beaten to blend
- ⅓ cup minced **green onions** (including tops)
- 3 tablespoons chopped **fresh cilantro** leaves
- 2 **fresh jalapeño** or other hot green **chilies** (about 2 oz. total), rinsed, stemmed, seeded, and diced
- 2 tablespoons **yellow cornmeal**
- 1 tablespoon **ground cumin**
- 2 teaspoons **salt**
- ½ teaspoon **pepper**

  About 2 teaspoons **salad oil**

Stir frequently until greens are slightly wilted, 3 to 4 minutes. Reduce heat, cover, and cook until greens are very wilted and tender to bite, about 15 minutes. Add salt and pepper to taste; serve at once.

Per serving: 144 cal., 54% (78 cal.) from fat; 3.5 g protein; 8.7 g fat (1.2 g sat.); 16 g carbo (4.2 g fiber); 24 mg sodium; 0 mg chol.

Apple Corn Muffins

Elsa Kleinman, Topanga, CA

Of all the baked goods that her grandmother made using home-grown apples, these muffins were Elsa Kleinman's favorite.

PREP AND COOK TIME: About 35 minutes

MAKES: 12 muffins

- ¼ cup (⅛ lb.) **butter**
- ⅔ cup **brown sugar**
- 1 pound **sweet apples,** such as Fuji, rinsed, peeled, cored, and sliced lengthwise
- 1 cup **yellow cornmeal**
- 1 cup **all-purpose flour**
- 3 tablespoons **granulated sugar**
- 1 teaspoon **baking soda**
- ½ teaspoon **salt**
- 1 cup **buttermilk**
- 1 **large egg**
- 3 tablespoons **salad oil**

1. Melt butter in a 10- to 12-inch frying pan over medium heat; stir in brown sugar until dissolved and bubbly. Stir in apples and cook until they are barely tender when pierced, about 5 minutes. Divide apple slices and sugar mixture equally among 12 buttered muffin cups (½-cup capacity).

2. In a bowl, mix cornmeal, flour, granulated sugar, baking soda, and salt.

3. In another bowl, mix buttermilk, egg, and oil to blend. Stir into cornmeal mixture just until evenly moistened. Spoon batter equally into muffin cups.

4. Bake in a 350° regular or convection oven until tops are lightly browned and feel firm when pressed, 15 to 20 minutes. Immediately run a knife between each muffin and cup rim and invert over a baking sheet to remove muffins (if any apple slices re-

Tender apple slices make a sweet topping for upside-down corn muffins.

main inside muffin cups, replace on muffins). Serve warm or at room temperature, apple side up.

Per muffin: 236 cal., 32% (75 cal.) from fat; 3.3 g protein; 8.3 g fat (3.2 g sat.); 38 g carbo (1.5 g fiber); 274 mg sodium; 29 mg chol.

Herbed Beer Bread

Cynthia Becker, Pueblo, CO

Cynthia Becker embellished a simple beer bread recipe with herbs and cheese. The resulting savory quick bread is a good way to round out a meal of soup or salad.

PREP AND COOK TIME: About 1¼ hours

MAKES: 6 to 8 servings

- 3 cups **all-purpose flour**
- 2 tablespoons **sugar**
- 2 teaspoons **baking powder**
- 1 teaspoon **salt**
- ¼ cup **shredded parmesan cheese**
- 2 tablespoons **dried onion flakes**
- 1 teaspoon **dried dill**
- 1 teaspoon **dried sage**
- 1 teaspoon **dried thyme**
- 1 teaspoon **dried rosemary**
- ¼ cup (⅛ lb.) **butter,** melted and cooled
- 12 ounces **beer**

1. In a bowl, mix flour, sugar, baking powder, salt, cheese, onion flakes, dill, sage, thyme, and rosemary.

2. Reserve 1 tablespoon melted butter for brushing on the top of bread. Add remaining melted butter and beer to flour mixture; stir just until evenly moistened. Scrape batter into a buttered 9½- by 5½-inch loaf pan and brush top with reserved butter.

3. Bake in a 350° regular or convection oven until browned, about 50 minutes. Serve warm, cut into squares or slices.

Per serving: 263 cal., 26% (69 cal.) from fat; 6.2 g protein; 7.7 g fat (4.6 g sat.); 42 g carbo (1.3 g fiber); 530 mg sodium; 19 mg chol.

Pork Chops Braised with Cider Vinegar

Lisa Pan, Hayward, CA

Lisa Pan's mother, who grew up in Shanghai, taught her this flavorful treatment for pork chops.

PREP AND COOK TIME: About 25 minutes

MAKES: 4 servings

- 1 tablespoon **salad oil**
- 4 **center-cut loin pork chops** (about 1 in. thick; about 7 oz. each)
- 1 **red onion** (about 10 oz.), peeled, halved, and thinly slivered lengthwise
- 2 cloves **garlic,** minced
- ¼ cup **apple cider vinegar**
- 1 tablespoon **soy sauce**
- 1 tablespoon **honey**
- **Salt** and **pepper**

1. Pour oil into a 10- to 12-inch non-stick frying pan over medium-high heat. When hot, add pork chops and cook, turning once, until browned on both sides, about 4 minutes total. Transfer to a plate. Add onion and garlic to pan. Stir frequently until onion is limp, about 5 minutes.

2. Stir in vinegar, soy sauce, and honey, and return pork chops to pan. Reduce heat, cover, and simmer until pork chops are barely pink in the center (cut to test), 3 to 5 more minutes.

3. Place each pork chop on a plate and top equally with onion mixture. Add salt and pepper to taste.

Per serving: 476 cal., 55% (261 cal.) from fat; 41 g protein; 29 g fat (9.2 g sat.); 12 g carbo (1.1 g fiber); 384 mg sodium; 133 mg chol. ◆

Spicy gingerbread in a pool of crème anglaise ends Christmas dinner on a homey note (recipe on page 254).

December

field day

Crisp winter
weather adds
spice to a
gourmet picnic

There's a lot to be said for picnicking in the off season: the air feels cool and smells of wintry things like smoke and wet leaves, the sun gleams brightly but benevolently, and parks and beaches are empty of crowds. Winter is a beautiful time to be outside, particularly when you've brought a thick blanket to sit on and a lunch that includes thermoses of hot soup and spiced apple cider.

Cool-season picnic fare can be hearty and assertive, like our saffron-spiced carrot and white bean soup, a warm accompaniment to Spanish ham and Manchego cheese sandwiches spread with tangy tomato jam. Crisp apple and persimmon slices with walnuts dressed in sherry vinegar make a delicious winter-fruit salad, and dark chocolate–fromage blanc brownies and dried figs are indulgent, portable desserts.

By Charity Ferreira and Jil Peters

Photographs by James Carrier
Food styling by Karen Shinto

Winter picnic menu

- Persimmon and Apple Salad
  with Walnuts
- Carrot and White Bean Soup
- Ham and Manchego Sandwiches
  with Tomato Jam
- Couscous Salad with Radicchio
  and Pistachios
- Chocolate–Fromage Blanc Brownies
- Dried Figs
- Hot Spiced Cider

Curl up with
a picnic lunch:
pearl couscous
salad and Spanish
ham and cheese
sandwiches.

Persimmon and Apple Salad with Walnuts

PREP AND COOK TIME: About 15 minutes

NOTES: Fuyu persimmons are the small, flat-bottomed variety that can be eaten when firm. Assemble salad just before packing.

MAKES: 6 to 8 servings

- ⅓ cup **walnut pieces**
- 2 tablespoons **orange juice**
- 1 tablespoon **sherry vinegar**
- 1 tablespoon **olive oil**
- 3 **Fuji** or other tart **apples** (about 8 oz. each), rinsed, cored, and thinly sliced lengthwise
- 3 **Fuyu persimmons** (about 4 oz. each; see notes), rinsed and thinly sliced lengthwise

  Salt and **pepper**

1. Bake the walnuts in an 8- or 9-inch baking pan in a 350° regular or convection oven, shaking pan occasionally, until nuts are golden beneath skins, 7 to 10 minutes.

2. Meanwhile, in a bowl, combine the orange juice, vinegar, and olive oil. Add the apples, persimmons, and toasted walnuts and mix to coat. Add salt and pepper to taste.

Per serving: 139 cal., 34% (47 cal.) from fat; 1.1 g protein; 5.2 g fat (0.5 g sat.); 25 g carbo (2 g fiber); .9 mg sodium; 0 mg chol.

Carrot and White Bean Soup

PREP AND COOK TIME: About 1 hour

NOTES: You can prepare through step 4 up to 1 day ahead; cool, cover, and chill. Continue with step 5 just before serving or packing.

MAKES: 2½ quarts; 6 to 8 servings

- 1 head **garlic** (3½ to 4 oz.)

  About 1 tablespoon **olive oil**

A warm bowl of carrot and white bean soup takes the chill off.

- 1 **onion** (about 8 oz.), peeled and chopped

  Salt and **pepper**
- ½ cup **dry white wine**
- 3 cans (14½ oz. each) fat-skimmed **chicken broth**
- ¼ teaspoon **saffron threads,** crumbled, or ⅛ teaspoon powdered saffron
- 2½ pounds **carrots,** peeled and cut into ½-inch chunks
- 2 cans (15 oz. each) **small white beans,** rinsed and drained
- ¼ cup **dry sherry**

1. Cut garlic head in half crosswise; rub cut surfaces with a little olive oil and wrap garlic in foil. Bake in a 400° regular or convection oven until garlic is soft when pressed, about 40 minutes. When cool enough to handle, pluck or squeeze garlic cloves from peel; discard peel.

2. Meanwhile, in a 6- to 8-quart pan over medium-high heat, cook onion in 1 tablespoon oil, stirring occasionally, until very limp, about 15 minutes (if onion starts to brown, reduce heat and add a few tablespoons of water). Sprinkle with salt and pepper. Add wine and stir often until most of the liquid is evaporated, 2 to 3 minutes.

3. Add broth, saffron, and carrots. Bring to a boil over medium-high heat, then cover, reduce heat, and simmer until carrots are very tender when pierced, about 20 minutes. Add roasted garlic.

4. In a blender or food processor, whirl mixture, in batches, until smooth.

5. Return purée to pan over low heat; add beans and sherry. Cover and simmer, stirring occasionally, about 10 minutes. Add more salt and pepper to taste.

Per serving: 252 cal., 8% (21 cal.) from fat; 15 g protein; 2.3 g fat (0.3 g sat.); 43 g carbo (4.7 g fiber); 101 mg sodium; 0 mg chol.

Ham and Manchego Sandwiches with Tomato Jam

PREP TIME: About 15 minutes

NOTES: Manchego is a firm Spanish sheep's-milk cheese. Make and wrap

Packing tips

It's important to pack foods at a bacteria-safe temperature: keep hot soup and cider in thermoses, and salads, sandwiches, and other drinks in a cooler with frozen gel packs. Use to-go containers to create individually boxed meals, which travel well. Prepare the sandwiches on round rolls so they fit neatly into empty soup bowls. Parchment paper wrapped around the sandwich can do double duty on your lap as a drip-catcher.

And don't forget to pack...
- A picnic blanket
- Forks, spoons, and napkins
- Serving spoons for salads
- Salt and pepper shakers

- Paper towels or other cleanup materials
- Plastic bags for trash
- Sweaters or sweatshirts for chilly weather

sandwiches just before packing.
MAKES: 8 sandwiches

- 8 **sandwich rolls** (3 oz. each)
  About 1 cup **tomato jam** (recipe follows)
- 12 ounces **thin-sliced Spanish cured ham** or prosciutto
- 4 ounces **Manchego cheese** (see notes), thinly sliced, or parmesan cheese, shaved
- 4 cups **arugula leaves** or salad mix (about 4 oz.), rinsed and crisped

Slice rolls in half horizontally and spread top halves generously with tomato jam. On bottom half of each roll, equally layer ham, cheese, and arugula leaves. Place top of roll on filling.

Per serving: 479 cal., 30% (144 cal.) from fat; 23 g protein; 16 g fat (6 g sat.); 63 g carbo (2.4 g fiber); 1,433 mg sodium; 49 mg chol.

Tomato Jam

PREP AND COOK TIME: About 1¾ hours
NOTES: Cover and chill any leftover jam for up to 2 weeks.
MAKES: About 2 cups

- 1½ pounds **cherry tomatoes** (about 4 cups), rinsed and stemmed
- 1¼ cups firmly packed **brown sugar**
- ¼ cup **cider vinegar**
- ½ **lemon** (3 oz. total), including peel, rinsed and very thinly sliced
- 2 tablespoons minced **fresh ginger**
- 1 teaspoon **ground cumin**
- ¾ teaspoon **ground cinnamon**
- ⅛ teaspoon **ground cloves**
- ½ teaspoon **salt**
- ⅛ teaspoon **pepper**

1. In a 3- to 4-quart pan, combine tomatoes, brown sugar, vinegar, lemon, ginger, cumin, cinnamon, cloves, salt, and pepper. Bring to a boil over medium heat, stirring often, 4 to 5 minutes.

2. Reduce heat and simmer, stirring occasionally, until mixture is reduced to 2 cups and has the consistency of thick jam, about 1 hour and 15 minutes. Add more salt and pepper to taste.

Per ¼ cup: 153 cal., 2% (2.7 cal.) from fat; 0.9 g protein; 0.3 g fat (0 g sat.); 39 g carbo (1.6 g fiber); 167 mg sodium; 0 mg chol.

Couscous Salad with Radicchio and Pistachios

PREP AND COOK TIME: About 30 minutes
NOTES: Israeli couscous, sometimes called "pearl couscous" or "toasted pea pasta," is a small, ball-shaped pasta available in some supermarkets and natural-food stores and in Middle Eastern markets; you can also order it

from the Pasta Shop (888/952-4005). If you can't find it, use orzo pasta instead. Preserved lemons are available in some well-stocked supermarkets and in stores that sell Middle Eastern ingredients. You can make this salad up to 4 hours ahead; cover and chill.
MAKES: 8 to 10 servings

- 1 pound **Israeli couscous** or orzo pasta (see notes)
- ¼ cup **balsamic vinegar**
- 3 tablespoons **extra-virgin olive oil**
- 1 head (about 8 oz.) **radicchio,** rinsed, cored, and thinly sliced
- ½ cup chopped **shelled roasted pistachios**
- ½ cup chopped **parsley**
- ¼ cup minced **preserved lemon** (see notes)
  Salt and **pepper**

1. In a 5- to 6-quart pan over high heat, bring about 4 quarts water to a boil. Add couscous and cook just until tender to bite, about 6 minutes (10 for orzo). Drain and rinse under cold running water until cool.

2. Meanwhile, in a large bowl, mix vinegar and olive oil. Add couscous, radicchio, pistachios, parsley, and preserved lemon. Mix gently to coat, adding salt and pepper to taste.

Per serving: 250 cal., 27% (68 cal.) from fat; 7.5 g protein; 7.6 g fat (1.1 g sat.); 38 g carbo (2.6 g fiber); 244 mg sodium; 0 mg chol.

Chocolate–Fromage Blanc Brownies

PREP AND COOK TIME: About 1 hour
NOTES: Fromage blanc is a tangy, fresh cheese available in some well-stocked supermarkets and in specialty cheese shops. If it is unavailable, substitute 4 ounces cream cheese, at room temperature, and 4 ounces sour cream; whisk or beat together until smooth before mixing with sugar and egg in step 2. Cool brownies completely before wrapping.
MAKES: 9 brownies

- ½ cup (¼ lb.) **butter,** cut into 1-inch chunks
- 6 ounces **unsweetened chocolate,** finely chopped
- 1½ teaspoons **vanilla**
- 2¼ cups **sugar**
- 5 large **eggs**
- 1 cup **all-purpose flour**
- ½ teaspoon **baking powder**
- 8 ounces **fromage blanc** (see notes)

1. In a 2- to 3-quart pan over low heat, stir butter and chocolate until melted and well blended. Remove from heat and stir in vanilla and 2 cups

Fudgy fromage blanc brownie is just a cream cheese brownie dressed up.

sugar. Transfer to a bowl and add 4 eggs, one at a time, beating well after each addition. Stir in flour and baking powder just until blended.

2. In another bowl, mix fromage blanc and remaining ¼ cup sugar and 1 egg until well blended.

3. Spread half the chocolate mixture level in a buttered and floured 9-inch square baking pan. Pour cheese mixture evenly over chocolate. Drop ¼-cup portions of remaining chocolate mixture on top, partially, but not completely, covering cheese mixture.

4. Bake brownies in a 325° regular or convection oven until a wooden skewer inserted in the center comes out with moist crumbs attached, 45 to 50 minutes. Let cool in pan on a rack for at least 20 minutes, then cut into 9 squares.

Per brownie: 497 cal., 43% (216 cal.) from fat; 9.3 g protein; 24 g fat (14 g sat.); 68 g carbo (3.3 g fiber); 220 mg sodium; 148 mg chol.

Hot spiced cider. In a 3- to 4-quart pan, combine 2 quarts **apple juice, 1 cinnamon stick, 6 whole cloves, 1 star anise,** and ⅛ teaspoon **ground nutmeg;** bring to a simmer over medium-high heat, stirring occasionally. Remove from heat and let stand about 1 hour or cover and chill up to 1 day. Just before serving or packing, pour through a fine strainer into another pan and reheat over medium-low heat until steaming. Makes 8 cups.

Per cup: 118 cal., 2% (2.7 cal.) from fat; 0.1 g protein; 0.3 g fat (0 g sat.); 29 g carbo (0.2 g fiber); 7.8 mg sodium; 0 mg chol. ◆

A welcome exchange

Friends come bearing cookies for a relaxed party—and sweet holiday supplies for all

By Charity Ferreira • Photographs by James Carrier • Food styling by Karen Shinto • Prop styling by Christina Ecklund

■ Heidi Haas and her friends and coworkers in the San Francisco Bay Area have made an annual tradition out of a practical excuse to get together at the holidays: a cookie-exchange party. Each guest brings five dozen cookies, which Haas displays on the dining room table. Amid much talking and tasting, guests make their way around the table, collecting several of each kind of cookie in the extra containers they've brought, until the platters are empty.

Haas's friends, many of whom love to bake, appreciate being able to focus their attention during this hectic season on one special cookie, and the whole group benefits from each person's efforts. "This way no one has to spend two or three weekends baking, but everyone goes home with a dozen different kinds of cookies," says Haas.

Since the theme is sweets, Haas keeps the rest of the fare simple, providing a few savory finger foods such as cheeses and crackers, along with mulled wine and apple cider.

Whether you're invited to an exchange party or want to host one yourself, these cookies will make great additions to any platter.

Gingerbread
pinwheels

Palmiers

Raspberry shortbread sandwiches

Peanut-chocolate macaroons

Chocolate thumbprints

Mint chippers

Orange butter shells

Gingerbread Pinwheels

PREP AND COOK TIME: About 1 hour, plus at least 1½ hours to chill

NOTES: This cookie is a spin on traditional pinwheels, made by rolling plain and chocolate doughs into a swirl. Store cookies airtight at room temperature up to 3 days; freeze to store longer.

MAKES: About 50 cookies

For gingerbread dough:

¾ cup (⅜ lb.) **butter,** at room temperature

¾ cup firmly packed **brown sugar**

¼ cup **light** or dark **molasses**

2 **large egg** yolks

2¼ cups **all-purpose flour**

2 teaspoons **ground ginger**

1 teaspoon **ground cinnamon**

½ teaspoon **ground nutmeg**

½ teaspoon **ground cloves**

½ teaspoon **baking soda**

¼ teaspoon **salt**

For plain dough:

1 cup (½ lb.) **butter,** at room temperature

1 cup **granulated sugar**

1 **large egg**

1 teaspoon **vanilla**

3 cups **all-purpose flour**

½ teaspoon **baking soda**

¼ teaspoon **salt**

1. *Make gingerbread dough:* In a bowl, with a mixer on high speed, beat butter, brown sugar, and molasses until smooth. Beat in egg yolks until well blended, scraping down sides of bowl as needed. In another bowl, mix flour, ginger, cinnamon, nutmeg, cloves, baking soda, and salt. With mixer on low speed, beat flour mixture into butter mixture until well blended. Wrap dough in plastic and flatten slightly; chill until firm but pliable (see tips, below), about 1 hour (or freeze for 30 minutes).

Make plain dough: In a bowl, with a mixer on high speed, beat butter and sugar until smooth. Beat in egg and vanilla until well blended, scraping down sides of bowl as needed. In another bowl, mix flour, baking soda, and salt. With mixer on low speed, beat flour mixture into butter mixture until well blended. Wrap dough in plastic and flatten slightly; chill as directed above.

2. With a lightly floured rolling pin on a lightly floured sheet of waxed paper, roll out gingerbread dough into an approximately 12- by 15-inch rectangle. Slide dough, on waxed paper, onto a 12- by 15-inch baking sheet. Repeat to roll out plain dough and chill both doughs until slightly firmer, about 10 minutes.

3. Carefully invert gingerbread dough over the plain dough, lining up edges as evenly as possible. Remove waxed paper from top of gingerbread dough. With a sharp knife, cut rectangle in half lengthwise to make two 6- by 15-inch rectangles. Transfer one of the rectangles to another sheet of waxed paper. Let stand about 10 minutes to soften slightly.

4. Starting at long edge of one rectangle, lift waxed paper to roll doughs into a tight, even cylinder. Repeat to roll other rectangle. Wrap rolls in plastic; freeze until firm, about 30 minutes.

5. Unwrap rolls and slice crosswise into ½-inch-thick rounds. Lay cookies flat, 1 inch apart, on buttered 12- by 17-inch baking sheets.

6. Bake cookies in a 325° regular or convection oven until edges just begin to brown, 15 to 20 minutes. If baking multiple sheets in one oven, switch positions halfway through baking. Transfer pinwheels to racks to cool.

Per cookie: 145 cal., 44% (64 cal.) from fat; 1.7 g protein; 7.1 g fat (4.3 g sat.); 19 g carbo (0.4 g fiber); 120 mg sodium; 31 mg chol.

Palmiers

PREP AND COOK TIME: About 30 minutes

NOTES: Thaw dough at room temperature for about 1 hour, or overnight in the refrigerator. Look for large-crystal decorating sugar at cake-decorating supply stores and some well-stocked supermarkets. Store palmiers airtight at room temperature up to 3 days; freeze to store longer.

MAKES: 36 cookies

About ½ cup **granulated sugar**

1 package (17.3 oz.) **frozen puff pastry sheets,** thawed (see notes)

Clear large-crystal decorating sugar (optional)

1. Sprinkle work surface lightly with granulated sugar. Lay one sheet of puff pastry flat on surface and sprinkle evenly with about 3 tablespoons sugar. Beginning at one side, fold in dough, ½ inch at a time, to the center of the square. Repeat to fold in the other side so the two rolls are touching.

2. With a sharp knife, cut roll crosswise into ¼- to ½-inch-thick slices. Lay cookies flat, 1 inch apart, on buttered 12- by 15-inch baking sheets. Repeat to fold and slice remaining sheet of puff pastry; arrange cookies on baking sheets. Sprinkle cookies generously with large-crystal decorating sugar (or more granulated sugar).

3. Bake cookies in a 375° regular or convection oven until golden brown all over, 18 to 22 minutes; if baking more than one sheet at a time in one oven, switch positions halfway through baking. Transfer palmiers to racks to cool completely.

Per cookie: 88 cal., 55% (49 cal.) from fat; 1 g protein; 5.4 g fat (0.9 g sat.); 8.9 g carbo (0.2 g fiber); 36 mg sodium; 0.6 mg chol.

6 tips for **perfect** cookies

1 **Start with soft butter.** If the recipe calls for butter at room temperature, it should be soft but not runny. You can soften it for a few seconds in a microwave oven or let it stand in a warm place, such as near the preheating oven.

2 **Chill the dough.** If the recipe directs you to chill the dough so it can be rolled or shaped without sticking to your hands or the counter, but your kitchen is warm, you may need to chill the dough longer than the recipe suggests. The dough should feel cold and firm but pliable. If it becomes sticky as you work, return it to the refrigerator to firm up again.

3 **Take your oven's temperature.** Ovens vary a great deal, so it's a good idea to check yours periodically with an oven thermometer on the middle rack to make sure it's baking at the temperature you set it for. Minimize opening and closing the oven door during baking to avoid lowering the temperature.

4 **Use cool baking sheets.** Never put cookie dough on warm pans. To cool pans quickly, rinse with cold water; dry before using them again.

5 **Rotate pans midway through baking time.** Cookies will bake more evenly if they spend equal time on the top and bottom racks of the oven.

6 **Try cooking parchment.** This paper is sold in rolls or sheets in well-stocked grocery stores and baking-supply shops. Advantages: cookies won't stick, baking sheets stay clean, and you can use the same piece of parchment for several batches of cookies.

Orange Butter Shells

PREP AND COOK TIME: About 1 hour

NOTES: Madeleine pans have shell-shaped indentations and are usually used to make a soft, spongy cookie traditional in France. You can order the pans from Williams-Sonoma at www.williams-sonoma.com or (800) 541-2233. If you have only one pan, you can bake the cookies in batches; be sure to cool the pan under cold running water and dry it thoroughly before baking the next batch. Store cookies airtight at room temperature up to 3 days; freeze to store longer.

MAKES: About 18 cookies

- 1 cup ($\frac{1}{2}$ lb.) **butter,** at room temperature
- $\frac{3}{4}$ cup **granulated sugar**
- 1 **large egg**
- 1 **large egg** yolk
- $1\frac{1}{2}$ tablespoons grated **orange** peel
- 1 teaspoon **vanilla**
- 2 cups **all-purpose flour**
- $\frac{1}{2}$ teaspoon **baking powder**
- $\frac{1}{4}$ teaspoon **salt**

  Powdered sugar

1. Lightly butter 18 madeleine molds ($1\frac{1}{2}$ to $2\frac{1}{2}$ in. long; see notes) or coat lightly with cooking oil spray.

2. In a bowl, with a mixer on high speed, beat butter and granulated sugar until smooth. Beat in egg, egg yolk, orange peel, and vanilla until well blended, scraping down sides of bowl as necessary.

3. In a small bowl, mix flour, baking powder, and salt. With mixer on low speed, beat flour mixture into butter mixture until well incorporated. Pinch off 1-inch balls of dough and press evenly into prepared madeleine molds.

4. Bake cookies in a 325° regular or convection oven until edges are lightly browned and centers feel dry and firm to the touch, 12 to 14 minutes. Immediately invert pans to release cookies onto racks and dust shell-patterned sides with powdered sugar. Let cool.

Per cookie: 190 cal., 52% (99 cal.) from fat; 2 g protein; 11 g fat (6.6 g sat.); 20 g carbo (0.4 g fiber); 154 mg sodium; 51 mg chol.

Raspberry Shortbread Sandwiches

PREP AND COOK TIME: About 1 hour

NOTES: Use a sharp knife, a $\frac{1}{2}$-inch cookie cutter, or the narrow end of a $\frac{1}{2}$-inch plain pastry tip to cut holes out of half the cookies before baking. These cookies are best eaten the day they are filled, but you can store cooled, unfilled cookies airtight at room temperature up to 3 days; freeze to store longer.

MAKES: About 20 sandwich cookies

- 1 cup ($\frac{1}{2}$ lb.) **butter,** at room temperature
- $\frac{1}{2}$ cup **granulated sugar**
- 1 teaspoon **vanilla**
- $2\frac{1}{2}$ cups **all-purpose flour**
- $\frac{1}{8}$ teaspoon **salt**
- $\frac{1}{2}$ cup **raspberry jam**

  About $\frac{1}{3}$ cup **powdered sugar**

1. In a bowl, with a mixer on medium speed, beat butter, granulated sugar, and vanilla until smooth. Add flour and salt and mix on low speed until dough comes together in a ball. Transfer to a lightly floured surface.

2. Divide dough in half. With a lightly floured rolling pin, roll each portion to about $\frac{1}{8}$ inch thick. With a floured 2- to 3-inch round or star-shaped cutter, cut out cookies. If desired, cut a $\frac{1}{2}$-inch circle out of the center of half of the cookies to make a window for the jam filling (see notes). Place cookies 1 inch apart on buttered 12- by 15-inch baking sheets. Gather excess dough into a ball, reroll, and cut out remaining cookies.

3. Bake in a 325° regular or 300° convection oven until edges are just beginning to brown, 10 to 12 minutes. If baking more than one sheet at a time in one oven, switch positions halfway through baking. Transfer cookies to racks to cool completely.

4. Spread the flat side of each of half the cookies (those without holes) with about $\frac{1}{2}$ tablespoon jam. Top each with a remaining cookie (with a hole), flat side toward filling. Sprinkle tops of cookies evenly with powdered sugar.

Per sandwich cookie: 192 cal., 45% (87 cal.) from fat; 1.8 g protein; 9.7 g fat (6 g sat.); 25 g carbo (0.5 g fiber); 116 mg sodium; 26 mg chol.

Peanut-Chocolate Macaroons

PREP AND COOK TIME: About 1 hour, plus at least $1\frac{1}{4}$ hours to stand and cool

NOTES: These French-style macaroons are easiest baked on cooking parchment (see "6 tips for perfect cookies," page 248). They're best eaten the day they're filled; however, you can make both cookies and filling up to 3 days ahead. Stack cookies carefully in an airtight container and store at room temperature; cover ganache airtight and refrigerate. Melt ganache over hot water and cool (as described in recipe, following) before filling cookies.

MAKES: About 18 sandwich cookies

- $2\frac{1}{3}$ cups **powdered sugar**

Choose a range of dishes, from cake stands to scalloped bowls, to highlight the variety of cookies at the exchange.

- $1\frac{1}{3}$ cups **unsalted roasted peanuts** (about 7 oz.)
- $\frac{1}{3}$ cup **granulated sugar**
- 4 **large egg** whites
- **Chocolate ganache** (recipe follows)

1. In a food processor, whirl powdered sugar and peanuts until nuts are very finely ground (no large nut pieces should be visible).

2. In a 3- to 4-quart pan over medium heat, bring 2 to 3 inches of water to a boil; adjust heat to maintain a very low simmer. In a large bowl or the bowl of a mixer, whisk sugar into egg whites. Set bowl over simmering water in pan (bottom of bowl should not touch water) and stir constantly until sugar is dissolved and mixture feels warm to the touch. Remove bowl from water and, with a mixer on high speed, whip egg white mixture until thick, stiff peaks form. Gently fold in nut mixture.

3. Spoon mixture into a pastry bag fitted with a $\frac{1}{2}$-inch plain tip and, with the tip almost touching the parchment, pipe into flat, 2-inch circles about $\frac{1}{8}$ inch thick, 1 inch apart, on two cooking parchment–lined 12- by 15-inch baking sheets.

4. Bake cookies in a 300° regular or convection oven until tops are shiny and dry and edges are cracked, about 15 minutes. Cool completely on baking sheets (about 1¼ hours), then remove cookies by gently lifting them up and peeling the parchment paper away from the bottoms.

5. Spread the flat side of each of half the cookies with about 1 teaspoon chocolate ganache. Top each with a second cookie, flat side toward filling.

Per sandwich cookie: 202 cal., 44% (89 cal.) from fat; 4.4 g protein; 9.9 g fat (3.2 g sat.); 27 g carbo (1.2 g fiber); 21 mg sodium; 3.6 mg chol.

Chocolate ganache. In a heatproof bowl set over (but not touching) barely simmering water in a pan, occasionally stir 6 ounces chopped **bittersweet** or semisweet **chocolate**, 2 tablespoons **whipping cream**, 1 tablespoon **corn syrup**, and 1 tablespoon **butter** until chocolate is melted and mixture is smooth. Remove from heat and let cool until thick but not firm, about 15 minutes. Makes about 1¼ cups.

Mint Chippers

PREP AND COOK TIME: About 40 minutes, plus at least 30 minutes to chill
NOTES: Store cookies airtight at room temperature up to 3 days; freeze to store longer.

MAKES: About 30 cookies

  1 cup (½ lb.) **butter,** at room temperature
1¼ cups **powdered sugar**
  ½ teaspoon **peppermint extract**
  ½ teaspoon **vanilla**
  2 **large egg** whites
  2 cups **all-purpose flour**
  ¼ teaspoon **salt**
  ⅔ cup **miniature chocolate chips** or 4 ounces bittersweet chocolate, chopped

1. In a bowl, with a mixer on high speed, beat butter, powdered sugar, peppermint extract, and vanilla until well blended. Beat in egg whites until incorporated. Reduce speed and mix in flour, salt, and chocolate chips. Cover bowl with plastic wrap and chill until dough is firm but pliable, about 30 minutes.

2. With powdered sugar–dusted hands, shape dough into 1½-inch balls, flattening each slightly between your palms to about 2½ inches wide. Place 1 inch apart on buttered 12- by 15-inch baking sheets.

3. Bake in a 300° regular or convection oven until cookies feel firm to touch and are barely beginning to turn golden on the edges, 10 to 12 minutes. If baking more than one sheet at a time in one oven, switch positions halfway through baking. Transfer cookies to racks to cool completely.

Per cookie: 128 cal., 53% (68 cal.) from fat; 1.3 g protein; 7.6 g fat (4.7 g sat.); 14 g carbo (0.4 g fiber); 88 mg sodium; 17 mg chol.

Chocolate Thumbprints

PREP AND COOK TIME: About 1 hour, plus at least 1 hour to stand and chill
NOTES: Turbinado sugar is a light golden brown, large-crystal sugar, sometimes labeled "raw sugar"

Reaping the rewards of the exchange: bring one kind of cookie, take home a collection.

or "Demerara sugar." It's available in some well-stocked supermarkets, at natural-foods stores, and by mail-order through the Baker's Catalogue: www. kingarthurflour.com or (800) 827-6836. If you can't find it, substitute additional granulated sugar.

These cookies are best the day they are filled, but you can make both the cookies and the filling up to 3 days ahead. Store cookies airtight at room temperature; chill ganache airtight. Melt ganache over hot water and cool (as described in recipe, left) before using.

MAKES: About 50 cookies

  1 cup (½ lb.) **butter,** at room temperature
  ¼ cup firmly packed **brown sugar**
  ½ cup **granulated sugar**
  2 **large egg** yolks
  1 teaspoon **vanilla**
  2 cups **all-purpose flour**
  ½ teaspoon **baking powder**
  ¼ teaspoon **salt**
      About ⅓ cup **turbinado sugar** (see notes)
      Chocolate ganache (recipe at left)

1. In a bowl, with a mixer on high speed, beat butter, brown sugar, and granulated sugar until smooth. Beat in egg yolks and vanilla until well blended, scraping sides of bowl as needed.

2. In a small bowl, mix flour, baking powder, and salt. With mixer on low speed, beat flour mixture into butter mixture until well blended. Cover bowl with plastic wrap and chill until dough is firm but pliable, about 30 minutes.

3. Place about ⅓ cup turbinado sugar in a shallow bowl. Shape dough into 1-inch balls and roll to coat in turbinado sugar. Place 1 inch apart on buttered 12- by 15-inch baking sheets. Press your thumb into the center of each cookie to make a ½-inch-deep imprint.

4. Bake cookies in a 325° regular or convection oven until lightly browned, 10 to 12 minutes. If baking more than one sheet at a time in one oven, switch positions halfway through baking. Transfer cookies to a rack to cool completely (if indentations have disappeared, make them again while cookies are warm).

5. Carefully fill each indentation with about ½ tablespoon chocolate ganache. Let cool until ganache is shiny and firm to the touch, about 1 hour (or chill for about 30 minutes).

Per cookie: 92 cal., 54% (50 cal.) from fat; 0.9 g protein; 5.5 g fat (3.2 g sat.); 10 g carbo (0.2 g fiber); 58 mg sodium; 20 mg chol. ◆

Baby clams show their affinity for garlic in this classic pasta.

occasionally, until barely tender to bite, about 10 minutes.

2. Meanwhile, in a 10- to 12-inch frying pan over medium-high heat, stir garlic in olive oil often until fragrant (do not brown), 1 to 2 minutes. Add wine, clam juice, and reserved liquid from clams and boil until reduced to about 1 cup, 6 to 8 minutes. Add clams and stir occasionally until hot, 1 to 2 minutes.

3. Drain spaghetti. Add to clam sauce along with parsley and chili flakes; mix, and add salt to taste. Divide equally among four wide bowls.

Per serving: 472 cal., 12% (56 cal.) from fat; 31 g protein; 6.2 g fat (0.8 g sat.); 71 g carbo (2.6 g fiber); 223 mg sodium; 49 mg chol.

Winter Greens with Olive Vinaigrette

PREP: About 10 minutes

NOTES: Prepared olive tapenade is a convenient way to add depth of flavor to a simple salad. Purchase it at many well-stocked supermarkets and delis, or substitute 2 tablespoons minced black olives, 1 tablespoon minced shallots, ½ teaspoon minced garlic, and ½ teaspoon Dijon mustard for the tapenade. Use a combination of whatever bitter winter greens you can find in the market, or substitute 1 pound of salad mix.

MAKES: 4 servings

2 tablespoons **balsamic vinegar**

2 tablespoons **prepared black olive tapenade** (see notes)

1 tablespoon **extra-virgin olive oil**

1 pound **bitter winter greens,** such as radicchio, arugula, escarole, and frisée (see notes), rinsed and crisped

Salt and **pepper**

In a large bowl, whisk vinegar, tapenade, and olive oil until well blended. Add greens and mix to coat. Add salt and pepper to taste.

Per serving: 80 cal., 68% (54 cal.) from fat; 1.6 g protein; 6 g fat (0.6 g sat.); 5.3 g carbo (1 g fiber); 220 mg sodium; 0 mg chol. ◆

Clam up

Bold flavors team up for an easy weeknight dinner

By Charity Ferreira

■ Spaghetti with clams is one of those deceptively simple dishes that is far more satisfying than its few straightforward ingredients would imply. Canned whole baby clams are more tender than the canned chopped variety, and they're in excellent company when combined with a good olive oil, noodles cooked just enough to maintain their bite, and lots of garlic and parsley. Toss peppery greens with a vinaigrette made from purchased tapenade, and slice pears for dessert.

Clam pasta dinner

Winter Greens with Olive Vinaigrette

Spaghetti with White Clam Sauce

Breadsticks

Ripe pears

Spaghetti with White Clam Sauce

PREP AND COOK TIME: About 30 minutes

MAKES: 4 servings

12 ounces **dried spaghetti**

3 tablespoons pressed or minced **garlic**

1 tablespoon **olive oil**

½ cup **dry white wine**

1 bottle (8 oz.) **clam juice**

2 cans (10 oz. each) **baby clams,** drained (reserve liquid)

½ cup chopped **parsley**

½ teaspoon **hot chili flakes**

Salt

1. In a 5- to 6-quart pan over high heat, bring about 4 quarts water to a boil. Add spaghetti and cook, stirring

JAMES CARRIER; FOOD STYLING: KAREN SHINTO

Beef tenderloin marinated in molasses and bourbon has an earthy sweetness to match sweet potato gratin.

FOOD STYLING: SUSAN DEVATY (2)

At home on the range

Colorado's Vista Verde Ranch inspires a high-country feast for your holiday table

Recipes by Linda Lau Anusasananan • Food photographs by James Carrier

Vista Verde, a guest ranch near Steamboat Springs high in the Colorado Rockies, is an irresistible place to hole up over the holidays. Although guests can enjoy cross-country skiing and snowshoeing, horseback riding and sleigh rides, some might just decide to come for the food. Jonathon Gillespie, the ranch's executive chef for the past five years, has an endless supply of menus up his sleeve—and he's happy to share his ideas. He offers cooking seminars where you can learn to make some of the ranch's most popular dishes, such as beef tenderloin marinated in molasses and bourbon. It makes the perfect centerpiece for this Christmas feast from Vista Verde Ranch. — *Amy McConnell*

Ranch Christmas Dinner

Mixed Greens with Fuji Apples and Walnut Vinaigrette

Seeded Rolls and Butter

Molasses-Bourbon Beef Tenderloin

Sweet Potato–Chipotle Gratin

Green Beans with Mushrooms

Cabernet Sauvignon or Zinfandel

Cholly's World-Famous Gingerbread Cake with Crème Anglaise

Coffee or Tea

Mixed Greens with Fuji Apples and Walnut Vinaigrette

PREP AND COOK TIME: About 30 minute

NOTES: Chef Gillespie overlaps the apple slices like wings on top of each serving. We've mixed in the apple slices for an easier presentation. I desired, toast the nuts (step 1) up to day ahead; store airtight.

MAKES: 8 to 10 servings

- ¾ cup chopped **walnuts**
- ⅓ cup **walnut** or salad **oil**
- ¼ cup **cider vinegar**
- 3 tablespoons minced **shallots**
- 1 clove **garlic,** peeled and minced
- 1 teaspoon **Dijon mustard**
- 1 teaspoon **raw** or firmly packed brown **sugar**
- 2 tablespoons thinly sliced **fresh chives**

  Salt and **pepper**
- 2 **Fuji** or other sweet **apples** (8 oz. each)
- ¾ cup thinly slivered **red onion,** rinsed

6 quarts **mixed baby greens** (1 lb.), rinsed and crisped

8 ounces **Maytag** or other **blue cheese,** crumbled

1. In an 8- to 10-inch frying pan over medium heat, stir walnuts often until lightly browned, 6 to 7 minutes. Remove from heat and let cool.

2. In a large bowl, whisk together oil, vinegar, shallots, garlic, mustard, sugar, and 2 tablespoons of the toasted walnuts. Stir in chives and salt and pepper to taste.

3. Rinse apples; quarter, core, and thinly slice lengthwise. Add apples, red onion, and mixed baby greens to dressing and mix to coat. Add half the cheese and mix gently. Mound salad equally on 8 to 10 plates. Sprinkle with remaining cheese and toasted walnuts. Add more salt and pepper to taste.

Per serving: 245 cal., 70% (171 cal.) from fat; 7 g protein; 19 g fat (5.4 g sat.); 13 g carbo (2.1 g fiber); 337 mg sodium; 17 mg chol.

Molasses-Bourbon Beef Tenderloin

PREP AND COOK TIME: About 1 hour, plus at least 4 hours to marinate

MAKES: 8 to 10 servings

1½ cups **light** or dark **molasses**

6 tablespoons **balsamic vinegar**

¼ cup **bourbon** or dry red wine

About 1½ tablespoons fresh-ground **pepper**

1 tablespoon minced **garlic**

1½ tablespoons minced **shallot**

1½ teaspoons minced **fresh ginger**

½ teaspoon **dried thyme**

½ teaspoon **hot chili flakes**

1 **center-cut beef tenderloin** (3½ to 4 lb.)

Parsley sprigs

Salt

1. In a large baking dish or roasting pan, mix molasses, vinegar, bourbon, pepper, garlic, shallot, ginger, thyme, and chili flakes. Trim any excess fat from tenderloin and discard. Rinse meat and pat dry. Set in marinade and turn to coat. Cover dish and chill, turning meat occasionally, at least 4 hours or up to 1 day.

2. Lift beef from marinade; discard marinade (or bring to a boil, cool,

Timeline

☐ **Up to 2 days ahead:** Make gingerbread and crème anglaise.

☐ **Up to 1 day ahead:** Marinate meat. Cook mushrooms. Toast nuts for salad.

☐ **About 1½ hours before serving:** Assemble sweet potato gratin.

☐ **About 1 hour before serving:** Bake sweet potato gratin and beef.

☐ **About 15 minutes before serving:** Heat water and cook beans; reheat mushrooms. Assemble salad.

☐ **Just before serving:** Assemble and garnish dessert.

DAVID ZAITZ

cover, and freeze for another use). If tenderloin is uneven, tie with cotton string where needed to make evenly thick. Set on a rack in a foil-lined 12- by 15-inch roasting or baking pan.

3. Bake in 400° regular or convection oven until a thermometer inserted in center of thickest part registers 130° to 135° for rare, 40 to 50 minutes. Let rest in a warm place at least 5, or up to 15, minutes.

4. Remove strings. Transfer meat to a platter and garnish with parsley sprigs.

To serve, slice ¼ to 1 inch thick. Add salt and more pepper to taste.

Per serving: 264 cal., 34% (90 cal.) from fat; 24 g protein; 10 g fat (3.8 g sat.); 18 g carbo (0.1 g fiber); 63 mg sodium; 73 mg chol.

Sweet Potato–Chipotle Gratin

PREP AND COOK TIME: About 1½ hours

NOTES: Garnet and Jewel sweet potatoes have moist, dark orange flesh; they are often labeled yams in grocery stores. If you use the drier yellow- or white-fleshed sweet potatoes, increase the cream used in step 1 to 2 cups and cover dish tightly before baking in step 3; uncover after 40 minutes of baking. You may assemble the gratin through step 2 up to ½ hour before baking. If you have only one oven, bake in same oven with beef.

MAKES: 8 to 10 servings

½ cup **milk**

2 **canned chipotle chilies** (about 1 tablespoon, including sauce on chilies)

About ½ teaspoon **salt**

1½ to 2 cups **whipping cream** (see notes)

3½ pounds **Garnet,** Jewel, or other **sweet potatoes** (see notes)

1. In a blender, whirl milk, chilies, and ½ teaspoon salt until smoothly blended. Stir in cream. Reserve ⅓ cup of the cream mixture.

2. Peel and rinse sweet potatoes; cut crosswise into ¼-inch-thick slices. In a shallow 2½- to 3-quart casserole, arrange about a third of the sweet potatoes in an even layer, overlapping slices; evenly drizzle with about a third of the remaining cream mixture. Repeat to make two more layers of the sweet potatoes and cream.

3. Bake (covered, if using drier, pale-fleshed sweet potatoes; see notes) in a 400° regular or convection oven for 40 minutes. Uncover, if covered, and drizzle top evenly with about 3 tablespoons of the reserved cream mixture. Continue baking, basting occasionally with reserved cream mixture or pan juices, until potatoes are tender when pierced and top of gratin is browned, 15 to 25 minutes longer. Let stand about 5 minutes before serving. Scoop out portions with a large spoon.

Per serving: 275 cal., 39% (108 cal.) from fat; 3.3 g protein; 12 g fat (7.2 g sat.); 40 g carbo (5.6 g fiber); 159 mg sodium; 42 mg chol.

Green Beans with Mushrooms

PREP AND COOK TIME: About 30 minutes

NOTES: You can prepare mushrooms through step 2 up to 1 day ahead; cool, cover, and chill. To reheat, stir over medium heat.

MAKES: 8 to 10 servings

- 12 ounces **chanterelle,** oyster, or common **mushrooms**
- 3 tablespoons **butter**

  Salt and **pepper**
- 2 pounds **green beans,** rinsed

1. Trim off and discard tough or discolored stem ends of mushrooms and any bruised spots or blemishes. If using chanterelles, submerge mushrooms in cool water and gently agitate with your hands to loosen any dirt. Drain, rinse thoroughly under running water, and gently pat dry with a towel. If using oyster or common mushrooms, rinse well and drain. Cut mushrooms into bite-size pieces or quarter lengthwise.

2. In a 10- to 12-inch frying pan over high heat, melt 2 tablespoons butter. Add mushrooms and stir often until liquid is evaporated and mushrooms are browned, 6 to 10 minutes. Add salt and pepper to taste.

3. In a 5- to 6-quart pan over high heat, bring 2½ to 3 quarts water to a boil. Trim off stem ends from beans, and remove any strings. Add beans to water and cook until barely tender to bite, 5 to 8 minutes. Drain. Return drained beans to pan with remaining tablespoon butter; mix to coat and add salt and pepper to taste. Pour green beans onto a platter and spoon mushrooms on top.

Per serving: 67 cal., 49% (33 cal.) from fat; 2.4 g protein; 3.7 g fat (2.2 g sat.); 8.1 g carbo (2.1 g fiber); 42 mg sodium; 9.3 mg chol.

Cholly's World-Famous Gingerbread Cake

PREP AND COOK TIME: About 1¼ hours, plus at least 1¼ hours to cool

NOTES: This dark, moist cake is a favorite of guests at the ranch, where it's cut into rounds and set on a pool of custard sauce. You can make cake up

Spicy gingerbread with crème anglaise ends Christmas dinner on a homey note.

to 2 days ahead; cool, cover, and store airtight.

MAKES: 9 or 10 servings

- 1 cup **dark molasses**
- 1 teaspoon **baking soda**
- 2½ cups **all-purpose flour**
- 1 tablespoon **baking powder**
- 1½ teaspoons **ground cinnamon**
- 1 teaspoon **ground ginger**
- ½ teaspoon **salt**
- ⅛ teaspoon **ground cloves**
- ½ cup (¼ lb.) **butter,** at room temperature
- 1 cup firmly packed **brown sugar**
- 2 **large eggs**

  Crème anglaise (recipe follows)

  Unsweetened cocoa and/or **powdered sugar** (optional)

  Fresh mint sprigs (optional), rinsed

1. In a 2- to 3-quart pan over high heat, bring 1 cup water to a boil. Remove from heat and stir in molasses and baking soda. After mixture stops foaming, stir in ½ cup cold water; let cool to room temperature, stirring often, about 10 minutes.

2. In a small bowl, whisk together flour, baking powder, cinnamon, ginger, salt, and cloves.

3. In a large bowl, with an electric mixer on high speed, beat butter and brown sugar until well blended. Beat in eggs until blended. Reduce speed to medium-low. Add flour and molasses mixtures alternately until incorporated, then beat on high speed until well blended. Pour into a buttered and floured 9-inch square pan.

4. Bake in a 325° regular or convection oven until a toothpick inserted in center of thickest part comes out clean, 45 to 50 minutes. Let cool in pan on a rack at least 1¼ hours.

5. Pour about ¼ cup crème anglaise onto each plate. Cut cake into pieces (see notes) and set them in sauce on plates. If desired, lightly sift cocoa and powdered sugar over each plate and garnish with a mint sprig. Offer remaining crème anglaise to add to taste.

Per serving: 378 cal., 26% (99 cal.) from fat; 4.7 g protein; 11 g fat (6.3 g sat.); 67 g carbo (0.9 g fiber); 526 mg sodium; 68 mg chol.

Crème Anglaise

PREP AND COOK TIME: About 30 minutes

NOTES: You can make this sauce up to 2 days ahead; cover and chill.

MAKES: About 3¾ cups

- 1 quart **milk**
- ⅔ cup **sugar**
- 8 **large egg** yolks, lightly beaten
- 2 teaspoons **vanilla**

1. In a 3- to 4-quart pan over medium heat, stir milk and sugar often until mixture begins to bubble around edges of pan, 10 to 12 minutes. Remove from heat.

2. Whisk about ½ cup of the hot milk mixture into egg yolks, then pour mixture into pan and whisk to blend. Stir with a flexible spatula over medium-low heat until custard coats the spatula in a smooth, velvety layer, 10 to 14 minutes. Remove from heat and pour through a fine strainer set over a bowl. Set bowl in a container of ice water and stir often until cool. Stir in vanilla. Serve cool or cold.

Per ¼ cup: 108 cal., 41% (44 cal.) from fat; 3.6 g protein; 4.9 g fat (2.2 g sat.); 12 g carbo (0 g fiber); 36 mg sodium; 123 mg chol. ◆

Briny oysters, spicy mignonette, and lemony martinis make a posh pre-dinner lineup.

Cocktail hour

Entertain in style with the ice-cold tang of martinis and oysters

By Paula Freschet • Photographs by James Carrier

Lately, it seems as if every chic restaurant offers its own house cocktail, together with that quintessential sophisticated appetizer, oysters on the half-shell. But who wants to battle the crowds at the hippest oyster bar in town? Move the pre-dinner scene to your home—all you need is one cocktail as the specialty of the house, a small group of friends, and a whole lot of ice. Our sweet-tart lemon martini comes with a twist, as do our oysters, which get a little zip from an innovative tangerine-chili mignonette. Together, they're the perfect starter for a glamorous night on the town—or *chez vous.*

Oysters on the Half-Shell with Tangerine-Chili Mignonette

PREP TIME: About 10 minutes

NOTES: You can make the mignonette up to 3 days ahead; cover airtight and chill. Have the oysters shucked at the market up to 1 day ahead; set, cup side up, on a rimmed tray; cover and chill.

MAKES: 24 oysters and ½ cup sauce; 8 servings

- 2 teaspoons grated **tangerine** peel
- ⅓ cup **tangerine juice**
- 3 tablespoons **rice vinegar**
- 1 **fresh red jalapeño chili** (about ½ oz.), rinsed, stemmed, seeded, and minced
- 1 tablespoon minced **shallot**
- ⅛ teaspoon **pepper**
- 2 dozen **shucked oysters on the half-shell** (see notes)

1. In a small bowl, mix tangerine peel and juice, vinegar, chili, shallot, and pepper.

2. Nest the oysters in crushed ice on a rimmed tray. Place bowl of tangerine-chili mignonette with oysters on the tray. To eat, spoon a little sauce onto each oyster.

Per serving: 36 cal., 28% (9.9 cal.) from fat; 3.1 g protein; 1.1 g fat (0.3 g sat.); 3.2 g carbo (0 g fiber); 48 mg sodium; 23 mg chol.

Frosty Lemon Martini

PREP TIME: About 10 minutes

NOTES: Look for lemon-flavored vodka and lemon-flavored liqueur (such as the Italian *liquore di limoni*) in well-stocked supermarkets, liquor stores, and wine shops. For extra frostiness, place sugar-rimmed martini glasses in the refrigerator for at least 10 minutes or in the freezer for 7 to 8 minutes.

MAKES: 2 servings

- 1 tablespoon **sugar**
  Lemon wedge
- 1 cup **crushed ice**
- 6 tablespoons chilled **lemon-flavored vodka** (3 oz.; see notes)
- 2 tablespoons chilled **lemon-flavored liqueur** (1 oz.; see notes)
- 4 teaspoons **lemon juice**
- 2 thin strips (3 in. long) **lemon peel** (yellow part only)

1. Pour sugar onto a small, rimmed plate. Rub rims of two martini glasses with lemon wedge to moisten, then dip rims into sugar to coat (see notes).

2. Place ice in a cocktail shaker. Add vodka, liqueur, and lemon juice. Shake until mixture is very cold, about 10 seconds. Strain into glasses. Garnish each with a twist of lemon peel.

Per serving: 162 cal., 0% (0 cal.) from fat; 0 g protein; 0 g fat; 11 g carbo (0.1 g fiber); 2.6 mg sodium; 0 mg chol. ◆

Market menu

How to put a fresh spin on a buy-and-serve holiday party

By Linda Lau Anusasananan

Sandwiches go Asian with this buffet: fill steamed buns with barbecued pork, roast duck, or chicken, and nibble on pickled vegetables, spring rolls, and roasted nuts.

Throwing a holiday party always sounds like fun—until you're whipping up the last batch of homemade mini-quiches and you realize that it's a labor of love, with the emphasis on *labor*. But putting together an impressive spread can be much simpler than it looks. The diversity of the West means that a great variety of delicious ethnic foods are widely available—often ready-made—and can be combined to make an easy and delicious menu.

Ethnic markets are a great place to start; if you live near the San Gabriel Valley's Little Beijing, Seattle's International District, or San Francisco's Mission District, you can find an array of delicacies just by heading out to the corner store. Explore those closest to you for theme ideas; you might find Indian, Mexican, Russian, or Vietnamese markets that offer delicious party food. But even if these resources aren't available to you, you may be surprised by the choices at any supermarket. We shopped at a large Asian grocery store to put together a lavish Chinese buffet; for an Italian table, we found great options at our local supermarket. Whatever you choose, you'll spend more time at the store than at the stove—which means that when the party rolls around, a good time can truly be had by all.

Chinese sandwich buffet

For an Asian spread, offer barbecued pork and roast duck as the main meats, with buns or pancakes to hold the sandwich fillings. (If you're shopping at a supermarket, buy roast chicken or pork tenderloin and serve the meats sliced, with hoisin sauce and green onions.) Set out a selection of snack foods and dim sum items (purchase them frozen or buy them from a local restaurant) and fresh vegetables. Accompany the menu with imported Asian beer, rice wine or sake, and tea, and finish with cookies or candy. Here are some choices to seek out—and where in the store to find them.

SNACK ITEMS
- **On the shelf:** Wasabi peas, seaweed rice crackers, roasted watermelon seeds, roasted mixed nuts, and fried peanuts

VEGETABLES
- **In the refrigerator case:** Fresh soybeans *(edamame),* kim chee, pickled ginger, and pickled daikon
- **At the deli counter:** Cantonese pickled vegetables, seaweed salad, and soybean–mustard green salad
- **On the shelf:** Canned assorted pickled vegetables and baby corn

BREADS
- **At the deli counter or in the freezer:** Sesame buns *(shao bing),* steamed rolls, green onion cakes, steamed green onion knots, and Mandarin pancakes (sometimes sold as spring roll wrappers; choose those with a crêpelike texture)

MEATS
- **In the refrigerator case:** Fried tofu puffs (drizzle with sweet hot chili sauce or peanut sauce)
- **At the deli counter:** Barbecued pork *(cha siu),* ribs, roast duck, soy sauce chicken, roast pork, and barbecued chicken wings
- **On the shelf:** Sweet dried beef and pork (jerky) and Chinese sausages (may be found in the refrigerator case)

SAUCES
- **On the shelf:** Hoisin, satay, ponzu, teriyaki, barbecue, plum, and peanut sauce; chili sauces and pastes; miso and sesame dressings

DUMPLINGS

- **At the deli counter or in the freezer:** Potstickers or *gyoza,* wontons, spring rolls, steamed meat- or vegetable-filled buns, and steamed seafood and meat dumplings

SWEETS

- **In the freezer:** *Mochi* ice cream balls; coconut, green tea, or mango ice cream
- **On the shelf or at the bakery counter:** Almond cookies, cookie rolls, sponge cakes, sesame crunch or peanut crunch candy, fortune cookies, candied ginger, coconut, and winter melon

Italian antipasto party

Assemble a selection of meats, cheeses, marinated vegetables, and purchased salads for an Italian appetizer party. Dress up a platter of fresh vegetables with a shallow dish of extra-virgin olive oil and balsamic vinegar seasoned with salt and pepper. Accompany the whole menu with wine and Italian sodas—flavored syrups poured into club soda over ice. To end the evening, serve *affogato,* a simple but sophisticated Italian dessert in which hot espresso is poured over vanilla gelato just before serving. Or offer gelato with cookies or cake. Italian foods are readily available in most supermarkets; seek out Italian markets for an even greater selection. Here's what to look for.

SNACK ITEMS

- **At the deli counter or in the freezer:** Bruschetta, mini-pizzas, and large pizzas (cut into bite-size pieces)
- **At the deli counter or on the shelf:** Olives and anchovies

VEGETABLES

- **In the produce department:** Fresh fennel, artichokes (steamed), red bell peppers, celery, cherry tomatoes, and zucchini; fresh rosemary or other herbs (for garnish)
- **On the shelf or at the deli counter:** Pickled vegetables *(giardiniera),* marinated mushrooms, marinated artichoke hearts, caponata, roasted red bell peppers, grilled or roasted vegetables, and white bean salad (or buy canned white beans, drain, and gently mix with olive oil, balsamic vinegar, chopped tomatoes, and chopped fresh herbs)

BREADS

- **At the bakery or on the shelf:** Crusty loaves, breadsticks, and focaccia

MEATS AND CHEESES

- **In the refrigerator case:** Pesto-mascarpone torta, mozzarella-prosciutto roll, and cheeses like asiago, bel paese, gorgonzola, taleggio, provolone, and Parmigiano-Reggiano
- **In the freezer:** Meatballs and frozen cooked, shelled shrimp
- **At the deli counter or in the refrigerator case:** Cured meats like prosciutto, coppa, mortadella, salami, and Italian sausage

SAUCES AND CONDIMENTS

- **On the shelf or in the refrigerator case:** Basil, dried tomato, or artichoke pesto; tapenade; marinara sauce; extra-virgin olive oil; and balsamic vinegar

SWEETS

- **In the bakery, refrigerator case, or freezer:** Tiramisu, polenta cake, cannoli, or *crostata*
- **In the freezer:** Gelato
- **On the shelf:** Biscotti and other cookies, panettone, panforte (fruitcake-like confection), assorted chocolates, and torrone (nougat candy)

Style and substance

Believe it or not, a store-bought party can look and taste just as good as a feast you slaved over for hours—or even better, since you'll have that much more time and energy to direct toward planning your menu and putting together a pretty table. Our tips for assembling a satisfying, appealing spread:

- **For a dinnertime party** with substantial options for grazing, provide about 1 pound of meat, poultry, or fish for every four guests. (If you're serving bone-in items such as ribs or Peking duck, allot 1 pound for every two guests.) Balance the meat with bread or other starches and plenty of crudités, salad, or marinated vegetables; round out the menu with hors d'oeuvres, cheeses, and dessert.

- **Look for a colorful variety of foods;** if most of your hors d'oeuvres are wrapped in pastry, for instance, choose bright vegetables for a crudités platter, or set out a beautiful bowl or plate of ripe fruit.

- **Remove all food from store containers** and arrange on attractive dishes or platters. Try combining different shapes and colors of tableware; assembled with restraint, an assortment can look beautiful and sophisticated.

- **Garnish platters** with sprigs of fresh herbs (reliable standbys such as parsley and cilantro, or uncommon varieties like *shiso* leaves, variegated sage, or stems of silver thyme), single flowers, or vegetables such as green onions or thinly sliced radishes. ◆

Dockside special: Dungeness crab teams up with fresh fish in a flavorful tangle of angle hair pasta swimming in sherry and butter.

Casual crab

A Mendocino expedition yields fresh, simple Dungeness dishes

By Sara Schneider • Photographs by James Carrier

We set out in search of crab aboard *El Patron,* which nosed away from the Rumblefish dock in Noyo Fishing Center, then lifted its prow into the white mist to plow past the black cliffs of Northern California's Mendocino coast. Mountainous swells and bitter wind questioned our judgment on this midwinter day. But a rainbow broke through the mist in favor of the mission. Temporarily distracted by a cry of "Pod off the port side!" we followed some whales, and the rainbow followed us. Crab isn't an urgent matter, after all; it's just part of the bigger rhythm here.

Finally, though, we pulled some crab pots, only to study their low-tech mechanisms for allowing undersize specimens and unwanted critters to escape—safeguards to help sustain the stock and surrounding marine life. Clearly it wasn't a great year for harvesting Dungeness, but there was hope: crabbers were spotting large numbers of "teenagers," which would soon be big enough to harvest. The cycle goes up and down, part of that natural rhythm.

In the end, we found the crab we were looking for—back on the dock, where Capt'n Bobino (Pete Huckins, in other settings), local seafood distributor, crab shack proprietor, and general character, took a machete to some crustaceans pulled in by savvier crabbers than we. He dropped them into a cast-iron skillet with olive oil and garlic, doused them with sherry and butter, and gussied them up with vermicelli. Even the baguettes went into the pot. Not a pretty dish, but the sauce dripping off our elbows as we dipped into it testified to the pleasure of casual crab. Here's our version of his recipe, along with those for a couple of other Dungeness finds.

Crab tips

- **As a shortcut** to purchasing live crabs and cooking and cleaning them at home, buy cooked crabs and have them cleaned and cracked at the market.
- **Crack crab**—or have it cracked—before adding to warm or cold sauces, so flavors can seep under the shell.
- **Provide crab crackers or nutcrackers** to break shells further, containers to hold discarded shells, and damp towels or bowls of water to clean messy hands.

Capt'n Bobino's Fisherman-style Crab

PREP AND COOK TIME: About 35 minutes
NOTES: Huckins uses live crabs in this dish: he cuts each in half lengthwise, then between the legs, into pieces that each include part of the body; cleans the crab; and then cracks the pieces slightly with a mallet or hammer. For less daring cooks, we start with cooked crabs. But if you want the freshest possible flavor, ask your seafood merchant to cut, clean, and crack the live crabs as Huckins does; add them after sautéing the garlic in step 3 and stir often for about 10 minutes before adding the fish.

Huckins also mixes the pasta—and even the baguette slices—into the pan once the crab and fish are cooked, and he serves the dish straight from there. Follow suit for a lively party, letting everyone dip into the common pot.
MAKES: 4 to 6 servings

- 2 **cooked Dungeness crabs** (about 2 lb. each), cleaned and cracked (see notes)
- 1 pound **boned, skinned, firm white-fleshed fish** such as halibut
- ¾ cup (⅜ lb.) **butter**
- ¼ cup **olive oil**
- ¼ cup minced **garlic**
- 1 cup **dry sherry** or dry white wine
- ⅓ cup **lemon juice**
- ½ cup chopped **parsley**
  Salt and **pepper**
- 8 ounces **dried angel hair pasta**
  Lemon wedges
- 1 **baguette** (about 8 oz.), sliced

1. In a 5- to 6-quart pan over high heat, bring 4 quarts water to a boil.
2. Rinse crabs and fish and pat dry; cut fish into 1- to 1½-inch pieces.

3. Add butter and olive oil to a 12-inch frying pan (with at least 2½-in. sides) or 14-inch wok over medium-high heat; when butter is melted, add garlic and stir just until fragrant, 1 to 2 minutes. Add fish and turn pieces occasionally until beginning to brown, 2 to 3 minutes.

4. Pour in sherry and lemon juice, then gently add crabs and sprinkle with parsley; cover and simmer until crabs are hot and fish is opaque but still moist-looking in the center (cut to test), about 5 to 6 minutes. Add salt and pepper to taste.

5. Meanwhile, add angel hair pasta to boiling water; cook, stirring occasionally, until barely tender to bite, 3 to 4 minutes. Drain pasta well and spread in the bottom of a wide serving bowl.

6. Pour crab mixture over pasta and garnish with lemon wedges. Serve with baguette slices to sop up the sauce.

Per serving: 751 cal., 44% (333 cal.) from fat; 39 g protein; 37 g fat (16 g sat.); 53 g carbo (2.3 g fiber); 723 mg sodium; 160 mg chol.

Mendo Crab Cakes

PREP AND COOK TIME: About 45 minutes

NOTES: The point of a crab cake is pure crab flavor, not filler, according to Nicholas Petti, chef-owner of Mendo Bistro in Fort Bragg. He won the 2002 Mendocino Crab & Wine Days Crabcake Cookoff with these simple cakes, based on that theory. The winning wine with crab at the competition, Handley Cellars' 2000 Sauvignon Blanc, is perfect with them.

As a shortcut for the tarragon aioli— or if you're concerned about possible

Crab cakes and a dollop of aioli top a four-ingredient cabbage salad.

bacteria in raw eggs—substitute 1½ cups mayonnaise mixed with ¼ cup chopped fresh tarragon, 1½ to 2 tablespoons minced garlic, 2 tablespoons lemon juice, and hot sauce and salt to taste. Start the cabbage salad first, then make the aioli and crab cakes.

MAKES: 8 first-course or 4 main-dish servings

- 1 pound **shelled cooked crab** (about 2¾ cups)
- 1¾ cups **panko** (Japanese dried bread crumbs) or other dried bread crumbs
- ½ cup finely chopped **green onions** (including green tops)
  Tarragon aioli (recipe follows; see notes)
  About ½ cup **salad oil**
  Champagne cabbage salad (recipe follows)

1. Sort through crab; remove and discard any bits of shell. In a bowl, combine crab, ¾ cup panko, and green onions. Gently mix in ½ cup tarragon aioli just until mixture holds together.

2. Press mixture firmly into eight equal patties about 3 inches wide; set slightly apart on a sheet of waxed paper or foil. Pour remaining 1 cup panko into a shallow bowl.

3. Pour ⅓ cup oil into a 10- to 12-inch frying pan over medium-high heat. When hot, set each crab cake in panko, then, using a slotted spatula, turn, pressing gently to coat. Transfer crab cakes to pan, working in small batches. Cook until golden brown on the bottom, 3 to 4 minutes; turn gently and cook until browned on the other side and hot in the middle, 3 to 4 minutes longer. Transfer cakes as cooked, in a single layer, to a 12- by 15-inch baking sheet in a 200° oven and add remaining cakes to pan, adding more oil as necessary to brown on both sides. Discard any remaining panko.

4. Divide champagne cabbage salad evenly among plates. Set crab cakes on salad, add a dollop of tarragon aioli, and serve immediately, passing remaining aioli to add to taste.

Per crab cake: 138 cal., 31% (43 cal.) from fat; 13 g protein; 4.8 g fat (0.6 g sat.); 9.2 g carbo (0.6 g fiber); 197 mg sodium; 57 mg chol.

Tarragon aioli. Combine 2 **large egg yolks,** 3 peeled cloves **garlic,** ⅓ cup **lemon juice,** and ½ teaspoon **salt** in a food processor or blender; whirl until mixture is smooth. With machine running, gradually pour in 1 cup **salad oil** (such as peanut) and ½ cup **extra-virgin olive oil** (or use all olive oil) in

a slow, steady stream, whirling until mixture is thick and smooth, 1 to 1½ minutes. Stir in ¼ cup chopped **fresh tarragon,** ¼ to ½ teaspoon **hot sauce,** and more lemon juice and salt to taste. Makes about 1⅔ cups.

Per tablespoon: 117 cal., 100% (117 cal.) from fat; 0.3 g protein; 13 g fat (1.8 g sat.); 0.4 g carbo (0 g fiber); 47 mg sodium; 16 mg chol.

Champagne cabbage salad. In a large bowl, mix 3 quarts **finely shredded cabbage** (about 1¼ lb.) with 1½ teaspoons **salt;** let stand 30 minutes. Mix with ⅓ cup finely chopped **fresh chives** (about 1 bunch) and ¼ cup **champagne vinegar.** Makes 1½ quarts.

Per ¾ cup: 19 cal., 5% (0.9 cal.) from fat; 0.9 g protein; 0.1 g fat (0 g sat.); 4.1 g carbo (1.8 g fiber); 449 mg sodium; 0 mg chol.

Cracked Crab Vinaigrette

PREP TIME: About 30 minutes, plus at least 2 hours to chill

NOTES: This easy party appetizer or cool, festive dinner-party entrée— almost a cracked-crab salad—comes from Peter Selaya of the New Moon Cafe in Nevada City, California. Serve it with good sourdough bread.

MAKES: 8 to 12 appetizer or 4 to 6 main-dish servings

- 4 **cooked Dungeness crabs** (about 2 lb. each), cleaned and cracked
- 1 cup **extra-virgin olive oil**
- ½ cup **red wine vinegar**
- ¼ cup **lemon juice**
- 1 cup thinly sliced **green onions** (about 1 bunch, including tops)
- ½ cup chopped **parsley**
- 2 tablespoons minced **garlic**
- 2 teaspoons *each* chopped **fresh basil, oregano,** and **thyme** leaves
- ½ teaspoon **Worcestershire**
- 2 cups thinly sliced **celery**
  Salt
  Coarse-ground **black pepper**

1. Rinse crabs under cool running water to remove any bits of loose shell; pat dry and put in a large bowl.

2. In a medium bowl, mix olive oil, vinegar, lemon juice, green onions, parsley, garlic, basil, oregano, thyme, and Worcestershire. Stir in celery and add salt and pepper to taste.

3. Pour vinaigrette over crabs and mix gently to coat. Cover and chill at least 2 hours or up to 1 day, gently mixing once or twice.

Per appetizer serving: 246 cal., 73% (180 cal.) from fat; 15 g protein; 20 g fat (2.8 g sat.); 2.8 g carbo (0.7 g fiber); 225 mg sodium; 72 mg chol. ◆

Polenta makes the meal

Italian-style cornmeal is great at lunch, dinner—or breakfast

By Kate Washington • Photographs by James Carrier

Don't tell anyone, but polenta is hardly more than plain old cornmeal mush. That said, it has a lot to recommend itself: it's versatile, easy to make, and delicious. Alone or topped with a simple sauce, polenta seems as warm and comforting as your oldest sweater. But drizzle it with truffle oil or turn it into crispy fries, and it dresses up for all occasions. What's more, contrary to myth, there's no need to stir it constantly. From breakfast to dinner, polenta makes life deliciously easy.

Basic Polenta

PREP/COOK TIME: 25 to 45 minutes

NOTES: When buying polenta, look for Italian brands or cornmeal labeled "polenta"; avoid instant (we found it unpleasantly gluey; when we accidentally dropped a bit, it bounced). Polenta's cooking time depends on the coarseness of its grind and your preference. In our tests, 20 minutes of cooking produced creamy polenta with tender, separate grains; after 40 minutes, the result was thicker, with less distinct grains.

MAKES: About 4 cups; 4 servings

- 1 cup **polenta** (see notes)
- About ½ teaspoon **salt**
- 1 tablespoon **butter** (optional)

1. In a 2½- to 3-quart pan over high heat, bring 4 cups water to a boil. Reduce heat so that liquid barely boils.

2. Stirring constantly with a wooden spoon, pour in polenta in a slow, thin stream, pausing occasionally and stirring to break up any lumps. Stir in ½ teaspoon salt.

3. Reduce heat and simmer, stirring often, until polenta is thick and creamy to bite and pulls away slightly from sides of pan when stirred, 20 to 40 minutes (see notes); adjust heat as necessary to maintain a simmer (if it's too high, bubbles may "spit" globs of hot polenta out of the pan). Stir in butter, if desired, and add more salt to taste.

Per serving: 250 cal., 1.8% (4.5 cal.) from fat; 6 g protein; 0.5 g fat (0 g sat.); 54 g carbo (7 g fiber); 290 mg sodium; 0 mg chol.

Polenta with Pancetta and Sage

PREP AND COOK TIME: 40 to 50 minutes

NOTES: Pancetta is available in many supermarkets and at Italian groceries. We like this aromatic, hearty polenta with roast game birds or chicken. Garnish the polenta with sprigs of fresh sage or with fried sage leaves (see page 265).

MAKES: About 4½ cups; 4 to 6 servings

- ½ cup chopped **pancetta** (3 oz.; see notes) or bacon
- 1 teaspoon **olive oil**
- 1 tablespoon chopped **fresh sage** leaves
- 1 cup **polenta**
- **Salt** and fresh-ground **pepper**

1. In a 2½- to 3-quart pan over medium-high heat, stir pancetta in olive oil until crisp and beginning to brown, about 5 minutes. With a slotted spoon, transfer half the pancetta to paper towels to drain.

2. Add chopped sage to pan and stir until fragrant, about 30 seconds. Add 5 cups water and bring to a boil.

3. Following steps 2 and 3 of basic polenta recipe (above), add polenta (omit salt in step 2) and cook until tender to bite. Add salt and fresh-ground pepper to taste (omit butter).

4. Ladle polenta into bowls and top with reserved pancetta.

Per serving: 252 cal., 33% (83 cal.) from fat; 5.2 g protein; 9.2 g fat (3.1 g sat.); 36 g carbo (4.7 g fiber); 97 mg sodium; 9.5 mg chol.

Creamy Breakfast Polenta

PREP AND COOK TIME: About 45 minutes

NOTES: We like this polenta on a cold morning, topped with jam and crème fraîche (or sour cream) or with butter and maple syrup. Alternatively, you can omit the sugar and serve the delicate polenta as a base for savory dishes like osso buco or a wild mushroom ragoût.

MAKES: About 6 cups; 4 to 6 servings

Follow directions for basic polenta (left), but use only 3 cups water and add 3 cups **low-fat (2%) milk** and 2 tablespoons **sugar** in step 1. Omit butter in step 3. Ladle cooked polenta (with a higher liquid-to-polenta ratio, it will be soft and creamy) into bowls and top each serving with 1 tablespoon **blackberry jam** and a spoonful of lightly sweetened, whipped **crème fraîche** or sweetened sour cream (optional).

Per serving: 292 cal., 8.2% (24 cal.) from fat; 8.2 g protein; 2.7 g fat (1.5 g sat.); 59 g carbo (4.9 g fiber); 262 mg sodium; 9.8 mg chol.

Oven-baked Polenta

In a shallow 2-quart baking dish, mix 4 cups water, 1 cup **polenta,** 1 tablespoon **butter** (optional; cut into pieces), and ½ teaspoon **salt.** Bake in a 350° oven for 40 minutes. Stir polenta and continue baking until creamy to bite, about 10 minutes longer. Remove from oven, stir, and let stand at room temperature for 5 minutes to thicken. Makes about 5 cups.

Per serving: 200 cal., 1.8% (3.6 cal.) from fat; 4.8 g protein; 0.4 g fat (0 g sat.); 43 g carbo (5.6 g fiber); 232 mg sodium; 0 mg chol.

Polenta Fries with Spicy Tomato Dipping Sauce

PREP AND COOK TIME: 2 hours, plus 1 ½ hours to chill

NOTES: Chef Ben de Vries of Andalu in San Francisco uses a scalloped cookie cutter to make polenta fries in frilly crescent-moon shapes; we've cut the polenta into batons for ease and to avoid waste. Instead of deep-frying, you can oven-fry the polenta: prepare the recipe through step 2. Pour enough oil into a 10- by 15-inch nonstick baking pan to coat well (use two pans for thin-cut fries); roll strips in oil to coat, then spread them out in pan. Bake in a 450° regular or convection oven, turning occasionally, until crisp and browned, 35 to 45 minutes. Continue with step 4.

MAKES: 4 appetizer servings

- ½ cup **grated parmesan cheese**
  Basic polenta (recipe precedes) or oven-baked polenta (recipe precedes), optional butter included
  Salt and **pepper**
  About ½ cup **all-purpose flour**
  Canola or salad **oil**
  Spicy tomato dipping sauce (recipe follows)

1. Stir cheese into hot basic polenta. Add salt and pepper to taste. Scrape mixture into a buttered 8-inch square

Crunchy polenta sticks are an addictive twist on classic french fries.

baking pan and, with a spatula that has been dipped in water, spread level, ¾ to 1 inch thick. Chill until very firm, at least 1½ hours and up to 1 day.

2. Run a knife around edges of pan to loosen polenta, invert onto a board, and lift off pan. Trim any rounded edges from polenta (save trimmings for another use). Cut polenta in half to form two equal rectangles (wipe knife with a wet paper towel as needed to prevent sticking), then cut each half into strips ½ inch wide and 3 to 4 inches long to produce thick, wedge-cut fries (if desired, cut strips in half through wider side to produce thin, square-cut fries). Trim away uneven edges. Spread about ½ cup flour on a rimmed plate and roll each polenta strip lightly in flour.

3. Pour 3 inches oil into a deep-fryer set at 375° (or medium-high) or a deep, heavy, 3- to 4-quart pan over medium-high heat. When oil reaches 375°, working in batches, lower polenta strips into oil in a deep-fry basket or a few at a time with a slotted spoon; fry until crisp and golden, 7 to 9 minutes. Remove with basket or slotted spoon. Drain briefly on paper towels, then transfer, in a single layer, to baking pans and keep warm in a 200° oven.

4. Sprinkle fries with salt and serve with spicy tomato dipping sauce.

Per serving: 473 cal., 32% (153 cal.) from fat; 12 g protein; 17 g fat (2.9 g sat.); 66 g carbo (7.4 g fiber); 476 mg sodium; 7.9 mg chol.

Spicy tomato dipping sauce. In a 10- to 12-inch frying pan over medium-low heat, frequently stir ½ cup chopped **onion** in 2 tablespoons **olive oil** until very limp, about 10 minutes. Add 1 **can** (14 oz.) **whole tomatoes,** ½ cup lightly packed rinsed **fresh basil** leaves, and 1 **dried bay leaf** to pan. Reduce heat to low and cook, stirring occasionally, until tomatoes have disintegrated and most of the liquid has evaporated, about 30 minutes. Let cool about 30 minutes. Remove and discard bay leaf. In a blender or food processor, combine tomato mixture, 2 tablespoons **sherry vinegar,** 1 tablespoon **extra-virgin olive oil,** and 1 teaspoon **cayenne.** Whirl until smooth. Use at once or chill, covered, up to 2 days. Makes about 1 cup.

Per tablespoon: 31 cal., 74% (23 cal.) from fat; 0.4 g protein; 2.6 g fat (0.3 g sat.); 1.9 g carbo (0.5 g fiber); 41 mg sodium; 0 mg chol.

Truffled Creamy Polenta

PREP AND COOK TIME: 30 to 45 minutes

NOTES: This rich polenta—wonderful with duck—is based on one served by chef Mark Purdy at Dry Creek Kitchen

Customizing polenta

- **Texture.** You can adapt any polenta recipe to the texture you prefer by changing the cooking time or the ratio of liquid to polenta. Our basic recipe has a 4:1 ratio (4 cups liquid to 1 cup polenta) and produces a thick, soft polenta that sets firmly when chilled. The breakfast polenta, however, has a 6:1 liquid-to-polenta ratio, which results in a loose texture.

- **Basic flavor.** Adjusting the flavor of polenta is equally simple. Using milk lends breakfast polenta and truffled polenta gentle creaminess; replacing some of the cooking water in basic polenta with broth—meat, chicken, or vegetable—adds savory depth. Any polenta recipe becomes more luscious if you stir in butter, olive oil, or cheese (shred or grate hard cheeses; cut softer cheeses into cubes).

- **Additions.** For variation, add herbs, spices, or aromatics such as garlic or caramelized onions, or stir in sautéed hearty greens such as kale, as chefs John Clark and Gayle Pirie do at their San Francisco restaurant, Foreign Cinema. Experiment to find your favorite combinations; polenta's versatility is a large part of its charm.

in Healdsburg, California. For Purdy's deluxe version, omit mushrooms and stir 1 to 2 tablespoons chopped black truffles into polenta with the cheeses. Truffle oil is available in specialty markets; use either white or black.

MAKES: 6 side-dish servings

Follow directions for basic polenta (recipe precedes), substituting 5 cups **milk** for the water in step 1 and omitting butter in step 3. While polenta cooks, melt 1 tablespoon **butter** in a 10- to 12-inch frying pan over medium heat. Stir in 1 cup finely chopped rinsed **black trumpet,** chanterelle, or common **mushrooms** (or use a mixture). Stir often until liquid has evaporated and mushrooms are browned, about 7 minutes. Stir mushrooms, ½ cup **mascarpone** or cream **cheese** (4 oz.), 2 tablespoons fresh-grated **parmesan cheese,** 1 teaspoon **truffle oil** (see notes), and 1 teaspoon **sherry vinegar** into polenta. Season to taste with **salt** and **pepper.** Ladle into bowls and drizzle with more truffle oil to taste.

Per serving: 408 cal., 42% (171 cal.) from fat; 13 g protein; 19 g fat (12 g sat.); 47 g carbo (4.8 g fiber); 360 mg sodium; 51 mg chol. ◆

Perfecting pasta

A few shortcuts make fettuccine
Alfredo a modern classic

By Jerry Anne Di Vecchio

Shower creamy fettuccine with prosciutto and pine nuts.

■ Researching a cookbook in Rome long ago, I received a serious amount of time and attention from restaurant staff when I ordered fettuccine Alfredo, where Alfredo himself had produced it. Before my eyes, tender ribbons of fresh pasta were lifted from a cauldron of boiling water and tossed into a silken sauce with lumps of golden butter, cascades of thick cream, and a blizzard of feathery parmesan cheese. It took three waiters in concert to produce this masterpiece in a shining copper pan on a tabletop stove. Rich to the point of indigestion; nonetheless, a landmark dish.

I bought a hand-cranked pasta machine to make the fresh fettuccine and headed home with the recipe for the sauce. Fettuccine Alfredo became a standard in our house. Even my young daughter and her friends loved it, especially if they could pull the impossibly long strands of fresh noodles, draped over their arms, from the machine while I turned the handle.

As the years rolled along, my taste for creamy pastas expanded, setting off a battle with the same shift in my waistline. A compromise was necessary. The pasta dishes I enjoy most now have far less butter and cream at heart but retain a vital level of richness. One of my favorite

recipes, in fact, showcases creamy, ripened cheeses, from blues to bries, and omits the butter altogether. The dish can be tailored to individual tastes, and any well-stocked supermarket or deli offers a tantalizing selection of cheeses to choose from.

This pasta is also incredibly easy—basically a one-pan affair. The fettuccine isn't boiled in water; it's cooked in wine and broth and absorbs most of the liquid (no draining). If it's too saucy for you, just wait a minute. Mix again, and the pasta soaks up more.

Traditional technique? No—it's missing three waiters. But traditional silky delectability? Definitely—and though it's rich, it shows decidedly more restraint with the cream.

Fettuccine with Gorgonzola and Prosciutto

PREP AND COOK TIME: About 20 minutes

NOTES: Instead of gorgonzola, you can use any creamy blue cheese or substitute brie (mushroom brie would be delicious), St. André, or another high-fat, ripened cheese.

MAKES: 4 or 5 first-course, 2 or 3 main-dish servings

- ¼ cup **pine nuts**
- 2 ounces **thin prosciutto slices,** separated and cut into slivers
- 4 to 6 ounces **dolce** (sweet) **gorgonzola,** regular gorgonzola, cambozola, or other mild blue **cheese** (¾ to 1 cup, packed; see notes)
- ½ cup **whipping cream**
  About 1½ to 3 cups fat-skimmed **chicken broth**
- 1 cup **dry white wine**
- ¼ teaspoon **dried thyme**
- 9 ounces **fresh fettuccine** or 8 ounces dried fettuccine
  About 2 tablespoons finely slivered **fresh basil** leaves or 2 tablespoons minced parsley
  Fresh-ground **pepper**

1. In a 4- to 5-quart pan over medium-high heat, stir pine nuts until lightly toasted, 2 to 4 minutes. At once, pour from pan into a small bowl.

2. Add prosciutto to pan and stir until slightly browned, about 2 minutes. Add to pine nuts.

3. In a microwave-safe bowl, break or cut cheese into small pieces. Add cream. Heat in a microwave oven on full power (100%) until cream bubbles, 1 to 2 minutes. Whisk mixture until smoothly blended, smashing any bits of rind from cheese. Let stand at room temperature until ready to use.

4. As cheese heats, pour broth (1½ cups if using fresh pasta, 3 cups for dried) and wine into pan; add thyme.

Bring to a boil over high heat, then reduce heat and simmer for 2 to 3 minutes.

5. Return heat to high; when liquid is boiling, add fettuccine (break dried pasta, if necessary, to fit into pan) and stir to separate strands. Cook, stirring often, until pasta is tender to bite, 2 to 3 minutes for fresh, about 7 minutes for dried. If pasta begins to stick, add ½ to 1 cup more broth; there should be a generous amount of liquid. Add cheese-and-cream mixture to pasta and stir for about 1 minute. Remove from heat and let stand for 1 to 2 minutes, stirring several times, to let pasta soak up more liquid.

6. Ladle into warm bowls. Sprinkle equally with pine nut–prosciutto mixture and basil. Season to taste with pepper.

Per first-course serving: 405 cal., 47% (189 cal.) from fat; 18 g protein; 21 g fat (11 g sat.); 30 g carbo (1.4 g fiber); 568 mg sodium; 93 mg chol. ◆

Golden state

Caramelized onions enhance hearty winter dishes

By Charity Ferreira

■ Everything tastes better browned—from the seared crust of a steak to the glassy burnt-sugar top of a crème brûlée—and caramelized onions are no exception. Transforming raw onions into a savory, jamlike mixture is simple: Cook them slowly in a little oil over low heat, so they melt into a sweet golden-brown tangle. Sweet onions such as Vidalia and Oso will caramelize a little faster, but all onions will eventually turn brown and take on a deep, rich flavor that enhances a variety of dishes (see box below). The delicious results are well worth the effort.

Sweet onions add depth to an earthy lentil salad topped with roasted fish.

Caramelized Onions

PREP AND COOK TIME: About 1 hour

NOTES: To double this recipe, use a larger pan and allow 10 to 15 extra minutes of cooking time. If making up to 3 days ahead, let caramelized onions cool, then chill airtight.

MAKES: About ¾ cup

- 1½ pounds **onions,** peeled, halved, and thinly slivered
- 1 teaspoon minced **garlic**
- 1 teaspoon **olive oil**

  Salt and **pepper**

In a 3- to 4-quart pan over medium-high heat, frequently stir onions and garlic in oil until onions start to become limp; reduce heat to medium-low and stir frequently until onions are very soft and browned, 40 to 45 minutes. If onions start to stick to the pan, reduce heat further and stir in 2 tablespoons water. Add salt and pepper to taste.

Per ¾ cup: 278 cal., 18% (50 cal.) from fat; 7.3 g protein; 5.5 g fat (0.8 g sat.); 54 g carbo (9.9 g fiber); 19 mg sodium; 0 mg chol.

French Onion Soup

PREP AND COOK TIME: About 45 minutes

MAKES: 4 cups; 3 or 4 servings

  Caramelized onions (at left)
- 1 tablespoon **balsamic vinegar**
- 2 cans (14 oz. each) fat-skimmed **chicken broth** or vegetable broth
- 2 sprigs **fresh thyme** (3 in. each)
- 1 **dried bay leaf**

  Salt and **pepper**
- 8 slices **baguette** (about 2 by 4 in. and 1 in. thick)
- ¼ cup sh redded **gruyère cheese**

1. In a 3- to 4-quart pan over medium-high heat, stir onions and balsamic vinegar often until liquid is evaporated, 1 to 2 minutes.

2. Add broth, thyme, and bay leaf; bring to a boil. Reduce heat and simmer, stirring occasionally to blend flavors, 10 minutes. Add salt and pepper to taste.

3. Meanwhile, place baguette slices in a single layer on a 12- by 15-inch baking sheet. Broil 4 to 6 inches from heat until lightly browned on top, 1 to 2 minutes. Turn slices over and sprinkle evenly with cheese. Broil until cheese is melted, 1 to 2 minutes longer.

4. Remove thyme and bay leaf; ladle soup into bowls. Serve with toasts.

Per serving: 265 cal., 22% (59 cal.) from fat; 11 g protein; 6.6 g fat (2.6 g sat.); 41 g carbo (3.9 g fiber); 430 mg sodium; 11 mg chol.

Roasted Striped Bass with Warm Lentil Salad

PREP AND COOK TIME: 40 minutes

MAKES: 4 servings

- 1 cup **small French green** or brown **lentils,** sorted and rinsed

  Caramelized onions (at left)
- ½ cup canned peeled **roasted red peppers,** cut into strips
- 3 tablespoons **sherry vinegar**
- 2 tablespoons chopped **parsley**
- ½ teaspoon **ground cumin**

  About ½ teaspoon **salt**
- ¼ teaspoon **cayenne pepper**
- 4 **boned, skinned striped bass** or other firm-fleshed white fish **fillets** (about 6 oz. each)

  Pepper

  Lemon wedges

1. In a 4- to 5-quart pan over high heat, bring lentils and 1 quart water to a boil. Reduce heat and simmer until lentils are tender to bite, 25 to 30 minutes. Drain and return to pan. Stir in caramelized onions, peppers, vinegar, parsley, cumin, ½ teaspoon salt, and cayenne.

2. Meanwhile, rinse fish and pat dry. Sprinkle lightly all over with salt and pepper. Arrange pieces slightly apart in a foil-lined 12- by 15-inch baking pan. Bake in a 400° regular or convection oven until opaque but still moist-looking in the center of the thickest part (cut to test), about 6 minutes.

3. Mound lentil salad equally on four dinner plates. Using a wide spatula, top each mound with a piece of fish. Serve with lemon wedges to squeeze over fish.

Per serving: 408 cal., 13% (53 cal.) from fat; 46 g protein; 5.9 g fat (1.1 g sat.); 44 g carbo (8.2 g fiber); 451 mg sodium; 136 mg chol. ◆

More ways to use caramelized onions

- Stir 2 tablespoons balsamic or cider vinegar into onions a few minutes before the end of the cooking time to make a tangy onion relish that's great on sandwiches, crostini, and pizza
- Mix into couscous or rice pilaf
- Fold into an omelet or a frittata
- Toss with cooked pasta along with a few ounces of blue cheese and some toasted walnuts

Fried potato turnovers are a Mediterranean take on Hanukkah food traditions.

Southern lights

Saffron Shores offers Jewish food traditions from North Africa

Joyce Goldstein wants to change everything you thought you knew about Jewish culinary traditions. Most of us in the United States associate Jewish cooking with Eastern European flavors (among them chicken fat, onions, and sour cream). But Goldstein's exhaustive research into Mediterranean Jewish food has opened up a world of different tastes.

Her newest cookbook, *Saffron Shores: Jewish Cooking of the Southern Mediterranean,* isn't for the novice cook; many recipes are challenging. But it is a beautiful treasure trove of dishes from the Jewish communities of North Africa. Some will seem familiar—spiced roast lamb with couscous and harissa from Morocco, for instance—whereas others are more exotic, like a green puréed soup of fava beans and cilantro, garnished

with chicken gizzards, for Passover.

Saffron Shores (Chronicle Books, San Francisco, 2002; $35; 800/722-6657) is full of fresh ideas for all the Jewish holidays. For Hanukkah, it is traditional to eat oil-rich foods in honor of the miracle of a Temple lamp that burned for eight days with only one day's supply of oil. Goldstein suggests serving sweet or savory fried pastries, such as classic North African *briks* (spicy filled turnovers). We found more than one reason to like her Tunisian pastries, filled with mashed potatoes and fresh herbs—first, because they're easy to put together (egg roll wrappers fry up beautifully, and the thick filling doesn't leak out), and second, because they taste like a subtle twist on comfortingly familiar latkes.

— *Kate Washington*

Tunisian Potato Turnovers

PREP AND COOK TIME: About 1 hour
MAKES: 4 dozen turnovers; 12 to 16 appetizer servings

- 2 **russet potatoes** (1 lb. total), peeled and cut into 1-inch chunks
- 1 **onion** (6 oz.), peeled and chopped
- 2 cloves **garlic,** peeled and minced
- 1 tablespoon **olive oil**
- 3 tablespoons minced **Italian parsley**
- 3 tablespoons minced **fresh cilantro**
- 1 tablespoon drained **capers,** rinsed and coarsely chopped
- 1 teaspoon **salt**
- ½ teaspoon fresh-ground **pepper**
- 1 **large egg,** separated
- 12 square (6 in.) **egg roll wrappers**
  Salad oil such as canola for frying

1. In a 3- to 4-quart pan over high heat, bring potatoes and 2 quarts water to a boil; cover, reduce heat, and simmer until potatoes mash easily, about 15 minutes. Drain and transfer to a bowl; mash with a potato masher until smooth.

2. Meanwhile, in an 8- to 10-inch frying pan over medium heat, stir onion and garlic in oil until onion is very limp, about 10 minutes (if onion begins to brown, reduce heat to medium-low). Stir into potatoes, along with parsley, cilantro, capers, salt, and pepper. In a small bowl, beat egg yolk to blend; add to potato mixture and mix well.

3. In another small bowl, beat egg white to blend. Cut each egg roll wrapper into four squares (keep covered with plastic wrap until ready to use). Place about 1½ teaspoons potato mixture in the center of each square. Brush edges lightly with egg white. Fold each square diagonally over filling to form a triangle; pinch edges to seal.

4. Pour 2 inches of oil into a heavy 5- to 6-quart pan over medium-high heat (or use a deep-fryer and follow manufacturer's recommendation for depth of oil). When oil reaches 375°, using a slotted spoon or a mesh basket and working in batches of 6 to 12 (pastries should fit easily in one layer), lower pastries into oil. Fry until golden brown, turning once, 3 to 5 minutes total. Transfer to paper towel–lined 10- by 15-inch baking sheets in a 200° oven and keep warm up to 30 minutes. Allow oil to return to 375° between batches.

Per serving: 123 cal., 36% (44 cal.) from fat; 3.4 g protein; 4.9 g fat (0.7 g sat.); 16 g carbo (1.3 g fiber); 240 mg sodium; 15 mg chol.

Sage advice

Crisp, delicious fried sage leaves are the kind of smart touch chefs love to use to dress up winter dishes. Why let them claim all the kitchen wisdom, though? It's shamefully easy to fry the leaves: it just takes 15 seconds in a tiny bit of hot oil—and sage is sturdy, so no worries about it crumbling. You can use the common variety, which darkens to a deep gray-green, or search out variegated sage for a more dramatic look. A few fried leaves are wonderful floated on a savory squash soup, garnishing an hors d'oeuvres tray, or planted on a bowl of polenta with pancetta (see page 260); for extra impact, fry up a big batch and arrange them around a lavish Christmas pork roast.

Fried sage leaves. Rinse about 20 large **fresh sage** leaves and lay flat on a double layer of paper towels; cover with more towels and press gently to flatten and dry leaves. Pour **olive** or canola **oil** into a narrow 1- to 1½-quart pan over medium-high heat to a depth of ¼ inch. When hot (oil will ripple), lower heat to medium and add sage leaves, a few at a time, in a single layer. Fry just until oil stops bubbling around leaves, 10 to 15 seconds (do not let brown), then remove carefully with tongs and drain on more paper towels. Sprinkle with **salt** to taste. Use at once, or store between layers of paper towels in an airtight container at room temperature up to 1 day. — *K. W.* ◆

Stylish endings

Fruit flavors for novel holiday desserts

By Linda Lau Anusasananan

H oliday desserts aren't following the rules this year. Lemons make their seasonal appearance in a refreshingly unseasonal sherbet, tangy with buttermilk. Limes follow suit in a simple sorbet. Either of these desserts would end a festive dinner on a delicious new note.

Double-Lemon Sherbet

PREP AND COOK TIME: About 1 hour, plus at least 2 hours for scoops to freeze

NOTES: This sherbet comes from Linda Wisner of Portland. It has a wonderful floral quality if made with lemon verbena and Meyer lemons (available in some farmers' markets), but the sherbet is also very good made with lemon grass and regular lemons. Up to an hour before serving, scoop sherbet, set scoops in a single layer in a cold metal pan, and freeze.

MAKES: 1 quart; 8 servings

 2½ ounces **fresh lemon grass** (about 2 stalks) or ⅔ cup lightly packed **lemon verbena** leaves, rinsed (see notes)

 1 cup **sugar**

 1½ tablespoons grated **lemon** peel (see notes)

 ⅓ cup **lemon juice** (see notes)

 1⅓ cups **buttermilk**

 ⅔ cup **half-and-half** (light cream)

1. Trim and discard root ends and tough tops from lemon grass; remove and discard tough outer layers. Coarsely chop tender inner stalks.

2. In a 2- to 3-quart pan over high heat, bring ⅔ cup water to a boil. Stir in lemon grass, remove from heat, and let stand for 15 minutes. Press through a fine strainer set over a bowl, then return liquid to pan; discard lemon grass.

3. Add sugar to lemon grass water and stir often over high heat just until dissolved, 2 to 3 minutes. Remove from heat and stir in lemon peel and juice. Nest pan in a bowl of ice water and stir often until mixture is cold, about 10 minutes. Stir in buttermilk and half-and-half.

4. Pour mixture into an ice cream maker (1-qt. or larger capacity) and freeze according to manufacturer's directions until dasher is hard to turn or machine stops. Package airtight and freeze until firm enough to scoop, at least 2 hours or up to 2 weeks.

Per serving: 142 cal., 17% (24 cal.) from fat; 2 g protein; 2.7 g fat (1.7 g sat.); 29 g carbo (0.1 g fiber); 53 mg sodium; 9.1 mg chol.

Lime Sorbet

PREP TIME: About 35 minutes, plus about 45 minutes to chill

MAKES: About 1 quart

 4 or 5 **limes** (about 2½ in. wide), rinsed

 1 cup **sugar**

 2 tablespoons **orange-flavor liqueur** (optional)

1. With a vegetable peeler, pare green part of peel from four limes. Put peel and sugar in a food processor and whirl until peel is very finely chopped.

2. Cut limes in half; ream enough juice to make 1 cup. Add to sugar mixture and whirl until sugar is melted. Cover mixture and chill until cold, about 45 minutes.

3. Pour lime-sugar mixture through a fine strainer into an ice cream maker (1-qt. or larger capacity), then pour 3 cups ice water through strainer into maker; add orange-flavor liqueur. Freeze according to manufacturer's directions until dasher is hard to turn or machine stops, about 25 minutes.

4. Serve softly frozen, or cover and freeze to store longer. If frozen hard, let stand at room temperature until soft enough to scoop, 10 to 20 minutes. If desired, cut one lime into thin slices (discard ends) and garnish portions with slices.

Per ½ cup: 106 cal., 0% (0 cal.) from fat; 0.2 g protein; 0 g fat (0 g sat.); 28 g carbo (0 g fiber); 0.7 mg sodium; 0 mg chol. ◆

Spiced garbanzos and tomatoes with rice and slaw make an easy meal.

Curry favor

Indian flavors help turn pantry staples into a warming weeknight dinner

By Linda Lau Anusasananan

■ Everyone needs an ace-in-the-hole dish, something wonderfully delicious to pull together for a quick dinner when the cupboard is almost bare. This vegetarian curry answers that need. It does a good turn to shelf-stable pantry basics by combining them with flavorful spices for a main course that tastes exotic and complex. Start by lightly browning onions, ginger, and garlic for the flavor base. Add spices, garbanzos, and canned tomatoes for a well-seasoned entrée to eat with rice or whole-wheat tortillas (similar to Indian chapatis). If you're serving rice, start cooking it just before you make the curry. The sprightly slaw and sparkling mango floats can be made in minutes.

Garbanzo-Tomato Curry

PREP AND COOK TIME: About 20 minutes

NOTES: If you prefer a very mild curry, reduce or omit the cayenne.

MAKES: 4 servings

- 1 **onion** (8 oz.), peeled and chopped
- 1 tablespoon minced **fresh ginger**
- 2 cloves **garlic**, peeled and minced
- 1 tablespoon **salad oil**
- 1 tablespoon **curry powder**
- 1 teaspoon **cumin seeds**
- ½ teaspoon **mustard seeds**
- ¼ teaspoon **cayenne** (see notes)
- 2 cans (15½ oz. each) **garbanzos**, rinsed and drained
- 1 can (14½ oz.) **diced tomatoes**
  Salt

  About 1 cup **plain nonfat yogurt**

MENU

Quick curry dinner

Garbanzo-Tomato Curry*

Cabbage and Cilantro Slaw*

Cooked Basmati Rice or
Whole-Wheat Flour Tortillas

Hot Tea or Beer

*Mango Floats**

*Recipe provided

1. In a 10- to 12-inch frying pan over medium-high heat, stir onion, ginger, and garlic in oil until onion just begins to brown, 5 to 8 minutes. Add curry powder, cumin seeds, mustard seeds, and cayenne and stir until fragrant, about 30 seconds.

2. Add garbanzos and tomatoes (including juice). Bring to a boil, reduce heat, and simmer uncovered, stirring occasionally, to blend flavors, about 5 minutes. If mixture is thicker than desired, stir in a little water to thin. Add salt to taste. Spoon into serving dishes.

3. Serve with yogurt on the side.

Per serving: 264 cal., 26% (69 cal.) from fat; 13 g protein; 7.7 g fat (0.7 g sat.); 37 g carbo (8.2 g fiber); 457 mg sodium; 1.1 mg chol.

Cabbage and Cilantro Slaw

PREP TIME: About 15 minutes

NOTES: To make this slaw more quickly, you can use purchased shredded cabbage or coleslaw mix.

MAKES: 4 servings

In a large bowl, mix 1½ quarts finely shredded **cabbage** (12 oz.; see notes), ⅓ cup chopped **fresh cilantro**, 3 tablespoons **lime juice**, 2 tablespoons **salad oil**, and ¼ teaspoon **hot chili flakes**. Add **salt** and **pepper** to taste.

Per serving: 84 cal., 75% (63 cal.) from fat; 1.1 g protein; 7 g fat (0.9 g sat.); 5.4 g carbo (2.1 g fiber); 18 mg sodium; 0 mg chol.

Mango Floats

PREP TIME: About 10 minutes

MAKES: 4 servings

Pour 1 to 1½ cups chilled **mango–passion fruit sparkling juice blend** into each of four tall glasses (12- to 16-oz. capacity; fill ¾ full). Add a scoop of **mango sorbet** or vanilla ice cream to each (about 3 cups total). Add more sparkling juice if necessary to fill glasses.

Per serving: 263 cal., 0% (0 cal.) from fat; 0 g protein; 0 g fat (0 g sat.); 67 g carbo (1.5 g fiber); 0 mg sodium; 0 mg chol. ◆

Island-style Morning

On Christmas Day, wake up to a Hawaiian brunch

By Linda Lau Anusasananan

On Christmas Day, wake up to a holiday permeated with Islands flavor—guavas and mangoes, coconut and macadamia nuts, and pungent kona coffee. A brunch of favorite Hawaiian foods will set the mood for a *Mele Kalikimaka* (Merry Christmas).

Guava Bellinis

PREP TIME: About 5 minutes

NOTES: Mix Bellinis just before serving. For a nonalcoholic version, use sparkling water instead of sparkling wine.

MAKES: 1 serving

In a 6-ounce champagne flute or wine glass, combine ¼ cup *each* **refrigerated guava nectar** and chilled **sparkling wine** such as Italian prosecco (or spumante) or Champagne. If desired, garnish rim of glass with a thin slice of **star fruit**.

Per serving: 78 cal., 0% (0 cal.) from fat; 0.1 g protein; 0 g fat; 9.9 g carbo (0 g fiber); 6.7 mg sodium; 0 mg chol.

Pineapple-Mango Platter with Ginger

PREP TIME: About 20 minutes

NOTES: If preparing through step 2 up to 2 hours ahead, cover and chill.

MAKES: 8 servings

2½ pounds **peeled, cored pineapple**

2 **firm-ripe mangoes** (¾ to 1 lb. each)

1 or 2 **limes** (3 oz. each), rinsed

3 tablespoons minced **crystallized ginger**

1. Cut pineapple crosswise into ½ inch-thick rings; arrange on a platter.

2. Peel mangoes. Slice fruit off pits and cut into ½-inch chunks; discard pits. Arrange mangoes over and around pineapple. Cut limes into wedges and place on platter.

3. Sprinkle ginger evenly over fruit. Squeeze lime juice from wedges over fruit to taste.

Per serving: 131 cal., 5.5% (7.2 cal.) from fat; 0.9 g protein; 0.8 g fat (0.1 g sat.); 34 g carbo (2.5 g fiber); 7.4 mg sodium; 0 mg chol.

Coconut-Orange Bread Pudding

PREP AND COOK TIME: About 1¼ hours, plus at least 2 hours to chill

NOTES: A soft, mildly sweet bread such as challah could be used. You can assemble this dish through step 3 up to 1 day ahead; chill.

MAKES: 8 servings

8 ounces **Hawaiian** or Portuguese **sweet bread** (a loaf or dinner rolls; see notes)

1 package (8 oz.) **neufchâtel** (light cream) **cheese** or cream cheese, at room temperature

1¾ cups **coconut** or maple **syrup**

10 **large eggs**

1 can (14 oz.) **coconut milk**

2 teaspoons grated **orange** peel

1 cup **orange juice**

¼ teaspoon **ground nutmeg**

¾ cup **sweetened shredded** or flaked **dried coconut**

⅓ cup chopped **roasted, salted macadamia nuts**

1. Tear the bread into ½-inch chunks. In a food processor, whirl the chunks into coarse crumbs (or finely chop with a knife); you should have about 1 quart. Pour into a buttered 3-quart shallow casserole; spread level.

2. In food processor, whirl cheese and ¼ cup syrup until blended; or in a bowl, with a mixer on medium speed, beat until blended. Spoon evenly over bread (it doesn't need to cover bread completely).

3. In a bowl, whisk eggs to blend with ½ cup syrup, coconut milk, orange peel, orange juice, and nutmeg. Pour evenly over cheese mixture and bread. Cover casserole; chill at least 2 hours.

4. Bake, uncovered, in a 350° regular or 325° convection oven until center barely jiggles when casserole is gently shaken, 40 to 50 minutes. Sprinkle top evenly with coconut and nuts; continue baking until coconut is lightly browned, 7 to 9 minutes.

5. Heat remaining 1 cup syrup in a microwave-safe pitcher in a microwave oven at full power (100%) until warm, about 40 seconds. Serve pudding at once. Add syrup to taste.

Per serving: 621 cal., 46% (288 cal.) from fat; 15 g protein; 32 g fat (19 g sat.); 71 g carbo (1.5 g fiber); 322 mg sodium; 297 mg chol.

Oven-browned Portuguese Sausage Slices

PREP AND COOK TIME: About 35 minutes

NOTES: You can use another cooked sausage such as kielbasa (Polish). About 30 minutes before the bread pudding is done, slide pan with sausages onto bottom rack of oven.

MAKES: 8 servings

1. Cut 1½ pounds **linguisa** (Portuguese sausages) diagonally into ¼-inch-thick slices. Arrange slices in a single layer in a 12- by 17-inch baking pan.

2. Bake in a 350° regular or 325° convection oven (see notes) until sausages are lightly browned, 20 to 30 minutes; turn slices after about 10 minutes. Drain briefly on paper towels, then transfer to a serving dish. Serve warm.

Per serving: 264 cal., 78% (207 cal.) from fat; 11 g protein; 23 g fat (8.4 g sat.); 1.8 g carbo (0 g fiber); 916 mg sodium; 57 mg chol. ◆

Hawaiian Brunch

Guava Bellinis*

Pineapple-Mango Platter with Ginger*

Coconut-Orange Bread Pudding*

Oven-browned Portuguese Sausage Slices*

Kona Coffee

Recipe provided

Baked acorn squash holds a savory filling of pork sausage, apples, and pecans.

a 9- by 13-inch baking pan and cover pan tightly with foil. Bake in a 350° regular or convection oven until tender when pierced, 45 to 50 minutes.

2. Meanwhile, in a 10- to 12-inch nonstick frying pan over medium-high heat, stir sausage until it is crumbly and just slightly pink, about 5 minutes. Drain off and discard fat. Add onion, apples, raisins, cranberries, and thyme; stir often until apples are tender when pierced, 8 to 10 minutes. Stir in pecans.

3. Uncover squash and turn halves upright; fill equally with sausage mixture. Drizzle equally with maple syrup and bake, uncovered, until filling is slightly browned on top, about 15 minutes longer.

Per main-dish serving: 400 cal., 27% (108 cal.) from fat; 8.4 g protein; 12 g fat (3.3 g sat.); 70 g carbo (12 g fiber); 356 mg sodium; 22 mg chol.

Chinese Three-Bean Chili

Alan Tobey, Berkeley

Alan Tobey likes to experiment with fusion dishes that are practical for the home cook, such as this pork chili flavored with Chinese seasonings.

PREP AND COOK TIME: About 50 minutes

MAKES: 4 servings

- 1½ tablespoons **cornstarch**
- 1 tablespoon **chili powder**
- 1 teaspoon **Chinese five spice**
- ½ teaspoon **salt**
- 1 pound **pork loin**, rinsed, fat trimmed, and cut into 1-inch cubes
- 2 tablespoons **salad oil**
- ⅓ cup thinly sliced **green onions** (white and pale green parts only; reserve green tops for garnish, if desired)
- 3 **fresh serrano** or other hot green **chilies** (about 3 oz. total), rinsed, stemmed, seeded, and minced
- 2 cloves **garlic**, peeled and minced
- 2 tablespoons **salted fermented black beans**, minced
- 1½ teaspoons minced peeled **fresh ginger**
- 1 can (14½ oz.) **kidney beans**, drained and rinsed
- 1 can (14½ oz.) **pinto beans**, drained and rinsed
- 1 can (14½ oz.) **diced tomatoes**

1. In a bowl, mix cornstarch, chili powder, five spice, and salt. Add pork and mix to coat.

2. Pour oil into a 4- to 6-quart pan over

Home cooking for the holidays

Readers' recipes, tested in *Sunset's* kitchens

By Charity Ferreira • Photographs by James Carrier

Stuffed Acorn Squash

Kathleen Moretto, Stockton, CA

Kathleen Moretto was in the mood for something simple and seasonal when she came up with this baked, stuffed squash. She serves the halves with cornbread as a main dish, or cuts the squash into quarters to serve as a holiday side dish.

PREP AND COOK TIME: About 1¼ hours

MAKES: 4 main-dish or 8 side-dish servings

- 2 **acorn squash** (about 1½ lb. each), rinsed

- 8 ounces **bulk pork sausage**
- ½ cup chopped **onion**
- 2 **sweet apples** such as Fuji (1 lb. total), peeled, cored, and chopped
- ¼ cup **raisins**
- ¼ cup **dried cranberries**
- ¼ teaspoon **dried thyme**
- 3 tablespoons chopped **pecans**
- ¼ cup **maple syrup**

1. Cut each squash in half crosswise; scoop out seeds. Cut a thin slice off the bottom of each half so it can stand upright. Place each half flesh down in

medium-high heat. When hot, add pork mixture and stir often until browned on all sides, about 4 minutes. With a slotted spoon, transfer pork to bowl. Add green onions, chilies, garlic, fermented black beans, and ginger to pan. Stir until fragrant, about 1 minute.

3. Return pork to pan and add 1 cup water, kidney beans, pinto beans, and tomatoes. Bring to a simmer, then lower heat, cover, and simmer (do not let boil), stirring occasionally, until pork is tender when pierced, about 25 minutes.

4. Ladle into bowls and top with sliced green onion tops, if desired.

Per serving: 411 cal., 33% (135 cal.) from fat; 36 g protein; 15 g fat (3.2 g sat.); 33 g carbo (9 g fiber); 1,050 mg sodium; 67 mg chol.

Radicchio and Smoked Cheese Risotto

Paul Franson, St. Helena, CA

Paul Franson discovered this dish—a creamy risotto made with radicchio and smoked scamorze, a cheese similar to mozzarella—on a trip to Italy and was determined to re-create it at home. We also enjoyed the dish with red cabbage, which turns the rice a surprising purple hue. Smoked mozzarella is available in well-stocked supermarkets and specialty cheese shops. If you can't find it, substitute another firm, flavorful cheese, such as fontina.

PREP AND COOK TIME: About 45 minutes

MAKES: 2 or 3 main-dish servings

- 2 tablespoons **olive oil**
- 1 **onion** (8 oz.), peeled and finely chopped
- 2 cloves **garlic**, peeled and finely chopped
- 1 cup **arborio** or other short-grain white **rice**
- 1/2 cup **dry white wine**
- 4 cups thinly slivered **radicchio** or red cabbage (about 8 oz.)
- 3 1/2 to 4 cups fat-skimmed **chicken broth**
- 1/2 cup shredded **smoked mozzarella** (see notes)
- **Salt** and **pepper**

1. Pour oil into a 5- to 6-quart pan over medium-high heat; when hot, add onion and garlic and stir often until onion is limp, 5 to 6 minutes. Add rice

No-bake rice pudding makes a creamy and elegant holiday dessert.

and stir until opaque, about 3 minutes. **2.** Add wine and stir until it has been absorbed, 1 to 2 minutes. Add radicchio and 3 1/2 cups broth and bring to a boil over high heat, stirring often. Reduce heat and simmer, stirring often, until rice is tender to bite, 15 to 20 minutes. If a creamier consistency is desired, stir in about 1/2 cup more broth. Stir in cheese; add salt and pepper to taste. Serve immediately.

Per serving: 453 cal., 30% (135 cal.) from fat; 19 g protein; 15 g fat (4.3 g sat.); 55 g carbo (5.8 g fiber); 195 mg sodium; 20 mg chol.

Bavarian Rice Pudding

Donna Storey, Berkeley

Donna Storey makes this mousse-like rice pudding every year on Christmas Eve.

PREP AND COOK TIME: About 1 hour, plus at least 2 hours to chill

MAKES: 6 servings

- 3 1/2 cups **whole milk**
- 2/3 cup **sugar**
- 1/2 cup **long-grain white rice**
- 2 tablespoons **butter**
- 1/4 teaspoon **salt**
- 1 teaspoon **unflavored gelatin**
- 2 tablespoons **light rum**
- 1 teaspoon **vanilla**
- 1 cup **whipping cream**

1. In a 3- to 4-quart pan over medium-high heat, bring milk to a simmer. Stir in sugar, rice, butter, and salt. Reduce heat, cover, and simmer, stirring occasionally, until mixture has thickened slightly and rice is very tender to bite, about 45 minutes.

2. Meanwhile, in a small bowl, sprinkle gelatin over 2 tablespoons cold water; let stand until soft, about 10 minutes.

Stir into hot rice mixture, followed by rum and vanilla. Chill uncovered until cool but not set, about 1 hour.

3. In a bowl, with a mixer on high speed, whip cream to soft peaks. Fold cream into rice mixture. Divide pudding evenly among six parfait glasses (at least 8 oz.). Chill until set, at least 1 hour, or cover and chill up to 1 day.

Per serving: 394 cal., 48% (189 cal.) from fat; 7 g protein; 21 g fat (13 g sat.); 43 g carbo (0.2 g fiber); 219 mg sodium; 74 mg chol.

Cranberry-Orange Scones

Linda Tebben, Menlo Park, CA

These cakelike scones created by Linda Tebben make a great holiday breakfast.

PREP AND COOK TIME: About 40 minutes

MAKES: 8 scones

- 2 cups **all-purpose flour**
- 1/3 cup plus 1 teaspoon **sugar**
- 1 1/2 teaspoons **baking powder**
- 1/4 teaspoon **salt**
- 2 tablespoons grated **orange** peel
- 1/4 cup (1/8 lb.) cold **butter,** cut into chunks
- 1/2 cup coarsely chopped **fresh cranberries** or frozen cranberries, thawed
- 1/4 cup coarsely chopped **pecans**
- 1/3 cup **orange juice**
- 1/4 cup **plain low-fat yogurt**

1. In a bowl, mix flour, 1/3 cup sugar, baking powder, salt, and orange peel. With your fingers or a pastry blender, rub or cut in butter until mixture forms coarse crumbs. Stir in cranberries, pecans, orange juice, and yogurt just until dough is evenly moistened.

2. Scrape onto a floured board and, with lightly floured hands, pat into a 7-inch round about 3/4 inch thick. Cut into eight wedges and place slightly apart on a 12- by 15-inch baking sheet. Sprinkle lightly with remaining 1 teaspoon sugar.

3. Bake in a 375° regular or 350° convection oven until lightly browned and a wooden skewer inserted into the center comes out with moist crumbs attached, about 20 minutes. Serve warm or at room temperature.

Per scone: 243 cal., 31% (76 cal.) from fat; 4.2 g protein; 8.4 g fat (3.9 g sat.); 38 g carbo (1.4 g fiber); 227 mg sodium; 16 mg chol. ◆

Articles Index

Index of Recipe Titles

Low-Fat Recipes

General Index

Walnut(s)
  persimmon and apple salad
    with, 244
  vinaigrette, with mixed greens
    and Fuji apples, 252
Watermelon ice cubes, 134
Wild rice, apricot, and bread
  dressing, 220
Wine
  for brunch, 54
  Cabernet with steak, 210
  Chardonnay, 120

Wine (*cont'd.*)
  hammock wines, 134
  memorable budget wines,
    27
  Mosel Riesling, 165
  mulled white, 234
  paired with roast pork and
    chicken, 229
  Pinot Noir, 206
  Rhône-style, 187
  from Santa Ynez Valley, 78
  Sauvignon Blanc, 123

Wine (*cont'd.*)
  seeking hard-to-find, 107
  Spanish favorites, 151
  sparkling, 162
  Syrah, the next big red, 184
  for vegetarian holiday menu,
    226
  warming reds for winter, 47
  Western Zinfandels, 237
Wine and herb marinade, 141
Winter greens
  sweet braised, 238

Winter greens (*cont'd.*)
  with olive vinaigrette, 251

Yogurt panna cotta, 55
Yogurt sauce, sesame, 85

Zucchini
  blossom–porcini orecchiette,
    186
  savory summer pancakes,
    143
  timbales, 176